The Canadair Sabre

The Canadair Sabre

Larry Milberry

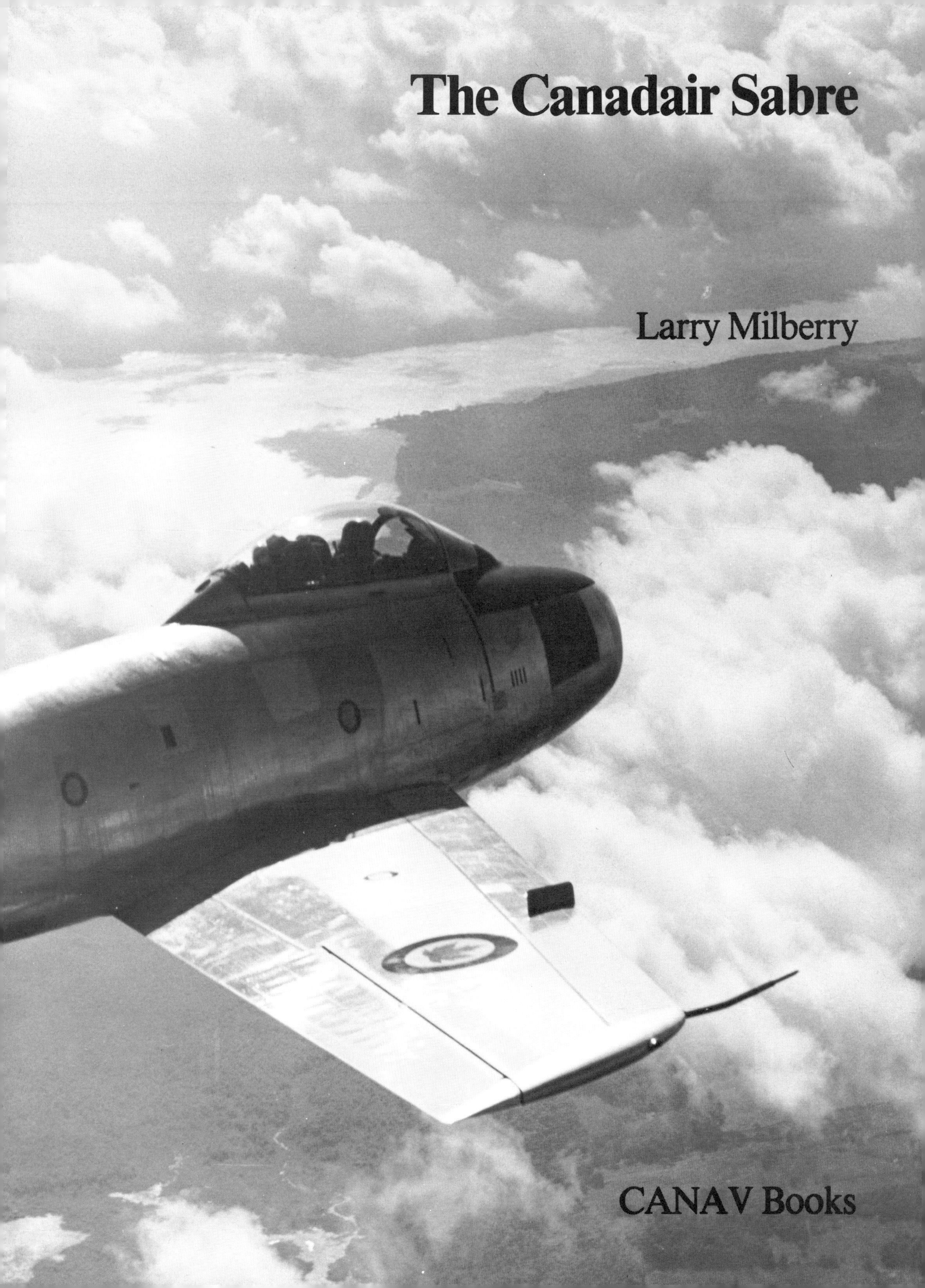

CANAV Books

Canadian Cataloguing in Publication Data

Milberry, Larry, 1943-
    The Canadair Sabre

Includes index.
ISBN 0-9690703-7-3

1. Canadair F-86 (Jet fighter plane) -
History. I. Title.

UG1242.F5M54 1986   623.74'64'0971
C86-093914-6

EDITOR AND DESIGNER
Robin Brass

TYPESETTING
East End Graphics and Second Story Graphics

PHOTO RETOUCHING
Stephen Ng, SNG Retouching Studio

REPRO ASSEMBLY
Ralph Clint

PROOFREADING
Ralph Clint, Frank Phripp, Ralph Heard

Printed in Canada by Bryant Press Limited,
Toronto

Published by
CANAV Books
Larry Milberry, publisher
51 Balsam Avenue
Toronto M4E 3B6
Canada

Front endpaper
Sabres from 400 and 411 (Aux) Squadrons
overfly the old Maple Leaf Stadium and Island
Airport in downtown Toronto in 1957. Photo by
Cpl Barry Herron. (DND)

Title page
A lone Canadair Sabre in its natural element.
(Canadair Ltd.)

Back endpaper
A pair of Downsview-based Sabre 5s nudge up
nice and close to Cpl Barry Herron's lens in
another of his classic photos from the fifties.
(DND)

F/O L.J. Redman flies VH-702 of 444 Squadron.
These markings were unique to 444's Sabre 4s.
(A.J. Bauer)

Contents

A newly refurbished Turkish Sabre 2 waits at St. Hubert, May 1955. Soon after the photo was taken, it was ferried to the UK by the OFU, thence on to Turkey. (Gordon S. Williams)

The Golden Hawks in Sabre 5s. This great
aerobatic team was *the* symbol of the RCAF's
postwar glory days.

Preface

The Canadair Sabre is one of the great success stories in Canadian aviation history. The Sabre, designed by North American Aviation in California just after the war, was destined to become *the* classic of the jet fighter age—what the Camel and Spitfire were in earlier days. It came along just in time too. As North American and the US military were making major design decisions, such as whether or not it should have a swept wing, the Soviets were pushing ahead with their own fighter, the MiG-15. The MiG got into the air in July 1947, several months ahead of the Sabre, and when revealed as a swept-wing design, fully justified the American decision to sweep the Sabre's wings. Before long these two impressive steeds were doing battle over the Yalu in Korea.

The Sabre soon joined the RCAF, whose top command was determined to enter the postwar era well equipped. In the day fighter realm, no better choice could have been made. Canadair quickly went to work mass producing Sabres, and adding improvements along the way. In the following decades for thousands of Canadians the best years of their lives would be their Sabre years—building, maintaining and, above all, flying this all-time beauty. With a Canadair F-86 strapped to his backside, there was no happier or more confident fighter pilot. Year after year in the fifties and sixties, Canada's Sabre pilots would walk off with NATO gunnery trophies. There can be little doubt that the presence in Europe of the RCAF Sabre squadrons had a sobering influence upon those across the Iron Curtain.

This book is the story of the Canadair Sabre, of nearly 2000 little "made in Montreal" fighters flown by thousands of pilots in a dozen air forces. My goal has been to provide a mixture of hard-core history, technical data and human-interest anecdotes. As with all previous CANAV efforts, this one is the result of much research and the cooperation of hundreds.

Much important research was done abroad. British aviation historian Roger Lindsay spent years digging up the story of the Canadair Sabres used by the Royal Air Force. Previously, Roger had published fine monographs about the Venom and Javelin, and his articles have appeared in various journals such as *Air International*. He's a long-time aviation fan and did a stint in the RAF as a radar tech. For a living, Roger is an advertising and marketing consultant in Cleveland, U.K.

The 1000th Sabre built by Canadair during pre-acceptance checks at Cartierville. (Canadair Ltd.)

JG 71 Sabre 6 at Buchel in July 1960.
(D.W. Menard)

Coverage of the Luftwaffe's Canadair Sabres is the result of similar years of digging by Gerhard Joos of Moerfelden-Walldorf, West Germany. He joined the Luftwaffe in 1957, doing ops on the RF-84F and G.91, though the Sabre remained his favourite fighter. In 1962 Gerhard joined Dornier, mainly as a G.91 test pilot. In 1967 he became a commercial pilot, flying Viscounts 707s, 727s and 737s with Condor and Lufthansa. Along the way he too produced some aviation journalism with, among other efforts, a monograph about the Canadair Sabre. Today he is captain on the Lufthansa Airbus A310.

Another key member of the research team is Ralph Clint of Toronto. A retired Air Canada radio man, he is a lifelong aviation keener and has helped on several CANAV ventures. This time he has carried out general research and proofreading, and has made the line drawings. Towards the end of things, he was pressed into service assembling the book for the printer. W/C Frank Phripp (ret.) also worked as a proof reader. No reader of *Sixty Years* will

forget his fascinating stories about WEE Flight and the NRC flying wing project. Also enlisted for proofreading was Ralph Heard. A veteran Sabre driver, Ralph flies helicopters these days for Ontario Hydro.

A.J. "Al" Lilly of Moncton was another big help in getting details of early Sabre days nailed down, and in helping me reach old-time Sabre personnel. Al was just as helpful some years ago when I was preparing the Canadair North Star book. Bob Baglow of Ottawa, recent publisher of a new book about the Avro CF-100, did some good scouting for Sabre history in and around Ottawa. As usual, the "Avenue Road" gang chipped in with plenty of moral support over noon-hour beers in the mess—S/L John Biehler, F/L Bill Meaden, Captain Harry Holland *et al.*

The late Ian Geddes of Canadair was always on hand to assist in the earlier years of this project. When he passed away, Ron Pickler made sure that all my queries to Canadair were well taken care of. Below are listed the names of others who helped in ways large or small, some by contributing their always-enjoyable Sabre reminiscences: Don Ackert, D.R. Alton, Ralph Annis, Giorgio Apostolo, Bill Bain, J.H. Barger, A.J. Bauer, Richard Beaudet, Capt D. Becker, Sheldon Benner, C.D. Bricker, W.B. Bristowe, A.C. "Al"

Brown, James W. Brown, Bruce Burgess, Alex Burnett, S.E. "Syd" Burrows, B.R. Campbell, I.F. "Scotty" Campbell, R.D. "Bob" Carew, W.H. "Bill" Casley, L.A. Cheek, R.J. "Chick" Childerhose, Lewis Chow, R.G. "Bob" Christie, Ed Coe, G.H. "Check" Collison, Mike Cooper-Slipper, Peter Cope, Peter Crampton, Hugh Crawford, J.H. "Denny" Den Ouden, Bob Durnan, Paul Duyns, J.F. "Stocky" Edwards, Christian Emrich, Ziya Ertug, F.W. "Fred" Evans, Bill Ewing, R.W. "Ron" Fentiman, J.W. "Jim" Fiander, Bob Finlayson, I.H. "Sam" Firth, George J. Fitzgerald, Michael Fitzgerald, J.D. "Jim" Fitzpatrick, Bruce Fleming, D.C. "Dave" Fletcher, R.J. "Bob" Flynn, Jack Forbes, Wm. C. Ford, Ron Found, Ernie Gardiner, Jean Gaudry, P.M. Gerhardt, E.A. "Ernie" Glover, Ron Gowe, Herb Graves, John Greatrix, Bill Gunston, Dan Hagedorn, Ken Hagarty, Deacon Hall, Bob Hallowell, Tony Hannas, Peter Hargrove, Paul Hartman, Fred Hatch, M.J. Herriot, J. Barry Herron, L.J. "Lou" Hill, Col Joel R. Hinlo, R.A. "Bob" Hoover, Fred W. Hotson, Joe Houlden, Harry Hrischenko, Fred Isaacs, Russ Janzen, Bob Jones, George W. Jones, A/V/M J.E. Johnson, W/O Vic Johnson, K.E. "Ken" Johnston, Michael J. Kasiuba, F.D. "Danny" Kaye, Peter R. Keating, Dean Kelly, S.L. Kent, R.M.

"Bill" Kidd, Robert Kirby, B.J. "Buck" Kirlin, Manfred Knopp, Albert J. Koshul, Alfred W. Krüger, G.E. "Gerry" LaGrave, Arnie Leiter, K.C. "Ken" Lett, J.A. Omer Levesque, Howard Levy, Leonard W. Lilley, J.D. Lindsay, Bob Liscum, W.S. "Bill" Longhurst, Bob Lording, Mel Lundy, Jim Lyzun, Norm Malayney, John Marion, Paul Marshall, G.P. "Gerry" McCully, Alf McDonald, David McEwen, Don McIlraith, W.H. "Scotty" McKay, G.T. "Scotty" McLean, Jack McNulty, Dave Menard, John Meuse, R.G. "Bob" Middlemiss, George E. Miller, Jay Miller, Charles Moffatt, Ray Moneta, F.A. "Fred" Moore, Bob Morgan, Red Morris, D.J. "Don" Morrison, Peter Mossman, Chris Nissen, W.H. "Bill" Norn, Ed Norsworthy, Tom O'Dowd, Michael O'Leary, Ken Orr, Al Paddon, P.S. "Phil" Perry, R.S. "Ron" Poole, H.W.D. Prince, J.R. "Jim" Pugh, D.A. Purich, Bob Raven, Hans Redemann, L.J. Redman, R.D. "Dick" Richmond, Jack Ritch, Rodger Ritchie, Ron Robinson, J.L.A. Roussell, Lynn de Sansoucy, Robb Satterfield, Bruno Schönweiss, Bud Scouten, Jack Seaman, E.A. "Al" Seitz, C.R. "Bob" Simmons, D.B. "Don" Simmons, Eric G. Smith, Ken Smy, J.D. "Red" Somerville, John H. Spratley, W.J. "Bill" Stacey, Bill Stewart, Jan Stroomenbergh, Turbo Tarling, Claudio Tatangelo, Chris Terry, Reg Thatcher, David Thompson, G. J. "Jerry" Tobin, G.A. "Gerry" Turner, Georges Van Belleghem, J.E. "Jerry" Vernon, Hank Volker, Seigfried Wache, Douglas Warren, H.F. Wenz, Dave Wicks, J.D. Wiebe, Tom Wheler, the late Gordon S. Williams, W.A.C. Wilson, Wilf G. White, Harry Whiteman, Graham Wragg, Ron Wylie and Roberto Zambon.

The Milberry kids each helped in keeping this project rolling along. Matthew did research at the Directorate of History, and used his computer to help streamline parts of my operation. Kathleen, Simon and Stephanie all assisted in such essential chores as stuffing envelopes.

In addition, Roger Lindsay wishes to thank Alfie M. Alderson, Robin A. Brown, J.D. "Buzz" Burrey, Derek Burton, Richard Butcher, Phil Butler, Denis Casper, George H. Cole, Geoff Cruickshank, J.G. Davies, David Dorrell (Ed. *Air Pictorial*), Ken Ellis (Ed. *Flypast*), John Finch, Leslie C. Glover, Peter Gosden, Jed Gray, Alan W. Hall (Ed. *Aviation News*), John Harrison, Reg Havers, Martin Horseman (Ed. *Aircraft Illustrated*), Bill Ireland, Paul A. Jackson, John G. Johnson, Charles Keil, Günther Kipp, Ian H. Laurie, Gordon Macadie, Bruce MacDonald, A.S. Mawman, Ron Mettam, Dick Millward, Roy Montgomery, Richard Moore, Riccardo Nobili, Brian Pickering (Military Aircraft Photographs), the late Stephen Piercey, John D.R. Rawlings, Bruce Robertson, Norman J. Robertson, Al Statham, Trevor Stone, Ray Sturtivant, Eric Taylor, Chris Thomas, G. Rennie Turner, Dick Ward, David Watkins, Ian White and David Williams.

Those who assisted Gerhard Joos include Gerhard Albert, Rolf Batz,

Cockpit view of JA-232, a Luftwaffe Sabre. (Peter Nolde)

A trio of factory fresh Sabres on a photo trip near Montreal and flown by OFU pilots. (DND)

Ernst-Dieter Bernhard, Hans-Ulrich Flade, Willi Hahn, Lutz Geissler, Kurt Kahl, Dieter Kelle, Johannes Meinke, Hans Meinking, Hansjörg Laudam, Jürgen Puls, Reinhold Puchert, Joachim Rack, Günther Zirngibl and Walter Kretzschmer.

Organizations, squadrons, etc. which helped with various details include the Bangladesh Air Force,

Canadian Aviation Historical Society, Condor Flugdienst, Department of National Defence (Directorate of Flight Safety, Directorate of History, Directorate of Information Services, Photo Unit), Flight Systems Inc., General Flugsicherheit, Luftwaffe (JaboG.35, 43, JG 71, E-Stelle 61, WS 10), MBB Flugzeuge, Pakistan Air Force, Rockwell International and the South African Air Force Museum.

The 413 Squadron Sabre 2 on the jacket was painted for CANAV by Geoff Bennett of Moncton. Geoff was born in the UK, where he attended art college and served in the RAF from 1948-1952, flying a bit on Vampires.

Later he worked as an architectural draftsman, then joined the RCAF in 1957. He instructed on Harvards at Moose Jaw from 1958 to 1964, during which time he flew with the Goldilocks aerobatic team. From 1966 to 1977 he was with Maritime Command where he piled up over 5000 ear-shattering hours on the Argus. Upon leaving the service, Geoff "retired" into the MOT as instrument standards inspector in its Moncton operation. He has been painting seriously since 1967—all sorts of subjects, but mostly aircraft, and, in that area, mostly Argus (over 400 Argus paintings to date!).

Larry Milberry

The Sabre Comes to Canada

Early Jet Aircraft

Research into jet power had been going on in earnest throughout the 1930s in several countries, with the first flight of a jet aircraft, the Heinkel He 178, taking place in Germany in August 1939. In April 1941 the He 280V, the first jet fighter, made its initial powered flight. Though eight were built, no production followed. In May 1941 the British flew their first jet, the Gloster G.40. In October 1942 the first American jet, the Bell P-59A Airacomet, flew, and by war's end the Japanese and Russians had their own entries in

the jet fighter stakes. Certainly the Germans had the practical lead in development of combat jets, with the Messerschmitt Me 262 their biggest success. Over 1000 were built, but the oft-related story of Hitler disagreeing with his experts about how best to use the Me 262 explains Germany's failure to capitalize on its technological superiority. While the air force wanted the 262 to break the back of the Allied bombing offensive, Hitler insisted on using it as a ground attack weapon. This squabbling, and the dwindling German ability even to fuel its aircraft neutralized the

262's impact as a weapon.

Meanwhile, the British had turned out two promising jets, the Gloster Meteor and the de Havilland Vampire. By war's end the Meteor had seen limited combat, and the USAAF's Lockheed P-80 was undergoing operational trials. The pressure of war had compelled the major powers to dig deeply and quickly into the potential of the jet engine, which, even in its early forms, was recognized for its simplicity and reliability. The Korean War, just around the corner, would reinforce its potential.

The Me 262 was the first mass-produced combat jet fighter. It had a mildly swept wing. A proposed development would have had a fully swept wing, but the project was abandoned. North American later developed this wing in its basic form for the P-86. The aircraft shown has been restored by the USAF Museum and is part of its collection at Wright-Patterson AFB. (USAF Museum)

The RCAF's first jet was this Meteor F.3. It had a pair of 2000 lb. thrust Derwent engines and could reach 475 mph. This photo was taken at the Victory Aircraft plant, Malton, in October 1945. (K.M. Molson)

LtCol David Schilling's group of F-80 Shooting Stars refuels at Dow AFB, Maine, while returning from Europe on August 21, 1948. They had earlier made the first west-to-east jet crossing of the Atlantic. (USAF Museum)

First Transatlantic Jets

The early post-war years were a time of turmoil in scattered "hot spots" around the world, from China, where Mao's forces were about to drive out those of Chiang Kai-shek; to the Middle East, where newly formed Israel was fending off an Arab onslaught; to Berlin. On June 22, 1948, the Soviets imposed a blockade of Berlin, bringing Europe once again to the brink of war. This brought about the famous Berlin Airlift with the USAF and RAF undertaking a massive supply operation into the stranded city.

As there was an ever-present threat of the Soviets attacking Allied aircraft flying the corridors into Berlin, the Americans had to beef up their air defences, thus speeding along their first tactical transatlantic flight by jet fighters.

In fact, the very first jet crossing occurred July 14-15, 1948, when six Vampires from 54 Squadron, RAF Odiham, flew from Stornaway to Goose Bay via Iceland and BW-1 in Greenland in 8:18 hours flying time. This was an operational training and goodwill undertaking, the Vampires putting on displays at several Canadian and US locations during their visit. They flew back "across the pond" on August 26. But the USAF jet crossing

S/L Cal Bricker wearing the USAF immersion suit. He was serving on F-84s at Shaw AFB at this time. (via C.D. Bricker)

was no goodwill visit. It was Cold War business, even if it had been planned in the pre-blockade days to show the mobility of short-range jet fighters. With preparations, including route surveys by C-47, completed, 16 F-80s fired up at Selfridge AFB, Michigan, on July 12, 1948. Under Col David Schilling, CO of the 56th FB Group, they took off on their first leg, to Dow AFB, Maine. Next stop was Goose Bay, where the F-80s rendezvoused with the westbound RAF Vampires. Then, on to BW-1 in Greenland, and Iceland, and on July 21 they touched down at Odiham. Final stop was Fürstenfeld-

bruck in West Germany, where the fighters conducted several training missions with B-29s, before heading home. En route, they again met the RAF Vampires, this time at BW-1. Back at Selfridge, Schilling and his men resumed routine flying, but their mission had a lasting effect—the USAF had demonstrated to the Soviets that its jet fighter units had the mobility necessary to meet Communist threats anywhere.

Sabre Beginnings

The ancestry of the F-86 Sabre goes back to the Second World War and German aeronautical research, though the actual beginnings were at North American in California, where in early 1945 work was begun on a jet fighter for the US Navy. The company had already done several months of jet research when the navy contract was awarded. The outcome for the navy was the XFJ-1 straight-wing fighter which first flew in November 1946.

At the same time, North American was preparing a version of this design for the USAF, the XP-86. However, those at the design end of the air force version decided to use the results of some German research, and, once USAF approval was obtained, this appeared in the form of a swept wing. The radical XP-86 prototype was first flown at Muroc dry lake, California, on October 1, 1947. George Welch piloted it on the occasion, and on April 26, 1948, he dived the prototype through the sound barrier for the first time. Within a year, production F-86As were coming off the production line. On September 15, 1948, Maj R.L. Johnson piloted a Sabre at Muroc to establish a new world's speed record of 670.981 mph. In early 1949 the 94th Fighter Squadron at March AFB, California, became the first unit to fly the F-86.

Sabres for the RCAF

Late in the war Canada was itself involved in jet engine research. Several Canadians had worked in England at Power Jets Ltd., which was developing jet engines under Frank Whittle. Trans-Canada Air Lines was interested in a jet airliner for post-war use, and the RCAF had requirements for modern fighters for its post-war squadrons. One of these was for an all-weather interceptor, which was soon under development by the new Avro Canada firm, headed by the famous Roy Dobson, that had taken over the Victory Aircraft plant at Malton, Ontario.

The RCAF would also need a new day fighter. While the all-weather design, soon to be revealed as the CF-100, would guard northern regions against the threat of Soviet bomber attack, the day fighter would protect cities and strategic installations in the south. Besides, planning was already under way to form an alliance between Western Europe and North America to assure a free Europe. Thus, on April 4, 1949, the North Atlantic Treaty was signed by 12 Allies, Canada included. It was early decided that part of Canada's NATO contribution would be in European air defence, and that a modern fighter would be needed. With such considerations in mind, the RCAF went shopping but quickly realized that this was a no-contest situation—the North American F-86 was the best day fighter in the free world.

Canada's post-war industrial reorganization was guided by Prime Minister Mackenzie King's famous minister, C.D. Howe. It was Howe who cleared the way for Dobson to acquire Victory Aircraft so that the CF-100 and Avro Jetliner projects could proceed, and who likewise approved the formation of Canadair at the wartime Canadian Vickers plant in St. Laurent near Montreal. In charge of Canadair then was Benjamin Franklin, and under his energetic and imaginative leadership Canadair began a profitable venture converting C-47s to airline use, and building Canada's first modern airliner, the North Star. The

North Star had flown in 1946, and orders were signed with the RCAF, TCA and BOAC to build over 70 aircraft.

In 1946, when the North Star program was well under way, Franklin retired and Howe brought his old friend, Oliver West of Boeing in Seattle, back to head the operation. In 1937 Howe had called West in as one of his key men in establishing TCA. Once things were running smoothly at TCA, West returned to the States. This time, several other top personnel from Boeing also came to Montreal, including T.V. Chandler, T.J. "Ted" Emmert, Ian Manley, Harry McKeown, R.A. "Bob" Neale, Dean Stowell and Charles Ulsh, Kelly Smith and C.J. Heine of Douglas also arrived at this time, and there were other important "imports" as well. These seasoned experts filled top posts in such areas as sales, engineering, tooling, factory management, procurement, inspection, estimating and contracts.

In September 1946 Canadair was sold to the Electric Boat Co. of Groton, Connecticut, under John Jay Hopkins. Hopkins, who wanted to have greater control of Canadair, retired West, and C.D. Howe then, in

In-flight view of the North American XFJ-1 Fury. First flown November 27, 1946, the Fury later served in the US Navy squadrons, though only 30 production aircraft were built. Top speed of this Sabre progenitor was 568 mph. (Rockwell Int'l)

The prototype XP-86, first flown October 1, 1947 by George Welch of North American. (Rockwell Int'l)

Mainstay of the RCAF's day fighter squadrons right after the war was the North American P-51D Mustang. The first of 130 were delivered in 1947, and they served with 416 and 417 squadrons and the Air Armament School at Trenton. Later, they equipped several auxiliary squadrons. This line-up is of AAS Mustangs at Trenton, June 19, 1951. (DND PL130165)

Actual jet ops in the RCAF began with the Vampire F.3. Eighty-five were procured in 1948, serving initially with 410 at St.Hubert. This shows 17036 of 400 "City of Toronto" Auxiliary Squadron quite literally firing up. (via Tommy Wheler)

1950, installed one of his "dollar a year" men, J.G. "Geoff" Notman, as executive vice president, something to which Hopkins agreed so long as his own power was not undermined. Notman, who would, in fact, later become president of Canadair, was cousin of the then-Minister of National Defence, Brooke Claxton. He served the company for many years and gained a reputation for his competence and wonderful ability to get along with everyone, whether on the shop floor or in the executive office. In 1952 Electric Boat was acquired by General Dynamics.

"Cost of U.S. Jets 5 Times Vampires"
When word got out that the RCAF was to re-equip with Sabres, there was a sudden, though short-lived fuss in the Toronto press. A buy-British campaign was mounted, and arguments for the Vampire against the Sabre made headlines. On April 16, 1949, the Toronto *Telegram* reported that for the announced price to be paid by Canada

for 130 Sabres, it could have a fleet of 800 Vampires! The paper continued, "That Canadair Ltd., the Montreal firm which is to build the F-86, can build only 100 units and keep the cost down to the level set by North American who built 600, is highly unlikely. To be charged against the order for 100 will be the tooling cost, which is estimated to be at least $1,500,000, and which will have to be amortized completely on the small production level . . . Experts question the cost and time to prepare tooling and equip staff to handle fighter construction which is so far removed from the 4-engine transport work now under way at the plant. . . .

"Another problem posed by purchase of the F-86 is that of conversion of pilots. Under the Vampire training program, pilots are being checked out on Vampires after a comparatively short familiarization course on Harvards, which features ground handling at high speeds and approach procedures.

"The F-86, which has a much higher

landing speed due to its heavier wing loading, proves a bigger problem which will probably mean purchase of new advanced trainers. . . . Unless the RCAF training program is stepped up in the next few months, the F-86 could suffer a fate similar to the RCAF transports now in storage."

The news item ranted about other reasons for not purchasing the Sabre, and actually had the gall to claim that the Vampire was "the world's top-performance fighter," stating that it could reach 40,000 feet faster than the Sabre, then easily climb through 50,000 feet. The *Telegram* reached its own absolute ceiling by stating that the USAF was interested in the Vampire!

Several such articles appeared in Toronto papers and were little more than frantic attempts on the part of Toronto interests to counter the attention lavished on Montreal-based Canadair by the federal government in awarding it the Sabre contract, the initial one being for 100 aircraft, signed in August 1949. Toronto would soon be able to do little more than look enviously at Montreal as Sabres began pouring off the production lines. None of the press's claims ever proved out, not even the training insinuation.

Setting Up for Production

The first F-86 program manager at Canadair was Bob Raven, and he recalls some of the early times on the project:

On May 14, 1949 we made a trip out to North American in LA in the company's DC-3, CF-DXU. Aboard were Bill Lowe, head of the Canadian Commercial Corporation, and his wife, and a man named MacDonald, a legal counsel, and his wife. There was also "Chan" Chandler, manager of production, Dal Russel from purchasing,

and me. Mr. Lowe had a cheque with him for $250,000, made out to North American. It was the first instalment of a million dollars payable within the first year of our arrangement.

By this time, Canadair had been informed by the Department of Defence Production that the Sabres we were to build would always have to be constructed exactly as those built by North American, i.e., no Canadian design changes. The program would be under control of Canadair Manufacturing Division, led by R.A. Neale, VP Manufacturing. However, this arrangement didn't last long, and the RCAF won the battle in Ottawa to institute design changes. I believe that they budgeted about 15 per cent of the dollar value of the program for such ECPs (engineering change proposals) they had in mind. As a result, Canadair's plans were revised to handle the

program in its standard departmental manner; and I returned to the engineering department as project engineer on the Sabre.

The licence agreement between the CCC and North American covered the F-86 and its derivatives. This included an all-weather version, the F-86D. Now, the USAF wanted so many of the

Aerial view of Cartierville on September 12, 1954. Below is the complex where the Sabres were built, formerly Noorduyn's wartime Norseman and Harvard production facility. Running along it is Henri-Bourassa which intersects Laurentien Blvd. At that corner is a double hangar where Curtiss-Reid built Rambler biplane trainers in the late twenties. A bit down Laurentien can be seen some light aircraft and small hangars, site of the original Curtiss-Reid flying school, and farther down is the huge main Canadair complex where North Stars had been built, and where the Argus was about to appear on the production lines in about two years. (Canadair Ltd. P1-1688)

Another view of the Sabre plant, this one looking northerly across a part of Montreal that is now fully built-up. (Canadair Ltd.)

"D" improvements incorporated into the "A" that the F-86E was born; and Canadair had the right to all the manufacturing data for these aircraft without an increase in the licence fee.

The first F-86 assembled at Canadair consisted of many subassemblies and parts purchased from North American. These were extremely useful in tooling jig verification, and compliance to be interchangeable with NA manufactured assemblies.

I seem to recall that in late 1950 or early 1951 the RCAF sent a contingent to North American to resolve the question of whether Canada wanted the F-86D or E. I believe they selected the "E" on the basis that the "D" was still in the production design stage and would not be available for some time. There would be serious enough delays in the "E" program.

To maintain continuity at Canadair, and retain our workforce, "A" Sabres were initially built, then entered a modification and retrofit program without leaving the premises. The first order was for a batch of 100 Sabres at a planned rate of five per month. Our tooling was always to be kept up with USAF changes incorporated into the NA production line.

The Korean War upset all our best laid plans, and we eventually went to a rate of 10 per month until the supply of GFE (engines, radar, communication equipment, etc.) improved. Production finally reached 50 Sabres per month. In 1951 I became project engineer for the T-33 and George Burlton took over from me on the F-86.

Bob Raven

C.D. Howe at Work with the Sabre
One incident reported to have taken place in the early days of the F-86 at Canadair concerned the inimitable C.D. Howe. For many years he had almost run the country—he had been indispensable to Prime Minister Mackenzie King. His hand seemed to touch every major area of national development. He instigated Trans-Canada Air Lines; the Jetliner, CF-100 and CF-105 at Avro; the North Star at Canadair, then the Sabre; and manipulated such mammoth projects in the fifties as the St. Lawrence Seaway, and the Trans Canada Pipeline. During the war he was sometimes called "minister of everything." Few leaders of Canada ever had such energy, imagination or determination as the immigrant from south of the border.

The shortage of GE engines in the early days of Sabre production was used one day by Howe to advantage.

Orenda was developing Canada's first jet engine in the late forties, and typical of many a Howe-sponsored undertaking, it was a costly venture. Parliament would likely have been monitoring expenses and raising eyebrows as the bills poured in. At one point, in order to impress the government that the Orenda was of great national importance, Howe arranged a tour of Canadair.

One Friday afternoon (as the story goes), everyone in the plant went home for the weekend, and when they returned, an amazing discovery was made. Sabres all around flight test and on the production line were found to be engine-less. Now, part of this could have been put down to the slow GE delivery rate, but some Sabres had had their engines Friday afternoon. What had happened? Well, it seems that Howe had made arrangements to have the engines hurriedly removed and stashed out of sight. As he showed his group around, Howe lamented that in spite of the miracle of production Canadair had achieved, it was stymied for a lack of engines. If only something could be done to accelerate things at Orenda then the air force would soon have its Sabres. Apparently this little ruse had the desired effect.

Early Flight Tests
First to fly the Sabre in Canada was Alexander J. "Al" Lilly, Canadair's

chief test pilot. Al Lilly had begun his flying career on the Prairies, soloing at Moose Jaw in 1927. During the 1930s he served in northern Saskatchewan with the RCMP, but when he read an Imperial Airways advertisement for pilots, he applied, was accepted, and went to England just before the war to fly the Ensign airliner. When war broke out, Lilly returned to Canada, flying briefly with Canadian Airways on the Rapide and Beech 18, then instructing RCAF student pilots at the Moncton Flying Club. In 1941 he became chief test pilot for Ferry Command in Montreal, flying a wide variety of aircraft from Hudsons to Liberators, B-26s, Lancasters, PBYs and Mosquitos.

After the war, Lilly flew for Maritime Central Airways, but in 1946 joined Canadair, where his experience in aircraft certification and test flying was a key asset. At the time Canadair was involved in a program converting C-47s for the airlines and was about to begin test flying the North Star. Lilly made his first flight at Canadair on June 24 aboard a C-47 renovated for a Swedish operator. On July 15 Douglas

The original Canadair F-86, No. 19101, but carrying a company-type tail number and its famous CK-R code letters. This aircraft was built up largely from US-made parts and was basically an F-86A. The picture was taken on August 15, 1950, a few days after first flight. (Canadair Ltd. D6560)

test pilot Bob Brush and Al Lilly took the prototype North Star on its first flight. Later, while on a North Star demonstration tour in Europe, Lilly flew his first jets, the Vampire and Meteor.

When Canadair was chosen to build the Sabre, Al Lilly and Bill Longhurst were quickly groomed to take on the test flying program. In July 1950 they were sent to North American in California to look over the plant and the Sabre systems. No flying was allowed, as there was a shortage of J47 engines at the time, making familiarization flights of low priority. On this trip, Lilly also visited the Northrop plant where he test flew the C-125 Raider trimotor which Canadair was interested in producing.

In August 1950 Lilly visited Wright Patterson AFB near Dayton, Ohio, for a short jet course under Col Dick Johnson. His first flight was on August 1 in an F-80 (N80437). Four other F-80 trips followed quickly, and on August 3 Lilly flew a Sabre for the first time, an F-86A (49-1170). On his third Sabre flight, two days later, he exceeded Mach 1. He returned to Cartierville August 7, having logged eight hours on jets.

By this time the first Sabre (the only Canadair F-86A) was ready for test flying and had been towed over to Dorval (the runways at Cartierville were not yet ready for jet operations). On Aug-

Al Lilly wearing an early type of hard hat procured in the US. (Canadair Ltd. 6538)

Al Lilly after the first flight of the Canadair Sabre. From the left are Mr. Claxton, A/M Wilf Curtis, Geoff Notman, Dr. Solandt of the NRC, and Eric Nelson, Commercial Sales Manager at Canadair. (Canadair Ltd. 6537)

ust 8 Lilly flew 19101 initially, a 30-minute shakedown flight. A flight next day was limited to 15 minutes by an electrical failure, and flight three on August 10 lasted 25 minutes. There was no more flying until August 18 when Lilly flew the Sabre to Malton, whence it was towed to the Canadian National Exhibition for two weeks of display. September 16 Lilly flew an airshow for the Toronto Flying Club, and next day returned to Cartierville, completing the trip in a record 23 minutes. Things were quiet for a few days then Lilly made five flights in 19101, October 4-6. During this period, he was also flying on the North Star and C-47, as well as doing many of the proving flights on the C-5 VIP transport.

Meanwhile, production of the F-86E (known in Canada as the Mk.2) was getting under way. The program was accelerating rapidly. Al Lilly's log book shows many new Sabres tested in the late months of 1950 and early 1951:

November 6, 1950	19138
15	19215
	19216
25	19219
	19224
	19218
27	19227
29	19226

In-flight portrait of an early Sabre 2 on a test flight near Montreal. (Canadair Ltd. D10554)

February 6, 1951	19266
	19277
	19259
	19113
8	19267
19	19112
20	19285
29	19288
	19291
	19291
April 3	19316
8	19316
	19312
	19322
	19323
10	19324
15	19324
25	19326
	19239

In just a few months since hand-assembling its F-86A prototype, Canadair had been able to establish its production line and complete over 200 aircraft. Standards were so high that North American sent some of its people to see just how Canadair was able to do such an exceptional job.

In 1953 Al Lilly went over to sales at Canadair. By this time, flight test had grown considerably, and many civilian pilots were to fly Sabres from Cartierville in the coming years.

Bill Longhurst
Canadair's key test pilot throughout the Sabre era was W.S. "Bill" Longhurst. In the late thirties he had completed the aeronautical program at Central Technical School in Toronto, and also took flying lessons at nearby Barker Field from Fred Gillies. In early 1939 he travelled to England and joined the RAF. By May 1940 he was with 502 Squadron, Coastal Command, flying from Northern Ireland. He completed two tours, mostly on Whitleys, and by that time he and the OC were the only members of 502 left since they had begun their first tour together. Barely a year had passed.

In early 1941 Longhurst was posted to Montreal ferrying Hudsons, Liberators and other types across the Atlantic. Next he joined RAF Transport Command flying Liberators on communications duties. Other ferry postings included Palm Beach, Natal and San Diego. While in San Diego he evaluated the RY-3 transport, recommended it for the RAF and ferried the first one back to Dorval. An interesting interlude occurred in the summer of 1943 when he piloted a Dakota towing a Waco glider from Montreal to Prestwick via Goose Bay, BW-1 and Reykjavik.

Following the war, Longhurst flew briefly with Don McVicar and on other minor ventures until 1948 when he was asked by Al Lilly to join Canadair. Before long he was involved with the North Star. With the decision to build Sabres in Montreal, he and Al Lilly checked out on the F-80 and F-86. Longhurst was soon busy at Canadair flying

production Sabres. His tasks were to be endless, as development proceeded. At one point, there was concern about asymmetric slat deployment on Sabres, with several incidents and accidents reported. Longhurst test flew a Sabre to evaluate this problem. The slats on one wing were taped down for the flights. When the one side deployed, sure enough, control was lost, but Longhurst discovered quickly that as soon as he eased off on the stick and G dissipated, the slat would retract and normal flight would be resumed. So it was a matter of training the pilots to handle another emergency situation coolly.

Test flying is usually routine and often boring, but Longhurst had his occasional thrilling flight. Canadair conducted first flights and much experimental flying on such Canadair types as the Argus, Yukon, CF-5, CF-104 and CL-84 VTOL aircraft. He finally left Canadair in 1971 and took a biology and computer science degree at Concordia University; then a posting at Queen's University in Kingston in cancer research.

Busy Test Pilots

Another of Canadair's long-time Sabre test pilots was G.T. "Scott" McLean. He had joined the RCAF in 1941, instructed at Borden, and flown Mosquitos with 107 Squadron, RAF. After the war he ran a small flying school at Uplands, then instructed at Amsterdam for KLM on the DC-3, DC-4 and Constellation. Before joining Canadair

Mach .96 range and found that by throwing out the dive brakes control could be instantly regained.

McLean and the other test pilots rarely had anything out-of-the-ordinary to report about the Sabre. Everything was so routine that on occasion they would go looking for trouble. One little "game" was to seek out the nastiest-looking thunderhead and fly right into it—just for the fun of it, you understand. That sometimes resulted in flameout, and a few good jolts to the airplane. But everyone had the greatest of faith in that sturdy North American airframe. The main thing McLean does remember is that the Sabre era at Canadair was one of tremendous activity, and work days meant flying from early morning till

Canadair's key test pilots during the Sabre era: Bruce Fleming, Bud Scouten, Scotty McLean, Bill Longhurst, Hedley Everard, Bill Kidd and Ian McTavish. (Canadair Ltd.)

instrument engineer Gordie Hicks recalled one such flight: "Bill Longhurst was to take 19200, the one and only F-86 Mk.3, to 40,000 feet, then pitch over for a high Mach dive. The resulting steep angle caused a spanner which had been carelessly left in the cockpit by a ground crew to jam the stabilizer hydraulic actuator. When he began pulling out, Longhurst reported that the elevator control was stuck but that he was staying with the aircraft as long as possible to try to free the controls. Success was reported only when the Sabre was down to minimum recovery altitude. Post-flight inspection showed that the spanner was freed only after it had been bent by stick pressure applied by Longhurst."

Later in his career, Bill Longhurst

in 1953 he flew a Lodestar from Malton for Canada Packers and worked for the DOT as a check pilot. At the DOT McLean met various pilots from Canadair and was soon lured away by them to fly Sabres. Although he had never flown jets, he made a quick transition (1½ hours on the T-bird) and went straight to work.

McLean notes that nearly all Sabre flying at Canadair was straight production work—very little test and development, as the aircraft was long since a proven design. There were the occasional special programs, though, including flight research into extended wingtips. On this, McLean and Bill Longhurst made numerous low-level runs, determining that at high speed the Sabre would run out of aileron control. These runs were harrowing at times, speed brakes being needed to dampen the onset of control loss. McLean and Hedley Everard also discovered the details leading to frozen controls while diving the Mark 6 in the

sundown, and often on weekends, sometimes flying six or eight different machines in a day. For, while the Sabres were coming down the line, so were hundreds of T-33s.

Just as the last Sabres were being completed, Canadair was launching several important projects, and McLean was soon involved with test flying on the Argus, Yukon, CL-44 and Convair 540. Later he took over the company's sales and service office in Ottawa, which he continued manning through 1986.

Sandford Bruce Fleming was also at Canadair through the Sabre and Starfighter years. Fleming, a Montrealer, had joined the RCAF in 1942, making his first flight at No.13 EFTS at St-Eugène, Quebec, on January 27, 1943. After further training at Uplands, Charlottetown and in the UK, Fleming was posted to 58 Squadron, RAF Coastal Command, where he flew a tour on Halifax 3s. At war's end, he converted to Beaufighters, and finished up overseas on Dakotas with 435 Squadron.

Back in Montreal, Fleming did some routine ferrying for the Babb Co. and joined 401 Squadron at St. Hubert. On May 30, 1949, he flew the Vampire for the first time. In early June he went to Canadair to fly DC-3s and North Stars, but before long found himself back in the air force, flying Sabres with 441 Squadron under S/L Andy MacKenzie. He volunteered for duty in Korea and in March 1952 joined the 336th FIS at Kimpo, flying F-86As and Es. On 82 missions, Fleming was to have several scrapes with the MiG-15. Later, he flew in the Air Division from North Luffenham and Baden. When the wing moved temporarily to Baden, Fleming had a decision to make about a good friend, Bijoux, his poodle. He solved this matter by tucking Bijoux behind him in his Sabre and flying to Germany. Once he landed, Fleming dropped Bijoux down onto the wing and as he taxied in, the sight of a Sabre with a white poodle loping along behind it must have caused a double-take or two!

Fleming left the RCAF in July 1955, not before he did a bit of flying with the OFU, and was one of the culprits responsible for tearing up the barracks at Goose Bay following some Random shenanigans. He rejoined Canadair in January 1957, flying the Sabre, Yukon, Cosmo, F-104 and other types, including the Challenger. Fleming's last Sabre trip was in 23102 on February 18, 1966, flying chase on CF-104 No. 701.

R.M. "Bill" Kidd joined Canadair in 1952. He had originally trained as an RNZAF cadet in Canada during the war. Later he flew Wellingtons and Stirlings, was shot down, evaded capture, and was then posted to Ferry Command at Dorval. Post-war he joined BOAC and became one of the early Comet captains, and one of the first to pass 500 hours flying jets.

Kidd recalls that the Sabre program was extremely busy but very smoothly run. One week the flight test department handled 180 flights, and there was often dawn to dusk activity. To Kidd, the success of the Sabre program at Canadair was a major feather in the cap of Canada's aircraft industry.

On August 14, 1961, the first two CF-104 flights were made in Canada by Bill Kidd (12703) and Glen Reeves of Lockheed (12704). Kidd later flew extensively on the CL-44 and Argus

A Sabre 5 pranged at Cartierville by CEPE test pilot F/L Ken Olson. (Canadair Ltd.)

before leaving Canadair for CAE in 1967.

Test pilot Bud Scouten started flying in Winnipeg in 1936. He flew in the bush for a while, then joined TCA on Lockheed 14s, first on the Prairies, then on runs out of Malton. In 1941 he went to Ferry Command in Dorval. After the war, as so many did at the time, he roamed from one job to another for a while—to Nassau, West Palm Beach, and finally to FAMA in Buenos Aires flying DC-4s. He was home in Manitoba in 1948 when Al Lilly called. Canadair needed a good pilot with DC-4 experience to help with the North Star program. That was the beginning of a career for Scouten that would last until 1971.

When the Sabre went into production at Cartierville, Scouten soon got involved. As he hadn't flown jets, Lilly sent him off to Scoudouc for a checkout on the T-33 under F/L Mac Graham. Then it was to work, keeping the flight test hangar from clogging up with Sabres and T-birds.

Ed Coe had begun his flying career in the twenties, soloing in California in

1929. He went to England in 1941 to ferry aircraft around the country, and in 1943 began working for Ferry Command from Dorval. After the war he returned to the US, running a small airport in Vermont. In 1950 Al Lilly enticed him back to Canada. Coe became one of the real "solid citizens" there, primarily flying Sabres and T-33s, though adding aircraft like the Argus and Cosmo later on. In 1965 Ed Coe retired and settled in Glen Falls, NY.

Over the years, many a test pilot would ply his trade with Canadair. One of these, Glen Lynes of Montreal, had attended a test pilot's course in England just after the war. He was an outstanding pilot and did much of the early Sabre demonstration flying for Canadair. He later moved to Avro at Malton, where he was killed October 20, 1955, flying a CF-100. Ian McTavish had been a Mosquito pilot in the war and later spent some years with Canadair. Les Benson joined the company after flying Sabres at North Luffenham and with the OFU. Besides, many Central Experimental and Proving Establishment personnel flew Sabres and T-33s at Cartierville, and even in 1986 some of the flight test personnel are pilots who flew Sabres. These include Doug Adkins (chief test

20

pilot) and Bob Flynn, a company Challenger pilot at the Windsor Locks, Conn., plant.

In the Forefront

Canadair had accomplished a major coup in establishing its Sabre operation almost overnight. Within months of Al Lilly's historic flight of August 8, 1950, the company had a production line running, an army of workers trying its best to keep up with activity. But Canadair was only part of the story. At Malton, Avro Canada was being even more innovative. In 1949 it had flown North America's first jet transport, the C.102 Jetliner. While North Stars and Sabres were big news around Montreal, the Jetliner was making headlines in New York, Chicago, Miami and Winnipeg, setting new records almost every time it took off. Alongside it was the mighty CF-100, for its time an awesome all-weather jet interceptor. And both had been designed and built in Canada. Avro's engine division was simultaneously developing engines that would be unrivalled anywhere and power the CF-100 and later Sabres.

Elsewhere in the Canadian industry things in the post-war years seemed bright. At de Havilland in North Toronto the Chipmunk, Beaver and Otter were attracting attention. Fairchild at Longueuil was building a rugged bushplane, the Husky. At Fort Erie the Canadian-designed Fleet 80 Canuck was being built. Though not all these ventures would prove out in the end, these were surely exciting days, and if those in the industry were optimistic, it was with good reason.

Hectic Times

The first Sabre 2 flew January 31, 1951, with Bill Longhurst at the controls. Development of the more powerful Orenda engine was meanwhile booming along at Malton. It was first test flown in a Lancaster in June 1950, then was fitted into an F-86A by North American in California and test flown initially by Maj R.L. Johnson at Edwards AFB that October. As Sabre 2s were being completed and Canadair's flight test department was hard pressed to keep up with the volume of work, things were being readied to switch production to the new engine; the first Orenda Sabre made its Cartierville debut September 25, 1952, Scotty McLean doing the flight. On June 30, 1953, Bill Longhurst flew the first production Orenda Sabre. By that time, with Sabre production barely three years old, some 800 aircraft had been turned out.

One of those on the scene during these hectic days was Hank Volker,

Sabre production line at Cartierville in the early fifties. Wings, front and rear fuselage sections, and aircraft taking shape can all be seen. (Canadair Ltd.)

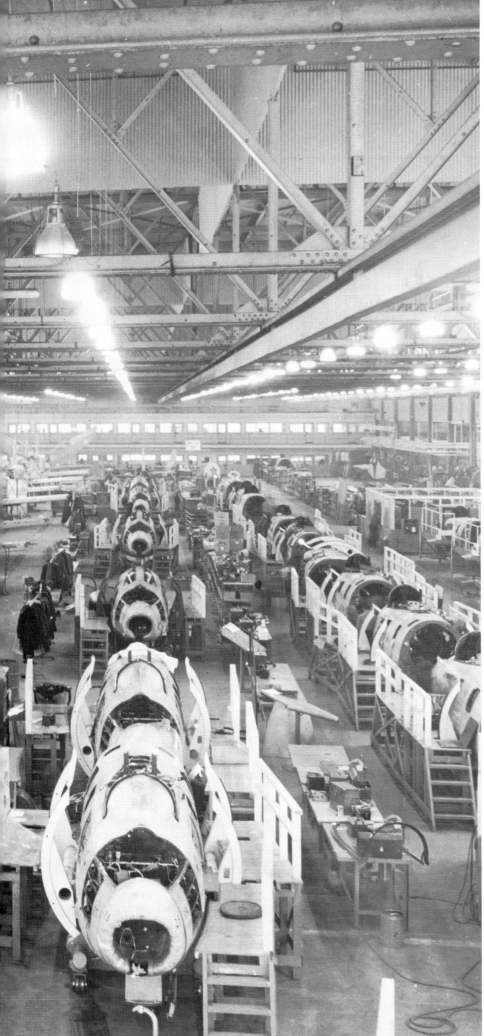

who writes, "I joined Canadair in the spring of 1952, working at first with the Service Department in Plant 2 on Bois Franc Road. My first impression of the Sabre program was when John de Vries, in charge of quality control, showed me the enormous production line in the main assembly shop. Most impressive was the wing assembly position—joining of the centre section and outer wing panels. This was accomplished with the individual panels suspended from a hoist while the operator installed the internal wrenching bolts and barrel nuts on the periphery of the spar box joint faces. Also impressive was the functional test area for landing gear and flight controls, especially the cycling of the landing gear and doors—brisk and noisy—in sequence: doors open, gear up, doors close, doors open, gear down, etc., etc. It was a great show for visitors and employees alike.

"Also great to watch was the regular test flying from Cartierville's two runways. Usually the tarmac around Plant 2 was packed with shiny new Sabres, often bearing interesting markings.

"Technically, the Sabre was a whole new venture for Canada's aircraft industry—the last word in the engineering sense; thus, quite a challenge with its fully-powered flight controls and advanced structure."

Tail No.	First flight
XB856	May 4, 1953
XB834, '857	5
XB836, '837, '838	7
XB861, '862, '864	8
XB858, '865	11
XB867	12
XB860, XD706	19
XB859, '866, '868, XD707, '708, '709, '710, '712, '713	20
XB863, XD711, '714	21
XD717	22
XD715, '718, '719, '720	25
XD716	26
XB839, XD724	27
XD723, '726	28
XD721, '722	29
Total first flights: 38	

First flight dates, May 1953, for a series of Sabre 4s indicates the rapid production pace at Canadair in the early 1950s.

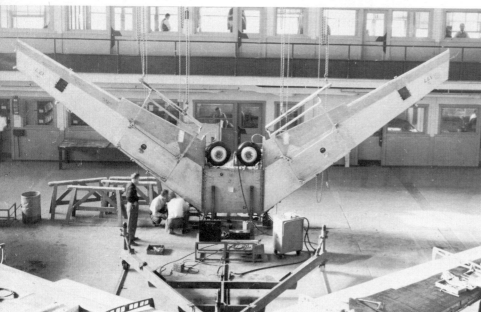

(Above and top right) Three more impressive views of production on the Sabre line. Note the rails along which major sections were easily rolled, and how the assembled product moves along a few inches above the floor. One can just about hear the din created by all this activity, and sense the exuberant feeling of the time.

(Right) Three views showing installation of a J47 into a Canadian Sabre. (Canadair Ltd.)

24

Sabre 1292 on jacks during the landing gear system check in the plant. (Canadair Ltd.)

The Red Indians Go Overseas

The RCAF's first post-war squadron to go overseas was 421, the Red Indians. It had formed at Chatham September 15, 1949, under S/L R.T.P. Davidson, a well-known wartime fighter pilot. 421 began with a few Harvards, but in September it started equipping with Vampires. The year 1951 was spent working up on the Vamps and late in the year word came of a move to RAF Odiham in Hants.

The squadron was transferred to Odiham January 16-29, 1951 on three North Star trips. The first arrived with S/L Davidson, three officers and 16 men. Back-up for the airlift was provided by RAF Hastings. No aircraft were taken overseas as the plan was to borrow RAF Vampires and Meteors. The first Vampires arrived January 23 and by February 2, 421 had a full complement of 24, and a few Meteor 7s for dual training.

Flying commenced immediately, with pilots doing some basic famil trips, then launching into the usual training flights and exercises. The point of the whole operation was to familiarize the RCAF with fighter ops in the post-war European air environment, and thus train a cadre of pilots before establishment of RCAF wings in NATO.

Typical activities took place May 14-15, 1951, with the squadron diarist writing: "First early readiness—breakfast at 0630 hours. Readiness at 0730.

Vampire 5s of 421 Squadron in May 1951 while the Red Indians were operating from RAF Odiham. (DND PL51833)

First section scrambled at 0750. Second section at 0820, third at 0830. This was an exercise with Royal Navy and 3rd Division USAF flying B-29s. HMS *Indomitable* and HMS *Swiftsure* cruised up the English Channel and were 'attacked' by B-29s. 421 Squadron was

S/L Davidson heads up a formal squadron photo. In back are Howie Tetlock, Ken Thorneycroft, Bruce Sheasby, Arch Debenham, Al Milne, Bob Vincent, John Greatrix and Hap Day. Seated are Bill Paisley, John Hicks, John Rainville, the OC, Fred Evans, Bud McKay, Lloyd Skaalen. In front are Jack Walton, Jack Newsom, Mark Sauder and Bob Wood. Most would soon go on to fly the Sabre. Davidson would also fly a tour in Korea. (DND PL50708)

scrambled to provide fighter protection. Many interceptions were made and much good experience gained in attack on heavy aircraft.'' On the 15th he wrote, ''Readiness at 0930 hours with the squadron airborne at 0940 to intercept Meteor VIIIs at 35,000. Scrambled again about 1110 hours to intercept B-29s. On immediate readiness at 1315 hours. Scrambled at 1330 hours but no interceptions carried out. Night flying—four shifts without incident. Heavy day for all pilots concerned.''

In August the squadron deployed to Celle, Germany, and the next month took part in Exercise Pinnacle, mainly on bomber intercepts. Flying during this time was busy—in August 502:35 hours on Vampires and 47:30 on Meteors. But in October things began to wind down as 10 Vampires were handed back to the Brits. Organization Order 114/51 spelled things out: ''421(F)Sqn RCAF has been located at

F/L C.J. ''Hap'' Day and F/O Mark Sauder, 421ers at Odiham, May 26, 1951. Day was killed later in a Sabre crash. (DND PL50932)

Getting ready for some flying activity at Odiham. (DND PL50937)

RAF Station Odiham since January 1951 for the purpose of obtaining training in operational techniques in close cooperation with RAF units. The tour of duty was planned for approximately one year's duration, therefore it has been decided that this squadron is to be returned to Canada by 15 December, 1951.''

The Red Indians stood down at Odiham on December 1. A few days earlier 410 Squadron had opened for business at North Luffenham as No.1 Wing began its build up. 421 went home, this time to St. Hubert, converted to Sabres, and later in 1952 was back in Europe.

F/L Omer Levesque, first Canadian to fly the Sabre (May 1950), is briefed at Canadair by Al Lilly in June 1951. (Canadair D5806)

Regular Troops Fly the Sabre

In 1950 the RCAF began preparing its regular fighter pilots to fly the F-86. Perhaps the first mini-course on the Sabre for squadron pilots took place at Larson AFB in Washington state, and it included pilots Ray Greene, John Marion, Don Morrison and Grant Nichols. Their course ran from November 22 to December 14 on the early F-86A. Along with Gil Guerin and Claude LaFrance, Morrison and Nichols were the first RCAF post-war pipeliners to fly jets. They had converted to the Vampire at the Central Flying School, Trenton, two years earlier. At Larson, Don Morrison logged 9:10 hours on the Sabre. He recently recalled: "We returned to Canada to do the initial acceptance and pilot training on the F-86s produced by Canadair. The first 20 aircraft built had a four-pound breakout force on the control column. These Sabres were difficult to fly in formation, but a modification to a reduced force with a built-in feel system improved later aircraft considerably. The original batch was updated by Canadair.''

Test pilot Paul Hartman, then flying with the RCAF's Experimental and Proving Establishment, confirms Morrison's contention: "The problem was

Checking out on the Sabre. Entries from F/O D.J. Morrison's log book show flights at Larson AFB in late 1950.

easily solved. Close adherence to design tolerances during manufacture, installation of rubber bungee cords of correct tension to provide stick forces commensurate with stick movement, and correct setting of aileron and elevator trim motor response and torque loads, resulted in lowering the aileron and elevator control stick breakout forces to two and three pounds respectively. The result was ex-

Certificate presented to RCAF pilots on the Sabre course at Larson.

Three of the early RCAF pilots to fly the Sabre did so while on course at the USAF Experimental Test Pilot School at Muroc Air Base (now Edwards AFB), California. From the left are Bob Christie, Gordon Bennett and Ray Greene. Christie reports, "Ray and I were on the course that started in early July 1950. About Christmas Gord joined us. Ray and I then went to Wright Field, Ohio. I worked at fighter test for Dick Johnson, and Ray worked with cargo test but also flew some fighters. When we returned to Canada in the fall of 1951, Ray and Gord went to Arnprior to work with the NAE, and I went to Rockcliffe with E&PE. I was supposed to fly at the CNE in 1953 but was working on a priority Sabre program, so Ray went down to do the air show there. He was killed when he crashed into Lake Ontario on September 19. His son, John, later became a pilot in the USAF, lately flying F-15s at Luke AFB." (via R.G. Christie)

Happy looking gang of Canadair flight test people with CEPE pilot Terry Evans. Note that this is one of the "two-seat" Sabres! (Ron Robinson)

cellent aileron and elevator control feel. Some of the first Canadair-built F-86Es went to the USAF in Korea for evaluation and pilots there were very impressed with the aircraft. I later spoke with a USAF pilot who reported that there was considerable competition among pilots in Korea to fly the Canadair Sabres because of superior handling qualities."

A number of other RCAF pilots were getting their introduction to the F-86 with the USAF in 1950. Actually, the first of all was F/L Omer Levesque who was sent on exchange to the 4th FIW at Langley, Virginia, in the spring. Another was E.G. "Irish" Ireland. He was a wartime Spitfire pilot, with a 109 and a pair of 190s to his credit in 1944. He was one of the originals forming No.1(F)OTU at St. Hubert in 1949 and in November 1950 was sent to Kirtland AFB, New Mexico, on a Sabre course. He logged 19:20 hours before returning to Chatham,

where he was CFI on Vampires. During this time other RCAF crews were also in the States preparing for arrival of the CF-100. Some were crewing on F-94s, others taking intensive airborne interception/nav courses. These were truly pioneering times.

Technical Training
With the advent of jet aircraft like the F-86, CF-100 and T-33, the RCAF had to adopt new means of teaching air and ground crew about their intricacies. Thus, the Mobile Training Unit (MTU) was established (later known as Field Technical Training Units, or FTTUs). Initially, 10 hand-picked air force techs were selected to get the MTU rolling, and F/L Dick Skuce was placed in charge. Sabre 19103 was dedicated to the cause, being ferried to St. Hubert from Canadair, and James W. Brown, one of the instructing techs, recalls how it served: "At St. Hubert, every pilot and aero engine tech had his chance to run up Sabre '03, and, though it had countless starts, it never flew while serving with us. In those days, the J47 was allowed five 'hot starts' (starts where fuel, pooled in the tail-pipe, ignited and could lead to damage to the engine or airframe). Our Sabre had arrived with two, and we immediately added a third. So we had an aircraft with two to go, and 12 squadrons of personnel to train! We soon learned that if our energizer was fully up to scratch we would always get a good start, and with attention paid to

that detail, our much-started Sabre made it in the end.

"In early 1952 our MTU moved to Chatham. There, along with the main systems, we taught the operation of the ejection seat. Later, we received some letters of appreciation from pilots who had had the occasion to use them."

Lester A. Cheek was involved in the early days of the MTU:

In the spring of 1946 Camp Borden was activated as a technical training unit. Personnel were transferred into No.1 Technical Training School and trained as instructors in the basic aircraft trades. When the Canadian government decided to equip NATO Squadrons with Sabres, the RCAF adopted the training method in use by the US Air Force, i.e., Mobile Training Units. RCAF Training Command had a large instructor establishment to draw on.

In the fall of 1949 seven instructors, WO2 Cheek, F/S de Maurivez and Stevens, Sgts Alford, Barton, Brown and Webster were sent on temporary duty to North American Aviation in Los Angeles, where they joined a larger group of RCAF personnel under S/L Jim Hemsley. The latter were to staff the Technical Services Unit at Canadair when the Sabre went into production.

The instructors spent six weeks on a company-sponsored Sabre familiarization and maintenance course. Unfortunately, training panels were not available and aircraft in various stages of production were used for instructional purposes. The aircraft at that time was the model 1A with a General

The RCAF's tech group is toured around the flight line at the North American plant in Los Angeles during their course there in 1949. (via L. Cheek)

Electric J47 engine. An interesting point was that the F-86 was originally designed with straight wings but information returned to the US at the end of World War 2 showed that the Germans had made considerable progress with swept wing research. As a result, North American decided to adopt the idea and the Sabre fuselage was lengthened approximately five feet and the wings swept back.

Following our course, the instructors proceeded to Otis Air Force Base on Cape Cod. There a squadron was in transition and a mobile training unit was on site to facilitate training. Three weeks were spent with the unit, gaining familiarization and experience on the use of the various panels and training methods. When finished at Otis, the instructors returned to Camp Borden. Technical publications, drawings, etc., given to each instructor had to be forwarded through our diplomatic channels because of the classified nature of

the material. This material was never delivered to the individuals; consequently nothing more happened until October 1950.

In October 1950, the seven originals were transferred to RCAF Station St. Hubert, and were joined by three additional instructors, WO2 Herriot (armament), F/S Kitchen (radar) and Cpl Barret (wireless). The plan evolved to the effect that the team would come under Air Defence Command for duty and discipline and under Training Command, Trenton, for instructional purposes. Our normal work day was to be spent at Canadair. To this end a vehicle (World War II ambulance) was supplied to transport the team from St. Hubert to Cartierville and return daily. One of the instructors doubled as the driver.

The winter 1950/51 was spent at Canadair, which by now had the Sabre in production and was also building the panels for the Mobile Training Unit. There were seven or eight major panels, each displaying a specific and vital aircraft system. Actual aircraft controls were employed and the components were sectionalized wherever

possible so that the selected action could be viewed by the student. During this time syllabi of training and instructional notes were produced for pilots converting from other types of aircraft to the Sabre, and others for technicians in maintenance and servicing for seven different trade specialties. Also during this period, ADC decided that it would be more advantageous to upgrade the squadrons at St. Hubert rather than move the training facility to other bases. As a result, semi-permanent classrooms were constructed on the second floor of the base workshop building by the Station Engineering Section.

The commencement date for the first course and number of personnel trained evades me, however the Air Division comprised 12 Sabre squadrons and to the best of my knowledge, few if any personnel participated in those squadrons without passing through the MTU. To show the support the school received from higher authority, I recount the following incident. On the Friday preceding the Monday opening of the school, G/C Somerville, commanding officer at St. Hubert, asked me if we were all set to go; I replied that we were, but I was a little concerned that we were all NCOs and our students would all be commissioned officers; there could be problems of punctuality and attendance. The G/C replied, "Don't worry, they will be there on time because I'll lead them in, I'm putting myself on the first course." He was as good as his word. As long as I was with the MTU I never had an instructor complain about any problem with an officer or airman on course.

The MTU staff was increased to 18 instructors plus a clerk and a commissioned officer. The late F/O Bill MacDonald was placed in charge. In June 1952, Herriot and I left the MTU for the Officers Training School in London, Ont. On being commissioned, I was transferred to No.1 Operational Training Unit, Chatham, N.B., to become the OC Servicing Flight. During my stay in London, the initial upgrading of the squadrons had been completed at St. Hubert and the MTU, and most of the staff moved to Chatham. My arrival there in October coincided with a very tragic event in that the first and I believe only airman

The RCAF's original group of Sabre technical instructors. In the back are Sgt Jack Alford, Sgt Jimmy Brown, Cpl Slim Barrett, FS Ron Kitchen and Sgt Ross Barton. In front are FS C.H. Stevens, FS de Maurivez, WO1 Lester Cheek, WO2 Murray "Doc" Herriot and Sgt Bill Webster. (via L. Cheek)

to do so lost his life by being sucked into the intake of a Sabre jet.

No.1(F)OTU became the upgrading unit for pilots selected to fly the Sabre. It had three flights. First, Conversion Flight, with T-33 dual training aircraft for conversion from Harvards to jets. Second was Tactical Flight, in which pilots were taught formation flying pertaining to combat tactics, and how to use the aircraft as a weapon. Third was Gunnery Flight. In this flight, aircraft were armed and then flown, usually in a section of four (instructor and three students) to a firing range where they could employ the tactical lessons learned and at the same time sharpen their skills as marksmen. To facilitate this operation a Mustang towing a "flag" would proceed to the firing range and present a target for the Sabres. The ammunition loaded into each aircraft would have been previously dipped in a wax-like substance of different colours and the colour of the ammo loaded on each aircraft was recorded. As the bullets penetrated the flag they left a distinct coloured ring around the hole. Following the exercise, the Mustang would fly over the aerodrome and release the flag, which would be retrieved by the armourers. It was then stretched out against a backdrop so the hits could be counted and identified. There was considerable excitement when the students landed and participated in the assessment.

Flying the Mustang was not without its hazards. On one occasion the pilot taxied into the hangar area, shut down and climbed out screaming, "Where is he? I'll kill him." It happened that the pilot was flying along, constant speed, nice and level as a good target tow ship should, when all of a sudden he felt a violent jolt and found himself staring straight ahead at mother earth. It seems that an overly zealous student, determined to present a high score, pressed his attack too close and in breaking away picked up the tow cable, standing the Mustang on its nose. Fortunately the cable broke and the Mustang returned undamaged. There was no difficulty in identifying the culprit—he brought back a Sabre with a damaged slat and a cut in the leading edge extending back to the front spar.

The Sabre was not considered supersonic. It lacked the engine power to attain such speeds in level flight, but in a dive it could break the sound barrier and produce a credible sonic boom. The Commanding Officer at Chatham received a letter from the CO at Trenton requesting Chatham to supply a Sabre to produce a sonic boom for Air Force Day 1953. Chatham's CO obliged and at a subsequent mess meeting read a letter from the CO at Trenton thanking him for his cooperation but now wanting to know if the officers at Chatham would contribute to the repair of all the television antennas and windows damaged on the station.

In July 1954, I left Chatham for No.4 Fighter Wing, Germany, to be OC Repair Flight. The Air Division, with its headquarters at Metz, had four wings, each with three squadrons of 25 aircraft, 300 Sabres in all.

At one time a Sabre was leased back to Canadair to facilitate a sales program for the Swiss Air Force. Although Canadair was unsuccessful in selling the Swiss, the aeroplane was returned to No.4 Wing bearing a Swiss mountain climber's badge. The Swiss airmen were reported to have said that the Sabre was the best damn mountain climber they had ever seen.

The Sabre was a rugged aircraft. Wrinkled and bent from overstressing, they usually came home. It was with regret that the famous aerobatic team, the Golden Hawks, had to be terminated to give way to the more economical Snow Birds, flying Tutors.

Lester A. Cheek

The Squadrons Take Shape

F/O D.J. "Moe" Morrison leads a flight of 410 Sabre 2s from St. Hubert just before the squadron set sail for England. (DND)

410 Squadron

The first RCAF squadron to equip with Sabres was No.410. It had become Canada's first jet squadron when it began equipping with Vampires under S/L R.A. "Bob" Kipp in late 1948. The squadron soon gained fame as it toured Canada and the United States putting on spectacular air shows with its Blue Devils demonstration team. In 1950 it was three months on the road with its Vampires on Exercise Sweet Briar, which centred in Alaska and the Yukon.

The squadron diary notes that on April 10, 1951, 410 had one Sabre at its temporary Dorval base. It had been flown over from Canadair by F/L Doyle, but had to go back to the plant next day on account of mechanical problems. Meanwhile, the squadron had to content itself flying two Harvards as it had relinquished its Vampires to the auxiliary. Finally, on May 19, two Sabres showed up; then three more on the 25th. Soon there was a full complement of Sabres and flying was beginning to build up.

In November 1951, 410 became the first squadron in No.1 RCAF Air Division and prepared to sail aboard HMCS *Magnificent* for the UK, where it would be based at North Luffenham. One of the young pilots to make the trip was F/O Robin "Red" Morris. He had joined the RCAF in 1949, making his initial flight April 11 at Centralia in a Harvard. In less than a year he was at Chatham where, on April 17, 1951, he made his first Vampire flight. He joined 410 the following month, and took a Sabre (19119) up for the first time on May 29. On September 4, 13 and 18 Red ferried 19151, 19163 and 19150 respectively to Norfolk, Virginia, where the squadron's Sabres were cocooned by the US Navy, then loaded aboard ship (24 above, 11 below decks). After these ferry flights, the 410 pilots took commercial flights back to Dorval. Some were reportedly indignant when refused permission to carry their parachutes aboard the airliners!

Life at North Luffenham was to be exciting, to say the least. It was a fighter pilot's heaven, with intensive flying whenever weather allowed. There were few restrictions, with almost any aircraft in the skies being fair game for the Sabres of 410 (and later 439 and 441). Red Morris was involved in air combat with two RAF Vampire F.B.5s on August 11, 1952, when the

A 410 Sabre is hoisted aboard HMCS *Magnificent* at dockside, Norfolk, Virginia. (via Bill Bain)

Under way. The "Maggie" steams on the open sea with her cargo of Sabres destined for 1 Wing, North Luffenham. (via D.J. Morrison)

F/O Tom Lauzon of 410 steers for the RCN. But fear not, Lauzon had been in the merchant navy during the war, so knew something about boats. (via Bill Bain)

F/O Morrison does some target shooting aboard ship heading for Scotland. (via D.J. Morrison)

Early 410 prang after a mission from Dorval. Although looking almost unscathed, 19145 was classed as a Category A prang. (via Red Morris)

potential for trouble in the fighter game became readily apparent. The Vampires brushed, and Red watched as one (WA189) suddenly turned into little bits of wood and aluminum fluttering earthward. No sign of the pilot. Then, far below, a parachute billowed. The pilot had been flung clear and landed safely in marshland. His memory, it seems, was totally blank regarding the whole incident.

Unfortunately, 1 Wing was to record many accidents during its three years at North Luffenham. The first fatal Category A (write-off) appears to have involved 19177 and 19181 in a mid-air on April 18, 1952, near The Wash. F/Os Kerr and Rayner were killed in the crash. Many another Cat.A was to follow— aircraft getting hung up in weather and running short of fuel, in-flight fires, short landings, etc. F/O D.G. Tracey had a fuel crisis December 16, 1953, and had to abandon his Sabre. For some reason he was unable to use his ejection seat, tried to get out on his own, but didn't make it.

One of the earliest Sabre crashes in the RCAF occurred at Dorval on June 20, 1951. F/O Ron Found relates what happened to him that day:

410(F) Squadron under S/L Larry Hall had moved from St. Hubert to Dorval as runway work was being carried out at St. Hubert. The squadron gave up its mighty Vampires and the pilots their white scarves, leather helmets and goggles. The new Sabres started arriving in May 1951. Dorval, an international civil airport, had long and well-marked runways and our pilots fell into the habit of approaching on the fast side and letting the aircraft float down the runway until it was ready to land. An excellent practice for clearing the runways quickly, but poor training for the type of runways we would soon be using in England.

S/L Larry Hall was not impressed with this habit we were developing and at morning prayers had all pilots rebriefed on correct approach and landing speeds. We were briefed to fly the correct approach and landing speed or to go around.

My accident occurred in late morning. I was on my fifth Sabre mission, had completed all mission items, and was returning to Dorval. Speed,

altitude and bank all seemed fine on the final turn, but by the time I hit the fence I was almost 10 Kts fast. As briefed, I commenced an overshoot with the intent of correcting the final approach speed on the next circuit. The initial part of the overshoot seemed normal, however about 1/3 down the runway it was obvious that acceleration was lacking. Thinking this was caused by drag I raised the undercarriage and flaps. No improvement was noted; in fact, airspeed and altitude (10 - 15 feet) began to slowly decrease. At about 2/3 runway I hit the emergency fuel switch, which resulted in a short, sharp push of thrust and then nothing. (I later learned that because I put the emergency fuel on with the throttle full open, the power had gone from whatever the engine stable condition was, say 60 per cent, to maximum instantaneously. This resulted in the engine melting out the tailpipe. The tower reported molten metal streaming out the tailpipe onto the runway.) I had very little runway left, the ILS shack was straight ahead, and I considered I had insufficient airspeed and altitude to turn safely. I set the aircraft on the ground just before the ILS shack. My expectation of a plywood building with a copper antenna proved untrue—it had a concrete foundation three feet or so above ground. The good old Sabre went through cleanly, losing its wings in the process and coming to rest 100 - 200 feet beyond. I shut the aircraft down, took my helmet off and placed it on the windshield. I then heard the fire behind and exited the cockpit in a great hurry. (Interestingly, the canopy was completely destroyed but I didn't try to open it.) When I realized that I had left my helmet on the windshield, I went back for it.

When the firefighters and ambulance arrived, which they did very quickly, I was leaning against a fence 100 yards or so away. The first firefighter out of the truck asked me

who I was. I told him, the pilot, but he seemed in doubt. F/L Mike Doyle, my Flight Commander, who arrived with the ambulance, had to provide confirmation.

The only injuries sustained were abrasions on my left elbow and over my left eye, both so insignificant that the doctor, besides providing a nice drink of brandy, only put on two band-aids, and those for sympathy.

One sad result of the accident was that the emergency fuel switch was wired OFF—an atrocious solution when all that was required was more information and training for the pilots. This condition remained for a considerable time, thus we lost a valuable emergency system for no good reason.

The most important and longest-lasting result was the use of the hard hat. 410 pilots were the first issued with protective helmets. They were the US Navy two-piece type. This meant the inner soft nylon mesh helmet could be worn by itself without the hard outer protective shell. Wearing of the shell was not mandatory and we were led to believe that they were probably just a nuisance and would soon be left in our lockers.

Just before impact with the ILS shack, I was leaning well forward to see over the nose. When impact occurred, the harness locked and my head snapped forward and down onto the top of the control column. My helmet took the total blow and had a very distinct scar front dead-centre. There is no question in my mind that without the hard hat I would not have survived the accident. The helmet was taken by G/C West, Director of Flight Safety, and was used in safety lectures. It took me six months to get it written off my kit, but I never saw a pilot fly a high performance aircraft without one after, certainly not on 410.

Ron Found

A trio of pictures showing F/O Ron Found's close call at Dorval. Neither Sabre nor ILS shack survived, though the pilot walked away, thanks to his "bone dome." (via Ron Found)

S/L Douglas "Duke" Warren took command of 410 at North Luffenham in May 1952. Warren was an ex-Spitfire pilot. He and his twin, Bruce, had joined the RCAF in 1940 and served together from then till war's end. Duke relates some of his early Sabre memories:

I first flew the F-86 at Chatham on April 18, 1952, when it was just being introduced into RCAF inventory. Chatham still had Vampires on strength at the OTU. I already knew a

good deal about the F-86, for my brother, Bruce, while a test pilot at Avro Canada, had visited Wright-Patterson AFB, where he flew a USAF F-86 on March 1, 1951. Bruce spoke highly of the F-86, telling me how easy it was to go supersonic with a little help from gravity. The comparison between the controls at speed of the CF-100 and F-86 found the former sadly lack-

The 410 gang during the first six months at North Luffenham. From the left standing are Larry Hall (OC), M.F. "Mike" Doyle, Don Broadbent, Al Robb, Bill Gill, Ken Johnson, Art Rayner, Colin Campbell (Adj), Wes McEwen Len "Speed" Bentham, Grant Nichols, Bill Bain, Sonny Haran, Pete Knox-Leet, D.J. "Moe" Morrison. In front are Ralph Biggar, Red Morris, Frank "Sly" Sylvester and John Marion. (*The Aeroplane* via D.J. Morrison)

ing. (Bruce had been test flying CF-100s so knew what he was talking about.)

Shortly after Chatham, I was transferred to North Luffenham as OC 410 Squadron. I was delighted with this, as our F-86s were the best fighters in the UK and Europe at the time. In spite of all the admin and paper work, I managed to fly 22 hours my first month at 410. On August 1, I had the squadron at Soosterburg, Holland, for the big air show at Ypenburg Airport, The Hague. Before we created any supersonic booms, I checked with air show organizers regarding all the local greenhouses. Did they really want the booms? I was assured they did, so we did. And, as expected, there was a lot of broken glass, but that was all taken care of by the air show people.

One flypast that gave me great personal pleasure was at Dieppe on August 19. I had flown a Spitfire at the Battle of Dieppe, shared in destruction of a Do 217, saw many aircraft, both friend and foe, shot down, watched with anxiety the Canadian army below, and lost several friends with whom I attended school in Alberta. And here I was, leading a squadron of supersonic fighters over the now-peaceful Dieppe shores. It had only been 10 years, and none of my fellow pilots on 165 Squadron that August day in 1942 would have believed that we would be flying overhead in 1952 had I been able to make a prediction.

I spent 13 months at North Luffenham, logging 190 hours, that in spite of admin tasks, standing in as COpsO when the Wingco was away, and shortages of aircraft because of the troublesome (at the time) situation with inverters and gun-plugs. It had been enjoyable, but I was very pleased when notified on July 1, 1953, that I was posted to Korea.

Douglas Warren

S/L Warren took his squadron to gunnery practice at RAF Acklington during 1953. Nearby there were excellent range facilities, even for the worst of UK weather. Included was excellent radar coverage over the North Sea off the Northumberland coast. Even the smallest vessels could be seen on the radar, and the air-to-air controllers were so experienced that they could simultaneously watch and position drogue and firing aircraft in very limited visibility.

Warren relates, "The squadron flew

In May 1952 Duke Warren became OC of 410, a post he held for over two years. This later edition of 410 shows (back row) Garth Cinnamon, Red Morris, Ron Poole, Ron Found, Sonny Haran, Bob Gibson, Bill Bain. In the middle are Lou Saveraux (EO), Speed Bentham, Frank McMullin (ADJ), Gordy Joy, Duke Warren, Moe Morrison, Pete Knox-Leet, Al Robb, J.L. "Denny" Den Ouden, Bob Lewis, Norm Flavin (EO). In front are Sly Sylvester, Tommy Thompson, Ron Potter, Ralph Biggar, Pat Mepham and Ken Young. (DND via J.L. Den Ouden)

to Acklington April 28. This was a famous World War II night fighter station, but now was the RAF's main gunnery camp. I knew several of the senior RAF officers at Acklington, and we got into some lively discussions about armament on the Sabre and the radar ranging gunsight. The RAF chaps were quite scornful of our light .50 guns compared to the much heavier cannons standard on British fighters like the Meteor, Hunter and Swift. I agreed with the effectiveness of the cannons, but pointed out what a fine job aircraft like the Mustang, with its .50s, had done against the cannon-armed Fw 190s and other Luftwaffe wartime fighters. Discussions were always very friendly and interesting— just fighter pilots airing their views about combat theory.

"One day a Meteor tow plane from Acklington was struck by a round of .50 calibre. It landed safely, but the canopy rail was damaged, preventing the pilot from getting out of the cockpit for some time. We immediately viewed the gun camera film from the Sabre involved. What we saw was that the attack had been normal, all angles-off within limits. But by mischance one

round glanced off the tow bar and ricocheted forward to strike the Meteor.

"When the Meteor was more closely examined, it was found that after striking the canopy, the round then penetrated the main spar, causing Cat.A damage! I now looked forward to meeting again with my RAF friends, and when we were well into it I said, 'I know our point fives are not as effective as 20mms, but one of our out-of-date rounds, by only ricocheting off the bar, cut the main spar of a Meteor. Imagine if a six-gun Sabre firing armour-piercing and incendiary ammo had unloaded at the Meteor?' Hereafter the controversy subsided considerably, but I must admit I took some delight in pushing the needle into my RAF friends, quoting their views about our 'relatively ineffective' point fives."

In the March 1954 issue of *Talepipe*, W. Hopkins and G. Gatro provided in verse a good-natured rapping of 410 pilots' knuckles. One assumes that the poets were among the ranks of the airplane fixers at North Luff:

Life Gets Dangerous

The sun gets up and the sun goes down,
410 kites go round and round.
They just get up and it's time to come
    down,
Drop tank leaking somewhere.

My mask is unplugged but I don't care,
I'm still getting lots of air,
The pins ain't even in my chair;
Life gets dangerous don't it.

The oleo legs get lower and lower,
Ain't been filled for a month or more.
I'll probably prang and that's for sure,
Just can't depend on nothing.

The tyres are low and the rudder leans,
The ground is all soaked with kerosene.
They can't even keep my windshield clean.
Just one durn thing after t'other.

Just sucked a groupie up the snout,
If I shut down he may get out;
And then I'd be in dutch no doubt
Sure got troubles ain't I?

Corrosion gnawing at the nose wheel door,
Been gnawing there for a year or more.
When it wears through they'll sure be
        sore...
Cause someone's got to change it.

Now old Joe Pilot's an awful sight,
Got to bed too late last night.
At twenty thousand he was turning white;
Smokey's must be booming.

The idling's high and the temp's too low
The hole in the flap is starting to grow;
I can't even get a good fuel flow.
Motor bikes are safer.

Flying is through and day is done,
But we'll be here with the morning sun.
Some ignorant people think it's fun,
But it's just wasted effort.

413 Squadron

No.413 Squadron formed at Bagotville in August 1951. The OC, S/L J.D. "Doug" Lindsay, recently noted, "I reformed 413 Squadron as the first all-weather unit at Bagotville, August 1950, with Vampires. Production difficulties with the CF-100 and a simultaneous, though temporary, surplus of Canadair F-86s warranted a change of priorities. Thus 413 was redesignated a day fighter unit with Sabres, following the conversion of 410, 441, 439 and 416 Squadrons. We received our Sabres in December 1951."

Before arrival of its Sabres, 413 also

had two Harvards (903 and 2780) and a T-33 (14685). Its early flight commanders were Phil Brodeur and Ken Lett, who both already had considerable experience on T-33s and Vampires. But most 413 pilots were sprogs, fresh from basic flying training and OTU at Chatham. One was W.A.C. Wilson. He had joined the RCAF in 1950, making his first flight in a Harvard at Centralia on May 2.

By April 1951 Wilson was at Chatham, where, on the 24th, he flew the Vampire for the first time. His total Vampire time for the course would be 78:10 hours. This he added to a total of 76:20 hours on Harvards and 33:35 on

Original 413ers at Bagotville in April 1952. In the back are W.A.C. Wilson, Lou MacDonald, Mark Sauder, Phil Brodeur, Slim Snider, Doug Lindsay, Dan Kaye, Ernie Glover and Len Fine. The others are Ken Lett, Bob Moncrieff, Ron Poole, Bill Paisley, Art Maskell and Ken Branch. (via Dan Kaye)

A nice view of Bagotville in the early 1950s. It shows the standard layout of runways and taxiways of a wartime training station in Canada. (G.H. Collison)

Expeditors. Now he was ready for squadron life and was posted to 413. Like the rest of the squadron, he at first had to be content flying Vampires, Harvards and the T-bird, but on January 8, 1952, he finally strapped himself into a Sabre (19224) and "went swept-back." By year's end his log would show over 132 hours in the Sabre.

The squadron logged many hours April 28 - May 19, 1952, on Operation Apple Tree. Lindsay describes it as a "tour of the Maritimes, Quebec and Ontario to show the Sabre to the Canadian public with flypasts over major cities, and static displays." 413 suffered its first loss on September 19, 1952, when F/O Moncrieff was killed. While flying from Bagotville to

Jean Gaudry, Gord MacDonald, Buzz Neilsen, Jack Turner and Norm Ronaasen, who delivered the first Sabres to Bagotville on December 3, 1951. (via Jean Gaudry)

Downsview to perform at the CNE, he dived into the ground after encountering duff weather.

K.C. "Ken" Lett notes some memories of early 413 days:

Our first pilots were an OTU course straight out of the training pipeline. When 421 Squadron returned from Odiham in the fall of 1951, we acquired Bill Paisley and Mark Sauder, at the time experienced fighter pilots. We converted to Sabres in December, and flew our Vampires to Montreal for the auxiliary wing.

In the spring of 1952 we were despatched by the Hon. Brooke Claxton, Minister of National Defence, to show the flag around eastern Canada. We did fly-bys with some basic aerobatics from Halifax to Toronto. In late spring Doug Lindsay left for Korea, Phil Brodeur became CAdO at Bagotville, and I ended up acting CO faced with organizing a continent-wide summer exercise, and a daily show at the Canadian National Exhibition, and the International Air Show at the CNE. In July we hosted 430 Squadron under W/C "Stocky" Edwards, and an F-94 squadron from Westover AFB under Maj "Chappie" James. We also had visits from the Vampires of 401 and 438 Squadrons under W/C Wendy Reid. I have vivid recollections of try-ing to be squadron commander, operations officer, and, at the same time, cater to a group of strong-willed COs, while trying to organize a flying program for all, and lead a squadron of very junior and inexperienced pilots—all at the same time.

We deployed to Toronto in mid-August for 19 consecutive days of fly-bys over the waterfront, followed by two appearances at the International Air Show. During the show we did a 12-airplane routine which included some basic aerobatics and live weapons firing against a float in Lake Ontario. I shudder to think what people these days would say about us doing circuits at the CNE with hot guns, coming around the corner pointing at the crowd as we lined up for our passes!

Since we flew each evening between 6:00 and 7:00, we were back on the ground to enjoy Toronto's social life, then sleep it off by the time we had to do the next day's show. The details of the activities of our band of hot-blooded Canadian lads away from home and loose in the big city are best left untold.

Doug Lindsay returned from Korea by year's end, was promoted to wing commander and posted to North Luffenham as COpsO. We then spent the early part of 1953 preparing for deployment to Zweibrücken, and were led to Europe by S/L "Rocky" Gordon, our new CO. Soon after our arrival at 3 Wing, I left 413 to form an instrument school for the Air Division.

K.C. Lett

Another of the early pilots on 413 was F/O Ron Poole. He had previously flown Vampires at Chatham, and Mustangs and T-birds at Rivers. Poole recalls that the squadron had wanted to be 431 Squadron. Doug Lindsay and his boys found the 413 motto a bit innocuous for a fighter squadron: "'We Watch the Waves"! Of course, 413 had been a distinguished PBY squadron during the war. The old 431 "Warriors of the Air" motto would surely have appealed more to the soon-to-be Sabre jocks. Nonetheless, HQ would not relent, and 413 it was.

August 5, 1951, Len Fine, Doug Lindsay and Ron Poole delivered 413's first aircraft, three Vampires. Shortly after, Andy MacKenzie's 441 lads arrived at Bagotville to give the 413ers some basic pointers on the Sabre, and by year's end Doug Lindsay's boys were merrily roaring over northern Quebec in their own F-86s.

414 Squadron

No.414 Squadron received its first Sabres in November 1952. The records describe some occurrences of the day, including one of the all-too-common prangs:

June 15, 1953
Good weather prevailed throughout the area and GCI exercises were laid on in coordination with Hornet. The target was a B-36. On returning from an exercise, F/O Giles, in Sabre F-86 643, experienced a flame-out on the break for landing. The engine failure was noticed when power was applied after wheels were selected down. F/O Giles attempted a re-light, which was unsuccessful, and manoeuvred his aircraft for the approach landing. Distance and airspeed could not allow 643 to reach the button, and the Sabre was set down straight ahead in the bush. The a/c smashed its way through heavy bush and medium timber, shearing off appendages right and left. The starboard wing was ripped from the fuselage and the a/c came to rest perpendicular to its path of approach. A fire started in the aft section by the speed brake wells. F/O Jim Giles jumped safely out of the aircraft, unhurt. The a/c is a complete wreck. The sqn extends a welcome to two new pilots from the OTU at Chatham, they are F/Os Merklinger and Bob Hughes. Our total pilot strength is now 25.

June 16

GCI exercises were carried out, using a Comet as the target, and the intercepts varied from good to poor. Hornet seems to be having trouble in determining proper heights for the interceptions. CAVU weather prevailed throughout, although only 19 Sabre hours were put in. The new pilots got off in the Sabre today and had a look around the general area plus a few pipelines. In the morning, W/C Yellowlees and S/L Allan gave the pilots a short briefing on the serviceability of the Sabres and stated that more care must be observed in the handling and reporting of unserviceabilities of the F-86s. Nothing is to be left to chance. F/O Hrischenko left for Toronto in the evening via C.P.A. to attend a dinner in Toronto. A total of 19 hours was reached for the day.

No.414 Squadron diary

No.414 participated in Exercise Tailwind, and July 10-12 it chalked up many ''kills:'' 18 Lancasters, 3 KC-97s, 2 Mitchells, 2 Comets, 2 Mustangs, and a B-36, Dakota, Norseman and Beaver. From August 22 to September 3 the squadron was on Leapfrog 4 to Baden.

416 Squadron

No.416 Squadron reformed at Uplands on January 8, 1951, under S/L D.C. Laubman and equipped with P-51s. Laubman, like many post-war fighter squadron OCs, had a distinguished wartime career that included 15 enemy aircraft shot down, seven

The rest of the Bagotville early birds were the 414 ''Black Knights,'' seen in this 1953-vintage photo. Up top is Harry Hrischenko. Sitting are Dick Leblanc, Chuck Stewart, Bruce Merklinger, Basil Smith and Lou Ally. The rest are Dale McLarty, Stu Millar, Gerry de Nancrede, Bo-Bo Stewart and Lou Mohan. (via H. Hrischenko)

Sample page from Harry Hrischenko's log in 1952 showing five different types flown in one month. The RCAF apparently had no qualms about letting its young pilots loose with the equipment!

in just two days in September 1944. Some of Laubman's pilots would soon go on to be well known Sabre drivers, including John Den Ouden, Ernie Glover, Jim Hanna, Ken Lewis, Doug Lindsay (7 kills, WW2), Bill Marsh and Chuck Steacy. Mustang days were full of action and lots of fun, with such activities as firepower demonstrations at Petawawa and Borden, and drogue towing at Chatham. There were the usual survival and escape and evasion exercises, but if these dampened the boys' spirits a bit they made up for it otherwise, as a note in the squadron diary for June 19, 1951, suggests: ''Complaints of low flying and dogfighting over the city of Ottawa were received.'' On an air defence exercise on June 22, 416 claimed 5 North Stars, 6 TCA DC-3s, a Lancaster, Anson and Norseman in its list of ''kills.''

By September, 416 was flying three T-birds (14681, 14687 and 14689), so its pilots were getting a little jet time. The following March, S/L Laubman was posted to Europe, and S/L John MacKay took over as OC. Flying with 401 Squadron during the war, MacKay had 10 7/10th kills, including part of an Me 262. He also had numerous damaged German aircraft to his credit, including three Arado 234 jets.

The squadron's first Sabres appeared in April 1952. On April 9, F/O

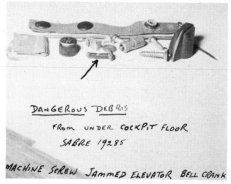

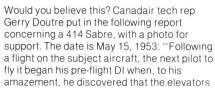

Would you believe this? Canadair tech rep Gerry Doutre put in the following report concerning a 414 Sabre, with a photo for support. The date is May 15, 1953: "Following a flight on the subject aircraft, the next pilot to fly it began his pre-flight DI when, to his amazement, he discovered that the elevators were missing on the aircraft. Upon questioning the pilot who had previously flown the aircraft, it was discovered that he had not found anything abnormal during his flight and was extremely surprised to learn that he had returned to base minus his elevators." (via H. Volker)

The Accident Investigation Branch had its hands full in the post-war years. Every day there were accidents to investigate, sometimes several on the same station. The board was always short of staff, and its investigators were overworked. Yet they somehow managed to get the job done. Causes of accidents/incidents were, of course, varied, and often difficult to pin down. In this case, the culprit was what would be called today "FOD"—foreign object damage. A screw jammed part of the control mechanism (the elevator bell crank). The second picture shows the FOD that was discovered when the AIB sleuths looked under the cockpit floor. (DND)

Harry Hrischenko became the first in the RCAF to save his life with an ejection seat. When his Sabre got into an uncontrollable spin over the countryside near Ottawa, he pulled the handles and his seat functioned as advertised. Hrischenko had been a flying "nut" since his boyhood. He had learned to fly on a post-war Air Cadet scholarship at the Windsor Flying Club. His Sabre flying was to include tours with 414, 416 and 421 Squadrons. Later he flew Neptunes and finished his flying career on Cosmos and Falcons with 412 Squadron.

On June 14, 1952, 416 participated in air shows at Uplands and St. Hubert, with highlights being a four-squadron flypast by 48 Sabres and solo aerobatics by 416's F/O Roy Howie. On more serious business, 416 conducted plenty of practice air firing to prepare for its forthcoming posting overseas.

421 Squadron

At 421 Squadron, F/L Fred Evans made the squadron's first Sabre flight in 19126 on January 29, 1952, the diarist noting, "The rest of the pilots continued studies into the intracies of the Sabre." February 4, 11 pilots, fresh from the OTU, arrived at 421. Their

Harry Hrischenko's 416 Squadron Sabre after Harry bailed out near Manotick on April 9, 1952; and one of 414's jets in the Bagotville boonies in January 1953. (via H. Hrischenko and D. Simmons)

A 416 Sabre at Trenton in the summer of '52. F/O Bill Worthy is at the controls, and the ever-competent ground crew are just finishing a fast turn-around. The gun plumber is buttoning up the gun panel. Three lads hold the Sabre from rolling away as it's under power. (DND U1001)

first day at the squadron was spent being introduced to the other members, being issued with new flying equipment, and eagerly scrambling over the Sabres in the hangar.

Soon each had his chance to "go swept back," as the phrase of the times went. Inevitably, the new Sabres were to acquire their first "wounds." February 14, 1952, the 421 diarist notes, for example, ". . . due to extenuating circumstances, Fulford missed the runway and damaged the nose wheel of his aircraft." February 26, F/L Buzik returned to base low on fuel. Traffic ahead forced him to go around, and in the process his tanks ran dry. He crash-landed short of the runway. The diarist later noted, "The Sabre was badly damaged, but, fortunately, Buzik climbed out unhurt. He was later awarded a reprimand and a $50 fine."

Some useful practice at intercepts was obtained two days later when a B-50 arrived from Tucson. Along with

five Sabres from 413, those of 421 flew missions against the SAC bomber, 421 logging 28.

The diary entry for March 3 shows further progress in getting the squadron into the swing of things Sabre-wise, as well as some gossip: "F/L Thorneycroft and F/O Skaalen finished their transition period on the Sabre, whilst Tobin, Young and Ackert came back from leave all keen to get swept-back. The next day's Sabre flying was curtailed due to inclement weather. The following day, the 5th, was also a stinker, so the ground-crew spent all the time servicing their a/c, whilst the pilots went and upheld the sporting tradition of 421, by shellacking AC&WU in a volleyball game."

On March 14 Capt Jorgensen (USAF) led a three-plane Sabre formation to Uplands, where the new 421 colour scheme was shown off. The squadron continued adding new personnel, with wartime veterans de Nancrede, Doyle, Thompson and Turnbull arriving. Ackert flew the Sabre for the first time March 17, "although a high nose attitude in his landing scraped the tail aspirator section." By early April,

421 had its two flights organized: A Flight, with F/L Evans as commander, F/L Thorneycroft deputy, and F/Os Fulford, Hallowell, Harris, Moore, Northrop, Thompson, Turnbull, Wagner, Young; and B Flight, with Capt Jorgensen commander, F/L Tetlock deputy, and F/Os Ackert, Buzik, de Nancrede, Doyle, Heard, Hogan, Pringle, Tobin, Weeks.

Sabre conversion was still not complete, and Sabres were still scarce. Much flying was still being done in the Yellow Peril (Harvard) at 421. April 4 USAF Sabres from Presque Isle arrived for a visit and the full Red Indian "treatment." According to the records of the day, "Despite bad weather, and equally bad heads, our friends from the south took to the air next morning on their return to Presque Isle."

The poor state of affairs as to aircraft availability in these early months can be appreciated by the diary entry for April 17: "Only 7 a/c left on the books of which only 2 are serviceable." However, by the 23rd, things were looking up: ". . .the squadron put up a personal record by logging 24 hours in the F-86. . . . But this record was broken next day when 38 jet hours were flown. As most of the ships now had drop tanks, it enabled the pilots to stay up much longer and carry out better exercises."

Attention was by this time being placed on weaponry, and 421 sent F/O Skaalen to Nellis AFB on a weapons instructors course, while the pilots began flying famil missions to the air-to-ground gunnery range at Winchester, south of Ottawa.

In preparation for 421's Leapfrog, several squadron pilots ventured to BW-1 in Greenland aboard a 426 North Star to inspect facilities there, but a big 421 "thrash" held May 23 seems to have been of at least as much interest: "The big event of the 23rd was the squadron party for both the ground crew and pilots held at 3486 Iberville Street in Montreal. With the help of a seven-piece orchestra, loads of free booze and eats, the party was a roaring success. What went over big was the invitation to and acceptance of the WDs from the station to attend the brawl. Despite far too many gate crashers, including civilians and members from RCAF Lachine, there were no scraps, although everyone was feeling pretty high. All the credit for the success of the brawl went to F/O Buzik, a past master at organizing parties."

Early June at 421 began with a

General view of the flight line at St. Hubert in 1953. (G.H. Collison)

gruelling escape-and-evasion exercise near Chicoutimi in the Saguenay. Such exercises were run occasionally, and on them pilots were set loose in "enemy" territory as if they had parachuted in during war. They were expected to use all their wiles to achieve objectives without being apprehended by local authorities. Usually they had few resources at their disposal and were operating strictly on their wits. Of this exercise the squadron diary notes: "Despite strenuous terrain and inclement weather the affair was considered a success, even though 50 per cent of the pilots were captured. This was not

considered ignominious because many lessons were learned about interrogation of prisoners, and pilots found they let slip too much evidence and information by many previously unthought-of manners and habits, as well as loose tongues."

On June 3-4, 421's pilots were at the Institute of Aviation Medicine in Toronto, having flown up in a Dakota. At St. Hubert the Dak crew was astonished when a 421 prankster boarded wearing his parachute. On the return flight, the same "hot shot" drove his point home by presenting the Dak captain with an aviation insurance policy! At the IAM, the Sabre pilots were put to the test in a centrifuge with and without G-suits, to determine their

Early days at St. Hubert with brand new Sabre 2s just in from Canadair and as yet unpainted. A Dakota and Expeditor wait down the line. (via Stephen Piercey)

YEAR 1952		AIRCRAFT		PILOT, OR 1ST PILOT	2ND PILOT, PUPIL OR PASSENGER	DUTY (Including Results and Remarks)	SINGLE-ENGINE AIRCRAFT DAY		NIGHT		MULTI-ENGINE AIRCRAFT DAY			NIGHT			PASSENGER	INSTR/CLOUD FLYING		LINK TRAINER
MONTH	DATE	Type	No.				DUAL	PILOT	DUAL	PILOT	DUAL	1ST PILOT	2ND PILOT	DUAL	1ST PILOT	2ND PILOT		St'f	CLOUD	
						TOTALS BROUGHT FORWARD	125/10	248/00	10/05	9/45	1/00							49/46	5/15	
MAY	15	F86E*	287	SELF	SOLO	FORM. 3A/c LETDOWN, LOW FL		1:20												
MAY	15	F86E*	271	SELF	SOLO	FORM. 3A/c - HU. OW. HU.		1:05												CLOUD PENETRATION: -2-35000
MAY	15	F86E*	287	SELF	SOLO	FORM. 3A/c -		:45												AIR/GROUND CIRCUITS
MAY	16	HARVARD	938	SELF	F/O ACKERT	HU - CV - HU		:40												
MAY	19	F86E*	271	SELF	SOLO	FORM. 4 A/c, GCI		1:10												"RAT RACE 2 F86S" BANG ON"
MAY	20	NORTH STAR	17520	PASSENGER		ROCKLIFFE, GOOSE BAY											4:30			
MAY	21	NORTH STAR	17520	PASSENGER		GOOSE BAY, BLUIE WEST 1											4:40			
MAY	21	NORTH STAR	17520	PASSENGER		BLUIE WEST 1, GOOSE BAY											3:50			
MAY	22	NORTH STAR	17520	PASSENGER		GOOSE BAY, ST. HUBERT											3:40			
MAY	22	HARVARD	938	SELF	F/O WELLS	LOCAL RECCE.		:25												
MAY	22	HARVARD	938	SELF	F/O KIENHOLZ	LOCAL RECCE.		:40												
MAY	22	HARVARD	938	SELF	F/O ADKINS	LOCAL RECCE.		:55												
MAY	23	F86E*	320	SELF	SOLO	FORM. 6 A/c		1:00												
MAY	26	HARVARD	3323	SELF	F/O HIND	HU - ROCKLIFFE		1:00												
MAY	26	HARVARD	3323	SELF	SOLO	ROCKLIFFE - HU		1:00												
MAY	26	F86E*	344	SELF	SOLO	CINE ¼ ATTACKS, LANCASTER		1:15												BLEW TIRE ON T/O
MAY	27	F86E*	333	SELF	SOLO	FORM. 4 A/c & LOW LEVEL		1:05												
MAY	27	F86E*	312	SELF	SOLO	CINE ¼ ATTACKS, LANCASTER		:45												
MAY	28	F86E*	292	SELF	SOLO	FORM. 2 A/c TAIL CHASE		:50												
MAY	28	HARVARD	3323	SELF	F/O HOGAN	INSTRUMENTS. GCA		1:15											1:00	
MAY	29	F86E*	292	SELF	SOLO	AEROBATICS		:50												
MAY	29	HARVARD	938	SELF	FORBES	LOCAL		:40												
MAY	30	F86E*	241	SELF	SOLO	AIR/GROUND		1:05												
					GRAND TOTAL [Cols. (1) to (10)] 411 Hrs. 45 Mins.	TOTALS CARRIED FORWARD	125/10	265/45	10/05	9/45	1/00							50/45	5/15	

Early flying at 421 Squadron as shown in the log book of F/O Ralph Heard.

tolerance. During the proceedings F/O Ralph Heard logged 9g (*sans* g-suit), thought to be a Canadian record at the time.

On June 24, 1952, F/O George Northrop ran short of fuel in 19292. He made a forced landing near Chateaugay, New York, where he was "royally treated by the peasants and brought back to the base in the comfort of the CO's car."

422 Squadron

On January 1, 1953, 422 Squadron was put back into business. Wartime, it had operated Sunderland flying boats, but now, under S/L John Buzza, was flying Sabres from Uplands. Initially equipped, as usual, with a small Harvard and T-33 contingent, it received its first Sabre January 12, ferried in from Canadair by Ernie Glover. A few days later Glover was awarded the US DFC in recognition of his successful

The Tomahawk gang at Uplands in 1953. Standing behind are Gerry Smith, Ken Harvey, Bill Christianson and Bill Weary. Squatting on the wing are Vern Cottrell, Ray Carruthers, Rod Pritchard, Jim McKay, Gord Ellis and Ernie Saunders. In front are E.J. Lister, John McLeish, Gord Brennand, Stu Smith, John Randle, Ted Bottoms, Al Adams, John Buzza, Fred Axtell, Ernie Glover, Don Parker and Nels Levesque. (via Al Adams)

Sancoucy Scrapbook

Likely the No. 1 aviation "keener" in the days of 421 and 427 Squadrons at St. Hubert in the early 1950s was LAW Lynn de Sansoucy—"Sou" to most. She was famous there for her tremendous air force spirit and her photographs. She writes of this February 1953 photo, "A number of 427 pilots had gathered outside the hangar one mild winter day to enjoy the sun. I asked them to group together so I could take a picture. They cheerfully did so, then two pilots suddenly picked me up and set me among them. F/O W.S. 'Stu' Deacon appropriated my camera and took the picture. Note the parka, worn even on a mild day to protect my uniform—hadn't been issued coveralls—and the large screwdriver carried by all line crew for 'buttoning up' the Sabre. Those in back are Jerry Blumenschein, Emil Zuber, Drum Laviolette, Bill Grip, Jim Pugh and Swede Larsen. In front are Jack Frazer, Sou, Ted Livingston, Tex MacDonald, Clem Tousignant and Ernie Gardiner, with Denny Turner down in the centre."

St. Hubert, June 1953—sometimes less energetic activity was preferred . . . or, none at all.

Vengeance of 434 Squadron during a 427 visit, for prior artistic effort perpetrated by 427 upon a 434 Sabre. The skunk is unloading on 427's lion!

Draining pooled jet fuel from the tail pipe of a 427 Sabre.

(left) F/O Doug Adkins. In recent years he has become chief test pilot at Canadair and winner of the McKee Trophy.

In this posed picture taken by F/O Rigby Stamison, Sou explains "I'm standing in a reverse position to face the camera; but this illustrates the way to climb into a Sabre. You snapped out the handhold lever by pressing on its lower end. Grasping it with your left hand, you placed your foot on the hanging door to the ammunition compartment, and pulled yourself up, to put your right foot on the wing root. Your left foot then went into the kick step (near the left edge of the picture) whose cover swung inward. You then slung your right leg over the cockpit's edge, pulled up your left leg and either stepped onto the seat or, if you were more graceful or athletic, braced your hands on canopy and cockpit and swung your feet straight down to the floor."

(Below) Faces around St. Hubert, FS Drakley, LAW L.T.M. Della-Vedova, LAC "Butch" Waugh, LAW "Dusty" Bok, F/O "Denny" Turner, F/O Keith Haise.

Aircraft were towed to and from the hangar by a tractor called a "shop mule." A mechanic always sat in the cockpit, ready to apply the brakes when necessary.

RAF Sabres on the line at St. Hubert in June 1953. On the left, the mechanic standing on the wing and kick step is readying the pilot. The other two planes are "buttoned up," their pilots awaiting the leader's signal to start.

Party time with 422 at Uplands. (via Al Adams)

No. 422 Squadron was mainly equipped with RAF Sabre 4s on loan before its Sabre 5s came along. The use of these Mark 4s has caused much consternation among markings freaks. 19632 is a typical case in point. It bears full RAF markings, including serial, then 422 has come along and added its own wild "Tomahawk" scheme and an RCAF tail number. (via Al Adams)

Korean tour—he had downed three MiG-15s. March 5 Glover led five 422 Sabres for a beat-up of St. Hubert, where 3 Wing was assembled for Leapfrog 3.

Many of the squadron's initial aircraft were Sabre 4s destined for the RAF, fresh off the production line. They were temporarily allotted to the RCAF to avoid any slowdown in wing formation, pending delivery of Mark 5s in early 1953.

July brought 422's first big exercise, Tailwind. It ended July 12, and 422 posted its tally of "kills:" 16 Lancasters, 3 B-25s, 3 Comets. Unofficially, it claimed a CEPE Sabre, 16 Vampires of 401 and 438 Squadrons, a North Star, 4 Dakotas (including that of the AOC) and a Harvard. The squadron explained its record on the basis of "shoot first, ask questions later." Did this also explain an incident the previous June 25? A 422 Sabre on an air-to-ground gunnery run shot up a house, narrowly missing one of the occupants? Oops!

427 Squadron

No.427 Squadron came back to life on August 1, 1952, at St. Hubert. First to show up for work was S/L Lyte Ger-vais, followed on the 2nd by F/L Bob Vincent from Chatham. In the following days the other personnel drifted in from here and there, and the squadron borrowed two rooms from 438 in order to get things rolling. As for aircraft, it

Sabres were known to be hard on the trees at times. 19689 tore up a few near Ottawa after F/O Carruthers of 422 leapt out when control was lost. A stuck slat and/or aileron hinge failure was suspected. (via Al Adams)

was the same old story—no Sabres. However, the diarist was able to record, "Two Harvard aircraft have been allotted to the squadron strength (to be kept as quiet as possible). . . . F/O Jack Charron, with F/S Scott as passenger, successfully tested our first Harvard. Jack reports it is really hot."

On August 25 Bob Vincent flew 427's first Sabre (19407) in from Cartierville, causing a near riot among the pilots. It was September 9 before the third Sabre showed up, so it was slow going on the swept-wing front during these early days. By now, however, the Lions did manage to put their hands on a T-bird or two. Along with the routines of training, there was sadness at 427 when F/O Jimmy Peterson was killed in 19411. His aircraft dived straight in near St-Mathias, Quebec. Such tragedies were rude reminders to the young Sabre pilots of a grim fact of life in their profession. But the fledgling squadrons all survived their setbacks and, come Leapfrog time, were ready.

430 Squadron

To W/C J.F. "Stocky" Edwards, the Sabre was one of the all-time great fighters. Edwards was a leading RCAF wartime ace and was OC of 430 Squadron when it formed with Sabres at North Bay in November 1951. Edwards writes, "The Sabre era gave a terrific boost to the RCAF in the fifties, especially after the post-war letdown. This was a 'gung ho' time, with the induction of so many young pilots and groundcrew who would man our Sabre wings. The Sabre was a beautiful, natural fighter plane, filling a place in the fighter pilot's dreams as had the Spitfire."

No.430 started Sabre flying in February 1952, and, as was usual in the squadrons training for overseas, these were hectic times. The original roster of pilots included W/C Edwards, S/L Paul Gibbs, F/L Jim Fiander, and F/Os R.H. Aitken, Arch Debenham, J.D. Fitzgerald, Gerry Gagné, John Greatrix, S.R. Keffer, M.R. MacGregor, D.K. MacKay, S.J.E. Newson, P.V. Robinson, H.B.W. Sheasby, George B. Shorey, Art Skidmore, R.R. Smith, Les Sparrow, L.J. Walter and A. Whyte. Ground crew and other support personnel numbered about

Commander of 430 Squadron, W/C J.F. "Stocky" Edwards. (DND PL55325)

another 200 people.

During the 430 build-up, one curious event took place. Large crates began arriving and were stacked in a hangar. When W/C Edwards enquired about them, his technical officer explained that they contained spare parts and were all being handled in a new "automated" supply system. Everything 430 would need, and all at the push of a button! As more crates arrived, the OC became more curious, but was always told not to worry—just more spares for overseas. One day, though, he insisted on having a look. There were lots of "But sirs" from supply people; but the boss prevailed. A crate was opened, and just as well. Inside, and in box after box destined for Grostenquin, were all the spares in the world that one

would need to keep a squadron of P-51 Mustangs running! Automation had failed its first big test so far as W/C Edwards was concerned. Edwards got right on the blower to Air Defence Command HQ, St. Hubert, and things were soon put right. From then on, ADC called him regularly to make sure 430 had everything it needed.

431 Squadron

One squadron from the early Sabre days was short-lived. That was 431. It was originally formed under Organization Order 67/53 as an all-weather unit to fly CF-100s. These plans were soon changed, and 431 was replaced by 409. 431 was then formed at Bagotville January 18, 1954, with four officers and 59 men. The first Sabre, 19108, arrived that month. OC of the squadron was S/L C.D. Barnett, with pilots being F/Os Frioult, Fulford, Hackett, LaFrance, Landreville, MacDonald, Maskell, McIlraith, Pugh, Rose and Villeneuve. By April 21, 1954, 431 comprised 14 officers, 80 men and 12 aircraft, including a T-33.

On June 10, 431 was in Toronto performing at the National Air Show, and it flew numerous other shows that summer at Torbay, Chatham (Ontario), London and Windsor. Then came its "big show," flying as the Sabre element on Prairie Pacific, the RCAF's trans-Canada air pageant. Pilots were F/Os Fulford, Landreville, MacDonald, McIlraith (spare) and Rudy. This operation involved 431 from August 12 to September 5, but was its swan song. October 1, 1954, it was disbanded and its Sabres ferried to Canadair. It would remain dormant until 1978 when the Snowbirds became 431 Squadron.

The first Sabre 2 built, 19102, during its brief attachment to 431 "Iroquois" Squadron. Fern Villeneuve readies for a flight. (via Wm. Balogh)

434 Squadron

P.S. "Phil" Perry relates some experiences from the early days of 434 Squadron:

My Sabre days began in 1952 when, as a corporal aero engine tech, I was posted from 422 Squadron at Sea Island to 434 at Uplands. At the time, 434 was a name only, and didn't even have a hangar, and we were loaned to 416, which was just completing conversion to Sabre 2s.

My new-found buddy, Cpl Bill Linden, an airframe tech, didn't like the dirty work any more than myself, so by playing cards with the CAdO, W/C Heggteviet, in the airwoman's canteen in the evening, he was able to volunteer both of us as lifeguards for the summer. This was great, as all we had to do was lie around the pool during the day and, as it was behind the airwomen's canteen, we kept it open late in the evening for the benefit of the girls.

Done by Childerhose. 19402 of 434 Squadron rests in a field outside Ottawa, totally ruined after the pilot managed to run out of fuel while on a mission from Uplands. Once again, the sturdiness of the Sabre saved what was left of the day. (via J. Biehler)

They showed their appreciation by keeping us supplied with the odd beer and, of course, their company. We had a lot of fun, especially with the new sprog pilots coming in to 434 who spent a lot of time at the pool, though we cut *them* off in the evening.

With the departure for 2 Wing of 416 we soon got busy building up 434 for our departure for 3 Wing early in 1953. Our first aircraft were what 416 left behind—two or three T-33s and a couple of Sabres. One of the Sabres was a hangar queen which had been robbed for parts and was up on jacks. There it stayed, and we continued the tradition of robbing it whenever parts were needed. After we left for Europe,

422 took what was left of the much-stripped Sabre, and it eventually went back to Canadair for a rebuild.

We had a great time at Uplands during our build-up. The OC, W/C Mitchner, was a very good sort, as were the pilots and ground crew. I received a promotion to sergeant and took charge of servicing, where I stayed until returning to Canada in 1956. The Uplands servicing crew stuck pretty well together the whole time—a great bunch who knew how to work and play hard. We were close and had a good relationship with our pilots.

Of course, there were the inevitable pranks. One day I was driving a tractor with LAC Tim Murphy beside me and

48

LAC Hank Henry riding the brakes in a Sabre we had towed off the runway with brake trouble (actually blew a tire from heavy feet on the brakes—another case of beer for the servicing crew . We were heading down the taxiway, enjoying the quiet away from the hangar line, when all hell broke loose. Unknown to us, F/O Syd Burrows was aloft and had overheard the tower notifying traffic of the towing operation.

Not one to miss a golden opportunity, Burrows requested a low pass down the active runway. The next thing I knew was the combination of a flash of aircraft, whoosh of air, jet blast and smell of burnt fuel. Tim and I bailed off the tractor, avoiding the aircraft in tow which carried on with Hank cowering in the cockpit. By the time we realized that we'd been had and started after the tractor, Hank applied brakes and stopped everything. We pulled ourselves together and carried on back to the hangar, a bit red-faced and still shaken. I got even with Syd later by commandeering him to be best man at our wedding in 1954 at Zweibrücken. And that was no easy job.

Like most ground pounders I used to take every opportunity to get a trip in our T-33s. Unfortunately the Sabre did not come equipped for two, though we did discuss having one of the pilots sit on my knee to give me a flight. These plans were normally discussed at the bar late at night; however, with the gang we had in those days it's a wonder that we didn't try it.

One of my most amusing flights was with F/L "Mate" MacDonald when we flew from Uplands to St. Hubert for some reason (probably to steal parts from the training Sabre at the FTTU). This was a few days before Christmas and we got stuck at St. Hu-

bert because of freezing rain. All we had was our flying suits, so I borrowed a set of hooks for Mate, and we had a great time in the sergeants mess for a few days.

But things got serious, as the weather just stayed. It didn't matter so much for me, a single guy, but Mate had a family in Ottawa. We ended up taking the Greyhound bus back, then a taxi from the bus depot, with a stop at a drug store so Mate could pick up some Christmas gifts. Mate just made it home in time. Like the good friend he was, he invited me in, but I thought it better to leave him to his family.

Our build-up on the Sabre 2 went well at 434 with the exception of a shortage of parts and aircraft. The latter because Canadair could barely keep up with the way our pilots were writing them off. Fortunately this was without any serious injury, and we were eventually ready for our trip across the Atlantic. I was to precede the squadron to Zweibrücken as the advance party NCO. We left Uplands by North Star in early February 1953, with the squadron to depart with 413 and 427 on March 5. We could have waited a couple of weeks as it took a month to complete Leapfrog 3. Our flight took us to Paris, where we were to stay over night, then carry on by train. Well, that was a mistake! On arrival at Orly airport, a young movements officer met us and got us to our hotel with orders that everyone was to be ready to depart at 0800 next morning.

After checking out rooms and trying to figure out which was the toilet, we all hit the town for the sights. It was a great night, but what a terrible job getting everybody together for 0800! What a sorry-looking group boarded the bus, then the train for

Zweibrücken. The trip to Homburg, France, where we departed the train and were met by the 3 Wing reception party, was uneventful except for one casualty. One of our airmen (who carried a navigator's wing and ribbons from the war) got together en route with some French air force types; while we slept off last night's hangovers, the LAC was getting sloshed again. This came to my attention just before we got in to Homburg, and with what little time remained I tried getting him shaped up and presentable for our arrival. We were met by G/C Chester Hull (the CO) and WO1 Earl Cooper (the SWO), who gave us a nice welcome before we boarded our bus for Zwei. I thought we had it made until our LAC, who was hidden by the rest of the group and bravely hanging on, gave a war whoop, drawing the CO's steely-eyed attention. The bus later stopped at the gate on arrival at the Wing and the LAC was escorted to the jug. Then I had to explain why to the CO next day. Such was our arrival at 3 Wing.

Phil Perry

439 Squadron

No.439 Squadron was reformed at Uplands on September 1, 1951, with S/L Cal Bricker in charge. When formed, all the 110-strong squadron had to fly were two Harvards. As was usual for a new Sabre squadron, there were frustrations. Even Harvard flying didn't commence until October 17, and a diary comment that month expressed

A beautiful line of 439 Sabres at Uplands awaiting the flight to North Luffenham. (DND PC81)

"Tiger" squadron members just before leaving Canada. In the back row are Rocky Laroche, Ray Conti, Ray Bedard, Frank Fowler, Frank Raymond, Herb Ruecker (hidden), George Fitzgerald. In the middle are Sherm Hannah, Laurie Hamilton, Blake Smiley, Harry Wenz, Cal Bricker, Bill Bliss, Dick Wingate, Charles Wilkinson. In front are Al Seitz, Ken Cheesman, Ken Jennett, Curly Reischman, Alf Everard, Tom Wheeler, Len Pappas, Tom Wilson. (DND PL54293)

a certain malaise: "Serviceability was poor because of the lack of tools and parts. Weeks after completing the MTU course at St. Hubert we were still not flying the Sabre." The first Sabre didn't arrive until November and the OC made 439's initial Sabre flight in 19128 on November 10 after being checked out by Don Simmons of 441 Squadron. From here on the pilots of 439 began training in earnest, and on April 15, 1952, the OC announced to them that they would become the first Sabre squadron to fly their aircraft overseas. This would be Leapfrog 1, and launch day would be May 30. Bricker himself went u/s en route (F/L Bill Bliss filled in as acting OC) and the weather made for slow going, but 439

was safely on the ramp at North Luff by June 14.

In July 1953, S/L Bricker was replaced by S/L K.J. Belleau. The diarist for July 26 made a rather daring com

Sabre 19240 was severely damaged in a prang at Uplands while with 439 Squadron. Later, in a "let's see if it works" bit of fireworks, '240 was used in a dummy ejection seat trial, also at Uplands. (DND via Al Seitz)

Ensconced at North Luff, 439ers Smiley, Everard, Pappas, Wheeler, Sills and Jennett take in the sun while waiting for some action. (G. Fitzgerald)

Some of the pilots of 439 at the squadron's dispersal hut at North Luff. Conditions weren't exactly ideal! (Bert Davis)

ment: "The station CO, G/C Hale, could not start his jet, and immediately claimed 439's APU was u/s. Our man looked in the CO's cockpit, pushed in his ignition circuit breaker, and successfully started the Old Man on his way. It appears 'finger trouble' knows no rank limitations." In August, 439 joined 410 and 441 in a major exercise, Momentum. On one scramble, F/Os Wenz and Wingate had a mid-air collision when attacked by an F-84, but damage was slight. August 19 the squadron flew 50 sorties on Momentum, and two days later 439 was suddenly ordered to Horsham. The two-week exercise ended August 23.

September 10, 1953, was an interesting day for 439, as F/O Fraser

tried to shoot down F/O Fitzgerald. Well, he didn't exactly do this on purpose. Fitzgerald was towing the flag, and on one of his runs on it Fraser somehow put four bullets in the tow ship. Meanwhile, F/L Bliss had been on exchange with the USAF in Korea, and when he returned in September was able to give 439 valuable briefings about fighting MiGs with the F-86. 439's demonstration team performed September 19 at North Luff's open house. The team had formed at Harry Wenz's instigation. With Dean Kelly getting all sorts of good publicity for 441, Wenz felt 439 should get involved, and, with Doug Lindsay's approval (he was COps O at North Luff at the time), a team was formed. Original members were F/L Wenz and F/Os Laurie Hamilton, Mack Giles and Len Pappas. The diary notes that at the open house F/Os Smiley and Hannah "were kept busy, especially by the youngsters who seem to know more than the pilots

about the Sabre." An unusual entry on October 14 refers to some skeet shooting: "F/O Wingate accidentally shot the airman who was setting the traps for us. The MO extracted 41 pellets from the chap's face and said he would be OK!"

Al Seitz of 439 recently looked back to his Sabre flying from North Luffenham:

My affair with this predatory bird began with a posting to 439 Squadron, newly formed at Uplands. Not yet a cynical veteran (total time on jets: 55 hours flying the Vampire), I was properly humbled and impressed at my first sight of the Sabre.

From the first flight, one appreciated the Sabre's completely straightforward handling characteristics. The Mark 2 was a sprightly performer to about 35,000 feet, but pretty much of a dog at 40,000, though occasional formations could struggle up a bit higher. These were usually exercises in futility since, in that thin air, the J47 had no muscle left for turning power. The Marks 5 and 6 had ceilings of 5000 and 10,000 feet higher respectively.

There were no speed restrictions in descent, though sonic booms were normally not appreciated. Sometimes, in low fuel situations following a tangle close to home, formations would descend with little more precision than a gaggle of geese. Normal IFR penetrations were carried out at 300KIAS. As to sonic booms, the '86 needed to dive nearly vertically to go supersonic. Then, its boom could be aimed with the gunsight, and would be heard only in a relatively small area 5 - 10 miles in diameter. It was a great way to open an air show!

Air shows! Singly, in formation fly-bys or in aerobatic teams the Sabre was a superb air show performer. It could make a pass just as low, just as noisy, and almost as fast as an F-100, F-104 or F-18. It could pull up and roll out of sight even without an afterburner. A pilot could pull up at something around 575K and do a vertical eight and double loop, one on top of the other.

Dean Kelly, while a flight commander with 441 Squadron at North Luffenham, was one of the legendary Sabre demonstration pilots. At a Fighter Command gathering at RAF West Raynham, Kelly put on his solo show, midst the Hunters, Swifts and the D.H.110, all there to strut their stuff. As did the others, he opened up with a low 600 mph pass. Then, instead of pulling up for vertical rolls, he hauled it around in a 7g turn, slowing to gear and flap speed, further slowing to just above the stall, and dragged it by with his jet blast scorching the grass. Throttle on and cleaning up, he came around in another 360, by the reviewing stand, no higher and apparently not much faster than the first time—and yanked it up!

Fighter pilots stopped breathing! Kelly's Sabre arced up past the vertical, continued over the top of the first half of a loop—very slowly. And as the nose came down, he very gently rolled out and accelerated away in the opposite direction. It had been below stalling speed over the top, but at zero g the controls still responded to airflow, so this seemingly impossible

The front gate at RCAF Station North Luffenham. (G. Fitzgerald)

piece of flying worked nicely. One of the RAF test pilots later admitted, "I've never seen an aircraft flown so close to the bone."

Easy to fly in all phases, the '86 was just as easy to land, and a usual jet fighter pattern was flown. The initial point, three miles back from the runway, was hit at 300K. On the pitch the speed was lowered to 185K for gear and flaps, and a minimum of 150K

maintained through base turn. Final approach was a minimum of 135K, or higher if heavy, until landing was assured. Touchdown at 115K. A piece of cake if recommended speeds were adhered to.

It was often a matter of pride for "tigers" to chop the throttle on the pitch and by careful playing of the turn, and timing of lowering gear and flaps, coast to the runway without using power. No big thing in itself, but a perverse wind or something unusual in the circuit requiring extra manoeuvring and power could lead to embarrassing moments. Axial flow engines can take a while to spool up, and a few Sabres squatted in the toolies because of that power lag.

Al Seitz

Fighter operations in the Air Division posed new challenges to RCAF air and ground crew. Flying-wise, there were new weather conditions; restrictions regarding such things as international boundaries between NATO partners and such neutral states as Sweden and Switzerland; the rather ominous buffer zone separating NATO and Soviet bloc countries; potential for language mix-ups; and congested airspace where vigilance against midair collisions was paramount. There was the exhilaration for the fighter pilots of daily dogfighting in these crowded skies; and politically, there was the sometimes tense drama when world war threatened, and everyone knew that the main battle ground would be Europe. Al Seitz has described some of his early experiences as a Sabre pilot, first in England with 439 Squadron, then on the Continent:

Before our arrival in England the Sabre had already made its presence felt— USAF F-86As were stationed there. The "A" had a slower roll rate than our "E". At the same time, the British had only Meteors, Vampires and Venoms in their day fighter operation. RAF fighter pilots were as aggressive as any of us, but also somewhat chauvinistic about their own aircraft. Many were reluctant to believe that the Sabre could actually ignore Mach and dive vertically to its heart's content. However, the RAF soon learned that the Sabre was faster in level flight than its straight wings. For our part, we learned that to get into a turning rat race with them was to invite humiliation.

Of course, we had more going for us—speed, and a rate of roll at least three times that of any RAF fighter— and they had controls which seemed set in concrete at high speed. As we learned our business, we found that if a Brit got into six o'clock position we could use rolling dives to get out of range. Or, if commencement speed was near the straight-wing's limiting Mach, we could scissor him from six o'clock to twelve o'clock in little more than a half dozen rapid reversals of turn directions. RAF pilots developed the arms and shoulders of wrestlers as they cursed their wing-heavy machines and watched Sabres zigzagging about with the gay abandon of swallows.

The Meteor 8s and Venoms could always outclimb the Sabre 2, as well as out-turn it. The Venom was a particularly agile performer within Mach limitations; the first time I experienced a tail slide was in trying to follow a Venom around a loop begun at over 35,000 feet. While the Meteor was limited to about Mach .80, the Venom went to .85. The Meteor could shed its tail exceeding its Mach limit. The Venom simply tucked its nose under and sought lower altitude regardless of the pilot's intentions. The Vampire could disintegrate altogether if pushed passed its Mach limit.

RAF formations often loitered near our known climb corridors and, with the help of radar ground control, positioned themselves in perfect attack perches. Their frustration was complete when, after the attack had started, the Sabres simply lowered their noses and pulled away, still gently climbing. Often, as the Brits returned to their bases, their formations were ripped apart by Sabres slashing through with overtake speeds in excess of 150K.

The RAF did get good film footage when they came across Sabres fighting among themselves with speeds well down. The film mostly showed Sabres diving away to recoup. Often the film showed evidence of the attacking RAF fighter undergoing Mach buffeting.

Flying in the UK was vastly different from flying in Canada. The weather, particularly in winter, was atrocious. I did more GCAs by radar for real—down to and below minimums—than I'd ever done before. The kind of CAVU day one can expect at any time in North America is rather rare in Britain, or much of Europe for that matter. Beacons were few and far between. Most navigation was done under radar control, which was excellent. IFR approaches were handled from the ground by CDRF (Cathode Ray Direction Finder).

Fighter pilots often pride themselves on their "mental dead reckoning" navigation skills, and are reluctant to admit uncertainty of position or ask for help. In the UK at that time a formation leader could ask radar for a fix when above 10/10ths cloud, hoping to hear that he was near some geographic position from where he knew his way home; or he could be honest and ask for "pigeons"—bearing and distance to base—thereby admitting he hadn't a clue where he was. RAF fighter controllers, ever keen to put a fighter pilot down, would provide very accurate fixes like, "Cypress Red, you are passing 400 yards south of Steeple Bumpstead, and approaching North Upper Middle Hampstead from the west." The next transmission from the flight leader would be a sigh and a resigned request for pigeons, usually followed by some remarks from his faithful followers, "It would appear that Glorious Leader has temporarily misplaced his marbles again!"

Barely three weeks after arriving in the UK, while on a mission over the North Sea, my aircraft (19112) suffered oil pump failure and subsequent engine failure. The Sabre's stand-by hydraulic system was electrically driven. Without a windmilling engine one had control only while battery lasted. I was over 10/10ths cloud (what else) when the controls stiffened in my hands.

My problems had begun 50 miles or so east of The Wash at 38,000 feet. I was steering towards a USAF base at Sculthorpe and had glided to about

7000 feet when I had to pull the handle. I was surprised to find that one can experience vertigo while descending through cloud under a parachute, and was more dismayed to find myself over water on breaking into the clear. But my section and radar had a good fix on my position when I ejected, and a large number of aircraft were soon searching for me. About an hour and 40 minutes after splashdown I was picked up by a USAF SA-16 Albatross, a beautiful amphibian. I was the second in the RCAF to successfully eject. Years later I was to have another over-sea ejection, this time from a CF-104.

Al Seitz

===

441 Squadron

Ralph Annis was to become one of the great all-time Sabre pilots in the RCAF. Besides being known for his famous Vancouver-Halifax speed

Andy MacKenzie, OC of 441 Squadron, chats with Air Marshal Curtis during the CAS's visit to North Luff, as MacKenzie's boys look on. Note the white carpenter coveralls-cum-flying-suit outfits being worn. (DND PL62200)

record in a Sabre, and as a Golden Hawk pilot, Annis was one of the originals with 441 Squadron. Some of his memories and impressions of 441 days follow:

===

I, along with several other pipeliners, joined 441 Squadron in early October, 1951, after completing our gunnery school on Harvards and our OTU on Vampires. It was quite an experience taking the swept-wing, flush riveted F-86 into the air for the first time. It

was the hottest airplane in the world in 1951 without any exaggeration. This thrill remained throughout my years flying it.

I initially flew out of St. Hubert and my last flight there was February 8, 1952, before the squadron was transferred to North Luffenham, England, aboard the *Empress of France* on February 13, 1952. Our aircraft had already preceded us on HMCS *Magnificent* and it didn't take long to start operations in England, my first flight being on March 4. Most of us had only 40 or 50 hours on the Sabre and our job in England was to work up battle formation, fly the aircraft to its limits and learn to be comfortable there.

While our equipment and personnel were the best in the world, there were a few things missing. When Air Marshal Curtis, Chief of the Air Staff, visited us about five weeks after our arrival in England, we naturally put on a Wing flypast and met him upon landing. I never will forget the startled expression on his face, as we were in all manner of clothing. Only three or four people in the squadron had proper flying suits. The rest of us had a mixture of whatever we could obtain. I flew that day in

53

a pair of khaki drill trousers and a T-shirt. It wasn't long until we were outfitted in carpenters overalls, which certainly weren't flying suits, but at least we now looked as if we belonged to the same air force.

The flying in England was superb. The war had ended only a few years earlier and the Russian threat was steadily increasing. We were all into the gung-ho attitude of the Royal Air Force and worked with them and the USAF on a daily basis. Our missions were everything from tree-top level to 40,000 feet. Our gunnery officer, Ray Jolley, worked to develop our cine camera program so that we could assess our capability in dogfighting. Each mission on which we used the cine camera (which was almost always) was followed by an in-depth review to determine whether we would have shot down the other guy or how well we did on air-to-ground strafing. We spent long periods of time sitting on cockpit alert, starting a half hour before dawn to a half hour after dawn. These boring periods were usually followed by a scramble and on many occasions we were assigned to "wake up" some RAF or USAF base by doing a beat-up over the air field. You can be sure that four screaming Sabres, at tree-top level, making multiple passes, woke everyone in the area up. I shall always remember one refuelling man jumping

from the wing of a B-29 as I was doing a simulated attack. I had him on cine film and often wondered how he made out on that long drop to the tarmac. The missions were supposedly designed for the air base defence forces but we loved them.

A mere three months after arrival in England, our boss, S/L MacKenzie, took three of us with him to visit an RAF wing at the old Luftwaffe base in Wunstorf, Germany. It was our first introduction to the Continent, and of the Sabre to that part of the world. It was quite an experience for us young people, but one of the things that sticks in my mind was the way the urinals were designed in the Officers' Mess, whereby you could lean your forehead on a specially designed release mechanism and flush as you threw-up. We called them honk-bowls. True German efficiency!

In June of 1952 our wing carried out trials in air-to-air fighting against the elite Central Fighter Establishment of the Royal Air Force. They flew Meteors, which were much inferior to the Sabre, but the pilots were probably the best in the world. At that time our pilots still had less than 100 hours in the Sabre. 439 Squadron flew the trials from 25,000 feet up, 410 Squadron, between 1500 feet and 25,000 feet, and 441 Squadron the high-G gut-wrenching trials from ground level to 1500 feet. We were supposed to maintain two-plane integrity but soon after interception the Meteors fought individually, which immediately gave them a two-to-one advantage. Flying

number two to Dean Kelly took about all I had as I tried to keep from blacking out even with a G-suit and still keep him in sight. It was only on our final flight against the Meteors that we dropped our two-plane attempts and took them on one-to-one. Over all, with our relative inexperience and our attempt to "play by the rules," the RAF made the decision to send the Meteors to Korea, where they performed adequately but proved no match for the MiG-15.

Our training continued in two-plane and four-plane and often large exercises where the entire wing of 36 Sabres would be launched on exercises against "enemy" bombers arriving from the Continent. I don't think there is a pilot from North Luffenham who doesn't remember the final day of a week-long exercise where nearly every fighter in southern England was launched against a tight box of 24 B-29s; not only was our Canadian wing involved, there was a wing of F-86As and at least three wings of Meteors, plus a few Vampires and Venoms. The air was full of airplanes making attacks on that poor bomber formation from every conceivable angle. Fighters were flashing by each other and the bombers without much regard for who might be in the way. Why we didn't have at least one mid-air is nothing less than miraculous.

Often we were asked to put on a demonstration of the Sabre's capabilities and these invariably included dropping a sonic boom. This phenomenon was new to the world and everyone was

F/L Dean Kelly beats up the flight line at North Luff. Note the trademark of the J47-powered Sabre 2, a trail of thick black smoke. (DND)

fascinated by the shock waves created when an aircraft flies faster than the speed of sound. One of our pilots was even invited to the Royal Aeronautical Establishment at Farnborough to drop sonic booms for the boffins of the RAF. We were cracking the sound barrier all over England at the time and in fact one of my log book entries reads, "North Luffenham to Horsham-St. Faith, boomed Horsham with 6 planes." I can't recall what the event was but we undoubtedly created some excitement. Unfortunately some damage did occur on the ground and dropping booms became a no-no. On September 20, 1952, I did a Battle of Britain Air Show at RAF Watton. Naturally they wanted me to break the sound barrier and I still have stapled in my log book a waiver signed by the Commandant declaring that he accepted "all responsibility in respect of complaints received or damage caused as the result of aircraft 19165 exceeding the speed of sound in the Watton Area."

All this high-intensity flying and training soon made the RCAF ruler of the skies in Europe. Nothing could touch us, including the USAF, who in their defence, flew an older model Sabre. Some of them tried, however, and to my personal knowledge we had three aircraft credited without firing a shot: one Meteor and one Vampire that broke up in mid-air while trying to stay with the Sabre and a Venom that ran out of fuel and couldn't make it home after tangling with us. Fortunately no one was hurt.

When Andy MacKenzie left for his ill-fated tour in Korea, our acting squadron commander was Dean Kelly, probably the best solo aerobatic pilot in the RCAF. One day Dean wanted to go to RAF Leuchars in Scotland to visit some friends and took me along as his number two. In those days it was standard procedure to do a low pass when arriving and departing from strange bases and, of course, the RAF was always happy to see the Sabre in action. As we approached the airdrome at approximately 500 kts, I was flying on the right wing and Dean was turning right so that I couldn't see the ground but we were low enough that I saw a pole of some sort flash by and I tucked in my formation as tight as I dared because I knew that my right wing wasn't far off the ground. During lunch our RAF host congratulated us on our close formation flying and this

A nice formation of 441 Sabres during aerobatic practice. (via Ralph Annis)

must have gone to Dean's head. On takeoff, Dean called for the inevitable low pass and I was quite comfortable since we flew across in a reasonably level attitude but then he pulled up and proceeded to do a slow roll with me hanging on for dear life. After landing in Luffenham he casually mentioned the roll and didn't think that I would mind but didn't want to tell me beforehand in case I was nervous. Casual, that was Dean!

This little incident probably was the seed that grew into the 441 Squadron formation aerobatic team and of course I volunteered. Our leader was Gar Brine, who was later killed in an F-86 in Chatham, N.B., right wing was Fern Villeneuve, who later flew with

the Golden Hawks, myself on left wing and John Gaudry in the slot. We did quite a few air shows in England and on the Continent but the two most important in my mind are one at North Luffenham for HRH the Duke of Edinburgh on May 21, 1953, and one for the National Air Races at Southend-on-Sea, on June 20, 1953.

The following incident will give you some indication of how our Wing was dedicated to flying. I was doing a low-level cross-country in mid-March 1953 at 300 feet and 360 kts (not very fast but 360 kts works out to 7 miles a minute which makes navigation pretty simple) when a bird flew through my

Overleaf
Nice view of 410 Sabres at North Luff. At the time, the squadron was using aircraft numbers on the slats, a short-lived practice. (DND PL62160)

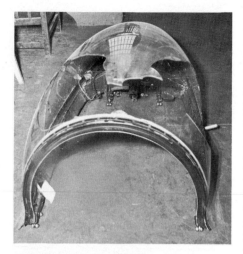

Shattered canopy and splattered helmet after an encounter with a sea gull. (via Ralph Annis)

HRH Duke of Edinburgh meets F/O Ralph Annis during a Royal Visit to North Luffenham. (DND)

canopy and hit me on the head. Fortunately at the time I had looked down to check my map and my crash helmet took the beating instead of my head. However, flying plexiglas cut me a bit around the eyes and sheared off my radio cord. I made a precautionary landing at Brize-Norton, got patched up by the M.O., who thought I had fallen off my motorcycle, and called home base telling them I needed a new canopy. Our ever-faithful ground crew arrived that evening, replaced the canopy, cleaned up the feathers, etc., gave me a throat mike, and I flew the machine home the next morning, where we were both back in business, the machine and I, in no time at all. Minor incidents like that were laughed off regularly.

I left North Luffenham and those wonderful days to become an instructor at the instrument flight in Zweibrücken, working for Ken Lett. We rarely flew less than 50 hours a month on a seat made of two-by-fours and a single layer of rubberized horse hair. Every new Sabre pilot in the Air Division went through our flight and every one of them became a hard-assed pilot. Maybe that's the reason the RCAF ruled the skies in Europe for 10 years.

Ralph Annis

F/L Dean Kelly

Among the early Sabre crowd, one was the RCAF's Sabre practitioner *par excellence,* F/L Dean Kelly. He had joined up early in the war, training on Fleets at St. Catharines. Next came Harvards at Dunnville, then overseas to a Spitfire OTU. A brief stint with 602 Squadron at Redhill, then Malta, in the thick of the desperate struggle there. Later, a year of instructing on Hurricanes in Scotland, and in April 1944 back on ops with 403 Squadron. A bail-out on May 7, then near-disaster on June 9 when hit and punched full of holes by shrapnel. Two months in hospital. January 1, 1945, was the last gasp of the Luftwaffe, as it hammered Allied bases all across Europe. Kelly was aloft, and bagged an Fw 190. He later stayed on with the occupation forces, and in 1947 was back in Canada on a refresher course at Trenton.

Dean Kelly never did leave the RCAF. As he puts it, "I never missed a day's pay." By December he was instructing at Centralia. That kept him busy for two years, and he next headed for Chatham. January 13, 1950, he made his first Vampire flight in 17071. In May 1951 he and two other pilots went to Williams AFB to collect the RCAF's first T-33s, Lockheed-built examples, pending production of the improved Canadair version. In August he flew solo aerobatics in a Vampire at the Detroit air races. There the Canadian fliers were toured like heroes throughout the city in open Cadillacs!

December 7, 1951, Kelly flew his first Sabre, 19125, and in February began his Sabre tour with 441 Squadron at North Luffenham, as a flight commander.

Kelly knew how to get the most out of the Sabre, flying it, as most who knew him claim, beyond its supposed limits. He soon became famous for his spectacular solo air shows, winning admirers like the Duke of Edinburgh and the King of Belgium. After watching Kelly's performance, the King sent his private aircraft to collect Kelly next day and fly him over for lunch. The Duke would have liked a check-out on the Sabre at North Luff, though this didn't happen. Dean Kelly was as much an ambassador of the RCAF as one of the regular troops.

All who served at 1 Wing in its early years seem to have a Dean Kelly story. It was said that Kelly would wear neither a hard hat nor a G-suit: a hard hat would keep him from seeing around the corners, and with a G-suit on he was afraid he'd pull the airplane apart! At least, so the story went.

April 1, 1953, Kelly performed at RNAS Ford. Afterwards, the CO invited him to try the navy's Attacker. Kelly was happy to have a go at the straight-wing jet fighter, took off, and put it through its paces, including spins. On landing, he was amused to find that the navy pilots were amazed that he had spun the Attacker and lived! Perhaps in appreciation for bringing the Attacker home, he got a "tip" on an upcoming horse race from the CO. He put down a pound and flew back to North Luff. A week later, an aircraft flew over from Ford. The nag had come in, and the navy courier had five pounds for F/L Kelly.

Later in his flying career, Dean Kelly instructed at Trenton and at Craig AFB, Alabama, and was OC of 414 Squadron on CF-100s and of 416 on Voodoos. He continued flying after he left the RCAF in 1967, spending several seasons on Avengers fighting fires in B.C. and budworm spraying in New Brunswick. This proved more hazardous than flying Sabres, Clunks or Voodoos. Twice the ancient Avengers tried to put Kelly out of business. An engine failed just after takeoff from Kamloops and Kelly set down in the Thompson River. A nearby boat picked up the pilot, who didn't even get his feet wet. Later, in New Brunswick, in

CF-IMW, he again had engine failure on takeoff. There was nowhere to land except in the trees. Into the trees he went, but Kelly kept his wits, consciously running through his escape drill as the Avenger, fuel tanks brimming, began to burn. He got out but 'IMW was burned to a cinder.

On December 1, 1971, Dean Kelly was visiting his old friend Jerry Billing in Windsor. Billing was flying Don Plumb's Spitfire CF-RAF at the time. It had been 25 years since he had touched a Spit, but that day Dean Kelly flew it again. In over 30 years Dean Kelly survived everything from the battle for Malta to the wild times at North Luff, even the battle of the budworms. His old CO from North Luff, G/C E.B. "Ed" Hale, probably summed up Kelly neatly when he said of him, "He's a perfectionist. He flies himself and the aircraft to the limits of tolerance. He frightens me sometimes."

F/L Dean Kelly while serving with 441 Squadron at North Luff. (via. E.B. Hale)

The "Silver Fox" squadron while at Acklington for gunnery in February 1954. S/L Gill was acting OC at the time. (via Dean Kelly)

Another of the 441 "originals" was F/O C.R. "Bob" Simmons. He and his brother, Don, had been flying in New Brunswick in the late forties and had their own light aircraft before both joined the air force. Bob Simmons joined November 11, 1949, trained at Centralia from January 1950, was at the Air Armament School at Trenton

No 441 SQDN R.C.A.F.
F/L Kelly F/o Abbott F/o Myles F/o Cunningham F/o Johnson F/o Eburn F/o Klein S/L Gill F/o Fik F/L Tolly F/L Borns F/o Mills.
F/o Webber F/o Raine F/o Bradley F/o McGregor F/o Berceil F/o Clayton F/L Atherton F/o Branch F/o Fine.

Dean Kelly hangs in alongside an RAF Dakota for some picture-taking. Of course, the slats are automatically hanging, though Kelly, unlike his wingman, isn't bothering with speed brakes. (via E.D. Kelly)

A motley bunch of Andy MacKenzie's boys at North Luff. Kneeling are Fern Villeneuve, Jean Gaudry and Gord MacDonald. The others are Murray Nielson, Bob Haverstock, Ian MacDonald, Jack Turner, Don Simmons, Ray Jolley, Gar Brine and Pete Cranston. The famous 441 crest, created by Bob Simmons in the squadron's early days at Dorval, hangs proudly behind. (via Ralph Annis)

in September, and flying Vampires at Chatham in December. March 19, 1951, he joined 441 Squadron at St. Hubert, as did the rest of his course. 441 was still flying Vampires and Harvards. Simmons made his first Sabre flight at Dorval in 19124 on July 13.

Soon 441 was busy ferrying its Sabres to Norfolk where the US Navy cocooned them for overseas transfer aboard HMCS *Magnificent*. The runway at Norfolk was short, about 4000 feet, so the Sabre crowd from St. Hubert practised at home using a line painted across their runway to indicate 4000 feet. On one flight from St. Hubert to Newcastle, Delaware, (the en route fuelling stop) a Sabre flown by

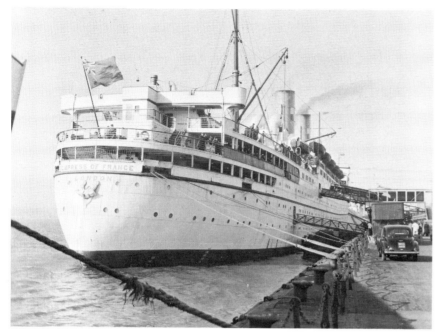

The *Empress of France* docked at Liverpool; and members of 441 Squadron coming ashore. (via E.B. Hale)

A 441 two-ship roars off at North Luff. (*Leicester Mercury* via Jean Gaudry)

John Marion flew through a flock of birds. Canadair had to send down tech rep Gerry Doutre to survey the damage. By the time he arrived, the chewed-up sea gulls were getting pretty ripe inside the Sabre, and the first item to appear on Doutre's expense account was a bar of deodorant soap.

Simmons arrived in the UK aboard the *Empress of France* along with the rest of 1 Wing and was soon flying from North Luff. July 1-2, 1952, he made several flights aboard a Bristol Sycamore helicopter as an observer trying to find any sign of F/O Conti, who disappeared at sea. On July 13 he flew with his mates at the big Brussels airshow where Dean Kelly was the star. Simmons still recalls part of Kelly's routine, which he describes as his "stupendous slow loop."

One of Simmons' mates on 441 at North Luff was Jean Gaudry. He had joined the RCAF in 1949, passed through Centralia, and did the Vampire OTU (Course 20) at Scoudouc, since Chatham was having runway construction. At 1 Wing, Gaudry, Ralph Annis, Gar Brine, Bob Haverstock, Norm Ronaasen and Fern Villeneuve began practising aerobatics to-

Steve Atherton and Jean Gaudry chat about a mission with one of their 441 crewmen. (via Jean Gaudry)

gether and putting on shows throughout the UK in what was perhaps the first organized Sabre "team" in the RCAF. Some years later, Villeneuve would lead the famed Golden Hawks. It all seems to have had its start at North Luff.

Gaudry had his own moments of excitement at 1 Wing. October 10, 1953, he was flying from Gutersloh, Germany, when he had radio failure above cloud. He managed to find a hole and drop through, but fuel was low and Gaudry was just lining up for an emergency landing on the autobahn when he spotted a runway. He altered course, touched down, then flamed out just as he was parking. June 12 he had been flying wing with the OC, Andy MacKenzie, when the boss had engine trouble and made a wheels-up landing in an open field. Gaudry was also involved in one of the early live television programs to feature the RCAF. He was lost one day, groping around in the haze, when he happened to stagger low across a nationally televised cricket match. His OC had only one comment about this little faux pas: "Gaudry, you're a piss-poor navigator!" Gaudry was also the culprit who led the multiple booming of Horsham St. Faith.

Early North Luffenham ops as illustrated in F/O Jean Gaudry's logbook in late 1952.

Salvaging S/L MacKenzie's Sabre from an English potato patch after an emergency landing brought on by a flame-out. (via J.H. Spratley)

C.R. "Bob" Simmons describes the origin of 441 Squadron's flashy Sabre 2 paint job. His item is reprinted from *Der Kanadier,* February 17, 1982:

During July of 1951, we were temporarily located at Dorval for initial flying of the newly acquired F-86 Mk.2 Sabres — our Vampires retired at St.

Hubert at the time of runway extension.

With the excitement of flying supersonic fighters for the first time in the RCAF, 441 Squadron members decided to propose a distinctive colour scheme. Following a few discussion periods at pilots' meetings, many design ideas were offered. Our CO, S/L Andy MacKenzie, left the choice to a majority vote. I can safely say that our checkerboard was an extension of those many checkerboard variations

YEAR 1952		AIRCRAFT		PILOT, OR 1ST PILOT	2ND PILOT, PUPIL OR PASSENGER	DUTY (INCLUDING RESULTS AND REMARKS)	DAY		NIGHT		DAY			NIGHT			PASSENGER	FLYING [incl. in cols. (1) to (10)]		LINK TRAINER
MONTH	DATE	Type	No.				DUAL (1)	PILOT (2)	DUAL (3)	PILOT (4)	DUAL (5)	1ST PILOT (6)	2ND PILOT (7)	DUAL (8)	1ST PILOT (9)	2ND PILOT (10)	(11)	DUAL (12)	(13)	(14)
						TOTALS BROUGHT FORWARD	95 25	321 45	6 40	8 45								52 10	18 45	
SEP	22																		
"	22	SABRE	165	SELF	-	¼ ATTACKS ON B-29 CAMERA		:45											:10	
"	23	SABRE	165	SELF	-	¼ ATTACKS ON B-45 T.C		1:00												
"	23	SABRE	147	SELF	-	DNCO - ⁴/₅ ⁴/₅ - 3 GCA.		:50												
"	25	SABRE	134	SELF	-	AIR TO GROUND - DNCO - STB		:45												
"	27	SABRE	165	SELF	-	LOW LEVEL - RATS - LAKENHEATH		:50												
"	29	SABRE	150	SELF	-	RC CROSS COUNTRY AT HOME		1:15											:10	
						TOTAL FOR SEPTEMBER 52 441(F) SQN SABRE		23:40												:45	
						30 SEPT 52 Hamburg½ TOTAL SABRE		164:00											1:50	8:15	
OCT	4	SABRE	183	SELF	-	"ARDENT" B-29		:35												
"	6	SABRE	151	SELF	-	BREAKS AND O/S		:40												
"	7	SABRE	163	SELF	-	AIR TEST AND AEROS		:45												
"	7	SABRE	163	SELF	-	GGH AND CLOUD		:50											:15	
"	9	SABRE	167	SELF	-	NL TO MANSTON		:40												
"	9	SABRE	167	SELF	-	MANSTON TO GUTERSLOH		1:05			(GERMANY)										
"	10	SABRE	167	SELF	-	AIR DISPLAY AT GUTERSLOH		:55												
"	10	SABRE	167	SELF	-	GUTERSLOH TO MANSTON		:45												
"	10	SABRE	167	SELF	-	MANSTON TO NL (NIGHT)				:25										
"	12	SABRE	146	SELF	-	"ARDENT" (VAMPIRES)		:45												
"	12	SABRE	146	SELF	-	"ARDENT" DNCO		:15												
GRAND TOTAL [Cols. (1) to (10)] 525 Hrs. 55 Mins.					TOTALS CARRIED FORWARD		95 25	334 25	6 40	9 10								52 10	19 20	

seen during the Second World War and, as well, those from the First World War when brightly coloured aircraft were in vogue.

The band around the nose appeared to be the logical area for a simple design. A width measurement was made and a layout of squares prepared. We decided on black and white because of our crest, the Silver Fox (head in black) on a white background. The first part was easy: surface preparation, masking, base coat and a smooth finish coat of white. Because of the multiple curve I remember the problem in sizing each square as the grid pattern was drawn from top to bottom. Each "square" took on a taper to retain the classic lines of the Sabre's snout. F/O Don Atherton joined in the marking, correcting and remarking of the first pattern on 19130, and together we painted in the black checkerboard pattern. A measurement chart was prepared for future use and, progressively, all squadron members who had a flair for brush-work took part.

Bob Simmons

Anything for a Laugh
The RCAF Sabre crowd was famous for pulling stunts. Sometimes these were spontaneous, sometimes deviously planned. Generally, they were the sort of things that are (and deservedly so) unprintable. But the horse-in-the-commander's-office gimmick can probably be retold for present-day readers. The accompanying photo and caption give the background, while Duke Warren, one of the perpetrators, provides some details about the presentation shown.

"There were always skits going on between the squadrons. When Andy MacKenzie was leaving for Korea, we had a mess dinner in his honour. I lived in a little village called Uppingham at the time and enquired around as to whether there was a local artist. I was directed to a small cottage, where I found the man I was looking for.

"I told him that I wanted a painting of a horse. He happened to have a book showing horses, and I selected an average bay. Then I explained that what I really wanted was a painting of a horse in an office, looking down at a desk where there was a name plate that said 'S/L MacKenzie.' This rather surprised the artist, but he had visited our base and was aware that MacKenzie

Outrageous is perhaps the best adjective to describe some of the pranks organized by the Sabre crowd. One Friday evening (after hours) at St. Hubert "certain individuals" from 410 Squadron procured an old nag and painted its backside with the 441 colours. It was then led into the boss' office (Andy MacKenzie) and left there with a bale of hay and a bucket of water. For no extra charge, the perpetrators left a large fish on the radiator. One can only imagine what all this added up to by the time the boss showed up for work Monday morning! Here, Duke Warren presents MacKenzie with a painting of the nag at a Mess dinner at North Luff just before MacKenzie left for Korea. (via Duke Warren)

and I were both squadron commanders there. 'Anything else?' he asked.

"Now I had to get into the finer details, and I explained that I wanted the hindquarters of the horse to be black and white checkerboard. This really floored the artist, but he got the connection as he had seen the 441 colour scheme before.

"The painting was ready in about a week, and the 15 pound fee was duly paid. The presentation went over big. Mac enjoyed every moment of the evening as we all laughed about putting one over on him back at St. Hubert."

In January 1954, 439 and 441 Squadrons flew to RAF Acklington. Each month this station hosted two Fighter Command squadrons for gunnery on its radar-controlled ranges. On this occasion, top score went to F/O Bergie of 441 Squadron with 35.3 per cent followed by F/O Morrison of 439 with 30 per cent.

The Canadians were happy to get some shooting in, and everything went well, much credit being due to the ground crew who kept the Sabres fully operational. The next edition of the

Wing magazine, *Talepipe,* included a few sentiments about the sojourn to Acklington:

TIGER TALK — 439

Hello Gang,
Now that we are settled down once again at "Luffenham," a name which this last month has been said with the utmost reverence, we can look forward once again to a fairly normal routine. At least we won't have to spend half of our lunchtime frying eggs and beans in the barracks, or if you prefer, beans and eggs.

Now that "Acklington" is becoming just a memory, we can look back over the last month and review some of the highlights with a carefree spirit. Most of us came back a little thinner but perhaps a little wiser. We learnt how other services operated, how they lived, and how they played.

We were introduced to a very ancient method of clearing snow from runways, each man being issued with an antique instrument called a shovel. We then lined up in a line-abreast formation and proceeded down the runway, clearing the snow as we went. Medical men tell us we have 206 bones in our bodies, but after three or four hours shovelling, some of us thought we had ten times that amount by the number of aches and pains we had. Still it was one way of keeping warm.

While we were at Acklington, most of the boys took the opportunity to visit nearby historical and beauty spots. The most popular of these were the "Dunn Cow," the "Crow's Rest," and the "Make-way Cafe." I believe quite a few of the gang managed also to visit the "Rex Hotel," at Whitley Bay.

No doubt when the name Acklington is just a vague memory, whenever the lads are shooting the guff over a few beers and such names as Morpeth, Ashington and the "Sweat Box" at Red Row crop up, they will bring smiles to many faces. And I know that any mention of the "Plough" and "King's Court Hotel" will bring peals of laughter from four airmen who enjoyed at least one evening of revelry.

Yours fraternally,
LAC "Al" Wood

Here is another piece of original North Luff "culture," created jointly by 410ers W. Hopkins and G.W. Gatro. Reprinted from the February 1954 *Talepipe*.

In the valley of heap big sunshine
Near the 410 pilots shack...
Lies a group of barren buildings,
Two are red, one is black.

In this place when wheels are gathered
Making plans for heap big joke...
Many airmen sit disheartened,
Weekend just shot down in smoke.

Pilot flies in heap big aircraft,
Him make smoke trails miles high...
Airman stand in smokey wheel-house,
Wait till dark then him D.I.

Airman him don't got no flashlight,
Pilot him go home to sit...
Airman make mistake in darkness,
Wait till morning, him get hit.

Xmas comes big revolution,
Airman him get drunk all day...
Pilot try to fly on Xmas,
Aircraft bound to ricochet.

Sun get up in sunshine valley,
Pilot him come down to fly...
When he get to sunshine valley,
Heap big cloud make sunshine die.

Pilot say his plane no good,
Send mechanic on the double...
Mechanic browned off when he find
Pilot just got finger trouble.

Airman him got motor-cycle
Just to prove that him heap brave...
Try to come too fast from Leicester,
Monday morning him in grave.

Pilot come to sunshine valley
Him just new, not very smart...
Him push throttle too far forward,
Now him known as Heap Hot Start.

Day dawns down in sunshine valley
Airman up before the sun...
Braves stay there from dawn to darkness,
Then D.I. when flying done.

(with apologies to Hiawatha)

More of North Luff

F/O Don McIlraith was one of the early Sabre pilots at North Luffenham. He had trained at Centralia, went on Course 13 (Vampires) at Chatham, then joined Andy MacKenzie's boys at 441 Squadron, St. Hubert. During McIlraith's North Luff tour, many a memorable event was logged. One night F/O Pete Knox-Leet landed short. From his disabled Sabre he called the tower, "Sabre 122. I'm on the button," but, before he got his situation explained, heard to his surprise, "Cleared for takeoff!" Another day, Les Benson and Dean Kelly leapt into their Swords to head out for some gunnery. Away they went, but Benson's trip was short — he had taken off in a Sabre that hadn't been refuelled since its last trip! A duff fuel gauge sealed Benson's fate for the day — his Sabre soon pooped out and he had to eject. Dean Kelly quickly spotted his sidekick bobbing around in the sea, and tried to catch the attention of some fishing boats to direct them to the downed pilot. When all else failed, Kelly fired a burst across the bow of one of the vessels. Whether this helped or not is not known, though the drenched Benson was eventually fished out safely.

Truly this was the school of hard knocks or, as McIlraith put it, "We learned as we went in those days. Few

F/O Knox-Leet's prang by night at North Luff. Having landed short and taken out a fence, he appears to have made it to the button. But poor 19122 had had the biscuit. (via Bill Bain)

of us had ever even had any dual in the T-33, and most had very little jet time of any description."

In the early days at North Luff, the RCAF had the hottest fighter in all Europe. The closest to it were the early USAF F-86As, while the RAF standard day fighters were still the Meteor and Vampire. But the RAF was about to introduce two new designs: the Hawker Hunter (first flight July 20, 1951) and the Supermarine Swift (August 1, 1951). It was a matter of strict pride to the British that the Canadians be kept in the background and that their easily supersonic fighters not be allowed to steal any of the thunder of the Hunter or Swift.

The "big thing" in 1952 was the sonic boom. It seemed to be all the press and public were interested in, especially at air shows. About the only sonic booms resounding in the English countryside at the time, however, were those caused by the troublesome Canadians with their Sabres. But the press was not discouraged, and every time a sonic boom let loose, it was reported proudly as coming from some RAF fighter or other. Actually, the Hunter and Swift were few in number, and struggling through some difficult test and development times. Especially so the Swift, which ultimately flopped.

It was a veritable free-for-all in the skies of southern England during 1 Wing's time at North Luff. As McIlraith recalls, the only restriction the Sabre drivers had was, "Don't bother the Royal Flight." Thus fighters mixed it up with total abandon

Mass Sabre formation with one flight each from 441, 439 and 410 Squadrons over the English countryside. (*Flight* via Al Seitz)

Outside 441 ops at North Luff: Bob Haverstock, Les Benson, Fern Villeneuve, Steve Atherton, Ian MacDonald, Buzz Neilson, with Dean Kelly at the window. (D.J. Simmons)

(weather permitting) day in, day out. But one RAF aircraft was deemed (by the RAF) to be untouchable, the high-flying Canberra bomber. It could thumb its nose at everyone. Well, almost everyone. One day Ralph Annis caught a Canberra at about 45,000. He edged up behind and recorded his "kill" on film, then quickly, and still undetected, flew home. The film was developed. The results were perfect. As Don McIlraith recalls, "I think the film showed about three rivets of the Canberra's belly." The film was then delivered by the RCAF to RAF Fighter Command. To this day, the RAF has maintained a "no comment" stance on the issue. In fact, it never even acknowledged receiving the film.

From North Luff, Don McIlraith went to the OFU for about 2 1/2 years, making 18 Randoms (ferry flights). Next were tours on T-33s at Portage and Trenton. At Trenton the Central Flying School had three Sabres, to McIlraith's utter joy: "Every day I could book myself 'a shot' in a Sword." Next came Saskatoon, then a tour with 427, where one truly sad occasion was the day he flew on the squadron's last Sabre trip, taking beautiful Sabre 6s to their doom at the scrapyard at Prestwick.

F/O Bill Bain was posted to 410 Squadron on October 9, 1951. Of course, one of his earlier memories of things at St. Hubert was the prank pulled on Andy MacKenzie—leaving the horse in his office after work one Friday. The 410 crowd was in Halifax by Monday morning to catch the *Magnificent* for Norfolk, and it was just as well for them. Nobody connected with the "joke" would have been safe were he still around Montreal when MacKenzie arrived at work that Monday.

At Norfolk, Bain recalls that the 410 Sabres were being towed down to the dock from the airport, and at what seemed to the OC, Larry Hall, and the engineering people, to be an excessive speed. However, after about a day and a half's work all aircraft were safely aboard ship—11 uncocooned below deck; the rest thoroughly sealed against the wind and salt spray of the Atlantic.

After safe arrival at the King George V Docks at Greenock, the 410 complement travelled by rail to North Luffenham. Bain made his first Sabre trip from there on December 7. He had arrived in the UK with the grand total of three Sabre flights to his credit.

As do many of those involved with the Sabres in the early days, Bain notes the incredible inexperience of all concerned. There were young pilots with little more than basic flying skills (though a great amount of desire and enthusiasm); and equally inexperienced technical people with few spare parts. Besides these limitations, those at North Luff had the poor British weather to fly in (at North Luff, a tall industrial smoke stack protruding from low cloud was more than once the main nav aid in saving a potentially disastrous return-to-base). The dampness played havoc with the Sabre's radar gunsight, making it unreliable.

And with or without the radar sight, the 410 pilots, with their limited gunnery experience, could rarely score a

F/O Speed Bentham, S/L Duke Warren, F/L Grant Nichols, F/O Al Robb and F/O Garth Cinnamon after a flight from North Luff. The Sabre was Nichols' and was the only one on 410 with the nose painted black. (*Flight International* via Stephen Piercey)

decent percentage on the range. Many a log book entry shows 0/100 for a day's shooting over The Wash. The Sabre's radios were also temperamental. Had Joe Stalin only known all this!

Bain also remembers the RAF ground controllers. Their equipment was basically old wartime issue, but the operators themselves were expert. They could take a Sabre up, vector him right to a target, then watch each Sabre and let the pilot know when it was time to head for home before fuel ran too low. Of course, one of Bain's most unforgetable memories is of the great fun had in practice air fighting. Even civilian aircraft were fair game, and any airport could be beaten up without advance notice. One day Bain was caught by a Meteor whose pilot certainly knew his stuff. He could do little to shake his adversary, that is, until he dived to low level. The battle continued until Bain spotted several of His Majesty's warships. He swooped in among them and finally got unglued from the pesky Meteor. By this time Bain's fuel was low, and he had to find a place to land. He spotted a runway and lined up on final. But as he got in closer, he saw that the runway was unserviceable, and being used to store bombs! Then another airstrip appeared, and Bain

made a quick landing. His engine flamed out soon after touchdown.

Bain immediately realized that this 'drome was abandoned. He climbed from his Sabre, then trudged to a farmhouse and was directed to the nearest town with a telephone. A trucker gave him a lift and even provided a swig of rum. From town, Bain called base to report his situation, and was instructed to return to his aircraft and secure it over night. This he did, spending a

F/O Bill Bain of 410. His helmet sports the 441 Fox, but on the side is the 410 Cougar nipping the Fox's ear! (via Bill Bain)

Early edition of 439's aerobatic team at North Luff: F/O Gillies, F/O Kerr, F/L Wenz F/O Hamilton. (DND)

66

cold, damp and generally miserable night in his cockpit. Next morning a fuel bowser arrived and Bain was soon back at North Luff. For the next few days he was obliged to wear a large metal pendant for everyone to see wherever he went—The Royal Order of the Inserted Digit, as it was called. It was his to wear until the next fellow made a dumb move and got to wear the pendant around *his* neck!

As 1 Wing was in England's first line of defence, it was some time before 410 was allowed to leave the country. The first such excursion was finally OK'd and 410 flew off to Holland for an air show. There the Canadians were treated like kings, and a great time was had by all. Bain especially enjoyed the terrific food which was provided in such variety—what a break from English rations!

Duke Warren relates some happenings in the latter part of his 410 days at North Luff:

1954 was a more or less routine year of F-86 flying—air-to-air gunnery, Canberra interceptions, dogfights with Meteors and USAF F-86s. I visited an RCAF exchange officer with the RAF at a grass training strip and turned up in a Sabre. My landing was normal, but getting stopped on the grass was a bit different. For a moment I thought I wasn't going to stop within the aerodrome boundaries, but things worked out. Takeoff was routine. I haven't heard since of a Sabre operating from a grass strip. On a visit to an RCN detachment at Gosport I was asked on departure to do a little air show to "show the RN what we can do." The weather was miserable, with a low ceiling, so I wasn't about to do anything foolish. The only thing I thought that might impress them was a good takeoff. I held it down and built up a good head of steam, pulled up and rolled over, getting into cloud upside down at 300 feet. Once inside, I smartly rolled right-side up. The Sabre's instruments were so good that this sort of thing was no problem.

In 1954 W/C Lindsay was posted away from the COpsO position at 1 Wing, and I became permanent acting till W/C Parks arrived. He was new to fighter ops and to the Sabre, and I worked closely with him as he got his feet wet. Unfortunately Parks was killed in a flying accident shortly after, and I was then appointed COpsO. In early 1955 the wing moved to Marville. As I

was placed in charge of the airlift, my F-86 flying was cut back. In the first four months of the year I managed just 16:25 hours flying it, but piled up countless hours in the C-119 going back and forth across the Channel. That June I was posted to staff college in Toronto, but the following year I was lucky enough to get back on Sabres, this time at Chatham as CFI. That was just ideal,

Brooklyns 25-foot glider tow-target (with F/O Bill Bain) recovered after being shot up by some 410 sharp shooter. At one point, 410 had three such gliders and towed them behind their Sabres for gunnery over The Wash. (via Bill Bain)

Results of compressor stall at North Luff, with the aft end of Norm Ronaasen's Sabre burned right through. Interestingly, 19183 made it back into service and survived for some years in Turkey, where it finally crashed in 1966. (via Bill Bain)

Service crew get their energizer plugged into a 441 Sabre. (DND PL62256)

as it meant lots of Sabre flying, working with a crowd of bright young officers coming along, and having the challenge of seeing them develop into promising fighter pilots.

Douglas Warren

Occupational Hazards

R.S. "Ron" Poole joined the RCAF in the early fifties and spent most of his flying career in the fighter business. He retired in 1977, his final posting being on Voodoos with 425 Squadron. In between, he flew Vampires, Mustangs, T-33s and Sabres. His first Sabre flight took place with 413 Squadron at Bagotville on December 20, 1951, and he remembers that things around the squadron in those days were not exactly "fully operational." For instance, at first 413 had but one flying suit and one helmet. When it came time for hero pictures to be taken, the gear was passed from pilot to pilot, regardless of whether it fit. In Poole's case, he was rather short, while the sole 413 outfit was made for a giant. In 1952 Poole and Len Fine were sent to 410 Squadron at North Luffenham as replacements for F/Os Kerr and Rayner, who had been killed.

Three incidents in three days point out that there was always some gremlin lying in wait to pounce on a fighter pilot. Call them occupational hazards. On July 27, Poole was operating from Fürstenfeldbruck. Recovering after a mission, his landing gear failed, and he had to land 19169 with the left main hung up. Next day he was flying 19176 on a radar tracking mission for the USAF when he had a triple bird strike—three crows. Fortunately, all they did was bang up his leading edge (to say nothing of themselves). They might have bashed in his canopy or ripped into the tail! July 29, Poole had more bad fortune. He was in 19161 about to make a formation takeoff. The Sabre ahead had problems and pulled out of the way. Poole roared

down the runway and leapt into the sky. Suddenly his radio went u/s and he came straight around to land. How fortuitous, for it was quickly found that he had more than radio trouble. The first Sabre to have problems had actually been spitting out bits and pieces of its insides; Poole's Sabre had ingested some of these and had started shedding turbine blades. Had Poole not come quickly around his engine would have failed within minutes.

North Luffenham Maintenance

Some details relating to Sabre maintenance at 1 Wing, North Luffenham, are mentioned here by LCol J.H. Spratley, who was OC Repair and Wing salvage officer commencing in December 1951:

The maintenance organization to handle the Sabres at North Luffenham was a modified form of central maintenance whereby the three squadrons would look after their own servicing (first line) and Wing Maintenance would be responsible for everything else, i.e. periodic inspections, repair and modifications.

The CTechO (Chief Technical Officer), W/C T.A. "Art" Spruston, and the OC Maintenance, S/L T.L. Byrne, introduced this idea. It is hard to believe that it was an innovation. There was, however, some muted objection at the squadron level, yet the reasons

No. 1 Wing pilots at a briefing during Ardent, one of the big air defence exercises held in the UK in the early fifties. (via E.B. Hale)

for the differing opinions were understandable. On the one hand, the squadrons were jealous of their autonomy and wanted to maintain a sense of identity and of belonging in every one of their members. This was particularly important if the squadron had to disperse. On the other hand, there was a shortage of spares, equipment and some facilities. The only reasonable way to use what we had to the best advantage was to pool them to the degree that was introduced. This included assigning squadron technicians to Wing Maintenance.

Apart from the jurisdictional differences, the major maintenance problem that I recall was the shortage of Sabre spares and ground handling equipment. For example, we had to resort to building inspection stands from wood, and the robbing of aircraft was a way of life in the early months. Since stored and reserve aircraft were also my responsibility, the unauthorized removal of "bits and pieces" was a major headache. I suspect the squadron technicians carried out midnight raids to the temporary hangars where our surplus Sabres were stored, but no one was ever caught at it. Obviously, the squadron maintainers were keen. There was always a healthy sense of competition and, as I recall, the results, i.e. serviceability rates, were outstanding.

J.H. Spratley

Bystanders Beware
An ever-present danger with jet aircraft in the early days was people too close to an air intake getting sucked into the engine. Two fatalities occurred with Sabres 19294 and 19451 in the Greek Air Force. An airman died at Oldenburg, December 22, 1954, when sucked inside 19504. In the RCAF, there were at least two such accidents with the Sabre. One occurred November 30, 1951, at Renfrew, Scotland. Aircraftman Al Richards was sucked into the intake while a mechanic was doing a run-up. F/O Winston Price reported that "before the engine had stopped completely, they had grabbed Richards and pulled him out. He was unconscious and his uniform was in tatters." Richards' injuries were minor, though his hat and coat were pulled off, chewed up, and spit out by the J47. Instrumental in saving Richards was LAC Roland Gelinas, who was later awarded the

G/C E.B. Hale, first CO of RCAF Station North Luffenham. (DND)

British Empire Medal for his quick action.

The Station Commander
When North Luffenham opened as home base for No. 1(F) Wing, the CO was G/C E.B. "Ed" Hale. He had begun flying with the Hamilton Aero Club, taking his first flight on June 5, 1936. Soon after, he had formed Peninsula Airways, equipped with a Puss Moth and one of the few Fleetwings Sea Bird amphibians. A Stinson Reliant was later added. There were adventuresome times for Hale during his time as a commercial flyer. In 1937 he had a charter to Florida and Havana with his Puss Moth. Such flights were still headline makers in the thirties. Another occasion his Reliant caught fire in Toronto harbour and burned to a crisp.

In 1939 Hale joined Imperial Airways in the UK, where he joined several other Canadian pilots including Al Lilly and N.E. "Molly" Small. At first Hale was on the Southampton-

Singapore flying boat service, then flew the Ensign airliner serving the Continent. When war broke out, Imperial Airways began using the Ensign for trooping. On one flight (September 16, 1939) into eastern France, Hale and his co-pilot observed a British Expeditionary Force barrage near Saarbrücken. They flew over to have a look but dived for home when some 109s showed up. Many years later, Hale learned from his friend, Johannes Steinhoff, later commander of the post-war Luftwaffe, that it had been Steinhoff himself who had scrambled the 109s that day.

Early in the war Hale returned to Canada. He commanded 161 Squadron on the East Coast on antisubmarine warfare, flying Cansos and Digbys. Post-war, two early assignments were OC of 412 Squadron at Rockcliffe, and CO of RCAF Station Chatham.

On January 21, 1949, G/C Hale flew the Vampire for the first time (17086) and soon also checked out on the Mustang and T-33. In 1951 he was made CO of the just-forming No. 1 Wing and arrived in Odiham that August. There he flew the Vampire and Meteor with 421 Squadron as he awaited his own three squadrons.

During a visit to North Luff by A/M Wilf Curtis, the subject of Korea came up, and Hale suggested that the RCAF should send some senior pilots there along with the younger ones to see

G/C Hale during a top-level visit to 1 Wing by A/M Wilf Curtis and Defence Minister Claxton. (DND)

what difference the experience factor might make. Curtis agreed and Hale immediately volunteered. Curtis was taken by surprise, and Hale quickly had a letter drafted, giving himself "carte blanche" in Korea, then had Curtis sign it. Hale was soon on his way to Japan on a 426 Squadron North Star.

In Tokyo, Hale met with Gen Partridge, who agreed that he could fly combat missions. However, when Hale met the wing commander, there wasn't such a welcome, as he was not too keen to have Canadians in his unit. All doubts were soon dispelled, though, as Hale proved himself a capable fighter pilot.

Hale joined the 51st Fighter Wing at Suwon, where he immediately began flying combat missions. Hale recalls a pattern of easy days when the Communists would lose many aircraft, then brief periods when the MiG pilots they met were clearly top notch. One explanation for this was that there were short periods between MiG OTUs in China when the instructors were free to head south into the fray, and at such times more UN aircraft than usual would fall victim to their more experienced ways.

On one mission Hale led his wing on an escort for F-84s which were to bomb an army depot. At the rendezvous he found that the F-84s had already gone in on the target, so the Sabres poured it on, trying to catch up. When they reached the target area, they found that the F-84s had been set upon by MiGs, so the Sabres got right to work. The MiGs were soon routed and no USAF aircraft were lost. For this action Hale later received the USAF DFC.

Another time, Hale's element was called in to escort a rescue chopper deep inside unfriendly territory. The Sabres spotted the downed pilot, and harassed nearby enemy troops while the chopper picked him up. But the chopper was low on fuel. A second one soon appeared. The first got a short jump on the pursuing troops, then landed. Its crew and the rescued pilot got out, and the chopper was set alight. The back-up machine then carried everyone home.

From May 1 to May 25, 1952, G/C Hale flew 26 combat missions in Korea

Line-up of 421 Vampires at North Luff. (via E.B. Hale)

Base defence—North Luff "irregulars" show off some prisoners who happen to be seasoned paratroops. (via E.B. Hale)

for a total of 38 hours. Though his stay was brief, it had been busy. Like others before him, he discovered the strengths and weaknesses of the Sabre vs the MiG-15. For example, he learned how to climb the Sabre to 40,000 + feet in the shortest time, then to stay there at speed—a tricky thing, as at such heights the Sabre would easily stall out. If the Sabre lost speed, it couldn't regain it up high. If jumped by high flying MiGs, Sabre pilots learned that a diving turn was best, as the Sabre could out-turn the MiG; and down lower the Sabre was much more competitive.

G/C Hale left North Luffenham in August 1953, replaced by G/C Red Somerville. Thereafter he held numerous positions in the RCAF before retiring in 1967.

The Old Sweats

Many of the "solid citizens" who flew the Sabre in the RCAF were veterans of the Second World War. In the expanding post-war air force, when the world was on the brink of another global conflict, the combination of skill and experience that these "old sweats" brought to the RCAF was indispensable. In fact, it gave the RCAF the edge it would have over all other NATO air forces, especially in gunnery. That, after all, was what the game was all about.

It is natural to find that the wartime crowd headed up No.1(F)OTU at St. Hubert and Chatham, and that the top instructors there were experienced pilots, often with kills in the European and North African theatres. And those who commanded the RCAF's first post-war fighter squadrons were from the same bunch. Thus, at Chatham were found such wartime types as Jerry Billing, Ernie Glover, Irish Ireland, Tom Koch, Omer Levesque, Gerry McCulley, Eric Smith, Stan Turner, Duke Warren and Tommy

The Duke of Edinburgh tries out a Sabre during a visit to 1 Wing in May 1953. (via E.B. Hale)

The Royal Party inspects 1 Wing at the Coronation Review, RAF Odiham, July 15, 1953. (via E.B. Hale)

Wheler. Leading the Sabre squadrons as they formed was a crowd of well seasoned combat pilots: Larry Hall (410), Doug Lindsay (413), Jack Allan (414), Don Laubman (416), R.T.P. Davidson (421), John Buzza (422), Lyte Gervais (427), Stocky Edwards (430), C.D. Barnett (431), J.D. Mitchner (434), Cal Bricker (439) and Andy MacKenzie (441). There is no question that it was the RCAF's wartime air and ground crew who made the Sabre operation and all other aspects of the air force work so successfully.

G/C J.D. "Red" Somerville was not only a wartime Mosquito pilot, but a pre-war flier from away back. He may be the oldest to have flown Sabres in the RCAF on a regular basis. He had soloed in 1929 from Toronto's famous de Lesseps field, and through the thirties did considerable barnstorming, and worked with 110 "City of Toronto" Squadron (Aux) as an aero engine mechanic. He spent the early war years instructing in Canada, and when finally posted overseas seemed "doomed" to Bomber Command. Doomed, for he had his heart set on Spitfires: "In an attempt to rectify what I deemed to be a serious error on somebody's part, I went to London to talk with Air Commodore Wilf Curtis, the senior RCAF officer there, and my former OC from 110 Squadron."

Curtis explained, "They're too hot, Red. The guys who fly Spits are 19 and 20 years old." Somerville was disappointed, but Curtis did agree to have him posted to night fighters. Somerville continues:

"My wartime operations were all on Mosquitos, first in the UK, then in France and Germany. I also checked out on such types as the P-47, P-51 and A-26. The 2800-hp engines on the A-26 were huge, and the noise unbelievable. Take off, wheels up, climb speed. Fifty feet up and I see a small T-handle labelled Control Lock. I think, the Americans have done it again: a mechanical device to hold the aircraft in a steady rate of climb while the pilot attends to more important things. I pulled the handle—it *locks* the flying controls and closes the throttles! My right hand is a blur as it snaps the T-lock and shoves the throttle open again."

After surviving various such shenanigans, Somerville decided to stay in the post-war RCAF. In 1948 he checked out on the Vampire and in 1951 was made station commander at St.

G/C Somerville during Sabre times. (DND)

Hubert. For Red Somerville, the timing of this posting couldn't have been better, for the Sabres were just beginning to appear:

The earliest Sabres at St. Hubert had at least two idiosyncrasies which only the first pilots to fly them experienced. The first was the hydraulic elevator control which was notable for removing any "feel" for the pilot. On takeoff, for instance, the fledgling Sabre driver would pull back on the pole. Nothing seemed to happen. Pull...nothing. PULL! Then he abruptly went flying.

The stick was fitted with a bungee spring device which allowed the pilot to overcome the hydraulic control, but it required several pounds of pull to do so. Responding to complaints from pilots, Canadair reduced the pull required to about a half pound.

The second curiosity was a toggle switch on the panel, used to prevent compressor stall. The pilot was to open this switch before slamming the throttle open from, say, idle to full bore. Sometimes this detail was overlooked, leading to engine flame-out.

The Sabre was a very strongly built fighter. One day Ronnie Found of 410

Squadron crash landed at Dorval following engine trouble. His Sabre slammed through the orange and white checkered ILS shack at the end of the runway. The Sabre was totally destroyed, but Found survived—saved by the solid framework around him, but also by his hard hat. Hard hats were a novelty in those days, and many pilots turned theirs into "objets d'art" with their names and various graphic designs painted on. Not everyone was sold on their effectiveness. Ron Found was glad he was wearing his, though. When he crashed, he was thrown forward. His hard hat took the brunt of the ensuing collision of man and machine. Some years after I experienced a strange feeling when I recognized Ronnie Found's battered crash helmet lying in a bin in a junk store.

As "station master" at St. Hubert, I could always find time to phone one of the squadrons and ask if there were any "spare" Sabres in need of a pilot. I often found myself test flying Sabres back from maintenance, or as wingman in formations, which allowed me all the fun of flying and none of the responsibility of leading. Perfect!

During this time, the RAF had a small unit at St. Hubert to handle the ferrying of Sabres to England. Each new Sabre required some 10 hours flying before delivery. Again, this was ideal for me, and I had all the Sabres to fly that I wanted.

I had the pleasure (with some anxiety thrown in) of making several trips in RAF Sabres as far as Goose Bay, a distance from St. Hubert of 673 miles. That was just about maximum range of the Sabres with their underwing tanks (100 gal.). Our track was down the north shore of the St. Lawrence to Sept Iles, then inland across Labrador to Goose. There were no alternates and weather was often marginal. Normally a pilot could hold over the beacon for snow showers to subside, but not with our RAF Sabres. We arrived at Goose with perhaps 10 minutes fuel remaining. It was scary. Later on, the Sabres carried the big 167-gal. underwing tanks and upped their reserve to 30 minutes on arrival at Goose.

My luck with postings continued and in August 1953 I was promoted to group captain and named station CO of North Luffenham. There I was reunited with many old friends from 410, 439 and 441 Squadrons, which had earlier formed at St. Hubert. On each squadron were 18 Sabres and 24 pilots.

But the actual number of drivers present always fluctuated; thus by having my name in three different flight rooms, I managed to log as much Sabre time as did squadron pilots. Later on, I did some extra flying testing Sabre 2s overhauled at Ringway, near Manchester, for the Greeks and Turks.

One day I was flying a solo trip in one of the refits. On the tail was the bright red and white Turkish flag. It was beautiful and sunny over eastern England and those were the days when air fighting was not a pre-arranged thing. Anyone was fair game. To be bounced was to be embarrassed, a terrible loss of face for the peacetime fighter pilot (in wartime he'd be dead!). All the more reason that I, a veritable "senior citizen" in the fighter business, should not be caught unawares.

For the day-fighter pilot, lookout was everything, and this day mine was better than that of the crew of a USAF B-57. They should have caught me before I turned in on them, but didn't, and they didn't even notice as I came up on their starboard wing. There I sat, waiting. Finally the navigator glanced over and gave a 'Hi, y'all!' wave. He looked back into the cockpit, then whirled in a classic double take. That red Turkish emblem! For certain it flashed through his mind, "That's a Russian out there!"

Every fighter pilot has his embarrassing moments. If you're lucky, nobody's around to see your mistake. But if you're leading a four-plane and three others and maybe the boys in the tower witness your gaffe, then you're apt to find yourself buying drinks-without-end afterwards. It happened to me.

When 1 Wing moved across to Marville, I was posted there as station CO. We were flying Sabre 5s, and the 6s were beginning to arrive. Everyone was anxious to fly the 6 with its beefed-up Orenda 14, but 1 Wing would be last to re-equip.

In 1956 I was vacationing with my family in the German Alps. There I happened to meet A/V/M Godwin, AOC of the Air Division. I asked him, "How about dropping off a Mark 6 at Marville?" and thought no more about it until, lo and behold, on the next delivery of Mark 6s, one spiralled down and landed at Marville. Naturally, I had my name on it and was ready to fly as soon as maintenance

completed the acceptance check.

Of course, the bathtub-size underwing tanks were removed, so I was to fly the Sabre 6 "clean." This was all I could have hoped for, as I roared away from Marville. What a rate of climb! Even better, I soon spotted and surprised a section of French Mystères, beautiful airplanes but, I can tell you, no match for the Sabre 6. The French were not too keen to mix it up so, after a short joust, I headed north for home.

Now I consulted my fuel gauges. I was low, so quickly called Marville. Tower came back with the runway in use. A few minutes later I called "Initial," pitched over the runway, dropped the gear on the downwind, and was on the final descending turn toward blessed asphalt. "Base, final..." I wanted final landing clearance. What I got back was, "Sir? We don't see you!"

I was seconds from landing at a French military airfield under construction. The runway heading and dispersal were just like our own. I rechecked my fuel and decided that the embarrassment of landing here would be less hard to take than landing in some farmer's field as I struggled back to Marville. So I transmitted, "I'm landing at this French base 20 miles south. You'd better send someone to get me." It cost me a fortune in drinks at the Mess that night.

By the time I ended my tour in the Air Division I had logged 625 Sabre hours. I loved that airplane.

J.D. "Red" Somerville

First Big Exercise

In July 1952 the RCAF participated in a continental air defence exercise, Signpost, stating, "It is necessary to carry out realistic training using the new equipment and techniques, and to obtain a careful evaluation of the overall effectiveness of the Air Defence system." One specific objective was to give the chance to auxiliary units to train alongside the regular forces, thus the timing of Signpost to coincide with annual summer camp for the auxiliaries. USAF fighter and bomber aircraft were to play a major part.

The scope of Signpost is clearly illustrated by the list of participants:

At Bagotville

413 Sqn	16 Sabres
430 Sqn	16 Sabres
401 Sqn(Aux)	10 Vampires
438 Sqn(Aux)	10 Vampires
58th FIS	3 F-94s

At Uplands

416 Sqn	16 Sabres
442 Sqn(Aux)	10 Mustangs
443 Sqn(Aux)	8 Mustangs

At St. Hubert

421 Sqn	16 Sabres
400 Sqn(Aux)	10 Vampires
411 Sqn(Aux)	10 Vampires
58th FIS	3 F-94s

At Rockcliffe

420 Sqn(Aux)	8 Mustangs
424 Sqn (Aux)	8 Mustangs

*Total: Sabres 64, Vampires 40, Mustangs 34, F-94s 6 (144 fighters)

This excerpt from the "game plan" of Signpost illustrates the parameters considered essential by Air Defence Command in the early fifties and shows the concern for keeping the exercise realistic yet safe:

8 *Aircraft Markings.* All B-29 and B-50 aircraft of the USAF will carry distinctive markings. Details of the markings are to be promulgated by the CCC to those concerned immediately prior to the Exercise.

9 *Aborting Strike Aircraft.* Aborting strike aircraft, when in or required to enter, an ADIZ or CADIZ, will request their position and flight plan be passed to radar.

10 *Night Aggressor Aircraft.* Aggressor aircraft operating at night will use nagivation lights at all altitudes.

INTERCEPTION AND COMBAT PROCEDURES

11 *Simulated Attacks.* Simulated attacks on aggressor aircraft are authorized in accordance with Air Staff Instruction 2/6 but the following additional safety precautions, required by Strategic Air Command, are to be observed during simulated attacks on *all* aircraft.

(a) Breakaways are to be carried out at a safe distance from the bomber aircraft. The actual distance will vary with the type of attack but is in no case to be less than 600 feet.

(b) No head-on attacks are to be made.

12 *Gun Checks.* Before making simulated attacks all pilots are to carry out a gun check as described in Appendix "M" to this order.

13 *Failure to Recognize Intercepted Aircraft.* Aircraft which cannot be recognized as "friendly" or "faker" are

to be treated in accordance with Air Staff Instruction 2/5.

14 *"Destruction" of Bombers.* In order to have a reasonably straightforward yardstick for estimating the number of bombers which would have been destroyed on a raid the following rules are to apply:

(a) To assure destruction of the bomber, it must be attacked by a minimum of two fighters, each of which must approach within effective range of the bomber. "Effective Range" is considered to be within 750 yards.

(b) Four attacks on the bomber, during which the fighters make *effective* attacks, are to constitute a "kill". This number may consist of one attack by one fighter and three by the other, or two attacks by each fighter.

(Special Note:— It is possible that some pilots in the Auxiliary squadrons may be considered insufficiently experienced to make attacks, although they may be flying as No. 2s. In this case, the No. 2 should stand off while the Section leader makes attacks. Two *effective* attacks by the section leader will then constitute a "kill" as it will be presumed that the No. 2 would have followed his leader in under war conditions. A sensible interpretation of this rule should be made and it should be clearly stated in the report whether the No. 2 was authorized to make attacks or not. If the No. 2 fails to make attacks although he is authorized to do so, this special rule is not to apply.)

(c) After a total of four effective simulated attacks, the fighter is to be assumed to have expended all ammunition. He is immediately to inform the controller that his ammunition is expended (Ammo Zero) and is to return to base under the instructions of the formation leader and controller.

(d) Fighter pilots are to keep the controllers informed of their progress, using the normal operational procedure, and are also to inform the controller when they have made four attacks and can be considered to have expended all ammunition. They are responsible for informing the controller also when their fuel

state will not permit further operations. The first aircraft of a formation is to report "sights on" at the commencement of the first attack.

(e) Specific identification of the bombers is required for assessment purposes. In the case of "faker" aircraft, this is to be obtained after attacks have been completed. For other aircraft the normal identification procedures laid down in Air Staff Instruction 2/5 are to apply. The identification of individual bombers is to be obtained by each formation of attacking fighters. In the case of a formation of bombers, the detailed identification of at least one of the formation is to be obtained. Care is to be taken to ensure that fighters obtaining the identification of bombers do not interfere with subsequent attacks by other formations. In order to assist in the identification of bombers, it is essential for pilots to note and report after landing the exact time of interception and attack and, if possible, the geographic position.

(f) Attacks are *not* to be made against civil and commercial aircraft *under any circumstances* or against service transport aircraft unless specific instructions are given.

(g) Unit commanders, formation leaders and controllers are to insist on the maintenance of strict R/T discipline. It must be emphasized that unnecessary R/T chatter may ruin the exercise. Disciplinary measures, including grounding for the period of the exercise, are to be taken against offenders in this respect.

15 All strike aircraft, on first entering the area of radar cover, will be heading for a specific target. An analysis will be made of the effectiveness of the defences in dealing with this initial attack. In order, however, that the maximum training value may be obtained from each raid, the bombers may not, on all occasions, withdraw after the first attack but will proceed to other targets. In such cases, the bombers may be intercepted again by fresh fighters, even though they may have been "destroyed", in order to provide as much training as possible. The raid will be assessed in addition as one attacking the second target and so on. On other occasions, a raid may with-

draw from radar cover and return as a new raid. In such cases, it is to be assumed that the raid consists of different aircraft and "kills" on the previous raid are to be disregarded.

ACTION TO BE TAKEN IN THE EVENT OF AN ACTUAL EMERGENCY

16 In the event of an actual emergency occuring during "Signpost," it will be necessary to take certain actions to ensure that the emergency can be met with the minimum amount of delay. The emergency may be caused by:

(a) The declaration of a military emergency.

(b) The detection of actual hostile aircraft.

(c) Information being received from intelligence sources that an attack is imminent.

17 If an emergency occurs the following action is to be taken:

(a) The command control centre will broadcast a code word, preceded by the word "emergency" on all tactical frequencies. This code word is to be promulgated to all operating units by the CCC just prior to the commencement of the exercise.

(b) On receipt of the code word all fighter aircraft are to land, refuel immediately and, on instructions from the CCC via the GCI come to operational readiness with guns fully armed.

EMERGENCY AIRFIELDS

18 Mont Joli and Ancienne Lorette airfields will be available for emergency use. The following facilities will be available:

(a) JP-1 fuel (refueling by hand pump)

(b) 100 Octane fuel (civilian sources)

(c) Energizers

(d) A skeleton crew will be available to carry out minor servicing. Facilities for major repairs and other maintenance services will not be available.

(Note: All pilots are to understand that the main runway at Ancienne Lorette Airfield (06-24) is only 3370 feet in length, and at Mont Joli, the main runway (06-24) is 6000 feet in length.

No.1(F) Operational Training Unit

RCAF Station Chatham

The heart of the RCAF's Sabre training program was at Chatham, New Brunswick on Miramichi Bay. It had been a BCATP training station during the war (No.21EFTS, Finches; No.10AOS, Ansons), and had then been reactivated with W/C Ed Hale as the first post war station commander. He arrived at Chatham on May 1, 1949. No.1(F)OTU, formed at St. Hubert September 1, 1948 to train jet fighter pilots on Vampires, reformed at Chatham November 15, 1949.

Students arriving at the OTU were wartime "retreads" mostly with fighter experience, and "pipeliners," young pilots fresh from basic training. When squadrons formed up, this provided an ideal set-up—all good pilots with a solid core of personnel who were veterans of modern air combat and important symbols for the young pilots to look up to.

RCAF Station Chatham in the summer of 1955, looking west and taken from the station's S-51 rescue helicopter. (via Ken Johnston)

Initially the OTU operated 25 Vampires and several Harvards. Check-out for the Vamp was a few high-speed circuits, landing flapless, in the Harvard. Then, away you went. Most students flew the Vampire at Chatham after two or three Harvard trips. A busy day was April 25, 1951, when 79:35 hours were flown on Vamps at the OTU. Of course, there was no such luxury until 1951 as a T-bird. So it was "survival of the fittest" and almost everyone panned out. Most of the pipeliners agree that this was mainly due to the excellent training they had received on Harvards at places like Centralia, Gimli, Macdonald and Trenton, where, once again, the instructors were nearly all wartime veterans. It appears that the first Sabre arrived at Chatham on February 20, 1952. It was 19281 and was ferried in by F/O Bruce Fleming.

Typical among the post-war trainees at Chatham was John L. Den Ouden. He had made his first flight in the RCAF in Harvard '688 at the Central Flying School, Trenton. That was on May 30, 1949, with his instructor, F/O Ovans. He soloed July 6. On February

19, 1951, he made his first flight at the OTU in a Harvard with Dean Kelly. March 6 he flew the Vampire. After graduating, he was posted to 416 at Uplands under S/L Don Laubman. There he had the joy of "owning" his own Mustang and recalls how on Sundays the boys would be out at the 'drome polishing and vacuuming their aircraft. Den Ouden's Sabre years began with a flight in 19289 on March 28, 1952.

Syd Burrows had first flown in Harvard 2903 at Centralia on April 18, 1951, with instructor F/O Bud McNair. He soloed May 9 and graduated January 29, 1952. Like hundreds of others in these years, he was shipped to RCAF Station Macdonald. It was home for No.1 Primary Gunnery School and operated Harvards that could carry underwing ordnance and had a .303 in the starboard wing.

Burrows arrived at Chatham in the spring, making his first flight in a Harvard on April 16. He flew the Vampire the same day and recalls it as "very basic and easy to fly." He graduated June 20 after a total at the OTU of

A pair of hero shots at Chatham, 1951. Doug Hogan with Vampire "28," and Ralph Heard. (via Ralph Heard)

Backbone of RCAF pilot training for decades was the Harvard. For fighter pilot training, the Harvard was where it all began, at places like Centralia, Macdonald and Trenton. DK-W, bomb racks fitted, is seen with the Air Armament School near Trenton in 1950. The lovely formation scene of Central Flying School Harvards is over Lake Ontario in September 1955. (H. Hrischenko, DND PL130175)

47:55 hours on the Vamp, 8:15 on the Harvard and 1:00 on the newly-arrived T-33. His first posting was to 434 at Uplands, where on August 19 he strapped into 19128 and made his first Sabre flight.

Training at Chatham was undertaken by various flights: conversion, gunnery and tactical. During his tour there as CFI, Omer Levesque introduced coloured bands painted on the aircraft according to flights (red for conversion flight, blue for TAC flight and black for gunnery flight), a concept he had brought back from Korea. In total, a student would need some 80 hours to complete Sabre training. Of course the ultimate goal was to graduate good combat pilots—men who could outfight any opponent. At the time, much centred on how best to deal with the MiG-15. The doctrine taught at Chatham is outlined in this OTU publication of November 22, 1955:

Year 1951-2	Aircraft Type	No.	Pilot, or 1st Pilot	2nd Pilot, Pupil or Passenger	Duty (Including Results and Remarks)	Single-Engine Aircraft Day Dual	Day Pilot	Night Dual	Night Pilot	Multi-Engine Aircraft Day Dual	Day 1st Pilot	Day 2nd Pilot	Night Dual	Night 1st Pilot	Night 2nd Pilot	Passenger	Instr/Cloud Flying Dual	Cloud	Link Trainer
					Totals Brought Forward	125 110	140 150	10:05	9:45	1:00							42:10	3:40	
DEC 28	VAMPIRE	17066	SELF	SOLO	ARMAMENT #2		1:00												
DEC 29	VAMPIRE	17066	SELF	SOLO	ARMAMENT #3		1:00												
DEC 31	VAMPIRE	17045	SELF	SOLO	ARMAMENT #4		1:00												
DEC 31	VAMPIRE	17054	SELF	SOLO	ARMAMENT #5		1:00												
DEC 31	VAMPIRE	17047	SELF	SOLO	INSTRUMENTS (:20)		1:00										:20		
			J. Levesque S/L	SUMMARY FOR DEC UNIT- #1 (F) OTU DATE- 31 DEC 51 SIGNATURE- R Heard	TYPES VAMPIRE HARVARD GRAND TOTAL	18:30 :30	:30										1:45 :25		
						125:10	145:50	10:05	9:45	1:00							42:30	3:40	
JAN 2	VAMPIRE	17077	SELF	SOLO	ARMAMENT #6		1:10												
JAN 4	VAMPIRE	17036	SELF	SOLO	INSTRUMENTS (:20)		1:00										:20		
JAN 4	VAMPIRE	17020	SELF	SOLO	INSTRUMENTS (:25)		1:00										:25		
JAN 4	DAKOTA	978	OPERATION "KYAK"	SEARCH F/L BILL RAWLINGS	"SPUN IN" ON AEROBATICS IN VAMPIRE 16304 JAN (NIGHT DAK 3:00)														
JAN 5	VAMPIRE	17045	SELF	SOLO	OP KAYAK		1:15				FOUND JAN 7 BY FARMER 13 MILES FROM BASE.								
JAN 5	VAMPIRE	17045	SELF	SOLO	OP KAYAK		1:00												
JAN 5	HARVARD	2804	SELF	F/O ROWE	OP KAYAK		3:20												
JAN 6	HARVARD	3318	SELF	F/O MONCRIEFF	OP KAYAK		3:15												
JAN 7	VAMPIRE	17021	SELF	SOLO	OPS KAYAK & BATTLEDRESS		1:15				OPERATION "BATTLEDRESS" F/O HOWE PRANGS F-51								
JAN 7	HARVARD	3318	SELF	F/O SHANNON	OPS KAYAK & BATTLEDRESS		3:20				ON AIR TEST JAN 6 - SEARCH GIVEN UP 10 JAN								
JAN 9	VAMPIRE	17065	SELF	SOLO	FORMATION #8		1:00				A/C FOUND JAN 17								
JAN 9	VAMPIRE	17065	SELF	SOLO	ARMAMENT #7		:30												
				GRAND TOTAL [Cols. (1) to (10)] 309 Hrs. 55 Mins.	Totals Carried Forward	125:10	163:55	10:05	9:45	1:00							43:15	3:40	

Vampire flying at No. 1(F)OTU, RCAF Station Chatham. These excerpts are from F/O Ralph Heard's log book.

Early Allison-powered T-33 seen at Chatham in the early fifties. The underslung tip tanks give the aircraft away as Lockheed, not Canadair-built. (Ralph Heard)

Course 15 at Chatham. In the back row are R.J. Moncrieff, Sam Moore, Al Young, W.H. "Scotty" McKay, Jack Nichol, Ron Barnett (straddling cockpit), Bob Hallowell (in cockpit), Stan Keffer, Neil "Rev" Pringle, P.V. "Pat" Robinson, Don Ackert, George Shorey, Frank Wagner, Les Sparrow. Standing are Brian Burns, Jerry Tobin, Ralph Heard, "Nat" Hogan, George Fulford, "Red" MacKay, F/L Petrin, Fern Potvin, George Northop, "Buzz" Buzik. Kneeling is Ian McMillman. (via Ralph Heard)

J.L. ''Denny'' Den Ouden while on course at the Vampire OTU. He joined the RCAF in 1946 and trained first as an aero engine tech, then remustered to flying in 1949. He first flew the Vampire March 6, 1951, then went on P-51s with 416. March 28, 1952, he finally got his hands on a Sabre. He flew it last on August 7, 1958, and totalled 809:35 hours on type. His final Sabre log book entry reads, ''Farewell to the sweetest aircraft ever built.'' (via J.L. Den Ouden)

Sabre Tactics—Fighter vs Fighter

GENERAL

1   The basic principles of World War II fighter tactics and air combat still apply to the employment of modern jet fighter aircraft in battle. Although certain basic rules remain unchanged, everyone engaged in the use of air

Sabre 19290 taxis at Chatham in the early fifties and displays the markings devised by Omer Levesque: nose and fuselage bands, and painted rudder, as well as large fuselage number in black. (Al Humphreys)

power today must be ready to evolve and evaluate, accept and reject new tactics more rapidly then ever before.

2   Experience on jet aircraft at high altitudes and high speeds proved that a larger number of smaller flights with a maximum of four aircraft in a flight, were much more effective than a smaller number of larger flights. The system of a maximum of four aircraft in a flight has many advantages and these are described as follows:

(a) *Fuel Economy* - Because the aircraft start up in fours, taxi straight out and employ a running take-off, a considerable amount of fuel is saved which would normally be burned up waiting for other aircraft to start and get formed up at the take-off position.

(b) *Surprise* - Because the aircraft are operating in small numbers they are more difficult to detect both by radar and visual sighting.

Survival course at Chatham. Gathered around the barbecue are Bernie Pannell, Gar Cinnamon, Bob Morgan, Pete Knox-Leet, Wes McEwen and Speed Bentham. (via J.L. Den Ouden)

(c) *Manoeuvrability* - A flight of four aircraft is much more manoeuvrable than the unwieldy squadron number of twelve or eighteen aircraft and because each flight operates on its own, it allows the flight leader and the element leader (No.3) more initiative.

(d) *Speed* - The smaller number of aircraft in the formation permits the leader to fly at a higher power setting, enabling him to keep the speed well up without giving the wing men too much difficulty in station keeping. This system eliminates the number of stragglers who are then in a vulnerable positon.

(e) *Area Coverage* - For a given number of aircraft in any one area, it is claimed that a large number of sec-

A real mob scene at Chatham. The boys seem to be whooping it up just a bit. How many went flying next morning? (via Gerry McCully)

tions of four give better area coverage than a smaller number of large groups of aircraft. Each of the smaller groups is free to initiate an attack or to take defensive action if bounced without waiting to be given clearance by a squadron leader who may be a mile or more away from the flight or section which has spotted the enemy aircraft.

(f) *Fire Power* - This system provides more number ones who are primary shooters.

FORMATION AT HEIGHT

3　The most effective formation at altitude was the 4-plane "fluid 4" with the element (No.3 and No.4) stepped up and away from the sun, with the element leader well up and almost line abreast with No.1, and No.2 and No.4 well up, staggered only slightly back (see diagrams). Since the best defence is good offence, aircraft should be flown at maximum performance, i.e., the slowest aircraft in the flight is flying at maximum performance and the leader adjusts his power so that formation may be maintained.

　The success of this "fluid four" formation described above relies on the four highly specialized individuals working as a *team*. Each member of the formation has a specific duty to perform and must carry out this duty if

the team is to fulfill its primary function of destroying enemy aircraft in the air. The duties of wingman, element leader, and flight leader are outlined as follows in an attempt to fully realize the importance of each.

4　*Duties of Wingman* - The wingman must hold a position on his leader to allow him to do two things:

　　(1) Cover the rear of the flight.
　　(2) Assume the offensive quickly.

He must have mastery of his aircraft and already have developed the ability to dogfight and look around at the same time. Approximately 75 per cent of the wingman's duties are defensive if the leader is to be effective offensively. He must be an aggressive, able and disciplined pilot to be a capable wingman.

5　*Duties of the Element Leader (No.3)* - The element leader in this type of combat formation is invaluable to the flight commander. He must take a position on the lead that affords him an advantage on any aircraft trying to attack that element. The primary function of the element is to allow the lead element to complete any attack begun. Any split of the element before this function is completed should not be tolerated. The tactical situation will determine when this split is to be made. Either element may be the lead element depending on direction of attack, position of enemy aircraft and who sees the enemy first. If time permits, however, the lead element should be directed until visual contact is made to allow the

flight to commence the fight with the element properly positioned.

6　*Duties of the Flight Leader* - The flight leader must be capable of manoeuvring his element into the firing position on enemy aircraft without unduly jeopardizing other members of the flight. A good flight commander must be a good fighter pilot in possession of all the basic requisites—Ability, Aggressiveness, Air Discipline and Air Gunnery. The flight leader must be able to think alone, possessing that essential ability of being able to assess a combat situation quickly and accurately. He must be aggressive or all his other capabilities are wasted and he must know the capabilities of enemy aircraft to be encountered in relation to the performance of his own aircraft.

ENGAGEMENT OF THE ENEMY

7　*Offensive Action* - As soon as it is known that enemy aircraft are in the area, whether through GCI control or visual sightings, all drop tanks in the flight should be jettisoned immediately. If a pilot is unable to get rid of one or both tanks he should withdraw immediately accompanied by one other aircraft. The two remaining aircraft in the flight may remain in the combat area since they are still considered a self-sufficient fighting team. During engagement with the enemy, aircraft should be operated at maximum power. Basically, a flight of four aircraft is briefed to operate as a unit as long as the tactical situation permits. On an in-

Pilots on Course 41 at Chatham, February 1955. In the back row are P/Os Marc Demers, Ron Adams, Barry Jones, Tom Bebb, Phil Coyle, John Taylor. In the centre are P/Os Bryan Doyle, Alan Brown, Cyril White, Bob Caskie, George Howarth, Ron Clarkson, Jack Muirhead. In front are P/O Bob Porter, F/L Jack Seaman, F/Os Bud Ballance and Ed Alto, F/L Bill Tibbett, F/O Bill Bayley. Missing were P/Os Jerry Westphal and Howie Jacobs. (via A.C. Brown)

itial attack on a flight of enemy aircraft the flight should remain intact even after the enemy split into sections of two, but when the enemy split into single aircraft the elements could separate. Throughout this action the wingmen are on the defensive and the element and the element leaders are primarily the offensive. No.3 should be permitted to take a bounce at any time that he is in a more favourable position to do so than No.1, provided that it does not jeopardize the flight leader's position and that he is cleared to do so by the flight leader. Similarly, when aircraft are operating as a pair, No.1 is the shooter and No.2 is the look-out, but No.2 can take a bounce provided that No.1 is not engaged in an attack and that the wingman is cleared to go ahead. When aircraft operate as pairs, No.2 should fly well up and change position from one side of the leader to the other during turns at any time that difficulty is encountered in maintaining the line abreast position. This cross-over should be executed very

quickly to avoid waste of searching time.

8   Pilots are to avoid rough erratic flying which would result in over-control of the aircraft, loss of speed, and loss of position. Flight and section leaders have very little time during which to fire on the enemy and once an attack is initiated, they have to be absolutely free to concentrate on this attack. It is essential to cut the corners and close the range on the enemy without losing sight of him for an instant. If an attempt is made to put the gunsight on the target at extreme ranges, valuable time will be lost which might be employed in cutting the corner and thereby decreasing the range to one where effective firing could be commenced. With the high speeds employed and small target size, it is essential to reduce the firing range as much as possible. The most effective attacks are made from almost dead astern and at ranges under 800 yards. When the leader initiates an attack he so informs his wingman by using the code word and the wingman then is required to inform the leader whether he is cleared or otherwise. Following this, if the wingman at any time loses contact with his leader or spots any aircraft which will interfere with himself or the leader's attack, he advises his No.1 who is to break off his attack immediately and assist in keeping the section clear. If at any time sections are split up into individual aircraft, pilots

should get their nose down, their airspeed up and withdraw from the combat area.

9   *Defensive Action* - All aircraft attacking from the astern position should be considered hostile until they are proved otherwise. Breaks should be called at the appropriate time and the warning called promptly. All breaks should be made in the downward plane to permit the aircraft to be pulled around in a maximum turn without loss of essential airspeed. If an enemy aircraft does not break off an attack after an initial bounce, a Sabre pilot should keep the nose down in a turn below 25,000 feet at which time the Sabre should be able to out-turn the enemy. If necessary, a maximum rate turn should be maintained to ground level to present a difficult target until the attacker disengages.

10   *Special Techniques* - Various techniques have been used by Sabre pilots to ensure that maximum cross-cover is given both to themselves and other aircraft. Some squadrons have completely removed the head rests to permit better rearward visibility. It is good practice to always position the seat so that the pilot's head is right up at or on the canopy. The seat and shoulder harness should be loosened generally right after takeoff to allow freedom of movement. In some cases, pilots prefer to remove the anti-glare visor from their helmets to allow better vision in the vertical plane. It is a general feeling among experienced pilots that any personal or aircraft equipment which restricts vision or freedom of movement is to be avoided.

11   *The "Scissors" Tactic* - One series of manoeuvres referred to as "the scissors" deserves comment. This tactic has been employed with considerable success to turn a defensive break into an offensive situation. Upon being attacked the Sabre should normally break into the attacking aircraft. *If* the enemy passes behind and slides outside the turning arc of the Sabre, the Sabre would execute a sharp reversal of turn back towards the attacker. If the attacker broke off the attack and went straight away the Sabre would be in the astern position and, depending on relative speeds, might be in a position to fire. If the attacker continued to turn with the Sabre in the break, the rapid reversal would set up the scissors with the opposing aircraft turning

toward each other from opposite sides of a circular pattern (see diagram B).

The Sabre would continue to turn, progressively raising the nose, gaining altitude and losing airspeed, reversing the turn each time a cross over with the enemy occurred. Speed brakes should not be used and full power should be employed, thus the loss of speed will be accompanied by an increase in height. After several reversals, depending on the ability of the attacking aircraft, a Sabre pilot will very often find himself on the tail of the attacker (see diagram C). If the scissors is not successful, the straight breaking turn could then be employed if the attacking aircraft was getting into firing position.

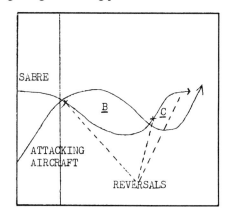

12 The important points of the scissors tactic may be summarized as follows:

(a) Do not attempt to set up a scissors if the closing speed of the attacking aircraft is not great enough to cause him to over-shoot and slide outside of your breaking turn.

(b) The reversal rolls must be made at maximum rate.

(c) The timing of the reversal is critical, and this timing must become instinctive through practice.

(d) The reversals must be accompanied by a gain in height and a corresponding deceleration to get behind the enemy.

(e) Because of the deceleration involved, aircraft in a scissors are temporarily susceptible to attack from other aircraft at a superior altitude.

Enemy Fighter Tactics

GENERAL

13 The only experience on which information was gained was on the tactics of the MiG versus the Sabre during the Korean War. Although the geographical location will affect tactics somewhat, the tactics practised by the MiG in Korea are outlined below for information of all concerned.

14 MiG pilots and the tactics employed by them varied from excellent to poor. Altogether the average pilot ability was considered to be lower than the average ability of the Sabre pilots in that theatre. However, it is apparent that there are many extremely competent MiG pilots, brilliantly led, employing tactics designed to make the most of every advantage which they enjoy or may encounter.

OFFENSIVE TACTICS

15 Action employed to engage Sabre pilots operating as a protective shield for the UN fighter bombers was initiated, usually, from north of the Yalu river. Formations of MiGs took off and climbed to operating altitudes up to 50,000 feet, often higher, and crossed the river at full speed. Formations varied from large gaggles of 30 or more to the basic fours. It was customary to find each apparently "lone" flight or section followed by another flight or section stepped well up behind, plus another up and behind, ad infinitum. Any attempt by Sabres to lock on one section would be thwarted by a return attack from the higher cover MiGs. As a rule once the attacking MiGs were spotted and a break commenced, the MiGs would break off the attack and, using their speed and height advantage, would pull up and reposition. Often another attack from this same section or another accompanying section would take place immediately. The Sabre pilots found themselves tactically embarrassed by this tactic and could do very little but break and turn to spoil the attack and foul up the position. This MiG tactic was termed the "Yo-Yo." Head-on attacks by the MiGs were numerous if position was favourable as the heavier armament presented quite an advantage in such an encounter.

DIVERSIONARY OFFENSIVE TACTICS

16 Almost always in conjunction with the above tactics, the MiGs used "Sucker Bait." Pairs or flights of MiGs would be sent through the area in the contrail level(s) to draw the attention and fire of the high cover Sabres while the other MiGs got set for a bounce and still other large numbers, carefully camouflaged, streaked through at lower levels to strike at the fighter bombers. Again, large numbers of MiGs would come across the Yalu at high speed, cut across the Sabres in full view, turn for home and continue letting down. The obvious intent was to draw the Sabres off their patrol line while counting on their high speed to take them safely across the Yalu river before the Sabres could close. Generally speaking, every known trick and manoeuvre was employed from time to time and a few new ones demonstrated.

17 Camouflage was used extensively in both an offensive and defensive role. High flying MiGs had a powder blue under-surface or an overall silver finish while those assigned to the lower levels had light and dark green upper surfaces.

DEFENSIVE TACTICS

18 Here again everything from brilliance to stupidity was demonstrated. Sabre pilots attacking large numbers of MiGs (6 or more) have been faced with a 3-way split of formation. If they continued to pursue those on the original course, they would soon find themselves bracketed by the MiGs which were detached from the formation. A break into either of the bracket groups would result in attack by the other. If, when the original MiG formation split, the Sabre pilots chose one of the turning sections, they would find themselves pursued by the main body.

19 Unless a very great height advantage was enjoyed by the Sabres, small numbers of MiGs would employ a full power steep climb straight away from the attack. Climbing at a lower speed than the Sabre is capable of, and having a higher ceiling, the MiG was fireproof under these conditions. If the Sabre pilot attempted to climb at the same angle he would soon stall out and leave himself in a very unenviable position "with his Mach down," at least temporarily.

20 If the Sabre pilots could close to an effective range before being spotted, the chances of a kill went up, provided that the attack could be pressed home without interference. Under these conditions the MiG would attempt to turn or run straight away toward the Yalu. In a diving run the MiG has a good chance of holding his own unless caught initially at a low cruising speed. Often a burst of tracer

fire from extreme range was successful in causing an otherwise safe MiG to initiate a turn. The Sabre then could cut the corner, close the range and go to work.

Under attack, some MiG pilots presented very difficult targets to the extent that UN pilots often expended all their ammunition without effecting a kill. Otherwise MiG pilots ejected at the first sign of fire before any hits had been registered. Low level pursuits sometimes resulted in the MiG spinning into the ground again without any apparent battle damage. From all reports the MiG seems prone to spin when the controls are mishandled and possibly has poor recovery characteristics.

22 Under attack, the MiG has been observed to fire its cannon, apparently in an effort to lighten its load. Likewise some aircraft have been observed to stream fuel under attack but prior to being hit. This may indicate a fuel jettison system to lighten the combat load.

In an article in *Aircraft* magazine, December 1957, R.J. "Chick" Childerhose, himself a veteran Sabre driver, described weapons training at Chatham:

A T-33 with a screaming luminous orange paint-job taxied out on the runway at RCAF Station Chatham. It sat there a few minutes, waiting for the armament vehicle to unreel the 1000 feet of thin steel cable. At the other end of that strand was a 30-foot long, 6-foot wide plastic aerial target. A groundcrew member ducked under the cigar-shaped fuselage to hook on. It was ready.

Flying the tow ship for this morning's exercise is Flying Officer "Tappy" Carruthers, one of the teaching staff of the RCAF's Fighter Weapons Instructors course. A long-time (three years) squadron pilot in the RCAF's Air Division, Carruthers takes his turn flying the tow ship with the other instructors at Weapons Flight.

Strapped in and watching him from the Sabre line-up on the ramp are the four pilots going up for the "shoot." Anxiously they watch the flag careening over the runway during the take-off run. Smoke pours off the two small rollers at either end of the steel tow bar. Finally it surges into the air after the steeply climbing T-bird. Leader calls:

"Okay Blackbird. Fire up, go Channel 14 for tower."

Takeoff is in pairs. As the wheels lurch into their wells and the final D-door snaps shut, the Three and Four crank into a starboard turn. By cutting

inside the leader's turn toward the gunnery range, the second pair can catch up.

The shark-finned Sabres climb swiftly, seemingly tied together in close formation. Leading Blackbird section is Captain Russ Miller, a USAF exchange officer who is presently in command of the Weapons Flight.

"Okay Blackbird, spread out." Then he adds: "Powder Puff Control, Blackbird here, request vector to Sailboat Tow."

The scope boys at the local radar shop have both Sabres and tow ship on their screens.

"Roger Blackbird, steer one-zero-zero, tow is at eleven o'clock for fifteen miles."

During the brief exchange on the R/T, the section has fanned out. Gunsight check completed, the Number Two begins sliding into the line astern formation followed by Three and Four.

Ahead, the leader starts a gentle diving turn to bring him out parallel to and astern of the flag. Eyes smart as the four pilots squint into the dazzling whitish haze of ocean horizon for the

An OTU Mk. 5 gets up and away at Chatham, headed for the range (note underwing 2.75-inch rockets), then fires off at its target on the water. Cpl Barry Herron captured both these exceptional views in July 1957. (DND PL108423, '415)

tow ship. Suddenly it appears, a min-iature T-bird with a tiny grey ribbon fluttering behind. The section closes with it, still in line astern.

"Blackbird Leader is off, going to perch."

You see a plan view of his Sabre as it flashes over the canopy of the T-bird. Then Number Two calls off, cranking it around in a climbing turn towards the land. One mile out, 3000 feet above the tow and parallel to him. That's the perch position.

"Blackbird Three is off."

Then it is your turn. Hurtling by the flag toward the tow ship, you sneak a glance at airspeed and needle-ball.

No trim required. You call: "Black-bird Four is off."

G-force squashes you down, drag-ging on arms and legs as you bend in 90 degrees to the tow ship. In the climb there is time to look around.

Below and behind now is the leader. A tiny silver Sabre sliding across a wrinkled black ocean toward a pos-tage-stamp target. Quickly you select the necessary armament switches. Red ammo in this bird; why you think of it you don't know.

A thrill of panic stabs in your chest as you fail to spot the flag, or the tow ship. Then it's there; that atrocious orange paint really helps. The Three-man is starting the reversing half-roll of the key position. It's time to go. You call: "Blackbird Four is in."

The horizon tilts as the smudge-sized target begins its slide from high on the canopy around to the front wind-screen. Then the pipper, a spot of reflected light projected on the wind-screen by the gunsight, becomes all-important. Ahead, Number Three is breaking over the T-33, heading back for the perch.

Now to fly that groove, the pay-off slot. Shaved seconds of time is all that's allowed. Agonizingly, the pipper remains above the flag. Then as the target begins its sudden and terrifying expansion, the pipper slides behind it. Break-off! Your mind screams the command.

The flag blurs under a wing as you level off. With almost 200 knots over-take speed, you quickly catch the tow ship and break upwards over it.

"Blackbird Four is off." Your words are squeezed out against G-force.

Now it is necessary to watch the tow ship over one shoulder, a neck-cracking task. Getting the 90-degree position for the climb out to the perch is paramount. Suddenly the tow pilot breaks in on the radio.

"Blackbird Four, you reversed your turn too soon on that last attack."

Occasionally the tow pilot will offer a word of advice to a student in the air, but not very often. You acknowledge:

"Four checks."

Back up to the perch again, this time vowing that you won't waste the next attack. Not that you have much time to brood, the timing of a four-plane gun-nery circuit is too fraught for that. Blackbird Three starts his reversal and it's your turn to go down.

"Blackbird Four is in."

This time you hold off the reverse for a second. Then as the Sabre rolls into that last turn you recall the in-structor's briefing: "Get the pipper on the flag in the last part of your attack and hold it there. You've got to track it smoothly."

Concentrate! Hold it on there. This time you're in luck, the white dot is on the flag. Not in the middle, but you'll settle for less. As the banner begins to swell under the dot you carefully squeeze the trigger. Two fifty calibres burst into life, remote but infinitely pleasing. Smoke trails waver ahead, an illusory indication of the path of the bullets.

The hammer of the guns is a morale-booster. Things are working out. You might even get some hits today. Four attacks later Sailboat Tow calls the leader.

"Last attack this direction."

You've reached the northern end of the range. As always, the tow pilot calls the signals. As Blackbird leader comes off the flag he answers:

"Blackbird leader is off, pulling up to the 2 o'clock position."

In turn, the rest of the section com-

plete their attacks and pull up to the right. As they did at the beginning, they fly a loose line-astern formation. The leader flies a gentle turn to the left, moving around to the landward side of the flag again. Inside the turn you can see the slower-moving T-bird bending it around to head back down the range.

"Blackbird section, check your fuel and oxygen. Don't press those attacks too close."

In this momentary lull, the leader passes a word of warning. You recall his words on the subject during the briefing:

"We had a guy a few months ago so anxious to get a good score that he came home wearing the flag."

It was good for a laugh too. Nobody mentioned the other pilot who pressed an attack too close. The flag wrapped itself around his canopy and he never got out before hitting the water 15,000 feet below. You push the thought away.

In succession, the first three Sabres peel off. Number Three shows an oil-stained belly as he rolls into the dive. You watch until he starts reversing his turn. Time to go.

"Blackbird Four is in."

And almost as an echo comes the transmission:

"Blackbird Two is off."

It means that the circuit is working right. With four aircraft in the gunnery pattern, good timing is essential. As the leader pulls off the flag, the Three-man should be coming off the perch. At the same instant the Two-man should be reversing his turn onto the flag. If anyone goofs, the whole pattern is fouled up.

Now you are nursing it around the last turn. Dragging the pipper toward the flag. Concentrating on holding it on the fluttering gray banner. Smoothly now, hold it there, gentle squeeze of trigger. Machine gun fire and a vibration. Smoke trails and a jumping pipper.

Thirty minutes is about par for actual time-on-the-flag. Thirty arm-aching minutes of violent manoeuvre and sweaty concentration. Roll-off the perch, roll-into the attack, roll-out of it again. Watch for the other guys. Bend your neck around to watch the tow ship. Keep your position in the circuit. Check your fuel, the dials, the trim.

Suddenly however, and always sooner than expected, the leader calls:

"Blackbird Leader is off and dry. This is your last pass."

That the leader has fired-out gives you a start. This last attack had better be good. From the perch you can see Number Two firing on the flag. You wonder if he's hitting it. Then Number Three is reversing his turn below, and it's time to go.

It's a good pass this one, pipper riding steady on the front part of the flag. You start firing out of range, holding the trigger down as the banner expands under the dot. Suddenly one gun cuts out, then the other. You break off the pass, turning towards the formation. Blackbird section returns to the landing circuit.

Afterwards, as always, they gather in the flight room for a de-briefing. This time Capt Miller gives the talk-down on the trip, but later the students themselves do the leading. It includes briefing and de-briefing, just as they will do when they return to their squadrons.

Somehow, the instructors at the FWI course manage to watch the students during the hectic moments of the gunnery pattern. They fly their own attacks and still come back with advice for individuals. Things such as:

"Number Three, I noticed that you were breaking-off out of range." Or perhaps, "Number Four, I think you were pulling a square corner on the last part of your attacks. Try more lead in the first part of it."

Usually by the time the de-briefing is ended, the flag has been retrieved from the centre of the field where the tow ship dropped it. The armament vehicle returns it to the hangar and it is hung up for scoring. The leader of the section usually handles the green chalk used to cancel the hits. As he marks them, he calls out the colour to the man marking the hits on the individual score sheet. Often there is a rhubarb over questionable hits, especially if the scores are close.

"Three red, one yellow. Another red, three green."

At which juncture an outraged voice might cry:

"Hey! One of those is a yellow! Look at it. That sure as hell isn't green!"

"Whatd'ya mean isn't green? Of course it's green."

And while the argument waxes warmer between the owners of the controversial colours, the man with the chalk continues on:

"Five blue, two yellow, two red. Another blue . . ."

But there is more to this fighter weapons course than this. The utilitarian Sabre fills an air-to-ground role as well, and students from Air Division get practice in dive bombing, skip-bombing, strafing and rocketry. At the up-to-date gunnery range near Chatham, various targets are used for each phase.

"For skip-bombing," says F/L Gerry de Nancrede, "we use a vertical target 20 feet long and 10 feet high. The idea is to hit it just at the point of ground and target."

F/L de Nancrede, an ex-Spitfire pilot of World War II and a gunnery graduate of the USAF Fighter Weapons School, has been instructing at Chatham for a long time. He is considered to be one of the best gunnery instructors in the RCAF. He went on:

"For rocketry we have pyramid-shaped targets, 15 feet at the base and 15 feet in height. Second-hand aerial targets sewn together and painted red are stretched over a frame. They take quite a beating."

Included with the actual weapons flying training, and an integral part of the FWI course, is the ground instruction phase. There is a total of 70 hours classroom time devoted to the intricacies of the gunsight, the study of ballistics and trajectories, the theory of pursuit curves, and more. All of this instruction is handed out by the same instructors who handle the flying end of the program. It's a big job.

And the results are greater than it first appears, for although these instructors only train a selected few, their work is reflected throughout the day-fighter operations of the RCAF. That fact makes these men responsible for making Canadian fighter pilots among the best in the world.

R.J. "Chick" Childerhose

One of Chatham's instructors, and later an Air Division sharpshooter, was F/L Bill Norn. He served in the RAF during the war as an instructor and joined the RCAF in 1951. In 1953 he went to Chatham on the conversion flight, flying the Allison-powered T-birds. He notes that two of them had no ejection seats and one day one had engine failure. The crew had to get out, so the instructor held the plane steady while the student went over the side, then struggled out himself. Little known facts!

In 1954, Norn moved from conversion to gunnery, and he writes:

A Sabre four-plane out of Chatham in the late fifties. By this time the Sabre 2s were long gone to Greece and Turkey, and the Mk. 5 reigned in the skies of New Brunswick. (DND PL95083)

In gunnery flight we flew in sections of four against a radar reflective banner target which we called "the flag." Towing was at 15,000 feet, weather permitting. Exercises were flown only when visual contact could be maintained with the ground in the range area off the New Brunswick coast near Tracadie. Firing was always from land toward sea. In these early years our tow aircraft was a Mustang, and the flag was attached to its underside by the flag crew on the runway prior to takeoff. Maximum speed for towing was 165K. We later progressed to the T-33, then the Sabre for towing. The speed remained at 165 for these types, as that provided a realistic closing speed for the firing aircraft and was within the limits of the flag material, which would shred at higher speed.

Towing with the Sabre was limited to right turns only to prevent burning the cable off, as it was attached to the right speed brake. In order to fly as many missions as possible, we flew whenever the weather at the range was safe enough to shoot, and this resulted in many bad weather departures and recoveries of the sections and tow-ship. The latter was quite often required to complete a GCA run, drop his flag to one side of the runway and then proceed with his landing. A lost flag resulted in eight lost firing sorties, as we fired two sections of four on each flag.

In January 1955 a weapons flight was set up at the OTU to train specialty instructors for weapons planning and delivery, and I was transferred there to instruct until April 1956 when I was sent back to gunnery flight till that October. During this period the OTU trained a number of Reserve pilots, as the Reserves were re-equipping with Sabres. We also trained NATO pilots including an intake of Turkish students. One incident following a gunnery mission led by F/O Hank Henry involved a Turkish student. He had only partial engine power and was returning to base with the section leader for a gradual descent and straight-in approach for landing. All went well until

85

a duty pilot in the tower to help in emergencies. This day it was F/O Al Seitz, and he saw the Sabre as it slid by the tower, eyeball to eyeball. Wow! But not to worry, as the Turk was still airborne and could come around for another approach. Hank Henry got him around in a treetop level circuit, wide and gentle, then lined up on the runway. But the Turk still didn't have his wheels down, and as his seat was right down by now his visibility was restricted. Again he was called to overshoot, and again he managed to get lined up nicely to fly through the tower. By now, F/O Seitz had had enough, for the Sabre was lower than ever. Together with the rest in the tower he dove for the stairwell in order to escape.

As it happened, there were two civilian painters at work in the tower. They were working with air force green, the only colour we ever seemed to have lots of. Everyone arrived in the stairwell together as the Turk wallowed past, in shock, with F/O Henry coaxing him around for yet another go-around. "This time land, wheels or not," Henry told his student. And he did, wheels up. He got away with it, but F/O Seitz didn't—his uniform was ruined, covered in lovely green paint.

Bill Norn

Two other old hands at Chatham in 1954 were W/C Stocky Edwards (OC of the OTU) and S/L Irish Ireland (CFI). Here Ireland displays some typical Miramichi salmon hauled from waters near Chatham. (E.G. Smith)

OTU Sabre No.210 with some off-beat markings. It bears the code RO, not seen before on an RCAF aircraft. Then, it has some personalized artwork of "the wheels": W/C Bill Smith, unit OC, and S/L Eric G. Smith, the CFI. The "1000" indicates that it was Sabre No.1000 built at Canadair. Someone later had the gall to leave '210 in the forests of New Brunswick. (via E.G. Smith)

the leader called the student to lower his gear using the emergency T-handle. It was located on the cockpit floor at the base of the centre console. But the student had locked his shoulder harness in preparation for landing and couldn't reach the handle. The leader called to him to lower his seat, and with the runway fast approaching called for an overshoot. The student put on all the power he had and staggered away to the right, heading straight for the control tower.

In those days we had an instructor as

Of course, as Chatham was a place to learn, there were bound to be mishaps. Most weeks there were several accidents causing minor to severe damage; and inevitably there were Category A crashes, with painful losses—some 34 fatalities, beginning with the first, F/O G. Collingwood, in August 1952. The unit diary records endless incidents: F/O Roy, lowered flaps inadvertently at 300 knots (sure to spoil one's day); F/O W.J. Chambers, nose-gear fairing door ripped off at 400 knots; F/O L.M. Eisler, aircraft damaged when collided with drogue; F/O J.B. Webber, aborted takeoff when unable to get nose wheel off runway; F/O Coulter, flamed out and made wheels-up landing; 2nd Lt Bener, crash landed after mid-air fire, etc., etc.

One of many serious Chatham prangs occurred with 19367 on May 21, 1953. The pilot was F/O L.J. "Rocky" Redman. He had been flying since his first ride at Centralia, February 5 the previous year, and had been at Chatham since March 1953, having first flown the Sabre April 22. Redman had just taken off in '367 and had the gear up when his power suddenly dropped to about 60 per cent. He switched immediately to the alternate fuel system and the power came back up momentarily. Then it began cutting in and out,

Two more wartime instructors at Chatham. G.L. "Gerry" McCully and Tom Koch. Both were 1941 RCAF recruits who flew Spitfires overseas. Koch even did a tour on merchant ship Hurricanes. Besides the rigours of combat, each also endured Cat.A prangs in the Sabre. (DND)

Sabre 5 23367 set down beautifully on a blueberry farm in New Brunswick. (via Ken Johnston)

and the pilot turned back for an emergency landing. He didn't make it. His Sabre crash landed, rolled over and exploded. The canopy was torn off, so Redman was able to crawl out, though he suffered serious burns. The crash was so spectacular that one witness recalls commenting to a bystander that

Flight commander (gunnery) at Chatham, F/L Tommy Wheler, in May 1952. Wheler was typical of the experienced instructors at the OTU. He had begun flying in the RCAF in 1941. Overseas, he spent a dangerous first year flying Hotspur gliders and associate tow-planes, then got onto Spits with 411 Squadron. Shot down in August 1944, he managed to escape after three tries. His wartime tally included two 190s and a 109 confirmed. Postwar, he rejoined the RCAF in 1948. May 22, 1950 he made his first jet flight in a Vampire at Downsview, and he began instructing at Chatham in September 1951. He first flew the Sabre (19278) on March 14, 1952. He joined 444 Squadron and was responsible for the cobra emblem being painted on the squadron's Swords. (DND)

Capt Fred Webster, USAF exchange officer, waits as his Sword is serviced at Chatham, 1953-54. Several US pilots instructed at Chatham in the 1950s, mostly Korean vets. Another was James H. Kasler, with six Korean kills. He served at Chatham July 1955-July 1957. He was later shot down on his 91st F-105 mission in Viet Nam and spent seven years as a POW. Kasler had started his career as a B-29 gunner in the Second World War—real tigers those Sabre lads! (via Gerry McCully)

87

the rescue crew shouldn't even bother going out, for who could live through that mess. Redman recovered after several months, went back on flying, and joined 444 Squadron in October 1954. The cause of his crash was quickly pinned down: fuel contaminated with water at the tank farm. The same day, a T-33 flown by Odey Levere flamed out and had to make a dead-stick landing. It had been refuelled from the same source.

Monthly flying rates at Chatham averaged in the 1000 hours range for the Sabre. Typical figures appear below:

December 1956	F-86	747:40 hrs
	T-33	326:20
	C-45	70:50
	S-51	9:50
January 1957	F-86	1369:10
	T-33	506:15
	C-45	73:45
	S-51	13:00

F/O Rocky Redman while converting to Sabres at Chatham in 1953, and a picture of his Sabre crashed there that May 21. (via L.J. Redman)

No.1(F)OTU would train thousands of Sabre pilots, including many foreign pilots from NATO countries. It operated for over a decade, but by 1958 the RCAF had decided to re-equip with a new fighter. A long search went on for the replacement, and was called by some "the search for the holy grail," with a team of people roaming from country to country looking for the best (yet cheapest) airplane. At last, the government decided on the F-104 and quickly ordered several squadrons-worth. The Sabre would be withdrawn from front line service by 1963 at the latest, so an all-new training system had to be devised and implemented. This, as it turned out, was to include the Sabre.

The OTU diary for November 1961 includes this entry: "The most significant change during the past six months was the disbandment of No.1(F)OTU effective 31 October 1961, and the formation of No. 1 Sabre Transition Unit effective 1 November, 1961. The role of the STU is to provide transition training for all pilots selected to fly the CF-104 aircraft."

In December 1961, with completion of the last OTU course, the guns on the Chatham Sabres were all removed. The air-to-air range was closed. On the STU there would be no use for gunnery, as the CF-104s were to be used as bombers and recce aircraft only. This move with the Sabres was to have a slightly ironic twist some time later when the Cuban crisis flared up. In discussions with the Americans, some

Canadian representative suggested that Canada could contribute to defence needs if things got out of hand by rushing Sabres to air bases in Florida. That the RCAF could do indeed, except that the Sabres would have been quite useless. They had been defanged!

In November 1961 W/C L.J. "Lou" Hill took over as OC of the STU, with old Sabre hand S/L Tony Hannas as CFI. A whole new era of Sabre flying in the RCAF had begun. For hundreds of Sabre-loving jocks there would be another seven years of heavenly bliss at Chatham.

Chatham Chopper

K.E. "Ken" Johnston of Saint John, New Brunswick, flew at Chatham in the early fifties, but not in the glamorous role of "jet jockey"—he flew the station's veteran Sikorsky S-51 rescue helicopter. He tells a few tales from his specialized vantage point:

While at Chatham I had a front-row seat for a lot of Sabre flying. I would see it at its best, with high and low speed passes, and formation flying; and at its worst, with Sabres lying broken or burnt in field or forest, or on the ice of Miramichi Bay.

Rescue equipment at Chatham in those days consisted of a high-speed rescue launch, and a large Bombardier snowmobile that could carry several people, such as a ground search party that had to get out on quick notice. During freeze-up in fall and break-up in spring, neither launch nor snowmobile could be used on the wide expanses of Miramichi Bay or Gulf of St. Lawrence, so at these times an S-51 from 103 Rescue Unit at Greenwood was temporarily detached to Chatham for rescue duty. This was the only RCAF helicopter in the entire Atlantic region in the early fifties. Normal crew on the S-51 was pilot and crewman. A hoisting device was installed outside the left passenger door and was operated by the pilot as the crewman gave him instructions.

The S-51 was comfortable but didn't have excess power; and the C of G movement was only about 4 inches. Usually, two 200-pound passengers, or three lighter ones, could be carried. Though lacking many refinements of later designs, the S-51 was enjoyable to fly. Its large windows provided an excellent view of the ground.

I seldom flew above 300 feet and

An OTU Sabre at Trenton for Air Force Day on May 28, 1960. This was the last Sabre to suffer a Category A crash. It was lost along with G/C W.R. Cole on October 23, 1967. (Larry Milberry)

most passengers really enjoyed a flight. There was always a waiting list of people wanting a ride. One day I took special delight in demonstrating a zero airspeed autorotation from 1500 feet to one of the jet pilots at Chatham. You could almost hear his fingers crunching the armrests!

I first arrived at Chatham in March 1953 along with my crewman, Cpl "Bull" Durham. Almost immediately, we were called out on the search for the pilot of a CF-100 out of Bagotville. We bogged off for Mont Joli, arriving there in inclement weather 3:10 hours later. We were turned around there, as the lost pilot had been picked up.

My first flight relating to a Sabre accident occurred in March when two Sabres crashed on the ice of Miramichi Bay. The searchmaster, myself and crewman flew out to the site once it was located, but there was no need for the MO. Both pilots had been killed. In April I returned on leave to Greenwood, and F/O Hal Hinton with crewman Cpl J. LeBlanc filled in. On April 30, following my return, the S-51 was ordered to the Quebec North Shore, to a point some 135 miles east of Havre St. Pierre to investigate possible survivors from the crash of a Ventura survey plane. This turned out to be a gruelling five-day trip, with no sur-

vivors located. Our 17:25 hours aloft included a long overwater trip straight across the Gulf of St. Lawrence from the North Shore to Gaspé. That June the S-51 was on standby during the annual budworm spraying season in New Brunswick, but there were no emergencies reported.

On January 4, 1954, a T-33 with two aboard went down south of Chatham. Aircraft and crew were spotted in the late afternoon, and it was just about dusk when my crewman, Cpl Baxter, and I took off. We were directed to the site by St. Margarets' radar station. The T-33 was in an open area of the forest. While my crewman kept a close watch on our tail, I gently eased the S-51 down into the restricted landing area. While I kept the helicopter idling, Cpl Baxter and the student pilot (who had ejected) assisted the pilot (who had ridden the T-bird down).

By the time the injured pilot was aboard, it was completely dark. I got on the radio (we had a useful UHF set rigged up by the tech people at Chatham on which we could transmit from the ground if necessary) and was told that a ground party was en route. The helicopter couldn't carry all four of us, so we left the student behind for the ground party to take care of. Away we went with the injured pilot.

This was my first helicopter night flight, and I was unprepared for what was about to happen. I did my run-up and pre-takeoff check and asked Cpl Baxter to advise an orbiting Canso that

The Fitter's Lament
I have just made my debut in Maintenance
    wing,
And what with Lent starting and all,
T'will be the ninth wonder if I do survive
The rigours that on me befall.

Of corporals and sergeants I haven't a gripe
One gets them regardless the place,
Some good and some bad, some tall and
    some short,
A menace in most any race.

All joking aside, they're not half as bad
As that monster that has all pipes.
I mean the Orenda, that giver of squirts,
That great instigator of gripes.

My fingers are punctured with lock-wire so,
They look like a mainliner's arm.
I have cricks in my joints from reaching
    for nuts,
That would cause a watchmaker alarm.

If you don't skin your knuckles on
    rigamajigs,
You get jammed in the awfullest place.
You loosen a pipe that's supposed to
    come off,
And get squirted all over the face.

While hydraulic fluids run way up your arm
You kneel in somebody's mess.
The toes of your boots get scraped
    on cement,
In the end you're no model for dress.

Just ask any fitter, if he likes his job,
He'll say, "I've no cause for remorse."
And ask him what pusher he thinks is
    the best,
He'll say, "The Orenda, of course."

LAC J. Bowie, *Chatair,* April 1956.

I'd be returning to base at 500 feet, and to keep an eye for us. I positioned our two adjustable landing lights, one straight up, one ahead, to help with visual contact with the ground. I overestimated the power of those small lights.

Gradually increasing rpm and manifold pressure to takeoff power, I did a jump takeoff to quickly clear any nearby trees, and immediately lost visual contact with the ground. I couldn't hover without ground reference, so my first reaction was to keep the collective-pitch stick at takeoff extension, and continue climbing while watching my rpm. I felt I was out of control, apparently climbing in a tight spiral, and the fuselage was probably turning as well. After what seemed ages, I finally got my pedals adjusted to slow down the compass's wild spinning and gained some semblance of control. Once we were straight and level and could breathe easier again I had the crewman call the Canso that we were at 1100 feet.

Everything outside was pitch black, and I hoped to catch sight of some lights as I flew north. After staggering along, I spotted some and headed straight for them. It turned out to be Chatham air base. There several cars had been arranged in a semi-circle to

F/O Ken Johnston with Chatham's rescue chopper No. 9603, summer 1955.
Note speaker attached to landing gear strut.
(via Ken Johnston)

floodlight a landing area set out with red flares. All the activity would have done justice to a Hollywood production! I landed alongside the waiting ambulance to end a far-from-average rescue flight!

In October 1954 the S-51 was transferred permanently to Chatham, with me as pilot. At Chatham I had hopes of getting in time on the Expeditor, T-33, and maybe even the Sabre, but this was not to be. On a local dual trip one day, a Mayday came in. We had to land so that I could get to the helicopter, and valuable time was lost getting it fired up and launched. It was clear that I would have to spend most of my time on stand-by with my S-51

No. 1(F)OTU shoulder patch. (via Wm. Ford)

A striking aerial view of RCAF Station Chatham in OTU days. (via Ken Johnston)

and forget about any other grand ideas. I never got so much as a ride in the T-33.

My flying was to be varied and always interesting at Chatham. There were searches at low level, transporting accident investigation personnel to crash sites, flying photographers around, even bringing in Santa Claus! In January 1955 the S-51 took part in a real "first." Overnight, a light snow had fallen—too light for the snow-blowers, but maybe a job for the helicopter. I taxied out to the end of Runway 28-10, then ran down the full 7500-foot length, blowing the snow away very effectively, and the day's flying then got under way.

Sabre crashes weren't restricted to remote areas. Several occurred right at Chatham. One was a mid-air of two aircraft in a tail chase. One Sabre crashed straight off; the other stalled turning on final as it staggered back in. I flew the MO out to where the second aircraft had gone in. He waded through deep snow to reach the aircraft, only to find the pilot dead. We then flew to the other crash site, which was nothing but a hole in the ground.

Another time, four aircraft were returning after practising formation aerobatics. They had a spectacular break into the circuit with two aircraft pulling up into the downwind leg, followed immediately by the others. As I watched, I thought Nos.1 and 2 were awfully close and that something had fallen from one of them. Then No.2 suddenly fell into a spin and didn't recover. The pilot was killed. Days like that, unfortunately, had to be expected. In spite of such accidents, No.1(F)OTU turned out many a fine fighter pilot, if we are to judge by the fame of the Air Division.

My role as helicopter pilot at Chatham was one of waiting around for something to happen; and when it did, to do my best to get moving in a hurry with the appropriate personnel to help. Although the waiting was tiring, sometimes nerve-wracking, it was certainly not dull. The Sabres coming and going and often putting on a bit of a show guaranteed that.

Ken Johnston

Standard cockpit of an RCAF Sabre. (DND)

91

The RCAF in Korea

Servicing crew works on a Canadair-built F-86E-6 Sabre, "Betty Boots." In the background is a typical sandbag revetment used to protect against any sort of enemy attack. As so often is the case with Sabre photos in Korea, underwing tanks are everywhere. (via H. Volker)

Soon after the Korean War broke out in June 1950 the RCAF made its primary transport squadron (426) available for United Nations service. Not long after, RCAF fighter pilots were taking exchange postings with USAF wings in Korea. The first of these was F/L J.A. Omer Levesque. In the spring of 1950 he had received a posting to the 4th FIW at Langley, Virginia, flying F-86As. The 4th was sent to Korea shortly after the war began and Levesque thus arrived in the war zone in December.

On March 31, 1951, Levesque's squadron, the 334th, was escorting B-29s on a raid along the Yalu. He was flying wing for Maj Ed Fletcher when MiGs attacked. The two Sabres turned in to a pair of MiGs, and Levesque pursued one of them down to 17,000 feet where he fired a long burst. The MiG began rolling and crashed in flames. Levesque thus became the first Commonwealth pilot to make a kill in jet-to-jet combat. He would complete

71 missions in Korea before returning to Canada in May to take up duties as CFI at Chatham.

The intelligence officer at the 4th FIG, Capt Arthur V. Beckwith, later reported on Levesque's kill: "F/L J.A.O. Levesque, 19794, RCAF pilot attached to the 334th FIS, 4th FIG, APO 970, is officially credited with the destruction of one MiG 15 type aircraft. On 31 March, 1951, F/L Levesque flew wingman in a flight of F-86 aircraft on a combat air patrol over North Korea. During a conflict with the enemy, F/L Levesque pursued a MiG 15 flight leader in a downward spiral. Attempting to evade F/L Levesque, the enemy pulled up into the sun. As the enemy aircraft came out of the sun, F/L Levesque made a deflection shot at 2000 feet, and observed several strikes on the left side of the fuselage. F/L Levesque then fired a one second burst at closer range and observed the left flap of the MiG 15 to split along the trailing edge. The MiG 15 snapped

violently to the right, paused abruptly in an inverted position, and continued in a long glide toward Sinuiju. F/L Levesque observed the MiG 15 to crash and explode."

In Korea, the Sabres were at a disadvantage. First of all, their opponent was the MiG-15, which had a higher service ceiling. While the Sabres were ready to fall out of the sky at 42,000 feet or so, the MiGs cruised handily at 50,000. Then, the USAF Sabre bases were over 200 miles south of the Yalu, where the MiGs operated. The Sabres had to expend much fuel just getting to the Yalu and home again. There wasn't much left for actual business. Then, there was no radar coverage for Sabres, as they were over enemy-held territory far from home. The MiGs, on the other hand, had radar to direct them. Finally, if "Charlie" (the MiG pilots) didn't like the looks of things, he could easily scoot across the Yalu to the Sabre-free sanctuary of China. (Officially, the USAF forbade its pilots to

(Left) F/L Omer Levesque gives the "V"-for-victory sign following his MiG kill.
(Above) Levesque's own sketch of the MiG crossing fatally in front of his Sabre. (via Omer Levesque)

cross the Yalu. That is not to say that the rule was always observed. Some MiGs were unofficially nailed over Manchuria but officially noted as falling south of the Yalu.)

In spite of the difficulties, the Sabre pilots in Korea had one all-important advantage—they were vastly superior to the enemy. So many were leading wartime fighter pilots, and it had only been a few years since they had last seen combat. Except for their Russian advisers, the Koreans and Chinese had little experience flying anything anywhere, let alone in combat. It is little surprise, then, that the Sabres chalked up a 14 to 1 kill ratio against the MiGs.

F/L E.A. "Ernie" Glover served in Korea between June and October in 1952. He had enlisted in the RCAF in December 1940 and trained on Fleets at Mt. Hope and Harvards at Aylmer. He went straight overseas following Wings Parade to fly Masters and Hurricanes at 56 OTU. He joined No. 1 Squadron flying Hurricanes on night fighter and intruder ops, and in July 1942 converted to Typhoons at Acklington. May 19, 1943, he was hit by flak near St. Omer while on his 98th op. From then until war's end he was a POW.

Back home, Glover worked in Toronto for Dominion Bridge and reformed 117 Air Cadet Squadron. November 24, 1948, he was back in the RCAF and went straight to Chatham for some refresher flying. For the next two years he ran the GCA unit at St. Hubert and Chatham. February 15, 1951, he checked out on the Vampire and he was posted straight away to 416 Squadron at Uplands. He volunteered to go to Korea, and, just before he did, checked out on the Sabre at 416 and at 413 at Bagotville.

F/L Glover arrived in Korea on June 20 and joined the 334th Fighter Squadron at Kimpo. He would fly 58 missions while there, the last on October 12. During that time he would become the RCAF's leading Sabre pilot in Korea, with three MiG-15s destroyed

F/L Ernie Glover with his crewman, SSgt Allan T. Reveley of Mimico, Ontario while both were serving with the USAF in Korea. (USAF)

Lt Pete Frederick of the 336th FIS flew the Canadair Sabre, "Glory Us." He downed 3 MiGs. This Sabre carries "Misawa" tanks, different in appearance from all others seen in this book. (Maj Gene Sommerich via Gordon S. Williams)

YEAR 1952 Month/Date	Aircraft Type	No.	Pilot, or 1st Pilot	2nd Pilot, Pupil or Passenger	DUTY (Including Results and Remarks)	S.E. DAY Pilot	S.E. NIGHT Pilot	INSTR/CLOUD
					— Totals Brought Forward — 111:20 / 741:35 / 10:05 / 26:20 / 61:05 / 187:45 / 312:40 / 6:45 / 56:25 / 98:45 / 117 / 72:15 / 63:45 / 85:00			
MAY 15	F-86E	50607	SELF	SOLO	C.A.P. UIJU-MIZU. B.3. MISSION #57.	1:35		
MAY 15	F-86A	491118	SELF	SOLO	C.A.P. ANGU-MIZU. W.3. MISSION #58.	1:25		
MAY 16	F-86A	491255†	SELF	SOLO	ARMED RECCE. J.HANCOCK 3. MISSION 59. MIG COUNT AT ANTUNG, TATUNG-KOU, & TA-KOU-CHAN. FLAK	1:00	:20	
MAY 16	F-86E	512767	SELF	SOLO	C.A.P. UIJU. MISSION 60.	1:15		:10
MAY 17	F-86E	50637	SELF	SOLO	LOCAL TRNG. CHECK OUT CAPT. LANE	:45		
MAY 17	F-86E	512800	SELF	SOLO	C.A.P. NAMSI-DONG-ANJU.Rd. MISSION #61.	1:25		1:00
MAY 18	F-86E	50607	SELF	SOLO	C.A.P. NAMSI-DONG-ANJU.Rd MISSION #62.	1:15		:30
MAY 18	F-86E	50607	SELF	SOLO	C.A.P. LONG-DONG. S.I. MISSION #63. COVER FOR PEDRO PICK UP CAPT. H.SHARP & 2 OTHERS. YALU MOUTH.	1:15		:20
MAY 19	F-86E	512792	SELF	SOLO	C.A.P. ANJU. W.3. MISSION #64.	1:10		:20
MAY 20	F-86A	491118	SELF	SOLO	ESCORT. MIZU. W.3. MISSION 65. MIG RPT ED & SHOT DOWN CAPT. LANE. 4th GOT FOUR.	1:25		
MAY 20	F-86E	512767	SELF	SOLO	C.A.P. UIJU. W.I. MISSION #66.	1:25		
MAY 21	F-86E	512824	SELF	SOLO	C.A.P. ANJU. B.3. MISSION #67.	1:40		
MAY 21	F-86A	491316	SELF	SOLO	C.A.P. NAMSI-DONG-W.I. MISSION #68. FIRED AT MIG. WIRED BY MIG. FIRED AT MIG. BACK ALIVE. FILM ASSESSMENT SHOWED MIG DAMAGED & 2 SHOT DOWN	1:15		
MAY 22	F-86E	512767	SELF	SOLO	C.A.P. P'YONG YANG R.2. MISSION #69.	1:25		
MAY 22	F-86E	512792	SELF	SOLO	C.A.P. UIJU. JOHN SPECIAL ONE. MISSION #70. LAST LIGHT PATROL AT ANTUNG. NIGHT LANDING.	:45	:30	:15
MAY 23	F-86E	512767	SELF	SOLO	C.A.P. P'YONG YANG. R.I. MISSION #71.	1:15		
MAY 23	F-86A	50679	SELF	SOLO	C.A.P. P'YONG YANG. G.I. MISSION #72.	1:05		
MAY 24	F-86A	491175	SELF	SOLO	C.A.P. ANJU. B.I. MISSION #73. TOP COVER FOR "EASTER" F9F's.	1:15		
MAY 24	F-86A	491175	SELF	SOLO	ESCORT. MIZU-ANJU. B.3. MISSION #74.	1:25		
MAY 25	F-86E	512747	SELF	SOLO	C.A.P. MIZU-UIJU. R.3. MISSION #75.	1:25		:15
MAY 25	F-86E	512824	SELF	SOLO	C.A.P. MIZU-UIJU-NAMSI. J.S3 MISSION #76. TEN BANDIT TRAINS AIRBORNE.	1:25		:45
MAY 26	F-86E	50607	SELF	SOLO	C.A.P. ANJU. W.I. MISSION #77. TOP COVER FOR "MIDAS" F80's	1:20		:20
MAY 26	F-86E	50607	SELF	SOLO	C.A.P. CHINAMPO. W.I. MISSION #78.	:50		
					GRAND TOTAL [Cols. (1) to (10)] 1692 Hrs. 15 Mins. — Totals Carried Forward — 111:20 / 770:15 / 10:05 / 27:10 / 61:05 / 187:45 / 312:40 / 6:45 / 56:25 / 98:45 / 117 / 72:15 / 67:10 / 85:00			

Bruce Fleming served a busy tour in Korea. "His" Sabre was "Lucifer," seen here in its revetment. The log book extract shows Fleming's latter missions, and includes various two-mission days. In the hero shot, Fleming is seen while working as a test pilot at Canadair. (via S.B. Fleming)

and three probables. The first kill (September 8) was not conventional, in that Glover was firing at another MiG at the time. As Glover attacked it, a second attempted to loop around and get into firing position. In the process it crashed.

The next day Glover was flying high cover for some F-84s. When he saw one of them getting plastered, he dropped onto the pursuing MiG and had a merry chase for some 80 miles. He scored hits on the MiG and its pilot finally had to eject. On September 16 Glover was leading the 4th Fighter Wing escorting a photo recce Banshee

covering enemy airfields. The Chinese put up some credible resistance but lost four MiGs in the process. When several broke in on the Banshee, Glover was successful in destroying one of them. Throughout his Korean tour, Glover's aircraft was F-86E-6 No.'833 built in Montreal.

On June 12, 1953, F/L Glover was awarded the only-ever RCAF peacetime DFC. He later flew Sabres in the Air Division with 422, then 421 Squadron, instructed weapons instructors at Chatham, and from 1963 to 1966 was the standards officer on the STU. For the following three years he was OC of 129 Test and Ferry Flight at Trenton. This was a choice spot for a flying buff, as it gave him a chance to fly all sorts of aircraft including the Sabre. In fact Glover was pretty well the last of

the RCAF/CF Sabre pilots. He and Amos Pudsey (OC of 6RD, Trenton), along with two other pilots, took four Sabres out of storage at Mountainview in late 1968 and flew them to the Sabre stand-down at Chatham. Even later, in 1970, he ferried Canadair's Sabre chase plane from Cartierville to Mountainview. This was perhaps the final official CF Sabre flight.

On November 26, 1952, S/L J.D. "Doug" Lindsay (formation leader) and Lt Harold E. Fischer (No.2) had a productive encounter with the North

F/L Doug Lindsay with the 39th FIS in Korea. (USAF)

Koreans, as reported in Fifth Air Force Daily Intelligence Summary No.205 of November 27: "At 261505/I, over BA 7859, altitude 46,000 feet, Python 1 and 2 (two F-86's flying counter air) attacked a flight of 12 MiGs that were heading 150 degrees. As friendlies attacked, two of the MiGs broke from the rest of the formation in a climbing right turn. Friendlies followed these two MiGs with Python 1 firing at the lead MiG at which time friendlies were attacked by another two MiGs that fired on Python 2. Python 1 broke into the attacking MiGs firing a 90 degree deflection shot at one of the MiGs from 300 feet range. The MiG pilot ejected his canopy and bailed out. The MiG was observed to crash at BA 8545. During the encounter Python 2, who had become separated from Python 1, pulled in behind one of the 12 MiGs, closing to within 1,200 feet and firing several bursts. Hits were observed on the tail and right wing and pieces began falling off the MiG, which made a diving turn, dropping to 5,000 feet. Python 2 rolled around the MiG and observed the cockpit to be empty with the canopy off. The MiG was observed to crash at BA 8545 and the pilot was observed descending in his chute. Total Claims: Two MiGs destroyed pending film assessment. Negative friendly damage.''

S/L Andy MacKenzie was the only RCAF pilot shot down in Korea. He was a seasoned fighter pilot with 8-1/2 wartime kills while flying Spitfires.

Notations by Eric Smith (right) during Korean days. He often flew with Bill Lilley, a seven-MiG ace. While in Korea Smith flew several E-6s: 52-2833, '834, '836, '841, '855, '860, '864, '875. The latter was his personal Sabre and he flew it on 16 missions.

Post-war he had assumed command of 441 Squadron, operating from St. Hubert and North Luffenham. He went to Korea in late 1952 and began ops with the 39th FIS/51st FIW at Suwon. Interestingly, the F-86Fs of the 39th carried a checkerboard paint scheme on the tail similar to that of MacKenzie's own 441 Squadron.

On December 5, 1952, MacKenzie was on a mission (his fifth) flying No.2 to Maj Jack Saunders. Near the Yalu, a swarm of MiGs was spotted. The MiGs attacked, and MacKenzie and Saunders became separated. In the ensuing melee, MacKenzie's Sabre was shot to pieces, apparently by one of his squadron mates. There was nothing

95

Canadair Sabres were ferried down to Fresno where North American readied them for sea-shipment to Japan. Sixty aircraft were involved in this deal. (via R.J. Childerhose)

to do but eject, and within minutes MacKenzie had been captured. He was to remain a Chinese POW for two years, mostly spent in solitary confinement.

F/L Claude LaFrance also flew with the 39th in Korea, completing 49 missions between May and October, 1952. On August 5 he downed a MiG, and he provides his own description of what happened: "We were ordered to Sariwan, North Korea, where some MiGs had been reported. We were still climbing through 28,000 feet when we spotted two MiG-15s heading back north. They had allowed their speed to fall off after a previous engagement, and after jettisoning our partially full external tanks, we were able to overtake them.

The MiG 15 was the Sabre's main opposition in Korea. This one was delivered intact to the Americans by a North Korean pilot who flew it into Kimpo in October 1953. Canadians downed at least nine MiGs in Korea. (USAF Museum)

My leader attacked the enemy wingman who immediately broke left. As I had anticipated, the enemy leader placed himself in a position to shoot down the attacker (my leader). I immediately got behind him. He then broke hard, and after several high-G turns I was in a position to shoot him down at very close range, and I did so with two short bursts . . . the pilot bailed out."

S/L John MacKay scored a victory on June 30, 1953. He downed a MiG-15, as reported by the USAF on July 23: "Leading a flight of four F-86 aircraft,

S/L MacKay sighted a lone MiG on the tail of four friendly aircraft. He closed to within range and fired, scoring hits in the tail section. The MiG pilot ejected himself near Yongsansi."

F/O "Bob" Carew served in Korea February 18 - July 6, 1953, flying Sabres with the 335th FIS from Kimpo. He had joined the RCAF in August 1941, being channelled into the fighter business. He served on Spitfires with 66 and 412 Squadrons, flying a total of 81 missions. He rejoined in 1950, first doing a two-week refresher course on Harvards at Chatham, then the Vampire OTU. Soon he was an instructor at the OTU on Vampires, T-33s and Sabres; and when volunteers for Korea were being sought, he put his name in, being accepted as the 16th RCAF pilot in that program. He would be the last to complete his 50 missions in Korea, and, after S/L MacKenzie, the only other RCAF pilot to eject in Korean action.

Carew flew out to Korea beginning February 8 with a TCA North Star trip from Dorval to Chicago; then United DC-6 to San Francisco; Pan Am DC-4 to Tokyo; and C-124 to Kimpo, arriving there February 18. He initially flew one T-bird famil flight with Lt Hall, then three F-86F local trips March 5 - 9. March 14 he went to Wonju on a C-119 on a week-long escape-and-evasion course. Several more Sabre training missions were then flown from Kimpo on what was called "Clobber College," all in aid of getting ready for the real thing. April 5 Carew flew his first Korean operational mission, 1:30 hours. Carew describes subsequent flying, including his bailout:

Most of our missions consisted of escorting fighter bombers (usually F-84s) or photo recce aircraft (RF-80s),

YEAR 1953 MONTH DATE	AIRCRAFT Type	No.	PILOT, OR 1ST PILOT	2ND PILOT, PUPIL OR PASSENGER	DUTY (INCLUDING RESULTS AND REMARKS)	SINGLE-ENGINE AIRCRAFT DAY DUAL (1)	PILOT (2)	NIGHT DUAL (3)	PILOT (4)	MULTI-ENGINE AIRCRAFT DAY DUAL (5)	1ST PILOT (6)	2ND PILOT (7)	NIGHT DUAL (8)	1ST PILOT (9)	2ND PILOT (10)	PASS-ENGER (11)	INSTR/CLOUD FLYING [Incl. in cols. (1) to (10)] Sim. (12)	Cld. (13)	LINK TRAINER (14)
					TOTALS BROUGHT FORWARD	139.15	1068.10	15.35	22.35	:30						137.25	64.20	21.50	55.00
May 29	F86-E	886	SELF	—	RECCE TO FIGHTER BOMBERS.		1.35				YAKU AREAS - BOMBERS MADE good hits.								
May 30	F86-E	766	SELF	—	WEATHER RECCE		1.20				YAKU AREA - Complete OVERCAST.								.20
	TOTAL F86 JET OPS MISSIONS 27	40.20 HOURS	TOTAL FOR MAY.			19.40										8.05	.35	.50	
	" SPITFIRE " " " 81	122.20	TOTAL F86 F			10.35											.35	.30	
	BRAND TOTAL. 108	162.40	F86 E			9.05												.20	
			C-124													8.05			
			BRAND TOTAL. 1249:00			139.15	1070.05	15.35	22.35	.30						137.25	64.20	22.10	55.00
June 1	F86-F	766	SELF	—	YALU SWEEP.		1.20				LOST RIGHT TANK ON TAKE-OFF - ENDED UP AS SPARE at CH-DO.					.20			
June 7	F86-F	945	SELF	—	YALU SWEEP.		1.40				LOTS of MIGS ABOVE - 40-45000'. 3 SHOT DOWN. BEST MISSION SO FAR.								
June 10	F86-F	831	SELF	—	ESCORT. TO FIGHTER BOMBERS		1.30				LOW OVERCAST. MAKING FOR POOR BOMBER RUNS.								
June 11	F86-F	856	SELF	—	YALU SWEEP.		1.30				COMPLETE OVERCAST NOTHING SEEN.								.30
June 13	F86-F	835	SELF	—	WEATHER RECCE		1.25				COVERED OVER MOSTLY LOW STRATUS.								.40
June 13	F86-E	856	SELF	—	WEATHER RECCE		.45				ABORTED MISSION.								
June 14	F86-E	760	SELF	—	ESCORT TO FIGHTER BOMBERS		1.25				CHON-CHUN RIVER AREA.								
June 14	F86-E	836	SELF	—	ESCORT TO PHOTO RECCE		1.00				CHON-CHUN RIVER AND YALU RIVER ANTUNG AREA.								
June 15	F86-E	886	SELF	—	YALU SWEEP. 43,000'.		1.40				MIZU AREA.								
June 16	F86-F	953	SELF	—	YALU SWEEP AND PATROL		1.25				MIGS REPORTED BUT NONE SEEN.								
June 19	F86-F	967	SELF	—	YALU SWEEP.		1.20				CLOUD BASE 8000' - SOME FLAK. MIGS REPORTED BUT NONE SEEN.								.20
June 22	F86-F	648	SELF	—	ESCORT TO PHOTO RECCE.		1.30				CHON-CHUN AREA.								.20
June 22	F86-F	967	SELF	—	ESCORT TO PHOTO RECCE		1.20				ANTUNG AREA RECCE of AIRFIELDS.								.30
June 24	F86-F	946	SELF	—	ESCORT TO PHOTO RECCE		1.05												.10
GRAND TOTAL [Cols. (1) to (10)] 1267 Hrs. 55 Mins.					TOTALS CARRIED FORWARD	139.15	1090.00	15.35	22.35	.30						137.25	64.40	24.10	55.00

Some of the action recorded by Bob Carew (left) during his Korean tour.

as well as patrols and area sweeps. Some MiGs were seen from time to time, usually high above us. During my tour, our wing shot down a number of MiGs, credit going mainly to the flight leaders. Wingmen like myself rarely got much chance to score as they were too busy covering their leaders.

My tenth mission, April 17, was to provide close escort for an RF-80 near the Yalu River. Near the end of the mission we were advised that 40 MiGs were heading our way, and to get the photo plane out of there. We were about to leave in any case and proceeded to climb.

Levelling off at 43,000 feet, I found my aircraft pulling ahead of the others despite throttling back. My instruments showed that I had too much power for my throttle setting. As I slowly advanced the throttle, I flamed out. I later learned that the previous pilot who had flown this aircraft ('838) had had the same problem, but near base. It had corrected itself as the pilot descended to land. Unfortunately that pilot failed to report the trouble. I believe a replacement fuel valve probably would have solved the problem.

In any case, the flame-out didn't bother me, as I expected to get a re-light at lower altitude. I set up a glide at 165 KIAS and the correct angle to get a 16:1 glide ratio (16 miles of distance for every mile of height). With the engine windmilling, and hoping the battery was in good shape, I had sufficient hydraulic pressure, but nevertheless used the controls with care.

As it turned out, the engine would not re-light using normal, then emergency procedures. By 11,000 feet I realized that I would have to eject. By this time I had glided about 130 NM and was approaching the island of

Chodo. Though controlled by our forces, it was about 100 miles inside North Korean waters on the west coast and was used as a bail-out position. I got the wind conditions from Chodo and pulled the handles at 7000 feet about a mile off shore.

I tumbled after ejection, but after kicking away the seat and pulling the rip cord things got straightened out. I spotted two rescue helicopters, a flying boat and rescue launch headed my way. I must say, the American rescue operation was excellent.

Seeing my shadow on the water gave me a good indication of where I was headed: over land, then into water beyond. There was a strong wind, but I managed, by pulling on the shroud lines, to control my heading, and landed backwards on the shoreline. I wasn't able immediately to collapse my canopy, and the wind dragged me over the turf. Helicopter 13884 soon picked me up and flew me to a base on Chodo. Later in the day, a C-47 landed on the beach at low tide and flew me back to Kimpo in time for supper.

Although my legs were black and blue for several days, I was back on operations April 24. I completed my 50th mission July 4, and July 9-14 I flew home aboard a 426 Squadron North Star.

R.D. "Bob" Carew

F/L Fred Evans of 421 Squadron served with the 334th at Kimpo and writes:

In Korea I flew a lot with the famous Pete Fernandez, who had over a dozen MiG kills. I also chased Jimmy Jabara more than once. Pete was the best there was—no argument. Jabara would always fly the fastest F-86 in the squadron, then give hell to his No.2 for not keeping up.

I don't think there was much difference between the US and Canadian Sabre. I got flak from some buddies because the Canadair Sabres had more than their share of electrical problems. Back in Canada, I met with Fred Kearns and some of his engineers at Canadair and mentioned this. They researched it and concluded that this was the result of our aircraft spending too much time sitting around docks on the way to Korea. Salt air was the culprit.

On February 1, 1953, I got off before dawn leading a flight of four to the Yalu. On the way home one of the controllers asked us to investigate a train. My reply was that we'd love to (pre-dawn sweeps were boring as hell and everyone knew damn right that no MiGs were going to be found floating around in the dark at that time of day).

We found the train and began to set up an attack pattern. I had Nos.3 and 4 stay high as top cover, while I went in with No.2. After the second pass coming off target I lost my radios. At first I thought I might have been hit, but everything was otherwise working OK. I gave No.2 the universal signal to take over lead. As we climbed out for home base I began to think that this was going to be close on fuel and started running over forced landing procedures in my mind. You have no idea how quiet the F-86 becomes when the fuel is all gone! The gauges all read zero, the nose drops and down you go.

At Kimpo, my circuit and approach were by the book. I had it made. Then I saw a picture on the runway as clearly as if it had been drawn there. The sun had just nicely come up, and there was a silhouette of a Sabre with only the left undercarriage down. I instinctively shoved the stick into the left corner, hit the runway positively, and held the left wing down as long as my strength allowed. The right wing slowly approached the horizontal and stayed there. I just couldn't believe such luck. I found out later that the undercarriage

F/L Fred Evans who flew a busy Korean tour in 1952-53. (DND)

touched the runway just as the wing came to the horizontal. My No.2 wasn't so fortunate—he landed about 200 feet short. I remember later hearing the wing commander say to the maintenance officer, "Go find a bullet hole in that airplane." That would make the accident due to enemy action, and therefore not his problem.

Another of my little adventures concerned a "maintenance fumble" and

Three famous Korean MiG Killers with whom several Canadians flew: Pete Fernandez, Jimmy Jabara and Bill Lilley. Seen at the 334th. (USAF)

near-disaster on January 28. The airplane had just had some major maintenance but hadn't been test flown. The cable connecting the control column to the tail plane had slipped off the pulley or hadn't been put on in the first place. It froze in a three-degree forward position, and lucky for me that I wasn't able to get airborne. The Far East Air Force flight safety magazine later reported the incident: "A flight of F-86s headed out for the runway and positioned themselves for two-ship element takeoffs. The flight leader ran his aircraft up to the required per cent power and gave the signal for takeoff. Upon observing 100 knots on the airspeed indicator, he began efforts to raise the nose gear on his smoke chariot. Not meeting with much success, he increased his efforts by really horsing back on the stick and still the ship acted like it was glued down. He told his wingman to pass him and take off and then turned his attention to aborting his takeoff. It didn't take very long for him to decide he needed more runway than he had left so he punched the panic button (external load salvo switch) and flipped the ground retract switch on the gear. After the ship came to rest he calmly called his group leader to say that he wouldn't be along for this trip. (Don't seem like this boy gets clanked-up very easy!) He then climbed out and surveyed the damage.

"Although the beginning of this lad's trouble was centred around a maintenance fumble, the Board still handed him the Primary on this accident because he neglected to comply with TO-01-60JLB-1 which calls for a thorough control check prior to takeoff.

"That's about the size of this tale. The moral of the story is obvious: Whether you're flying the Noon Balloon for Rangoon or one of Uncle Sam's sky wagons—Buddy, you better check those controls before you try leaping off in that bird!

The Ole' Man sez: 'If those flippers and flappers don't flip and flap like they're supposed to, best you keep that bird on the deck til they do!' "

Had I been afforded the opportunity to appear before the Board, I would have staunchly denied that I neglected to comply with the technical order. Rather, I believe that when I checked the forward and aft controls, that caused the cable to jam. To this day I swear I had a green light for fore and aft trim for takeoff. Some good came of all this though—from then on no airplane was put on operations after major maintenance without a full test flight.

Fred Evans

On a later posting to Staff College, Evans lectured about combat in Korea. He explained how much superior a plane the MiG-15 was to the F-86. This raised a few eyebrows, but as Evans put it: "Any fighter that could fly faster, higher, with greater fire power, and comparable manoeuvrability was a better airplane."

S/L Duke Warren arrived in Korea on July 21, 1953, and flew his first mission with the 39th FIS at Suwon two days later. The war was just winding down and the truce about to be settled. Although he flew 67 missions, Warren would see no combat. He describes some of his Korean flying:

On July 27 my flight commander notified me that I was to take three other pilots over to Tsuiki, Japan, and return with four Sabres from the maintenance depot there. I briefed my flight, and we then waited at the AMU for a C-47. A USAF major arrived with ten other pilots in tow. "Are you Warren?" he asked. I acknowledged, and he surprised me by simply turning the nine over to me, saying that I was in charge.

Just then the C-47 flight was called and off we went. On arrival at Tsuiki I assembled the pilots and briefed them —get lunch, then we would see which aircraft were which for the ferry flight, and get airborne as soon as possible. While briefing, one pilot picked up his gear and wandered off. I enquired of the group and someone replied, "Oh, that's so-and-so. He's in a rush to get back to Korea to get in a MiG mission before the truce."

After lunch, while we were getting organized with the Sabres, one taxied quickly by. I soon determined that it was our keener, having helped himself to an aircraft. My immediate reaction was to call the tower and have the runway blocked, but as the operation had started so hurriedly in Korea, I let it go. But I must admit, it did give me some satisfaction when the tower called me a few minutes later: "Are you in charge of the F-86 pilots? Well, the fellow who just took off has bailed out over the strait. We think the Japanese are picking him out of the water right now."

I got my whole group away that afternoon, except for myself. I was still there at nightfall and was set to go (the USAF was not much in favour of flying the F-86s at night). But I was anxious to get back. It was rumoured, and later confirmed, that each side would only be able to keep the number of aircraft in Korea that it had when the truce was signed.

At 2200 I climbed aboard my Sabre and cranked up, only to have a crew chief signal with a flashlight to shut down. My state of mind after a gruelling day was such that I felt like taxiing straight out regardless. However, I complied, climbed out and found that one of the drop tanks had been leaking. That was that, and it was back to the officers' club till things got squared away.

After the truce, I flew a few patrols east-west along the buffer zone. I also did many ferry trips to Japan. I enjoyed those, as did the young pilots I flew with. I viewed the flights as training missions, having the new pilots do the flight planning, navigation and leading under my direction. The USAF had certified me as an instructor, and I also checked pilots out when they first joined the squadron from the States. I was also being checked out as a C-47 pilot and flew as co-pilot on several trips. One of them ended as a "wild west" scene. After we landed, a group of Koreans under a US Army NCO came to unload us. It turned out that the NCO was a renegade with a Korean gang and was dealing in the black market.

Later, I was transferred from the 39th to 51st Wing HQ working in operations. This gave me a wider view of USAF procedures at the wing level. Here I worked closely with BGen Benjamin O. Davis, the commander, and the first coloured man to reach general rank in the USAF (his father was the first in the US Army). While working in ops at the 51st, one of our C-47s was stranded at K-2 (Taegu) with a faulty starter. K-2 was a hell-hole to be stuck at, so, as no other transport was available, I volunteered to fly the spare down in an F-86. I was at K-2 in 30 minutes and didn't shut down as the C-47 crew chief removed the starter from my radio compartment. I then had him run over to ops and tell them that I'd not be shutting down, but returning immediately to base. A minor incident then erupted which I later reported to Wing HQ: "Upon taxiing

out to the runway, the major in charge of Base Operations came out in a jeep and got up on the wing to tell the under-signed it was required by USAF Regulations to refile a DD-175. The following factors were brought to his attention: a) Sufficient fuel existed for return flight; b) Pilot had left K-13 20 minutes ago and was familiar with route and weather; c) In no way was return flight endangering property or personnel of US government; d) Pilot was aware of AF Regulation but requested clearance for this flight due to circumstances."

I also sent a message to Gen Davis explaining the incident (I had taken off in spite of the snarly major). He was sympathetic but reminded me that I had, in fact, violated flying regulations, and that was that. I got a bit more consolation from one of the pilots who declared, "We have too many chicken shit regulations, and I'm glad someone showed us how foolish

Duke Warren (left) with his flying buddy, Tex Monague, USMC, while on duty in Korea. (USAF)

some of them can be." At the end of November I left Korea, returning to the UK. I was back on 410 on December 15.

Duke Warren

Upon his return to RCAF duties, S/L Warren submitted a candid, personal summary of his Korean tour. It provides hitherto unpublished insights into this period of RCAF/USAF cooperation:

REPORT ON KOREAN TOUR
WITH 51 FIGHTER INTERCEPTOR WING
22 JUL 53 - 22 NOV 53
BY
26237 S/L D WARREN, DFC,
OC 410 (F) SQUADRON

Introduction

1 The following report covers the period during which the writer was attached to 39th Fighter Interceptor Squadron at K-13 AF Base Suwon, Korea. Those subjects which have already formed basis for previous reports by RCAF pilots are omitted in order to keep the summary brief.

Operations

2 The writer arrived on 21 Jul 53; the next day was spent drawing flying gear, intelligence briefing and interview with the Base Commander and Group Commander (C Ops O) plus Squadron Commander. On 23 Jul 53, three sorties were flown in the F-86F for local familiarization and to get accustomed

Ed Hale (left) with an American pilot, during Hale's Korean tour. (via E.B. Hale)

to the aircraft. The 24th had marginal weather and flying was strictly limited. The 25 and 26 Jul the weather was completely down. On the morning of 27 Jul the writer was placed in charge of 10 other pilots and sent to Tsuiki which provided central maintenance for all Sabre aircraft in Korea with instructions to ferry back as many aircraft to Korea as possible that day. That evening hostilities ceased.

Whereas there was a rather lengthy program of approximately seven days termed "Clobber College" this seemed to be used for inexperienced people and the writer was not detailed to attend this. However it was understood at 4 FIW all pilots new to Theatre were required to attend.

Post Hostility Period

3 Immediately the USAF began its training program which is quite similar to the RCAF requirement, at the same time a repatriation program to send pilots back to United States was organized, a sliding scale was devised incorporating missions flown and time in Korea. In some cases people were sent home within two weeks, others were due to go but were held up for shipping space. A good deal of uncertain confusion existed re this program and the Squadrons suffered for a period of approximately four months due to this. Squadron's strength was reduced from approximately 50 to 32 at time of leaving.

Gunnery

4 Air to Air firing training commenced; this was practically nonexistent during the operational phase. At first scores were very low 3% - 5% with a fair number of NIL scores but a steady improvement was noted with practice.

Only major difference in USAF methods was the fact that:

(a) Gun sights were "pegged" at 1000 feet.
(b) Sight was re-harmonized to give better flag results at particular speed of firing.
(c) Centre guns were not fired as it was felt these caused dispersed bullet patterns and gave low scores.
(d) No attempt was made to fire using radar.

A mobile training unit concerning the A-4 sight was located on the unit and all pilots were lectured on the sight and encouraged to visit this trailer. However the personnel that were operating this were not of the level of experience the "Fire Bird" project technicians were and some benefit was lost due to this.

Regarding the actual serviceability of the sight itself whereas accurate figures are not available from a pilot users' point of view the A-1 sight serviceability was about the same as that at 1(F) Wing and the A-4 some 20% better. Under the arrangements existing at 51 FIW no one man was responsible for both sight and radar and some control was lost due to this. There was no Squadron Armament Officer but rather a Wing Armament and broken down into the two phases, those worked on aircraft independently of each other though a certain liaison did exist.

Other Training

5 This took the form of lectures on ground subjects for everyone and air work for newly arrived pilots. Because of rapid turn-over of pilots the experienced pilots were constantly engaged in "checking out" sorties. Instrument flying, which the average newly-joined pilot was quite weak in, was considered important but it was difficult to effect as there was no "cloud flying" area designated and airways had to be used entailing flight plans. Because these had to be filed across the field and transport was poor 2 hours had to be allowed for this, then if the land line connections failed, which often happened, no practice flights were accepted. Taken overall the average pilot's Instrument Flying ability on 51 FIW was well below that of his RCAF counterpart.

The radio beacon network was well thought out for jets, each main base having two beacons sited and frequencies so arranged that only band change was necessary to change beacons without retuning by pilot.

GCI

6 The equipment furnished to the radar units in Korea was not the latest, furthermore pilots who were surplus to requirements or considered unsuitable for fighters were given a three week course at Johnson AFB Japan and then sent out as controllers; for these reasons the standard of interception and controlling was very much lower than that in England at the present time. The Base Commander stated the controlling was not as good as that he had experienced in England in 1944 and the writer agrees. Although there was a fixer VHF/DF network pilots quite rightly had little confidence in it and so used it as a last resort and the operators did not get enough practice.

Patrols and Alerts

7 Four patrols were flown each day weather permitting, two up each coast by 51. The west coast patrol went as far as the mouth of the Yalu and the east coast the range of the F-86F was the limiting factor. Pilots were instructed to remain three miles offshore and precautions were taken to prevent flying over land; if undercast existed, patrol skirted edge or aborted sortie.

Alert was continuous with 4 aircraft on ORP with pilots in cockpit plus 4 aircraft with pilots standing by. Eight aircraft were on 5 minutes availability

Canadair-built F-86E-6 of the 334th FIS in Korea. (via H. Volker)

in dispersal area. A further 8 aircraft were available on 15 minutes notice one hour before dawn and one hour before dusk. Unfortunately it was felt although the numbers of aircraft that were available for scrambles and interceptions was ample, their effectiveness was considerably reduced by the poor controlling, lack of immediate R/T instructions on getting airborne and poor warning.

As an example of this, the defecting NK MiG pilot was first noticed when he landed at K-14 (down wind); he then rolled up to ORP and got out and started talking to pilots on alert duty.

Morale

8   The morale of the American fighter squadron was felt to be lower than that of its RCAF counterpart. This was due to a large percentage of personnel being in the USAF as the lesser of two evils, the army being the other.

The compulsory military training scheme also affected the ground crew

A Canadair Sabre in post Korea days. Survivors of the 60 that went to Korea were distributed among Air National Guard squadrons, in this case the Michigan ANG. (Wm. Balogh via D. Menard)

and it was exceptional to meet an airman of Sgt rank or below who wanted to make the USAF a career. Senior USAF officers called their junior pilots "GI Pilots" and treated them as such. Of 34 squadron members of 1st Lt and 2nd Lt rank only three were interested in the service as a career. RCAF and RAF exchange officers were highly regarded by USAF Squadron Commanders at 51 F Wing and were specially sought after.

The younger pilots also felt the Sabre or any jet was dangerous to fly. This was not due to battle casualties as these were practically non-existent. (74 MiGs shot down in Jun 53 against NIL Sabre losses.) The squadron commander was aware of this and when questioned said he felt it was a partial result of recruiting information which led one to believe a particularly outstanding man was required to fly jets. This feeling seemed to be decreasing just prior to writer being returned.

The senior USAF officers such as Squadron Commander, Operations Officer and above were extremely able, well-qualified men who did their very best under difficult circumstances. The same applies to the senior NCO ranks who were career men. (A fuller appreciation and explanation of some of the morale problems appeared in 31

Oct. 53 *Saturday Evening Post*.)

In addition, all functions of command seemed to be up at least one rank in USAF, the Joint Operations Centre entered far more into the detailed operation of Wing flying than is customary for RCAF or RAF procedure. Squadron and Wing Commanders complained bitterly of this.

Other Activities
9 The writer spent five days with Canadian Army and 14 days with the Canadian Navy aboard HMCS *Iroquois* on a trip to Hong Kong. The return trip to Japan was made via USN Neptune from Kai Tak to Kadena on Okinawa. This island has been tremendously built up by the American Forces, four lane routes similar to Queen Elizabeth highway connect various installations. Speaking generally one of the most impressive items on the tour was the build-up of American power in Japan.

An additional four days were spent at "Freedom Village" during repatriation of POW's in the expectation of S/L MacKenzie's return.

Items Considered to be
of Specific Value to RCAF
10 (a) The "barrier" arrangement which prevents excessive damage to aircraft leaving runway. This has

been thoroughly discussed elsewhere.
(b) The system of radio beacons and network set up specifically to facilitate jet operations in Korea and Japan.
(c) While it is a round-about way of arriving at a conclusion the writer feels strongly that the USAF in Korea demonstrates the value of RCAF training and selection to produce both officers and pilots.

Summary
11 The original reason for sending RCAF officers to Korea ceased five days after writer's arrival.

There was still knowledge to be gained however and it is felt the tour was of benefit. However the same result could be obtained in 90 days temporary duty tours as the USAF practices instead of six months. All USAF officers encountered were very friendly and especially those who previously served with RCAF or RAF during WWII; the latter seemed to go out of their way to speak highly of their former service.

A total of 72:25 hours was flown in F-86F and 189:50 hours passenger time in 8 different types of aircraft.

D. Warren S/L
OC 410(F) Sqn.

RCAF Sabre Pilots in Korea

Name	USAF Squadron	Period	F-86 Sorties	Kills	Probables	Damaged
Bliss, S/L W.H.F.*	334th	March-August 1953	31			
Carew, F/O R.D.*	335th	February-July 1953	50			
Davidson, W/C R.T.P.*	335th	September-December 1952	51			
Donald, F/O J.D.		April-May 1952	0			
Evans, F/L F.W.*	334th	December 1952 - March 1953	50			
Fleming, F/O S.B.ˣ	336th	March-June 1952	82		1	2
Fox, S/L*	(51st FW)	May-October 1953	29			
Glover, F/L E.A.ˣ•	334th	June-October 1952	50	3		3
Hale, G/C E.B.ˣ	16th	April-May 1952	26			
LaFrance, F/L J.C.A.ˣ	39th	May-September 1952	49	1		
Lambros, F/O A.*	39th	October 1952 - March 1953	50			2
Levesque, F/L J.A.O.*ˣ	334th	November 1950 - June 1951	71	1		
Lindsay, S/L J.D.ˣ	39th	July-December 1952	70	2		3
Lowry, F/L R.E.*	25th	July-December 1952	50			
MacKay, S/L J.*	39th	March-July 1953	50	1		
MacKenzie, S/L A.R.	39th	December 1952, POW	5			
Mullin, F/O J.B.	335th	June-November 1953	55			
Nichols, F/L G.H.*	16th	January-May 1953	50		1	
Nixon, F/0 G.W.*	16th, 25th	March-July 1952	50			
Smith, S/L E.G.*	334th	August-December 1952	50			
Spurr, F/L L.E.ˣ	25th	April-July 1952	50	1		
Warren, S/L D.	39th	July-December 1953	67			
		Totals	1036	9	2	10

*Awarded US Air Medal
ˣAwarded US Distinguished Flying Cross
•Awarded RCAF Distinguished Flying Cross

Leapfrogging the Atlantic

First across the Pond

The first RCAF pilot to jet across the Atlantic was S/L C.D. "Cal" Bricker. He had been a photo recce pilot on Mustangs and Spitfires during the war and had commanded 430 and 443 Squadrons in 1945-46. Post-war he flew Mustangs with 417 Squadron at Rivers, but in 1949 was posted on exchange to the 20th FB Group, 79th Squadron, at Shaw AFB, South Carolina. The 79th was flying the Republic F-84 Thunderjet. He arrived at Shaw in January 1950, and after some quick T-6 time, it was on to the F-84, his first jet. Bricker remembers that "mentioned throughout my briefings was the warning that the Thunderjet needed a very long takeoff run, but not to worry—she'd come unstuck near the end of the runway."

Solo day came, and after another warning about the roll and the F-84's slow rate of climb, away went Bricker: "As I soared over the gatehouse, just off to the side past the end of the runway, I saw doors fly open and people dash out. I was sure I had really pulled a poor takeoff. Not so, I was later told; it happens nearly all the time. A month earlier, an engine failure on takeoff had led to near disaster, and the guards were taking no chances with low-flying Thunderjets."

Just after the Korean War broke out in June 1950, the Shaw group was deployed to Manston, Kent. Bricker flew one of the F-84s across, thus recording a first for a member of the RCAF. His log shows the following legs:

July 20	Shaw AFB-Otis AFB	2:10 hrs
22	Otis-Goose Bay	2:20 hrs
23	Goose Bay-BW-1	1:50 hrs
25	BW-1-Keflavik	2:15 hrs
26	Keflavik-Kinloss	2:05 hrs
	Kinloss-Manston	1:20 hrs

In December 1950 Bricker's F-84 group retraced its steps to South Caro-

lina. In March 1951 he was back in Canada to brief the RCAF on what he had learned about transatlantic jet flights, and that fall was made OC of 439 Squadron, the first RCAF unit to fly the ocean with Sabres.

Leapfrog 1 and 2

In 1951 the RCAF began establishing itself in Europe, first with 421's brief sojourn at Odiham flying RAF Vampires, then at North Luffenham. The first squadrons ensconced there were 410 and 441, and they had made the trip from Canada aboard ship—aircraft and personnel aboard the aircraft carrier *Magnificent* in the case of 410; aircraft on the carrier and personnel on the *Empress of France* for 441. But it was clear by then that single-engine jet fighters could be flown across the Atlantic. Logistically it was quite straightforward, using the famous wartime route from Goose Bay to Bluie West I, Kefla-

vik, and Kinloss or Prestwick. Tactically, this made more sense as, weather permitting, there was little to interfere with a fast crossing—two or three days even. In time of emergency, this was a vital consideration. Shipping aircraft across took weeks of preparation (cocooning, loading, etc.) and perhaps two weeks at sea and offloading. Thus, after experiencing the seaborne operation, the RCAF switched to direct overflights, calling these operations "Leapfrog."

The feasibility of flying jets on the

Leapfrog 2, about to depart from Uplands on September 23, 1952, is inspected by Brooke Claxton, Minister of National Defence. Here he checks over 430 Squadron. From the left are W/C Bud Malloy, CO of Station Uplands; W/C Stocky Edwards, W/C Flying, 2 Wing; A/M Curtis, the CAS (hidden); Claxton; and F/Os Zeke Walter, George Shorey, Bruce Sheasby, Les Sparrow, Stu Banks and John Greatrix. (DND)

Famous overview of Uplands on the day of 2 Wing's send-off to Grostenquin. Count the Sabres. This gives a good picture of Uplands, a typical wartime station. Some of the old buildings are still in use today. (DND PL55471)

Pilots S. Hannah, Harry Wenz and George Fitzgerald sojourn at Keflavik during Leapfrog 1, June 1952. (via G.J. Fitzgerald)

North Atlantic had been proven by the 1948 crossings with Vampires and F-80s. Soon such trips would be routine with Leapfrogs, Bechers Brooks (RAF) and High Flights (USAF). Leapfrog 1 was ready to leave Uplands in late May 1952. S/L Cal Bricker would lead, and his first job was to get his boys ready: "I became involved in the planning—many, many meetings on all aspects of the operation, air and ground support, facilities, routes, techniques, flight safety, training—to fly the squadron to England, with logistical support from Air Transport Command.

"No pilot could make the trip with less than 75 hours on Sabres. All met the requirement and were well prepared. The emphasis was on safety. We adopted the code name 'Leapfrog' as our ground support, split in two, was leapfrogged to supply constant despatch and reception servicing for the Sabres.

"I insisted that each pilot be equipped with an exposure suit. These were designed to afford some protection short as it would be, to any pilot down in the sea. Time went by, and no suits arrived. Although we could have borrowed them from the USAF, the RCAF was designing its own. The day arrived for this 'better' suit to be demonstrated to 439. We all gathered around the pool and watched as an expert wearing the suit leapt into the water. Held up by his Mae West, he expounded on the suit's virtues, in spite of the rush of bubbles coming up at the back of the suit (which had split). His rescue was rather slow, as most of us were roaring with laughter. We used USAF suits for the crossing."

Defence Minister Brooke Claxton saw 439 on its way May 30, with the planned four-day trip scheduled to refuel at Bagotville, Goose Bay, BW-1, Keflavik and Kinloss before reaching North Luffenham. Weather, though, disrupted plans, and the trip took 16 days. En route, Cal Bricker was laid low by appendicitis and command was temporarily handed to F/L Bill Bliss. The squadron got into North Luff on June 15 where station CO, G/C E.B. Hale, had a welcome prepared. The boys were happy, if weary, and one reported, "Our morale is at an all-time high and our finances at an all-time low." A week's leave in London got the 439 Tigers off to a happy start in No.1 Air Division.

Flying soon got under way and, of course there were some teething problems and, sadly, losses. An early diary entry for July says, "Due to recent cases of pilots becoming lost, the flying for the first few days of this week was devoted to low-level map reading of the eastern sector." July 1, F/O Ray Conti was killed; he had run out of fuel

421 Squadron lined up "on parade" at Uplands, ready for Leapfrog 2. Venturas of Spartan Air Services and a US Army Beaver are in the background. (DND PL55446)

and crashed at sea. He had been on his first North Luffenham mission.

For each of the Leapfrog departures there was a grand send-off, focusing, in true fighter pilot tradition, on the bar in the Mess. One sometimes wonders how, within a day or so, everyone was "ready" for the 3500-mile trip across the pond. As if the rigours of the trip weren't bad enough, more than a few Swordsmen must have strapped on their jets to a pounding in their skulls caused by over-indulgence the night before.

No.427 Squadron helped send off 421 on Leapfrog 2. A September 23, 1952, diary remark described plans to assist in the festivities: "A small wooden row boat was decided upon as a presentation to 421(F) for those pilots who would be forced to bail out over the water."

S/L J.W. "Jim" Fiander participated in Leapfrog 2, being a flight commander at the time. He had joined the RCAF in 1940, training at St. Catharines and Dunnville, then going on Hurricanes and Spitfires with 401 Squadron, and later instructing at Uplands. He stayed on in ground jobs after the war, but in August 1951 got

The 2 Wing "brass" for Leapfrog 2: S/L John MacKay, OC 416 Squadron; S/L R.G. "Bob" Middlemiss, 421 Squadron; W/C Stocky Edwards, W/C Flying, 2 Wing; and S/L Paul Gibbs, 430 Squadron. (DND)

back on flying at Chatham, making his first Sabre flight on February 2, 1952 (19223). He soon joined 430 Squadron at North Bay and on Leapfrog 2 took 19238 across the pond:

Sept. 28 '52	North Bay-Bagotville	1:00 hrs.
	Bagotville-Goose Bay	1:15
30	Goose Bay-BW-1	1:30
Oct. 3	BW-1-Keflavik	1:36
	Keflavik-Prestwick	1:40
11	Prestwick-Grostenquin	1:15

Poopy suit practice for 4 Wing prior to Leap-frog. (via Al Adams)

F/L Fred Evans, a wartime fighter pilot, first flew the Sabre on January 29, 1952, at 421 Squadron, St. Hubert. His last flight would be many years later—November 15, 1965, with the STU at Chatham. He relates some memories of his early years and Leap-frog 2: "When 421 returned from England in 1951, I stayed behind brief-ly to complete the Day Fighter Leader Course with the RAF, then rejoined

Goose Bay, last stop outbound for all Sabres on Leapfrogs, Bechers Brooks, and Randoms. (G.H. Collison)

421 at St. Hubert. I read 'the book' quickly, and when the first Sabre came aboard I grabbed it. All was routine at St. Hubert until we started getting ready for Leapfrog 2. Pretty well everything has been written about that, except about the 'clean-up' flight. Six-ty Sabres don't leave point A and ar-rive at point F at the same time without a great deal of planning. I was ap-pointed clean-up flight commander, and would stay behind with anyone who couldn't get off for one reason or another. All went well until point C, Bluie West 1, where we all arrived together on September 30, 1952. Most went on to Prestwick the same day.

"Life at BW-1 was a bitch for a whole week. Just when we got the u/s aircraft fixed, the weather closed in. Every morning we were up for a brief-ing. Our clothes were getting a bit high, but we were afraid to launder them in case we were cleared to go and they were still not dry! We finally got into Keflavik on October 8, left next day for Prestwick, but had to turn back because of a u/s bird. We made it the same day, took two days to clean up and rest, had a beer or two, then on to Grostenquin October 11."

Squadron OCs on Leapfrogs
413 S/L W.I. Gordon
414 W/C J.F. "Jack" Allan
416 S/L John MacKay
421 S/L R.G. "Bob" Middlemiss
422 S/L W.J. "John" Buzza
427 S/L C.L.V. "Lyte" Gervais
430 W/C J.F. "Stocky" Edwards
434 S/L John Mitchner
439 S/L C.D. "Cal" Bricker
444 S/L John MacKay

439 Prayer
Look down, O CAS, on these thy pilots, bowed before thee, and bring in the wandering from the wilderness of Quebec. Give the Met observers wisdom so that there be no widows and orphans. Deliver the JP-1 and repair the parking brakes. Succour all who require beer, smugs or SOSs. Remember our last compass heading so that we may be found in the days to come, even before 416 follows. Unworthy as we are, we pray for them. And those who have forgotten their computers, stop watches, and green tickets, do thou, O CAS, protect through thy duck boats and Danish weather ships. For thou art the helper of the sprog and retread, the demoter of the lost, the granter of short service commissions to the wanderer. Thou knowest each man's need (spare the daughters of these foreign lands), for it was ever thus. Grant unto each according to his ability and the capacity of thy dun-geon and eternal lashes; through AOC, our constant adviser, and Lord of the Salt Mines.

Duke Warren's boys at 410 Squadron put up a bit of a skit in honour of 439 crossing the Atlantic.

Leapfrog 3—The 30-Day Grind
The most famous of all Leapfrogs was number three. it took a month to com-plete (March 7 - April 7, 1953) and left many a Sabre driver frazzled by the time the three squadrons (413, 427, 434) staggered into Zweibrücken. Some Leapfrog 3 anecdotes appear in the 427 Squadron diary:

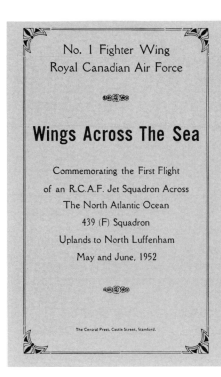

No. 1 Fighter Wing
Royal Canadian Air Force

❀❀❀

Wings Across The Sea

Commemorating the First Flight

of an R.C.A.F. Jet Squadron Across

The North Atlantic Ocean

439 (F) Squadron

Uplands to North Luffenham

May and June, 1952

❀❀❀

The Central Press, Castle Street, Stamford.

The Cast

(In Order of Twitch)

S/L. C. D. BRICKER, Goose Bay Star and Bar
F/L. W. J. BLISS, Order of The Greenland Garter
and Undies
F/L. H. F. WENZ, Distinguished Iceland Ice Cube
F/O. J. R. BEDARD
F/O. K. A. CHEESMAN
F/O. R. J. CONTI
F/O. A. J. EVERARD
F/O. J. G. FITZGERALD
F/L. J. L. HAMILTON
F/O. J. S. HANNAH
F/O. K. J. JENNET
F/O. J. R. LAROCHE
F/O. H. N. MACKERACHER
F/O. L. PAPPAS
F/O. F. RAYMOND
F/O. H. F. REISCHMAN
F/O. H. C. RUECKER
F/O. E. A. SEITZ
F/O. M. SILLS
F/O. D. A. SMILEY
F.O. T. D WHEALER
F.O. C. F. WILKINSON
F/O. H. T. WILSON
F/O. H. R. WINGATE
F/O. H. G. FOWLER

The North Atlantic Squadron

Old Man Bricker scans the sky,
Comes back in with a tear in his eye
And says, my boys you've got to fly
As the North Atlantic Squadron.

They spent 10 days in Labrador,
And many more on Iceland's shore,
Then took off with a sickening roar
As the North Atlantic Squadron.

The pilots all have got the twitch
They'd hate like hell to have to ditch,
The water's cold as a son-of-a-bitch,
'Neath the North Atlantic Squadron.

The ground crew they all moan and groan
They've never been so far from home,
But 439 is on the roam
As the North Atlantic Squadron.

Now they're on old Blighty's shore
And here they'll spend a long time more,
Looking around for a little score
As 439 Squadron.

Eject Yourself *(Tune, Enjoy Yourself)*

Cal Bricker's boys with bags of noise have said they fly the sea.
That may be fine for four three nine, but not for you and me.
Far out from Goose, when on the loose, a weather ship they spot.
From where they sit they're in the shit, and things don't look so hot.

Chorus
Eject yourself, it's later than you think,
Eject yourself, and end up in the drink.
The fuel goes by as quickly as a wink,
Eject yourself, protect yourself, it's later than you think.

Some make it past the weather ship, some haven't any luck,
Some now are getting chilblains from swimming like a duck.
They're almost in to Bluie, but Bluie's down in fog,
Press on, dear chaps, an "A" class prang you'll enter in your log.

Some try a rocky GCA and one or two get in,
The other boys aren't worried 'cause it isn't far to swim.
One poor sod tries to overshoot, and ends up on his back,
And pieces from his cartwheel go aflying round like flak.

The band is out at Prestwick, and the brass stands all around,
When one poor lonesome Sabre comes and crumps onto the ground.
Cal Bricker looks out of the wreck, he feels a little grim,
The brass come up and shake their heads, and say these words to him:

Enjoy yourself, we have to have a goat,
You've proved a point, the Sabre will not float.
A message came from which we'd like to quote,
We see it now as clear as mud, you should have come by boat.

F/O Al Seitz of 439 Squadron about to touch down at BW-1 during Leapfrog 1. Notice the rugged terrain and the icebergs. (DND PL54923)

glasses in her pocket and wept.

Mar. 8 Aircraft with minor unserviceabilities are being checked by ground crews. Seat packs changed from inland winter to maritime in preparation for the actual crossing. Latest word is that 427 will lead the wing out of Goose at 0800 tomorrow.

Mar. 9 Persistent layer of cloud based at 500 feet lies along the fiord at BW-1 and postpones our operation for today. 427 pilots, attired in immersion suits, sat sweating in their a/c all morning waiting for the word to go, which never came. Time is spent playing "Stook," logging sack time, and movies. One party of five set out to dig holes in the ice to lure unwary fish onto outsize hooks. They had the foresight to take along refreshments, which alone was responsible for the success of the party, since the fish declined the offer of meat.

Mar. 10 Our two leading sections sat and panted in their a/c while the met men at both ends dickered and doubted. Postponement again today.

Mar. 11 A deep low has descended on Bluie while perfect flying weather prevails at Goose. A short horror film this a.m. showing how to get into Bluie.

Mar. 12 More low weather at Bluie . . . Weather prophets say we should get away in the morning.

Mar. 14 And the weather prophets were wrong.

Mar. 13 427 led the wing on the 95-minute trip to Greenland. . . . Weather ship was 40-45 miles off position, but no navigation difficulties were experienced.

Mar. 15 Met men say the next leg of the operation, Greenland to Iceland, will be the most difficult to forecast. A US F-94 pilot also waiting for the good weather to fly to Iceland, tells us he has been here 51 days!

Mar. 16 A day of rest. No major unserviceabilities among our a/c.

Mar. 17 A school of lows ganging up in Iceland postpones our operation. Outlook for tomorrow poor. In the afternoon the wing went on foot to a nearby glacier.

Mar. 18 Weather still poor and we remain at BW-1. We hear that Soviet

No.3 Wing at BW-1 whilst en route to Zwei in March 1953. Besides Sabres, this picture features several other fifties-vintage aircraft: a North Star, C-46, C-54, C-82, C-119s, A-26 and F-94s. The bleakness of Bluie chills the bone, even for those who were never at the place! (J.R. Pugh)

Vincent (19437), F/Os Mullin (19409), Hind (19415), Rowe (19418), Pugh (19422), Tousignant (19450), Livingston (19430), Larsen (19432), Adkins (19438), Frazer (19443), Deacon (19451), Bain (19445), Laviolette (19447), Gardiner (19444).

Mar. 6 Weather is still not good enough for the first leg of Leapfrog, St. Hubert to Goose Bay. Goose is reporting low visibility and snow. A North Star with an advance party left for Germany (via Paris) at 1130 hours. 427 Squadron will lead the wing over and the line up is as follows: S/L Gervais (19427), F/L Sinclair (19433), F/L

Mar. 7 The squadron left St. Hubert today in 4 sections and arrived at Goose Bay without incident . . . Soucy, the shy airwoman at St. Hubert who has been everyone's friend with her needle and thread, her willingness to run errands, and her devotion to 427 Squadron, clicked her camera all day at departing Sabres, then put her

planes have shot down two allied planes over Germany.

Mar. 19 Perfect day at Bluie, the reverse at Keflavik.

Mar. 20 Still at Bluie, we were joined by 14 Sabres of RAF operation Bechers Brook under S/L Cole.

Mar. 21 Lows breeding and multiplying over Denmark Straits and Iceland keep us in Bluie. Met men say there is an 80% chance of going tomorrow.

Mar. 22 Bad weather at BW-1—and met men say no chance of going tomorrow which raises hopes all round!

Mar. 23 Still at BW-1.

Mar. 24 300-foot ceiling and 3/4 mi. visibility at Keflavik. Improvement in the afternoon too late for us to get away. Met men say we should go tomorrow.

Mar. 25 More bad weather!

Mar. 26 The majority of squadron personnel rose at 5 a.m. to fight their way through a blizzard to the briefing room, there to be told that the weather was unsuitable for takeoff.

Mar. 27 Bad weather at Iceland.

Mar. 28 After early reports of good weather at Iceland, the squadron took off in four sections from BW-1. The last section was at the point of no return when Kef reported snow showers and lowered visibility. They landed through the 500-foot ceiling with 2-mile visibility.

Mar. 29 All the a/c left behind at

Senior officers at St. Hubert for Leapfrog 4's departure for Baden, August 27, 1953: A/V/M A.L. "Art" James, Commander No. 1 Air Defence Group, Air Defence Command; S/L John Buzza, OC 422 Squadron; A/M C.R. Slemon, the CAS; S/L John MacKay, OC 444 Squadron; W/C Jack Allan, OC 414 Squadron; and W/C "Bud" Malloy. (DND via Al Adams)

Sabres sweep low over the hangars at St. Hubert, then turn for Goose Bay, leg number one of Leapfrog 4. (DND PL58302)

having radio channels recrystallized for European operation.

Apr. 7 Led by 427, the wing moved out of Prestwick at 1130. By 2000 the squadron was established at Zweibrücken, having taken one month to the day to reach here. Our average ground speed is thus less than impressive. However, stories of the fabulous quarters and 40-foot bar in the mess are all based on fact. 1 Wing has not displaced us, and the only immediate danger seems to be from the demolition crew sent over from Grostenquin (2 Wing) to aid in the welcome ceremonies.

Another minor hazard is the number of motorcycles which appear at high speed from nowhere, and disappear in the same direction pushing Mach 1. We hear that two airmen of our advance party have distinguished themselves by walking over a cliff in the darkness.

Apr. 8 We have been given 5 days off, and what happens between now and 5 days hence, dear diary, is none of your business.

427 Squadron Diary

Bechers Brook: RAF Sabres on the North Atlantic

RAF pilot "Check" Collison started flying in 1944 and received his wings in 1949. He spent the next few years flying Vampires and Meteors, but when the RAF needed crews to ferry Sabres from Canada to England he joined that operation. All along he was flying as a lowly sergeant pilot, but finally decided to move up in the ranks. He switched to the RCAF in 1954 and first flew CF-100s with 433 Squadron, then instructed at No.3AW(F)OTU at Cold Lake. Next he joined 414 on Clunks and later Voodoos. In 1964 he was posted to Lahr test-flying CF-104s. Then came a stint in Flight Safety, and retirement in 1971.

Collison here tells of his experiences as a Sabre ferry pilot with 147 Squadron, RAF. The squadron was involved in Operation Bechers Brook in 1953, moving hundreds of Sabres across the pond:

Summary of Leapfrogs

One	439 Sqn	May 30 - June 14, 1952	To North Luffenham
Two	416,421,430 Sqns	September 28 - October 10, 1952	To Grostenquin
Three	413,427,434 Sqns	March 7 - April 7, 1953	To Zweibrücken
Four	414,422,444 Sqns	August 27 - September 3, 1953	To Baden-Söllingen

BW-1 arrived here today, closely followed by US F-84s.

Mar. 30 Weather at Prestwick and along route poor.

Mar. 31 More bad weather at Prestwick.

Apr. 1 Bad weather at Iceland, and strong headwinds.

Apr. 2 Iceland weather poor.

Apr. 3 Headwinds again.

Apr. 4 Kinloss. Headwinds made it necessary to stop here for fuel.

Apr. 5 Prestwick. Remaining a/c of 3 Wing arrived here from Kinloss and Iceland without incident. We hear, however, that S/L Cole is missing in his Sabre.

Apr. 6 3 Wing a/c are on the ground

My association with the Sabre began early in January 1953. I was in the last days of my rehab leave following a three-year tour on Vampires in the Middle East when I received an OHMS requesting my presence at Adastral House in London. Upon my arrival I was directed to a small office not much larger than a broom closet. The occupant, disguised as a civilian, didn't fool me for a minute.

"Ah, yes, Collison. Here's just the job for you. We are taking delivery of some Sabres in Canada. How would you like to help ferry them over?"

Despite visions of the cruel sea, and Harry Hawker, I responded with the time-honoured, "Yes! Sir!" and consequently found myself taking a Sabre conversion course at RAF Abingdon in Oxfordshire. I was not too sure that I had been posted to the right place since Abingdon's main activity appeared to be paratroop training. Every day, hundreds of enthusiastic brown jobs hurled their bodies at the ground from scaffolds, towers, balloons and aircraft. I noticed that a basket balloon was almost continuously in operation in the centre of the airfield, disgorging its eager contents. This activity, as well as flying, went on simultaneously without apparent conflict.

It soon became clear that the Sabre was quite different from anything I'd seen or flown before. Compared to the Vamp, it was enormous, and built like a tank—solid metal! It was the first aircraft I'd ever seen that had all the EOs

Serene view of a RAF Sabre 4 overflying the Greenland icecap on a Bechers Brook in July 1953. (G.H. Collison)

stencilled on the fuselage: STEP, NO STEP, FILL ONLY WITH COKE— MIL SPEC 1066-55BC, ACTUATE ONLY ON SUNDAYS, etc., and all those mysterious lights in the cockpit! The cockpit would take some getting used to with all that room and visibility. Very un-British. The ground school also provided something new with its hydraulic, electrics and fuel systems training stands.

Whatever our misgivings, we were soon blasting off into the blue with reasonable confidence. I found the aircraft was a pleasure to fly. A bit sensitive in pitch, stable and very positive in roll, a good rate of climb, and very quick to pick up speed when pointed at the ground. It also covered the ground at a great rate of knots. On my third or fourth trip I tried to find my parents'

house just outside London. I headed east, but soon was over the English Channel. A smart 180 and a few more minutes put me over the Bristol Channel. I gave up. You needed more than a rate-one turn to stay over land. (Throttling back a bit more after takeoff would also have helped.)

We were considered experts after amassing 10 hours and so set out from North Luffenham in an RCAF North Star to join 147 Squadron at St. Hubert. Staging through Prestwick, Keflavik and Goose Bay, we arrived at Dorval after a relaxing 18 hours of flying. My subsequent trips in the North Star were also just as relaxing. There

RAF ferry pilots head for their Sabres at Bagotville. Fourteen Sabres were involved in this flight across the pond. (DND PL55688)

(Overleaf) Sabres arriving from Leapfrog 2. 430 Squadron is in front, 416 in the back row and 421 appears to be in the circuit. The scene at Grostenquin is one of excitement, but it looks as if there's still lots of getting-ready to be done. (via John Greatrix)

A tremendous crowd of RAF types, all of 147 Squadron, photographed in front of the fire hall at Goose Bay in July 1953. (RAF)

Nicely composed photo of Sabre 4s in Canada awaiting delivery to the RAF. Photographer Don Tansley writes of some of the legs flown by the RAF pilots: "These hops were quite long for Sabres. Tail winds were welcomed, navigation precise, the cardinal rule was *no* separation-visual contact all the way. Some aircraft barely made it, and some had to be towed around the peritracks after running dry after their landings. Some mornings we had 20 Sabres waiting to go, pilots strapped in. The first five were plugged into generators awaiting the final met and the green light. If all went well five carts roared and five Sabres started, then a mad rush for the next five and so on. Soon the sky would be blackened with the dense kerosene smoke as Sabre after Sabre took off." (G.H. Collison)

must be many who have shared my experiences and understand exactly what I mean. After landing in a strong head wind, the pilot apparently had great difficulty in remembering how to get the aircraft off the runway. Obviously, this was not the first incident of its kind, for those clever Canadians had it all figured out, and had an SOP: "Everyone in the back end crowd forward into the front end." Having all those RAF pilots peering over his shoulders and breathing down his neck seemed to have the desired intimidating effect, because he taxied off the runway in no time flat.

Next day we were off from St. Hubert in a Dakota, bound for Chatham to learn the mysteries of the simulator.

In my case, this included the experience of trying an inverted takeoff. Somehow or other, someone had contrived to park the simulator upside down, so that on takeoff, my attempt to get the thing into the air was greeted by a screech of brakes, and a loud guffaw

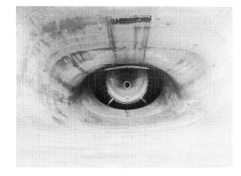

Looking straight down the intake of a RAF Sabre. This picture was taken by Don Tansley, at the time a technician in the RAF.

BW-1 in March 1953, with Sabres from Bechers Brook 3.

Taking care of the final detail before taking off from Kef.

FS Ray Stead, F/L Dave Blair and F/O Bob Sowery in immersion suits at Kef.

Survival exercise near Bagotville. RAF ferry pilots trek off across the unfriendly snows of northern Quebec; and the local Bombardier flies along with its load of Brits.

from outside the cockpit. My persistence produced increasingly louder and louder noises. Those coming from outside would best be described as hysterical.

Then followed a quick trip to Bagotville for high altitude indoctrination, a run through the pressure chamber with explosive decompression and the inevitable anti-social consequences. "Why are you grinning like an idiot, Collison? Phew! You're disgusting." We then started shake-down flying with Sabres that had been flown over to St. Hubert from Cartierville. This was interrupted by a further trip to Bagotville for a three-day winter bush survival course. After classroom instruction, we clambered on board a Canadian contraption called a Bombardier and set out for the wilds beyond Chicoutimi. The driver of the bobsled-cum-tank, no doubt inspired by our unique presence, attempted to keep the vehicle airborne most of the time. It eventually died of heat exhaustion, and we had to trek in by foot the remaining couple of miles. There were about 10 in our party, and we each bivouacked separately about 50 yards apart on the banks of a lake. Since it was almost dark, there wasn't much time to build a lean-to, and most of us simply stamped out fighter trenches in the deep snow, using spruce boughs for bedding and roofing.

Our attempts to build fires met with varying success. Sudden flare-ups of birch bark followed by pitch black darkness, and curses as axe heads departed their handles, never to be seen again. I got a reasonable fire going, but it gradually disappeared down in the snow. It's amazing how much snow you have to melt to get a can full of water, but the hot chocolate and cinders was worth the effort. Amongst other goodies, our survival food ration

gave us our first taste of "the oatmeal bar" and the "concentrated meat bar." These, despite the derogatory comments at the time, were in fact not that bad. The temperature overnight was about minus 15, which, by our standards, was cold. However, I think we coped quite well without too much discomfort, and benefited from the experience.

Within a few days of returning to St. Hubert we were off to Goose Bay to pick up the Sabres positioned there for our first ferry across the pond. Our route would be Goose-Bluie West 1-Keflavik-Kinloss-Kemble. Since there was no alternate for BW-1, and the situation at Keflavik was little better, these legs were the most critical as regards weather, and we had to wait for good VFR conditions at both ends before proceeding. Ferrying single-engine jet aircraft to Europe at that time was no recent innovation. The USAF High Flight reinforcement operation (F-84, F-86, etc.) had been in progress for some time; the Canadian Leapfrogs 1 and 2 had gone over in 1952; as well as Bechers Brook 1 and 2 with the initial batch of RAF Sabres.

Consequently, procedures were pretty cut and dried. During ferrying, ocean weather ships moved to position on track about half way along each water leg, and "duckbutts" (Albatross or B-17 search and rescue aircraft) filled in the gaps between. The ships and aircraft all carried radio beacons, thus providing navigational assistance as well as air/sea rescue backup.

BW-1 is sited some 50 miles up a fiord I can pronounce but not spell (a new twist!), on the gravel bench of the receding Narsarssuak Glacier. The comprehensive pre-flight briefing included a USAF movie showing the unique low-level approach to BW-1 which might become necessary should the

Unofficial version of 147 Squadron's crest!

ceiling drop below 5000 feet. The approach called for a let-down out to sea using the Simutak beacon at the entrance of the fiord. Once visual, the idea was to proceed up the fiord at low level towards Narsak Mountain, deke right, then keep to the left wall of the fiord, pass the rocks and grounded ship, turn down the left arm, and the airfield would appear to the right. In theory, a duckbutt would be scrambled off to escort any aircraft in. Luckily, none of the RAF Sabres had to use this type of approach.

If all failed, there was also a procedure for landing wheels-up on the ice cap using the Narsak beacon. Apparently some USAF aircraft had earlier been caught out and were obliged to use this procedure. They were picked up without much trouble by an Albatross.

For the over-water legs, we wore immersion suits which, I believe, were ob-

A classic view at Goose Bay in May 1953 with Bechers Brook Sabres in the foreground, one of 434's, then three T-birds and another line of further RAF aircraft. Someone's Canso is taxiiing out in the distance. (RAF)

RAF Sabres crowded into the hangar at Goose Bay in March 1953.

G.H. "Check" Collison in sunny Greenland, April 1953.

tained from the Royal Navy. The two-piece garment, consisting of blouse and trousers, was made of lightweight canvas with rubber seals around neck, wrists and waist, and had rubber boots. It even had a small sealable sleeve located in a strategic position on the trousers should you get caught short just before takeoff. While the suits were uncomfortable, they looked effective. Anyway, they didn't have to be used in anger. By comparison, the USAF "poopy suit" seemed very cumbersome. The wearer always looked like he was being devoured by a dinghy.

On March 20, 1953, BB3, with 10 Sabres, blasted off for BW-1, arriving

there without incident. The place was crowded, since Leapfrog 3, which had left Goose Bay five days previously, had been unable to stage on to Keflavik because of weather. On March 29, after seemingly endless morning no-go weather briefings at the Polar Theatre, we all managed to press on to Keflavik in sections of three or four, every 10 minutes. We were again delayed at Keflavik, but got to Kinloss in the north of Scotland on April 5, where we parted company with our Canadian cousins whose destination was Zweibrücken. Ours was Kemble, in the south of England, which we reached next day.

Nine days later we were coaxed aboard another dreaded North Star and set out for Canada to do the whole thing again. This time it would be with a difference as we were each to shuttle two aircraft across. After completing one leg, we would backtrack in a Hastings (simply heaven compared to the North Star) and pick up the second Sabre. In this manner, and leaving Goose on April 20, we moved across about 50 aircraft in 12 days.

From here on, the flights that followed, while never dull, became a matter of routine. Our pilot strength was

Striking photo taken at Kinloss on May 1, 1953 following completion of the second shuttle from Keflavik. S/L Stevenson, the OC of 147, had arrived just minutes earlier with the last section of four. The known pilots in this picture are: Sgt George Lovett (2nd from left), F/L Budd (4th), F/L Richie (5th), FS Ray Stead (6th), FS Frank Burney (9th), FS Johnny Howard (11th), Sgt Vic Wallace (13th), FS Jack Meacham (14th), S/L T. Stevenson (15th), Sgt Check Collison (17th), FS Tubby Capp (19th), F/L Bunny Harvey (21st), F/O Mike Cross (23rd), F/O Hind (27th), F/L Dave Blair (29th), Sgt Vic Burrows (30th). (RAF Kinloss)

Hangar scene at Goose Bay during RAF ferry operations in July 1953. A Hastings awaits outside the doors. Hastings were the backbone of the Bechers Brook support operation. An RCAF Canso sits beyond. (G.H. Collison)

nearly 50 officers and NCOs by the end of July, and by the close of 1953 we had ferried well over 400 Sabres across. Unfortunately this fine achievement was marred by three fatal accidents: one on approach to Prestwick, one on the beacon approach at St. Hubert during shake-down flying, and one after departure from Kinloss while climbing up through heavy cumulus. We also bent at least three other aircraft. At Goose Bay, during an attempted start following engine maintenance, there was an exceedingly loud woof, followed by clouds of whitish smoke. After

the usual frantic activity that attends these matters, it was discovered that the tail pipe and some other vital bits of engine had parted company with the aircraft, having been blown some distance into the infield. I never did hear what the exact cause was, but suspect that a turbine blade had let go. A second aircraft touched down in the rough, a bit short of the runway at Keflavik, resulting in a somewhat buckled gear and airframe. I believe it was the good ends of these two aircraft that were later mated into a hybrid, XB829. A third aircraft landed short in Scotland after a flame-out when the unfortunate pilot pulled the throttle around the detent during the break and was unable to get a relight before running out of airspace.

Many little things come to mind when I think back to Bechers Brook. St. Hubert—the hospitality of the Canadian mess members and their families; the smashing-looking WDs; our much-appreciated 24-plane Battle of Britain flypasts at Ottawa and Montreal; and the inadvertent low-level one at St. Hubert that was less appreciated by the preoccupied couples in the rooms on the top floor of the Aviation Hotel at the end of the runway. Goose Bay—the crackling and banging of the steam pipes in our quarters; the tropical temperature of the rooms; and the incessant shocks from static electricity. Bluie West—the iceberg off the end of the runway; the brave USAF airman, poised for a fast get-away, standing at the top end of the runway, waving his bloody great flag like mad, to warn us that there was only 1000 feet of runway left; and the mosquitos the size of small birds. Keflavik—the horizontal snow storms, and trying to catch, without success, an escaped hat; and the sweet young Icelandic girl who would climb aboard the transport aircraft each time we arrived and attempt to deliver her carefully-rehearsed address of welcome, but which we would give instead, since this was our umpteenth trip and we knew every word by heart. And lots more. I'd do the whole thing again tomorrow given the chance.

Check Collison

Excerpt from Check Collison's log from Bechers Brook days.

Year 1953 Month Date	AIRCRAFT Type	No.	Pilot, or 1st Pilot	2nd Pilot, Pupil or Passenger	DUTY (Including Results and Remarks)	SINGLE-ENGINE AIRCRAFT DAY Dual (1)	Pilot (2)	NIGHT Dual (3)	Pilot (4)
—	—	—	—	—	— Totals Brought Forward	214·00	941·35	16·25	57·00
APR 4	SABRE 4	XB673	SELF	—	RED 3. 3a/c. KEFLAVIK - KINLOSS		1·55		
APR 5	SABRE 4	XB673	SELF	—	YELLOW 2. 2a/c KINLOSS - KEMBLE		1·10		
APR 5	VALETTA	170	F/L DOSSETT	SELF	KEMBLE - ABINGDON				
APR 13	NORTH STAR	17518	W/CMDR. MORRISON	SELF	LYNEHAM - KEFLAVIK				
APR 14	NORTH STAR	17518	W/CMDR. MORRISON	SELF	KEFLAVIK - GOOSE BAY				
APR 16	SABRE 4	XB680	SELF	—	BLUE 2. 2a/c FORMATION. R/c LETDOWNS		1·40		
APR 16	SABRE 4	XB680	SELF	—	BLUE 1. 2 a/c FORMATION. R/c LETDOWNS		1·40		
APR 16	SABRE 4	XB680	SELF	—	BLUE 2. 2 a/c FORMATION. A/c LETDOWNS		1·40		
APR 20	SABRE 4	XB697	SELF	—	BLUE 4. 4a/c GOOSE BAY - NARSASSUAK		1·40		
APR 20	HASTINGS	WD483	F/L WRIGHT	SELF	NARSASSUAK - GOOSE BAY				
APR 24	SABRE 4	XB736	SELF	—	BLUE 4. 4 a/c GOOSE BAY - NARSASSUAK		1·40		
APR 25	SABRE 4	XB736	SELF	—	BLUE 4. 4 a/c NARSASSUAK - KEFLAVIK		1·40		
APR 25	HASTINGS	WD483	F/L WRIGHT	SELF	KEFLAVIK - NARSASSUAK				
APR 28	SABRE 4	XB646	SELF	—	BLUE 4. 4 a/c NARSASSUAK - KEFLAVIK		1·45		
APR 30	SABRE 4	XB646	SELF	—	BLUE 4. 4 a/c KEFLAVIK - KINLOSS		1·40		
APR 30	HASTINGS	WD491	F/O HABGOOD	SELF	KINLOSS - KEFLAVIK				
	SUMMARY FOR APR. 1953				SABRE 4		16·30		
[signature] S/LDR	UNIT: 147 SQDN.			AIRCRAFT TYPES	PASSENGER				
O/c 147 SQDN.	DATE 1.5.53 SIGNATURE. [signature]								
MAY 1	SABRE 4	XB736	SELF	—	BLUE 4. 4a/c KEFLAVIK - KINLOSS		1·40		
MAY 1	SABRE 4	XB646	SELF	—	BLUE 4. 4a/c KINLOSS - KEMBLE		1·00		
MAY 1	VALETTA	WD168	F/L ELLIOT	SELF	KEMBLE - ABINGDON				
MAY 2	HASTINGS	WD491	F/O HABGOOD	SELF	ABINGDON - KINLOSS				
GRAND TOTAL [Cols. (1) to (10)] 1789 Hrs. 55 Mins					Totals Carried Forward	214·00	960·45	16·25	57·00

On the Continent

A fabulous sight, Sabres from Nos. 2 and 3 Wings mix it up right over Grostenquin. This is something that the Air Div did over the skies of Europe for over a decade. (Bob Hallowell)

Grostenquin

While No.1(F) Wing continued to operate at North Luffenham till the spring of 1955, four new fighter bases were readied for the Air Division wings: Grostenquin and Marville in France, and Baden-Söllingen and Zweibrücken in Germany. The first to start up was Grostenquin, home of 2 Wing, which arrived in early October 1952. At the time, Grostenquin was still a mud hole, with many facilities unfinished or unequipped, and mud, mud everywhere. The base was being built from scratch, and, it would seem, the wing, (416, 421 and 430 Squadrons) was a bit early. They found bare-bones

quarters, no hangars, and such surprises as contaminated fuel and runways so slippery that the Sabres had to de-camp the first summer to temporary bases while the runways were re-surfaced. G/C J.K.F. MacDonald was the first base commander at Grostenquin, but in November 1952 was replaced by G/C M.E. ''Mike'' Pollard.

One of those who winged into Grostenquin on Leapfrog 2 was F/O John Greatrix, who remembers, ''Mud was everywhere and deep water-filled trenches lined the roads. There was no street lighting, so after dark it was not unknown for personnel to tumble into

these ditches. The contractor had thoughtfully installed wooden ladders for those unfortunates. Otherwise there was no way out! For daily use we were supplied with rubber boots. These were so essential that they were actually authorized as fit for the mess. Our barracks had no heat, often no water, and the lights were famous for failing. We kept Herman Nelson heaters outside hooked up to big canvas tubes. These were fired up at night and poured heat into the corridors of our 'H' huts. But the heaters would invariably run out of fuel long before morning. We'd wake up huddled in our great-coats and buried in our

120

blankets, frozen stiff. In spite of all these wonderful features of camping in the wilderness, our spirits were always high.''

From early August to late October 1953, 2 Wing was dispersed pending runway improvements at Grostenquin. 416 at first deployed to Marville and later to Zweibrücken. In between it visited bases in Denmark and Norway. In December 416 participated in a mass flypast as Grostenquin celebrated its first anniversary of RCAF ops. In early 1954 it went on its first deployment to Rabat Salé in Morocco, recently established as the Air Div's gunnery centre. Rabat was an old French base, which France was happy to let the RCAF use. For some years, until the opening in July 1957 of the range on Sardinia (Deci), Rabat would serve as a much-liked place to get away for some sun, not to mention the business of live firing by the Sabre boys.

Many a Sabre incident, from close call to Cat.A accident, was the result of weather. Though a flight may have launched into fair skies, on return to base, or arrival elsewhere, weather was sometimes near or even below minimums. July 13, 1955, F/L G.W. Patterson of 416 Squadron found himself in this situation. He was an old hand on the Sabre, with over 540 hours on type at the time. Patterson described what happened:

"I took off at approximately 1605 local as number two of a four-aircraft section, Catfish Charley. The exercise

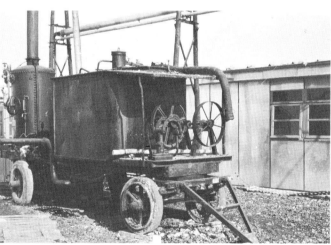

Early views around 2 Wing: the station (runway in background); F/O Dusty Keinholz of 421 with pants appropriately rolled up; early PMQs (permanent married quarters); and, looking like some artifact from the early industrial age, a rig used to heat buildings at the wing. (DND PL81724, Ralph Heard, last two Bob Morgan)

Air Division HQ at Metz, France. HQ had at first been in temporary quarters in Paris. (DND)

was carried out as briefed, with #3 and #4 being sent home early. With 1300 pounds #1 and #2 returned to base at 43,000 feet and were required to orbit once to allow separation for another element ahead, before commencing descent. At this time #1's radio failed, and I took control of the element for letdown and landing. In procedure turn, I was instructed to contact GCA on 'A' channel. My transmitter elicited no response, so I returned to approach frequency, visually signalling channel changes to #1. The letdown and approach were

Pilots of 416 over the summer of '53: F/Os Clements, Swede Evjen, Herbie Graves, John Hutt, unknown, Frod Rudy, Pudgo Marshall and Bill Marsh. (Bill Worthy)

carried out under ADF control. No contact was made with the aerodrome or ground* on first passage at 2500 feet, so a circular pattern was set up, reducing altitude to minimum safe, still under ADF control and made a new approach, missing the aerodrome. On my third attempt GCA cut in and gave direction, and it was while under GCA direction that #1 left me. I continued my approach, informing GCA that #1 had broken away, and further reduced my altitude because I was instructed that I was south of the field, and consequently clear of obstacles. With GCA aid, I arrived over the aerodrome approach lights at 150-200 feet. Realizing a visual approach was impossible I asked GCA for a square circuit, and it was while I was downwind at 175K IAS at 2000 ft.

*This was my first indication that weather had deteriorated, and that it was below aerodrome limits.

indicated that GCA informed me that his precision scope had failed. I informed GCA I was climbing for bailout, and climbed as instructed on a heading of 140°. I undid the seat harness and all connections but the radio, and when the engine failed at 10,000 feet, at 210K IAS, from fuel starvation, I informed GCA that I was abandoning, and did so forthwith.

"After freeing myself from the seat, I pulled the ripcord, and the parachute streamed, but did not open. The second attempt to billow the canopy was successful and I noted the time at 1706 local."

W/C W.M. Foster, then acting CO of 2 Wing, summarized what caused Patterson's predicament: "The three other aircraft of Catfish Charley Section and one other aircraft which was airborne at the same time managed to land at 2 (F) Wing, Grostenquin, only by the narrowest of margins. The principal reason for the loss of this aircraft was an amazingly quick deterioration in the weather, which decreased from an indefinite ceiling at about 2600 feet, visibility 1½ miles, to a ceiling of 300 feet, visibility ¼ mile in heavy snow, in the space of about 7 minutes, after all aircraft were on the let-down or in the circuit and were committed to land."

F/L E.C. Tuckey of 416 Squadron describes his own weather crisis and inevitable bail-out 20 miles north of 2 Wing:

"On the 9 September '55 at approximately 1530 hours I took off in Sabre 23086 as number two man in a two-plane formation. The leader was F/O G.F. Gower, and our exercise was phase training #14. After climbing to height (45,000 ft.) and executing several practice turns we engaged in combat with two Sabres. During the ensuing hassle the leader was kept well in sight and the fuel was passed to him as laid down in the briefing. The code word "bingo" denoting 1200 lbs. left, and the code word "joker" denoting 700 lbs. left were used. Our initial altitude of 45,000 ft. was rapidly lowered during the hassle until we were fighting just above the cloud top. My leader made one last pull up with an aircraft on his tail. It was at this point that I gave my fuel state as "joker." I positioned myself behind the second aircraft and followed both of them straight down in a dive into the cloud. I would estimate the top of the cloud at 15,000 feet. I was a sufficient distance

Officers of 416 Squadron circa 1955. In front are Bob Weber, Herb Graves, Eric Tuckey, Chuck Cherewick, Jack Stout, G/C Buck Newson, S/L Joe Roussell, Dave Tinson and Joe Houlden. In the middle are Eric Chappell (armament officer), Bob Caskie, Don West, Ian Morrice, Bill Mills, Ray Goeres, Red Willett, Pete Caws, Al Nichol, Jack Gatto, Bob Marion, Jim Fitzgerald, Bob Paul. In the rear are Art Fay, Bill Wilson, Jerry Copp, Bernard Beaulieu, Jerry Gower, Eric Elliasson, Tex MacDonald, and (standing on wing) Jean Parrott. (via H. Graves)

behind that I did not fear collision. Therefore, I maintained the same course in the cloud and pulled out of the cloud on the same heading. While in the cloud my leader informed that he had broken clear of cloud at 9000 feet and very shortly after this I did likewise. I could not see either of the other aircraft. I heard my leader call 2(F) Wing homer for a check steer to base. He was given a heading of 240 degrees. I realized that I must have been in the same immediate area as my leader and as my heading was also 240 degrees, everything appeared O.K.

My radio compass being tuned into 2(F) Wing and placed on the compass position read off 90 degrees to the left, thus showing a relative bearing of 2(F) Wing at 270 degrees. I checked my stand-by compass and found it reading within 10 degrees of 240 degrees. At

AS-250 in full 416 regalia waits in front of the main hangar at 2 Wing, July 9, 1953. (DND PL80304)

this time I contacted 2(F) Wing homer and was given an identical steer of 240 degrees. My fuel by this time was reading slightly less than 500 lbs. Knowing there were CBs in the vicinity I chose to follow the steer course and ignore the radio compass. I immediately throttled back to 75%. Also at this time I passed over an airfield with a black top runway and a large hospital building to one side with a huge red cross painted on the roof. I thought at the time this was Zweibrücken and therefore pressed on feeling that I had ample fuel to reach base. I continued

to call 2(F) Wing homer and obtained at least two more check steers, these steers were within several degrees of the original. I think I can recall one as being 250 degrees. This course was held for several minutes with a gradual deterioration of the weather occurring. During these minutes the radio compass continued to read a full 90 degrees off to the left. I was down to 5000 feet indicated with occasional rainy patches being flown through. By this time my fuel gauge showed approximately 250 lbs. I realized things were getting desperate. At this time I received

19405 of 416 Squadron lifts off at Grostenquin during Exercise Coronet, July 24, 1953. (DND PL80360)

instructions from 2(F) Wing tower to go over to channel "C" and declare "May Day." I complied and requested a check steer to 2(F) Wing as I realized I was somewhere in the vicinity. Cornbeef or Yellowjack replied, asked for my call sign, asked for a long count, and gave me a course of 160 degrees to fly to 2(F) Wing. I am not at all positive of this course but I am positive that I turned on the course given. After a second long count they confirmed my course and placed my position as 11 miles out of 2(F) Wing. At this time I was 4500 feet indicated flying through patches and eagerly glancing ahead for 2(F) Wing. The engine coughed two or three times, the fuel gauge read empty. I noticed de-acceleration taking place, I informed my controlling agency that "she" was quitting and that I was getting out. I pulled the nose gently back to 5000 feet (just below ceiling) and ejected."

Countless technicalities plagued the Sabre during its years in service, and the following incident is typical. The pilot involved was F/O L.B. Marion: "On the morning of 27 Jan. '56 I was flying Sabre 5 23168 as a No. 2 in a

two-plane training flight. We were returning to base with 800 lbs of fuel. We did a normal pitch-out, and on base I called tower advising them I had three wheels down and locked as the indicators showed. On final I was advised by runway monitor to overshoot because my right main wheel was not down. On the overshoot I selected wheels up, but all that happened was the indicators for nose and left wheel showed down. The undercarriage light came on and the right wheel showed unsafe. The utility hydraulics showed 3000 lbs. Despite pulling all undercarriage circuit breakers and replacing them and trying the emergency handle for 20 seconds, the indicators and undercarriage warning light remained the same. I then tried bouncing the aircraft on the runway with no success. I dropped the drop tanks on the downwind leg and was advised by the Commanding Officer 2 (F) Wing to bail out. I climbed to 5200 feet and did a normal ejection. The rest of the trip was uneventful."

A mid-air occurred in 1955 when three Sabres from 2 Wing got badly tangled up. F/O G.L. Howarth's pilot's statement gives some details of what happened: "The section was signed out and briefed for phase training #15 and #17 on 21 Jul. '55. F/O

Donald as #1, F/O Allingham as #2, F/O Noel as #3 and myself as #4. The section took off and climbed to 40,000 feet for practice battle formation. After completing the exercise we descended in loose line astern at 80% power setting and speed brakes out. The leader called the section into box formation. While joining up, #3 was slow in moving forward to his position on the port and told me to move ahead. As I was approaching my position #3 passed in front of me giving me quite a scare. I then proceeded to take my position in the formation. At this time we were at 85% power setting, airspeed of 320 to 340 knots, and approximately 1000 feet above ground. The section then did a 180-degree turn to starboard and was flying parallel to the railway tracks at Faulquement heading west.

"I noticed that #3's flying was quite erratic, although his flying previous to this had been quite smooth. Suddenly #3 disappeared below my range of vision. After an interval of 5 to 8 seconds #1 seemed to explode. I saw a bright flash of flame and ducked my head. I felt a few jars as I flew through the debris. Then I noticed I had approximately 100 degrees of starboard bank and was near stalling. I then recovered from this position and had started to climb when I noticed I

In the early years with the Air Division few pilots had any formal instrument training. It was soon clear that, in the often grim weather of western Europe, pilots would have to get their ratings. The first three pilots trained as Air Div IF instructors were Gerry Gagné, Ralph Heard and Chuck Steacy. They got their tickets with the RAF at No.210 AFS, RAF Tarrant Rushton, and at the CFE, RAF West Raynham. The course ran May 5-June 15, 1953. Here Ralph Heard prepares for an instrument training flight in a Meteor belonging to 210. His instructor in the back is F/L Kesserling. The first Air Div instrument flight formed at 3 Wing under Ken Lett, with the first course going through in September 1953. In short order, every Air Div pilot earned his ticket with this flight, and each wing was soon running its own flight equipped with T-33s. (via Ralph Heard)

Meteor 3, the ancient EE492, at Tarrant Rushton, where Air Div pilots Gagné, Heard and Steacy got their instrument tickets in 1953. (Ralph Heard)

was flamed out and my canopy was shattered. I could also hear a deep rumbling and gathered that some of the debris had entered my engine. I then saw what looked like the aerodrome. I headed towards it and confirmed this steer with an ADF homing. By then my airspeed was very low and I saw a field, so I locked my harness and force-landed. When I had stopped I smelt smoke, so I blew my canopy and departed in great haste. I then left some airman to guard the aircraft, stopped an Air Force vehicle that was passing on the road and reported to the Station hospital."

The aircraft involved in this incident had been finishing up their exercise with a flypast over the local railway station to salute some friends. The flypast turned to disaster as Howarth (in 23130), Noel (23099) and Donald (23154) all went down. Noel and Donald didn't make it. Allingham's Sabre suffered considerable damage but he did get back to base. The Air Div lost another Sabre that day when F/L E.L. Fine of 441 Squadron pranged while landing in 23109. Fortunately Fine got away with it.

During the first days at Grostenquin there was no flying to speak of, as heavy rains added to the mess there. The Red Indians (421) quickly flew off

A 421 Sabre 2 taxis out at Grostenquin. (Stan Hegstrom)

Course 1 of the Air Division's instrument flight, September 14, 1953. In back are Ralph Annis, Arch Debenham, Sherm Hannah, Howie Rowe, Gerry King and Gerry Gagné. In front are Bill Peterson, W.H. "Scotty" McKay, Ralph Heard, W.A.C. Wilson, Bill Paisley and Ken Lett. (via Ralph Heard)

On March 24, 1953, F/O Gerry Tobin was executing an overshoot from final at 2 Wing when his aircraft began spewing flame and parts from the tail end. At the same time, power dropped right off and Tobin had to make a forced landing. The Sabre crumped in, splashing through a water-filled bomb crater. It's believed that water rammed through the intake doused the fire and saved the day for Tobin. He sustained minor injuries and his boss, Bob Middlemiss, gave him a few days off to rest up. His Sword was a dead loss. (via G.J. Tobin)

to North Luff for a gunsight mod program to their Swords, and while there the squadron had its first overseas Cat.A. F/O Buzik suffered an electrical failure in flight and had to make a forced landing at the USAF base at Sculthorpe. As his Sabre barrelled along the turf it apparently broke up a card game and sent airmen scrambling for their lives. Nobody was hurt, but AX-350 was a write-off. Several other prangs followed, but there were no fatalities until June 9, 1953, when F/O Cloutier ejected too low from 19365. The minimum safe height for ejection from the early Sabre seats was 3000 feet. Below that, pilots were taking their chances, as the escape process, other than actually getting fired out, was manual.

Regular air defence exercises kept 421 and the other squadrons busy in the early years at Grostenquin. A big one in 1953 was Coronet, and Rebound followed in October. In between, 421 had to deploy to Zweibrücken pending

Early 2 Wing prangs: AX-350 done at Sculthorpe by F/O Buzik; and AS-304 bent by F/O Morgan at Grostenquin. (via Bill Bain, Stan Hegstrom)

further runway refinishing at GT. Magna Flux was flown in February 1954, with 421 and other Air Div units deployed to the French base at Cambrai.

F/O Don Ackert writes of one Magna Flux happening. "We took off en masse on the first sweep, and in sections of four penetrated England at 35,000-40,000 feet. A fantastic battle ensued involving Meteors, Vampires, Venoms and our own magnificent Sabres. Although we routed the

English defence force completely, our enthusiasm precluded disengagement with adequate diversion fuel. As a result, 36 Sabres arrived over Cambrai with emergency fuel. The French controller was unprepared for what followed as he could barely speak English. A snow squall was moving through at the time, reducing ceilings to less than 1000 feet and visibility to less than a mile. The R/T erupted with calls for immediate letdowns. Cursing and disorder followed. My own section

Not looking especially ferocious, these 2 Wing Sabre pilots talk shop: George Foster, Ed Dyck and Stan Hegstrom; and in a more ''professional'' setting, the same sort of hero talk goes on, with F/Os Ashworth, Hudson, Nordick, Faulds, F/L Windover and F/O Sullivan. (via Stan Hegstrom, DND PL127788)

lead, F/O Des Peters, calmly directed us to our squadron frequency and, homing in on the unreliable Cambrai beacon, carried out a rapid innovative letdown in a 'relatively' safe quadrant. This quick action put us over base for a tight but safe circuit and landing. This recovery smozzle was over quickly, but two 4 Wingers descended by parachute following flame-out, and one flamed out on final. Needless to say, other orders of battle (including approach

A 430 Squadron Sabre blasts off during Coronet. This aircraft later went to the Turks and met its fate there in a mid air collision. (DND PL80362)

procedures) were implemented for ensuing Magna Flux operations.'' On March 19, 1954, 421 flew to Rabat via Istres and Oran on its first Weapon Fire (gunnery camp) at the newly opened RCAF range in Morocco. CO at Rabat was a former 421 boss, W/C R.T.P. Davidson.

In March 1954 Sabre 5s began arriving at 2 Wing, and the 2s were quickly ferried to the UK for overhaul under MAP for the Greeks and Turks. During the shake-down period with the new Sabres, there was a total grounding for replacement of defective fuel pumps. In 1955, 2 Wing formed the first edition of the Sky Lancers aerobatic team, with two pilots each from 421 and 430 Squadron, and the spare from 416. The team was a roaring success, and plans were made at HQ to continue it in 1956, with a team from 4 Wing. Later in 1955 421 Squa-

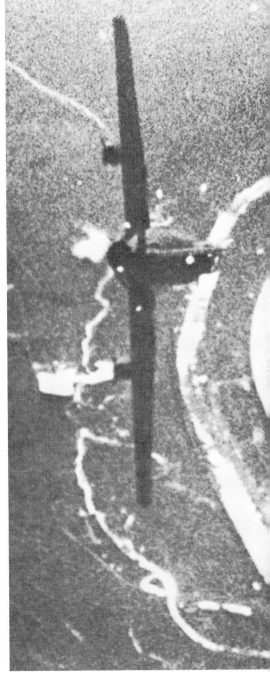

F/O Bernie Reid of 421 Squadron waxes an F-86H of the 138th FIS, USAF Air National Guard (New York) on TD in Europe in January 1962. (via B. Reid)

127

Action on the flight line at 2 Wing during Coronet, July 24, 1953. (DND PL80361)

dron undertook its first Zulu Alert—the NATO readiness alert whereby eight Sabres were committed, four fuelled and armed for immediate takeoff, the others on short standby.

Sabre 6s began arriving in April 1955, so the 5s were shortlived at GT and were soon being shipped back to Canada for use with the auxiliaries and

May 26, 1954, and the first Sabre 5s arrive at 2 Wing. In the greeting photo are A/V/M Campbell, F/O A.N. Pringle, G/C Bill Woicer and G/C Mike Pollard. (DND PL80939,80930)

YEAR 1953		AIRCRAFT		PILOT, OR 1ST PILOT	2ND PILOT, PUPIL or PASSENGER	DUTY (INCLUDING RESULTS AND REMARKS)	SINGLE-ENGINE AIRCRAFT				MULTI-ENGINE AIRCRAFT						PASS-ENGER	INSTR/CLOUD FLYING [Incl. in cols. (1) to (10)]		LINK TRAINER
							DAY		NIGHT		DAY			NIGHT						
MONTH	DATE	Type	No.				DUAL (1)	PILOT (2)	DUAL (3)	PILOT (4)	DUAL (5)	1ST PILOT (6)	2ND PILOT (7)	DUAL (8)	1ST PILOT (9)	2ND PILOT (10)	(11)	DUAL (12)	PILOT (13)	(14)
						TOTALS BROUGHT FORWARD	115:25	301:55	10:10	14:10							49:15	7:15	21:00	
		Rm Wood A FLT CMDR			SUMMARY FOR:	JANUARY 1953 TYPES:													
					UNIT:	421(F) SQN. 2(F)WING 1 SABRE II	1:05				TOTAL JET: 177:15 HRS.									
		R. Middlemiss S/L OC 421(F) SQN			DATE:	20 JAN 53														
					SIGNATURE:	R. Hallowell F/O TOTAL SABRE	117:30													
FEB	3	SABRE	312	SELF	/	GUNSIGHT CHECK, OGH, GCA (WOODY)		1:05											:15	
FEB	3	SABRE	312	SELF	/	AEROS, GCA FORCED LANDINGS (R-263)		:48												
FEB	12	SABRE	298	SELF	/	FORM TAILCHASE, OGH GCA (DUSTY)		:50			-SANS DROP TANKS AGAIN!							:1	:15	
FEB	16	SABRE	271	SELF	/	FORM, OGH, GCA (REV)		1:00												
FEB	16	SABRE	333	SELF	/	FORM, OGH, GCA (REV)		1:10												
FEB	17	SABRE	349	SELF	/	SIGHT CHECK, AEROS, FORCED LANDINGS IN ROUET, REV (ZWEIBRÜCKEN)		1:00			-FUN AVEC F-84's									
FEB	17	SABRE	333	SELF	/	BLUE II - BATTLE FORM, TAIL CHASE		1:05												
FEB	17	SABRE	298	SELF	/	BATTLE FORM - BLUE I - THORDEY		:45												
FEB	17	SABRE	333	SELF	/	BLUE I - TRACK CRAWL - THORDEY		1:00												
FEB	23	SABRE	333	SELF	/	AEROS, OGH, GCA		1:00											:15	:15
FEB	26	SABRE	333	SELF	/	BATTLE - 40,000 (SL DUSTY, SELF + WX NER)		1:15											:10	
		Rm Wood F/L A FLT CMDR			SUMMARY FOR:	FEBRUARY 1953 TYPES:													
		R. Middlemiss S/L OC 421(F) SQN			UNIT:	421(F) SQN, 2F WING (1) SABRE II		10:50			TOTAL JET: 188:05 HRS.									
					DATE:	1 MAR 53														
					SIGNATURE:	R. Hallowell F/O TOTAL SABRE -		128:20											:55	:30
MAR	2	SABRE	377	SELF	/	FORM 35,000, TAILCHASE (DUSTY)		1:00												
MAR	5	SABRE	377	SELF	/	FORM 40,000, OGH (DES, SL RLWYATK SELF, BOB)		1:20												
MAR	5	SABRE	377	SELF	/	1/4 ATTACKS - FR. 84S (DUST)		1:15												
					GRAND TOTAL [Cols. (1) to (10)] 462 Hrs. 45 40 Mins.	TOTALS CARRIED FORWARD	118:25	322:00	10:10	14:10							50:10	7:35		

CERTIFIED THAT F/O R. HALLOWELL HAS RECEIVED INSTRUCTION FROM A MEDICAL OFFICER IN THE PHYSIOLOGICAL ASPECTS OF HIGH ALTITUDE FLIGHT WITH OXYGEN, AND IS FAMILIAR WITH THE MECHANISM AND THE CONDITIONS UNDER WHICH THE MECHANISM IS TO BE USED. R.G. MIDDLEMISS S/L OC 421(F) SQN

the OTU. Meanwhile all usual activities continued, including squadron exchanges. In October 1956, 421 deployed to RAF Celle, Germany, while a RAF Vampire squadron visited Grostenquin. In late 1956, 416 began gearing down, as it had been reassigned as a NORAD CF-100 squadron. Meanwhile, the NATO policy of adding all-weather fighter capability began taking shape. In November 1956 W/C Irish Ireland led 445 Squadron's CF-100s into Marville, and in February 1957 the Clunks of 423 Squadron descended on Grostenquin to replace 416's Sabres.

The CF-100s brought a new element to the Air Division and new competitiveness. This often took the form of

Sabre ops at 2 Wing from the log of Bob Hallowell of 421 Squadron. Hallowell was later the "Red Knight" T-bird solo aerobatic pilot.

Sabre and Clunk crews totally ignoring each other, that is, when they weren't busy insulting each other. Trained all-weather boys, the Clunk crews were amazed at the foul weather in which the Sabres actually flew. Many a Clunk driver was soon angling for a ride in a Sabre. Not many Sabre chaps lined up to fly the homely straight-winged Clunk, though at least two came close. Perhaps the first Sabre pilot in the Air Div to try his hand on the Clunk got as far as the taxi strip, then promptly totalled it by driving into a ditch. Sharpshooter Bob Paul didn't even get

A close brush with real trouble. 23421 tangled with Clunk 18320 of 423 Squadron. Damage was severe to both aircraft, but they made it down safely. (DND)

An Air Div Bristol disgorges a 421 Sabre at Langar. (Bert Davis)

129

that far. While he was sitting in a Clunk the ejection seat fired. Paul was hurled out. In some kind of one-in-a-million chance, he landed in the seat on the tarmac and lived to tell about it!

Armament technician, Bob Jones, served at 2 Wing in the fifties, and looks back on a few of the events he experienced:

In March 1954 I was transferred from the Central Experimental and Proving Establishment, Ottawa, to 430 Squadron at 2(F) Wing, Grostenquin as a weapons mechanic. For some reason the Armament Officer came to believe that my previous posting had

A 416 Sabre bearing special tail and wing markings of Carte Blanche. (DND)

made me an expert on the 50 calibre machine gun and shortly after my arrival he outlined to me an interesting problem.

Evidently the Eastern Bloc had been sending a photo plane across the Iron Curtain at about 45,000 feet on a regular basis. Since our old Mark 4 Sabres could not operate much above 42,000, the spy plane felt safe enough. Even so, our pilots thought we should take a crack at this invader. The main problems were altitude, and the fact that the guns of our F-86s had a piece of T-shaped aluminum inserted in the breech of each gun which prevented them from being fired, even though ammunition was fed right to the gun. This "T" piece could only be removed while the aircraft was on the ground, effectively stopping any hot headed

One of NATO's big air defence exercises in the 1950s was Carte Blanche, involving hundreds of aircraft. Here pilots of 414 Squadron dash for their Sabre 5s on a Carte Blanche scramble June 22, 1955. (DND PL82210)

Air Division AOC, A/V/M Hugh Campbell, visits the troops during Carte Blanche at Metz. (DND PL82213)

439 facilities at Toul AFB during Carte Blanche. (Bob Morgan)

Support personnel at work during Carte Blanche: engine techs LAC J. Normoyle and FS Tom Simpson; refuellers LAC J.W. Rintoul and Sgt P. Klem; armourers LAC J.F. Zimmer and M.L. McLeod; radar techs LACs René Thériault and Gordie Graves; and fire fighters Cpl Red Sweeney with LACs George Cowan, Anson Savage and Eric Gallant. (DND PL82300, 82307, 82295, 82231, 82278)

pilot from shooting down another aircraft, either friend or foe. The armament officer proposed that I try to find a way for a pilot to clear the "T" piece while airborne, and therefore be able to get at least one firing pass at the spy plane before it could get away.

I was given a small space in an equipment tent to try my experiments, but I soon realized that the problem was hopeless. The Sabre gun installations had been designed so that a pilot could advance ammunition to the guns and clear stoppages by means of activating switches in the cockpit which, in turn, activated pneumatic "gun chargers". With the "T" pieces inserted, the gun chargers would not operate properly and only managed to jam the guns.

Obviously, the engineer who designed the "T" pieces knew what he was doing!

After a day or two I admitted defeat and advised the armament officer; he accepted my results with good humour and I never heard any more about the Russian spy plane. I never did figure out if he was just testing my ingenuity or whether he really wanted me to help him start the Third World War!

The Mark 2 and 4 Sabres had a mechanical linkage to fire the canopy ejection cartridge. The canopy rails pointed right at the aircraft tail and we always wondered if an ejected canopy would hit the tail; one day we found out.

In order to insert the ground safety pin for the cartridge the armourer had to kneel on the pilot's seat, facing aft. He then had to jam his head, one arm, a shoulder and the upper part of his body between the head rest and the inside of the canopy in order to insert the safety pin in the ejection cartridge —all the time being very careful not to touch the mechanical linkage which would fire the canopy ejection cartridge. At 430 Squadron dispersal one day a careless armourer hit the linkage while trying to insert the safety pin. The canopy was fired straight back, but either from hitting the airman who was still kneeling on the seat, or whether through design, it sailed over the port horizontal stabilizer and landed in the grass. The unhappy airman was not hurt.

The pilots of Air Division were a mixture of wartime veterans and new members, some of the latter barely a year or two out of high school. These young pilots sometimes had experiences of what would later be called "the generation gap" in exchanges with some of the older NCO ground crew. In a daily maintenance log for a Sabre one entry by a pilot read, "Strange noise behind seat, please check". A grizzled NCO entered the following rectifying comment, "Noise okay, that's the engine".

On another occasion, at Rabat a young 430 pilot was asked to perform a flight test to check the fuel flow on some newly installed drop tanks. The aircraft took off, did a climbing turn and then flew back over the flight line, doing slow rolls, with the fully loaded external fuel tanks flexing the wings on each roll. It was said that the line Flight Sergeant nearly swallowed his coffee cup while witnessing this display. The

pilot was made to fly the damaged Sabre back to Grostenquin where it was discovered that the main spar was cracked.

I know of only one occasion when an airman was "sucked in" by a Sabre and lived (Jeff St. Germain of 430 Squadron). At FTTU everyone was warned to stay at least 25 feet from the front of a Sabre with its engine running. During operations this distance was largely ignored and it became normal for ground crew to duck under the nose of active Sabres in order to get aircraft scrambled. Jeff forgot that sometimes aircraft engines are running although the aircraft might not be ready to fly.

An engine test was being done at the squadron dispersal area with an LAC fitter at the throttle. The first indication he had that something was wrong was a terrific bang, followed by a belch of black smoke from the tail pipe. The fitter immediately shut down the engine and dismounted. He quickly determined that someone was up the intake and a brave soul crawled in and pulled St. Germain out. His winter parka had wrapped over his head and prevented his lungs from collapsing but he had severe injuries to his head and back; after a period in hospital he was posted back to Canada. The engine was a write-off.

In early 1954, 430 Squadron was playing War Games from the French Air Force base at Cambrai. It was there that it was proved that a Sabre could land without a pilot. A flight of four was caught in a snow squall, and what with language problems at Cambrai and a low fuel situation with the air-

Armament tech Bob Jones while on detachment with 430 Squadron at Rabat in 1955.

craft, a disaster was fast approaching. Three of the Sabres managed to land but the fourth ran out of fuel and the pilot ejected close to base. The pilotless Sabre disappeared into the snow flurries at about 2,000 feet altitude. It was later found in a farmer's field. It had made a flat, straight-in approach, skidding across the snow covered field on its drop tanks. It was only necessary to install a new seat and a canopy and the aircraft was ready to fly again.

Bob Jones

A 430 Sabre 5 in pre-camouflage colours crosses the runway threshold at Rabat. (Bob Jones)

John Greatrix reports on three incidents which occurred during his 2 Wing Sabre-flying days:

In early 1953 Red McKay and I were on a mission near Metz—practice GCI under control of the French Air Force's 'Menthol Red' GCI. We met a two-plane element of FAF straight-wing F-84s at about 35,000 feet. With Gallic élan, the 84s took us on in an air fight. As element leader, I made the mistake of slowing down and trying to turn inside the F-84's radius. As expected, one of the Thunderjets got behind us, so Red and I rolled over and dove away supersonically to escape. One of the F-84 pilots, seeming not to have read his pilots notes, tried to follow us down. He quickly exceeded his maximum permissible air speed, and his tail came off. Although we didn't witness the incident, a few minutes later we were advised by 'Menthol Red' that a 'friendly' had crashed. Back in our Ops room, we got the details: the Thunderjet pilot had ejected and reported that his aircraft had come apart while pursuing two RCAF Sabres. It seemed to Red, myself and the rest of 430 Squadron that, if we were sent to Europe to bolster 4ATAF, we were not exactly off to a great start!

On September 27, 1953, we were on an air defence exercise, Operation Heads Up, at Aalborg, Denmark. W/C Stocky Edwards led us to Aalborg for the joint RDAF, RCAF and RNoAF activities. The station had one main runway with a squadron of Danish Meteors on readiness at one end, and 430 Squadron at the other. The Danes were scrambled from the Ops centre, we from the control tower. One morning we were on two-minute alert: George Shorey leader, Gord MacDonald No.2, myself No.3 and Red Hetterick No.4. Suddenly we were scrambled. We got good starts except for No.2, who had a "hung" start and delayed our taxiing out. George, however, quickly taxied to the button, and as soon as he saw us pulling out of the line, he started his takeoff roll. What none of us knew, however, was that the Danish Meteors had also just been scrambled.

Gord, Red and I were trying to catch up with our leader and were just about to taxi onto the runway when we saw the heat waves rising at the far end—two Meteors were already barrelling towards George, who was well into his takeoff roll. Suddenly the Meteors rose, on the judder, just over the Sabre, and whistled by us in split formation, wings wobbling. George was long since committed and there in front of him was the second element of Meteors. At this point he barely managed to get airborne, almost on the stall, slats extended to the stops, as the Meteors flashed by on the runways beneath him. We were all scared witless by this turn of events and looked on in disbelief that no one had crashed. I watched George disappear straight and level into the sunrise, gear and flaps still down with, I imagined, one owl-eyed, petrified fighter pilot coming to the slow realization that he had just experienced a considerable miracle. If our No.2 had had a good start, usual for the J47, we would all have been on the runway on time and Aalborg would have been a mess of smoking craters. Oh yes, scramble procedures were amended forthwith, lest another incident of "chicken" arise.

In May 1955 430 deployed to the USAF base at Chaumont, France. G/C Bill Weiser, our station CO, and S/L Ken Lett flew in in a T-33 from Grostenquin to see how we were doing and stayed overnight. Our hosts decided to have some fun. They painted the T-bird up in Russian markings. When the time came for the CO to fly home, the USAF provided a fighter escort, lest his plane be "molested" by any quick-shooting NATO pilot.

John Greatrix

K.C. Lett, former OC of 416 Squadron, gives further details of the "pink" T-bird story:

We at 2 Wing had a very close and friendly relationship with our USAF friends at Chaumont in eastern France. Among other things held in common, we agreed that we suffered from a lack of amenities compared with our brothers in Germany. To brighten things up a bit over the winter of 1955, we invited the Chaumont wing to Grostenquin. They arrived on a Friday afternoon with their trusty F-86s and, what with partying and other factors, I regret to say that they were still with us a week later. To say the least, the visit had been a resounding success, with appropriate entertainment imported from France, fabulous food, and beer brought in from Bavaria by the keg. Our CO, G/C Bill Weiser, and the USAF commander were both taken somewhat aback by the entertainment and shenanigans of their boys but, good leaders that they were, did the "grin and bear it" thing and did nothing to spoil the fun.

Our Chaumont friends soon prevailed upon their commander to have us over for a return engagement. That got under way on Friday, May 24, 1955. As a result of trouble they had had getting all their aircraft back home and serviceable from 2 Wing, our commander, A/V/M Hugh Campbell, decided to limit the number of aircraft we could take to Chaumont. To offset things, he loaned us his personal Dakota. Along with our own Expeditor, flown by G/C Weiser, the Dakota filled the gap. Everyone was satisfied, except a certain Sabre squadron commander. For him, nothing less than a T-33 would do.

As I recall, I found something to keep me terribly busy until the transport aircraft had departed, then created something of a crisis as a pretence to borrow a T-bird to catch up with them. I was accompanied by F/O Tex MacDonald of 416. The trip down was routine, except that on arrival I was directed to a spot in the dispersal area. This was odd, as these were normally very secure areas and not used for parking transient aircraft.

Only the next day did I discover why I had been directed into a secure area, well hidden from the base complex. It seems that the USAF had done some detailed planning on how to "one up" the RCAF following our winter thrash. The idea was to swap a J47 from one of their F-86Fs for an Orenda from one of our Mark 5s. Apparently engine mounts etc. were similar, and the USAF was prepared for whatever adjustments were necessary. So, with a crew of high-priced technicians standing by and no RCAF Sabres, their plan went down the drain. Instead they decided on a lesser scheme—to repaint my T-33. This was beautifully accomplished in US Navy blue, complete with all the detailed decals. Tip tanks and speed brakes were done in pink, with

Hard Start

The writing is on the wall. An early CF-104 visits 2 Wing and formates with a 430 Sabre 6. (DND PL147910)

the Russian hammer and sickle emblem on each wing tip.

My recollections of the Friday night bash are somewhat vague, but of course it had all the ingredients popular for the time. Next morning, I clearly recall walking across the barren sandy area between the officers' club and the dispersal and noticing this beautifully painted aircraft. I didn't recognize it as my own T-33 until quite close, and then "the lights went on!"

First I assumed that this was a quick water-colour job that could soon be scrubbed off. But not so. It was good old enamel and quite permanent. Nonetheless, we prepared to depart. The USAF CO was Maj Bill Dillard, leader of the Sky Blazers, the USAF's European aerobatic team. One of his pilots, John Reynolds, suggested that they could wind up three of the Sky Blazers to escort me home, lest some over-zealous NATO pilot spot our Russian markings and shoot us down! The escort was organized in great style, regardless of the fact that they were on UHF and I was on VHF, so we were

unable to communicate.

We lined up on the runway in a diamond shape—true aerobatic style. The tower advised us to take off singly, but as I let the brakes go the three Sabres followed. They were superb formation pilots, so Tex and I got quite a thrill leading our own aerobatic team! We had one incident on the way home when a nosy stranger tried getting too close. He was soon sent on his way by two of our Sabres. On arrival at Grostenquin, with hand signals, gut feel and whatever else we did, we completed a reasonable beat-up. I then landed, and my escort went home.

No.2(F)Wing Station Commanders (Sabre Era)

G/C J.K.F. MacDonald	Oct. 1952	Nov. 1952
G/C M.E. "Mike" Pollard	Nov. 1952	May 1953
G/C W. "Bill" Weiser	Jun. 1953	Sept. 1955
G/C W.F.M. "Bill" Newson	Oct. 1955	Jul. 1957
G/C A.B. Searle	Jul. 1957	Jul. 1961
G/C R.E. MacBride	Aug. 1961	Jul. 1963

No.2(F) Wing Squadron Commanders (Sabre Era)

416 Squadron

S/L John Mackay	Mar. 1952	Aug. 1954
S/L K.C. "Ken" Lett	Oct. 1954	Mar. 1956
S/L J. "Joe" Rousell	Mar. 1956	Jan. 1957

421 Squadron

S/L R.G. "Bob" Middlemiss	Nov. 1951	Sep. 1953
S/L E.P. "Eep" Wood	Oct. 1953	May 1954
S/L J.R.F. Johnson	May 1954	Apr. 1956
S/L Claude Bourque	May 1956	Jul. 1958
S/L L.D. Allatt	Jul. 1958	Jun. 1959
W/C R. "Ray" Van Adel	Jun. 1959	Jul. 1962
W/C A.J. "Arnie" Bauer	Jul. 1962	Aug. 1963

430 Squadron

W/C J.F. "Stocky" Edwards	Nov. 1951	Jan. 1953
S/L P.L. "Pappy" Gibbs	Jan. 1953	Jan. 1955
W/C C.D. Barnett	Jan. 1955	Mar. 1955
S/L W.S. "Bill" Harvey	Mar. 1955	Oct. 1955
S/L C.W. White	Oct. 1955	Mar. 1958
S/L R.V. "Bob" Virr	Mar. 1958	Dec. 1960
W/C J.T. Mullen	Dec. 1960	Jun. 1963

The sequel was not quite as pleasant as it might have been. Not only was I in deep shit with G/C Weiser for daring to take a T-33 for the weekend, but I had brought it home as unfit to operate. Come Monday morning the T-bird was back in original shape, courtesy of a delighted squadron. The fellows enjoyed the incident so much that stripping all the paint off, then repainting the T-33 was easily worth all the trouble.

K.C. Lett

Various squadron exchanges continued as the years passed at GT. In May 1958 421 visited Kleine Brogel, a Belgian base, while the *Belgiques* flew into GT with their swept-wing 84s. October the following year 421 spent a week at another BAF base, Florennes. Gunnery continued year after year at Deci. All this activity kept the pilots and squadron organization in good trim. The exchanges provided valuable cross training, especially for the ground crew who had the opportunity

Astounding photo of at least 15 Sabres taking off from Volkel on July 19, 1953. (DND PL80349)

of getting familiar with fighters of other NATO partners. In time of war this training would have paid off, with aircraft dispersed hither and yon throughout Europe, away from home and familiar hands.

In the late fifties it was clear that the Sabre would be replaced, and in time the F-104 was chosen as the Air Div's future fighter. 421 went to Deci for the last time in November 1962, and on July 10, 1963, W/C A.J. Bauer flew 421's last official mission. The squadron stood down on July 31, and on August 12 421 ferried its Sabres to Prestwick to be scrapped (Exercise Sal Siesta). In November 1963 it was back in business at Grostenquin, flying the CF-104.

Zweibrücken

The RCAF base at Zweibrücken was ready for No.3(F) Wing in the spring of 1953. Personnel began arriving early that year. For example, a group of four officers, three corporals and 20 men of 427 Squadron arrived March 10 by train from Paris. But the vagaries of weather over the North Atlantic delayed Leapfrog 3, and the early birds could well have enjoyed a few more

days in "gay Paris." By April 4 there was word that 43 of 46 Sabres had made it into Kinloss. Two days earlier there had been a near-disaster at Zwei when A/V/M Hugh Campbell's Expeditor crashed on takeoff. The aircraft (No.1522) had just departed for Paris with F/L R. Gooder the captain and F/L W. Unruh navigating. Besides the AOC, other passengers were Air Commodore Hodson, G/C Cox and W/C Ashman. Both engines quit shortly after departure, and the wreck was soon located in an orchard near Boechweiler. It was a disastrous scene to those who first arrived to help. The plane was in pieces, but no fire had started. All aboard were badly injured but survived. This was hardly an auspicious beginning for Zweibrücken! The crash was traced to water in the fuel.

On April 6 Leapfrog 3 finally got into Zwei—Nos. 413, 427 and 434 Squadrons. After the gruelling month-long crossing from St. Hubert, the pilots were given a well-earned few days leave. Soon, though, it was down to work. In 427's case, flying commenced April 15. On April 26 the base was officially handed over to the RCAF by its previous tenants, the

High and lower level views of Zweibrücken in the mid-fifties. The second shows the distinctive pattern of the "Marguerites"—the aircraft dispersal pads. (DND PL81729, S.E. Burrows)

French. June 22 many 3 Wing dependents arrived at Le Havre aboard the SS *Atlantic*.

BGen R.W. "Ron" Fentiman, in 1986 Deputy Commander, Fighter Group, CFB North Bay, flew the Sabre in its heyday with 413 Squadron at Bagotville and 3 Wing. Later he instructed on T-birds, then with the RAF at Little Rissington on the Jet Provost and Gnat. Staff College and various ground postings followed, then Fentiman converted to helicopters, commanded 408 Tactical Helicopter Squadron, and even checked out as a parachutist. He attended the National Defence College, was base commander at Chatham, and since 1980 has held senior postings in NORAD. Here

BGen Fentiman looks back on his 413 days and two out-of-the-ordinary missions:

In retrospect and considering the comprehensive training programs of today, going through the F-86 OTU in 1952 was a bit of an adventure for those of us who were "pipeliners," that is, straight out of basic flying training, "advanced" training, and bombing

and gunnery—all on Harvards—to the Fighter OTU at Chatham. Right from Harvards, we had 10 trips in the T-33 (USAF models on loan to the RCAF), all dual, and then flew the F-86 solo—there were no two-seat versions for famil rides or dual instruction. However, it all seemed normal and natural for a bunch of 20-year-olds at the time. Those "older hands" who had flown the Vampire before us must have had an even more exciting time, because many went from the Harvard or Mustang straight into the Vampire—their first trip in a jet was solo! I went through Course 21 at 1(F) OTU, which I believe was the second F-86 course at Chatham, from August to December 1952, and was then posted to 413 Squadron at Bagotville.

F/O Ron Fentiman during 413 days. (DND)

PR ''set up'' shot taken at 3 Wing. Pilots in the foreground are on alert as one of the squadrons executes a lovely formation flypast. (DND)

Being among the most junior pilots on the squadron, I did not get to fly an F-86 across the Atlantic when, with 427 and 434, we opened 3(F) Wing, Zweibrücken, in the spring of 1953. Instead, I travelled by North Star in charge of a group of 413 airmen to Paris, and we went by train from there to Zweibrücken, arriving on March 12. I flew my first trip at 3 Wing on April 14 after the aircraft took a month to get across the Atlantic in Leapfrog 3. Then followed ''area famil'' flights and daily battle-formation and dogfighting (today called air-combat training) missions. We flew in the infamous Paris International Air Show fly-past at Cambrai in July '53 and in Exercise Coronet in the same month. Other highlights were the fly-past, in December in abysmal weather, for the NATO hand-over ceremonies at 2 Wing, Grostenquin, which was attended by Brooke Claxton, Minister of National Defence, and Air Marshal Slemon, Chief of the Air Staff. 2 Wing had been built in a swamp, and heavy rains

that fell had turned the place into a quagmire of mud and water. Some wag named and signed the two medium-sized lakes, one at either end of the runway, as ''Claxton's Brook'' and ''Slemon's Slough.'' The station was commonly known as HMCS *Grostenquin*. In March 1954, 413 flew to Rabat in French Morocco for a month on Weapon Fire—air-to-air gunnery ''on the flag.''

My first Sabre accident was in 19149 on June 23, 1954, following our return to 3 Wing from Rabat. A new CO had been posted in to take over 413. F/L Bill Paisley had been CO for several months after S/L ''Rocky'' Gordon had returned to Canada. Our new CO was S/L E.P. Wood, a wartime Spitfire veteran. ''Eep'' announced on arrival that his plan was to fly with every one of his pilots to get to know us and how we handled ourselves in the air. Mine was the first name drawn out of the hat, and in accordance with the plan I briefed Eep as my number two. We took off, climbed to altitude and flew some battle formation, then ''bounced'' another formation and ''hassled'' with them for a bit, then rejoined for an instrument let-down and approach to landing in formation with me in the lead and my new CO on the wing. We throttled back to 80 per-

Ron Fentiman's two Sabre prangs. First, the Turkish aircraft left on a beach in Italy; then, 19149 after taking out some fencing at 3 Wing. (via R.W. Fentiman)

cent and popped the speed-brakes at altitude over the beacon, and everything went well during the descent until we levelled off at the bottom to set up for a GCA approach with undercarriage down and half flap. That was when I discovered that my engine had "hung-up" at 80 per cent. No matter where I moved the throttle, from idle to full power position, it had no effect on the engine rpm, which then started to slowly decrease. I waved my number two off and called "switching to tower" (from GCA frequency) on the radio. I declared an emergency and said that I could make it to the runway. At the same time, I retracted my speed-brakes and raised the undercarriage. I knew I could make it to the runway "clean" with the power I had available, and I planned to lower the undercarriage at the last minute for landing.

At this point I noticed that my number two was still with me, although he was having a bit of trouble station-keeping on a lead who was raising undercarriage and retracting speed-brakes without benefit of the usual signals. We were now on different frequencies and could not communicate

by radio, and I was too busy with my emergency to attempt to regain radio contact with him; in any case, I had already waved him off. I waved at him again to "go away," but he didn't budge. At about 1½ miles from the button of the runway, I selected undercarriage down and was just lowering the flaps when the engine quit without warning. I was too low to bail out at that point as the post-ejection seat-harness release and parachute opening was a manual operation (not automatic as the systems are now), and the "book" read that 3000 feet above ground level was the minimum altitude for a successful bail-out. I had no option but to go straight ahead as a glider. Being careful not to stall by attempting to stretch the glide, I touched down at minimum speed at the same time as I went through the aerodrome fence. Eep overshot at the last minute, having flown with me almost to the fence which he barely cleared! I hit one of the reinforced concrete fence posts on the nose and that collapsed the nose gear, and for a few seconds I thought that the nose would dig in and the aircraft would flip over on its back.

The posts on either side mangled the leading-edge slats and tore the wings back to the main spar. Approach lights seemed to be flying everywhere as '149 sheared them off and ploughed its way to a stop just short of and to the right of the approach end of the runway. The first one to arrive at the scene was F/O Bruce Farquharson, a GCA operator who, after watching my aircraft descend off the bottom of his scope, ran for his truck and raced for the end of the runway. He asked if I was all right, and I replied yes, but thought that the aircraft might be unserviceable. A few days later, the chief air traffic controller told me that he was going to violate me for landing away from base without filing a flight plan—the main wheel tire marks started two feet outside the aerodrome fence line!

My next "exciting day at the office" occurred three weeks later on July 15, 1954, in 19298. Canada was providing F-86s to Greece and Turkey under a NATO mutual assistance program. They were Chatham OTU aircraft which were overhauled at Canadair, fitted with "hard" leading edges, and then flown to Grostenquin by the Overseas Ferry Unit. Pilots were gathered from the wings in Air Division to continue the operation to Greece and Turkey—eight to each in the first delivery.

We assembled at Grostenquin and flew our assigned aircraft on a local check flight before departing on the ferry trip. I was in the group going to Turkey, and our route was to be via the air force base at Istres near Marseille and Ciampino airport at Rome for refuelling stops, then on to Athens for an overnight stop. The next day was to be a one-hopper from Athens to the Turkish Air Force base at Eskisehir. Our refuelling stop went as planned at Istres, and we were en route to Rome at 33,000 feet when my troubles began. About halfway between Corsica and the Italian coast, I felt a momentary vibration in the aircraft, rather like a shudder. This was repeated after a couple of minutes, but the vibrations became heavier and more definite. A check of the engine instruments showed all to be normal at first; however, after several minutes, I noticed that the jet pipe temperature (JPT) was climbing. Shortly after informing the formation leader of the situation, I had to start throttling back to keep the JPT within limits. Eventually I had to throttle back to the idle stop, and still the temperature continued to climb above the red line. Then the inevitable happened—the engine seized with a bang, and once again I was in an F-86 glider. F/Os Bill Hind and Danny Kaye, who had been descending with me, later told me that my aircraft had given out a thick stream of white smoke at the time of the engine seizure, a combination of fuel and the hot engine, and Danny said that he stayed with me after that to have a ring-side seat for the bail-out.

However, after I announced my intentions over the radio, our formation leader advised me to force-land if I could. I then saw an airfield two or three miles inland, and judging that I had enough altitude to make the runway, announced my intention to force-land there. Bill and Danny radioed that they would go down to have a look at my intended landing spot, and I proceeded to drop my external fuel tanks over the sea to reduce drag and give me a better glide ratio. After a few moments, they called up to say that the runway was unsuitable for my landing—it was under construction and had men and machinery all over it. Again I called that I was bailing out and turned the aircraft towards the sea. But again our flight leader advised a forced landing, this time wheels-up beside the runway or on another suitable area. I never found out why he did that, and taking his advice was the dumbest thing I ever did—I should have told him to do something appropriate in his hat and bailed out immediately; although the forced landing was successful, it very nearly cost me my life. As later investigation revealed, the airfield which Danny and Bill recced for me was not the one that I had seen, and I was set up for a wheels-up forced landing in the mud beside 8000 feet of clear black-top on a different field. The field I had chosen was under construction and the runway had been finished, but nothing else had been built other than a mess hall and a couple of construction shacks. As a footnote, it was at this point that I noticed a flying boat crossing the beach and heading out to sea. As I later learned, the very efficient Italian air sea rescue service had been alerted to

my predicament, and they were on their way to pick me out of the sea if necessary.

The significant factor in this piece now was the emergency flight control system on the F-86. Without a wind-milling engine to drive the normal hydraulic pump and generator, the flight controls hydraulic system was pressurized by an emergency electric pump, powered by the battery which the aircraft operating instructions said would last 15-20 minutes under such conditions. Without hydraulic pressure, none of the flight controls (except the rudder, which was cable operated) would move. As I turned over the "low-key" point in my forced-landing pattern, I saw that the runway was clear and suitable for a wheels-down landing. However, I decided that it was too late to try to get the wheels down and adjust my pattern, so I carried on with my plan for a wheels-up beside the runway, and that saved my life. I had just completed my final turn and raised the nose to check my descent when the battery gave out and the flight controls locked up where they were. I was "along for the ride" at that point with no control over the aircraft, which continued straight ahead, and after what seemed like a surprisingly soft belly landing, my aircraft slid along, turning on its vertical axis about 110 degrees before coming to a stop in a great cloud of dust. Although the engine was now quite cold and the battery dead, training and/or habit induced me to complete a shut-down check, turning various switches off before I replaced the seat and canopy ejector safety pins and left the cockpit. My first action then was to take a picture of the aircraft with the Rolleiflex I had with me; that and my shaving kit were my only travelling possessions. Our baggage was on board a Bristol Freighter, along with several ground crew and aircraft support spares, which had gone on to Athens, our first intended overnight stop.

Although I was now safely on the ground, my tribulations had not yet ended. I had landed on an Italian air base under construction, and it was staffed by a caretaker unit. Shortly after I climbed out of the cockpit of '298, a truck-load of security troops arrived and proceeded to surround the swept-wing, silver jet (with Turkish marking, a red square with a white border on the fuselage, and a red rectangle with a moon and a star in the centre on

the tail) and its pilot, all the while pointing their submachine guns in the general direction of my stomach. I had my hands in the air and was unsuccessful in my attempts to establish communication with this group, which didn't seem to have a leader. After a few minutes of mutual staring—it seemed much longer—a staff car arrived with an officer who spoke English, much to my relief. My first order of business was to inform him of the dangers associated with aircraft seats and canopies which could go bang if the right things in the cockpit were pulled. He shouted something in Italian at four of the guards who were busy poking around in the cockpit. They took off at high speed to a distance of about 100 yards and then stood staring at the F-86 as if they expected the whole thing to explode before their eyes.

I was taken to one of the several small buildings on the base, where I was subjected to an interrogation right out of a movie scene. I stood in front of a desk at which was seated an Italian Air Force colonel, complete with two rows of WW II ribbons. The colonel asked me through an interpreter (the officer who had met me at the aircraft) over and over again why I had landed there. I repeated over and over that my engine had quit and that I could not go on to Ciampino, my intended destination. He then switched to asking why I had not bailed out instead of landing at his base. The futility of trying to answer that question (I was asking myself the same thing at that point in the proceedings) and, I suppose, some degree of shock from the preceding events, caused me to come to rigid attention and declare that I was an officer of the Royal Canadian Air Force based in Germany, and I was ferrying an F-86 to Turkey. I then shouted my regimental number, rank and name, and shut my mouth, refusing to respond to any further questions. At a sign from the colonel, I was seized from behind and held while the pockets of my flying suit were emptied onto the desk, and the questions started again. I remained silent, refusing to say anything more, and suddenly the atmosphere changed completely. The colonel stood up, shook my hand and gave me a cigarette. All the other officers smiled and shook my hand, and my possessions were returned. We then went to a small mess where I was treated as a guest of honour. After several beers, I had lunch with the Italian officers and was then driven in a jeep to Rome, where I hoped to meet the other members of the flight I had unceremoniously left a few hours before.

I arrived at Ciampino just as Danny and Bill and the others were departing for Athens. I was left in the company of a Canadian Army colonel; I believe he was our military attaché in Rome at the time. He seemed quite amused by my story, and after the others had departed for Athens, he took me to a hotel somewhere in Rome and made arrangements for a room for me, and then he left. I spent the next three days in that hotel in my flying suit, complete with camera and shaving kit. Dress regulations and the expected standard of officers' conduct and decorum at the time dictated that I should not go out of my room, or certainly not out of the hotel, with nothing but my flying suit to wear. At noon of the third day, the co-pilot of the Bristol Freighter called to say that they were in Rome on return from Eskisehir and would be departing the next morning for Grostenquin. There was room on the Bristol if I wanted a ride. I accepted the offer and made arrangements to get my bag and clothes so that I could go out and see some of Rome on the night of my last day there. Next day, I rode back to Grostenquin while my buddies spent a week in Eskisehir and Ankara being royally entertained by the Turkish Air Force. The Turkish authorities were very nice about the whole thing—they awarded all of us honorary Turkish pilot wings which were later presented to us on parade back at our home stations. At Zweibrücken the presentations were made by G/C Chester Hull, the first CO of RCAF Station Zweibrücken.

Life continued with exercises; Dividend was a big one at the end of July. By then we had received the Mk.5 Sabre which carried the larger drop tanks. These allowed a considerable range—for example, we acted as bombers in Dividend, taking off from Zweibrücken, flying to various IPs and targets in England while the RAF tried to intercept us with Meteors and Hunters, and then returning non-stop to home base.

The runway at Zweibrücken had not been properly surfaced when it was built, and it became very greasy when wet; the downhill slopes at both ends of the runway from the hump in the middle didn't help either, and occasionally during rain showers, one or two F-86s would slide off the end of the runway. So the runway was resurfaced in August and September of 1954. The squadrons deployed to other airfields while this was done, with 413 moving to Volkel in Holland for part of the time, and then to Grostenquin before returning to 3 Wing. All in all, it was a great time to be in the RCAF and to be flying the Sabre in Europe.

I returned to Canada in January 1955 to instruct on Harvards. Later I had the opportunity to fly the F-86 again at Macdonald, where I instructed on T-33s, and following that tour, at Central Flying School, Saskatoon. The Sabre was a great aircraft in her time, a dream to fly and a delight to the eye. It will always be my favourite aircraft.

R.W. Fentiman

November 15, 1953, 413 Squadron recorded another bit of excitement. F/Os Coulter, Nichol, Prescott and Wilson were letting down into Speke. As they passed through cloud, Nichol collided with a Miles Hawk, a small two-seat trainer. Both aircraft were damaged but were able to reach safety. No matter how vigilant they were, the Air Div pilots were in a dangerous profession, and knew it.

Certainly one of the key sources of historic information about the RCAF is squadron diaries. It seems that a squadron was either blessed with a keen diarist or not. The keenly maintained diary is usually a wealth of information—the basic goings-on, day by day, laced with tidbits reflecting the human side of squadron life. In other diaries some chap made the barest of entries which, 30-40 years later, are of little use or interest to either historian or reader. In the mid-fifties, 427 Squadron had a diarist who recorded all the "gen" in a neat mixture of fact and wit. Here is a selection of his offerings from early 1953 to late 1955:

Apr. 22, 1953 Weather still good, and routine flying took place. Only snag to spoil perfect weather is the heavy industrial haze from the Ruhr.

Apr. 25 Practice parade today in readiness for tomorrow's ceremony. The station is to be officially handed over to the RCAF by the French, who occupy this zone of Germany. 427 made its presence felt by driving a dummy general in front of the parade, complete with a motorcycle escort. The guard of honour provided by the French was unaware that it was a joke,

and seemed undecided whether to present arms or open fire. Cooler weather today.

Apr. 28 Tex MacDonald writes off his motorcycle and is unhurt after a collision with a car. Number of motorcycle accidents is increasing, and the general feeling is that "the boom" will soon be lowered on their use.

July 13 Volkel, Holland. The squadron arrived here at 1500 this afternoon ... We are here to fly past at Soesterberg for the 40th anniversary of the Netherlands Air Force.

434's servicing shack at Zwei. Nothing much to write home about. (P.S. Perry)

July 23 Commencement of Ex.Coronet. Fantasia and the Westonia are at war, and today is set aside for reconnaissance trips by both sides. 427 is on airfield defence, and our aircraft are on the button of the runway at 2 and 5 minute readiness. As one section takes off, the next moves up in 2 minute readiness, and another section comes out to the button from the dispersal areas. There is little activity today from the enemy, although their aircraft are reported in the vicinity, and 8 sections are scrambled.

July 24 The station got plastered by a lone Meteor which arrived at dawn from nowhere. Another plastering at dusk from a single F-84. 427 claims a Boxcar and a DC-3 (probably the property of KLM) among its day's trophies.

July 25 We meet a flight of F-84s over Belgium, and a hectic dogfight results.

July 26 One section of two tangles with F-84s which came over with the apparent intention of creating a disturbance at Brooky. Instead, they were given a personal demonstration of the advantages of flying a Sabre ... Everyone on the station is keenly inte-

Scenes from 3 Wing times: pilots of 413 catch some rays while waiting for some action; pilots Al Hunter and Gerry King head out on a trip; Sam Firth of 434 explores the mysteries of aerodynamics; Pete Cunningham and Henry "Smitty" Smith home from a mission; "Boomer" Booth relaxing at Istres after a flight from 3 Wing, destination Rabat; Bluenose pilots Ralph Metzler, Bernie McComiskey and Bill Thorleifson "at work" in the 434 crew room; Syd Burrows (self portrait); 434 servicing personnel with one of their fuel bowsers. (R.W. Fentiman, next seven S.E. Burrows, P.S. Perry)

NATO friends: a "Dog" (F-86D all-weather) Sabre of the Royal Danish Air Force, and a Norwegian F-86F, both visiting 4 Wing 1963-64 period. (Harry Tate via K.M. Molson)

rested in the exercise. One hardy little band, led by Nursing Sister Rowan, is camped out on a small mound by the mess to watch and advise about the air activity going on overhead.

July 27 An RAF Meteor lands at Zweibrücken. The pilot states he was low on fuel, but our wing intelligence personnel regard his visit with suspicion, and he is questioned in the style he might expect if he landed on the other side of the Iron Curtain ...

July 28 The wing is still on the offensive and 427 attends to a large number of F-84s defending an enemy airfield in Belgium ... The RAF pilot is loaded on his Meteor ... He is none the worse for his experience, suffering nothing worse than severely ruffled dignity and a lack of esteem for Canadians ...

July 29 We meet quite heavy opposition from Vampires over the airfield which we are constantly attacking in Belgium. Very spectacular dogfight ensues, with lessons in the turning radius of the Vampire.

July 30 Coronet ends with a day of attacks by 427 on the enemy base at Florennes.

Aug. 3 Today is a holiday and, after the long working hours of Coronet, it is welcomed by everyone. Very few people go away for the long weekend. Most just sleep in ...

Feb. 1, 1954 Gardiner and Ayres set off for a flight to Wildenrath. Gardiner has gear trouble and stays in Zweibrücken circuit. He is in the mess eating supper when he hears that a search is under way for his remains.

Feb. 5 The Expeditor en route from Gibraltar to Marseilles lands in the sea off San Remo. Everyone on board OK.

Feb. 12 Advance party of pilots and ground crew leaves by North Star for Rabat. 427 is to spend two weeks there for air-to-air firing.

Feb. 16 Main party leaves with 12 Sabres, support party travelling in North Star. Bill Bain flames out over the Alps above cloud and makes an emergency landing at Geneva. He lands short of the runway because of a landing Constellation, and writes off the nose wheel and nose section of '432.

Feb. 20 Air firing commences. We are towing our drogues with Sabres. While one flight does air firing, the other flights tow the drogue.

Feb. 22 Squadron members are to be seen staggering back from town heavily laden with handbags, carpets, hassocks and other local products.

Feb. 23 Scores are improving with every trip. Bill Grip is high man for the day, probably because Les Pringle, tech rep of Gen. Electric, has offered a bottle of rye to the first man who scores over 50.

Feb. 27 26 trips are flown for a total of 32 hours in the air. Scores are still improving—Bob Ayres gets 57 hits. Les Pringle bragging consistently about the good serviceability of his J47 engine.

Feb. 28 Swede Larsen is violated by an Air France pilot flying something that looks like a small Constellation and an Oozlum bird. The Air France machine is cleared for takeoff at the same time Swede was cleared to drop his drogue. Both a/c took evasive action. Flying control at Rabat is not too positive, mainly through language difficulties ...

Mar. 19 Dusk flying cancelled due to thunder showers. A stag party for Bill

Republic did well in the fifties with NATO, with most air forces using one or all of the F-84G, F-84F and RF-84F. These were generally good sturdy aircraft but decidedly underpowered. The G-model, for example, grossed out at over 18,000 lb and had a 5600-lb-thrust Allison J35. The F-84F weighed over 26,000 lb but had only a 7220-lb-thrust J65. The Sabre 6 tipped the scales at about 16,000 lb all-up, but had 7275 lb thrust. The joke was that the G didn't take off till its specially installed "gravel sniffer" sensed the dirt at the end of the runway. Others referred to it as "Allison's time bomb" after some mid-air engine explosions. Nonetheless the skies over Europe were always full of Republic fighters. Seen here is an F-84G of the Dutch Air Force visiting 2 Wing in 1955, a Belgian "F" (UR-U) and a French "RF" (33-CU) with its sleek photo recce nose. (Bob Jones, Harry Tate via K.M. Molson, via J-P Hoehn)

high-level bombers. In spite of the low overcast in England, we are intercepted by Meteors and Venoms.

Aug. 27 The station shuts down operations for approximately three weeks for the servicing of runways.

Sept. 29 We take 12 a/c to Rabat in three sections of four. The trip is accomplished this time in only two stages. This is possible because of the new a/c and their large drop tanks. We go first to Istres and then direct to Rabat, whereas with our old Mk. 2s we had to go to Oran from Istres to refuel.

Dec. 21 F/O Peters caused the squadron considerable anxiety this morning. He was flying alone when he experienced a loss of oil pressure and engine vibration. He commenced a GCA to come in to base through a ceiling of less than a 1000 feet. GCA then called F/O Ayres (who was Ops Officer), and said that F/O Peters' a/c had disappeared from the radar scope. Sembach search and rescue was alerted, and they located the wreckage of a Sabre near Bitache. In the afternoon we heard that F/O Peters was OK—he had started the GCA when the engine seized up completely. He was then only 1500 feet above ground and in cloud. He pulled back and climbed until he felt that the a/c was stalling, then he bailed out. He had a stiff neck, but otherwise was unhurt. As if all this wasn't enough to strain our nerves, F/O Ayres then launched himself in a Sabre and climbed to 40,000 feet. Here he experienced the same symptoms as F/O Peters had earlier, i.e. snarling and growling noises, no oil, no power, no engine. He got an ADF homing to base, sans compass, and let down through the cloud, still based at 1000 feet with a scattered layer at 600 feet.

Grip, who is being sacrificed on the altar of matrimony.

Apr. 3 No flying this morning. Most pilots walking around with unhappy expression, some with swollen jaws. This is not the result of last Friday's stag party, but due to the enthusiasm of Bob Fell, the station dentist, who has reserved this morning to demonstrate his powers to 427 pilots.

Apr. 5 Deacon and Gardiner go to Baumholder, the American shooting ground, to try and arrange our use of their range for rocket firing.

Apr. 9 Some of our aircraft have been cleaned of drop tanks, and there is a general scramble to grab a clean Sabre—the first we've had for six months or so.

Apr. 12 The sky over 3 Wing is almost completely overcast by old contrails from the almost continuous dogfight going on over the station. 38:50 hours of flying. Somebody boomed Zweibrücken and shattered the biggest plate glass window in town.

Apr. 26 Keith Firth surveying the

damage done to a/c and hangar when '409 jumped the chocks during an engine run-up, and ran into the hangar wall. Lou Cadieux was sitting in his office minding his own business when a Sabre suddenly popped in on him.

May 26 Squadron party held outdoors by the control tower. Coincides with the arrival of our first Mark 5 Sabres.

Jun. 12 Hard Times party in the mess attended by 1 horse, 3 pigs, 1 calf and 10 chickens, courtesy of 427.

Jun. 23 Fentiman of 413 Squadron loses his engine on GCA final approach and flies through the airfield fence 200 yards short of the runway. He is unhurt.

Jun. 25 Weather continues hot, and a certain ripe odour is detectable in the locker room where the G-suits hang.

Jul. 2 S/L Burke, F/O Deacon, Corning and Diamond ferry old Mark 2s to England.

Jul. 16 Along with bad weather comes Ex.Dividend in which the UK is the target for our Sabres, acting as

He broke cloud over base with the engine completely dead and turned in towards the runway. His wheels did not lock down, and the nose wheel collapsed shortly before the starboard main also gave way. F/O Ayres was unbent and the damage to the a/c has been assessed as "C" category.

Dec. 23 427 dropped 20000 Christmas cards from an Expeditor over

Zweibrücken ... F/O Ayres flew the a/c and made several passes over and through the town.

Mar. 1, 1955 Have new machine called the "Flight Simulator." Everyone is being checked out.

Mar. 5 Weather duff, so no flying today. Big game tonight between the Canadians and the Russians.

Mar. 7 Weather poor in the a.m., but managed to do some flying in the p.m. Canucks shut out the Russians 5-0 last night—a smooth victory.

Mar. 10 Station put up a nine-plane fly past for the Canadian hockey team ... The 3 Wing team is playing them tonight in Mannheim.

Jun. 29 For the past week and a half 427 Squadron has participated in Exercise Carte Blanche ... The squadron flew well over 200 sorties, with as many kills if not more than the rest of the squadrons at 3 Wing. The whole wing put out a very good show, and the station did not receive an atomic attack until Monday the 27th at which time everyone was wiped out.

Jul. 6 Everyone is making preparations for the trip to Rabat, including shots in the arm, and dental attention ... Now we are putting the heavy jugs on so that we will have little opportunity for further pre-Rabat practice.

RAF day fighters: a Supermarine Swift FR.5 heading uphill; and a flight line photo of the ever-glamourous Hawker Hunter. (Air Ministry)

Sep. 14 Random arrives with Mk. 6s—19 for 413 Squadron and 427 Squadron.

Sep. 23 Squadron discovers where RAF Hunters fly. Many sorties flown towards Jever. Some successes, although RAF a/c not too apt to play.

Nov. 25 Some concern for Ken Williams when he announces to F/O Leiter over R/T that his tanks will not drain. All concern forgotten when leader announces Williams is carrying no tanks.

427 Squadron diary

F/O Arnie Leiter of 427 Squadron relates a little incident which occurred when one of his squadron mates was taking a Sabre into Scottish Aviation for maintenance: "In the mid-fifties we began ferrying Sabres to Renfrew, Scotland, for overhaul. On one such trip F/O Bud Ballance, after a less-than-perfect approach and landing, decided to overshoot. He rammed the throttle forward, then decided he could salvage it. Now it was throttle idle, maximum braking. The runway was short for a Sabre at the best of times, and quickly Bud realized he might not stop in time after all. So it was throttle forward (once more!); but now it was a sure thing that even if he got airborne he would never clear the forest of cranes that lined the River Clyde and which were rushing towards him.

"This time Bud closed the throttle, pointed his Sabre to the left where he

Fair look-alikes were the ever-impressive F-100 Super Sabre (this one operated by the USAF's European demo team, the Sky Blazers) and the Dassault Mystère IVB(5-NL), France's front-line interceptor. Neither, as a rule, could out-fight the Canadair Sabre, though each had an afterburner and was supersonic in level flight. The Danes, French, Greeks and Turks also used the F-100 in NATO. (ECP Armées)

assessed his survival chances as being good, and raised the gear. He slid to a stop on a golf course. Soon he noticed a Scottish bobby pedalling his bicycle furiously towards him. Without a word of condolence or greeting the police-man, producing a pencil and note-book, began, 'Now, then, Sarrr! Could I see yourrr pilot's licence.' "

The varied and hectic pace of a Sabre squadron continued into 1956, with 427 involved in Argus, an on-going intercept exercise, and having the usual string of "incidents"—F/O Corning ejecting February 11 when his engine seized, F/O Ballance tearing off his gear at Renfrew, F/O Griffith ejec-ting too low and not making it, F/L Frost making a successful deadstick landing on a taxiway at Lahr. August 27-September 19 the squadron was off to Rabat, where, by the time the last round had been fired, not one decent score had been tallied. On October 16 F/O Noga intentionally spun Sabre 23567. This was a no-no, as the pilots had always been warned the Sabre was not readily salvaged from a spin. Noga punched out near Hahn AFB. F/O Pennycock found his way to a Belgian emergency field after hydraulic failure the following month. On May 31, 1957, W/C Stewart fatally crashed on the runway at Zwei and his Sabre cartwheeled into a hangar. Stewart had been making a check of Sabre 23463, which had a nose gear hang-up. The other Sabre landed safely midst the chaos of the accident.

No.427 went to Deci for the first time in August 1957. Eighteen Sabres were sent down, but the overall average was nothing to write home about—14.58 per cent. Shortly after its return to Zwei, 427 participated in Counter-punch and one day set a new daily

flying rate record for the squadron—88 hours. A visit to Deci the following spring produced a 25 per cent average score. Two years later the squadron was still struggling with low scores—22.6 per cent in February 1961. Such scores were typical throughout the Air Div, and with other NATO units.

Many squadron exchanges were recorded in the latter days of 427 before phase-out of the Sabre, inclu-ding to places like Bodø in Norway, the USAF base at Bitburg, Kleine Brogel in Belgium, and Skydstrup in Denmark. On a visit to 3 Wing, a Norwegian

Sabre pilot ran into trouble on February 9, 1962. He parachuted right on the station. That June, 427 deployed to Marville, where it re-mained until December when it held its last Zulu alert. The first CF-104 arri-ved (via C-130) at 3 Wing on December 12. Two days later, 427 became the first F-86 squadron to disband since 414 had done so in June 1957. On December 16 the OC, W/C St. Louis, handed over the squadron records to W/C Middlemiss, who was reforming 427 with CF-104s.

RAF all-weather Gloster Javelin WD804. The Javelin was faster than the CF-100, and armed with 30mm cannons and air-to-air guided missiles. But like most British fighters of the era, it was restricted in range. (Hawker)

Line-up of 434 Sabres at Volkel on July 19, 1953. They were visiting Holland to celebrate the 40th anniversary of the Dutch Air Force. (DND PL80348)

Phil Perry recently provided these reminiscences of life at 3 Wing, where he served with 434 Squadron:

One of our major problems in maintaining the Sabres during the early days at 3 Wing was the shortage of engines. We were forever removing the engine

Shining up the Swords. 434 Bluenosers all pitch in to clean their aircraft out on the 3 Wing dispersal (via P Perry)

from one aircraft for use in another to maintain a maximum of serviceable aircraft. Often what happened was that the engine would be pulled from one Sabre, then the aft section would be placed back onto the Sabre (minus its engine), and the aircraft would be placed out on one of the dispersal hard stands until we could get it back into the hangar once an engine became available. As the NCO of servicing, this often griped me as I required serviceable aircraft to maintain our flying and keep the pilots happy—not aircraft without engines.

It was while I was staring at one of these engine-less Sabres one day that it

suddenly dawned on me how to get even with F/O Bill Thorleifson for a prank he had pulled on me back in Ottawa. I got some of my crew together and we made as if to ready one of our Sabres for a test flight, but making sure to leave the engine intake and exhaust plugs in place. I then called the flight commander, F/L Chuck Keating, let him in on our upcoming skit, and had him send Bill out to air test the Sabre. Right on time, he came tramping up from the hangar, griping about how we always waited until the last thing Friday afternoon (around beer call time) to spring an air test.

Anyway, Bill came in and signed out the L14 form and I handed him the test card, which stated that a test flight was required regarding an engine change. I accompanied Bill to the dispersal, giving him the VIP treatment by carrying his parachute. He began his walk-around, and right off the bat complained about the oleos being too high. So I got a couple of the crew to jump up and down on the wing to drop them down, saying that they must be stuck up because of uneven refuelling. Then, when he got to the nose and complained about the damned nose plug being left in, I quickly moved to the tailpipe. As Bill pulled out the nose plug, I pulled out the tail plug. He

looked down the engine intake, but all he saw was empty space, and Phil Perry staring at him from the other end of the tunnel, giving him the big five—only my hand wasn't quite at my eyebrow, more like at my nose! I thought old Bill would come straight down through the airplane after me, but he quickly realized he'd been had and retreated to the hangar mumbling, "I'll get even with Chuck Keating!"

The three Sabre squadrons at 3 Wing were always competing with each other. This was especially evident in aircraft maintenance. Many long hours were spent by the technicians to put the maximum number of aircraft on the line. In the early days spare parts were in short supply and a lot of wheeling and dealing was carried out between Supply and our stalwart NCOs to get what was needed to get that extra aircraft on the line. Once the aircraft were on the line our servicing crews took over to make sure each Sabre provided the maximum flying time possible. We always had more pilots than aircraft and you could only get one pilot into a Sabre (though more than once I saw more than one pilot trying for the same aircraft).

Maintenance crews under FS Tommy Harper, Sgts Joe Madder and Bill Irwin, Cpls Archie Conner and Bill

Linden, armourers under FS Bob Mulley and Sgt Bill Smith, supported by the best all-round technicians in the business, kept the aircraft on the line. Then it was up to the servicing crews to keep them flying, and, believe me, they knew and took pride in their business. The fast turn-around was the name of the game. That was where others really shone—fellows like Cpl Scotty Stevenson, LACs Tim Murphy, Hank Henry, Jim Fayant, Whitehead, Isenor, Big Cliff Adams (for hot brake changes) and many others. Many a time it was "Where's the *@-*! pilot? This thing's been ready for five minutes."

We of 434 shared the maintenance hangar with 427. That caused a lot of good rivalry, especially when one was short of parts. One day one of our Sabres left the hangar with a 427 tail section, lest a graphic sample be needed. We would certainly have gotten it airborne had a sprog pilot not spilled the beans when he noticed that nose and tail numbers didn't match.

One morning I was in the hangar discussing the weather with our warrant officer, "Teach" Walker, when all hell broke loose—boom, crash, thunder! Then the nose of a Sabre came bashing through the corrugated iron wall next to the main doors. It knocked things all over the place, including several big

Herman Nelsons. When the noise and dust settled and the Sabre's engine was shut off, out from the cockpit crawled the most shaken young engine tech anyone ever saw. "Boy, what a ride," he gasped.

What had happened was that the Sabre was being run up in front of the hangar. My good friend, Sgt Bill Elderkin, was on the wing doing a generator voltage regulator trip. Being short of wheel chocks, a couple of sandbags were being used, but they simply didn't

BR-273 flown by F/O Gerry King, had its nose gear collapse at Istres when it hit wet snow on landing. (S.E. Burrows)

147

Two angles on the 427 Sabre that got loose at 3 Wing while on an engine run-up. (S.E. Burrows)

Bluenose Sabre 2s on the tarmac at Istres, on the way to Rabat. (S.E. Burrows)

stand the power of the Orenda. The next thing Bill knew there was a bump and he was on his way (without the tail attached there were no brakes). Fortunately Bill leapt from the wing before the Sabre-cum-battering ram went through the side of the hangar. And that's how we ended up with the spare tail section mentioned above.

With 434 we had many deployments around Europe, with the ground crew following the Sabres around in the old Bristol Freighter. The Bristol was slow but dependable, especially on our trips to Rabat for weapons training. Those were great trips indeed—hard work, but lots of fun, and real comradeship among everyone in the squadron. I can't remember higher morale in any other unit I served in over my 32 years in the service. It all came to the fore at Rabat, where flying was a dawn-to-dusk business. Maintenance there was under FSs Tommy Harper and Joe Madder, with men like Cpl Scotty Stevenson and LACs Cobill, Fayant, Godsal, Hathaway, Mork and Murphy assuring fast turn-arounds. Armourers FS Bob Mulley and Sgt Smith made sure of rapid re-arming between flights. Hell, the pilots couldn't keep up with us. It was only at Rabat that I can recall the

A 434 two-ship from Zweibrücken. (S.E. Burrows)

pilots actually dragging their asses because there were too many aircraft available (though the late nights down at Madina no doubt played a part in that). The French Air Force at Rabat thought we were all just plain crazy!

Phil Perry

On June 20, 1953, F/O S.E. "Syd" Burrows graduated from the OTU at Chatham and was posted to 434 Squadron at Uplands under W/C J.D. Mitchner. At the time he had 47:55 hours on the Vampire. On August 5 F/L Keating took him up for a checkout on the T-bird and on August 19 Burrows took up his first Sabre (19128). In all, he made four Sabre flights that day and four the next, on one of which he clocked Mach 1.03. September 11 his log notes a climb in 19347 to 48,000 feet. By the end of October Burrows had made 55 Sabre flights and already had 43:15 hours on type. Like all the young pilots on squadron, he was getting lots of opportunity to learn his trade: GCAs and letdowns, aeros, formation flying, cross-countries, air fighting, low-level nav exercises, gunnery, etc. Burrows' log for the end of 1952 shows his total times to date: Harvard 178:25 hours,

Texan 76:20, night Harvard 13:30, Expeditor 1:45, Vampire 47:55, T-33 5:05 and Sabre 79:20.

These were the early days of Sabre gunnery, and Burrows was scoring no better than most. On practice firing January 7-8, 1953, with 200 rounds per trip he scored 7½, 25, 16 and 20 per cent. With improvements in the gunsight and experience, scores gradually rose, and in time figures near 90 per cent were recorded.

On February 23 Burrows passed 100 hours on the Sabre and couldn't resist a brief log book entry, "No sweeter airplane." March 7-April 6 he was part of Leapfrog 3, flying 19421 from Ottawa to Zweibrücken. April 20 he commenced flying at 3 Wing with a sector recce, Frankfurt-Stuttgart-Baden, and on April 26 was part of a

F/O S.E. "Syd" Burrows while serving with 434 Squadron. (DND)

Sabre instrument panel as seen by pilot Syd Burrows. At the time Syd was towing the flag at Rabat, moving along at 140KIAS at over 8000 feet. (S.E. Burrows)

Series of gun camera frames taken from Syd Burrows' Sabre during a raid on Florennes in Belgium. Syd writes, "I got too low and ran my port wing through the antennas atop the GCA unit. Put a big hole in the slat and even brought home a hunk of metal inscribed 'Fabriqué en Belgique.' G/C Hull was not impressed, but our gallant metal bashers soon had things straightened out and the bird was flying next day."

1953 MONTH DATE	Type	No.	Pilot, or 1st Pilot	2nd Pilot, Pupil or Passenger	Duty (Including Results and Remarks)	SE Day Dual (1)	SE Day Pilot (2)	SE Night Dual (3)	SE Night Pilot (4)	ME Day Dual (5)	ME Day 1st Pilot (6)	ME Day 2nd Pilot (7)	ME Night Dual (8)	ME Night 1st (9)	ME Night 2nd (10)	Passenger (11)	Instr/Cloud Dual (12)	Instr/Cloud Pilot (13)	Link Trainer (14)
					Totals Brought Forward	113·00	357·05	5·30	7·40		6·55					67·45	67·55	10·20	22·15
JULY 21	F86E	347	SELF	—	FORM - T.C.		1·00				F86 163.20								
23	"	431	"	—	EX. CORNET - GCI		1·00												
23	"	394	"	—	" GCI BRAVO TL.		1·15												
24	"	274	"	—	A/C TEST		·30												
25	"	421	"	—	OP. CORNET - L.L. WK		1·10				FIRST 500 HRS								
25	"	421	"	—	OP. CORNET - SWEEP		1·15				L.L. TO EINDHOVEN CHUCK HIT FLOCK OF BIRDS								
26	"	434	"	—	" LL STRIKE		1·05				HIGH L 35000 BRUSSELS, EINDHOVEN SHOOT UP METEOR DAMAGED								
26	"	434	"	—	"		·55				WEATHER CLAMPED AT FLORENNES LANDED AT BITBURG 1 F84								
26	"	434	"	—	"		·55				WEATHER STILL DUFF RETURNED TO XP.								
27	"	434	"	—	" MISSION #5		1·05				STRAFED FLORENNES CLOBBERED ECA UNIT ANTENNAE, NINE DOOR								
28	"	239	"	—	" PATROL		1·10				FLORENNES -10 VAMPS METZ 2+2 PROBS. - ME 2 BIG GAGGLE								
28	"	439	"	—	" MISSION #3		1·25				CHUCK -1896 WITH WHEELS AND FLAPS DOWN								
30	C45	1518	F/O AL SEITZ	SELF	XP - SPAGDALEHM - XP						8 A/C PATROL 35000' BOUNCED BY 4 RAF 86's F86 175.05								
31	F86G	424	SELF	—	LET DOWNS		·55				1.15 PICKUP CHUCK								
31	"	270	"	—			1·00									20	10		
31	"	270	"	—	FORMATION - SNAKE		·50									20	20		
			OC 434 (F) SQN		SUMMARY FOR JULY UNIT 434 (F) SQN DATE 31 JUL 53 SIGNATURE S.E. Burrows F/O TYPES 1. F86E 2. C-45		25·05				F86 177.50 / 1·15 A FLT COMMANDER					2·25	·30		
AUG 1	F86E	429	SELF	—	LOCAL		·55												
1	"	"	"	—	ZWEI - FURSTENFELDBRUCK		1·00										·15		
1	"	"	"	—	FURSTEN - ZWEI		1·00										·15	·20	
					GRAND TOTAL [Cols. (1) to (10)] 510 Hrs. 10 Mins. Totals Carried Forward	113·00	375·20	5·30	7·40		8·10					67·45	69·05	11·10	22·15

Sabre flying at 3 Wing from F/O Syd Burrows' log.

27-plane flypast at the station handing-over ceremonies. Now began the usual hurly-burly life of a fighter pilot in Europe during the 1950s. There was all the routine flying, many exercises, and endless opportunity to hassle with a sky full of "enemy" targets. May 22 Burrows notes a B-29 and two F-84s "destroyed," a battle with 10 Vampires on July 22, bounced by four RAF

A sign of the changing times. The first 104 to come snooping around 3 Wing gets wired by Bob Hallowell flying Sabre 6 No.23598. The 104 driver later cried foul, claiming that Hallowell and his buddies had ambushed him from out of cloud. (via Bob Hallowell)

Sabres the following day, and on and on. On March 10, 1954, less than a year after he first flew the Sabre, Burrows passed 300 swept-wing hours.

About this time, Chuck Keating, Jack Frazer, Rick Mace and Burrows began practising formation aerobatics and were soon putting on air shows all over Europe as the Fireballs, the Air Division's official 1954 demonstration team. Their first shows were June 6 at Tours and Rennes. A busy program followed, with shows at places like Lyon, Volkel, Nancy and Sedan. The air show season seemed to be working out beautifully when, for Burrows, it came to a shocking end. On September 13 he was flying 23187 on a mission from Baden. Bruce Burgess was lead-

ing the section; Keith Booth and Len Stephens made up the rest of the flight.

The four Sabres did a mock attack on Zweibrücken and were just reformating when Burrows had a mid-air with a hawk. The bird smashed through the canopy, blinding him. He quickly decided that "this was it"—he'd have to get out; but then things seemed to look up. Burrows could see with his right eye, and by getting well down was protected from the wind blasting through the windshield. Burrows' mate, Stephens, came alongside to guide him and his wounded Sabre home. Within minutes, Burrows

An interesting 434 intercept. The bogie is a USAF B-47. (S.E. Burrows)

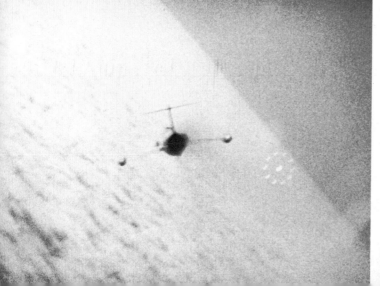

Armament officer F/O "Doc" Herriot instructs some 413 pilots on the Browning .50 machine gun. The pilots are F/Os Jack Nichol, Stu Oliver, Glen Younghusband, Lou Loubert, George Smola and Ron Fentiman. (DND)

Sgt Purcell of 413 helps in draining the tailpipe of a Sabre following a wet start. (R.W. Fentiman)

was braking to a stop. He was soon patched up and itching to get back flying, even though he knew he was permanently blind in his left eye. To show his competence, he flew Sabre 23093 for 35 minutes on October 10. But AFHQ was not easily convinced, and Burrows was yanked off flying. On November 1 he was on his way home. On July 29, 1955, he was awarded the Air Force Cross for bravery in saving his aircraft, but it would be some 15 years before HQ would rein-

F/L Larry Nelson of 413 Squadron lands at Volkel, Holland, while on exercises in August 1954. (via R.W. Fentiman)

state him as a pilot. He went on to command 440 Squadron (Dakotas) and a UN unit in India-Pakistan (Caribous and Twin Otters).

Bill Ewing was a 3 Wing tech on CF-100s during the heyday of the Air Division. There was always a certain amount of good-natured ribbing (even a bit of rancour) between the Sabre and "Lead Sled" people. Ewing writes "We of 440 'Foul Weather Interception Squadron' used to take pleasure in waiting until our birds were flying in the lousiest crud Germany had to offer. Then we ground types would wander into the club and in loud voices wonder as to the whereabouts of the Sabre crowd—the 'Sunshine Flying Club'—then duck out quickly as one of our number yelled, 'Hiding in the hangar!' That was fine by us, but the prank was seldom taken very well by the Sabre boys—the majority of Sabre

prangs in Germany in those days were related to said lousy weather."

The fair-weather Sabres routinely made mincemeat of the CF-100s, though Clunk drivers learned a few survival tricks. In one, the pilot with a Sword coming up his tailpipes would haul back, idle one engine and, as he stalled at the top, let his Clunk rotate 180 degrees so that it was now headed downhill, much to the surprise of the Sword pilot, who now found himself looking straight at an oncoming Clunk, or even with the straight-winged beast on *his* tail.

In their efforts to save face in the never-ending Sabre vs CF-100 competition, the Clunk crews would try anything to gain a few points. Once a

Officers of 413 Squadron at 3 Wing, August 1953. In the back are F/Os Lou Loubert, Ron Barnett, Ken Hagarty, Gene Nixon, Art Maskell, Lyle Coulter, Danny Kaye and Nick Mulikow. In the centre are F/Os Jack Nichol, Ron Fentiman, Bob Henderson, "Wac" Wilson, Arnie Cavett, Judd Killoran, Marcel Plouffe, Al Shaw, Bob Prescott, Bill Pettit. In front are F/Os Murray Kelly, Rick Mace, Bill Paisley, S/L Rocky Gordon, F/O Doug Williams (EO) and F/L Larry Nelson. (via R.W. Fentiman)

When 413 shut down at 3 Wing in 1957 it soon reopened for business, this time as a NORAD Clunk squadron. (Larry Milberry)

Zulu Alert at 3 Wing, with 434 Sabre 6s on stand-by. (DND PCN1840)

3 Wing Days from F/O Ken Hagarty's album …

Counter-clockwise from the left: Sabre 2 of 427 Squadron at Zwei; Korean veteran Gene Nixon gets ready for a flight with the help of his crewman; notice of a 3 Wing social event; hero shot of F/O Hagarty (413 Squadron); 3 Wing bikers-cum-Sabre pilots: Ron Fentiman, Bob Prescott, Brian Burns, Ron Barnett, Nick Mulikow, Ken Hagarty, René Loubert and Lyle Coulter; an outing at a German fair with pilots Bill Hind, Ken Hagarty, Bill Thorleifson, Ernie Gardiner, Stu Corning and Dave Alexander; T-bird '018 pranged by Annis and Hagarty after a fuel pump failure.

The Fireballs climbing straight up. (S.E. Burrows)

Before and After

There's a flugplatz in Deutschland,
  Zweibrücken is its name,
And all was very peaceful there,
  before the squadrons came.
Its hospital had no patients,
  no sick, no halt, no lame.
The staff was very comfortable,
  before the squadrons came.

Headquarters was a quiet place
  (they wish it was the same),
And business was BF'd each day,
  before the squadrons came.
Accounting was a simple thing,
  no shortage to explain,
You see, they had no money here,
  before the squadrons came.

All AOGs were met on time,
  supply folk were quite sane,
With lots of spares on every shelf,
  before the squadrons came.
Maintenance ran like clockwork,
  it was really just a game,
They had no qualified personnel,
  before the squadrons came.

The SPs had a pleasant time,
  with no one here to blame,
Their lovely cells were empty,
  before the squadrons came.
Flying control ran smoothly,
  no planes, no climb-out lane,
No noise, no fuss, no bother,
  before the squadrons came.

Then one sunny April day,
  with roar of might and main,
The place was rent asunder,
  'twas the day the squadrons came.
The situation's now a busy one,
  and making quite a name,
It's mostly work, with little play,
  since the squadrons came.

Headquarters has a paper war,
  Accounting is a pain,
The Admin Wing's turned upside down,
  since the squadrons came.
AOG is just a word,
  all things are "on next plane."
And Maintenance is in a whirl,
  since the squadrons came.

The hospital is crowded,
  the cells are just the same,
But things have only been that way,
  since the squadrons came.
The moral of this poem,
  if moral there's to be,
It takes all kinds to make a Wing,
  even you and me.

from *Flugplatz,* September 1953

Over the Flugplatz

No.1 came in to land,
He grasped the throttle in his hand,
The Orenda 10 refused to run,
That's how we lost No.1.

Refrain
Over the Flugplatz, over the Rhine,
Fuel's running short and so is my time.
Show me the runway, lead me home,
Back to the base I love.

No.2 was high and hot,
Bags of air he had got.
Touchdown came by GCA,
"X" marks the spot where he does lay.

No.3 was low and slow,
He tried to crank it, but it wouldn't go.
We heard him holler as he hit the ground,
"Cartoon Tower, I should have gone
  around."

No.4 on GCA
Flamed out when he was far, far away.
He tried to stretch it to Hugelsheim,
He flicked and spun at Iffezheim.

No.3(F) Wing Station Commanders (Sabre Era)

G/C A.C. Hull	Feb. 1953	Jan. 1956
G/C J.K.F. MacDonald	May 1956	Jul. 1960
G/C V.L. Berg	Jul. 1960	Jul. 1963

No.3(F)Wing Squadron Commanders (Sabre Era)

413 Squadron

S/L J.D. "Doug" Lindsay	Aug. 1951	Mar. 1953
S/L W.I. Gordon	Mar. 1953	Sep. 1953
S/L E.P. "Eep" Wood	Jun. 1954	Jul. 1956
W/C H.C. Stewart	Aug. 1956	Apr. 1957

427 Squadron

S/L C.L.V. Gervais	Aug. 1952	Aug. 1953
S/L D.K. Burke	Jun. 1954	Sep. 1955
W/C D. Laidler	Sep. 1955	Jul. 1956
W/C W.R. "Bill" Tew	Oct. 1956	Mar. 1958
W/C H.R. "Hal" Knight	May 1958	May 1960
W/C P.B. St. Louis	Dec. 1960	Dec. 1962

434 Squadron

W/C J.D. Mitchner	Jul. 1952	Feb. 1953
S/L J.W. "Jim" Fiander	May 1953	Nov. 1954
S/L A.L. Sinclair	Nov. 1954	Apr. 1956
S/L E.R.B. Gray	Apr. 1956	Apr. 1957
W/C H.C. Stewart*	Apr. 1957	May 1957
S/L J.F. Dunlop	Jun. 1957	May 1959
W/C H.F. "Harry" Wenz	May 1959	Jul. 1962
S/L John Ursulak	Jul. 1962	Sep. 1962
S/L K.C. "Ken" Lett	Sep. 1962	Jan. 1963

*Killed in flying accident

month the Sabre pilots had to log a bit of night flying. On occasion, as the Sabres flew their nav courses (as the Clunk people had it, from one brightly lit city to the next) the night sky would suddenly light up as a Clunk flicked on his lights to illuminate the little Sabre it had so easily stalked and "killed."

Baden-Söllingen

No.4(F)Wing made a fast Atlantic crossing, getting into Baden-Söllingen on September 4, 1953. Normal squadron activities soon began. 414 deployed five Sabres to North Luffenham October 6-7. Its first "Weapon Fire" at Rabat took place June 16-July 8, 1954, where the average score of 21.3 per cent was considered better-than-average. Some 94,176 rounds were expended during this shoot. The following month the squadron headed off with 14 Sabres on Operation Keystone, a deployment to sunny Greece via Rome. This was claimed by 414 to have been a reward for scoring so well at Rabat. Keystone commenced September 1 and involved the Greeks, Turks and Americans as well. 414 was busy on intercept missions for the duration and recorded these kills: 2 F-84s, September 1; 2 TBMs, Sep-

(Top right) The 1956-57 414 hockey team. (Above) On detachment at Damblain, France, August 1956, 444 pilots Ev Gill, Bill McMurray, Gin Smith and Al Brown try out a four-holer. (via R.J. Flynn and A.C. Brown)

tember 3; 5 USN Skyraiders, September 6. The squadron took off for home on September 8. A note in the diary for October 8 refers to a Sabre jumping the chocks and crashing into a second aircraft with much damage done.

A 414 Sabre blasts off from 4 Wing. (H. Hrischenko)

General view at Baden-Söllingen. Dispersal areas can be seen in the foreground. The effectiveness of natural camouflage (hardy Bavarian evergreens) is apparent. (DND PL81733)

Maintenance of 414 Swords at Baden. These are Mk. 4s on loan from the RAF. (H. Hrischenko)

Bob Flynn of 414 relates an incident that occurred June 10, 1957. "Bill Stacey as lead, Chuck Paine as 2, Davie Walker as 3 and I as 4 received a mid-morning live Zulu scramble and were directed towards the area of Fulda on the East-West Germany border. It appears that some reconnaissance was taking place, and 'easterners' were chasing same out, but were themselves getting a bit far into our air space. Walker and I sighted one of the easterners and gave hot pursuit, but to no avail. We lost the enemy and the game was over. This sortie was the closest I ever came to any type of 'action' during my European tour."

The trips to Rabat were not without the occasional casualty, not always to

414's crew shack at Baden. Sabres at the ready in the background, as "the boys" wait for some flying. (H.Hrischenko)

156

A bit of a motley crew. Bob Massier, John Ursulak, Barry Smith, Otto Ulrick, Jack Breffit and Bud Lawrence camp out at Damblain. (via A.C. Brown)

die. The American service police found him and rushed him to a military hospital in Casablanca.''

Ray Carruthers of 422 had his second Sabre ejection on February 1, 1955. He was flying 23193. At the time, there had been several engine malfunctions when engine time was in the 80-100 hour range. Carruthers' machine was in that danger zone, but the squadron was going on detachment to Rabat and '193 had a reliable weapons system, so it was decided to take a

Standard Sabre-pilots memorabilia is the Mach Buster's certificate.

chance with it. Carruthers was heading for Rabat and cruising at 39,000 when his engine packed up. There was an explosion, then another on the way down at 12,000. At 6000 feet it was time to get out. Carruthers came down safely off Valencia. He was adrift for 11¼ hours before being picked up by the steamer *Sahara*. The sea had just about claimed him by that time. In later years he flew 104s, F-105s in the USAF, and even checked out on the F-111.

do with flying either. There were instructions to the air force about dealings with the locals, not travelling alone when off base, etc. On January 21, 1955, F/O Hoogen of 422 Squadron fell victim to some less-than-friendly Arabs. The diarist put it this way: ''He was badly beaten and left to

Later that spring, F/O Filyk was practising some spins. He had a few successful goes at it, then got into one that was stubborn. At 8000 feet he thought it best to depart and blew the canopy. But before he could pull the handles his aircraft came out of the spin on its own. Sabre and pilot came home safely after all.

Triple Four Squadron had prepared to leave on Leapfrog 4 under S/L Gene Heggtveit, but illness prevented him from keeping that date. Instead, S/L MacKay, just returning to 416 from his Korean stint, led 444 across. Once in Germany, MacKay continued to 416, and F/L Mark Sauder took over 444 as interim boss until W/C F.H. Darragh arrived as OC on January 15, 1954. Sadly, Darragh was killed shortly after taking command. His Sabre 5 had engine failure during a GCA. Sauder

A couple of 422 prangs. TF-029 after a wheels-up episode, and 19619, sure never to get back to its rightful owners, the RAF. It went down in Belgium, but F/O Smith ejected safely. (via Al Adams)

The whole outfit—444 at Baden in the mid-fifties. (via L.J. Redman)

again filled in until S/L "Bud" Lawrence took charge May 17. That month he led the squadron to Rabat for its first Weapon Fire.

On December 30, 1954, the squadron had its first bail-out when F/L A.J. Bauer parted company with 23163. His seat became entangled in his chute, causing Bauer some consternation. He and the seat eventually alighted in a tree and Bauer came to no harm. Most of 1954 had been spent at 444 converting and getting used to the Sabre 5. The last of its 4s had been ferried to Speke on March 26. The 5s were soon supplanted by 6s, 444 being the first squadron to re-equip with them (May 1955). Also in 1955, 444 adopted its mascot, Cecil the Snake. Cecil, an all-metal cobra, had been spotted in a shop window by A.J. Bauer, who proposed him as mascot to S/L Lawrence. The boss concurred and Cecil was "in." He was shortly to festoon the tails of the squadron's Sabres, the ideal symbol to complement the unit's "Strike swift, strike sure" motto.

A frequent pastime among Air Div members was skiing, and pilots were periodically sent on ski courses to make sure they knew what they were doing. The *Schwarzwaldflieger*, 4 Wing's monthly magazine, reported on one skiing escapade involving a pair of 444 pilots, F/Os Brown and Fitzsimmons: "... after a short training session of skating one night (with refreshments) the two heroes took to the slopes the next morning. Feeling rather courageous, young Al took on the Big Hill, and soon found (about halfway

Summary of flying, 444 Squadron, No.4(F)Wing, 1962		
Month	*Sorties*	*Hours*
January	556	684:45
February	423	486:40
March	550	633:25
April	512	660:35
May	503	615:25
June	465	555:25
July	559	749:25
August	497	501:55
September	401	500:00
October	352	499:20
November	349	499:50
December	351	500:00

down) that he was out of control. Spying a helpless-looking member of the opposite sex, he steered towards her shouting 'Fore' and 'My dive brakes won't hold,' while all the time secretly hoping for rescue. However, just as collision seemed imminent, Al did a steep turn and spun in, receiving a twisted ankle for this gallant gesture. F/O Fitzsimmons, who had been lurking nearby, applied first aid and led Al, still rigged on the boards, back to the dispensary for examination. Moral: he who skis slow, skis best."

Events from the 444 Squadron diary for 1962 show more typical Air Division life in Sabre days. By this time all the wings were awaiting the CF-104 and realized their beloved Sabres would shortly be laid to rest in the scrapyard at Prestwick. On January 1, 444 led 4 Wing into the skies. A happy day, but not so the 13th, as Cpl G. Mitchell was sucked into a Sabre during a run-up. He died a few days later of his injuries. Most of the squadron's flying for the month was to practise cine in aid of a forthcoming deployment to Sardinia. In February the squadron sent 25 Sabres off to Deci, but bad

weather deterred the boys from getting in much shooting. This was especially annoying as 444 had its sights set on the highest 20,000-foot trophy shoot ever for the Air Div. No firing was undertaken until March 3. No good results were noted until March 5 when a 33 per cent average was recorded, indeed the sought-after record.

A May diary entry describes more "socializing" at 444: "There was only one major social event for the month, and this was the fighter pilots night sponsored and hosted by the members of the USAF Air Base at Phalsbourg. Twelve Snakes were in attendance and after a fine round of cocktails and an excellent meal, the party really got under way. Guest speakers included Chief Snake, W/C J. Roussell, and the guest of honour, General Adolph Galland ret., former Commander-in-Chief of Luftwaffe fighter operations during WW II. The party ended at an undetermined hour amidst slowly

"Lyrics" to a Triple Four song composed by members of the squadron maintenance unit whilst on detachment to Sardinia, c. 1962.

(Tune: "The Battle of New Orleans")

We took a little ammo and
  we took a little gas,,
We flew an hour twenty just
  a sitting on our ass.
We got down to Deci in the
  middle of the day
And the Wing Co said, "OK now boys
  you have to make it pay."

Chorus
We fired our guns and the pipper
  kept a slidin',
It isn't quite as easy as
  it was awhile ago.
With all six guns and the
  pipper kept a-slidin'
On across the beaches to the
  town of Decimo.

We took a little readin' and we
  found our sights were bad,
The ammo started jammin' but
  we got the best they had.
They used it in the first world war
  and in the second too,
The only ones that left a mark
  were orange, red and blue.

We went to thirty thousand and
  the scores were not the best
But we started hittin' better

now we're up there with the rest.
We lost the flags and shot the flags
  and even dropped them short,
There were seven sections in a row
  that needed to abort.

We tallied up our totals and
  we found them kind of low,
Cause 422 had beat us bad
  and so had 430.
So we power packed a section and
  we flew at 20 thou
And when the scores were added
  only one had beat us now.

We took them back to our Wing and
  we parked them by the Rhine,
The 104's are comin' but we know
  they'll take some time.
So we'll fly ours till they fall apart
  and hope to get some more,
And the first ones that will get them
  will be good ol' Triple Four.

We packed our guns and we
  haven't got a pipper,
The missiles are a comin' and
  the guns have gotta go.
Triple Four will get 'em and we'll
  know just how to use 'em
And we'll never have to prove it
  down in torrid Decimo.

Some Sabre scenes around Triple Four in the late fifties. 23722 is refuelled; techs attach a tow target to a Sabre's dive brake; VH-635 gets some attention to guns and canopy; VH-743 under tow by a Unimog; one of Cecil's best with a broken nose; and "secondary reserve" aircraft cocooned against the weather. (Harry Tate via K.M. Molson, DND PL84732, 81760, 84764, Harry Tate via K.M. Molson, DND PL84724)

fading squadron songs and cheers". The squadron stood only one alert in May. Late in the month an escape and evasion exercise was conducted throughout the Air Div. Alert commitment was quite the opposite for July when 17 days were spent on Zulu.

Also in July, 444 went on detachment to Belgium for nine days. And, that month, it experienced one of the more mysterious events of Sabre

days—the disappearance of F/O Ray Baltins. The diary notes for July 4: "Ray took off as a member of a four-plane section. He experienced gear trouble immediately after takeoff and left the section to burn off fuel before returning to land. He did not come back. Members of the RCAF, GAF and USAFE and US Army all took part in an extensive search for the missing aircraft. The results of this search proved to be negative." To this day, no trace of Baltins or his aircraft has turned up.

Bad news reached the Air Div in August 1962: a government austerity kick included limiting Air Div flying hours to 500 hours per month per squadron. For August, 444 logged 501:55.

fall by an immovable high pressure system that ups and sits right on top of us for a week or more. During November, a classic example of this phenomenon occurred. Every day for more than a week our schedulers plied their wits against the elements in an effort to completely utilize our 500 monthly allocated flying hours." Even so, 444 managed to eat up its quota. Bad weather dogged the wing in December too, but life was brightened up considerably by a visit on the 14th by Prince Philip.

F/O Strang summarized the dying days of Triple Four and the Sabre in his March 1963 diary entries:

"0001 hrs 1st March 1963 marked the beginning of a new era. 444 IDF

The 4 Wing instrument flight in 1957: T-birds and an Expeditor. (via R.J. Flynn)

Was that extra 1:55 a statement of how the squadron felt about this restriction on its activities? At Deci in August, the squadron recorded a 29.7 per cent average score. F/O Dargent had the high score at 81 per cent, and a high average of 60 per cent. The fitness bug hit 444 in October, as noted by diarist F/O J.T. Strang: "Lean, sinewy, alert and physically fit aircrew is the objective of the recent fitness program undertaken on the wing. Twice weekly, all squadron aircrew grunt, groan, strain and sweat their way to physical perfection. The results so far have proved beneficial to most, and we now find ourselves almost looking forward to the next PT period."

November was a fly-boy's nightmare at 4 Wing: "Unfortunately, here at 4 Wing one is often pestered late in the

Sqn ceased to exist and 444 ST/R Sqn was formed. The 1st was a Friday and with the exception of those ground crew preparing the aircraft for Sal Siesta, the squadron was closed down for the weekend.

"Bright and early Monday morning (the 4th) all Cobras had assembled and were eager to begin our last operational

CF-JJC and 'JJB were Sabre 6s "borrowed" from 4 Wing by Canadair in 1956 to demonstrate to the Swiss. The operation was a success in that the Sabres really wowed the Swiss, but in the end, the Hawker Hunter won the day. The Swiss preferred its heavier weaponry over the Sabre's .50 machine guns. Note the Swiss mountain climber's crest applied on 'JJC. (L.A. Cheek)

Reunions keep RCAF history very much alive, and there seem to be more of them than ever before. These keen fellows attended 444's reunion at Lahr in June 1982. Standing from the left are Len Harrison, Brian Bell, Willy Wilson, Sam Allingham, Con Platz, Bob Longhouse, Egan Agar, Ed Tann, Reg Heard, Tom McIntyre, Al Jenkins, Pete Davis, Win Corbett, Ralph Gallinger, Doug Dargent, Dusty Miller, Rod Violette, Jake Newlove, Mal Joyce, Len Novakowski, Trev White, Neil Coward, Al Brown and Chet Randall. In front are Arn Bauer, Pete Armstrong, Barney Marsh, Lea Archer, Gene Heggtveit, Gus Garry, Bud Lawrence, Jack Regan and George Ellerbeck. (DND LR82-283-1)

commitment. After a short delay due to dubious weather conditions at Prestwick, W/C Roussell and F/O Strang were airborne at 1020 hrs and the operation was under way. A total of 24 pilots and aircraft were involved and all were soon flying high over Europe's landscape for the last time. En route the weather conditions at Prestwick became unreliable and necessitated the diversion of six aircraft into RNAS Lossiemouth in northeastern Scotland and ten aircraft into RCAF Stn Langar, England. Only the first eight to take off of the 24 aircraft landed at Prestwick.

"Tuesday (5 Mar.) was a typical western Scotland day with low cloud and gale-force winds. The 16 diverted aircraft were unable to reach Prestwick. Finally on Wednesday the weather broke and by 1300 hrs all Triple Four birds had flocked in and were awaiting their horrible fate.

"Later in the afternoon as we boarded the Bristol, all took one last melancholy look at the durable old birds that had served us so well. They were standing like a group of old convicted generals awaiting a firing squad—noble, upright, but with no teeth, victims of two incurable diseases: time and obsolescence.

"We were soon airborne and roaring southward at a breakneck 160 kts.

No.4(F)Wing Squadron Commanders (Sabre Era)

414 Squadron

W/C J.F. "Jack" Allan	Nov.	1952	Feb.	1954
S/L J.R. "Jack" Ritch	May	1954	Apr.	1956
S/L L.J. Liggett	May	1956	Jul.	1957

422 Squadron

S/L W.J. Buzza	Jan.	1953	Jun.	1955
W/C C.C. Lee	Jul.	1955	Jan.	1956
S/L C.C. Magee	Jan.	1956	Dec.	1956
W/C G.G. Wright	Dec.	1956	Jul.	1959
S/L R.G. Murray	Jul.	1959	Aug.	1960
W/C F.J. Kaufman	Sep.	1960	Feb.	1963
W/C P.J.S. Higgs	Mar.	1963	Apr.	1963

444 Squadron

S/L E.R. "Gene" Heggtveit	Mar.	1953	Jul.	1953
S/L John MacKay	Jul.	1953	Sep.	1953
W/C H.F. Darragh*	Jan.	1954	Mar.	1954
S/L J.B. "Bud" Lawrence	May	1954	Jun.	1957
S/L D.F. "Doug" Archer	Jul.	1957	Jan.	1959
S/L E. "Gus" Garry	Jan.	1959	Sep.	1960
W/C R.V. "Roy" Smith*	Sep.	1960	Feb.	1961
S/L Jack Regan	Feb.	1961	Jun.	1961
S/L J. "Joe" Roussell	Aug.	1961	Mar.	1963

No.4(F)Wing Station Commanders (Sabre Era)

G/C R.S. Turnbull	Jul.	1953	Apr.	1955
G/C B.E. Christmas	Apr.	1955	Jul.	1957
G/C R.W. "Buck" McNair	Aug.	1957	Sep.	1961
G/C J.J. Jordan	Sep.	1961	Jul.	1965

*Killed in flying accident

Many an interesting automobile made its appearance among the Air Div wings back in the fifties. Often these were pure status symbols, and various characters became associated with their choice of "style." It is said that more Canadians were killed and maimed with the Air Div in their cars or motorcycles than in airplane accidents. Here is a selection of car photos from those halcyon days: 434 lads, Burrows and Firth, with their lovely Studebaker; a quartet of Swordsmen with their VW; Dale McLarty with a lovely old Mercedes; the inevitable prang, in this case Bob Hallowell's Renault in which he tried to carry 421 mates Dusty Keinholz, Doug Hogan and Scotty McKay to premature graves. Everyone survived, but not without some serious injuries. Finally, 416's "staff car"—a stately old Rolls. (S.E. Burrows, Gerry McCully, H. Hrischenko, via Scotty McKay, Bob Morgan)

Home in Söllingen at 2000 hrs, Sal Siesta was complete. All that remains now is for old Cobras to find their new places in the sun. A large number of our ground crew will be retrained on 104 aircraft and will be remaining at 4 Wing to support the new operation in the same excellent manner as the old. The remainder have returned or will soon be on their way to Canada, populating the new frontier from coast to coast."

Marville

No.1(F)Wing, formerly of North Luffenham, opened for business at Marville April 1, 1955. In anticipation of the move, two squadrons had already left the UK: 410 going to Baden (November 1954-April 1955) and 441 to Zweibrücken (December 1954-March 1955), while 439 remained at North Luff until March 18, 1955. Shortly after settling in at Marville, the wing joined in a vast NATO exercise,

Carte Blanche, June 20-27, with individual squadron participation as follows:

Squadron	Hours Logged	Serviceability
410	294:45	80.2%
439	219:10	80.6%
441	257:20	74.8%

The stated object of Carte Blanche was "to exercise all formations in the type of operations encountered in a major war."

For July, 1 Wing logged 1123:05

BT-495 caught in this outstanding view by F/O Ken Morash. (via L.J. Hill)

A 439 Sabre 6 banks over Marville, home of 1 Wing. (via B. Bristowe)

re-equipping with Sabre 6s, and the first of its 5s were ferried off to Langar pending shipment back to Canada. With 445 about to set up shop at 1 Wing, all 410 pilots were merged with 439 and 441 Squadrons, effective October 1. For September, its last month on Sabres, 410 logged what was perhaps its highest MFR—756:10 hours. Obviously, everyone was going mad to pile up a few last hours on his favourite airplane!

In October 1956, 410 "Cougars" packed up and left Marville, to be replaced by 445 "Wolverines" and its Clunks. The venerable Sabres of 439 and 441 would soldier on into 1963 when replaced by 104s. For the last year of Sabre ops, 1 Wing noted a grand total (including T-bird flight) of 9230 sorties/11,047 flying hours. Of these, 6833 hours were on training and test flights, the remainder on opera-

hours of flying and recorded a serviceability rate of 62 per cent. Wing strength for August was 142 officers and 989 other ranks. Early on, the wing noted its first serious losses, the first appearing to be 23360 in which F/O Easson (439) pranged on landing June 7 (but got away with it). F/O Johnson (441) wracked up 23302 turning final at Marville a few days later. F/O McCallum (410) died June 25 in 23328. He was on a Carte Blanche trip and crashed whilst tangling with a Vampire. He was the wing's first Marville flying fatality.

In June 1956, 410 Squadron began

Sampling of Air Movements, Marville, 1957						
	June	July	August	September	October	November
Takeoffs	1383	1234	1760	1310	1537	1507
Landings	1372	1247	1761	1294	1568	1498

410 "Cougar" Stats, June-November, 1955						
	June	July	August	September	October	November
Aircraft to Strength	15	15	22	24	25	27
Hours Flown	543:55	439:15	439:45	705:50	534:05	546:15

tions. No.1 Wing was the last Air Div wing to visit the Air Weapons Unit at Deci as its Sabres (439) and Clunks closed the base with their visit of November 13-29, 1962. The wing stood its last Zulu alert September 15, 1963. On November 4 that year 439 ferried all its Sabres to Prestwick, and in December a C-130 arrived with Marville's first CF-104.

An example of monthly sorties flown by an Air Division squadron appears in the 410 Squadron "Detail of work carried out" record for July 1955 when 410 was based at Marville flying Sabre 5s.

2 July	2 local training sorties
4 July	13 local training sorties
	1 ferry Hooten Park to Marville
5 July	1 sortie air test
	19 local training sorties
6 July	10 sorties air test
	18 local training sorties
7 July	11 sorties Exercise Barrage
	4 sorties engine derating test
	8 local training sorties
8 July	5 sorties air test
	22 local training sorties
15 July	5 sorties air test
	1 ferry Hooten Park and return
	23 local training sorties
16 July	17 local training sorties
18 July	27 local training sorties
19 July	21 local training sorties
21 July	2 sorties engine derating test
	20 local training sorties
22 July	16 local training sorties
	2 sorties air test
23 July	14 local training sorties
25 July	28 local training sorties
26 July	30 local training sorties
27 July	2 sorties air test
	13 local training sorties
28 July	23 local training sorties
29 July	1 sortie air test
	1 ferry Hooten Park to Marville
	20 local training sorties
30 July	7 local training sorties

Total Sorties: 387

View of part of the 1 Wing complex. (Bill Meuse)

Change of command ceremony at Marville, with 441 and 439 Sabres and personnel smartly lined up to greet VIPs arriving aboard a 412 Squadron Comet. (John Meuse)

The squadron historian best related some of the keynotes of 439's stay at 1 Wing:

The squadron remained in North Luffenham flying their F-86 Mk. 2 Sabres until March 1955, when it was moved to 1(F)Wing Marville, and refitted with new Mk. 5s. This completed the RCAF's build-up of four fighter wings at Söllingen and Zweibrücken, Germany, and Grostenquin and Marville, France. The only major problem encountered was to find a suitable location for the squadrons to carry out their required air-to-air firing practice, and this was initially solved when agreements were completed to use the base in Rabat, Morocco. On August 3, 1955, 439 deployed to Rabat for their first gunnery camp at this new location. The RCAF found that although flying facilities were adequate, it was rather hazardous for Canadians to mix with the seemingly uncivilized Moroccans in Rabat and nearby Casablanca. Since it appeared inevitable that sooner or later a serious incident would occur, negotiations with the Italian and German air forces commenced, and it was decided that the RCAF would pay 25 per cent of the cost to prepare the Italian base in Decimomannu, Sardinia, for air-to-air gunnery.

On August 29 the Canadian Ground Control Radar Interception site commenced operation under the name "Yellow-jack," and until January 1963 was to provide most of the control for the Canadian fighter squadrons during NATO exercises and normal proficiency flying. Although by NATO agreement, the official language to be used in the air was English, it was quite a relief to Canadian pilots to finally have a reliable control agency, which could understand more than the normal English phrases used by all pilots when flying. Also, the controllers at Yellow-jack became extremely proficient in their job, and it was with real regret that the squadrons said farewell to them when the agency

Sabre 5s on a busy January 27, 1956. This snowy scene is a Marville. IG-182 later went to the Luftwaffe, eventually to be broken up in 1961, while '034 survived to become N1046G on the US civil aircraft register. (DND PC1201)

Pilot's view of things as a 439 Sabre starts its takeoff roll at Marville. (B. Bristowe)

closed down in 1963, because the CF-104 aircraft were to be strictly low-level, and thus would not require radar control.

In January 1956 S/L Belleau was transferred back to Canada and S/L Fisher became OC of the squadron. The last refitting with new aircraft was completed in July 1956, when the Sabre 5s were replaced with Sabre 6s. These new aircraft were more powerful, had slatted wings, and at that time were the best day-fighter aircraft in the world. The Tigers in their "Sixes" were kings of the sky in Europe, and much to the disdain of all other air forces in Europe, were practically invincible. Over the remaining years it became almost a status symbol to others if they had photos to prove that they had "wired" a Canadian "Six." The pilots in Air Division were well aware of this fact, and it quickly developed into a point of smudged honour if one of them did get theoretically "shot down" by any aircraft other than another Canadian Sabre. Competition grew fierce among our squadrons. Zulu alert status was held continually throughout the year by two squadrons at a time, meaning that of the eight squadrons each held Zulu one week in four, and normally the same two squadrons were on duty at the same time. For instance 439 was usually on Zulu at the same time as 427 based at Zweibrücken, and practice intercepts with sections of four aircraft from each squadron opposing one another were regularly carried out; destroyed and damaged were kept on film, and at the end of each Zulu the two squadrons compared their claims

with great glee. Since this was the only way in peacetime that the pilots could assess their ability in the airfighting role NATO had given the Canadians, it was with all seriousness that intercepts were carried out, and a high state of proficiency was necessary if a pilot wanted to remain on the squadron, and not be sent back to Canada as unsuitable for day-fighter operations.

By June 1957 the gunnery range in Sardinia was completed, and on the 26th of that month 439 had the distinction of being the first RCAF fighter squadron to go to No.1 Air Weapons Unit Decimomannu for air-to-air firing practice. A minimum average score of 20 per cent was imperative for each pilot according to Air Division rules in order to be considered combat-ready as a day-fighter pilot. There were some misgivings among the squadron pilots as to whether this was possible or not, but everyone managed to hack the program and it was a jolly group of Tigers that returned from their first "camp" to welcome their newly arrived OC S/L Cannon ....

Normal flying commitments included practice intercepts, Zulu, exercises, deployments, night flying, and phase training for new pilots. The following is an excerpt from the squadron diary for the first week of February 1959. "The weather was generally good again this week. The squadron commenced Zulu on Wednesday for another week. The new requirements mean that at best almost every pilot on the squadron is on all day every day, and that aircraft requirements are high. To make it worse this week, six pilots are sick with the flu. Flying was general during the week with the bulk being made up of practice scrambles and night flying. The section of four that went to Renfrew, Scotland, for the weekend finally got back on Wednesday, after being fog-bound for six days. On Friday morning a surprise exercise was laid on. The five-minute Zulu section was scrambled after rejugging with big drops; their mission being to fly to Deci, Sardinia, rendezvous with the flag on the range, and fire all guns. Each aircraft had 260 rounds per gun, and after 12 passes at the flag, the remaining rounds were fired into the ocean. The score was 9.5 per cent with several gun stoppages. The aircraft landed, were turned around and returned to Marville on the same day. F/Os Tidball, Rice, Burke and Coles participated. F/O Jones was able to start phase training with single trips, and F/Os Pope and Jolly became combat-ready after completing their high-level trips. F/O Jim Foy and his wife arrived from Chatham to join the squadron. The week ended with a total of 110 sorties, 137.50 hours.

In April the squadron participated in the full-scale NATO exercise Top Weight, with many different air forces

A neat 24-plane formation flypast at 1 Wing. (Bill Meuse)

and aircraft types taking part. Flying started at noon and continued from dawn to dusk for four days. Maximum effort was achieved with 100 per cent aircraft serviceability throughout. On each of two days all pilots flew four sorties, and the squadron flew 138.10 and 143.45 hours, a record for

a day fighter squadron. Kills were claimed on many types of aircraft, with most of the trips consisting of fighter sweeps and aerodrome defence. The OC, S/L Cannon, came down from one trip, all smiles, and claimed 10 C-119 Flying Boxcars destroyed all by himself, causing numerous caustic comments from the rest of his boys.

S/L Cannon was replaced as OC on June 1, 1959, by S/L Day, DFC, who was to hold office for only a month and a half before tragedy struck. On Friday morning July 19 he took off as number two on a practice scramble, crashed just after getting airborne and was killed. The accident took place approximately two miles off the end of the runway and the aircraft burned. The investigation resulted in an obscure classification, and with much deep regret the squadron pilots attended his funeral in the town of Marville the following Tuesday. F/L Lewis, a flight commander, took over the squadron until October 19, when W/C MacKay reported from Chatham after taking a quick refresher course on Sabres, which he had not flown since a tour of duty in Korea with the USAF, where he scored one MiG destroyed.

Apprehension filled the air in squadron operations again on April 10, 1960, when word was received that F/O Bob Hallworth had been involved in a midair collision with a Sabre from 421 Squadron based at No.2(F)Wing. The accident occurred during an air fighting sortie, and both pilots managed to eject safely, were picked up within minutes by helicopter, and Bob was back on the wing in time to fill out the necessary forms and make it to Friday night beer call.

In July, W/C MacKay left the squadron to become Chief Operations Officer at No.4(F)Wing, the job he had originally been slated for, and S/L J.P. Bell took over control as the new OC. In the same month F/O Jerry Tremblay, the second 439 pilot to be selected for the RCAF's team in the NATO Trophy Shoot, was top man on the team as the RCAF soundly defeated all other air forces for the third year in a row, to further establish Canada's excellent reputation in Europe for producing top-notch fighter pilots .....

In the spring of 1962, No.439 were informed by Air Division, that they had been chosen as the RCAF's ACE Mobility Squadron. This was a NATO commitment (ACE standing for Allied Forces Central Europe), and the squad-

ron was to be prepared at all times to deploy to any NATO country in Europe with as little as 24 hours notice. This news was accepted with much excitement in the squadron, but when rumours of a deployment to Greece continued on for the whole summer, enthusiasm waned quickly. The rumours were finally confirmed in October and on the 4th 20 Sabres took off for Nea Ankhialos, Greece, supported by three Bristols, two Dakotas, 60 ground crew, and five spare pilots. Upon arrival in Greece the squadron was briefed, and told that this was a full-scale NATO exercise involving German, Canadian and Greek air forces, and some 3000 army troops from England, Germany and Greece. The exercise simulated a border skirmish between Greece and the Soviet satellite country Bulgaria,which touches on the northern border of Greece. The day after arrival, the squadron took up alert state from dawn to dusk, and flew fighter sweeps near the border and practice intercepts between their own aircraft. Maximum effort was carried out for eight days, and when the exercise was completed, a weary bunch of pilots climbed onto a Bristol to go to Athens for a relaxing (?) two days before firing up for the return trip to Marville.

The squadron remained the ACE Mobility Squadron until operations ceased in November '63, and although rumours grew of a deployment to Turkey, the only thing that came of it was that every two weeks a section of four Sabres was required to fly to Greece one day and return the next, in order to keep all squadron pilots current on the route at least as far as Nea Ankhialos, which would be a staging base in the event of an exercise in Turkey.

New Year's Day 1963 brought with it the beginning of a scheduled change of aircraft in Air Division with the replacement of the now-obsolete F-86 and CF-100 with new CF-104s. All four CF-100 squadrons were officially disbanded on New Year's Day, followed by Nos. 427 and 434 Sabre squadrons based at Zweibrücken. This posed a tremendous manpower placement problem for Air Division, and it was decided that all the CF-100 pilots would return to Canada, except for a few who were given jobs at headquarters in Metz. Since the Sabre squadrons would be disbanded gradually from January, when the first two went, until November, it was decided that pilots

Air transport support for the Air Division in the fifties was provided first and foremost by the Canadair North Star (these two seen over Montreal), the ungainly-looking Bristol Freighter, the venerable Dakota (this one at Toul) and, later on, the C-130 Hercules and the Yukon. This Herc is seen about to alight at Marville, the Yukon at Trenton. (DND via J.S. Parmelee, Harry Tate via K.M. Molson, D.W. Menard, Bill Meuse, Larry Milberry)

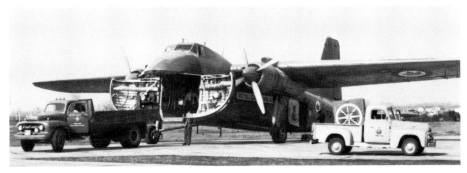

would be shifted about from squadron to squadron in an attempt to transfer pilots who had been serving with a squadron for three years back to Canada, and replace them with pilots who had been in Europe for only a short time.

No.439, which was to be the last squadron to disband, was thus destined to finish its operational role with a combination of pilots from every other squadron in Air Division. The "Tigers" received this news with numerous misgivings, because they felt that with competition among Sabre squadrons as high as it was, there was a good possibility that the high morale, which 439 had always been proud of, might suffer considerably. This small fear was quickly dispelled, however, with the arrival of W/C St. Louis (ex. 427 Sqn. OC) in January as the new commanding officer replacing W/C Bell. He immediately informed other new squadron pilots that they were not to forget that they were now an integral part of 439, and that their utmost co-operation was fully expected and demanded. Morale over the last 11 months of operation remained very high indeed, and as it turned out, the feared defeat turned into a rousing victory, because the combination of fresh blood and new ideas kept everyone on their toes right to the end. The standard operating procedures were placed under close scrutiny by every new pilot, and it became impossible to "spout" procedures without being able to back up a statement with logical fact. Many improvements were introduced right to the end, and if anything, morale soared rather than diminished.

Fang

F/L Bill Norn reports on some of his Air Division days while serving with 439 Squadron:

About 3:30 one afternoon two Sabres were ready for air tests. This meant a functional test, not a full check. I

439ers with Fang, the squadron mascot. Seated are F/O Johnson, F/O Wilkinson, F/L Bourgeois, S/L Sauder, W/C St. Louis, F/L McIlraith, F/L Keith and F/O Barrett. Standing are F/L Jacques, F/O Simons, F/O Speltt, F/L Palmer, F/O Armstrong, F/O Saunders, F/O Houston, F/L McGrath, F/O Schaan, F/O McKibbin, F/O Dun, F/O Charles, F/L DiMarco, F/L Christensen, F/O Bristowe and F/O Groskorth. Such was the squadron's pilot strength in the autumn of 1963. (via B. Bristowe)

booked the aircraft out, and F/L Norm Smith came along as my wing man. The Sabres were clean (no tanks) and we headed out towards Paris. We were approaching Rheims and still in the climb when we spotted a section of four Sabres at about 42,000. We switched to a quiet radio channel so we wouldn't be heard as we moved in. Building our speed, we pulled up beneath the section and dropped into firing range at six o'clock. Suddenly our quarry spotted us and called for a break to starboard. We were on an adjoining channel, and there was sufficient feed-through for us to overhear their chatter. Their lead and No.2 maintained their heading, and Nos.3 and 4 pulled hard right and down out of the fight. We continued and took film of our two targets. We then broke off in a steep dive to the left, and rolled over at reduced power to drop into line astern with Nos.3 and 4, who were struggling to regain altitude to assist Nos.1 and 2.

Nos.3 and 4 were carving around in a right turn as we took a quick pass at them, then broke off and headed for home. The noise on the R/T was terrible from the other section as they tried to figure out what had happened, and the leader called, "Get those bastards, follow them." Of course, we overheard that too, and I signalled my No.2 to lead and take us home.

We had taken off at full throttle and left our power at max. cruise, continuing at full power in our return to base. There was a cloud deck at about 4000 feet, extending about 40 miles between us and base, and we headed for this cover. We picked up our speed and could hear our pursuers behind. They were falling back, unable to keep up on account of their drop tanks. We were now dusting along at about .93, and as we flattened out for our approach we called for clearance to a circuit for landing. At the same time we popped our speed brakes. The ride down to circuit height was pretty exciting as we dropped under the cloud cover. At high speed we entered an area of increased moisture which produced an envelope of cloud over both aircraft. It was neces-

A flight of "Sabre Tooth Tigers" skims the cloud tops. F/O Bill Bristowe flying 23704 (DND)

No.1(F)Wing Station Commanders (Sabre Era)				S/L C.J. Day	Jun.	1959 - Jul.	1959*
G/C E.B. "Ed" Hale	Nov.	1951 - Aug.	1953	W/C J. MacKay	Oct.	1959 - Jun.	1960
G/C J.D. "Red" Somerville	Aug.	1953 - Jul.	1956	W/C J.P. Bell	Jul.	1960 - Dec.	1962
G/C D.J. "Blacky" Williams	Jul.	1956 - Jun.	1959	W/C P.B. "Pete" St. Louis	Jan.	1963 - Nov.	1963
G/C D.P. Hall	Jun.	1959 - Aug.	1963	*441 Squadron*			
				S/L A.R. "Andy" MacKenzie	Mar.	1951 - Nov.	1952
No.1(F)Wing Squadron Commanders (Sabre Era)				S/L W.T.H. Gill	Feb.	1953 - Mar.	1954
410 Squadron				S/L D.R. Cuthbertson	Mar.	1954 - Sept.	1956
S/L L.A. "Larry" Hall	Dec.	1949 - Apr.	1952	S/L A.W. Fisher	Oct.	1956 - Dec.	1956
S/L Douglas "Duke" Warren	May	1952 - Aug.	1954	S/L L.J. "Lou" Hill	Dec.	1956 - Aug.	1959
S/L A.W. Fisher	Aug.	1954 - Oct.	1956	W/C H. McLachlan	Aug.	1959 - Jul.	1961
439 Squadron				W/C D.A.B. Smiley	Jul.	1961 - Jun.	1963
S/L C.D. "Cal" Bricker	Sept.	1951 - Jul.	1953	S/L E.L. Arnold	Jun.	1963 - Aug.	1963
S/L J.H.M. Belleau	Jul.	1953 - Apr.	1956	S/L L.C. Price	Aug.	1963 - Sept.	1963
S/L D.J. Bullock	Apr.	1956 - Jan.	1957				
S/L R.Y. Cannon	Jul.	1957 - May	1959	*Killed in flying accident			

sary to hang on closer than ever. We broke into the downwind leg of the circuit, slowed to 185K, dropped our gear and called for landing clearance. We spaced ourselves in the final turn and landed. Total trip time was 18 minutes. As we touched down and taxied in, we heard the tower call for someone to get the numbers of those aircraft now cutting through the circuit. They belonged to 441, our companion squadron at the wing.

We parked our aircraft, charged into the mess and had a beer. After a short time, the leader whose section we had bounced came into the bar and asked who had been hassling them. We burst out laughing as he told us he'd been up with a section on phase training, that is, with new squadron pilots. They had really had some trip! It turned out that

two of their Sabres had been over-stressed, and two split their drop tanks in the ensuing dive and chase behind us.

In November 1958 the Prime Minister visited 2 Wing, and each squadron in the Air Div provided 12 aircraft. We lined up in impressive fashion on the taxiway as the PM made his drive past. After the review, we were all off again and, of course, made an air fighting exercise out of our return to base. As many power units as could be mustered were hauled out to start 96 aircraft. As we started, we pulled onto the runway in sections of four. There were 12 aircraft on the runway at a time as the lead sections rolled ahead for takeoff and the next four pulled into position to follow.

All 96 aircraft started and took off. Not a single one went u/s or had to abort. There was cloud at 5000 agl and when we climbed through it we were fair game for those already airborne. It was a most exciting day, and I don't think it was ever repeated—96 aircraft launched in about 20 minutes.

In those days we at 439 used to say to

other squadron pilots, "How would you like to see our squadron crest? You've probably never seen it before since it's on our tails and we're usually on your six o'clock!" We Sabre pilots were a different lot. Flew hard, played hard. We were extremely competitive, loyal squadron supporters, and were backed by professional ground crew. We flew in the best squadrons, in the best fighting unit, No.1 Air Division, in the best air force in the world. And we enjoyed every minute of it.

W.H. "Bill" Norn

On February 4, 1957, 23581 crashed on a routine flight from Marville. F/O F.P. Luettger of 439 Squadron made a miraculous escape at low level just before his Sabre ploughed in. His narrative of the event makes exciting reading: "On a recent engine failure I was forced to eject at very low altitude. I feel that by writing exactly what happened and what I feel made my ejection successful I may in some way ease the minds of some pilots on ejection, mainly at low altitude.

A Clunk (445 Squadron) and Sabre (441 Squadron) bracket a 96 Squadron Meteor N.F.11 from RAF Ahlhorn *circa* 1957. The N.F.11 was a stop-gap all-weather fighter, pending arrival on squadron of the Javelin. It didn't even come with ejection seats. By comparison, the Clunk was a real Cadillac! (via Lou J. Hill)

"I was number one in a two-plane formation and upon returning to base followed number two around on a practice forced landing. The practice forced landing was carried out successfully and I told number two to overshoot and we would join up and pitch. I came over the end of the runway at approximately 140 knots, applied full power and cleaned the aircraft up. At approximately three-quarters of the way down the runway at approximately 220 knots I started a steep climbing turn to the left. At approximately 50 to 100 feet above ground my engine exploded and caught on fire. At this time I lost all my thrust. I immediately informed my number two that my engine had quit and that I was bailing out.

"I ejected the canopy by the alternate ejection handle. I have always believed that this would force me to lower my head. I was struck very heavily by the canopy due to the over-shoulder radio cord which has since been removed from Sabre aircraft. I pulled up both handles and was very surprised when I did not get ejected. I realized instantly that I had to squeeze the trigger, which I did with my right hand. I released my lap strap before ejection and placed my left hand in the parachute 'D' ring. I did not have an automatic parachute. I did not have my feet in the stirrups. I was doubled over at the time of ejection to make sure that I could find the trigger. I do not remember the actual ejection but eyewitnesses say that I was parting from the seat when the seat was leaving the aircraft and that my chute was streaming while I was still going up from the force of ejection. My parachute was open before I realized what had happened.

"From the time my engine exploded till I hit the ground everything I did was automatic. It was four seconds from the time my engine quit till my chute opened and there isn't any time to think."

In the 1 Wing move to the continent, the 441 "Silver Foxes" went initially to Zweibrücken in November 1954, sharing facilities with 434. They didn't get into Marville, until March 1955, and it was another month before 441 was completely settled. Meanwhile the first 441 Sabre 5 had been flown January 3 by F/L Fine. Throughout spring and summer, aircraft were being ferried to Hooten Park for camouflaging. No more the gaudiness of Sabre 2 days!

Some 441 types: Kurt Barlow (EO), Roy Barnes, Bud McLeod, Larry Sutton, Dan Lambros, Casey Chapman, Larry Spurr, Scotty Campbell and Lou Hill. (DND)

In August 441 was on temporary detachment at Florennes, Belgium, 12 aircraft being involved, but midway through the exchange 441 was ordered home. Polio had broken out with two pilots affected. The visiting *Belgiques* were quarantined for 30 days at Marville. In the fall there was a deployment to Rabat, where 441 registered the top trophy shoot for the Air Div for 1955—34.88 per cent. The first 441 Zulu alert was stood in December. The following July, 441 again went to Rabat. The diary notes that on the 18th a North Star flew to Rabat but that the Swords couldn't get in that day due to headwinds and didn't arrive till the 22nd.

In August the first Sabre 6s arrived on squadron. As usual, there was an interim period with 441 when it flew both 5s and 6s, until the last 5 was ferried away. With the opening of Deci there were no more Rabat trips, and 441 made its first visit to Sardinia in September 1957. The trip was made non-stop, thanks to use of the "big jugs"—the 167-gal. drop tanks.

The 441 squadron book contains a reminiscent look at Deci:

Aside from the operational aspect of this twice yearly trip to Sardinia it was a welcome relief from the ever present Zulus at Marville, and seemed to be sort of a regular holiday by the Mediterranean Sea. It was true that the climate would be hot and tropical during the summer, damp and miserable in the fall and downright cold and uncomfortable in the winter. Bedding seldom dried out, hamburgers were made from old donkeys, local farmers guarded their tempting lemon field with cactus fences and loud shotguns and work started early in the morning and ended sometimes late at night. Off-duty hours, though, presented an opportunity to board an Italian bus (an experience in itself) and go into the capital city of Cagliari. There one could eat spaghetti, drink Chianti, shop for sweaters, lie on one of the nicest beaches in Europe and acquire a marvellous sunburn in the summer. Sitting on the Via Roma watching the short Sardinians stroll by we could while away hours, especially when sitting behind a large bottle of the dubious Ichanussa beer. Few people will ever forget these deployments. Those who were fortunate to have participated in these camps for the past several years will remember when the housing area was situated two or three kilometres from the airfield at a place christened "Old Barrack Village" and when early morning shifts were escorted to work by a not-so-fierce-looking but ever-present armed guard, supposedly to scare off roaming Banditos.

Amongst the old timers, Old Barrack Village has probably produced more fond memories than any area or part of the camp. First let's have an outside view of this haven. Try to picture a group of grey stucco buildings settled amongst a grove of grey bitter olive trees, surrounded by an ever-alert fence of prickly pear cactus, cut here and there by the odd dusty path or roadway. Add a half a dozen hammocks strung between the trees plus two or three empty beer cans in every spot of shade along with empty Chianti bottles decorating the window sills. Maybe a few scampering lizards in view at all times. A half dozen garbage pails overflowing most of the time seemingly left at random.

Do you have a sort of picture now? Okay, if so take a few airmen and place them lying about in the dress of the day. This usually consisted of a dusty pair of boots topped by a pair of heavy grey wool socks, fatigue pants cut at various lengths, yellow, blue or white tee-shirts and shielded by a pith hat that could have the name or initial of every character who has worn it since the camp originated. All this and more, guarded night and day by the ever *trustworthy* Italian guard who impressed you with inexperience, irresponsibility and a general carefree attitude that would sober you up at the sound of the bolt of his gun being repositioned.

441 Squadron history

441 participated in on-going exchanges as the years passed. From time to time it shipped four Sabres to Rygge, Norway, as four Norwegians took their place on the ramp at Marville. These were one-week stints; on longer ones ground crew were also exchanged, thus becoming familiar with NATO counterparts. Various countries were involved. On June 30, 1958, for instance, 441 deployed to Pferdsfeld, Germany. In October 1961 it spent a week at Rocroi, France, an RCAF alternate airfield where everything was under canvas.

Summary of Flying, 1 Wing Instrument Flight (T-33s), August 1957

	hours
T-33 air tests, comm flts, local flying	53:05
T-33 instrument flying with 439	42:25
,, ,, ,, ,, 441	40:00
,, ,, ,, ,, 445	24:25
,, ,, ,, ,, Wing	33:00
C-45	16:25
Simulator	58:00
Aircraft on Strength: 7 x T-33,1 x C-45	
Pilots on Strength: 6	
Total Flying Time: 209:20	
Instrument Ratings Renewed: 7	
Accidents: nil	

Two mishaps of 441 Sabres. On May 2, 1957, F/O H.A. Davidson suffered a flame out in 23530 and attempted a glide back into base. When he realized that he wasn't going to make it, he ejected, but too low, and was killed. His Sabre then landed intact by itself. The second photo shows the ruins of F/O Tom Koch's Sabre after his landing accident at Marville in late 1959. (via Jim Lyzun, T. Koch)

Air Division Sabre Squadrons Replaced by CF-100 Squadrons

Sabres	Wing	CF-100 Replacements	Misc.				
410 Squadron	1	445 Squadron	410 to NORAD with CF-100s, Nov. 1956				
416 ,,	2	423 ,,	416 ,, ,, ,, ,,			Feb.	1957
413 ,,	3	440 ,,	413 ,, ,, ,, ,,			May	1957
414 ,,	4	419 ,,	414 ,, ,, ,, ,,			Aug.	1957

Air Officers Commanding No. 1 Air Division (Sabre era)

A/V/M Hugh L. Campbell	Dec. 1952	Aug. 1955
A/V/M H.B. Godwin	Aug. 1955	Aug. 1958
A/V/M L.E. "Larry" Wray	Sep. 1958	Jul. 1963

A Rabat Portfolio

Gunnery camp snaps. From top left: maintenance on a 413 Mark 5; a French Hellcat and P-47 with Air Div Sabres in two ''time warp'' snaps; F/Os Cliff Zacharias, Stu Oliver, Harry Stroud and Johnny Johnson at the beach; a 421 mob scene; 434 at volleyball; and Bob Henderson and ''WAC'' Wilson, WAC in running shoes just down from drogue-towing over the Med. (W.A.C. Wilson, Ken Hagarty, Wilson, Wilson, via Charles Moffat, P.S. Perry, Wilson)

More of Rabat. From the right: "T-Bar" Millar; standard issue to pilots, Arab "blood chit"; Cobra pilots Trev White, Rocky Redman (with mascot, El Moghrabi), Barry Smith, Al Brown, Len Fitzsimmons and Ken McLeod; 414 turn-around, with F/O Harry Hrischenko; F/Os Redman and Brown with little "Elmo", who was later fatally stung by a scorpion; and Sgt Phil Perry with one of the Rabat kiddies. (S.E. Burrows, next two via A.C. Brown, DND, via Brown, P.S. Perry)

RESTRICTED

الحكومة البريطانية   BRITISH GOVERNMENT

الى كل عربي كريم

السلام عليكم ورحمة الله وبركاته وبعد ، نحامل هذا الكتاب ضابط بالجيش البريطاني وهو
صديق وفيّ لكافة الشعوب العربية . فنرجو أنْ تعاملوه بالعطف والاكرام ، وأن محافظوا على
حياته من كل طارىء . ونأمل عند الاضطرار أن تقدموا له ما محتاج اليه من طعام وشراب ، وأن
ترشدوه الى أقرب معسكر بريطاني ، وسنكافئكم مالياً إسخاء على ما تسدونه اليه من خدمات .
والسلام عليكم ورحمة الله وبركاته

القيادة البريطانية العامة في الشرق الاوسط

To All Arab Peoples — Greetings and Peace be upon you.   The bearer of this letter is an Officer of the British Government and a Friend of all Arabs. Treat him well, guard him from harm, give him food and drink, help him to return to the nearest British soldiers and you will be rewarded. Peace and the Mercy of God upon you.

The British High Command in the East.

SOME POINTS ON CONDUCT WHEN MEETING THE ARABS IN THE DESERT.

Remove footwear on entering their tents. Completely ignore their women. If thirsty drink the water they offer, but DO NOT fill your waterbottle from their personal supply. Go to their well and fetch what you want. Never neglect any puddle or other water supply for topping up your bottle. Use the Halazone included in your Aid Box. Do not expect breakfast, if you sleep the night. Arabs will give you a mid-day or evening meal. Always be courteous.

REMEMBER, NEVER TRY AND HURRY IN THE DESERT, SLOW AND SURE DOES IT.

A few useful words.			
English	Arabic	English	Arabic
English	Ingleezi	Day	Yome
American	Amerikani	Night	Layl
Friend	Sa-hib, Sa-deck	Half	Nuss
Water	Moya	Half a day	Nuss il Yome
Food	Aki or Mungarea	Near	Gareeb
Village	Balaad	Far	Baeed
Tired	Ta-eban		
Take me to the English and you will be rewarded.		Hud nee eind el Ingleez wa fahud Mu-ka-fa.	
English Flying Officer.		Zabit Ingleezi Tye-yara.	
How far (how many kilos?)		Kam kilo ?	

Distance and time: Remember, Slow & Sure does it.

The older Arabs cannot read, write or tell the time. They measure distance by the number of days journey. "Near" may mean 10 minutes or 10 hours. Far probably means over a days journey. A days journey is probably about 30 miles. The younger Arabs are more accurate.
GOOD LUCK.

FRENCH

Cher Ami,

Je suis aviateur britannique. Je ne suis pas venu ici pour vous faire du mal, à vous autres qui êtes mes amis.

Je suis ici par hasard parce qu'un accident est arrivé à mon avion.

Si vous voulez bien m'aider mon gouvernement vous recompensera suffisament aussitôt que je serai retourné sain et sauf.

F/O A.C. Brown 444 (F) Sqn.

RESTRICTED

Air Div sharpshooters at RNAS Brawdy in Wales for a gunnery shoot in April 1955: Unknown, RN with dog, Bill Stewart, Gerry Westphal, Bill Norn, Bob Paul, John Ursulak, RN Station Commander, George Miller, Hank Henry, Gerry McCully, RN, Bill Casley (EO). (RN via Gerry McCully)

Sharp Shooters

When you come right down to it, the best fighter pilot is the one who can shoot best. In Europe during the fifties, with every country, "good guys and bad guys," fairly bristling with fighter squadrons, the very best were the Canadians. Year after year in NATO they walked away with whatever gunnery trophies were going. In particular, they seemed to have a monopoly on the coveted Guynemer Trophy, named for France's great First World War fighter ace, Georges Guynemer.

For several years starting in 1958, NATO's best fighter pilots would meet at a French base, Cazaux, near Bordeaux, for gruelling shoots to determine the Guynemer winner. There were Hunters, Super Sabres, Thunderstreaks, Mystères and, to the dismay of all, the Canadair F-86s flown by the pilots of the Air Division, ready, willing and consistently able to "wax

the fannies" of all challengers. It got so maddening for other NATO teams that one NATO air force spent an entire year especially training a team to compete at Cazaux but still was whipped by the Canadians. After one day of firing on the drogue, a lone Canadian pilot had personally scored higher than the entire team from one of the other NATO air forces.

Not only were the Canadians merciless in the air. On the ground they were "bad actors." Apparently one day at Cazaux the French gun plumbers had been harmonizing the guns of one of their Mystères and had knocked off for

lunch, when some Canadians drove by the butts and noticed the Mystère sitting unattended. One of them hopped out, dashed over to the target in front of the Mystère and moved it, ever so slightly but just enough to make sure that the hapless French pilot couldn't hit the proverbial barn door later that afternoon.

The 1959 Guynemer Trophy is presented by A/V/M L.E. "Larry" Wray, AOC No.1 Air Division, to Ron MacGarva. Others from the left are Dave Barker, Bill Norn, Bill Casley (EO between Wray and MacGarva), Unknown, Alf McDonald and Bill "Kiwi" McArthur. (DND PL122715)

The 1959 edition of the Air Div's Guynemer team included F/O David Barker (4 Wing), F/O Bill McArthur (spare 4 W), F/L Alf McDonald (3 W), F/L Ron MacGarva (team leader, 1 W) and F/L Bill Norn. McDonald notes that the rules were simple: "Each pilot flew three trips. Each trip he carried 100 rounds in two guns only, and was allowed two passes only on the drogue. Two twizzle manoeuvres were made at 35,000 feet to record tracking consistency. These were, of necessity, recorded on camera, and if the film magazine jammed you got a goose egg."

Competing that August at Cazaux were seven other teams, two RAF, two French, one each Belgian, Dutch and USAF. In the end, Barker won top individual score for the entire competition. Norn took second, and McDonald third. Final team scores for the leaders were: 1st, RCAF, 1697.8 points: 2nd, RAF, 1427.2; 3rd, RAF Germany, 1075.2; 4th, French Tactical Air Command, 973.05. The others in order were the Belgians, Dutch, French ADC and USAF Central Europe.

The Air Div reigned supreme again at the 1960 trophy meet. They made it three in a row so far as the Guynemer went, scoring 1397.7 points. Second place went to the RAF Germany (1257.8), third to RAF Fighter Command (1240.5) and fourth to the Belgians (1234.5). The three top individual scorers were F/O McMullen of 427 Squadron (355.3 points), F/O McArthur of 422 (352.5) and Adj. François

Bedard of Belgium (344.6). Also at Cazaux in 1960 were teams from Denmark and Holland.

F/L Bill Norn was on three Air Div gunnery teams and relates some events of that period:

I was posted to 439 Squadron in November 1956. At the time, S/L D. Bullock was OC. We flew endless training missions, and most were air fighting exercises against other RCAF squadrons. Having been at Chatham, I knew most of the Air Div pilots at the time. As squadron weapons officer, I prepared and worked the pilots into our gunnery deployment exercises which we carried out at Sardinia. 439 would deploy there as a unit and be ready for live firing the next morning. Overnight the big ferry tanks had to be removed and stored, guns sighted and checked, and fuel and support facilities readied. Besides our yearly deployment to Sardinia, I also worked with 445, our Marville Clunk squadron, to qualify its pilots on gun firing as per the F-86 deployments. The Clunk proved a good and stable gun platform.

In March 1957 the Air Division was invited to compete in a gunnery shoot with 4ATAF, and F/L John Ursulak was chosen team leader. The others on the team were F/Os Hank Henry, Bob Paul, Gerry Westphal and myself. Gerry was spare. We would be competing against French and USAF teams at Cazaux. Just before deployment, we had an eight-day work-up at RNAS Brawdy in South Wales, the only live-firing range available to us at the time. We were able to get in an average of only 12 live shoots before the actual meet. That really wasn't enough to check out the sights and harmonization.

The Air Div, having cleaned up at Cazaux in 1958 and 1959, continued their winning ways in 1960. Here (kneeling) in front of a 422 Sword are Bill McArthur (422 Squadron), Richard Spencer (430), Alan McMullen (427) (team leader). Behind are Gerard Tremblay (439) and Neil Granley (444). (DND PL127960)

At Cazaux we were very well cared for by the French and Americans. The Americans were really taken by our aircraft, and the French were in awe of our scores. When one of our flags was being scored—and it showed a good score—a French pilot asked John Ursulak how he had managed to register so many hits. He answered that he just put the pipper on the bottom left corner of the flag and slowly slid it ahead of the bull as he completed his pass. The Frenchman replied that he felt lucky if he was even able to get the pipper on the flag at all, let alone track the aiming point!

Quick turn around. Pilots wait as the ground crew services a Sabre at Cazaux. Everyone who flew the Sabre is unanimous that it was their ground crew who were the heart of the RCAF's outstanding day fighter operation in the fifties and early sixties. (DND PL127953)

The three shoots I took part in were the 4th ATAF and 1st and 2nd AIR-CENT international firing competitions. With these meets, all sorts of rules were included by the various teams so that each might gain some advantages here and there, but basically four aircraft had to complete a mission, then be scored by target hits vs rounds loaded. So for a good score all rounds had to be fired, and gun stoppages were critical. All missions had to have cine film back-up to determine opening firing range and closing range so that no fouls were made, and to show that the angle-off the target at the time of firing was within limits. A film breakage or misfeed could cost the mission.

The second and third shoots were for the Guynemer Trophy. On them, in addition to the live shoot, we flew a cine tracking exercise. This was scored as a separate mission and was included in the pilot's average for the meet. The actual shoot was judged by a T-33 trailing the flag at a safe distance. The T-bird was there mainly to observe that all firing rules were adhered to. Fifty rounds were loaded for each of two

The Air Div team's tail logo as used at the 1957 gunnery meet at Cazaux. It was designed by the team's EO and ground crew. (Bill Norn)

guns to be fired during the 4th ATAF meet. The other two in which I participated carried 25 rounds in each of two guns. We were allowed three passes at the flag, one being a spacer pass. My first two shoots were done at 20,000 feet, the third at 30,000.

The key factor at each meet was our ground crew. They took a very personal interest in all activity, and it was indeed a pleasure to work with such dedicated specialists. The EO on all three shoots was S/L Bill Casley from 1 Wing.

W.H. "Bill" Norn

BGen W.H. "Bill" Casley served as EO and EO/team leader on three Guynemer meets and writes:

I went to the Air Div in 1956 after five years in Ottawa as RCAF project engineer on the Orenda engine, being involved in its development and installation in CF-100s and Sabre 5s and 6s. Soon after joining 441 Squadron, I checked out on the T-33 and Sabre and subsequently did a fair amount of maintenance test flying on the Sabre, so that I knew the aircraft pretty well. And what a beautiful flying machine it was, especially the Mk. 6.

With this background, I was asked

to pick a team of 36 technicians from the four wings, while Johnny Ursulak chose the team of eight pilots. We formed up in 1957 at Marville for initial shakedown, then deployed to RNAS Brawdy for live firing (at the time the RCAF had moved from Rabat but had not yet opened the Deci range). The RN came through in spades—our stay there was enjoyable and productive, and we deployed over to Cazaux in good form.

For the 1957 meet our pilots and ground crew put up a highly professional show. Each event required a team of five aircraft to taxi out at a precise time, with four taking off to complete the shoot. The spare was probably the most frustrated person, as he spent his time taxiing to the runway, then returning to the flight line as his compatriots took off.

Our support crew took great pride witnessing the RCAF Sabres returning in a tight box, then making a precise formation landing. Most of all, we experienced much satisfaction as the RCAF flag was displayed for the judges to make the official score count. It quickly became clear that the Canadians were the team to beat, and, as the competition progressed, they became the leaders in terms of aircraft readiness, air-to-air gunnery and overall professional ability.

In these shoots, though all our pilots were outstanding, F/O Hank Henry stood out. He was "a natural" in the

Sabre and, regardless of which aircraft he flew, his scores were always impressive. I remember the flag on which the Canadian team of four averaged 54 per cent, with Henry shooting an unbelievable 95 per cent. Henry remarked to F/L Bill Norn that, as low gun (something over 40 per cent), it was his duty to roll up the flag!

To me, the performance of these pilots was typical of the effectiveness of the Air Division. With the Sabre 5s and 6s they rode the best fighters in Europe, and each squadron was blessed with a number of very experienced pilots, backed by a competent support organization. Truly, those were the Golden Years and everyone who was involved looks back on them with great fondness.

The subsequent shoots followed essentially the same pattern as the first, except for the introduction of air-to-air

cine gun work at high altitude. This was undoubtedly introduced to offset the advantage the RCAF had with the Sabre, but once again our pilots came through with outstanding performances. I well recall attending a meeting

F/O Burnell Reid, F/O John Swallow, F/L Carl Bertrand, F/O Douglas Dargent, F/O Charles Winegarden and (team captain) F/L Russel Challoner—the 1962 Guynemer Trophy team while practicing at Deci. (DND)

Air Div Swords during the 1961 shoot at Leeuwarden, Holland. (Archiv G. Joos)

Sabre and CF-100 overhaul for the Air Division was carried out mainly by Scottish Aviation at Prestwick. Here both types are seen. On the dolly (centre left) is a CF-100 belly gun pack. Later, the same contractor was to scrap most Air Div fighters. A good, all-round package deal! (Scottish Aviation)

of the rules committee chaired by Air Chief Marshal Sir Harry Broadhurst (RAF) where the various team representatives asked for rules changes that would be to their advantage. The RCAF rep remained silent until Sir Harry asked if he had any request. All the Canadian cared to know was, "Sir, what time tomorrow is the first flag?" This collapsed the whole meeting! The RCAF, under F/L Ron MacGarva, won comfortably in both 1958 and 1959.

Looking back with the benefit of hindsight, there is no doubt in my mind that the tremendous performance of the Canadian team resulted from the use of a superb aircraft flown by very experienced fighter pilots supported by a well trained and disciplined ground crew—each man on the team proficient in his trade and dedicated to winning. It was a combination which proved unbeatable.

W.H. "Bill" Casley

In July 1960, S/L Duke Warren was transferred as COpsO to Decimomannu.

Deci was a tri service gunnery base on Sardinia used by the Italians, Canadians and Germans. It seems that the AOC of the Air Division thought I was just the man for the job, and he

put it this way: "You got along well with the Germans. Now let's see how you do with the Italians." In my first month at Deci I managed 13 sorties in the F-86 and three in the T-33. It was at this time that the RCAF squadrons in Europe had the finest gunnery teams.

The position had its problems, and I often felt caught in the middle with both Italian and German personnel coming at me with flying problems. My CO, W/C W. Middleton, had similar problems with the Italian base commander and German detachment commander. One persistent technical problem we had was with the radio failures. When the tower was u/s you had Sabres, F-84s, G.91s and even the occasional North Star all milling around and acting like mid-air collisions looking for a place to happen.

The chief controller had early on assured me that whenever the power failed there was a stand-by generator that would automatically cut in. One day we had a North Star which had been forced to circle extra long. I became impatient and stormed up to the tower to protest. "Show me what happens when the power fails," I insisted. The controller explained, "We send a man out to start the generator." "But you said it was automatic," I protested. "Yes," he said, "we automatically send a man out to start the generator."

I am telling the truth when I say that the failures were directly the result of the tower radios and the expresso machine in the canteen being on the same circuit. When they were both in use, the circuit-breaker popped! In

August 1961 I returned to Canada to a posting in Flight Safety. I was able to get the occasional Sabre trip from Uplands, but the Sabres there were eventually withdrawn. I finished my Sabre flying days with 840 hours on type.

I often look back to my Sabre career, to the days when the RCAF Air Division was *the* foremost fighter force in Europe, and when RCAF pilots were renowned for their gunnery, and when to be CO of a Sabre squadron was the highest honour a fighter pilot could have.

Douglas Warren

Controller 10: The GCA Story
In 1952 Bob Durnan of Toronto joined the RCAF. At first he trained as a firefighter, then changed to the air frame trade. Finally, in 1954, he took the flying control course at the old BCATP station at Grand Bend, Ontario. His first posting was to Downsview, and in 1957 he was transferred to Marville, where 439 and 441 Squadrons were based with Sabres, and 445 was flying CF-100s. Durnan, who was Controller 10, describes the importance of GCA (ground controlled approach) to the RCAF in Europe:

GCA is a landing aid whereby a controller uses radar to talk pilots down in bad weather. The GCA unit consisted of two trailers situated beside the runway about halfway between the approach ends. One trailer housed the auxiliary diesel generators, the other the radar and controllers. There were

A mixed bag of RCAF Sabres at Prestwick for servicing in the late fifties and early sixties. Each carries its distinctive squadron badge: AP-580 of 413, 23548 of 421, 23429 of 422, BB-560 of 427, BH-668 of 430, and 23640 of 441, showing slats deployed for landing. (all via Roger Lindsay, except 23548 Wilf G. White)

three controller's positions, each with two radar scopes. One scope was the PPI (plan position indicator), the other the PAR (precision approach radar). The PPI was atop the PAR and gave a plan view of the area surrounding the station. Its scale could be changed from 5 miles to 30 miles for solid returns (blips), and 200 miles for electronic returns (squawks). We used the PPI to direct aircraft onto the PAR for final approach, but it could also be used for a non-precision approach. On a PPI final the pilot was given steers to maintain a centreline, and he was told his distance from the runway and the altitude he should be passing through. Using this information the pilot would adjust his rate of descent to maintain a three-degree glidepath. As it was not as accurate as PAR, the limits were higher. If he was not visual at 500 feet/1 mile, the pilot was required to carry out a missed approach procedure by climbing to a prescribed altitude and homing to a radio beacon. He could then try again or land elsewhere, depending on his fuel. Because of its limitations, the PPI approach was only used when the PAR was unavailable. The PAR was so accurate that we often brought aircraft in well below limits of 200 feet/$1/2$ mile.

The PAR consisted of two scopes in one. The upper indicator had an electronic inscribed glidepath, and range marks, while the lower had a centreline and range marks. At 10 miles from the runway and a few degrees either side of the centreline, the aircraft would enter the PAR. The controller would give the pilot steers to maintain the centreline, tell him when to start down, then ask for changes in rate of descent to maintain the glidepath. Once on the glidepath, the controller would begin a con-

Always a sad sight for old timers in the Sabre business. A few tons of scrap is all that these once splendid RCAF Sabres ended up as on the British scrap metal market. Seen at Prestwick on August 13, 1963. (Gordon Macadie via Roger Lindsay.)

tinuous talkdown which, if interrupted for five seconds, would require the pilot to execute a missed approach procedure.

Periodically, the controllers had to undergo flight tests. These consisted of two normal approaches and one emergency. If he was not sharp, the controller could be assigned higher limits or have his limits taken away. Unfortunately a few controllers could not take the strain and were taken out of Europe.

We called an approach "a run," and used three letdown procedures: a beacon approach, a GCI/GCA handoff and a square pattern. On the beacon approach the pilots would descend from the beacon, start a turn toward the runway at a prescribed altitude and call GCA. We would pick them up on the PPI and direct them to the PAR for a final approach. The GCI/GCA handoff required coordination between the GCI (ground controlled intercept) controller and the GCA controller. GCI would position the aircraft on the PPI scope, report its position, heading and altitude to GCA, and hand it off. We would begin the approach from that position.

Square patterns were usually used for practice or to direct the aircraft around to the other end of the runway for a PPI approach if the PAR was not into wind. A square pattern had the advantage of allowing the pilot and/or controller to practise many approaches without necessity of the pilot climbing to high altitude for a beacon letdown.

The PAR could only serve one end of the runway. Someone came up with the idea of turning the trailers 180 degrees so that the PAR could serve whichever runway was into wind. We began to experiment with towing the trailers onto the runway, U-turning and positioning them facing the other way. This required teamwork on our part, because the trailer had to be levelled with jacks and the radar calibrated. We got quite proficient at quickly changing runways. Then, one day the station CO arrived with a distinguished visitor to show off this innovation. Everything went well until the tow truck broke down, stranding the trailers on the runway. This effectively closed Marville, with its one runway. The embarrassed CO turned to a corporal. Perhaps with dreams of promotion dancing in his head, off ran the corporal toward the stranded trailers, but he abruptly stopped when it came to him that he likely didn't have the muscle required to move the mighty GCA trailers. Despite this fiasco, we continued to turn the unit when required by wind direction.

One day we were caught with our PAR turned the wrong way. One of our Sabre squadrons was returning from Sardinia, and Europe was socked in. We were barely at minimums and the Sabres, which seemed to be chronically low on fuel, were reporting fuel states which would allow one approach and little more. We brought them in on PPI and prayed that there would be no missed approaches. Everyone was recovered without a hitch, and we sat back to wait for our "pat on the back." What we got instead was a blast for not having PAR available.

Because of our training and the high calibre of the pilots we controlled, our task was not normally difficult. It did require steady nerves because of emergencies and unusual situations. I recall one "hairy" day when we were at limits. I was traffic director, which meant that I directed all aircraft on the PPI to the PAR where I would hand them off to two final controllers. The Sabres were streaming off the beacon; GCI was handing off a section of CF-100s; and I was trying to fit an Expeditor into the pattern. Then GCI had another handoff for me, a T-33 towing a target that could only turn in one direction. At times like this we earned our pay.

I brought aircraft in under all sorts of emergencies, including an engine fire. It could be rather difficult to talk with your heart pounding, and realizing that an error could cost lives. Such was the case with a Sabre one day. The pilot had been practising square patterns when a fog bank moved in. He radioed that he'd land on his next approach if it looked too bad. At three miles from touchdown I reported to him that the pilot ahead of him landed with a half mile visibility. He then decided to land immediately.

At half a mile on final, the Sabre blip was on the glidepath, a shade left of centreline. I had just given a two-degree correction to the right when I saw the blip turn sharply left, so sharp that it couldn't possibly be corrected for and complete the landing. I told the pilot to overshoot and acknowledge, then watched in horror as the Sabre swung back right and left again where its blip merged with that of the operational readiness point hangar. The ORP was just to the side at the end of the runway and housed a pair of CF-100s on alert. I dashed to the door to see the results, expecting a fireball, but the fog was so thick I couldn't see beyond our own antennas.

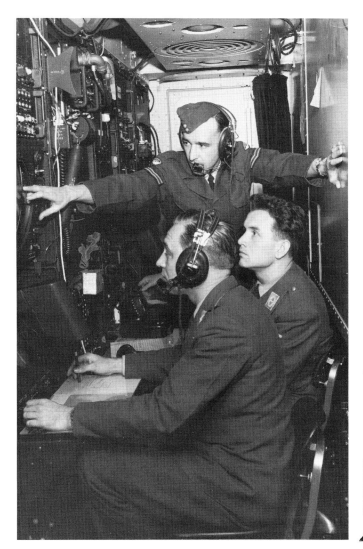

RCAF Cpl Melvin Splane instructs 2 German students in a typical GCA unit, January 20, 1959. (DND PL122092)

ON THE GLIDEPATH THREE MILES FROM TOUCHDOWN. SLIGHTLY RIGHT OF THE CENTRELINE CLEARED TO LAND CHECK WIND IS ONE THREE Z ON THE CENT TWO MILES F ADJUST YO SLIGHTLY BELOW THE GLID ONE AND A HALF FROM YOU OWN TUR HEADING TO TWO FOUR THE CENT LINE. NOW TEN...

DURNAN

Original artwork done by Bob Durnan on the GCA theme.

As the tower couldn't see the runway, they were unaware of anything unusual until I called them. I was soon relieved to hear that the Sabre had missed the ORP—it had crashed, but the pilot had survived. He had looked up at a half mile and by the time he got back onto instruments had gotten disoriented. He just missed the ORP and struck the ground heavily, bouncing and breaking apart. The last bounce may have saved the pilot's life, as he ended up atop an embankment instead of striking it head on. The Sabre had flown below GCA limits, but that was not uncommon. He just happened to get caught. Had we known just how bad the fog had become, the pilot would likely have stayed on the gauges and landed OK.

I once told the pilot of a Dakota that if he was not going to take my correc-tions he should go back to tower for a visual approach. The Dak was all over the sky and to continue the approach would have been useless. The pilot apologized, saying that he had been flying a desk too long. I later learned that he was a senior Air Div officer, but he was also a gentleman.

The highly trained radar technicians were an important part of our team. They kept the equipment working and put up with our nagging. One day a new tech, who was fresh from his course, told me that he couldn't get the radar to come on and that he was going to call the sergeant since he had tried everything he knew. I took him into the trailer, where I turned on the high voltage power supply. I then kicked it and the radar came on immediately. Some things just weren't covered in the manuals.

After my tour at Marville I returned to Canada, working at training stations on the Prairies. After Europe, both this work and the landscape were boring, so I left the RCAF in 1963 and took up a career as a police officer in Toronto. In 1979 I revisited Marville, and although the control tower and barracks were still there, this once-vibrant fighter base was now just a public works yard. On a 1981 visit to Trenton I toured the air traffic facilities. To my surprise I discovered that the same equipment I had worked at Marville in the fifties was still in use. Like me, it was 30 years older, but its modifications were an improvement. I couldn't say the same for my own! Today I hold a pilot's licence with an IFR rating, and often wonder about those pilots in their single-engine Sabres flying in all that bad weather. I'm glad that we in the flying control business were there to help them with their job.

Bob Durnan

Sabre Flying at Home

Experimental Flying: Early CEPE Days

Soon after the war the Experimental and Proving Establishment (EPE, later CEPE) at Rockcliffe began flying jets. In 1946, the first of three RCAF Meteors arrived, and pilots like E.L. "Shan" Baudoux, J.R. "Jack" Ritch and Bill McKenzie flew them. These were the RCAF's first jet pilots, and each had flown the Meteor in the UK late in the war. Vampires next arrived at EPE, and in 1951 the first Sabre. Once production was under way, EPE posted its first acceptance pilot, S/L Terry Evans, to Cartierville, along with F/Os Duyns and Robinson. Paul Duyns looks back to those days:

Ron Robinson and I were the first two resident RCAF pilots transferred to Canadair for the Sabre program. That was in June 1951. S/L Evans, CEPE pilot at Rockcliffe, came down to Canadair on an "as required" basis and test flew the majority of Sabres until Robbie and I were considered proficient to carry out acceptance testing.

Robbie and I were both retreads, coming back into the RCAF late in 1950. We did refresher courses on Harvards at St. Hubert before proceeding to Chatham for the Vampire OTU. Next we joined 410 at St. Hubert. It was just re-equipping with Sabres. We flew Harvards and attended the FTTU while waiting for the first Sabre to arrive.

Robbie and I were the last transfers into 410, so last in, last to fly the Sabre. My first trip was in 19117 on June 11, 1951. Then the two of us were offered the transfer to Canadair. We accepted, and with about four hours each on Sabres reported in to CEPE. To build up time we ferried Sabres to squadrons after acceptance by S/L Evans. Finally, after reaching about 20 hours we were ready to begin acceptance flying. My first test was in 19173

The RCAF's first Sabre acceptance pilots in a picture taken at Cartierville in the summer of 1951. From the left are F/O Paul Duyns, S/L Terry Evans and F/O Ron Robinson. (via Paul Duyns)

on October 9, 1951, my last on May 27, 1954. During this three years, we were at one time five resident pilots headed by F/L Bud Heck, but he left soon after promotion to S/L, and F/L Fred Moore took charge. The others were F/L Ken Olson, Robbie and myself. When we two left, it was to join 129 A&FF at 6RD, Trenton. Our replacements were Diz Deans and Don Simmons from 129. As CEPE and 129 were both under Air Materiel Command, it was a straight switch of pilots.

The early Sabres, while not completely snag-free, never had any major problems, e.g., engine or hydraulic failures. I recall making a dead-stick landing one day when the throttle jammed in the idle position. All in all, it was a great tour, but nice to get to 6RD and "re-join" the RCAF.

Paul Duyns

CEPE Records and Antics

In early 1955 S/L R.G. "Bob" Christie was on the West Coast with Sabre 19423, flying on air defence system tests. He would take the Sabre as far as 250 miles offshore so RCAF Station Holberg could evaluate their long-range radar. One day he flew four two-hour trips. Come April 11, Christie was pretty well wrung out, and having completed his duties, decided to beat it for home in Ottawa. He recently reported, "I just strapped the old Sword to my ass that morning and, with the forecast of good winds, bored straight down the CPR mainline to Ottawa. Being a Sunday, the servicing at Calgary and Winnipeg was done by the Reserves, who did a splendid job of almost instant turnarounds. This added to the pace."

Christie had taken off from Vancouver (Sea Island) at 10:30 EST and landed at Calgary 38 minutes later. Next stop was Winnipeg, a 1:17-hour leg; then on to Ottawa in another 1:51. Total flying time was 3:46, giving Christie a good edge over the previous 4:25-hour record time set by an RCAF Comet.

The trip made headlines, and Christie explains how this came about: "Bill Lee with whom I had been in public relations a few years before, called me the night I got home and said he'd like to do a story to partially offset the publicity the RCAF was getting as a result of the tragic collision of an air force Harvard and TCA North Star on April 8. Thus, an otherwise insignificant event got a lot more publicity than it deserved. When asked, I just replied, 'I was in a rush for dinner.'"

On June 12 Christie opened Air Force Day at Rockcliffe with a boom upon completing a record 15-minute run from Montreal in 23239: "The Montreal affair was set up for Air Force Day with a new Sabre which had been 'tweaked' for maximum allowable tailpipe temperature by one of the greatest aero engine mechanics we had in those days, Don Barckley. Not only was he good, but he cared—something

184

Test bed Sabre '069 awaiting fitment of an
early-model Orenda at Malton on May 1, 1953.
(Hawker Siddley 45386)

not always seen in sevicemen these
days, I'm afraid. As it was a clear day
we had just enough fuel to take off
from Uplands, make a pass by the
tower at Rockcliffe, fly down the
Ottawa River on the tree tops, call Cartierville and make a low pass there,
then flat out for Rockcliffe and
Uplands, with about five minutes fuel
remaining on landing. It was a bumpy
day—much plus and minus g along the
way—took weeks for all the bruises to
heal. 'They,' who calculated the speed,
claimed 732.5 mph for the round trip. I
doubt if the FAI would use the same
formula but, as it was again for the
publicity, we just went on pretending
that it was true.''

Bob Christie had first flown a jet in
March 1950 at Rockcliffe (Vampire
17007). He recently looked back on his
Sabre flying days:

My first encounter with the Sabre was
in December 1950 at Wright Field in
Ohio. I flew the F-86E models, and
was working alongside such renowned
North American test pilots as Jim
Brooks, Dan Darnell and J. Ray Dono-
hue. I made many test flights and recall
one of the spin trials that resulted in
near disaster. Stuck in a spin, I applied

full power in final desperation. Very
quickly, speed built up, my spin recovery action worked, and I landed
safely. We were all at a loss to figure
out what happened. Later, when I was
back in Canada, we lost a Sabre near
Uplands. The pilot ejected safely, and
we later discovered that the leading
edge slats could jam when side load
was applied in the open position, as in
a spin. With the slats on one side closed
and on the other side open, one wing
was stalled, the other not, and that
overcame the opposite rudder effect.
Recovery was possible only when speed
could be increased to force the open
slat closed, thus re-establishing control. Almost certainly, these two incidents had a common cause. The
phonolyte blocks acting as bearing surfaces in the slats were more closely
adjusted, and I never heard of the
problem again.

Another project of interest was
fitting the Orenda engine into an
F-86A borrowed from the USAF. This
aircraft was the first aircraft to be
powered by the Orenda, and was redesignated F-86AO. I flew a lot of
trials on this Sabre, and our biggest
problem was getting enough cooling air
around the engine because of its increased girth.

After the trials, the USAF wanted its
Sabre back, even though it was to be
scrapped. There were no tech orders

for the aircraft, many of the engine
gauges were of questionable calibration and working order, and the old
''AO'' just sat around Canadair, then
Avro at Malton, getting older and less
care. Still, the USAF wanted it back,
and delivered to its depot in Mobile.
So, after being ''bugged'' for weeks to
get someone to fly it south, I finally
decided to do it myself. At the time,
CEPE was part of Air Materiel Command and controlled ferry operations.

When I arrived at Avro, I found the
Sabre to be a true orphan. Nobody
seemed to even know how to start it, let
alone tell me about some of the weird
gauges that adorned the instrument
panel. Even the fuel gauges seemed
frozen and needed a good bash with
the fist to start reading. If there was
ever an accident about to happen, it
was Sabre '069.

Having promised to be back in
Ottawa in two days, and having used
up one day gathering info on starting
and operating the Sabre, I decided that
February 10, 1954, was the day. I did
one air test and found most systems
''go,'' but when I went to file a flight
plan I found the weather to the south
to be too unsettled. Early next day it
looked better, except for Mobile,
which was in thunderstorms. I managed to get the old bird fired up and in
and out of Wright Patterson and Nash-
ville, then took off for Mobile where

the weather was worsening.

The Nashville-Mobile leg was the longest, and while still 30 minutes out, my fuel gauges were showing low readings. Being over storms, and the destination looking better, I decided to press on. The "town finder" radio compass was homing on every thunderhead, but I could occasionally make out the "idents" of Mobile through the static. With the tanks running down, and being at 41,000 to save fuel and extend the glide if need be, we kept moving, and at last made contact with the tower at Mobile. The word was that another 15 minutes would see the area

CEPE personnel at the Air Armament Evaluation Detachment, RCAF Station Cold Lake, June 1957: Tony Gunther-Smith, Bob Christie (OC), Harry Jenkins, Jack Lumsdaine, Johnny "Whipper" Watson, Ron Pratt and Jimmy Dyer. (DND)

CEPE acceptance pilots Fred Moore and Bill Bliss at Canadair in 1956. (Canadair Ltd.)

CEPE trio on a flight from RCAF Station Namao, near Edmonton: Supermarine Swift F.4,WK276; Hunter F.2,WN891 and Sabre 6,PX-559. The latter two carry the CEPE polar bear crest. (via Russ Janzen)

cleared of storms, but I was down to five minutes fuel. I was given permission for a straight-in emergency descent. With the ceiling at 800 feet, I managed to make it over the beacon at about 450k at 700 feet, saw the field ahead, did the damndest tight turn to

almost killed off me, the bird and who knows who else. And for what! Lessons learned lasted me the rest of my service life.

Bob Christie

In 1954 Christie set up the Air Armament Evaluation Detachment (CEPE) at Cold Lake, mainly to assist in development of the CF-100's weapons system. Of this period he has one

CO, G/C Bill Newson, for a recommendation for test pilot's school. HQ turned down Newson's request and Janzen was shipped to the FIS at Trenton. But Newson soon became Chief Staff Officer, Training Command, and before long Janzen was off to Edwards AFB, arriving there in September 1951. The course lasted until June 1952, by which time Janzen had flown such types as the B-25, B-29, F-80, F-86E (first flight May 19, 1952), T-28 and T-33. One day, while sitting in a Sabre, he witnessed a tragic crash: Neil Lathrop was doing a roll as he flew down the runway in the XB-51. Something went wrong and Lathrop crashed fatally. This pretty well signalled the end of the fascinating XB-51 light bomber program.

Back in Canada, Janzen was posted to CEPE Climatic Detachment at RCAF Station Namao, near Edmonton. There he flew many types, including the Attacker, Hunter, Swift, Vampire and Venom. Hence, he had ample opportunity to compare each

PX-559 in the bone yard at Mountain View, south of Trenton, August 8, 1965. (Jack McNulty)

Two views of the Sabre 5 used to investigate area rule flight characteristics. The fuselage was "moulded" with bulges to create the desired results. (DND PL102711,'173)

keep it in view in the poor visibility, then ran out of fuel. I would have put out a May Day but was too busy keeping the field in sight. I used the emergency gear extension and landed without further incident—wrong runway, but who cared! Only the laundry knew how close it had been.

I had to be towed in, and after turning the paperwork over to the "breakers" who told me that the Sabre would be no more within a few days, I was called to the commander's office for a "chat." Seems I had landed on the runway closed for being a hazard to the Officers' Club. I apologized and explained, then off we went to the Club. I still wonder if all this was worth the effort, considering that I

interesting comment: "Canada never knew how fragile her air defences truly were in the fifties and sixties." Of course, it is only now being learned just how fickle a system the CF-100 actually was. Christie was early involved in the CF-104, commanded 1 Wing at Marville 1966-67 and was base commander at Lahr.

Another of the RCAF's early post-war test pilots was Russ Janzen. He had been ground crew in 1940-42, but remustered to air crew, instructing till 1945 on Harvards and Cranes. He then transferred to the navy to fly Seafires. In 1949 he did a refresher course at Trenton, finishing with an A2 category instructor's rating. He was posted to Centralia and while there asked his

with the Sabre, though his specific work was in cold weather trials. One day CEPE was hosting some air cadets, and the Swift (flown by Janzen), Hunter (Lee Volet, USAF), and Sabre (Pinky Stark, RAF) were to be demonstrated. The pilots organized something a little different—a race! Janzen writes, "We started about 20 miles from Namao, flying line abreast. We headed for the airport at about 400 knots at 1000 feet above ground. At my signal the three of us opened up the taps and headed for home. As we crossed in front of the cadets, the Hunter was about 100 feet ahead of the Sabre, with the Swift perhaps 150 feet behind the Sabre. Needless to say, we were all near critical Mach and were all experiencing buffeting.''

Commenting about the Swift, Janzen adds, ''It required use of the afterburner to stay with either the Hunter or Sabre. That was very costly in terms of fuel used.'' He felt that the British penchant to design a hydraulic control system that had aerodynamic feedback probably caused its operational delay and notes, ''The Americans solved the hydraulic control problem with bungee cords, i.e., the control force to move an F-86 control system was the same while taxiing as while flying at Mach 1.''

The Swift
Some interesting comments about an RAF contemporary of the Sabre appear in a history of the Supermarine Swift by Bill Gunston: ''It is impossible to overstate the influence of the Sabre at this time. Though the Air Staff seemed to find it an embarrassment, the Supermarine engineers and test pilots were intensely interested, and naturally wanted to find out how North America had 'done it' so many years earlier. Test pilot Morgan took a party of senior engineers up to North Luffenham, where the first Sabres in Europe were operated by the RCAF. The occasion evoked mixed feelings, because as well as being extremely instructive, studying an F-86 showed the magnitude of the leeway that British industry had to make up. Nothing remotely like the Sabre existed in Britain, nor could it then have been built. In the words of another Supermarine pilot, 'The cockpit seemed like something out of the 21st century, whereas the cockpit of the 535 (early Swift) was much like that of a Spitfire.'

''Even the pilot's anti-g suits and bonedomes were items then unobtainable in Britain, and the large clear-view blown canopy was something British industry could not make. Later a Canadian Sabre visited Chilbolton so that the canopy could be examined more closely. On departure, the visitor (F/L Dean Kelly) took off but returned at once, explaining that his left ammunition re-arm panel was not secured. A member of the ground crew locked the panel in seconds with a half-turn on each of six fasteners. The Canadian thanked him, roared off on his sooty trail, and a few minutes later shook

that part of Hampshire with a resounding bang. This kind of thing made a deep impression.

''On Supermarine aircraft, panels were held on by bagsfull of ordinary screws. Even more telling was the effortless ease of the American machine. You pressed a button and the engine started. You pressed a button and the canopy shut. There were many buttons, and the really impressive thing was not that they all worked, but that this was taken for granted.''

In the end, Swift production was cut short, and its service career petered out in the mid-fifties, but for a few FR.5s. Its contemporary, the Hawker Hunter, though, saw wide use in numerous air forces and was well regarded. Some remain in service today.

Women's Speed Record
In 1953 famed woman flier Jacqueline Cochran flew the Orenda-powered Sabre 3 development aircraft to set a new world record. Cochran was married to industrialist Floyd Odlum, and both he and Cochran were nuts about fast airplanes. With jets all the rage, and fliers like Chuck Yeager setting new records all the time, and

especially with French pilot Jacqueline Auriol having flown jets, Cochran was determined to get her hands on a jet fighter and crack the speed record. But the US military wasn't keen to have civilians flying its aircraft, forcing Cochran to make an end run.

Cochran was finally able to get hold of the airplane she needed. She used the influence of Odlum (who controlled Convair), and his friend, John Jay Hopkins (head of General Dynamics which by this time owned Canadair). In May 1953 Odlum and Hopkins were to cement their relationship as Hopkins bought control of Odlum's Atlas Corp. Cochran was even able to intimidate General Vandenburg, USAF Chief of Staff, by hinting that if he didn't cooperate with her scheme she could go over his head to her friend, ''Ike''— President Eisenhower!

Meanwhile, a scheme to have Cochran make her speed run between Montreal and Ottawa was abandoned because the stretch wasn't instrumented, whereas a completely instrumented facility existed at Edwards AFB in California. Cochran did come up to Montreal for a T-33 check-out, though. Bill Longhurst got her squared away with the T-bird, with one flight November 26, 1952, and four the following day. Plans were quickly made to ferry the Sabre 3 to Edwards along with a select Canadair crew under R.D. ''Dick'' Richmond and T.A. ''Tom'' Harvie. For official purposes, the object of the venture was to obtain an airspeed position error calibration, so the Sabre 3 could be used as a high-speed pace aircraft. Meanwhile,

Canadair had 16 personnel involved in the Edwards operation: pilot Bill Longhurst, eight engineering men, and seven ground crew. Those shown here along with Jacqueline Cochran are (in front) mechanics Bill Gyuricsko, Norman Frechette and Leo Lahaye, inspector Bert Waal. In the rear are Jack Jones (engine performance engineer, Avro), Ian Renwick (instrumentation engineer), Barry Gilmour (instrumentation mechanic) Lewis Chow (chief experimental engineer), Art Child (crew chief) and George MacFarlane (radio technician). (via L. Chow)

Cochran could get in her own flights.

Dick Richmond recalls that upon arrival at Edwards the Canadair team was not warmly welcomed by base commander, BGen Stanley Holtner. There was no hospitality laid on, and it was even pointed out that if the Sabre pranged, Canadair would be fully responsible and would have to clean up the mess. It is surmised that the USAF had its nose out of joint, with Cochran having "gone over heads" to obtain her clearances. Meanwhile, she was much at home at Edwards, being among her old flying cronies like Fred Ascani (whose 635 mph speed record she was out to beat), Jack Ridley and Chuck Yeager. In off hours she made up for the USAF's cool reception by going all out to entertain. One weekend she flew into Edwards with her Lodestar and took the Canadians over to Odlum's ranch for a big barbecue.

With Chuck Yeager looking over her shoulder, Cochran was soon familiar with the Sabre and making her initial flights, Mach runs included. On May 18, 1953, she set a new 100-km speed record of 652.552 mph. On June 3 she flew a 15-km circuit at a record 670 mph. She also became the first woman to break the sound barrier.

During the stay at Edwards, 19200 completed many flights: calibration, 20-plus flights; check flights by Longhurst and Yeager, and training and speed record flights by Cochran, 30 flights; ferry flights, 5. Cochran flew the Sabre 13 times between May 12 and June 3. Yeager flew it on May 6 and 15.

One of the Canadair technical crew

involved in the Edwards episode was engineer Lewis Chow. He recalls: "Jacqueline Cochran was a lady of great influence, and smart to boot. How else could she have gotten her hands on the Sabre 3 and access to the most classified air force base in the US! But a lady she was, and treated all of us from Canada splendidly. Chuck Yeager helped her a great deal on her record-breaking flights. He flew wing on all her flights."

The Overseas Ferry Unit

One of the best known (and likely the most infamous) of all Sabre units was No. 1 Overseas Ferry Unit, based at St. Hubert. Formed in late 1953 with the task of ferrying Sabres and T-33s across the North Atlantic, the OFU was under Air Transport Command, a fact which alone should have warned

(Below) Jacqueline Cochran with Canadair's Bill Longhurst, then with Chuck Yeager, both at Edwards. Her aircraft is seen being readied for a flight. It carried no national markings, only the tail number. The front fuselage was painted in fluorescent red. (Canadair Ltd. via L. Chow)

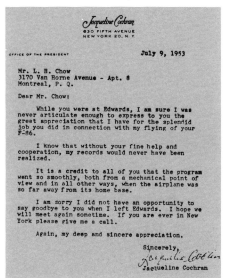

the RCAF that trouble lay ahead. How could ATC, with its tradition of sober professionalism, ever hope to deal with an impossible crowd of young fighter pilots?

The initial OFU pilots, all "hardened" Air Division veterans, arrived at St. Hubert in late October 1953 under their OC, S/L R.G. "Bob" Middlemiss, former commander of 421 at 2 Wing. Very little was ready for the OFU, certainly no aircraft. This seems to have chaffed the lads a bit, and during a drinking bout in the mess with a crowd of RAF ferry pilots, a scheme to get flying was soon hatched. It seems that the RAF was short of pilots to take a flock of Sabre 4s over to the UK from St. Hubert. "Piece of cake," one can just hear the RAF pilots saying, as they described the trip across the pond. The OFU pilots were not hard to convince and were soon part of the RAF formation cruising over the Greenland icecap on a rather unofficial "swan." This was the first of endless cases of Bob Middlemiss' lads going astray one way or another.

The OFU's operations were to be

known as Randoms, and Random 1 departed St. Hubert on February 11, 1954, in the following sections:

Red

1 F/L	J.E. Ecker	23004
	Deputy Op Commander	
2 F/O	M.W. Sills	23006
	Safety equipment	
3 F/O	K.A. Cheesman	23017
	Navigation	
4 F/O	A.C. Young	23020

Yellow

1 F/O	M.R. MacGregor	23029
	Navigation	
2 F/O	S.V. Hegstrom	23030
3 F/L	H.A. Clements	23032
4 F/O	J.L. Den Ouden	23036

White

1 F/O	G.J. Fitzgerald	23038
	Navigation	
2 F/O	J.E. Hutt	23013
3 F/L	J.D. Donald	23033
	Radio facilities	
4 F/O	L.W. Worthy	23045

Blue

1 S/L	R.G. Middlemiss	23052
	Operation Commander	
2 F/O	J.M. Simard	23078

F/O Den Ouden's trip went as follows:

Feb.		hours
11	St.Hubert—Goose Bay	1:45
15	Goose—BW-1	1:40
21	BW-1—Keflavik	:30
	(forced by weather to turn back)	
22	BW-1—Keflavik	1:45
23	Keflavik—Kinloss	1:45
24	Kinloss—Baden	2:00

Random 1 was what would become an average OFU operation. S/L Middlemiss' report included the following comments: "Departure (from Goose) was delayed almost one hour because of a very sporadic departure of approximately 20 High Flight aircraft who went out first. The interval between Random sections was reduced to eight minutes because remaining daylight time was getting short. ... Random 1 was delayed for six days at Greenland due to weather at Keflavik and long periods of communications blackout between Narsarssuak and Keflavik. On 21 Feb. an attempt was made to fly to Keflavik. All aircraft were airborne when a report of deteriorating weather was received from Keflavik. The Operation Commander recalled all sections .... A weather actual at the time of the cancelled ETA reported the sky obscured at 300 feet, visibility 1/2 mile."

Middlemiss' final comments were, "No departures were delayed because of unserviceabilities. No takeoffs were aborted. No aircraft turned back because of unserviceability in the air.

190

Random 1 just arrived at 4 Wing. The AOC A/V/M Hugh Campbell, is greeting the OFU boss, S/L Bob Middlemiss. Standing around waiting to be let loose on the mess are Middlemiss' boys: Clements, Hegstrom, MacGregor, Fitzgerald, Simard, Hutt and Den Ouden. G/C R.S. Turnbull, 4 Wing CO, is also present here. (DND)

General flying discipline of all pilots was excellent during the operations.''

Accompanying the 14 Sabres on Random 1 was a North Star carrying support personnel, such as service reps from Orenda under Bill Staines. The North Star carried all spares needed to keep the operation running smoothly. Some light is shed on the technical end of Random by Orenda rep Bill Sanders:

Prior to the commencement of the operation, four aircraft were flown to Goose Bay to be held there as spares, and, likewise, all the maintenance bases also held two spare engines each. A limited number of spares and consumable items such as "O" rings were also held by these bases .... The second hop from Goose Bay to BW-1 was delayed until Monday, February 15, owing to adverse weather conditions prevailing at BW-1. The particular hop was almost delayed again owing to USAF Operation High Flight taking precedence over Random 1. At scheduled TO time 10:30 hours, High Flight had several aircraft (F-84s, F-86s, F-94s) iced up. This resulted in Random's first section getting airborne after High Flight by 12:45 hours and the last section by 13:15 hours, only

just leaving the requisite $1\frac{1}{2}$ hours daylight search time after landing at BW-1.

Arriving at BW-1 we found that all the aircraft had arrived satisfactorily and 50% of the "A" checks were completed. I understand from Bill Staines that completion of the checks revealed one or two more tail cones had developed minor spot weld cracks....

On Saturday, February 20, all sections of Random 1 were airborne from BW-1, but were called back .... It was fortunate that Random was recalled because that night a 90-knot gale hit Keflavik ... a Globemaster that happened to be at Keflavik was moved about 18 feet and all four propellers had been windmilling.

Eventually the 14 aircraft arrived at Keflavik on February 22. Completion of the "A" checks revealed all centre

bearing scavenge screens to be clean, though engines in aircraft 23006, 23031 and 23038 were found to have further cracking of the tail cone bullet spot welds, and cracks at the trailing edge of the streamline supports. Engine No.1054 was the worst, having all four supports cracked, but they were considered to be within acceptance limits; and since all attempts to stop-drill these cracks resulted in a handful of broken drills, it was decided to centre-pop the cracks and call for the drilling to be done at Söllingen.

No.1 Party arrived at Keflavik later that evening after about 10 days in BW-1. The party generally appeared a little tired and bewildered. Making one or two enquiries from the boys about their bewilderment I was given the impression that it was quite normal for people to look that way when they had been subjected to more than seven days of Bluie West's climate and isolation, and was informed that this was what the USAF called "shook."

At some unearthly hour in the morning of February 23, No.1 Party left Keflavik for Kinloss by North Star .... Our return journey was started on the 26th from Söllingen, and after about 29 hours elapsed time we were back again in Montreal feeling very proud at the safe and successful completion of Random 1, but very tired and weary from the suspense of the operation and over 19 hours flying from Söllingen, *not* under Trans-Canada Air Lines conditions.

Bill Sanders

Denny Den Ouden "taxis" into St. Hubert January 13, 1955 on the first delivery to the OFU of a Sabre 6. Due to ice on the runway, a mule was required to get the plane in. On June 7 that year, 23372 pranged with 297 hours total time. The OFU diarist noted: "Red Hettrick up in clean Canadair 6 late in the afternoon. Flamed out and pranged in a field west of St. Hubert traffic circle. In hospital for the night but OK. A/c a write-off."

J.L. Den Ouden completed many a Random, including No.18, which was one of the fastest ever. It left St. Hubert September 8, 1955, for Goose, and got into 3 Wing September 11. Den Ouden flew 23501, and on the 11th took off with the flight from Bluie and went all the way through to Germany in 5:15 hours of flying. Back home, Den Ouden dragged 23474 all the way up to 55,100 feet on a test flight October 28. Here he relates a little anecdote which occurred over mid-Atlantic one day:

As you know, on the Overseas Ferry Unit on each ferry trip called a Random, the aircraft were flown across the

A Sabre 6 on Random 20 refuels at Kinloss, February 1956. (R.J. Childerhose)

Atlantic commencing at St. Hubert with stops at Goose Bay, Bluie (Narsarssuak) in Greenland, Keflavik in Iceland, Kinloss or sometimes Prestwick in Scotland, and then into Germany, France or England, wherever the aircraft were to be delivered. Anywhere from 30 to 70 aircraft would be taken on each operation flying sections of four aircraft 10 minutes (approximately 60 miles) apart. Normally upon reaching top of climb, the four aircraft in the section would spread out into "Finger 4" formation with each aircraft 500 or more yards apart for relaxed formation flying.

On one of the Randoms we had climbed out of Keflavik, Iceland, on a rare, beautiful cloudless morning. From 35,000 feet the ocean below looking eastward into the sun looked like hammered copper. The visibility all around was hundreds of miles. The four Sabres in my section were like little silver models suspended in the dark blue sky at that altitude. The radio had been absolutely silent for approximately half an hour. All was serene and the only thing that kept me from thinking that I was suspended inanimate in another world was the

soft hum of the turbine behind me and the very soft hiss of the air conditioning system in the cockpit.

All of a sudden, in a voice that sounded a long way away and with a broad Dutch accent, I heard the pilot of a Royal Dutch Airlines plane. I have never forgotten the exact words spoken, "Ocean Station India, this is KLM 567 over." Silence again for about a minute then, "Ocean Station India, this is KLM 567 over." Again silence for about another minute. Then, "Ocean Station India, this is KLM 567, do you read me over." Then very promptly in a voice from a radio that was obviously much closer and with a "Newfie" accent came these words, "Obviously not you silly bastard." Then for a period of about two minutes one could hear the transmit buttons of the Random pilots all along the line pressing their radio transmitter buttons momentarily and emitting a brief chuckle. Then all was silence once more in this surreal world for 20 minutes before the first section were heard to change frequency for the letdown into Kinloss, Scotland.

S/L Bob Middlemiss was a holy terror for radio discipline and I am sure since Gerry Tobin was the only Newfie on the Overseas Ferry Unit that he had to know who had made the remark, but as far as I know nothing was ever said or done about it by the "Boss."

We had a lot of characters on the Overseas Ferry Unit.

J.L. Den Ouden

OFU Diary

The OFU daily diary is surely one of the most entertaining ever compiled in the RCAF. It is one of the most explicit exposés on paper of the personal foibles of RCAF pilots. If one digs deep, he can actually find, intermingled with the "macho" reportings of boozing and sex, useful bits of aviation history. Much cannot be reprinted here, but the following excerpts provide a sense of what it was like flying a flock of little Sabres on the long and danger-fraught route between Montreal and Scotland. First, Random 11 of February-March 1955:

Feb. 5 Six pilots to ZD for Mk.2 pickups. OFU sponsored party at mess. Skits, Liberace (Bain) and assorted drunks. Successful do. Tobin's birthday. Flying:5:20.

The aftermath of the near-disaster at Keflavik on February 21, 1955. Sabre 23218 has been totalled. '356 has a badly crumped wing, and was later listed as a Cat.A. (via Bill Worthy)

Feb. 9 Test flights on Mk.2s and 5s. Burgess, Den Ouden, Vaesen got green ticket rides. Flying:11:50.

Feb. 12 Wx poor. Stood down. Random departure delayed til Wednesday.

Feb. 17 Wx poor. Runways 7 inches snowed under. Goose Bay wx good but no alternates. Baggage collected by North Star. Random delayed TFN. Four air tests due, but wx duff. Flying:3:45.

Feb. 18 Wx good, outlook for Random good. Sabre 2s, 5s, T-33s land at Goose. Gaudry, Hutt, Poole and Young returned St. Hubert.

Feb. 19 Wx marginal at Goose, good at BW-1. Finally off after 0700 knock-up. Clear all the way over to Bluie. Small party, poker game, etc.

Feb. 20 Wx good. Simmons remained with Fitzgerald who had u/s fuel pump. Tobin's a/c no start. GCI approach with GCA at Kef.

Feb. 21 Poor wx at Kinloss. Aerodrome u/s, snow and ice there. LAC MacKinnon while running up an a/c, jumped the chocks and froze to the full-open throttle. Aircraft careened left and ran into a parked a/c which burst into flames. A third a/c was damaged. Airman suffered shock after being helped out of cockpit which Hyatt, Heffern and St. Marie cracked with a fire extinguisher.

Feb. 22 Wx poor at Kinloss and aerodrome still closed. Takeoff to land at Prestwick. Benson, Turner, Hagarty remained to investigate crash. Hallowell struck a bird while in the circuit at Prestwick and lost his canopy. Made recovery from inverted position. Everybody lodged at Marine Hotel at Troon (27s a day!).

Feb. 23 Wx poor at continental bases. Stood down.

Feb. 24 Still closed. Stood down. Moved to USAF officers' club at Prestwick. Emergency pay parade courtesy SAO Langar.

Feb. 26 Continent clamped. Hallowell, Vaesen, Haran, Annis, McIlraith and Haverstock delivered Mk.2s to Ringway. Returned same nite.

Feb. 27 Clamped. Stood down.

Feb. 28 Clamped. Graham and McIlraith return to Canada.

Mar. 1 Still nothing. Vaesen returns to Canada via sked.

Mar. 2 CO and Hallowell flew to Grostenquin via North Star yesterday. A/c left for bases on continent.

Mar. 3 Finally, away we go. Five to 2 Wing, four to 3 Wing, 4 to 4 Wing. Sonny Haran pranged at 2 Wing, nose gear trouble ... Haverstock remains to deliver Mk.2 which was fitted with new canopy.

Mar. 4 North Star picked up pilots from Söllingen and flew to Zweibrück-
(continued on page 222)

OFU Briefing at Keflavik. From the left are Bob Hallowell, Gerry Tobin, Gord MacDonald, Ben Simard (behind MacDonald), Bill Worthy, Ike Gilhuly, and "Tweedy" Vaesen. Unidentified F-89 crew. Also unknown is the chap behind Vaesen. (DND)

Canadair Sabres in Colour

(Right) S/L Duke Warren about to taxi his Sabre 2 at North Luffenham in this 1952 photo. Duke added the red flash to distinguish this as the 410 commander's aircraft. Next is a refuelling scene at North Luff, June 27, 1952. Below are 439 Sabre 2s at North Luff. (via D. Warren, DND PC100, G.J. Fitzgerald)

Sabre 19594 of Triple Four cranks up for a mission from St. Hubert in August 1953. It's one of the RAF's Mk.4s on loan to the RCAF, so carries the British fin flash. (Bottom) VH-135 of 444 is seen at Baden with F/O L.J. Redman's new 1954 Austin-Healey 100. For many Air Div pilots, a decent set of wheels was simply part of one's proper kit. (Llyn de Sansoucy, L.J. Redman)

Sabres of 427 ''Lion'' Squadron at St. Hubert
in February 1953. Compare the markings with
those on BB-445 (facing) which appeared a
few months later at 3 Wing. Note the RAF
Hastings and the Dakota down the line.
(Llyn de Sansoucy)

Badly dinged Sabre of 427 Squadron awaits
the salvagers after a heavy landing at Rabat.
(Ken Orr)

A 427 Sabre taxis at Zweibrücken bearing the full colours *circa* 1953. (Ken Orr).

Sabre of 430 "Silver Falcon" Squadron, Grostenquin. (Bob Morgan)

"Red Indian" Sabre 2s at Grostenquin the day Prime Minister Louis St. Laurent visited 2 Wing in 1954. (Ralph Heard)

(Facing page) Canadair-built F-86E-6 Sabres of the 336th FIS while serving in Korea in 1952. No.875 was usually flown by S/L Eric Smith. (E.G. Smith)

"Bluenose" Sabre with nose painted up for an exercise over the summer of 1954. (S.E. Burrows)

All-red Sabre 5s painted for the September 1955 Toronto air show. They are seen on the tarmac at Trenton. (DND)

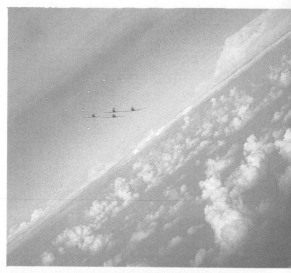

(Top left) Sabre 5s of 434 Squadron at Zwei.
(Top right) Beautifully "wired"—four Sabres sit in the sights of F/O Ed Welters six-gun Sabre. The centre photo shows 414 Sabre 5s in full regalia (pre-camouflage days).

(Below) "Thanks, OFU" Sabre pilot Bert Davis noted on this picture that he snapped of just-arrived Sabre 5s at 2 Wing, 1955.
(S.E. Burrows, via H. Hrischenko, Bert Davis)

The 1955 Sky Lancers in flight, then a view
on the tarmac of the ill-fated 1956 edition
of the team. (DND, L.A. Cheek)

In the top photo Sabre 23604 of 439 Squadron carries the fifties-vintage IG designator code, but unpainted tanks. (Above) Outstanding portrait of a 439 Sabre 6 on detachment in Greece during 1962. 23512 was scrapped at Prestwick some time later. (Gerry McCully, Bill Bristowe)

(Top left) F/O Bill Bristowe and ''friend'' in
a typical hero shot. (Top right) A 441 Sabre 6
shows its unit markings, February 1, 1957.
(Above) Sabres of 439 lined up at Grostenquin for the Prime Minister's review. (via
Bill Bristowe, DND PC2014, W.H. Norn)

(Above) Lloyd Hubbard banks away in a 427 Sabre as F/O David Wickes snaps his shutter. (Left) LAC George Ryder refuels a 439 Sword at Rabat in 1955. (Bottom) F/O C.T. Paine and LAC Empey pose for a PR shot at Rabat on July 15, 1956. Note the red-tipped ammunition. (David Wickes, Bert Davis, DND PC1323)

(Facing page) Flocks of sheep often did grass-cutting duty for the Air Div, in this case at Marville. The centre is an impressive scene at 2 Wing, with "Red Indians" lined up for action. Then, a 439 jet, tail festooned for Carte Blanche, taxis out at Marville with F/O Castle at the pole. (DND PCN1972, A.J. Burnett, Bert Davis)

206

(Top) Not the Twilight Zone! An actual Junkers 52 trimotor of the French Air Force taxis along as 434 Squadron Sabres await in the background in this Rabat scene. The view at the beach in Sardinia is sure to rouse a few old memories among Air Div types. In the other picture F/Os Tatton, Pickering and Nilsen head out for a mission with 439 during gunnery at Rabat in 1955. (Right) A lone Sabre on its way ''across the pond'' with the OFU. Quite the contrast with Rabat. (P.S. Perry, Gerry McCully, Bert Davis, via Ralph Heard)

(Facing page) Nattily painted Sabre 5s with the auxiliaries: AB-315 of 401 Squadron, and BQ-110 of 438, photographed at St. Hubert by George Fuller on March 29, 1958, shortly before they were exchanged for Expeditors. AM-331 of 410 Squadron is seen at Marville on March 13, 1956. It was on the US civil register as recently as 1984. (DND PC1182)

(Above) Activity on the flight line as 441
visits Sardinia in 1958. (Left) An Air Div F-86
with the ''Sabre Salvo'' tail flash designed
by the team's EO. (Below) General view of the
dispersal at Zweibrücken. (Lou J. Hill,
H.W.H. Casley, Gerry McCully)

(Right) A Sabre 4 of 234 Squadron, RAF, in full squadron markings as of spring, 1956.
(Below) An RAF Sabre visits 2 Wing.
(R.A. Brown, Ralph Heard)

(Top left) A 441 Sabre in a beautifully serene setting above cloud. (Bottom left) BB-148 of WS 110 visiting 3 Wing on a snowy March 11, 1958. (Lou J. Hill, Turbo Tarling)

(Above) An RCAF instructor prepares for a flight from Oldenburg. (Below) A fully painted Sabre 6 of 1/JG 72 carrying Sidewinder rails. (Bernhard, D. Kelle)

(Facing page) JC-105 of the 1.Staffel of JaboG.42 displaying the red and white drop tanks ordered by high command as an aid in identifying low-flying Sabres. JC-239 and JC-116 of JaboG.42 are seen during one of their last flights with this Geschwader before replacement with G.91s. Note the addition of a small white band atop the unit emblem. (Bernhard)

(Above) Four Condor Sabres seen late in their careers before being replaced by G.91s. (Below) An ex-Luftwaffe Sabre 6 of the Pakistani Air Force at Masroor near Karachi, March 25, 1981 soon after the Sabre had been withdrawn from PAF service. (Dornier, Lindsay Peacock)

In 1955 plans were in the works to form a Sabre aerobatic team at Chatham. The pilots were working up, but things came to a disastrous halt on May 13 when Swede Evjen and Garth Cinnamon had a mid air collision. Evjen was killed, and all plans were curtailed. One aircraft had been painted, and appeared later that summer at the Toronto air show flown by S/L Eric Smith. It was later written off in a training accident near Chatham. (E.G. Smith)

Standard Sabre markings "at home": 23238 of the Central Flying School, seen at Trenton in March 1959; and 23028, also at Trenton, but on June 11, 1966. (Turbo Tarling, Larry Milberry)

(Facing) Six of the Golden Hawks during a photo session with an RCAF Lancaster. (DND PCN183)

Golden Hawk crest.

(Above) The Golden Hawks visiting Trenton on June 1, 1963. (Left) The main hangar at No.1(F)OTU, RCAF Station Chatham with the base rescue S-51 hovering over the ramp. (Below) An OTU Sabre 5 being towed at Chatham. (Nick MacDonald-Wolochatiuk, K.E. Johnston, Lou J. Hill)

(Facing) An STU Sabre 5 wearing Canada's centennial year crest. Then, PX-506 of CEPE (Climatic), seen at Namao in September 1962. Finally, Sabre 5s in the boneyard at Mountain View on June 26, 1971. (Rae R. Simpson, Robert Kirby, Larry Milberry)

(Left) Sabre 4 of the Frecce Tricolori at Ahlhorn in September 1961. (Below) A variation on the same team's colour scheme. (Bottom) One of several Sabre 6 purchased in South Africa and now in the US. This one was seen at Briggs Army Airfield, Fort Bliss, Texas on October 5, 1985, still in SAAF colours. (Facing) Two outstanding in-flight views of a South African Sabre 6 taken by Herman Potgieter who, along with Willem Steencamp, produced the marvellous book, *Aircraft of the South African Air Force*. (G. Joos, Roberto Nobile, Herman Potgieter)

(Top) A lovely scene near Cold Lake, Alberta in the summer of 1977. Boeing's chase Sabre turns to follow a gaggle of T-birds. (Rae R. Simpson)

(Above) Standard colour scheme for drone Sabre 5s. This aircraft was seen at Flight Systems' Mojave base in the spring of 1978. (Rae R. Simpson)

(Facing page) Ex-Luftwaffe Sabre serving with Flight Systems, seen here at Hollman AFB, New Mexico on February 1, 1981. And a Sabre pilot's idea of heaven—Boeing's Sabre performs over the clouds near its Seattle base. (M.J. Kasiuba, Boeing K15491)

The "boys from the stable" (i.e. OFU) at one of their three favourite pastimes—boozing it up. Looks like chug-a-lug time, with Bill Worthy being egged on to show them how to do it! (DND)

Brothers Bob and Don Simmons pose at Cartierville for a PR shot under the tail of a newly refurbished Sabre 2 in Greek markings. Don, a CEPE acceptance pilot, had just completed test flying the aircraft, and was handing it over to Bob, working with the OFU, to ferry to the UK. (Canadair Ltd.)

en to pick up rest of gang. Into Prestwick for supper, then off to Keflavik for a nite's stopover.

Mar. 5 Goose Bay for lunch, then back to HU direct having cleared Customs at YR. Gang stood down until Thursday.

Random 15, July 1955

July 1 Heat wave continues. Everyone but OFU take off on long weekend. Pilots lay out in chairs amid clutter of baggage waiting for North Star. Hear over news that 8 Portuguese F-84s pack into a mountainside en route to an air show. Expensive air show.

July 2 Random takes off for Goose at 1025 hrs, 29 a/c led by Boss. Wx at BW down. Spend afternoon drinking a couple of cases of cans at Dave Newell's home in PMQs. Hard times dance in evening, free drinks. Some of the boys invite the entire crew of a German ship to the dance. The SDO kicked them out, so the Boys from the Stable invite the sailors into the barracks for a party.

July 3 Quiet day given over to recuperation. Wx still bad in BW.

July 4 Wx remaining duff in BW. Briefing in morning. Nothing moves. Pea pool, bridge and pocket books. That's all.

July 5 Random cancels out again. First really warm day at Goose. Have a softball game against OFU airmen with Bill Worthy pitching. Pilots win 11-8.

July 6 Entire day spent at hangar waiting for the word to go. Communications breakdown between BW-YR. Final blow comes when Duckbutt craps out in p.m. with inverter trouble. Boys

from the Stable terrorize hangar with buckets of water hurled down from balcony. Water fight continued intermittent throughout afternoon. Retiring to Mess, some of the lads attacked wine stores.

July 7 After a false alarm, Random was away for BW. Double hop precluded by bad wx at Kef. Baggage was waiting in the barracks so everyone dressed in civvies for supper.

July 8 Sudden improvement in forecast wx for Kef produces small panic when Boss calls quick briefing at 3 p.m. Stable boys are finally rounded up but too late to take off ahead of High Flite T-birds. Arrive in Kef at 11 o'clock at night in broad daylight. Most of the lads adjourn to the Officers' Club ... an all night party for some.

July 9 Briefing at 0800 hrs. Fog in Kinloss prevents early takeoff. Big warm front system moves in with bags and bags of rain. Everyone returned to the pad.

July 10 Briefing at 0600, takeoff at 0800. Land in Prestwick for lunch. While waiting to leave for Germany, APU escapes from tractor and prangs into drop tank of Frank Raymond's a/c. He, along with Bill Weary and Gilhuly, stay behind with u/s a/c. Random arrives at 4 Wing evening. Welcomed by hordes of Rhein River mosquitoes. Turkey supper, and a long bar to celebrate arrival.

July 12 5 a.m. departure via North Star for London. Everyone badly hung over.

Old time OFU driver Tommy Thompson who flew fighters during the war. (Ken Hagarty)

Year 1953 Month/Date	Aircraft Type	No.	Pilot, or 1st Pilot	2nd Pilot, Pupil or Passenger	Duty (Including Results and Remarks)	Single-Engine Day Dual (1)	Pilot (2)
	—	—	—	—	Totals Brought Forward	119 / 45	43 / 35
Nov 3	SABRE 4	XB852	SELF	—	TABLE 1 FORM FUEL FLOW 10ST		1:30
6	"	852	"	—	OBOE II ST.HUBERT → BAGOTVILLE		:45
6	"	852	"	—	BAGOTVILLE → GOOSE BAY		1:20
7	"	852	"	—	OBOE III GOOSEBAY → BLUE WEST ONE		1:45
8	"	852	"	—	OBOE III BW1 → KEFLAVIK		1:30
9	"	852	"	—	OBOE III KEFLAVIK → KINLOSS SCOTLAND		1:45
10	"	852	"	—	OBOE II KINLOSS → LYNEHAM		1:05
17	C-45	1525	F/O GAUDRY		DORVAL → HU (RETURN FROM UK)		
19	"	1525	F/O GAUDRY		LOCAL CIRCUITS		
21	"	1525	F/L CREIGHTON		HU → DORVAL		
23	SABRE 4	XB126		—	TABLE II FORMATION FED LANDINGS (3)		1:35
23	T-33	086	F/O M-WAY	SELF	IF PRACTICE HU → UL	1:25	
25	C-45	1525	SELF	—	AIR TEST DORVAL		
25	"	1525			UL → HU		
29	SABRE 5	23005		—	FAMIL CRUISE, LETDOWNS		1:35
4	SABRE 2	19102		—	GCI - OTTAWA (EMERGENCY LANDING HU)		1:05

SUMMARY FOR:- NOVEMBER 1953
UNIT:- 1 OFU
DATE:- 30 NOV 53
SIGNATURE:- R. Hallowell F/O

TYPES:- C-45 —
T-33 1:25
SABRE J,5 — 13:25
TOTAL SABRE — 263:25

GRAND TOTAL [Cols. (1) to (10)] 623 Hrs 40 Mins

Year 1954 Month/Date	Aircraft Type	No.	Pilot, or 1st Pilot	2nd Pilot, Pupil or Passenger	Duty (Including Results and Remarks)	Single-Engine Day Dual (1)	Pilot (2)
	—	—	—	—	Totals Brought Forward	114 / 45	262 / 20
JUL 4	T-33	308	F/O WORTHY	SELF	IF		1:10
4	SABRE 5	188	SELF	—	HU LOW LEVEL TO BAGOTVILLE		1:00
4	SABRE 5	188	SELF	—	BG → HU		:40
6	SABRE 5	144	SELF	—	LOCAL P/C TEST		1:05
7	SABRE 4	XB761	SELF	—	A/C TEST + AEROS		1:05
7	SABRE 5	195	SELF	—	ENGINE TEST		1:15
8	SABRE 5	198	SELF	—	LOCAL LOW LEVEL		1:10
12	T-33	195	SELF	—	LOCAL P/C AEROS		1:10
12	SABRE 5	167	SELF	—	A/C TEST BEFORE RANDOM #6		1:20
13	SABRE 5	083	SELF	—	P/C GCA CIRCUITS AEROS		1:15
15	T-33	127	SELF	—	A/C TEST		1:15
16	SABRE 5	167	SELF	—	ST. HUBERT TO GOOSE BAY		1:50
16	SABRE 5	167	SELF	—	GOOSE BAY TO NARSARSUAK		1:45
20	SABRE 5	167	SELF	—	BW1 TO KEFLAVIK		1:45
20	SABRE 5	167	SELF	—	KEFLAVIK TO KINLOSS		1:40
21	SABRE 5	167	SELF	—	KINLOSS TO ZWEIBRÜCKEN		1:40
26	SAT-33	308	SELF	F/O HEGSTROM	IF GCA		1:25
27	SABRE	188	SELF	—	4L's GCI #HELLS DOWN 2GCA		1:15
27	T-33	195	F/O SIMARD	SELF	LET DOWNS 2 GCA		1:30
28	T-33	116	SELF	—	2000 LOCAL AEROS - CLOUD		1:10
28	SABRE 5	201	SELF	—	HUBERT TO BAGOTVILLE		:40
28	SABRE 5	201	SELF	—	BAGOTVILLE - ST. HUBERT		:40
28	T-33	191	SELF	F/O DONALD	IF, LE GCA,		1:05

GRAND TOTAL [Cols. (1) to (10)] 964 Hrs — Min
Totals Carried Forward 114 / 05 | 265 / 10

Early OFU flying from Bob Hallowell's log, including the first OFU Atlantic trip, a Bechers Brook operation.

July 13 Nobody missing when a/c leaves London airport. Good spirits all the way to Kef.

July 14 The 2 a.m. takeoff produced a last-minute scramble for some of the boys since the hotel clerk neglected to awaken everyone. The usual deadly North Star monotony. Arrived home at noon hour. Given long weekend to recover.

OFU diary

An OFU Thrash

Much of the spare time of a fifties fighter pilot was spent at the bar. Drinking was serious business, and every opportunity to "hang one on" was seized enthusiastically. A standard OFU thrash was held the last weekend of September 1955, with the "Boys from the Stable" being the guests of the USAF's overseas ferry operation in Dover, Delaware. The proceedings were noted by the OFU diarist.

After a false start from Dorval, occasioned by a surge in No.3 fan, our plush-seated North Star finally was off

More activity from St. Hubert with the OFU, this time from Jean Gaudry's log. Random 6 shows up.

for Dover. The two-hour trip stretched into a 5 1/2-hour marathon as IFR conditions caught us in three different stacks along the way. Baseball pool won by John Gaudry.

Arrive at dusk to be met by three Hawaiian dancing girls and four cases

Much flying was logged by the OFU "herd" in its T-33 flight. Here Mac Graham, Bill Worthy, John Hutt (on ladder) and Les Benson pose with a nicely painted 21299. (via R.G. Middlemiss)

of beer served up by half-lit hosts. A caravan of cars whisked OFU boys to barracks to get rooms. Immediately repaired to Mess. Impossible to buy a drink—American hospitality was overwhelming. Steak supper finally over with about 10:30 and skits began.

CO "Centre Post" Middlemiss was decorated with monster medal. Ribald ode to Canadians sung by Yanks. Narsarssuak hymn sung by all. Party continued long into the night. Much talk and much noise ....

[Next day ...] By 1 p.m. most of the Canadians were back at the bar ... Later, the Americans began trickling in and many animated comparisons of hangovers ensued. TV room for ball game in p.m. Evening began slowly, everyone pacing themselves admirably well .... OFU wheels show up finally in company with Col. Manda and too many women for Yank members of the party ...

[And finally, Sunday ...] Leisurely breakfast and a bus out to the North Star. Big surprise to find the Star freshly painted and decorated up. On one side "Royal North Texas Airforce." On t'other, "Royal Can Co. No Force at All." And splattered down the length of the fuselage, "Go Home Canucks."

While waiting for a/c to become serviceable, Ralph Annis daintily bent over and evacuated his stomach to the cheers and plaudits of an appreciative OFU audience. This was followed by a dual act wherein Joe Hurley and Bill Christianson honked in formation.

OFU diary

In 1956 the OFU distinguished itself with a record-breaking trans-Canada flight between Vancouver and Halifax. The flight was made in two sections. Ralph Annis and Chick Childerhose flying the 2740 miles in 5 hours 30 seconds, with one fuel stop at Gimli;

Bob Hallowell flies a Turkish Sabre 2 on Random 11, February 18, 1955. On his wing is a Greek Sabre. Under other-than-OFU circumstances, these aircraft would likely have been shooting at each other! Hallowell later took a bird strike in this aircraft as he landed at Prestwick on February 22. His boss put him up for a gong for saving the day, but never heard back about the matter. (via Bob Hallowell)

and Bernie McComiskey and Bruce Merklinger, forced to make a last-minute fuel stop at St. Hubert, making it across in 5 hours 12 minutes. Thirty years later their times still look good.

In June 1957 Random 30 was flown out of St. Hubert—24 Sabres and 6 T-birds. Bob Middlemiss had stepped down as CO at the end of 1956 and S/L Cuthbertson had taken over. It was "Cuppy" who had the regretful job of leading the OFU into history. Random 30 was the end, and on July 31 the OFU was disbanded. In over three years the unit had ferried more than 800 aircraft across the pond. Not a single aircrew had been lost, and but a handful of aircraft (including one of Jean Gaudry's—he was blown off the runway one day by the winds of Hurricane Hazel). The OFU had lived up to its motto of "Deliverum Non Dunkem." Oddly, not a single decoration was handed out to any of "the herd." S/L Middlemiss had recommended some of his boys, but he never heard back from those in charge of gongs at HQ. So the OFU, with its madcap gang of jet fighter pilots-cum-boozers-cum-lovers, simply drifted into history.

Random En Route Distances	
St.Hubert—Goose Bay	673 nm
Goose-Bay—Narsarssuak	711
Narsarssuak—Keflavik	674
Keflavik—Kinloss	677
Kinloss—Marville	639
—Grostenquin	642
—Zweibrücken	654
—Söllingen	690

OFU Annual Flying, 1954	
Expeditor	449:35 hrs
T-33	1753:55
Sabre	6719:10
Total	9120:10

OFU Annual Flying, 1955	
T-33	1746:30 hrs
Sabre	5899:00
(Mk.2,	826:10;
Mk.5,	494:00;
Mk.6,	4578:50)
Total	7645:30

removed when Spike Stevenschnook and his 147 mob were deported last year ... Speculation is running high as to where these monsters will strike next. The job done on the bar at the mess last Saturday night had all the appearances of their work ..."

Auxiliary Sabres
In the mid-fifties the RCAF began equipping its auxiliary fighter squadrons with Sabre 5s drawn from Air Division squadrons, which were by this time taking delivery of Sabre 6s. The air force for some time had hoped to upgrade the auxiliaries with CF-100s and/or Sabres. Eventually CF-100s

were ruled out, but a timely surplus of Sabre 5s meant that by 1956 squadrons in Vancouver (442 and 443), Toronto (400 and 411) and Montreal (401 and 438) could have a first-class fighter to replace their obsolete Vampires.

While many Sabre 5s were scrapped in the UK rather than transported all the way back to Canada, where there simply was no work for them, enough to supply the auxiliary squadrons were loaded aboard HMCS *Magnificent* on the Clyde and brought home (though others were ferried back by the OFU). By the fall of 1956 they were in service with the six squadrons. At St. Hubert, for example, the official handing-over

(Left) No.411's pilots March 1957. Back row: Garry Fraser, Pat Sheridan, Evan Schulman, Chick Childerhose, Armand Hollinsworth, Jim Lumsden, Gordie Mansell, Fred Mills and Ron Richardson. The front row includes Doug Evans, George Smola, Hal Davis, Bill Draper, D.K. Burke, Eric Lane and George Seymour. Next, Sabre 5s are loaded aboard ship in Scotland, February 2, 1957 for return to Canada for the auxiliaries. (Below) Sabre 5s of 401 (Aux) "City of Westmount" Squadron and 438 (Aux) "City of Montreal" Squadron over Montreal March 1957. The AB code designated 401 while BQ represents 438. Mount Royal is below '028 with the University of Montreal at its base. St. Joseph's Oratory is just left of centre. Taken by Barry Herron. (DND PL108129, 71195, 108151)

West Coast auxiliary Sabres: SL-036 of 442
Squadron is seen at Comox during a 1958 open
house. PF-301 sits in the snow at 6RD, Trenton
in December 1960 after being retired.
(Jimmie White, Larry Milberry)

ceremony took place October 28. (OFU diary entry: "Montreal's donkeys were strengthened by the formal presentation of six clapped-out Fives. "Mac" Gregor puts on very credible solo air show. Three of the elder drivers blacked-out just watching!")

Of course, the auxiliaries were already jet operations, and converting to Sabres was not difficult. They had been flying Vampires since 1948 and their own T-birds since 1954. Local air and ground crews were bolstered by regular force support personnel who were old hands from the Air Division, men like S/L D.R. Cuthbertson, ex-OC of 441 Squadron at Marville. F/O Chick Childerhose, formerly of 434 and the OFU, and F/O Rocky Redman, who flew with 444, all of whom helped staff the auxiliary at Toronto.

But the "weekend warriors' " affair with the Sabre was short-lived. Changes in policy soon brought an end to their fighter status, and by the summer of 1958 the auxiliaries had been ordered to turn in their Sabres. They had been redesignated as transport units and were soon flying Beech Expeditors—quite a shock for those getting used to being the hottest bunch of reserve fighter pilots on the continent! Their Sabre 5s were ferried off to be scrapped or to fly at Chatham with the OTU. In their two years of flying, the auxiliary squadrons posted a creditable safety record, with only one fatality recorded: F/L J.V. Karr, a TCA pilot with the Montreal reserves, who crashed in 23340 on February 16, 1957.

Air Force Photographer
Some of the finest RCAF photographs taken in the 1950s were the work of Barry Herron. As a young photographer he worked for the *Daily Province* in Vancouver, then joined the RCAF in 1953. After basic training, he came under the influence of S/L Roy Wood, F/L Lou LeCompte and F/L Ken Coleman in the PR office at HQ in Ottawa and, under their guidance, as he puts it, "my career blossomed."

Herron explains further:

Wanting desperately to fly but lacking the educational background to be able to re-muster, I figured the only way into the air was with my camera. For-

Downsview as it was in March 1957, and captured on film by Barry Herron. A 400 "City of Toronto" Sabre 5 taxis in under the nose of a just-retired Vampire. A T-bird tears off, likely for some instrument training, while a 436 Squadron C-119 and some Clunks (in storage) can be seen in the background.
(DND PL108122)

tunately I had no one restricting the crazy ideas I had to shoot photographs of aircraft in flight. Roy and Ken particularly were staunch supporters of my efforts to progress in this area and even fought AFHQ on my behalf.

In those days our basic camera was the 4 x 5 Speed Graphic. With one lens, a 135mm standard, we did everything. We finally received the updated Graphmatic packs that held nine shots and were semi-automatic. By today's standards, of course, all this was antiquated. However, I must admit that the results with the 4 x 5 format were outstanding, though getting in and out of a jet fighter or trainer with all that gear left something to be desired. Yet, if I was going to fly I had better adapt.

In those days there were two schools of thought about air-to-air shooting. Traditionally, one shot from a B-25 or a North Star. But I wanted more action and wanted to be right there, side-by-side and close in. At Avro at the time there was a young staff photographer, Hugh MacKechnie, working towards the same end as I. He was coming in with some excellent results, and one day I saw one of his photos on Roy's desk. I said, "If Hugh can shoot like that, so can I." Roy agreed. But after a mid-air collision between two CF-100s in which Hugh was involved, it became harder to get a ride in such aircraft.

Getting a sequence of photos such as a loop was a real challenge with our bulky equipment. You would get your straight and level shots first, then change the 4 x 5 slide manually, cock the front shutter, check the focus, and prepare for the next shot. Shoot the up vertical position and repeat the first procedures, and be ready to shoot

(Top) Childerhose dives straight for Niagara, T-bird and photographer in pursuit. Then, a less harrowing view of GW-204. (Below) Herron (left) and Childerhose plan their mad mission to The Falls. (DND)

F/O Chick Childerhose hangs his Sabre 6 right in close to the North Star photo plane carrying Cpl Barry Herron. Our intrepid camera man got so carried away shooting this photo that he nearly fell out of the airplane! The scene is over the St. Lawrence River east of Quebec in September 1956. (DND)

coming over the top upside down. Again, go through the change-over of the film, cock the shutter, and be ready for the vertical down angle. Once this shot was in the can you had to get the camera gear ready in your lap for the pull-out before the g-forces hit and sent the equipment flying. I have to tell you—it was one hell of a challenge. Today, the photographer sits there with compact 35mm camera complete with zoom lens for sizing, auto focusing, auto exposure and motor drive. The hardest part of the shooting would be in getting the ride!

From 1953 to 1958 I pursued aviation photography vigorously and logged over 2500 hours in the air. I was 23 years old, and suddenly there was no position any more for a flying PR photographer, and I left the air force. I'll never forget what Chick Childerhose once told me about flying. He was one of my great backers, and when I told him that I wanted to be a pilot he said, "As a pilot, you fly the machine to the maximum, enjoy it, then land. As a photographer you fly with the machine, and capture it to the maximum. When you land you can look back at that magic moment and still have it to cherish over and over again."

I recall one flight involving Chick. F/L Reg Smith of the OFU and I mustered up a T-33 to go to Toronto on business. Reg had to do some squadron stuff and I wanted to shoot the reserve

Sabres at Downsview where Chick was then flying. S/L Doug Harvey had already asked that I get a photo of a Sabre over Niagara Falls, saying "Shoot it diving straight into the falls. It should look spectacular, better than that T-bird thing you did at the falls for Training Command."

Organizing it with Chick and Jim Lumsden we set up with Air Traffic Control on both sides of the border. Everything was easily cleared, Chick flying the Sabre and Jim the T-bird with me running the camera. The plan was for the T-bird to fall in behind Chick line astern, descend, start pulling up, roll over the top, and head straight into the falls. A problem was that Jim (in the back seat) was short and I was tall, so all Jim could see was the tip of Chick's tail.

We started our first run, with me banging away. Jim focused on Chick's

AB-209 of 401 Squadron dives over the countryside near Montreal. Cpl Barry Herron took the rather dashing photo. It's typical of the outstanding work he did for the RCAF during the post war years. (DND PL108140)

Nearly three decades later: J. Barry Herron, leading Hollywood cinematographer.

tail, while all I could see was the falls rushing up at us! Chick wasn't pulling out as soon as I had hoped, so I anxiously told Jim that I had the shot and to go ahead and pull up any time. "Chick is still going in, so we should stick with him," was Jim's reply. Those falls looked awfully damned close by the time we pulled up through the mist just above Niagara! Things got hotter on our second run, as a little Piper Tripacer roamed straight across in front of us. When we didn't reply to Chick when he called us after his run, he thought we must have hit the little guy. But we were just too busy pulling g and getting the heck out of there.

The Sabre was one of the most graceful, photogenic aircraft I ever knew. I would jump at a chance to get up on a photo trip with one. One day the first Mk. 6s arrived, and I was so anxious to shoot them that I ended up scrounging a Dakota as the photo ship. F/L Doug Adkins would fly the Sabre, but was surprised about the Dakota part of the operation. Full out, our "Dak" could reach the speed where the Sabre pretty well fell out of the sky! But things worked out, as Doug hung the Sabre right under the door I was shooting from. We got some great shots of the Sabre clean. I still don't know how Doug managed to pull it off. On another job, three photographers, one shooting black and white, one colour and the other movies, all crammed into the tail turret of a Lancaster flying between Quebec and Montreal. We were to shoot a flight of Sabres, but before we did we got into some very heavy turbulence that bounced plane and contents around severely. But we were all young and having a ball. We laughed like hell about it all.

One day Chick called to see if we could get together to shoot a Mk. 6 he was about to take across the Atlantic. I wandered down to Ops to see what was around to shoot from. The ops officer soon had me lined up with my very own North Star photo plane! Soon Chick was formating on us and I was shooting away. I felt pretty good for a kid of 21 pulling off stunts like that. I stood there in the open door and for the last shots got a bit carried away and leaned too far out. Fortunately the crewman was there to pull me back in. I believe to this day that he actually saved my life.

I left the RCAF in March 1958. And there were reservations. I had had a fantastic life and had been doing what I loved—photographing and flying. My parents had moved to Los Angeles and I decided to join them and pursue my career. It would never be as exciting again, but over 30 years I eventually rose to be a director of photography in the motion picture industry specializing in aviation and underwater cinematography. I'd have to say that my whole career has added up to one of fulfillment at its highest. To the RCAF famous motto *Per ardua ad astra* ("Through adversity to the Stars") I'd like to add "On the wings of a jet with a camera in hand."

Barry Herron

Two nice "mixed bag" formations. In one, an early Sabre 5 joins a T-bird, and a CF-100 Mk 3 of No.3(F)OTU. In the other, taken in September 1955, we have an air show grouping: one of that year's all red Sabre 5s, a T-bird, a 425 Squadron Clunk, and an RAF Canberra. (DND PL87152, 135010)

to duty, skill, and courage have served as an inspiration and splendid example to fellow aircrew. He is highly recommended as being most worthy of the Air Force Cross."

Historic Landmark

On April 20, 1954, Canadair officially rolled out its 1000th Sabre, a Mk. 5, less than four years since the first Sabre 2 left the assembly line. The previous year production had reached its peak of some 40 Sabres a month, or two a day. Officiating at the 1000th Sabre celebration was Defence Minister Brooke Claxton, who noted, "It is the first time in Canada's history that an aircraft company has produced 1000 front-line planes." His speech writer had apparently not done his homework—during the war, Canadian Car had built over 1400 Hurricanes at

George Medals

On July 21, 1955, Sabre 23109 piloted by F/L E.L. Fine of 441 Squadron crashed near Marville while landing. F/L R.G. "Bob" Morgan, who was on runway control duty, sprinted to the wreck immediately and, though it was aflame, began working on the canopy to get it open. LAC Harry J. Waters arrived to help. Using a fire axe, they were able to smash the canopy and lift Fine from the burning Sabre. For their bravery in saving Fine's life, Morgan and Waters were awarded the George Medal.

In an incident at Chatham on August 6, 1957, F/L W.J. "Bill" Marsh, with the help of four airmen, got S/L L.P. Frizzle out of Sabre 23217, which had crashed off the station. Marsh also was awarded a George Medal for bravery.

The Air Force Cross was awarded to F/O Clive C. Batcock for which the citation reads: "On March 2, 1960, while taking part in a practice air fighting mission in a Sabre aircraft, F/O Batcock's aircraft suffered an engine failure. At that time, he was positioned about 50 miles from base at 42,000 feet with the sky completely undercast beneath him. The cloud extended from an uneven base from 1,000 to 5,000

feet and was unbroken to 30,000 feet. Beneath the cloud, visibility was limited by rain and fog. Under these conditions, F/O Batcock, with serious risk to his life, completed a superb forced landing at his home base. Throughout the descent, he remained calm and collected and followed all recognized procedures to cope with the emergency situation with precision and accuracy. F/O Batcock could have, without condemnation, abandoned the aircraft. However, a free-falling aircraft would have been a definite menace to his home base and other populated areas in the vicinity. F/O Batcock's skill, courage, and sense of responsiblity saved a costly aircraft and the lives of others who might have been endangered by a falling aircraft. His devotion

Fort William. Sabre 1000 became RCAF 23210. It made its first flight on April 5, 1954, and seems to have spent its flying career at Chatham with the OTU. It crashed near Bathurst, New Brunswick, on May 22, 1956, after the pilot ejected safely. It had accumulated 364 hours aloft.

The 6-3 Wing

From its earliest days it was clear that the F-86 was inferior to the MiG-15 in more than one respect. The MiG was faster at altitude, climbed faster and had a higher ceiling. Introduction of the F-86E closed the gaps, particularly with a wing mod. This was easy to effect and could be done as a field mod to older aircraft. The leading edge of the wing from the front spar forward held the section that carried the slats. These slats deployed at low speed to improve control. In the new "E"'s the leading edge section was removed and replaced with a one-piece section with fixed leading edge. A leading-edge wing fence 145 inches out from the aircraft centre line and a longer wing-tip fairing were also fitted. These mods increased wing chord and area (chord by 6 inches at the tip and 3 inches at the root—hence, the "6-3" wing), enabling the Sabre to climb higher, and have a decreased turning radius at altitude, as somewhat higher "g" could be pulled. Speed also increased as the wing's critical Mach was raised. Unfortunately there were penalties at the lower end of the speed range, as stall speed increased without the slats.

Canadair manuals give the following figures for the two wings:

Lovely view of the ever-pleasing Sabre. SU-350 of the Central Flying School (Trenton) is just over downtown Kingston. (DND PL95875)

Senior personnel at the completion of Sabre 1000 at Canadair: C.D. Howe, Geoff Notman, Brooke Claxton and Chief of the Air Staff, A/M C. Roy Slemon. (Canadair Ltd.)

Early slatted wing: chord (width of wing) at theoretical tip (223 inches from aircraft centre line) is 63 5/8 inches; and 123 5/8 inches at wing root. Wing area 287.9 sq. ft.

6-3 wing: chord at theoretical wing tip is 66 5/16 inches; and 130 3/16 inches at wing root. Wing area 302.26 sq. ft. (Variously known as "6-3" wing, hard-edge wing, slick wing).

On Canadair Sabres the 6-3 wing started at c/n 701 and ran to c/n 1400. With c/n 1401 a revised wing came into use. It had the increased chord and area of the 6-3 wing, but the slats were re-introduced, thereby giving the Sabre back its low-speed handling characteristics. At this time it was planned to increase the span by 1-foot wing-tip extensions, pushing it to 39 feet 1 3/8 inches and area to 313.33 sq. ft., but this idea was dropped. All Canadair Sabres had the single-store wing, with the wing tanks mounted at the wing station 99.5 inches from the aircraft centre line. Light stores such as rockets could be carried on other unstressed points.

Tech Rep Anecdotes

Canadair's field tech representatives could be called the company's front-line troops. Once Sabres left the plant for squadron service, it was the civilian tech reps who were the trouble-shooters between the operator and the manufacturer. As a rule, they were experienced "old hands" in the business who, for years on end, led noma-

dic lives serving the RCAF, RAF, Turks, Greeks, Yugoslavs, Colombians—whoever flew Canadair Sabres. One rep spent so many years abroad with the company that his stock reply when asked about goings-on at Canadair was, "Gosh, I couldn't tell you. I've been away for 30 years."

One of Canadair's long-time reps was Reg Thatcher. Before the war, he and his two brothers had built the "Porcupine Clipper," a Pou-de-Ciel homebuilt. They flew it around their home turf near Timmins, and on one occasion had to pay a $5.00 fine for flying without a licence. In the pre-war years all three brothers went to work for Fairchild at Longueuil, and early in the war Reg moved to Ferry Command at Dorval as a crew chief, and as a flight engineer on several Atlantic crossings. He joined Canadair in 1945, first on DC-3s, then North Stars, and when the first Sabre was being assembled at Cartierville he became involved with that project. His first field job was with 430 Squadron at North Bay, where he quickly learned the ropes of Sabre operations, being kept busy with field mods and repairs, organizing inspection schedules and giving lectures on the Sabre's "anatomy." In general, the tech reps' role was to be as helpful as possible to the operator.

Later Thatcher served at 3 Wing and Metz (1953-56). An interlude in Switzerland followed. The Swiss were re-equipping and wanted to evaluate the Sabre, Hunter and Mystère. Two Sabre 6s were borrowed from 4 Wing and given civil registrations, CF-JJB and 'JJC, and Hedley Everard was assigned to do most of the demonstration flying. As the demostrations would include firing and dropping dummy bombs, Thatcher and the rest of the Canadair team had to truck a large amount of ordnance from Germany to Switzerland. When the German trucks and Canadian crews arrived at the border, the Swiss were incredulous, and much palaver ensued. Finally the

Jack Forbes and Bob Lording were two other old-time Canadair tech reps. They too had started their careers with Fairchild before the war, working on such types there as the 71,82, Bolingbroke and Helldiver. Lording served overseas on a Spitfire squadron. They both joined Canadair at war's end, and one of their early tasks on the Sabre was at the Canadian National Exhibition in 1950. Al Lilly flew the first Sabre to Malton, and Forbes, Lording and company had the job of towing it the 15-odd miles to the CNE grounds. These were the days before modern wide highways, and though the project got under way around midnight, the Sabre didn't roll into the CNE till noon. Along the way were various adventures involving knocking down

temporary storage was necessary. The new Sabres were flown to Downsview and quietly left there until the company could schedule the mod. Bob Lording had the job of supervising run-ups of these Sabres over a period of several months. The situation had to be kept out of the press in the meantime to avoid adverse publicity.

Jack Forbes later served with the RAF, Luftwaffe, South Africans and Turks. He's in agreement with many others that the RAF Sabre squadrons included some of the wildest characters. He remembers, for instance, a dining-in night at Wildenrath which rapidly deteriorated into a full-fledged soccer game played in the mess. Next someone started a fire, and when a fire truck arrived the Sabre drivers snatch-

Tech rep Jack Forbes while serving with Canadair in Turkey. (via Jack Forbes)

Tech rep Bill Staruch and his boss from Cartierville, Tim Simms, and Sabre pilot Danny Kaye with his technical partner, Phil Perry, while all four were assisting the Turks with their first Sabres. (via D. Kaye)

foreigners with their wares were allowed in.

The Swiss officer in charge of this program was Col. Frye, an enthusiastic flying veteran. He made sure that the Canadair party was well cared for and even given a tour through one of the Swiss secret mountain fighter bases. He flew the Sabre and was extremely impressed, especially by its manoeuvrability in the tight mountain environment.

Although the Sabre was a hit during this tour, in the end it was the Hunter that the Swiss chose. It appears that the deciding factor was its heavy cannon armament vs the Sabre's .50 guns. Initially 100 Hunters were purchased, with many remaining in service today. Following his days as a Sabre tech rep, Thatcher spent 1958-65 at Greenwood on the Argus.

fences and overhead wires, with disbelieving residents startled out of their sleep by the commotion. Two weeks later came the reverse operation, and it ran into a snag at the very start— during the CNE, a flagpole had been erected in front of the Sabre display. The pole had to be bashed down before the Canadair crew could get things moving back towards Malton.

When plans were made to set up the Air Division, it was initially decided to knock down and crate Sabres for shipment overseas. Forbes recalls that the first few aircraft were crated and in storage at Scoudouc, awaiting shipment, when the plans were changed and Leapfrog was devised. He was soon at Scoudouc, reassembling the Sabres and sprucing them up for ferry flights. Another minor episode involved storage at Downsview of some 125 new Sabres. Spar trouble required a quick mod before the Sabres could be delivered, but a backlog meant that

ed the hose and turned it on the firemen! Clearly Bob Middlemiss' OFU boys had no monopoly on nutty behaviour.

Apparently the station commander at Wildenrath during Sabre years was very proud of the well-manicured grounds. One night some visiting Sabre pilots poured fuel onto the nicest of the CO's lawns, spelling out their squadron numbers, then branded the station by setting the works alight! Another night at Wildenrath one of the squadron leaders, after a heavy session at the bar, decided that he was going Sabre flying—in his mess kit. Nobody seemed willing to deter this Korean veteran, who took off and carried out a regular beat-up of the station. The

The RCAF's Accident Investigation Branch had its work cut out for it through the Sabre era. There were almost daily accidents or incidents involving the Sabre, and the small AIB contingent was hard pressed to keep on top of things. Yet, in spite of the odds, it did. Left, an AIB team is seen about to trek into the woods near Bagotville to investigate a Sabre prang. Often all that was left after a Sabre crash was a smouldering hole in the ground. In the close-up scene, AIB personnel study the aftermath of the crash of 23218 of the OTU. The aerial view is of the crash of an RAF Sabre out of St. Hubert. (Bottom) Two views of 19113 after F/O Ray Peterson put it into the woods out of Bagotville, April 7, 1952. The fir was flying! (first 3 via John Biehler, last 2 via Ken Hagarty)

Built for the Luftwaffe, Sabre 6 c/n 1815 comes off the production line at Canadair. Behind is the now-empty line. Eight years of frantic Sabre times at Cartierville have just come to an end. (Canadair Ltd.)

The Sabre 6's mighty power plant—the 7275 lb thrust Orenda 14. (Hawker Siddeley Canada 59548)

escapade won him a job flying a desk.

Of course, the tech rep posting gave a chap much experience with bent airplanes. Jack Forbes recalls that after one RAF mid-air collision, in which both Sabres made it back, the best way to salvage the situation was to make one good machine from the two bent ones.

One of the famous pranks remembered by Forbes from his Luftwaffe days involved Erich Hartmann. One day Hartmann was complaining to his young pilots that they simply didn't have the spirit of his wartime lads. Now he had recently been given a new white Porsche sports car. That night Hartmann couldn't find his car when he left the mess and one of the boys suggested he check out back. There

was his Porsche—at the bottom of the swimming pool. Spirit restored!

B.C. "Buck" Kirlin was another of Canadair's tech reps. He had joined the RCAF in 1941 and eventually got overseas flying Typhoons with 438 Squadron. Weeks after the war ended he was on course at the Fighter Leaders School, RAF Tangmere, where he flew the Meteor 3. Back home in Montreal, he spent several years with the auxiliary at St. Hubert, flying Harvards and Vampires, then joined Canadair in 1952. His tech rep postings as far as

Sabres went were at Chatham, St. Hubert, Grostenquin, Zweibrücken, Linton-on-Ouse, Chivenor and in Greece. He recalls the Greeks as a definitely competent bunch of fliers. Mainly because of the build-up of heat through the day, they did most of their flying in the morning. Kirlin remembers the day a Sabre crashed on takeoff. The ailerons had been incorrectly rigged and were not checked out prior to flight, and with the pilot's first application of bank, both ailerons went down.

End of an Era

What Al Lilly had in a sense begun on August 8, 1950, came to an end on October 9, 1958, when the 1815th and last Canadair Sabre rolled off the production line at Cartierville. The aircraft was turned over to the Luftwaffe, and the bays were cleared for other work. Important projects like the CL-44 would soon be the big talk around Canadair, but the Sabre would never be forgotten. It had brought in $560 million in sales revenue for Canadair and its 2000 or so suppliers and subcontractors; and $190 million besides in salaries and wages. During the Sabre era, employment at Canadair soared from 5000 in 1950 to some 16,000 eight years later. Canadair's policy of seeking procurement of raw materials and parts from Canadian sources further strengthened the country's steadily developing aircraft industry. At the start of the program, 90 per cent of components had been US-made, but by 1956, 85 per cent

Famous Canadair shot of its aircraft finishing operation at Cartierville. Shiny new Sabre 6s, some old 2s, and some T-birds are shown.

were being made in Canada. Raw materials were 83 per cent Canadian. While Sabre operators, especially of the Orenda-powered versions, were flying one of the finest day fighters of the times, it's clear that the country as a whole had also been a major beneficiary. And it would be another full decade before the Canadair Sabres would be retired from air force duties.

Sabre 1815 later went to Pakistan and fought in the 1971 war with India. In 1986 it was still in storage in Pakistan awaiting final disposal.

Stan Russell, who was superintendent of the F-86 project, noted when the last aircraft rolled out of the plant: "When they handed me the job of superintendent of F-86 production it was a great thrill to be in on the groundwork of the first jet fighter to be built in Canada. My job was to lay out the line in Plant 2 and organize the work in general. The Sabre was far removed from any aircraft we had ever worked on. The intricacy of design and construction was of an order far higher than we had been used to, but the men met the challenge.

"The high rate of production we reached called for special planning and

superior quality of workmanship. The two-a-day rate that was attained would not have been possible without excellent teamwork."

Bob Lording was assistant foreman on the final line and noted, "Since I was able to work on the first Sabre I feel badly about the line coming to an end. It is an amazing airplane and has proven itself in many battles. It is the Spitfire of this era. Jack Forbes, Frank Clarke and I nursed the Sabre through many trials and tribulations that come with building a new airplane and I think we all feel a deep sense of regret that it is gone."

Perhaps the Sabre was gone from Cartierville, but Canadair's production lines would soon be packed with even more exciting fighter planes—CF-104s and CF-5s.

Canadair projects during the Sabre era		
Period	*Type*	*No. Built*
1946-50	North Star/Argonaut	71
1950-58	F-86 Sabre	1815
1952-59	T-33 Silver Star	656
1953	Beech T-36	None (227 cancelled)
1957-60	Argus	33

(Top left) Avro photographer Hugh Mackechnie captures a Mark 5 in a pair of nice diving shots; then (below) shows its lovely outline in a plan view. (Above) Gun harmonizing at Uplands, January 19, 1953; then an engine run at night. (left page via Bill Kidd, DND PL55762, Canadair Ltd.)

(Top) Canadair chase Sabre formates with the CL-41R and a 104. (Right) A Sabre tucks in behind an Argus flight at the Toronto air show, *circa* 1960. (Below) The Queen chats with John Jay Hopkins during a tour of the Sabre line. Then, a snap of Canadair pilots Scotty McLean, Don Simmons (CEPE) and Ed Coe. (Right) T-bird and Sabre 5, a pair of great Canadian products; and the glamorous "missile-with-a-man-in-it" CF-104, the RCAF's replacement. It is flown here by Bill Kidd. (via S.B. Fleming, Larry Milberry, Canadair the rest)

Sabre 5 Acceptance Procedure
Flight Test

Climb
(98% rpm. JPT Max 700°C)
1. Cabin pressurization:
   11,000-13,200' at 2.75 ratio to 21,200'
   11-000-13,200' at 5.0 ratio to 31,000'
2. Oxygen system: Check pressure demand operation
3. Controls—alternate and normal
4. Canopy heat, defrost and de-icer
5. Instruments, temps. and press.
6. VHF and radio compass

35,000' Level
1. Max JPT at 98% rpm 700°C
2. Cabin pressurization
   (After 3 to 5 minutes, rpm 85% cabin 14,500 + 1000')
3. VHF
4. Radio compass
5. Engine acceleration control (throttle open from 65% in 2 to 3 seconds)
6. Oxygen system

High Mach Dive
1. Dive Mach No. 95
2. Wing roll (above .93)
3. ASI and barber pole (12 kts. diff at .95)

25,000' Level
(Trim at 85% Mach No. approx .84)
1. Lateral trim
2. Alternate controls (trim change)
3. Emergency alt. control override (pressure 34-3600 PSI)
4. Aileron roll back
   Stick centering

5. Flight instruments
6. Temps and pressures
7. Oxygen system

Stalls, Low Speed Flight
(10,000-15,000')
1. Lateral stability: 130-150 kts
2. Stalls:
   Clean:— 110-115 kts
   Dirty:— 100-106 kts
3. Undercarriage operation:
   Extension 6-10 secs
   Retraction 5-8 secs
4. Flap operation

High Speed Run
(100% rpm, 10,000')
1. Mach No. 92 + .005
2. Temps and pressure
3. Fire warning lights
4. ASI, barber poles
5. Extend dive brakes: Min. utility press 1500 PSI. Check closing (time 2.5 secs)
6. Subject a/c to 4½ to 5 g. (Rolling pull-out) Check g-suit valve.

Remaining Checks
1. Gun sight, and ranging
2. Radio compass-Stn. passage
3. Fuel quantity gauge
4. U/c warning horn light and horn on between 58-64% rpm at 2000 ft, at IAS of 185 kts
5. Gyrosyn compass

Sabre on loan from the RCAF flies chase on the second pre-production CF-105 Arrow. (Hawker Siddeley)

Sabre 6 23440 flying "clean" during its time as a chase plane with Avro at Malton. (Hawker Siddeley 61847)

Test Flying at Malton

From the early days of the Orenda engine, Avro made use of the F-86 for test-bed purposes. At first the F-86A ('069) was the workhorse, then various Canadair Sabres were used. One of these was destroyed in a devastating hangar fire at Malton. Later on, Avro used a Sabre 6 (23744) as its prime chase plane during Arrow test flights.

Orenda test pilot Mike Cooper-Slipper recalls flying the F-86A. It had an improvised power control for its early Orenda engine. On takeoff the pilot had only one setting! Even so, he was thrilled to be able to fly an airplane that was "king of the skies." He remarks that "the Sabre was very easy to fly. You just pointed it and opened up. Things then happened very fast and you were flying. The ailerons were exceptional and you could do three or four rolls in a flash. But much above 500 knots (when flying low) the aircraft could start to roll, caused, we determined, by a minute difference in wing incidence. You had to be very

careful correcting, and could get a lot of aileron on to counterbalance. This was mainly a problem when doing low-level high-speed demonstrations." On one flight to Montreal from Malton, Cooper-Slipper covered the distance in 28 minutes, still very fast by today's jetliner standards.

Sabre flying from the log of Peter Cope. Most Avro test pilots logged some time on the Sabres on loan to their company. Of course, these pilots were mainly flying CF-100s except for those who were assigned to testing the CF-105 Arrow. Peter Cope made five Arrow flights for a total of 5:25 hours.

Orenda test pilot Mike Cooper-Slipper aboard '069. (Avro Canada 37933)

Date	Sabre	Time	Notes
21-9-51	FU-069	:30	Initial famil.
21-9-56	23283	1:15	Elevator control assessment
	23283	1:05	" " "
10-1-58	23744	1:30	Check flight and GCI cooperation
23-4	"	1:05	Arrow chase
23-4	"	1:15	" "
1-8	"	1:50	" " RL202 first flight
16-9	23539	1:15	" "
22-9	"	1:40	" "
16-10	23744	:45	" "
19-10	"	1:30	" "
28-10	23539	1:25	Fuel consumption check
11-11	23744	1:40	Arrow chase

Aerobatics

Early Jet Aerobatics

The first Vampires for the RCAF arrived by ship in late 1947. They were freighted to Toronto where they were assembled by de Havilland. On January 7, 1948, Russ Bannock of DH, a well-known wartime Mossie pilot, flew the first one, No.17014. January 19 the first Vamps were taken on strength by the RCAF, and in December 410 Squadron at St. Hubert under S/L R.A. Kipp became the first Canadian squadron equipped with them.

Meanwhile Vampires had entered service at Trenton with the Central Flying School, and through 1948 the CFS instructors toured throughout southern Ontario and the bordering states doing air shows. One was on June 27 at Selfridge AFB near Detroit, where CFS pilots S/L Barrett, F/L Irish Ireland and F/L Jack Phillips performed. There was a performance at the CNE in Toronto in August and another at Niagara Falls, N.Y., in September. On the way back to Trenton from there, pilot Les Banner had a fatal crash near Oshawa.

The following year 410 Squadron formed a full-fledged aerobatic team under F/L D.C. "Don" Laubman with Bill Bliss, Mike Doyle, Bob Kipp, Omer Levesque, Joe Schultz and Bill Tew, and put on a summer's worth of scorching air shows. The team, called the Blue Devils, was made up of solid wartime fighter jocks. There were appearances in 1949-50 at such events as the Michigan Air Fair, Cleveland Air Races and the CNE, and at Boston and Chicago. The Blue Devils did much to promote Canada's fledgling post-war air force and instilled a sense of pride among Canadians, and perhaps a bit of envy in the flying community south of the border.

Although the RCAF began forming Sabre squadrons in 1951, it was some time before team aerobatic flying with the new fighter began. There was simply no time for it, as build-up of the squadrons had top priority. Besides, most of the pilots were young and inexperienced. But as squadrons began settling down to routines, there was time to think about some fancy stuff, especially as the public was so keen to see the Sabre perform. It was by far the biggest air show attraction among the new fighters.

At North Luffenham, No.1 Wing formed an annual demonstration team which toured the UK and Continent. Pilots in 1954 were F/Os H.R. "Dick" Wingate (leader), A.M. "Mac" Gillies (No.2), E.N. "Norm" Ronaasen (No.3) and G.J. "Jeb" Kerr (box). Other pilots would learn the fundamentals of precision flying while at

North Luff, flying with the semi-official wing team.

Once the Air Division moved to the Continent there was a drive to establish an official Air Div team. After all, most other European air forces had a national team, and the USAF in Europe had its Sky Blazers. The RCAF team came into being in April 1954 and included F/L C.E. "Chuck" Keating (lead), F/O S.E. "Syd" Burrows (No.2), F/O J.L. "Jack" Frazer (No.3) and F/O E.R. "Rick" Mace (No.4). It had to do all its work-ups in off hours, morning and evening, as the pilots were expected to fulfil their normal duties as squadron jocks.

At first the team hadn't a name, but one day W/C Lyte Gervais suggested the boys paint their Sabres red and adopt the name Fireballs. That was that, and the paint job was soon applied. The Fireballs conducted their

Chuck Keating, Rick Mace, Syd Burrows and Jack Frazer—The Fireballs. Mace was killed in a T-bird in September 1954. (via S.E. Burrows)

Sky Lancers Tony Hannas (421 Squadron), "BR" Campbell (430), L.M. Eisler (421), Gerry Theriault (430) and Herbie Graves (416) pose with External Affairs Minister Lester B. Pearson. (DND via H. Graves)

first practice formation aeros on April 23 and on June 6 put on their first shows at Tours and Rennes. There followed a busy schedule, with one wild day being September 6 when shows were flown at Nancy, Sedan, Metz, Grostenquin, Zweibrücken and Baden.

On September 13 Syd Burrows was knocked out of the team following a mid-air with a hawk. Syd lost the use of one eye, and F/O L.W. "Bill" Grip took his spot. The season closed on September 29 with a show at 4 Wing. Along the way, AFHQ got wind of the brightly painted Sabres and someone hit the roof. The red scheme was considered to be unseemly and a stern order arrived at the Air Div that the paint was to be removed. This was quickly done, and the team lost part of its glamour.

In early 1955 the Air Div formed a new team at 2 Wing, the Sky Lancers, led by F/L Tony Hannas with F/Os B.R. Campbell (No.2), L.M. "Len" Eisler (No.3), G.C.E. "Gerry" Thériault (No.4) and H.L. "Herbie" Graves (solo). The first practices began in mid-April with two sessions a day thereafter, and the air show circuit soon got under way with displays at Chaumont (April 25), Auxerre (July 17), Volkel (August 19), Marignane (August 24), Blackbush (September 8), Tours (September 11), Düsseldorf (September 17), Grostenquin (Septem-

ber 20), Dortmund (October 2) and Cambrai (October 6). The shows ran 15-20 minutes and included the usual diamond formation fly-bys, loops, rolls, cloverleaf turns, various formation changes, and closing bomb bursts. The shows in Germany were a special hit, as the Germans were only beginning to reform their air force and jets were still a novelty.

On one practice session, "BR" Campbell had a bit of a scare. Pulling out at the bottom of a loop, his plane began to shake violently. Campbell got down OK, but found that he had taken 11g. The Sabre behind had precipitated things by bumping Campbell's

The Sky Lancers doing their stuff. (DND via H. Graves)

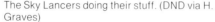

and taking a large chunk off the starboard stabilizer. Another item from Campbell's log was a flight August 24 of 2:45 hours, surely one of the longer RCAF Sabre trips recorded. This was done between Marignane and Grostenquin, and was the result of a bet between Campbell and Thériault that it was possible. In October 1955 the first edition of the Sky Lancers was disbanded.

In January 1986 Tony Hannas recorded a few of his Sky Lancers recollections. He begins with a reference to a mid-air collision:

First of all, the collision occurred on a practice run which we used to make two or three times a day. Before we had aircraft specifically assigned to us, we had to scrounge them from the squadrons. The easiest way of doing this without creating animosity was to do one sortie in the early morning, before squadron ops began, and one in the evening, after they terminated. This made it easier to get four Sabres for our other sortie around midday.

When we finally got our own aircraft, we maintained a similar routine. Additionally, in the evening we could practice over the airfield—most shows would be at airports, and thus we could use the runways as references. Otherwise, I had found a small lake about 10 miles south of Grostenquin which we used as a simulated airfield.

The day of the incident (July 13, 1955) was quite bumpy, so instead of doing our routine at low level over the lake, I decided to do it at 1000 feet. During a line astern pass (four a/c line astern) somebody touched somebody starting a chain reaction in which Nos.2,3 and 4 were each damaged. We used to fly a very tight formation, one of the tightest of all European teams, and in line astern, the noses were directly below the tail pipes in front; and in box formation, the wings of the wingmen and the leader were overlapped by at least three feet. Our metal-to-metal separations were probably 24 - 30 inches, so our margin for error was little. We felt comfortable with things, and felt compactness presented better unity, and a better picture from the ground.

No.3 (Eisler) suffered the most with the nose of his Sabre damaged, his pitot head lost (hence no airspeed reading) and most elevator lost. BR Campbell, who was No.2, received tail damage; and Gerry Thériault, No.4,

had a dent in his nose. I immediately picked up No.3 on my wing and returned him to base where he landed flying formation right down to the runway. I then did the same with No.2. Gerry felt safe in coming in by himself.

When the collision occurred, I was checking the positioning of the three behind me in my rear-view mirror. Suddenly, two aircraft broke violently up and to the right and left, and the third violently down. Doing the practice at 1000 feet certainly saved at least one aircraft.

One thing that this reinforced was the image of the Sabre as a sturdy

machine. From my first trip in it, I always had the sense that it was like a powerful horse. I suppose the way you got into it supported this feeling—you climbed up the side not unlike stepping into a stirrup, and then into the cockpit which was like the saddle. The damage suffered by Eisler's Sabre showed what a tough "old horse" the Sabre was.

July 31 we did a show at Metz at which RAF Hunters and USAF T-birds participated. Both teams spent Sunday night at 2 Wing, and on Monday a

The "instant" aerobatic team mentioned here by Tony Hannas. (DND LR82-433-1)

make-up aerobatic team was put together with a Hunter leading, two Sabres flying wing, and a T-bird in the slot. They did a couple of loops and rolls over the field, and some pictures were taken.

I recall that at Metz my mike failed, so I was not able to give lead-in instructions or directions during manoeuvres. We were working in a confined area, so I had to pull more g than usual. This, coupled with doing the show in silence, made for some extra sweat. The other time we suffered damage was at Düsseldorf. The day was cloudy with drizzle. One of the performances was by a very skilled glider pilot. His show ended in disaster as he smashed into Herbie Graves' Sabre just as we were getting ready to fire up. Thus, Herbie had to be left behind.

The Sky Lancers was the first team to take off and land in box formation, and we were quite proud of that. Other teams used to take off in formations of four, but No.4 in an echelon right position off the wing of No.2, and he slid into the box position after takeoff. Gerry used to sit with his nose just right of my tail, and as soon as the wheels came off the ground he moved over a few inches into truly line astern. On landing, because he was lower than the rest of us, he would touch down first, and when he did, would advise me so I could cut the power and the rest of us could land. This seemed to baffle the other teams more than anything else. They couldn't see how Gerry could control his aircraft directly in the wake from my tailpipe. They

couldn't see from a distance that he was slightly off centre on takeoffs and on landing, and only his rudder was in my wake.

You might get the impression that we were a travelling circus, and I suppose we were in a way. Practically every weekend over the summer the aerobatic teams of Canada, the UK, US, France and Italy would meet to put on an air show. We got to know the other teams well, and there was camaraderie and much discussion of techniques over many wines and beers. There was keen competition to be innovative and produce something new. I think we had a fine team, and we were always in demand and very welcome wherever we went.

Tony Hannas

Sky Lancers L.C. "Stretch" Price, E.H. "Ed" Welters, F.D. "Dale" McLarty, J.H. "Jake" Adams and F.K. Axtell. All but Price died in a training accident near Strasbourg. (DND)

In early 1956 the Sky Lancers were reformed, this time at 4 Wing. The team comprised F/Os J.D. "Dale" McLarty (lead), J.H. "Jake" Adams, F.K. "Fred" Axtell, L.C. "Stretch" Price and E.H. "Ed" Welters. The team got busy with its practising and the Sabres were painted in an attractive scheme, but all preparations were for naught. At about 2:20 in the afternoon of March 2 near a village close to Strasbourg the Sky Lancers' four-plane formation thundered straight into the ground as it came out of a loop. Everyone except for F/O Price was killed, and he hadn't been flying.

Albert Falderbaum swoops along upside down at the Düsseldorf air show, September 18, 1955; then has the gall to crump into Herbie Graves' Sword. Albert survived OK, and the Sabre, after some minor repairs, was OK too. (via H. Graves)

The funeral of F/Os Adams, Axtell, McLarty and Welters. (DND)

Thus, with great sadness, the Air Division terminated its involvement in team aerobatics.

The Golden Hawks

In 1959 Canada celebrated the 50th anniversary of manned, powered, heavier-than-air flight. It had been on February 23, 1909, that J.A.D. McCurdy had first flown the *Silver Dart* at Baddeck, Cape Breton Island. But 1959 had added significance, being the 35th anniversary of the RCAF, formed April 1, 1924. So it was appropriate that Canada celebrate its aviation heritage in a big way in 1959, and the highlight would be a team of gleaming Sabres performing aerobatics from coast to coast—the Golden Hawks.

The RCAF had a solid 10 years of experience in jet aerobatics when the CAS, A/V/M Hugh Campbell, gave his wholehearted support to a 1959 team. The Golden Hawks were authorized to operate for one year only, and HQ named S/L J.A.G.F. "Fern" Villeneuve team leader. He was a leading Sabre pilot who had flown aerobatics from North Luff. Other pilots picked were F/L Ralph E. Annis (solo), F/O J.T. Holt, F/L G.J. "Jeb" Kerr, F/L J.D. "Jim" McCombe, F/O J.T. Price (solo), F/L E.J. "Ed" Rozdeba and F/O W.C. "Bill" Stewart. Home for the Golden Hawks was to be Chatham. In charge of engineering was F/L Ray Grandy. Villeneuve

reported in at Chatham on March 2, 1959, and began getting his team ready for a busy season. In March, April and May the Hawks logged 271, 422 and 108:10 hours in the air, for 801:10 hours of training, an average of about 100 hours for each pilot in little over two months. On May 11 the team put on a dress rehearsal at Rockcliffe, with AFHQ personnel looking on. Next day it departed for the summer's work and on May 16 performed its first public

The Hawks' famous bomb burst, this time over English Bay, Vancouver on July 11, 1959. (DND PL64504)

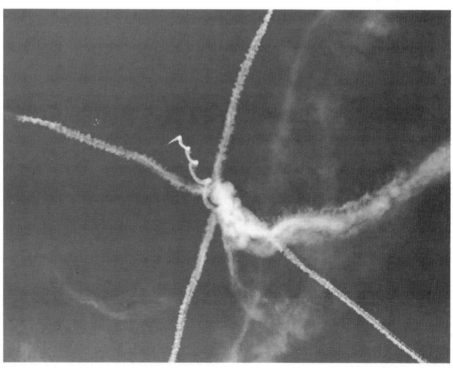

show for the crowd at Air Force Day, Torbay, Newfoundland. The Golden Hawks were to repeat their glittering 25-minute show 65 times in 1959. Their sequence of loops, rolls, crossovers and bomb bursts would be the talk of the town everywhere they went until their last show at Windsor on September 20.

The season had been a great success, but the lid was put on everyone's enthusiasm with the loss of Jeb Kerr. While in the circuit for a landing at Calgary on August 10, his Sabre (23073) collided with a Piper Tripacer. He and two doctors in the Tripacer were killed. In another incident, J.T. Price had a bird strike near Halifax while in the midst of a show. With his windscreen and canopy shattered and visor torn away, Price was in a pickle but kept his Sabre under control. Annis joined up with some encouraging words, and Price soon had everything sorted out and made a safe landing at Shearwater. Annis then returned and finished his solo flying routine.

The popularity of the Golden Hawks made disbanding them seem unthinkable, so the CAS agreed to keep them flying. For 1960, the same pilots were on the roster, except that F/O Holt was replaced by F/L D.V. "Dave" Tinson. F/L Dan McKinnon took over engineering. The following season was another success and included shows across the border in the US. The next season, McCombe became leader, with Rozdeba and Stewart staying on, and

The 1960 Golden Hawks. In the back are W.C. "Bill" Stewart, E.J. "Ed" Rozdeba, Jim McCombe, Fern Villeneuve. The others are "JT" Price, Ralph Annis, and Dave Tinson. (DND PL64728)

the rest being replaced by F/Ls B.R. Campbell, J.L. "Jack" Frazer, Lloyd J. Hubbard and A.F. "Alf" McDonald. Bob Dobson was commentator.

Late in 1960 Fern Villeneuve had a serious mishap at Chatham. On a local night training mission on November 7 he experienced severe engine trouble, and the citation for his later award of the Air Force Cross describes what followed: "At this time Squadron Leader Villeneuve, having just completed an overshoot, was between Chatham aerodrome and the town of Newcastle. He chose to turn away from the built-up area before ejecting rather than risk having the abandoned aircraft crash in the town. After completing his turn he noticed sparks coming out through the tail area together with a strong burning odour, and he had to flame out the engine. As Squadron Leader Villeneuve was now approaching another built-up area he again made the decision to remain with the aircraft rather than to eject. The controls then switched automatically to the alternate system, and the pilot selected the undercarriage down, dive brakes out, and flaps down. Just prior to landing at Chatham aerodrome the

The Hawks in one of their "crazy" formations. (via Bill Stewart)

Fern Villeneuve tries out the F-100 Super Sabre at Nellis. (DND PL64673)

controls seized, which resulted in the aircraft hitting hard and bouncing, and he levelled the wings with coarse use of rudder before the second impact. As the aircraft skidded along the runway on fire the pilot ejected the canopy and escaped, but he sustained a compression fracture of the spine. Squadron Leader Villeneuve's skill, courage, and determination in landing his aircraft rather than ejecting precluded the possibility of the aircraft crashing into a built-up area with tragic results."

In 1961 the Golden Hawks flew a busy season, with performances as far away as USNAS Pensacola, and the media everywhere acclaimed them as second to none in the aerobatic business. 1962 found Hubbard leading, with holdovers Campbell, Frazer and McDonald, the additions being F/Ls N.J. "Norm" Garriock, George E. Miller and E.J. "Ed" McKeogh. The Hawks' final year was 1963, Hubbard again leading, with veterans Garriock

and McKeogh. Joining new were F/Ls D.J. Barker, L.W. "Bill" Grip, C.B. Lang and A. Young. The season ended in Montreal with the 317th Golden Hawk air show. The Hawks had become the pride of the RCAF, and of Canadians young and old everywhere.

On February 7, 1964, the team was formally disbanded. The government claimed this would save $750,000 that year, money that was needed in other more vital areas. They had no idea what a bargain in publicity alone the Golden Hawks had been—cheap at several times the price. Some also claimed that the Sabre was getting too old for its role and there was no suitable replacement yet. Few in the know would have agreed.

Engineering Officer for the Golden Hawks in 1961-1962 was Phil Perry. He had completed a tour at 3 Wing in 1956, had been posted back to Trenton, then been commissioned in 1958. While stationed at Sea Island, he was asked by Jim McCombe to join the Hawks. Of these glory years, Perry writes:

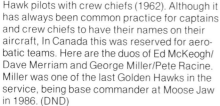

Hawk pilots with crew chiefs (1962). Although it has always been common practice for captains and crew chiefs to have their names on their aircraft, In Canada this was reserved for aerobatic teams. Here are the duos of Ed McKeogh/Dave Merriam and George Miller/Pete Racine. Miller was one of the last Golden Hawks in the service, being base commander at Moose Jaw in 1986. (DND)

Get that fella's number! Golden Hawk '551 fairly staggers past the crowd as the pilot takes his eyes off the road to do a bit of waving. This photo was snapped at Mount Hope on September 3, 1961. (Jack McNulty)

23037 heads downhill. (DND)

This was probably the highlight of my air force career. I was involved with a simply wonderful bunch of highly skilled professional servicemen doing what they loved. We had top priority when it came to support and equipment, and were treated strictly first class everywhere by everyone.

On the Hawks I had some 48 ground crew carrying out all aircraft maintenance during winter when the pilots were training at Chatham. When we were on tour (May to September) the team was broken down with 20 ground crew on the road and 28 at Chatham (if we were in the east) or Gimli (if we were in the west). Many of our techs were to stay with the team from beginning to end. My right hand man was FS "Tousie" Tousignant, who supervised our elite group of NCOs and airmen. I cannot say enough about our technicians. Being on the road and working out of pack-up boxes to maintain seven Sabres for five months was not easy. But they did it, and we never flew a show with less than six aircraft, and very seldom without the seventh as a flying spare. It took a lot of work over long hours, but, above all, teamwork. At the same time, our base maintenance crew backed us up with inspections and always had things ready to go when needed.

Morale was always very high, as the boys were so proud to belong to the Golden Hawks, and of the job they were doing. And some of our fellows were real characters. LAC Neuf Faulkner seemed to know everyone everywhere we went and could scrounge, beg or steal whatever was required. This took explaining sometimes, but we didn't always have time to go through normal channels. Once at Edmonton, there were no trucks to offload our equipment when we arrived, and we had a show to fly. So I called Neuf over and told him to find us a stake truck, which he promptly did. But soon I had a raging warrant officer after me, looking for a stake truck "stolen" from the motor pool. Good old Neuf! Sadly, he passed away recently after a long fight with cancer.

A real highlight was our appearance at Pensacola to help celebrate the 50th anniversary of US naval air. There we were, performing alongside the Blue Angels with their Grumman Tigers, and the Thunderbirds with their Super

Two of the world's most famous and successful fighter types, both designed by North American, team up on a photo mission: Golden Hawk Sabres and a P-51 Mustang. The Mustang is CF-LOR, one of the early Canadian civil warbirds. (DND PCN7040)

Three indispensable Hawks at Chatham in 1961: F/L Rocky Van Vliet, PRO; F/O Phil Perry, EO; and FS "Tousi" Tousignant. (DND)

The Hawks team up with the F-100s of the Thunderbirds during the CNE air show. In this case, September 15, 1959 out of Trenton. (DND PL64549)

Pilots of the Golden Hawks, Thunderbirds and Blue Angels in a historic photo taken at the Pensacola air show in 1961. (via Bill Stewart)

ber seeing Lundahl there, sweating blue and red through his white shirt, but having a ball. But I knew that we had a big job ahead of us in a few hours. The mixers would have to be on the ball. That morning I was on the flight line bright and early, and it was already 90°. I went over to see how the mixing was going on, and there was poor old Lundahl. He could hardly hold his head up, and he had been sick—right into the barrel.

We put on one of our finest shows that day, with the best smoke you could ask for. W/C Allan was elated, saying, "Whatever your boys did, Phil, tell them to keep it up." I relayed this to Lundahl, but all he had to say was, "To hell with you!"

When I joined the Golden Hawks they had a Beech 18 for the OC, PR officer, commentator and EO to use getting around from show to show. This was poor, as you can imagine we were always late. But we were somehow able to get our hands on two T-33s and one, 21500, we painted in our gold and red colour scheme. This one was for the OC and EO, while 21616, your basic T-bird, was for the PRO and commentator. During my tour with the Hawks, I put in over 300 hours on these aircraft. A lot of this was in the front seat, especially when flying with lanky Jack Frazer, who liked the roomier back cockpit. For a ground pounder I became very adept on the T-bird. Of course, I had the best of instructors.

The golden T-33 was a real crowd pleaser, so there were many low passes on arrival and departure. It made the front page of the Timmins newspaper when the Hawks put on a show at the airport opening there. We came in

Sabres. We spent five days there, and there was a real sense of competition among the teams both at practice and during the show.

It was very hot in Pensacola, and we had real trouble with our smoke. The white was OK, as it was made from straight 1010 engine oil, but the red and blue were different. They were a mix of oil, tryclorethelene, and waxoline dye from England. The mixing was as dirty a job as one could imagine, done in 45-gallon drums away from the flight line, as the stuff seemed to spread over everything. If one of our golden Sabres developed a leak in the smoke system, it pretty well required a re-paint (which we did on the road). The mixers would get the dye on them, and sweat red and blue for a month! Chief mixer was Cpl Lundahl, a great big armourer.

The heat was causing our smoke

systems to plug, so we tried varying our formula as a remedy. In practice sessions, this could give us pink, sometimes purple, instead of red and blue. Well, our OC, W/C Jack Allan was on my back over this, I was on Tousie's, and poor old Lundahl was ending up with it all!

The night before the show there was a great party for all three teams. It lasted into the wee hours, and I remem-

The Hawks' showy T-bird. (Larry Milberry)

The entire complement of Golden Hawks in 1961. (DND)

ahead of the team so I could check the parking area, etc. After landing and turning 180° to taxi in, the nose wheel collapsed, right in the middle of the runway. This made us quite popular. We blocked the runway for two hours and managed to delay the departing TCA flight. That afternoon, the local paper headlined us (with a photo of our broken T-bird) to the effect, "Golden Hawks Arrive to Open New Airport."

Our last show for 1961 was at Dow AFB at Bangor, Maine. Outside the officers' quarters there were three almost-antique surreys on cement pedestals with the wheels strapped down. These had been loaned by some local farmers. I don't know who got the idea, but we thought it would be a great skit to swipe one, take it home to Chatham, paint it gold, and mount it outside our Hawk building. This took some planning as Dow, a SAC base, had top security. To get the surrey out

The Golden Hawks at Trenton in 1961: in front, George Miller, Alf McDonald, Ed McKeogh, Jim Giles; in back, Phil Perry, Bruce Lebans, Norm Garriock, Jack Allan, Lloyd Hubbard, "BR" Campbell and Jack Frazer. (DND)

The Golden Hawks' infamous souvenir from Dow AFB. Some of the trouble makers seen here are Jim McCombe and Phil Perry (in the "cockpit"), LAC Neuf Faulkner (foreground). The others are innocent members of the C-119 crew. (DND)

of there we had to get it through hangar line security where our C-119 was parked.

About 2:00 a.m. a group of us dismounted the surrey, wheeled it away from the mess, loaded it into a stake truck and covered it with a tarp. We then backed the truck up against a wall, so nobody could see inside. We were to depart next morning, so our crew took the truck and stacked all our bags so as to conceal the surrey. The truck was then driven to the security gate, was inspected and passed. But all hell was already going on back at the mess! We wasted no time loading the surrey onto the C-119 and camouflaging it with all sorts of equipment and bags. Security again inspected us, to no

avail. Away we went to Chatham, where we unloaded our prize and stored it in our hangar. That was Sunday afternoon. Next morning Jim McCombe and I had to go to Montreal, so, mercifully, we missed the fireworks which followed.

The base commander at Dow called our base commander Monday and gave him what for. I guess we had created an international incident, and that surrey was ordered back intact to Dow—like yesterday! Tuesday morning, BR Campbell and Jack Frazer headed for Bangor in a yellow pick-up with the surrey in back. They had a hell of a time explaining their business to the Customs officials at the border, but finally succeeded, and got to Dow. There was no welcome for them there, so they quickly offloaded and hightailed it for home. Those Yanks just couldn't take a joke!

Phil Perry

251

(Top left) The Hawks, led by Fern Villeneuve, prepare to taxi out from Nellis AFB. Then, they are seen alighting in typical formation style. Finally, six Hawks overfly Bill Stewart's Mark 5 at Calgary on July 13, 1960. (DND)

(Top) Head-on view of one of the Hawks. Next, a Hawk four-plane, seen near Chatham on June 21, 1960. Then (arrgghhh!) Sabres 23455, 410 and 066 in a dreadful state at Mountain View on November 6, 1965. (first two DND, Harry Tate via Jack McNulty)

The Golden Hawks over the years

1959
W/C Jake Easton, OC
S/L Fern Villeneuve, lead
F/L Jim McCombe, right wing
F/L Ed Rozdeba, left wing
F/L Jeb Kerr, slot
F/L Ralph Annis, lead solo
F/L "JT" Price, second solo
F/O Bill Stewart, spare
F/O Jim Holt, spare
F/L L. "Sammy" Eisler*
S/L Russ Bowdery, PRO
F/L Ray Grandy, EO
F/O George MacDonald, commentator
F/O Lorne Johnson, Adj.

1960
W/C Jack Allan, OC
S/L Fern Villeneuve, lead
F/L Jim McCombe, right wing
F/L Ed Rozdeba, left wing
F/L Bill Stewart, slot
F/L Ralph Annis, lead solo
F/L "JT" Price, solo
F/L Dave Tinson, second solo
F/L Rocky Van Vliet, PRO
F/L Dan McKinnon, EO
F/O George MacDonald, commentator

1961
W/C Jack Allan, OC
S/L Jim McCombe, lead
F/L "BR" Campbell, right wing
F/L Lloyd Hubbard, left wing
F/L Ed Rozdeba, slot
F/L Bill Stewart, lead solo
F/L Alf McDonald, solo
F/L Jack Frazer, second solo
F/L Jim McCann, second solo
F/L Rocky Van Vliet, PRO
F/L Phil Perry, EO
F/O Bob Dobson, commentator

1962
W/C Jack Allan, OC
S/L Lloyd Hubbard, lead
F/L "BR" Campbell, right wing
F/L Norm Garriock, left wing
F/L Jack Frazer, slot
F/L Alf McDonald, lead solo
F/L George Miller, solo
F/L Ed McKeogh, second solo
F/L Jim Giles, PRO
F/O Phil Perry, EO
F/L Bruce Lebans, commentator

1963
W/C Frank Hatton, OC
S/L Lloyd Hubbard, lead
F/L Al Young, right wing
F/L Norm Garriock, left wing
F/L C.B. Lang, slot
F/L Ed McKeogh, lead solo
F/L Dave Barker, solo
F/L Bill Grip, second solo
F/L Jim Giles, PRO
F/L Carl Peterson, EO
F/L Bruce Lebans, commentator

*Killed in flying accident.

Swept Wings for the RAF

In the first four years following the Second World War, Britain's aircraft industry suffered a drastic decline from its position of world leader, thanks to economic and political circumstances. One result was the protracted development of swept-wing trans-sonic interceptor fighters, prototypes of which were being developed by both Vickers Supermarine and Hawkers, but at a pace which made their original intended service entry date of 1951/1952 quite remote.

Politics of another sort were to have even greater impact on this situation. Worsening relations between East and West, stemming from the Soviet Union's ambition to impose its Communist ideology throughout Europe, resulted in the formation by the Western Allies of the North Atlantic Treaty Organization and a collective military stance against the growing threat. With it came the realization that defences so rapidly run down after the end of the Second World War would have to be increased. If further impetus was needed it came on June 25, 1950, with the sudden Communist invasion of South Korea, something which rapidly involved the US, supported by some of its allies, including Britain, under the banner of the United Nations.

The appearance early in the Korean War of a new Soviet-built jet fighter was soon to exert immense influence over those responsible for equipping the Western air arms. That aircraft was the MiG-15, which soon outclassed and out-performed every type of Western fighter that it opposed, save one—the North American F-86 Sabre.

If it was not obvious before the outbreak of the war in Korea, it became crystal clear to Britain's defence planners during the latter part of 1950 that the RAF could not afford to wait a further three or four years for the arrival of indigenous swept-wing fighters of comparable performance to the MiG-15, which was already being mass-produced and in large-scale service with the Communist forces facing

Sabre F.4s of 234 Squadron going into a loop in this striking photo from *The Aeroplane* in 1955. (via J.D.R. Rawlings)

NATO in Europe. At that time the standard home-defence interceptor in RAF Fighter Command was the Gloster Meteor, the performance of which was inferior to the MiG-15 on several counts. Most notably, it was about 80 mph slower. The RAF's standard ground-attack jet fighter, only then coming into widespread service with tactical squadrons based in West Germany, was the de Havilland Vampire. Though quite nimble, pleasant and easy to fly, the Vampire was at an even

greater disadvantage compared to the MiG, being almost 140 mph slower, and was out-performed in every other department.

By the late summer of 1950 the RAF decided that it must try to acquire the North American Sabre, and in October that year a preliminary assessment of the F-86A was made, involving a total of nine flights by four British pilots. Their evaluation was summarized thus: "The aircraft handles beautifully and has normal take-off and landing characteristics. Its climb to height compares to the Meteor F.8 but of course at higher forward speed. 2 snags: (a) Instrumentation presentation is bad and would make all-weather flying un-

duly difficult. Possibly overcome by fitting of standard RAF (blind-flying) panel. (b) More importantly, starting procedure is highly complicated and a single mistake may necessitate engine change." Air Marshal Sir Basil Embry, then Air Officer Commanding-in-Chief, Fighter Command, was emphatic that the F-86A was not acceptable as an interceptor until the latter difficulty was overcome.

Notwithstanding these reservations, the RAF clearly wanted the Sabre, but finding a source of supply was likely to prove difficult because demand from the USAF was absorbing total production in the United States. It was at this juncture, on October 26 at a meeting of the Western European Air Advisory Committee, that the Canadian representative stated that manufacture of the F-86E by Canadair in Montreal, from which deliveries were scheduled to begin for the RCAF in January 1951, could be increased from the planned rate of 10 aircraft per month if there were requirements from other NATO countries.

Discussions in Washington early in November resulted in the recommendation that Canadair should build Sabres for the RAF, and that 84 aircraft could be delivered in the latter half of 1951 with approximately 300 more in 1952. Although RAF airframe requirements could be met from increased Canadian production, the manufacture of the General Electric J47 engine in the USA in 1951-52 was inadequate to meet the combined needs of the USAF, RCAF and RAF due to increased USAF demands resulting from the Korean War. As this lack of engines was likely to delay deliveries to the RAF until the latter part of 1952, consideration was given in February 1951 to substituting the Rolls-Royce Avon engine, which would have enhanced performance, on a scale comparable to that of the Orenda-powered Canadair Sabre. The Avon was shorter and wider than the J47, and the Sabre's fuselage would have required considerable modification to accommodate it. However, the Avon was already planned to power the Australian-built version of the Sabre, and Rolls-Royce tried to persuade not only the RAF but also the RCAF to adopt the Avon, though neither did. Despite the urgency of the RAF's requirement to obtain Sabres, there were to be many more meetings and not a few frustrations and administrative prob-

255

Ferry Training Unit Sabres in December 1952, just arrived at Abingdon where they were used to convert over 70 pilots to fly Sabres from Montreal to the UK. (*Flight International*)

lems in the ensuing 18 months. Initially the RAF wanted to use the Sabre for UK air defence, but funding under the Mutual Defence Assistance Program could only be authorized for the supply of *tactical* fighters, which influenced the RAF's decision to deploy most of its Sabres in Germany as part of the 2nd Allied Tactical Air Force.

While the RAF had to wait longer than expected for its Sabres, plans were nevertheless drawn up for the conversion of pilots and for ferrying more than 350 aircraft across the Atlantic. First deliveries were to commence in September 1952, drawing on the experience gained by the first large-scale ferry flight of Canadair-built Sabres, when 21 aircraft of 439 Squadron RCAF flew the Atlantic at the end of May to join Canada's No.1 Fighter Wing, then based at RAF North Luffenham in Rutland.

Three experienced jet pilots were sent by the RAF for conversion training on the Sabre at No.1 OTU at Chatham, New Brunswick, during August 1952, and it was they who ferried the first three Sabres for the RAF in October. They were included in the mass ferry flight, Operation Leapfrog 2, which left St. Hubert on September 28 and consisted of three RCAF Sabre squadrons which arrived in Grostenquin, France, on October 10, where they formed 2 Fighter Wing. The three RAF Sabres, designated F.2s to conform with Canadian mark numbers, received British serials XB530-532 (RCAF serials 19378, 19384 and 19404 respectively). They were delivered to North Luffenham, where they were

used to convert a dozen more pilots in preparation for the first all-RAF delivery flight of Sabres, scheduled for December. In addition to pilots, the RAF detached about 50 ground crew to North Luffenham to service their Sabres and undergo maintenance training on the type under the guidance of the RCAF, with the majority of these men forming a nucleus of training technicians, supplementing others who received instruction in Canada. Thereafter, for as long as the RCAF remained at North Luffenham, the base was to be a focal point of considerable collaboration with the RAF involving both operational and technical support for the Sabre.

In November 1952 the RAF was offered 60 more Sabres by the USAF in addition to the 370 which had been funded under MDAP. These new aircraft, also Canadair-built and MDAP-funded, were surplus to US and RCAF requirements, and were scheduled to be delivered at the rate of 20 per month from June 1953. Furthermore, the US indicated that it would be acceptable for Britain to use these Sabres for the air defence of the United Kingdom by RAF Fighter Command, and that there would be enough aircraft to form three complete squadrons (66 aircraft) by supplementing the new batch with a few Sabres from those allocated to 2nd TAF in Europe. Strangely only two months later, in January 1953, the RCAF made a request to "borrow" 60 Sabres from the RAF order for a period of 12 months from March '53— coincidentally exactly the same number of aircraft that the Americans had offered Fighter Command. This the RAF agreed to do, actually lending 71 aircraft, giving rise to the sight of some Sabres adorned in full RCAF squadron markings (mainly those of Nos.414,

422 and 444) yet retaining RAF serial numbers and national insignia. On December 4, 1952, the first trio of RAF Sabres left North Luffenham for RAF Abingdon, where they were assigned to No.1 Overseas Ferry Unit (later becoming No.1 Long Range Ferry Unit), under the control of RAF Transport Command, where they were used to convert ferry pilots on to the Sabre. Pilots were needed in substantial numbers for the forthcoming transatlantic delivery program, which the RAF named "Operation Bechers Brook" and modelled on the earlier mass delivery flights by both the RCAF and USAF, with whom operations were coordinated.

The first Bechers Brook delivery flight departed St. Hubert, Quebec, on December 9, 1952, and followed the established 3100-mile route via Goose Bay, thence to Bluie West One, Keflavik and Prestwick, before finally arriving at Abingdon on December 22. In fact this was rather an inauspicious start, because of nine RAF Sabres, one, XB534, crashed near Prestwick on the 19th. In common with all subsequent aircraft delivered to the RAF these Sabres were Mk.4s and differed from the Mk.2 in having various internal refinements concerning the canopy release, type of compass fitted and pressurization controls.

On March 1, 1953, Bechers Brook 2 departed Quebec, this time involving over 30 RAF Sabres, the majority of which arrived at 5 Maintenance Unit, RAF Kemble, Gloucestershire, 16 days later. 5 MU became the final destination of most Sabre deliveries, though other MUs were also used, notably No.23 at RAF Aldergrove, Northern Ireland, and No.33 at RAF Lyneham. Having flown the Atlantic in their natural metal factory finish, to which

"Arctic red" paint was usually applied to wing tips and tailplane to aid recovery in the event of a crash landing in the wastes of Greenland, most RAF Sabres were camouflaged upon receipt at the MU. The vast majority, comprising all the XB-serialled aircraft, were painted gloss dark green and medium sea grey on upper surfaces with cerulean blue under surfaces, the then-standard camouflage scheme for fighters allocated to the RAF's 2nd Tactical Air Force in Germany. The 60 XD-serialled Sabres allotted to Fighter Command in the UK differed from this scheme by having silver instead of blue under surfaces and a lower demarcation line. In addition to being camouflaged, the newly arrived Sabres received minor modifications and the replacement of some American radio and navigational instruments with British equipment. In most cases they were then test flown and delivered to operational units or stored at the MU as reserves. Bechers Brook 2 was unusual in that six aircraft concluded their ferry flight by flying on to the RAF base at Wildenrath, in Germany, where they formed the initial establishment of the Sabre Conversion Flight (SCF); having "missed" the MU in England these six Sabres remained in natural metal finish for many months. The job of the SCF was to train the senior pilots of the first operational 2nd TAF squadrons to convert from the Vampire FB.5 to the Sabre 4, and the flight also ran a ground school to train maintenance crews. One Sabre was lost on Bechers Brook 2.

On February 1, 1953, No.1 LRFU was redesignated No.147 (Ferry) Squadron, and in early April the unit moved from Abingdon to the nearby base of RAF Benson. Derek Burton was one of the first ferry pilots to undergo Sabre conversion training at Benson, which he recalls was rather basic: "The course consisted of ground-school lectures on the Sabre and 10 hours flying. I had flown Vampire 5 aircraft prior to my first solo in the Sabre (XB538/F) and did not find the transition difficult. That first, hour-long familiarization flight was followed by eight further flights, covering stalls, steep turns, high-speed runs to Mach 0.9, cross countries, radio compass let-downs and formation flying, the whole course lasting only two weeks!" Derek subsequently spent the next three years flying Sabres in Canada, across the Atlantic and

within Europe. He took part in six Bechers Brooks and some of his abiding impressions are recounted here:

The 147 pilots were taken by RCAF Expeditor from St. Hubert, where we were based, to Cartierville on the other side of Montreal, where the Canadair factory was. We picked up a Sabre, flew it for between 1 and 1-1/2 hours and landed back at St. Hubert. Each Sabre was given 10 hours "shakedown" flying before being certified fit for the Atlantic crossing. The number of aircraft in each convoy varied; the

Sabre bases and other centres of Sabre activity in the United Kingdom. The AAEE was at Boscombe Down, and the Central Flying School Examining Wing was at Little Rissington. Subcontractors Airwork General operated at Gatwick, Manchester and Liverpool, and Aviation Traders at Stansted. Hawker was at Dunsfold and Westland at Merryfield. Scottish Aviation at Prestwick did overhaul work for the RCAF. Major cities are shown for reference.

largest I remember consisted of 36. We took off in pairs and joined up to fly in fairly loose "finger four" formation, coming in close if there was any cloud, levelling out at 35,000 feet and optimum cruising speed because each leg of the trip was about the same as the

Sabre's maximum range with drop tanks, 750-800 n.m. My longest flight time was 1 hour 50 minutes from Goose to Bluie. Each four-ship formation took off at five-minute intervals. Unfavourable headwinds sometimes forced us to refuel at Bagotville or Chatham rather than fly non-stop from St. Hubert to Goose Bay. There was a direct H/F radio link between Goose Bay and Bluie West and Keflavik, so the CO would speak directly to the liaison officer to obtain weather actual and forecast before we took off. Because there were no diversion airfields, we had to have *guaranteed* good weather. When a convoy was in progress, ocean weather ships were positioned on each leg of the crossing as an aid to navigation, and as a reserve point if you had to eject. USAF Grumman Albatross amphibious SAR aircraft also used to get airborne while a convoy was in progress and set up a patrol orbit half-way between the weather ships and the staging posts. Personal survival equipment consisted of an immersion suit and a dinghy, and we had all been on a winter survival course. Thankfully none of these precautions were needed owing to the Sabre being such a damned good aircraft.

Navigation consisted mainly of working out a flight plan as accurately as possible, based on forecast winds on the climb, cruise and descent. As far as I remember there were virtually no approach aids at Bluie, and Keflavik was little better, although all the staging posts had good accommodation facilities, which is just as well, because weather could and did often hold us up, so that the whole delivery flight could take anything from one to three weeks! At Bluie and Keflavik I found it almost impossible to sleep in the summer, as it was daylight for 24 hours! From Keflavik we flew to either Kinloss (RAF) or Lossiemouth (RN). Servicing throughout the whole route was provided mainly by detachments of RAF ground crew at each staging post, though the Sabre had excellent serviceability and there was little else for them to do other than refuel, and the usual post and pre-flight checks. I later went on to fly the Swift F.R.5 and most marks of Hunter, and in my opinion the Sabre was streets ahead of them, especially considering the fact that it pre-dated them by years! It was a delightful aircraft to fly.

Derek Burton

Praise indeed, and by no means unique among RAF pilots privileged to fly the Sabre.

As the Bechers Brook program gathered momentum in the summer of '53, over 70 pilots were engaged in the ferry operation and it became common to use a double shuttle system, whereby half the aircraft in a convoy were flown one stage, with the pilots returning to the previous staging post to collect another batch of aircraft. This allowed twice as many aircraft to be ferried as pilots involved. Four-engined RAF Hastings transports were used to ferry the pilots between stages, and also from the UK to Canada, supplemented on occasion by Boeing Stratocruiser airliners of BOAC. The final transatlantic ferry flight of Sabres to the RAF departed St. Hubert on May 16, 1954, and comprised a small batch of aircraft which had been on loan to the RCAF and kept in Canada, and their arrival at Kemble on May 26 marked the completion of this tremendous achievement.

The protracted delays in the acquisition of Sabres had only served to heighten the frustration among most RAF fighter pilots, eager to fly this interceptor and envious of their North American counterparts, whose Sabres were increasingly encountered in British and European skies. Sabres had been based in England as early as August 1951 when the F-86As of the USAF arrived at Shepherds Grove to bolster RAF Fighter Command. Numbers were subsequently swelled by the arrival of further US Sabre squadrons and those of the RCAF at North Luffenham. More than two dozen volunteer RAF pilots flew and fought (and some died) with USAF Sabre squadrons in the Korean War, and a few examples of the F-86A had been lent by the USAF for evaluation by RAF test pilots at Farnborough and Boscombe Down between 1950 and the autumn of '52. However, it was not until the spring of 1953 that the first trickle of Sabres, soon to swell into a flood, began to reach the RAF's own units, which were destined to comprise 12 operational squadrons, 10 of which were to be based in Germany within the 2nd Tactical Air Force, the other two with Fighter Command in the UK. Additionally, a further half-dozen or so second-line units were equipped with Sabres to varying degrees. Despite the long anticipation of its arrival the Sabre was destined to see comparative-

ly brief operational service with the RAF, between May 1953 and June 1956, by which time indigenous fighters were available in substantial enough quantities to supplant it. Brief though its tenure may have been, the Canadair Sabre played a vital role in bolstering British air defences and the fighter was held in high esteem by most pilots fortunate enough to fly it in RAF service.

No.1 Long Range Ferry Unit/ 147 Squadron

As mentioned, this was the first RAF unit to operate Sabres, from October 1952, being responsible for ferrying the aircraft from Canadair to the United Kingdom. Renumbered 147 Squadron on February 1, 1953, it was also responsible for the delivery of Sabres (and other types) from MUs to operational units and vice versa. From the outset it included a training element, the Ferry Training Unit (FTU), which was primarily, though not exclusively, concerned with providing Sabre conversion flying for pilots selected to ferry these aircraft. 147 and the FTU moved to Benson in April 1953, by which time it had an establishment of about a dozen Sabres. With Bechers Brook in full swing and other units fulfilling the Sabre conversion task, FTU strength dwindled after midsummer, with only two or three Sabres being retained during 1954; thereafter examples were borrowed from 5 MU whenever the need arose.

BASES: North Luffenham 10.52-12.52 (attached to RCAF); Abingdon 12.52-4.53; Benson 4.53-6.56.
SABRE SERVICE: 10.10.52 (XB530/A)-22.6.56 (XB758, on loan from 5 MU).
REPRESENTATIVE AIRCRAFT: XB537/E, 544/H, 547/K, 601/P.
UNIT MARKINGS: Single black individual code letter forward of the fuselage roundel. Several aircraft remained in natural metal finish for many months.
CO: S/L T. Stevenson, AFC.

Sabre Conversion Flight

RAF Wildenrath, a newly constructed NATO airfield in Germany close to the Dutch border, became the main conversion training centre for 2 TAF squadrons with the formation of the Sabre Conversion Flight (SCF), tasked with giving tuition on the new fighter. Initially the "pupils" comprised the flight commanders and more experienced pilots of the squadrons earmarked to re-equip with Sabres, usually from Vampires. Training comprised

XB673 of the Sabre Conversion Flight at RAF Wildenrath in August 1953. Pilots, from the left, are P/O Neil (3 Sqn.), P/O Purdue (3 Sqn.), F/L Martin Chandler (SCF), G/C Nichols (station CO), F/L Roy Watson (SCF), P/O Smith (3 Sqn.), F/O David Williams (APS Sylt), P/O M. Anderson (67 Sqn.) and F/L Henson (GCS). (via Roger Lindsay)

ground lectures on the aircraft's systems, organized by F/L Martin Chandler and the CO, S/L Steele, followed by about two weeks flying, which hopefully amounted to at least 10 hours in the air, though this depended on the weather, and some pilots managed only one or two Sabre sorties before going back to their squadron. There they were automatically Sabre "experts" and helped in conversion of the remaining squadron pilots until all had attained operational status on the plane, which most found easy as well as exhilarating to fly.

The first six Sabres for the SCF were delivered direct to Wildenrath on March 13-14, 1953, and remained in their natural metal finish for much of their service, and indeed the sight of a "silver" RAF Sabre was almost synonymous with the flight, which also later acquired camouflaged examples. In total 26 different Sabres were used by the SCF with average strength being about 18, and in spite of its training role the flight achieved an excellent safety record, with only one aircraft lost due to a flying accident, which oc-

curred on June 15, 1953, when XB603 suffered a loss of power during an overshoot at Wildenrath, and crash landed. The SCF began to run down in June 1954, much of its work done or transferred to 229 OCU, though it continued to hold familiarization courses on the Sabre until the spring of 1955, using aircraft borrowed from 67 and 71 squadrons.

BASE: Wildenrath.
SABRE SERVICE: 13.3.53 (XB602, 616, 618)-13.10.54 (XB592, 618, 934).
REPRESENTATIVE AIRCRAFT: XB542, 673, 738, 874.
UNIT MARKINGS: None.
CO: S/L Steele.

Air Fighting Development Squadron
The AFDS was a component of the Central Fighter Establishment, and one of its main duties was to evaluate the combat capabilities of every new type of interceptor fighter entering RAF service and to devise the most effective tactics for its use, details of which were then made available to the operational squadrons. CFE staff pilots were invariably highly experienced and included several who had flown Sabres in combat over Korea.

BASE: West Raynham.
SABRE SERVICE: 4.5.53 (XB622, 666, 677)-11.2.55 (XD781).
REPRESENTATIVE AIRCRAFT: Only five Sabres were used by the AFDS, XD780 plus those listed above.

UNIT MARKINGS: None recorded. First three aircraft were delivered direct to W. Raynham in natural metal finish, as was XD781, which retained bare metal, with arctic red tailplane and wing tips throughout its RAF service.

67 Squadron
No. 67 had the distinction of being the first operational RAF squadron to take delivery of Sabres and also the last to retain one—though this is not to dispute the claim of No. 3 Squadron as the first to fly it! The former event occurred on May 8, 1953, with the delivery of XB586/Y from 5 MU, and by the end of the month 16 of the eventual establishment of 24 Sabres had arrived at the Squadron's Wildenrath base, enabling the phase-out of its Vampire 5s to proceed.

Although there was a nucleus of experienced and distinguished pilots at Wildenrath at that time, the squadrons were mostly composed of very young pilots, first tourists with an average age of about 21, whose eagerness to fly the fastest fighter available in the West was unbounded. John Harrison was typical; an ex-Cranwell cadet, he had turned down a posting to the Central Flying School as an instructor to fly fighters, which he achieved via Meteor and Vampire OCUs, and a very brief familiarization course at the SCF, to become the 13th pilot on 67 Squadron to convert to Sabres. "The Sabre was a joy to fly," he recalls, "but it could be tricky, especially at low altitude, when you had to watch out for the stall." Although the transition from Vampires to Sabres went smoothly, there was later a spate of accidents which caused considerable concern. "I remember attending three funerals in almost as many weeks; the reasons were difficult to compound—maybe it was partly due to youthful exuberance. Anyhow the top brass in RAF Germany were summoned to the Air Ministry in London and told that the Sabre accident rate was unacceptably high and it had to be drastically reduced—and it was, initially by cutting down on the flying hours! I seem to remember that for a while we were down to about 10 hours a month per pilot, which wasn't enough to keep our hand in." (Nothing changes!) There was another reason for the lack of flying hours, however, and that was poor serviceability, confirmed by John Harrison: "To begin with we had virtually no spares and it only needed the absence of quite small parts to ground a Sabre. The spares situation did improve, but not much. It's amazing, though, how we always seemed to find enough aircraft for the formation flying!"

67 Squadron was still working up to operational pitch on Sabres when the unit participated in the massed flypast of over 600 RAF and Commonwealth aircraft on July 15, 1953, before HM the Queen at Odiham, Hampshire, on the occasion of the Coronation Review of the RAF. For this event the Sabres of both 67 and 3 Squadrons were temporarily detached to RAF Duxford, near Cambridge, from June 20 until July 16. With so many aircraft in the air at once the flypast required considerable organization to perfect the split-second timing demanded of the review and for several days before there were practice flights over the route. John Harrison recalls an incident which occurred during one of them: "The weather could have been better during this particular formation flying rehearsal and one of our guys whose call-sign was 'Siamese 19' radioed to say that he had become separated from the formation and was lost. Someone asked him to describe the scenery over which he was flying, and from this description deduced (correctly) that he must be flying near Reading, and we were able to guide him back. It was one of his first flights in a Sabre!" John went on to describe

another ceremonial flypast in Germany that almost ended in tragedy: "It was for Princess Margaret and there were 48 of us in the formation; I led the last pair. The bad weather deteriorated until the cloud base was only 200 feet. Imagine 48 Sabres doing a QGH—it was a complete shambles with the murk full of Sabres, all trying to get down. Amazingly we all did, and without bending anything."

John Harrison has pursued a career in aviation and still flies, though now senior captain with Dan-Air on 737s and his commentary on Sabre operations 30 years ago makes an interesting comparison.

Flying was comparatively undisciplined in those days. There was a tremendous feeling of living life to the full, and flying that way too. The "cold war" was fairly warm at that time, and being based in Germany you were always aware that the whole thing could blow up at any minute and you would be in the thick of it. I say "undisciplined" but that's not quite true, because there was a very high standard of formation flying and battle tactics were taken very seriously, but there were virtually no restrictions.

The Americans had Sabre wings at Spangdahlem and Hahn, and the Canadians at Zweibrücken and Grostenquin; they used to fly north and we used to fly south and we all used to meet somewhere near Spangdahlem in a huge whirling dogfight—great stuff! Occasionally there were collisions and I remember two of our chaps collided over Munchen Gladbach, when they broke the wrong way, into one another during a battle formation—one ejected OK but the other was killed (XB690 and 730, respectively, November 6, 1958).

Our squadron boss was Squadron Leader W. "Paddy" Harbison, who had flown Sabres in Korea, where he had collected the American DFC. There he learned to fly and fight the Sabre in the vertical plane and he taught us accordingly—but this was in contrast to our station commander, Group Captain "Johnny" Johnson, the leading RAF fighter ace in the last war, who as an ex-Spitfire pilot and wing leader believed in fighting in the horizontal.

We were meant to be tactical, to be mobile, and the whole squadron had to be ready to be up and away in 15 hours

or less to operate from other bases. We often used to operate from the south side of the airfield at Wildenrath, living in tents, and quite independent of the station's facilities. It was cheaper to do that than actually deploy to another base, but not nearly so much fun. We also used to do "swap overs" and send detachments to the Canadians at Zweibrücken and the Americans at Spangdahlem, and they used to stay with us. We used to go to Sylt for armament practice camp. Tugs were Tempests. One guy shot the tug pilot in the bum! Yes, he put a point five into his backside, and would probably have pumped more into him if he hadn't yelled to call it off! He was invalided back to the U.K.

We wore early bone domes, heavy and ill-fitting, and anti-g suits which weren't very effective. You could pull 8g in a Sabre without any problems. The record is supposed to be 13g, held by a chap called Oakford on 71 Squadron, part of our wing at Wildenrath. You're not supposed to look at your instruments while flying in formation, but Oakford knew things were wrong and they were all in too steep a dive—so he glanced at his altimeter and got a fright! He yanked back on the stick as hard as he could and broke cloud at 400 feet. He pulled out just above the ground, popped all the rivets and momentarily blacked out as he reputedly pulled 13g; the other guys went straight into the deck.

John Harrison

John Harrison was invalided to the UK with back trouble resulting from 8g stress, at that time a common symptom among Sabre pilots. After his departure the Wildenrath Sabre Wing (67 and 71 Squadrons) was split up and redeployed to other bases, partly as a result of a mid-air collision between Sabre XB634 and Anson C.17 TX238 on approach to Wildenrath on April 5, 1955. Because of its proximity to the staff headquarters at Munchen Gladbach the airfield was much used by communications aircraft and it was felt wiser to base the fighters elsewhere, so in the interests of flight safety No. 67 moved to Bruggen in July 1955. Less than six months later the first Hunter F.4s were received, and between January and March 1956 most Sabres were flown back to the UK, although the last example, XB693/C, did not leave until August 21 that year.

BASES: Wildenrath, then Bruggen from July 1955.
SABRE SERVICE: 8.5.53 (XB586Y)-21.8.56 (XB693/C).
REPRESENTATIVE AIRCRAFT: XB598/R, 664/B, 682/V, 706/U, 730/Y, 737/A.
UNIT MARKINGS: Initially the only markings consisted of a narrow band across the top of the fin. This band was painted in the flight colour, red for A Flight, covering aircraft coded between A and about M, or blue for B Flight, aircraft N to Z. In most cases the band was thinly outlined in yellow. The individual aircraft code letter appeared immediately below, usually in white, thinly outlined in black, and often repeated in black on the nose-wheel door. Unusually, the squadron badge was often applied to the centre, white, portion of the national insignia fin flash. In 1955 colourful squadron markings were added on each side of the fuselage roundel, comprising a yellow-outlined red bar within which was a blue triangle, also outlined in yellow.
CO: S/L W. "Paddy" Harbison.

3 Squadron

No.3 Squadron had been the first in Germany to be equipped with Vampire F.1s in 1948, later exchanging these for the Mk.5 fighter-bomber variant. In 1952 the squadron had been notified that it would be the first to receive the new de Havilland Venom, and there was great disappointment when this failed to materialize, so there was great joy at the news that No.3 had been chosen as the first squadron in the RAF to fly the Sabre and change roles from ground attack to interceptor.

In fact the first Sabres to be received at Wildenrath were delivered direct from Canada on March 13, 1953, and were for the Sabre Conversion Flight, as mentioned. However, No.3 Squadron "borrowed" these for the purpose of beginning their own conversion from Vampires—with only a few sets of RCAF Pilots Notes for reference, since the SCF was itself just in the process of formulating a Sabre training program. George Cole was among the youngest pilots on 3 Squadron at that time: "I flew my first Sabre, XB616, on April 7 for an initial 30-minute familiarization flight, and thereafter had very little Sabre flying until after May 11, when the first of 3 Squadron's own Sabres were delivered. I adopted XB590 as my personal aircraft whenever it was available, and flew it for the first time on May 19, 1953, the day after its delivery, in the

'box' slot of the first four-ship squadron Sabre formation, hastily organized to pre-empt our rivals on 67 Squadron!" Together with 67, No. 3 Squadron deployed to Duxford for almost a month to prepare for the Royal Review flypast, in which the two squadrons put up a crisp combined formation of 24 Sabres, even though pilots averaged less than 25 hours on the type. Immediately after their return from Duxford No. 3 Squadron moved to its new base at Geilenkirchen on July 20, and was soon given its first taste of "combat" in the NATO air defence exercise, "Coronet" held July 23-30.

George Cole was chosen to demonstrate the Sabre at the annual Battle of Britain "At Home" at RAF Biggin Hill on Saturday September 19, 1953, and flew XB667 via Manston and Duxford, where he stopped the previous night. The aircraft was the star of the show, representing the RAF's first operational swept-wing fighter, and George gave flying displays with sonic booms that afternoon at both Biggin and Hornchurch. At that time there were no restrictions on such activities, though towards the end of his tour on 3 Squadron, George recalls that pilots were advised to avoid banging the larger German towns! George Cole has more recently been piloting RAF Hercules to the Falkland Islands yet his impressions of flying Sabres remain as fresh as ever: "The aircraft was grossly underpowered, taking over 20 minutes to get to 35,000 feet, but once there it coped well. Handling was good at low level, but performance fell off at altitude. Occasionally one slat would come out and stick out, producing some interesting manoeuvres! In mock combat the Sabre was good against the opposition at the time—Meteors, Vampires and Venoms. Venoms could go higher but nobody could perform like the F-86 at high Mach numbers. Hunters could out-accelerate the Sabre every time, but the confidence given to the pilot knowing that at the high-speed end of the performance envelope the Sabre simply reached terminal velocity with no awkward handling problems and no fear of spinning gave one an edge over aircraft with a theoretically superior performance. Handling in the circuit and during landing was excellent and viceless; you could do an approach without ASI by riding the slats at about 185 knots—it happened once to me, and to several other people."

"I sometimes used to fly No.2 to G/C Johnny Johnson, the station commander at Wildenrath, and later at Geilenkirchen, whose Sabre, like his Vampire before it, had a red fin and carried his initials "JEJ" in large letters. He was quite keen on leading "wing dings," seldom less than 24 Sabres, and we would often whistle low over other fighter airfields to encourage them to come up for sport, or get into furious dogfights with anyone foolish enough to be airborne at the same time. More usually we flew in "finger fours" and the majority of the flying was either air/air combat (ciné) or firing on the flag, or ground attack for which the Sabre was not really suited with its 0.5 inch guns."

George Cole completed his tour with 3 Squadron in October 1954 but continued to fly Sabres in the UK with 92 Squadron. 3 Squadron began to phase out its Sabres in favour of Hunter 4s in the spring of 1956, and there was a special ceremony at Geilenkirchen on June 22 of that year with the departure of XB670/S, billed as the last RAF Sabre in Germany, although this was actually not true.

BASES: Wildenrath, then Geilenkirchen from July 1953.
SABRE SERVICE: 11.5.53 (XB614)-22.6.56 (XB670/S).
REPRESENTATIVE AIRCRAFT: XB536/Z, 590/V, 617/C, 703/Y, 869/J, 938/D.
UNIT MARKINGS: Bright (apple) green rectangles, thinly outlined in yellow on each side of the fuselage roundels. Nose cones were also green, edged in yellow. Code letters were in flight colours (red for A Flt., blue for B Flt.) outlined in white, on the fin, and repeated in black on the nose-wheel door of some aircraft. Most aircraft had the squadron badge in a white disc below the cockpit. XB984/K differed in having a broad green band across the fin, edged in white, within which the code letter was painted in red, thinly outlined in white.
COs: S/L W.J.S. "Black Jack" Sutherland, to Dec. '53. S/L R.C.H. Simmons, Dec. '53-1956. S/L T.H. Hutchinson 1956-1957.

71 Squadron

Like its predecessors, the third Sabre squadron re-equipped from Vampire FB.5s, and began conversion in the autumn of '53, becoming operational early in the New Year. John Finch was newly posted to the squadron fresh from training with the USAF, where he had flown T-33s and straight-winged F-84E and G Thunderjets. His first Sabre familiarization sortie took place on January 19, 1954, courtesy of the

SCF, yet by February 1 he was fulfilling "Battle Flight" duties with 71, and therefore assumed that he was considered operational! "Battle Flight" was maintained at most RAF Germany fighter bases as alert duty to intercept and investigate incursions into Allied airspace by unidentified aircraft, as John Finch explains: "One squadron, on rotation, provided four aircraft (armed) on the ORP (Operational Readiness Platform, at the end of the runway). Usually after a one-hour stint pilots and aircraft, if available, were relieved. On a scramble one would work with a GCI unit (Ground Controlled Interception radar), which in 71's case was at Wildenrath, and not necessarily return to home base until later in the day—fine for the pilots who took the aircraft!"

John goes on to mention his other recollections during his spell on 71 Squadron Sabres. "High-level battle formations, PIs (practice interceptions) culminating in a tail chase, plus an awful lot of ciné attacks on other aircraft comprised the majority of sorties. There was plenty of unscheduled 'bouncing' and we considered any available aircraft as fair game, so most days saw our contrails heading south in search of the USAF and Canadian squadrons, We went on several detachments, apart from the annual live gunnery camp at Sylt, including: Schleswigland for air/air gunnery, Fassberg to work with the Venom

A 71 Squadron Sabre refuelling at Athens, June 16, 1955 while en route for Cyprus. (F/L J. Finch)

ground-attack squadrons, Aalborg and Florennes on squadron exchanges with the Danes and Belgians respectively, and Nicosia, in Cyprus. This detachment, from June 15 to July 6, 1955, also involved air-air firing practice, but had more significance because it was 'route proving' and because a bottle of whisky fitted into the cockpit fire extinguisher bracket!" John Finch also remembers one of the Sabre accidents that befell the squadron. "It occurred when two of our Sabres had a mid-air collision near Krefeld (XB628 and 729 on October 26, 1954). Both pilots survived. One landed in a field being ploughed by a very stoic German who just ploughed on unperturbed, with bits of aircraft falling all around him!"

Another accident afflicted 71's very first Sabre, XB691/A, when ground crew pushed it into a hangar soon after delivery and discovered the hard way that the fin was taller than the doorway. Thereafter all Sabres had to be pulled tail-down to negotiate the hanger doors. The technique is described by Denis Casper, who as an electrical fitter (air) completed the final part of his two years National Service as a member of 71 Squadron's ground crew, from September '53 until he was demobilized in August the following year, and has many memories of maintenance work on Sabres.

We could get about eight aircraft into the hangar but we had to be extra careful in easing them in because the doorway was about six inches lower than a Sabre's fin. The technique was for at least six airmen to pull down on

the aircraft's tailplane, thus raising the nose and lowering the fin, whilst another working party pushed the fighter forward from behind the wings; one of the most frequent cries to be heard in the vicinity of the hangars was therefore "two-six on the tail" (roughly translated as "jump to it").

There was a good deal of man-handling the aircraft, which were quite easy to move, and Land Rovers were used to tow the Sabres to the more distant parts of the flight line, where the majority of the first-line servicing took place and where the Sabres spent most of their lives. For starting our Sabres we were equipped with about eight Houchin starters—basically a trolley-mounted Ford V-8 engine driving a 24-volt generator. These produced 1600 amps on engine start, reducing to about 900 amps when the engine ignited. The Sabre did seem prone to "wet starts;" I don't know whether this was a characteristic of the General Electric J47 or attributable to heavy-handed pilots. The wet start drill was to shut off the Houchin supply to the aircraft, signal this to the pilot, who was supposed to wait three minutes to allow the excess fuel to drain from the jet pipe before attempting to re-start. However, few pilots would wait longer than a minute, particularly if their colleagues were already taxiing out for takeoff. The usual result was a huge flame from the jet pipe which enveloped the fin and tailplane and had to be extinguished by the ground crew—very spectacular, especially at night.

71 had a good servicing record but we never managed to get our full war complement of 24 Sabres airborne at one time, though we did achieve 23, in addition to the single Meteor T.7 and Vampire T.11 which were used for instrument ratings, dual checks and general "hacks." Sabre spares were a constant problem and a good deal of cannibalizing took place. On one occasion we were congratulated by G/C Johnny Johnson for putting up over 400 flying hours in a month, which was considered quite an achievement in view of the lack of spares and adverse weather. The whole squadron atmosphere was one of hard work and hard flying, busy but happy.

As far as my job was concerned I found the Sabre easy to service, with the cockpit instruments well arranged; many of the circuits had warning lamps to alert the pilot if a problem arose, and they also had a "push-to-test"

No.20 Squadron at Oldenburg in 1955. XB900 is the CO's kite as seen by the name on the canopy frame, and pennant below. (via J.D.R. Rawlings)

20 Squadron's aerobatic team in 1955: "Moose" Davies, Nick Jack Gulpin, David Williams, Dennis Lucy, "Screech" Leech and (kneeling) F/O Crowe. (via Roger Lindsay)

facility. On each side of the cockpit, roughly by the pilot's elbow, was a panel containing 10 or 12 miniature circuit breakers instead of the usual fuses. These MCBs were new to me, and I doubt whether any contemporary British aircraft was so equipped. One of my colleagues caused the accidental release of the fully-fuelled under-wing drop tanks on a hangared aircraft on which he was working. This happened while he was repairing a circuit behind the cockpit instrument panel and accidentally bridged two terminals with his screwdriver. When the resulting flap died down, an order was issued that drop tanks had to be emptied before aircraft entered the hangar!

Some of the inspection and access panels on the Sabre were too small and changing various components inside the fuselage could become very demanding, especially on cold days with numb fingers. Perhaps the weakest servicing aspect of the Sabre compared to British aircraft was the method of checking the fuel pump. We had to do this by operating a switch inside the port wheel bay and then *listening,* but it was often impossible to hear anything because of the noise of Houchin starters and other aircraft taxiing by!

Considering the intensity of flying each week, from Monday to midday Saturday, there were very few accidents, and I saw only two which occurred on the airfield at Wildenrath. On one occasion a 67 Squadron pilot couldn't lower the undercarriage, and after releasing the drop tanks he did an

excellent belly landing on the grass, without sustaining any personal injury or much damage to the Sabre. A more spectacular lucky escape happened when another pilot (from either 67 or the SCF) failed to become airborne during takeoff; he jettisoned his drop tanks at the end of the runway, which erupted into two fireballs, then retracted the undercarriage before hitting the soft ground of the overshoot area. The aircraft finally came to rest against an approach light post, which unhinged the nose section. Miraculously the pilot staggered from the wreck with nothing worse than a cut forehead and a shaking. To us onlookers it seemed that the cause of the crash was a ground stall. The aircraft involved was among the first to be modified with the 6-3 "solid" leading-edge wing, which required a slightly different takeoff technique and may have been a contributory factor to the accident.

Denis Casper

71 removed to Bruggen in July 1955 and re-equipped with Hunter F.4s in March 1956, with the last Sabres departing by early summer.

BASES: Wildenrath, then Bruggen from July 1955.
SABRE SERVICE: 2.10.53 (XB608 and 691)-5.6.56 (XB631/F).
REPRESENTATIVE AIRCRAFT: XB630/P, 700/M, 796/O, 896/L, 974/O, 987/H.
UNIT MARKINGS: Black diamonds on a rectangle, the upper half being white, the lower yellow, on each side of the fuselage roundel. Code letter white, or yellow above the fin flash. The squadron motif, an American eagle, was painted in black, all within a white disc positioned on the nose just behind the gun ports. Initially red (A Flt.) or blue (B Flt.) bands were painted around the nose cone.
COs: S/L E. "Ted" Trees to 1954. S/L L. Cherry, '54-'55. S/L Barnes, July '55-1957.

20 Squadron

This unit was the first Sabre recipient of the Oldenburg Wing and began to rapidly re-equip from Vampire 5s at the beginning of November 1953, with no fewer than 17 Sabres being delivered the first week. Operations followed a similar pattern to those already established by the first German-based RAF Sabre squadrons and are recalled by W/C Leslie Glover, who was CO from October 1954:

"Following a tour as a ground instructor at Cranwell I did a refresher and instrument rating course on Meteor 4s and 7s, then further refreshing on Vampire 5s and T.11s before converting to the Sabre. I had no difficulty with the transition, my main impressions being the sensitivity of the power controls, and the rapid build-up in the dive. Main day-to-day training was in pairs and 'finger fours' at 30-plus thousand feet, with occasional low-level recces and live firing on the air-to-ground ranges at Ströhen and Meppen at about monthly intervals. In addition to the annual visit to Sylt, the squadron deployed to Nicosia, Cyprus, for live air-to-air firing in May/June '55. During that time I took a detachment of four aircraft to Amman, Jordan for three days in early June and by popular request ran the first sonic boom over Amman. We converted to the Hunter 4 in December '55 and immediately felt the increase in power, rate of climb, manoeuverability and ability to achieve Mach 1 in a shallow dive, as opposed to the vertical dive in the Sabre. The only thing we missed was the radio compass."

AEROBATIC TEAM: Led by F/L Williams.
BASE: Oldenburg.
SABRE SERVICE: 28.10.53 (XB594/V)-30.5.56 (XB914/S).
REPRESENTATIVE AIRCRAFT: XB575/Q, 645/W, 731/J, 815/N, 888/T, 900/A (used by the CO).
UNIT MARKINGS: Medium blue rectangles each side of the fuselage roundel, divided by thin red, white and green horizontal stripes. White code letter above fin flash. Most Sabres also carried the squadron motif on the nose, just aft of the guns, comprising a white shield, thinly outlined in black, containing a black eagle on a blue sword, set against a yellow and red rising sun. The pilot's name was often painted in white on the cockpit canopy sill (port side).
COs: S/L I. MacDonald, DFC, 1953-Oct. '54. S/L Leslie C. Glover, from Oct. '54.

26 Squadron
Less than a week after 20 Squadron received its first Sabres, No.26, also at Oldenburg, followed suit and by mid-November 1953 the wing had almost 40 of the new fighters. Thereafter the histories of the two squadrons ran in parallel for the following 18 months, even to the extent of having a four-man aerobatic team, and rivalry was intense. Charles Keil, now an advertising executive, was a 20-year-old pilot on 26 Squadron when it re-equipped with Sabres.

Flight of 26 Squadron Sabres. (via Al Statham)

A 26 Squadron 16-plane flypast in 1955. (Al Statham)

I decided to join the RAF largely as a result of a talk given by a former senior boy at my school, Newbury Grammar School, who later became top student at Cranwell, and went on to serve with 26 Squadron, where he flew Tempests and Vampires. He then volunteered to serve in Korea, where he was killed while flying Sabres with the USAF.

I trained in Canada at 1 FTS Centralia and while there, flying Harvards, I recall the arrival of two RCAF Sabres whose pilots gave a talk to us on their combat experiences in Korea with the Americans. After the talk we were invited to sit in the Sabre's cockpit, and I clearly remember thinking, "My God, I hope I'm never expected to fly a plane as complicated as the Sabre," because the cockpit seemed so full of dials! Perhaps that's why, as a young inexperienced pilot with 26 Squadron I found the transition from Vampire 9 to Sabre more difficult than from the piston-engined Harvard trainer to the Vampire jet fighter!

My first and most abiding impressions of the Sabre were the American cockpit—roomier than any comparable British fighter, with a different, but better, layout of the instruments, which were also further forward and required more stretch to reach them.

The power controls were also a big change from the Vampire and Meteor, where the pilot had to exert a definite physical movement of the stick, whereas with the Sabre a similar physical force was enough to push the fighter into a max rate roll . . . one only needed a finger-light touch to make the aircraft respond. Another thing I associate with the Sabre was the paraphernalia one wore—the bone dome with inner helmet, G suit, and back 'chute which fitted into the ejection seat.

Once you became familiar with it the Sabre was very easy to fly and the most fantastic aeroplane around at the time, with beautiful handling qualities. Nevertheless for a while there were a lot of Sabre prangs in RAF Germany, due to inexperience and various malfunctions, notably hydraulics failures, and too many of these accidents were fatalities,

Pilots of 26 Squadron. The CO, S/L K. Smith, is wearing the beret. (via Al Statham)

mostly attributable to the (poor) North American ejection seat, which we didn't consider worked very well. It was unstabilized, so the chap who ejected became completely disoriented as he spun around, and you had to unfasten the straps manually to extricate yourself from the seat—which was comfortable, rather like an armchair. In the squadron we pilots often discussed the best ways to get out of the seat, and some guys used to fly with the straps undone—until one chap had to eject in that condition. He went forward, out of the seat, and was then swept back and got smashed up on the fin. For all practical purposes we reckoned the seat was of little use below 2000 feet because there wasn't time to orientate yourself and undo the straps to separate from the seat.

Charles Keil

Another former 26 Squadron Sabre pilot, Al Statham, who converted after training on F-84Gs in the USA, also regarded the ejection seat as being inferior to the British designs from Martin Baker. "Three movements were needed to activate the ejection sequence and there was no face blind. It was even referred to in a song we used to sing:

We are flying swept back Sabres,
We are supersonic,
We must give up cigarettes and no
   more gin and tonic,

We have a gunsight to give us the
   right deflection,
Trim tab to give us the right correction,
Hot seat to give a quick ejection,
Right, left, right, bang, bang!

American instruments, in my opinion, were not as good as British. The compass had no fast slave or quick erection button. The only method was to pull a circuit breaker under the left-hand coaming—very awkward as it was next to the undercarriage circuit breaker and if the wrong one was pulled the gear remained up in spite of 'down' selection. Enough said!"

Al Statham was among the 26 Squadron pilots who deployed to Plateau airfield at Habbaniya, Iraq, for a few days while the squadron's Sabres were on detachment at Nicosia for air-air armament practice in May 1955. Shortly after the return to Oldenburg the following month No.26 began to re-equip with Hunters.

BASE: Oldenburg.
SABRE SERVICE: 4.11.53 (XB623)-30.8.55 (XB588/P).
REPRESENTATIVE AIRCRAFT: XB543/Z (Al Statham's aircraft), 609/X, 708/T, 832/E (CO's aircraft), 862/R, 883/A.
UNIT MARKINGS: 18 inch-diameter white disc, thinly outlined in pale blue, containing a brown, white and black buck's head, positioned above the fin flash. Individual code letter, usually yellow outlined in red, (but red on XB832/E) forward of the fuselage roundel. On some aircraft the red outline was in the form of shadow-shading, e.g. XB767/Y.
COs: S/L K. Smith, March '52-Sept. '54.
S/L J.A.G. Jackson, Sept. '54-

234 Squadron

This was the third Oldenburg Vampire Squadron to re-equip with Sabres, commencing November 1953, and the majority of its full establishment of 22 aircraft had been delivered before the squadron moved to its new home base of Geilenkirchen in January 1954.

It soon built up to operational status and assumed the routine tasks of its day fighter role, but on October 29, 1954, an incident occurred which was anything but routine; one of 234's younger pilots, F/O Pete Underdown, was flying XB860 near Wintraal, Holland, when the aircraft exploded beneath him, causing him to fall several thousand feet into an apple tree without the assistance of a parachute. He suffered back injuries and spent some time in the RAF hospital at Hedley Court in England before rejoining 234 to resume his Sabre flying early the following year. Another 234 pilot lucky to get away with it was F/O Shrimpton, who flew his Sabre rather too close to terra firma while engaged in live gunnery practice at the Monschau range and mushed into the ground in the pull out, severely damaging the rear fuselage but miraculously managing to keep the aircraft airborne to make a safe, if shocked, landing back at base.

During the early part of 1955 234's four-ship aerobatic team led by F/L B.N. Byrne established quite a reputation in 2 TAF for its tight formation flying. It gave several displays at air shows on the Continent that "season." It was about this time that Robin

Sabres of 234 Squadron at Geilenkirchen on October 10, 1955. They were about to fly to Sylt for the squadron's biannual gunnery camp. The first aircraft has been modified with the hard wing, including wing fences. (via Robin A. Brown)

F/O Pete Underdown recuperating in hospital after being flung from XB860 when it exploded on October 29, 1954. Trouble began two minutes after takeoff at 1500 feet when a fuel pump failed. A comment by the Canadair tech rep reads, "seat charge, not exploded, found in vicinity of seat." Underdown fell into an apple tree, *sans* parachute, and survived. The incident occurred over Holland. (234 Squadron)

Brown joined the squadron; he was unusual among RAF fighter pilots then (and now!) in that he kept a detailed diary of squadron life and also took plenty of photographs which combine to provide an accurate and valuable record of those halcyon days. Previously a pilot with 79 Squadron in Germany flying Meteor F.R.9s, Robin Brown graphically describes the satisfaction of Sabre flying and conveys the atmosphere of 234 Squadron in these extracts:

F/L Robin Brown prepares for a mission in XB872 of 234 Squadron, Geilenkirchen. (via Robin A. Brown)

My conversion to Sabres was done at the Conversion Unit at RAF Wildenrath and consisted of ground lectures on the aircraft as was normal at that time, so that you knew what to do in the event of emergencies, how to handle things like hydraulic failures, bailing out, forced landings, etc. Then you were put in the cockpit and told to take the machine away and fly it! All very simple and straightforward. What isn't mentioned in my log book is that my very first Sabre solo flight, taking off from Wildenrath, to do an hour's famil flying in the local area and one landing, was enlivened by my doing my landing at RAF Bruggen instead of Wildenrath! Two very similar NATO airbases, about 10 miles apart, both with single east-west runways.

Realizing that I had boobed when I was about halfway down Bruggen's runway, I taxied round the perimeter track and simply took off again—the only acknowledgement of my error being a sarcastic wave from the runway controller in the caravan! When I landed safely at Wildenrath the fellow who had been watching out for me remarked, "Nice landing!" or words to that effect, at which I couldn't help but reply, "Not as good as the one I did at Bruggen!"

To fly the Sabre at that time was the epitome of every pilot's desire. The RAF had too long been equipped with the Meteor/Vampire stable and pilots on supersonic Sabres were the envy of lesser mortals. It is difficult to describe adequately the pride and delight one felt on being competent to fly a "swept-wing" aircraft and to have done the miraculous Mach 1.

A Christmas card produced by 112 Squadron at that time (who were flying Vampires) showed a cartoon of squadron personnel vainly trying to force the

F/L Bill Watford, OC "A" Flight, 234 Squadron. He wears the inner helmet typical in the RAF at the time, while his outer "bone dome" rests on the windscreen. (via Robin A. Brown)

F/O "Tex" Scrambler strapped into his 234 Sabre while on alert in 1955. (via Robin A. Brown)

Vampire's wings into a swept-back configuration with ropes and tractors. The sub-title was "All we want for Christmas is our wings swept-back!"

Apart from the machismo in being a supersonic pilot there was the huge American logistic back-up of the Sabre squadrons. You had a G-suit, a "bone dome," "Sabre boots" and a lot of other bits and pieces which marked you out as something special. In the Vampires and Meteors you still flew with a soft leather helmet and in normal shoes, and a lightweight flying suit over your battledress. In Sabres you were, as it were, dressed to kill!

One wore one's Sabre boots everywhere possible, with the tops of one's trousers tucked nonchalantly into the boots so that everyone could see them. As it happens they were extremely comfortable boots, with soft leather uppers, like the wartime RAF "escape boots." In civvies people also sported either the little gold-metal Sabre buttonhole badge, or the "Mach-buster" badge. These little goodies were handed out by the Canadair rep on the squadron after you had done your first supersonic run, and came with a certificate that stated you had flown faster than the speed of sound.

In those days, at least to start with, there was no regulation saying you shouldn't "aim" your sonic boom at the ground, and one tended just to happen to pull through while over HQ Rheindahlen so as to wake up the staff chappies! Eventually, of course, this was forbidden as too many windows were being broken.

In those days (something of a cliché, sorry) you were also at liberty—mainly because no one said otherwise—to decorate your bone dome with the squadron insignia or crest. I still have my bone dome from 234 Squadron days and I carried the 234 crest (a dragon rampant) on either side of the helmet at about ear position, while from rear to front across the crest of the helmet I sported my previous squadron's insignia, 79 Squadron's red arrow. I remember the aircrew medics at Rheindahlen complaining that RAE Farnborough had spent thousands of pounds to get a silver colour for the helmet to reflect heat and light away from the head, only to have squadron pilots cover the helmet with their personal graffiti!

To fly, the Sabre was a joy, especially after the old Meatbox and the Vamp. You were seated in a wide, roomy cockpit, with the cockpit sides seemingly very low compared to the RAF machines. The colour scheme in the Sabre appeared to have been designed with an eye to making life easy for the pilot—emergency lights so you could see them immediately and so on. We had a radar gunsight, of course, which is reflected in my decent scores (for once) at the RAF Air Firing camp at Sylt—although they had their share of unserviceability of course. We didn't like the American ejector seat too much and preferred Martin Baker's design, mainly because of the face blind. The Sabre's ejection seat was worked by handles adjacent to the arm rests, which was good when you were trying to eject from an aircraft subjected to high G forces, but we missed the (apparent) protection of the face blind, I think.

We had leg-restraining straps for the first time, and once again these were an improvement on the RAF design in that (I think my memory is correct here) the metal loops were part of the flying suit, and one didn't have to strap on a special strap round each leg as you did in the Hunter.

On 234 Squadron we had both "hard" and "soft" aircraft, i.e. the ones without and with leading-edge slats. With a swept-wing aircraft you were vulnerable to a flick when turning finals if you let your speed get too low or you were pulling it round too tight. The "soft-edged" Sabres compensated for this by the automatic opening of the slat.

The other thing that I liked about the whole Sabre business was the massive technological back-up that the aircraft had—special tools for every job, a ladder for the pilot to enter the cockpit, special intake guards, etc., etc. When we converted on to Hunter 4s we were back to makeshift RAF arrangements where things were made in station workshops.

234 Squadron gained brief notoriety by getting an air-to-air gun camera shot of the Soviet Badger that was allowed to fly over 2 TAF airspace on the occasion of the visit of Bulganin and Khrushchev to the U.K. They arrived at Portsmouth in the battle-cruiser Sverdlov but returned to the USSR in the Badger. Although the 2 TAF aircraft were supposed not to go anywhere near this machine, 234 got behind it and, as it were, shot it down! Rheindahlen got to hear about this and when the Russian VIPs returned over 2 TAF every squadron was grounded until they had safely passed. The photo of the Badger was in 234 Squadron's scrap book.

We didn't see much of the RCAF Sabres. They were based rather far away. The USAF by this time were equipped with the Sabre Dog and later the F-100, which out-manoeuvred us. Herewith a quotation from my diary of Wednesday, November 30, 1955.

"... nevertheless I was obliged to go off again, this time leading a formation of four aircraft. However, there was a short time for a breather, while the aircraft were refuelled, and then it was discovered that one aircraft was no good, so there would only be three.

"My No.2 was Denis Mayous, and my No.3 was Dicky May. I decided to do an operation takeoff, which means that each batted out to the runway as fast as was safe and lined up and took off without waiting for the others to formate on him. Once airborne I turned on to south and climbed to about 25,000 feet. I was leading my formation south to the American Zone, hoping to find some excitement in the way of American aircraft, so that we could have a battle.

"At 25,000 feet I levelled off, and cruised around over the Rhine and Koblenz for a while, then turned west and made my way up the Moselle

towards Trier as there were signs of contrails in that direction. We climbed to 30,000 feet so as to be in the contrailing area so that they might see us and come for us.

"It was only when I turned south, that we found ourselves anywhere near 'hostile' aircraft, and then everything happened at once. There were contrails everywhere and suddenly we were in the middle of about 16 gyrating, weaving, tumbling aircraft, all Sabres, but mostly ones with more powerful engines than ours. It was hard work for about 10 minutes, pulling around all the time in an everlasting circle, trying always to pull tighter than the man in front to get closer and on to his tail; so tiring that your head is driven slowly into your shoulders with the continuous G forces, and the arms get so heavy on the stick that you would like to drop them and rest them in your lap.

"Round and round we went until we had all lost each other and everyone had been shot down at least twice. Eventually, tiring of it, I called that I was clearing, and flew off to the south where I was joined by my No.2 and 3. Even then we were pursued and we had to break again to avoid them. We flew north again, until we saw Aachen lying under the smoke and haze, when I put the others into line astern and gave them a few minutes quite tough tail-chase. I threw the aircraft about as much as I could and watched them in my mirror as they milled and weaved about in my wake. Once, when I was diving vertically at the ground, I saw that a few thousand feet below me there was a little helicopter whirling along!

"Eventually I brought them into battle formation again, the time being about 10 minutes past midday, and having located the airfield I flew out the Kleine Broghel and then turned for the run in. As we descended the visibility began to decrease and it was only because of my radio compass, which has an arrow that always points directly at the airfield, that I was able to find my way back."

We rarely had liaison visits with

(Top) A 234 Squadron Sabre being wheeled into the hanger. Next, an overall view in 234's hangar at Geilenkirchen. The view of XB838 shows ground crew at work. Note the protective screen at the intake to prevent ingestion of foreign objects (people included!). Finally, a picture at RAF Sylt as armourers begin a quick turnaround after a Sabre has returned from a gunnery flight. (via Robin A. Brown)

268

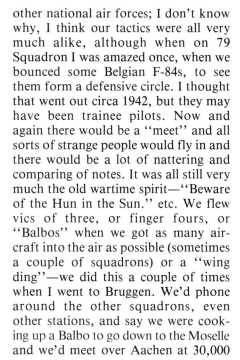

(Top left) XB891 is refuelled, April 1956. Oxygen cylinders, a start trolley, and an interesting German refuelling truck make up this scene. (Below) An RAF salvage crew takes a tea break from the task of retrieving a downed 234 Squadron Sabre (thought to be XB819). (Above) Sabre damaged after low-flying on the Monshau weapons range in Germany. The pilot was F/O Shrimpton of 234. A close one! (Robin A. Brown, 234 Squadron)

Flight about this time when I claimed that on an occasion when a vic of three Sabres was making a rapid descent, I could see the shock-wave, like a very long whip-aerial, emanating from about halfway down the upper fuselage. No one ever replied to my letter so I don't know whether I was imagining it.

Robin A. Brown

Robin Brown's reference to "soft" and "hard" winged Sabres respectively describes aircraft with the original wing with leading-edge slats and aircraft on which these had been replaced by a fixed leading edge, increased in chord by 6 inches at the wing root and 3 inches at the tip. A few of the later Sabre 4s had been delivered to the RAF with the hard wing, also identified by a small fence about midway along the upper leading edge, but the majority of RAF Sabres were modified while in service from about August 1954 by working parties from MUs and from the Bristol Aeroplane Co. Ltd. at Filton, which acted as a subcontractor for Canadair, who provided the modification kits. Although most RAF Sabres had the hard wing by the summer of '55, a few remained unmodified until withdrawal from the Service. One such machine on 234 Squadron was XB891, received from 4 Squadron on March 2, 1956, and destined not long afterwards to be the recipient of a splendid scarlet fin adorned with a black panther motif, courtesy of the 494th Fighter Bomber Squadron, USAF, during an exchange visit in which some of the 494th F-86s stayed

other national air forces; I don't know why, I think our tactics were all very much alike, although when on 79 Squadron I was amazed once, when we bounced some Belgian F-84s, to see them form a defensive circle. I thought that went out circa 1942, but they may have been trainee pilots. Now and again there would be a "meet" and all sorts of strange people would fly in and there would be a lot of nattering and comparing of notes. It was all still very much the old wartime spirit—"Beware of the Hun in the Sun." etc. We flew vics of three, or finger fours, or "Balbos" when we got as many aircraft into the air as possible (sometimes a couple of squadrons) or a "wing ding"—we did this a couple of times when I went to Bruggen. We'd phone around the other squadrons, even other stations, and say we were cooking up a Balbo to go down to the Moselle and we'd meet over Aachen at 30,000

feet in an hour, and then we'd see who turned up. They weren't *vast* formations, perhaps about 16 aircraft, but it was a big enough swarm to bring the F-100s and F-86s clawing up from Bitburg and Spangdahlen.

When we converted on to Hunters, people were very disappointed with the new machine. It didn't seem to have anything that the Sabre didn't, and was cramped in comparison. The USAF were, of course, converting on to Sabre Dogs, which outmanoeuvred the Hunter, so we felt that we were marking time instead of progressing. Naturally these were initial impressions; everyone who flew the Hunter grew to love it, but at first it was a disappointment.

In comparison to the Vampire and the Meteor the Sabre was like another era. It was a docile aircraft, very few vices, easy to land and very pleasant at Mach I and above. I wrote a letter to

269

No.66 Squadron in April 1956. It was re-equipping with Hunter F.4s, but, oddly, as the Hunter was not yet available in quantity, Meteors were flown on an interim basis. Hence, the Meteor F.8. The coastline below is in East Yorkshire. (MOD Air)

at Geilenkirchen and 234's Sabres went to the Americans' base of Chaumont, in France. For some while later XB891 retained its red fin, but by May '56 the first Hunter 4s had arrived for 234 and within a month all its Sabres had gone.

BASES: Oldenburg, moving to Geilenkirchen in January 1954.
SABRE SERVICE: (XB898/A-W)-4.6.56 (XB827/H).
REPRESENTATIVE AIRCRAFT: XB536/N, 642/S, 748/F, 807/Z, 867/E, 984/K.
UNIT MARKINGS: Initially the individual aircraft letter appeared ahead of the fuselage roundel, and the squadron code letter W appeared aft of the roundel, most letters being red, outlined in white. After a short while the squadron code letters were dispensed with and replaced by a white disc above the fin flash containing the unit's black dragon badge, embellished with red tongue and claws. At the same time the nose cone was adorned with black and red chequers, and the whole marking was thinly edged in yellow where it bordered the aircraft camouflage. In early summer 1955 the markings were again

revised: the nose cone was changed to red only, retaining the thin yellow edging; the white disc containing the squadron dragon was moved from the fin to the nose, just aft of the gun ports; markings were applied on each side of the fuselage roundel comprised of a black rectangle thinly outlined in yellow, containing 2 rows of red diamonds; individual aircraft letter was applied to the upper fin, initially painted in red, outlined in white, and laterally in white only. The code letter was repeated on the nose wheel door in black on white; most aircraft carried the "assigned" pilot's name in black on the cockpit canopy sill, e.g. XB872/R — FLT. LT. R.A. Brown.
COs: S/L R.M. Chatfield, DFC, Aug. '52-Mar.'55. S/L Roger Emett, Mar.'55-

66 Squadron
The "extra" 60 Sabres provided by the USA under MDAP funding were sufficient to equip two UK-based squadrons and the two units chosen were Nos.66 and 92 Squadrons, previously flying Meteor F.8 day fighters, which together with the Meteor NF.11 night fighters of No.264 Squadron comprised the Linton-on-Ouse Wing, in North Yorkshire. Deliveries commenced on December 1, 1953, to No.66, enabling it to claim the distinction of being the

first squadron in RAF Fighter Command to operate swept-wing interceptors and the first with supersonic capability—which fuelled the ego of its pilots to even higher levels, especially when it is remembered that the command at that time was large and still expanding, with a strength of 24 regular and 20 auxiliary squadrons, all of them equipped with straight-winged, subsonic Meteors and Vampires.

These Sabres for Fighter Command could be distinguished from those of the main RAF consignment used in Germany by having silver, instead of blue, undersurfaces, and XD-prefix serial numbers as opposed to XB serials. It was almost as though the delivery of the first two aircraft on December 1 took No.66 by surprise, because no one on the squadron had received any conversion training. Steps to rectify this situation were taken the following day when the CO, S/L Dennis Usher, and the squadron's instrument rating examiner, F/L Gerald "Jed" Gray, were flown by Anson from Linton to Wildenrath to take a familiarization course with the Sabre Conversion Flight (SCF). This consisted of three days of ground school and, because of bad weather, only three Sabre sorties apiece. One of the SCF instructors was F/L Martin Chandler; several years earlier as a flying instructor in Rhodesia, Jed Gray had sent Martin off on his first solos in both the Tiger Moth and the Harvard, in each case with a pat on the back and the entreaty to "land the thing carefully if you don't want to break your neck!" Naturally, Martin couldn't resist the opportunity to return the compliment when it was Jed's turn to make his first Sabre flight.

After the receipt of the first two Sabres no more were delivered to 66 until mid-January '54, and conversion could not begin in earnest until the end of the month. There was a considerable breadth of experience among the squadron's pilots at that time, which included several with Second World War combat experience, including the CO, Jed Gray and F/L "Bush" Barrey, the Australian A Flight Commander who held the DFC, AFC and DFM. The RAF still had a large number of NCO pilots in the '50s, and they tended to do more flying than some of their commissioned colleagues and also served with a squadron for longer tours of duty. This was certainly true for No.

On the line at Linton in 1954 as 66 Squadron Sabres are readied. All carry the unit's blue and white bar, rattlesnake crest on the nose, and pilot's name on canopy frame. (via J.D.R. Rawlings)

XD730 of 66 Squadron. On July 22, 1954 it crashed in the Pennine mountains. (via Eric Taylor)

66, among whose complement of young sergeant pilots was Ian Laurie, who had joined the squadron straight from an OCU in April 1950 and only left it in March 1955 to be commissioned, during which time he successively flew Meteor F.4s, F.8s and Sabres. Ian was a member of 66 Squadron's Meteor F.8 aerobatic team which gave a superlative display in 1951 culminating in a sensational cross-over from six points of the compass—the squadron was the first in the RAF to operate an aerobatic team of more than four aircraft. Notwithstanding his affection for the Meteor, Ian has equally fond memories of the Sabre: "This was a really beautiful aircraft, and once one got

used to the American instrumentation and the power controls, a joy to fly. Up to about 20,000 feet the Meteor 8 would always hold its own with the Sabre, but above 20 grand then the Sabre took over. To go supersonic in the aircraft it was necessary to climb to 40,000 feet then dive vertically with full power on. If you hadn't gone supersonic by 35,000 feet then that was it, but you had to start the recovery by 25 thousand otherwise the airframe would be overstressed by 15,000 feet. We used to 'bang' the airfield, when Air Traffic would leave their transmit button open so that you could hear your own sonic boom. One pilot was a bit off target and hit the city of York; it is reputed that the only window that was broken

was in the RAF recruiting office in the High Street!"

Like Ian Laurie, who was recently captaining VC-10 transports with No.10 Squadron, a surprising number of former Sabre pilots are still serving in the RAF, including a one-time A Flight colleague on 66 Squadron, then Sergeant, now S/L Bruce Macdonald, who joined the squadron in 1949 flying Meteor 4s and 35 years later was still flying the RAF's last Meteor T.7 as part of the CFS "Vintage Fair" with the last Vampire T.11 as the other half of the display duo. In 1954 sonic bangs were not only permissible, but became the high spot of air shows wherever the Sabre was the star attraction, and for the annual Battle of Britain "At Home" day on September 18 that year, Linton Sabres were much in demand at the RAF stations in England. On that day Bruce Macdonald was detailed to

271

Some pilots of 66 Squadron in 1954. Ian Laurie is second from the right in the rear. Front and centre is F/L "Bush" Burrey, while right behind him is the CO, S/L Dennis Usher. (via Ian Laurie)

fly XD772/H some 35 miles north of Linton, to Middelton-St. George, a former RCAF bomber base near Darlington, and now Tees-Side Airport. There the Sabre formed part of the static line-up until the afternoon's flying display, when Bruce climbed eight miles above the airfield to plant a sonic bang and then give a sparkling aerobatic show. After landing to refuel, he was off again to give a repeat performance over the nearby fighter airfield at Thornaby, before refuelling and returning to Linton, only 10 minutes flying time away.

66's Sabre sorties were seldom so short, as Ian Laurie recalls: "In the Sabre we used to run patrols over the English Channel from Linton (about 300 miles distant). To enable us to have sufficient time on the patrol line we used to shut down the engine and glide back to Linton, relighting over York at about 5000 feet. The relight procedure was very simple and happily very reliable." Jed Gray wouldn't entirely agree with Ian's comments about easy relights, especially after an episode while he was flying XD722/J off the Norfolk coast, which he graphically describes:

"On May 6th, 1954, I was flying as No.3 of a four-aircraft battle formation when I experienced flame-out at 18,000 feet. We were in close formation at the time and in a descent to starboard at 350 knots. The leader called for dive brakes out and reduction in power to 80 per cent.

I kept my R/T on and attempted a relight firstly without switching on emergency fuel. This was unsuccessful and so I attempted further relights with emergency fuel on at 180 knots. Since I was unable to effect a relight and was approaching cloud, I decided to abandon attempts and to concentrate on a forced landing.

My No.4 was detailed to remain with me, whilst No.2 was detailed to descend below cloud to check the cloud base and position. I broke cloud at 2,000 feet and saw a disused airfield straight ahead into which I considered I could glide. When short of the airfield I lowered my undercarriage, but when realizing I was undershooting raised it again and pressed the override. I tried to jettison my tanks by depressing the salvo button, but the circuit breaker must have been out and the tanks remained with the aircraft. Being unable to control a rapid sink I landed the aircraft rather heavily in a field 500 yards short of the airfield.

The aircraft did not catch fire, but

during the rapid deceleration, which took place over a distance of 150 yards I received a double compressed fracture of the back, a smashed ankle and nose, and several cuts.

The Court of Inquiry and the subsequent strip examination of the engine by the manufacturers showed that possible causes of the flame-out were a union between the oil filter and the main fuel regulator being crossthreaded, which could have conveyed air to the latter with resultant loss of thrust, and a faulty main fuel regulator in which the altitude control mechanism was in some way unsatisfactory. This meant that at the time of the flame-out there was a small degree of throttle movement due to the changing conditions of formation flying and that if the altitude control mechanism was sticking, the response following the movement of the throttle might have been erratic. This in turn would cause a change in fuel pressure and fuel flow to which the engine would endeavour to respond but might result in the engine stalling.

The accident classification was Major Unavoidable and the aircraft was Category 5.

Jed Gray

The scene of the accident was the disused airfield of Langham in Norfolk, and Jed was taken to the nearest hospital of any size, in nearby Cromer, where one of his first visitors was Martin Chandler, who had just been posted from Wildenrath to the Day Fighter Leader School (DFLS) at RAF West Raynham not far away. Chandler later rose to the rank of at least group captain.

Sadly, Jed Gray's accident was only the first of many for 66 Squadron during its time with Sabres, and not all the prangs ended without tragedy. Exactly a week later, on the unlucky 13th, XD773/C suffered a loss of engine power and ploughed into the runway undershoot area at Linton. On June 16 XD711/L and 716/K collided above Hornsea on the East Yorkshire coast, with both pilots managing to abandon their fighters. Little more than a month later, on July 22, during Exercise Dividend to test UK air defences, 66 Squadron lost three Sabres and two pilots within a few hours. The double tragedy occurred when four of the squadron's Sabres were letting down to Linton in bad weather from the west, and one pair (XD707/ and 730/) flew into high ground at Kinder Scout, Derbyshire, killing both pilots. This was almost a carbon copy of a similar multiple-crash three years previously when the squadron operated Meteors. The third Sabre to crash on the 22nd was XD758/L which was abandoned over Helmsley in North Yorkshire after a warning light indicated an engine fire.

During the first few months with Sabres, aircraft from both 66 and 92 Squadrons at Linton would frequently fly south to North Luffenham, often combining with the Canadians, to practice large-scale Sabre formation flying, usually as a prelude to a flypast over London for such occasions as the Queen's Birthday or other ceremonial events. North Luffenham had been the intended destination of Jed Gray on May 6 before his unscheduled crash landing at Langham. Finally recovered from his injuries, he returned to 66 Squadron at the end of July, and a month later on August 27, 1954, he was again detailed to lead a section of three Sabres to North Luffenham. As Jed walked out to his aircraft, XD776/Z, one of his colleagues, mindful of his previous misadventure, jokingly called to him, "Hope you make it to Luffenham this time!" Jed describes the flight which followed:

Some 16 weeks later, on August 27, 1954, I was detailed to lead a section of three Sabres to RAF North Luffenham, refuel, and then take part in a rehearsal for the Battle of Britain flypast.

After starting up, R/T check, taxiing and emergency fuel system check, we took off from Linton-on-Ouse. After takeoff I set course for North Luffenham and Nos.2 and 3 joined up in wide "vic" formation. As the aircraft were fuelled for a long-range detail, and the flight was to be of short duration, we proceeded to North Luffenham with dive brakes out and engine revolutions at approximately 93 per cent. During the flight to North Luffenham, my aircraft was functioning normally and all instruments and controls were normal. I tuned my radio compass to Linton-on-Ouse beacon shortly after getting airborne, to obtain back-bearings, and to the North Luffenham beacon at approximately halfway through the flight. My cockpit heating system was on "Auto" and the rheostat control about one quarter of the way from the "Cold" position, the

pressurization system switch being set in the "Pressurization" position shortly after takeoff.

On arrival in the North Luffenham area and flying at 2000 feet I ordered my section to line astern and flew around the local area to burn off excess fuel, since I considered it wiser to reduce the "all-up" weight of the section aircraft before attempting to land.

After being airborne for approximately 25 minutes I heard a banging noise coming from my aircraft. I did not consider this noise to be coming from the aircraft engine and on checking the instruments all were normally indicated. There was no rough running of the engine or vibration on the aircraft. I instructed my No.2 to come in closely to inspect my aircraft and see if all appeared to be normal. This he did and reported that all appeared to be normal. Just as this was taking place my cockpit began to fill with smoke and as there was no indication of fire from the fire warning lights I checked all instruments and controls, re-set the cockpit pressurization selector switch to "Ram" and reduced power. There was no indication in the cockpit that anything was abnormal, other than the smoke and the banging noise.

I then informed the section that I was going to land immediately and that as my visibility was reduced by smoke instructed my No.2 to lead me to North Luffenham airfield. I opened my cockpit canopy to try to disperse the smoke, but after an initial slight dispersal this persisted and then increased in volume. The noise that I could hear also increased in frequency, but not in volume. Suddenly flames appeared in front of me, appearing to come up from the seat area, and to the port side of me in the port console and throttle quadrant areas. There was still no indication of fire on the fire warning lights.

By this time, the heat in the cockpit was becoming unbearable and I felt a considerable heat around my eyes, left hand and left leg. The flames were steadily increasing and I realized I would never be able to remain in the aircraft long enough to reach North Luffenham and land. I informed my section that I was going to abandon the aircraft and then proceeded to carry out the emergency procedure for doing so.

I jettisoned my canopy, but could not operate the port arm rest handle to lock my harness due to excessive heat

and burns, so I fired the ejection seat trigger after closing down the engine and raising the nose of the aircraft to reduce speed and slipstream.

The ejection went normally and I cleared the aircraft at about 2000 feet. After a certain amount of tumbling, I released my harness straps, kicked the seat free and after a slight pause operated my parachute. This developed normally, and I landed successfully in a grass field in the grounds of Laxton Park Gate, near Corby, Northants. The aircraft crashed about three-quarters of a mile away in a field.

I then telephoned from a farm house to North Luffenham to give them details of the incident. As I was informed by a passer-by that the ammunition was exploding at the scene of the aircraft crash, I proceeded there on the pillion of a passing motor-cyclist and kept back spectators until the arrival of the police, fire brigades and ambulance from North Luffenham. I handed over responsibility of supervision to the CTO North Luffenham and showed him the area where I had landed by parachute and the ejector seat, starboard drop tank and pitot head, which I had located about three-quarters of a mile from the crashed aircraft.

I received burns on the left wrist and arm and singed eyebrows and parts of my flying overalls and clothing were burned.

The Court of Inquiry found that the cause of the fire was due to the ammunition compartment overheating, which then caused some of the ammunition to explode from time to time. Whilst the overheating warning light had not apparently operated, it was subsequently decided to introduce a modification to reposition this in a more prominent position at eye level.

Jed Gray

Jed Gray was one of only a very few RAF pilots to have the misfortune to suffer two Sabre write-offs and the good luck to escape serious injury. The second Sabre crash was Jed's fourth major accident; he had previously been shot down in a Spitfire by German flak and survived a mid-air collision in a Meteor 8 while with the Day Fighter Leaders School. Happily, after he left 66 Squadron in April '55, he continued an interesting but accident-free career which included promotion to squadron leader and command of 222 Squadron, equipped with Hunters. Jed now lives

Eleven Sabres of 112 Squadron in echelon over north Germany in 1955. (MOD Air)

in France. Unfortunately Jed Gray's second Sabre prang was far from being the last on 66 Squadron, which lost nine Sabres in its first 12 months with the type, which rose to a total of 12 write-offs before Hunter 4s began to supplant Sabres in March 1956, a record which for a while rather tarnished this famous fighter squadron's otherwise impressive history.

BASE: Linton-on-Ouse.
SABRE SERVICE: 1.12.53 (XD706/D and 702/N)-16.5.56 (XD706/D with three others).
REPRESENTATIVE AIRCRAFT: XD710/B, 725/X, 735/T, 765/E, 778/R; XB941/S.
UNIT MARKINGS: White rectangles, outlined in royal blue on each side of the fuselage roundel. Code letter in red (A Flt.) or blue (B Flt.) outlined in white, above the fin flash, often repeated in black or Flight colour on the nose wheel door. Initially most aircraft carried the Squadron's "rattlesnake" crest on each side of the nose, just aft of the guns. Pilot's name was often painted on the canopy sill in white. XD753/AFO used by the CO, S/L A.F. Osborne, had a blue fin and rudder, with a lightning flash containing his initials in yellow; it also had a blue nose cap ringed in white.
COs: S/L Dennis C. Usher, DFC, DFM, to Nov. '54, S/L A.F. "Sammy" Osborne, DFC, Nov. '54-1957.

112 Squadron
Another 2 TAF ground-attack squadron, No.112, began to replace its Vampire FB.5s in January 1954, having moved from Fassberg, only five min-

utes flying time from the Soviet zone of East Germany, to Bruggen, a new NATO airfield close to the Dutch border. This reflected the policy change resulting from the introduction of faster aircraft types by 2 TAF: Venom, Sabre, and later the Swift and Hunter. As G/C Crawford-Compton, the station commander, said at that time, "It's a disadvantage for present-day fighters to be up near the front line, for on the climb their forward speed is so great that at one time they must turn their backs to the enemy as they gain height. From Bruggen, on the other hand, it's possible to do a straight climb; moreover, the army are no longer embarrassed by having to look after the squadrons in the front areas."

Deliveries of Sabres to 112 built up quickly, and almost 20 were on strength by the end of the month, though the majority of these machines,

all soft-winged, were passed down to other squadrons (notably Nos.20, 26 and 93) in April and May, and were replaced on 112 with hard-winged examples from a later production batch with serials in the XB900 series.

Tactical exercises, designed to test the mobility of the Allied air forces on the Continent, were very much in vogue and usually concluded with a major "show" at least once a year, in addition to many smaller scale sector exercises. Late September '54 saw the major Exercise Battle Royal during which 112 and other squadarons at Bruggen, destined to briefly become the RAF's biggest Sabre base, operated under canvas from a grassy corner of the airfield to simulate war conditions as closely as possible. Many top cover sorties were flown in support of Venoms, and there was plenty of "trade" in the form of other NATO fighters, and B-47s and Canberras "attacking"

A Sabre of 112 Squadron with its successor, a Hunter F.4. (RAF Museum P11961)

Continental targets from their bases in England, while low-level strafing attacks on "enemy" airfields were also made by the Sabres.

The arrival in April '56 of Hunter 4s for 112 marked the imminent departure of the Sabres, and by June they were gone.

BASE: Bruggen.
SABRE SERVICE: 29.12.53 (XB576) 6.6.56 (XB920/K)
REPRESENTATIVE AIRCRAFT: XB649/C, 772/P, 917/A, 934/X, 978/N.
UNIT MARKINGS: Large red and white shark's mouth, edged and shaded in black, painted beneath the nose just ahead of the wing root, with the "eyes" in the same colours, beneath the cockpit (these markings originated with the squadron's P-40 Tomahawks in the Middle East in 1941). The aircraft code letter was painted in white high on the fin.
CO: S/L F.M. Hegarty, Nov. '53, '55, S/L A.R. Wilson '55-'57.

130 Squadron

This was a new squadron, only reformed with Vampire FB.5s on August 1, 1953, at Bruggen as part of the expansion of RAF fighter units both in England and overseas. It began to re-equip with soft-winged Sabres in February 1954 and its history with these aircraft paralleled that of its neighbour and rival at Bruggen, No.112 Squadron. This even included the replacement of its first batch of Sabres with the hard-winged version in April and May '54. Bill Ireland, who flew Sabres with 130 Squadron and continued to serve in the RAF, reaching the rank of

A 130 Squadron flight during Exercise Battle Royal in 1954. "V" (XB927) later undershot at Bruggen after engine failure, and was wrecked. (*Flight International*)

at least wing commander, described his memories of the aircraft, some 20 years later:

I was converted to Sabres at the Conversion Flight at Wildenrath. The transition, at least for chaps like myself who were trained in the UK, was by no means straightforward. Compared with the Vampire the Sabre was a very complex animal and, of course, many of the systems and virtually all the instrumentation was alien to us. I seem to recall that the Ground School preceding the first flight at Wildenrath was at least three days and I also recall that this was the most difficult part of the conversion. Flying the aircraft presented little difficulty to squadron pilots. There was, of course, the "Piccolo Syndrome" which caused some early confusion. This was a term applied to having the numerous controls on the stick and throttle. The one thing which did seem to catch many people out was the critical speed for lowering the flaps. The flaps were friction mounted and could be lowered at speeds below 160 knots. At 161 knots they blew up and had to be reset on the ground.

130 Squadron was a DF/GA (Day Fighter/Ground Attack) outfit when I joined and it took us some time to be weaned away from this and converted to the HF/DF role. Indeed, I am not sure if we ever did because I recall that we always maintained a JSLO at Bruggen—invariably a Belgian—and we kept up our relations with the various army formations in the corps area. We did, however, do a lot of interception exercises, many of them down into "Indian country," which is

what we used to call the areas protected by the F-86s from USAF Bitburg and Spangdahlem. Most of these exercises were carried out at about 35,000 feet and duration was from 40 minutes where the drop tanks were not filled up to an hour or even an hour and fifteen minutes when they were. For some time we had a delightful mutual exchange scheme with the Americans and would drop in to Bitburg or Spangdahlem, top up with fuel and take off again.

Regarding Battle Flight, I seem to recall that it was on a rotational basis around the fighter wings in Germany with wings being on it for two or three days and squadrons drawing the duty for part of this period. For the life of me I cannot recall what state of readiness we maintained though I have an idea that at the end of the Sabre's time we were on cockpit readiness. However, I may be confusing this with the Hunter period.

Regarding the 6-3 winged aircraft, my recollections are a little stronger. We started with the slatted version and must have had them for three or four months before the hard edges came along. Incidentally, until I looked at the Profile Publication on the Sabre I had never heard the 6-3 extension referred to. I see, also in that publication, that the fixed leading edge raised the stalling speed from 111 knots to 125 knots, but I do not recollect it being such a large margin. Sadly, on the Bruggen wing there was great competition for tight circuits after formation breaks. I say sadly because in one week a squadron commander gave one of his junior pilots an Orderly Officer duty for passing his boss on the approach;

the week after, the squadron commander crunched in about 400 yards off the western end of the Bruggen runway. Perhaps it was just a lack of experience but I do not think we made very much of the change from slatted to hard edges.

You ask what virtues and vices I recollect about the Sabre. As a pilot's aeroplane it really was fairly forgiving. As a war plane it was perhaps another matter. There was good control at all speeds and even when one was supersonic it was still possible to keep a target in the ring. However, it was a bit of a beast in dogfights, mainly because the radar gunsight was so subject to G loadings. If one came in for a beam attack on a pursuit curve which was at all tight, the display disappeared off the bottom of the screen altogether.

We conducted live air-to-air gunnery at Sylt at about six-monthly intervals. (This is not quite true because I recall one detachment in December where we were not able to fire once.) We did not do live air-to-air anywhere else and it was invariably against banners. I can only recall one occasion when we used a glider target and this must have been well to the end of my time on 130 Squadron, possibly even after we got Hunters. We did, however, do a fair amount of air-to-ground, though never at Sylt. We used to use the range at Monschau in the Eiffel and once or twice we used a range over in Belgium. I am afraid I have forgotten the name.

In comparison with the Hunter, I think we were all disappointed when we converted because, compared with the Vampire/Sabre step, the transition to the Hunter was a small one. Things we missed on leaving the Sabre were the very comfortable seat and superb view and also the possible duration one could obtain. We used to have a squadron cross-country called the "Capitals Limited" where the route overflew Bonn, Basle, Luxembourg and Brussels and thence back to Bruggen, and if you did this at 40,000 feet you still had enough fuel for a couple of circuits at base. The Hunter was, however, a superior air-to-air fighter; apart from the Sabre's gunsight projection disappearing off the screen, the aircraft could not be hauled as tight as a Hunter, particularly when you used the Hunter's flap to help you tighten the turn—the Sabre's flap would have ridden up, of course.

W.S. Ireland

A lovely 92 Squadron echelon in the Linton region, spring of 1954. (RAF Wildenrath 47646)

130 also replaced its Sabres with Hunters in April 1956, and like so many more 2 TAF squadrons, was destined to keep them for barely a year, as the unit was disbanded in 1957.

BASE: Bruggen.
SABRE SERVICE: 29.1.54 (XB790)-7.5.56 (XB949/Z).
REPRESENTATIVE AIRCRAFT: XB682/V, 800/F, 918/R, 922/X, 928/G, 933/W.
UNIT MARKINGS: Squadron marking was applied each side of the fuselage roundel and comprised a red rectangle, edged in white, containing a blue triangle, also outlined in white. Code letter was white, in a black disc above the fin flash.
CO: S/L Megor '53-'54. S/L F.C. Ellis '55-5.57.

92 Squadron

Stablemate of 66 Squadron at Linton-on-Ouse, No.92 followed its rival by re-equipping with Sabres in late February 1954, the two units combining to form the only UK-based fighter wing to operate the type and, until the service debut of the ill-fated Supermarine Swift later in the year, the only units in RAF Fighter Command to operate swept-wing aircraft capable of supersonic flight.

92's Commanding Officer at that time was S/L Rennie Turner, an experienced fighter pilot, with almost 2500 flying hours to his credit, which included combat experience during the war, when he flew the Mustang Mk.1 ("Low level recce role, down to 500 feet—lovely aeroplane"), the Hawker Typhoon ("Proved useless as a recce aircraft, very heavy, lots of engine problems, especially the coolant. Not very pleasant. Used to call them brick shit houses!") and the Tempest 5 ("Improved Sabre engine—much nicer and more reliable than the Typhoon"). The early 1950s may have been tame by comparison, but the RAF was expanding again, and it needed the professionalism and leadership of pilots like Rennie Turner to maintain its highest standards during the influx of young aircrew, which even included a few conscripts who qualified as fighter pilots during their two years of National Service.

Following the procedure adopted by 66 Squadron, Rennie and a senior pilot spent a week at Wildenrath with the SCF, at the beginning of February 1954, where he logged six hours on the Sabre, before returning to Linton to implement the conversion process from Meteor F.8s, which for him began on 23rd of that month with an air test in Sabre XD710 which had been delivered to 66 Squadron but soon "found its way" to 92. Rennie Turner summed up the transition as follows: "They were a very experienced bunch of boys, and the whole conversion process went swimmingly; you see we had former flying instructors on the squadron, and also one or two ex-Ferry Squadron boys who had flown the Sabres over from Canada. In fact Rex Knight, one of my flight commanders, had flown the Sabre operationally in Korea with the Americans.''

Rennie Turner had previously served with the Air Fighting Development Squadron, part of the RAF's Central Fighter Establishment at West Rayham, in the latter part of 1950 when the Commandant of the CFE had asked for volunteers to fly Sabres in Korea. ''We all stepped forward, and they simply chose the five or six chaps they needed. I think they selected five pilots led by a wing commander, who subsequently got the chop. They came back, except for the wingco, after about six months on ops and I remember ''Paddy'' Harbison recalling how he had chased a Chink MiG-15 halfway across North Korea before he shot it down.''

In common with his contemporaries, Rennie's recollections of the Sabre are slightly dulled after more than 30 years: ''After all this time it's not easy to remember every feature of the aircraft's handling, but the two main impressions of the Sabre for me are, firstly, that it was built around the pilot (as distinct from previous RAF fighters) and, secondly, the lightness of the controls. The only thing you had to watch out for was the hydraulic warning light. If that went on, you knew it was time to hit the silk—but fortunately the aircraft hardly ever suffered hydraulics failure. In some respects the Sabre was easier to fly than the Meteor—you didn't have two engines to look after for a start.''

During that first summer with Sabres there were many occasions

Pilots F/L D.N. Yates, F/L V. Woods, S/L R.W.G. Freer, F/L A.W.A. Wright, F/L D.A. Arnott (kneeling) and F/O R.P.V. Woodward. They flew the 92 Squadron Sabres for the photo session out of Linton. (RAF Wildenrath 47656)

when the Linton Wing aircraft would migrate to North Luffenham. S/L Rennie Turner explains why the Canadian base seemed such a favoured destination. ''Just so happened we were much in demand for formation flypasts, with 66 Squadron and the Canadians at North Luffenham, so we used to operate from there, since most of the flypasts were over London—for the Queen, Battle of Britain Day, that

sort of thing. Also when we had just received Sabres it was felt that the Canadians could show us a thing or two, since they'd been flying 'em for a couple of years longer than we had. In fact, I don't think they taught us much! Indeed, later, we went down there to show them our technique for rapid takeoff and assembly of formations, which was much quicker and better organized than their procedure. However, it was useful to talk to them about the aircraft, and sometimes we used to borrow spares from them.''

Rennie Turner describes typical tactics of those Sabre days: ''All the usual things, same as we did when we had the Meteors. Apart from the staple diet of PIs (practice interceptions) mostly out over the North Sea off the eastern seaboard, we had regular ''Rats and Terriers'' exercises for the benefit of the ROC (Royal Observer Corps), in which the 'terrier' (fighter) would be vectored on to the 'rat' (target), all at very low level, to give the ROC practice in plotting us. Jolly good fun, because we flew damned low—hedge-hopping stuff, following the contours. There was another thing called 'Treasure Hunt,' basically a map-reading exercise. You'd normally go out and do a

S/L Rennie Turner astride a 92 Squadron Sabre, and some of his pilots during a visit to North Luffenham on April 15, 1954. (via G. Rennie Turner)

recce, make a note of features on the exercise route, for example a farm house with six windows at a particular cross-roads. These instructions (clues) would be placed in a sealed envelope and off the chap would go.''

And of squadron rivalry he notes: ''Of course there was continual rivalry; that's normal. On 92 we considered ourselves far superior, and thought of them as bums! There's no doubt they thought the same of us, but we had far fewer accidents, and better pilots. In fact I remember some of the younger 66 pilots hanging around our crew room trying to learn all they could from our more experienced boys. Our aircraft were also kept in a higher state of preparedness, better maintained and in better condition.''

Esprit de corps certainly flourished on RAF fighter stations and was manifest in many ways, such as the special paint schemes with which several COs embellished ''their'' personal aircraft. Rennie Turner had bedecked his silver Meteor F.8 WK799/A with the squadron's red and yellow chequer markings across the entire fin, rudder and tailplane in addition to their standard position on each side of the fuselage roundel. Selecting Sabre F.4 XD779/A as his personal aircraft in April 1954, he soon distinguished it by the addition of three rows of red and yellow checks around the nose. Even during Meteor days he had bought his own black flying suit, in preference to the standard RAF pale blue/grey issue, plus a scarlet silk scarf as his personal garb. The newly-issued RAF (silver) ''bone dome'' helmets quickly became targets for squadron insignia, and in 92's case most were liberally covered in red and yellow checks. Not content with decorating the aircraft and flying clothes, Rennie Turner went one step further: ''Dating from the Meteor days, I instituted a red and yellow chequered squadron flag, beautifully made by the wives, which was mounted on the windscreen of our aircraft whenever we landed away from Linton. I used one on my motor car for many years!''

May 10, 1954, saw the Linton Sabres deploy to Luffenham for five days, and while there they participated in a series of practice interceptions against aircraft flown by the DFLS at West Raynham, which included some of the first Swifts. (Bruce Macdonald of 66 Squadron was among the Sabre pilots involved, and his log book entry on the

12th aptly describes the nature of these mock combats, ''Hoolie with DFLS!!!''—a sequel to his claim of one confirmed Swift which he had bounced the previous day.) The main reason for this stay at Luffenham was to practice formation flying with the Canadians, as a prelude to providing an aerial escort for Her Majesty the Queen's return to the UK on the 15th. The latter half of July enabled 92 to pit its Sabres against the handful of Hunter F.1s, operated by the CFE at Raynham, which made their debut during the UK's major defence exercise, ''Dividend,'' but encounters were few and inconclusive. Apart from Meteors and other Sabres, the main quarry in these exercises were the RAF's Canberra bombers—high fliers and always tough targets—and USAF B-47s—larger, less manoeuvrable and easier meat. During the 1950s SAC used to deploy complete bomber wings of B-47s to Britain for 90-day periods, and sometimes the giant B-36s would also operate from British bases and provide the Sabre with a target they could hardly miss.

September is synonymous with Battle of Britain celebrations, and while S/L Rennie Turner was content to demonstrate XD779/A at his home base that sunny Saturday, the 18th, Roger Lindsay was among the crowds further north, at RAF Ouston, in Northumberland, to witness a superb display by another 92 Squadron pilot, F/L A.W.A. ''Lefty'' Wright:

=====

As a young schoolboy, ''mad on aeroplanes'' since early childhood, Battle of Britain ''At Home'' day was the highlight of every year, providing, as it did in those days, the sole opportunity to gain access to an RAF station. Few families owned cars, certainly mine didn't, and the long trek from home by train and bus only served to heighten the anticipation of what types of aircraft might be on view. Armed only with a haversack containing sandwiches (hastily prepared before dawn), a bottle of lemonade, a copy of the current *Flight* magazine and, most important of all, pencil and notebook, I hurried through Ouston's gates that Saturday morning and clearly remember the surge of delight which gripped me as I caught sight of the tall camouflaged fin of XD759, ''S'' of 92 Squadron, standing proudly among the line of parked aircraft which made up the static display; it was the first RAF Sabre I had seen at close quarters. I was not the

only one to be impressed; Ouston was the home base of 607 Squadron, Royal Auxiliary Air Force, equipped with Vampire 5s plus a pair of Meteor 7s, and a succession of the squadron's ''weekend'' pilots took turns to clamber into the cockpit and try the Sabre for size, while ''Lefty'' Wright showed them the controls. The Sabre and its pilot were the undoubted stars of the show, even before the afternoon's flying display began, so when the Sabre took off and commenced its smoky climb to 40,000 feet, before its well-publicized supersonic dive over the airfield, there was an unusual hush over the crowd. Despite the craning of thousands of necks into the deep blue sky, by now sprinkled with white cauliflower cumulus clouds, there was neither sight nor sound of the Sabre for what seemed, to me at least, a lifetime. Suddenly there was a loud yet muffled ''bang,'' and the commentator's voice crackled over the Tannoy directing the attention of the crowd, by now nervously murmuring after exposure to the strange new phenomenon created by an aircraft flying faster than the speed of sound. Almost at once the Sabre appeared, low and fast, the impression of speed greatly accentuated by its silent approach and by the trail of black exhaust smoke behind it, before pulling up into a rolling climb, as its thunderous sound reached us. There followed a superb display of aerobatics before ''Lefty'' Wright gently coaxed XD759 on to Ouston's runway and taxied back to the hardstanding now thronged by hero-worshippers, not least myself. Photography at RAF airfields, even at air shows, was banned until August 1956, so I had to content myself with the sketches I had made of the aircraft with its markings, supplemented by a picture which was published in our local newspaper. Twenty-nine years later I was fortunate enough to obtain a print of that picture, from Richard Moore, whose father had been the press photographer at Ouston that day in 1954.

Roger Lindsay

=====

Just as RAF fighter squadrons in Germany used to spend several weeks every year at Sylt engaged in live air-to-air gunnery, their Fighter Command counterparts used to deploy to the Armament Practice Station at RAF Acklington, on the Northumberland coast, for the same purpose, firing at banner or glider targets towed by Meteors fitted with a simple winch attached to the ventral drop tank. In addition to the annual trip to the APS, the squadrons used to practise live gunnery over the nearest North Sea ranges to their home bases, and for the Linton squadrons these ranges extended off the East Yorkshire coast, only a few minutes flying time away. The Sabre could also be quickly and easily adapted as a target tug as described by George Cole, who, like "Lefty" Wright, joined 92 Squadron after having flown Sabres with No.3 Squadron in Germany.

The well-photographed 92 Squadron five-ship, this time over East Yorkshire. (MOD)

The towing hook on the Sabre was in fact a fuselage-releasable hook fitted about half to two-thirds of the way back and could be opened from a switch in the cockpit to jettison or release a target. Because of the low towing speed, maximum 180 kts, the aircraft sat at a very high angle of attack and a combination of friction around the back end of the fuselage and heat from the jet pipe caused a lot of cable failures in the early days. To counteract this, the front end of the cable was fitted with about 20 feet or so of very agricultural-looking chain with 1-1/2-inch or 2-inch links which bore the brunt of the wear and tear. It certainly solved the problem. The target itself was the standard banner or flag as still used today, starting life about 30 feet long by 6 feet wide and gradually fraying down to a usable minimum of 20 feet or just over. To cope with the radar ranging gunsight which was new to the RAF, the target flight at Sylt in northern Germany used to sew a large bag of tin cans to the front end of the banner to provide a reflector for the gunsight in order that the radar ranging would in fact work. By the time I reached 92 Squadron the targets had been fitted with proper radar reflectors on the spreader bars, much more effective. As a matter of interest the Germany squadrons never did tow their own targets to the best of my knowledge as they did all their air-to-air firing at Sylt at formal armament practice camps once a year for a month. I can't even remember if the Germany Sabres were fitted with towing hooks though I imagine they must have been.

The take-off with a flag fitted was fairly standard. The flag was attached at the end of the runway with the cable laid out at the side of the runway. The climb away had to be pretty steep to avoid dragging the banner through the approach lights and great care needed to be taken not to exceed 180 kts as the cable tended to snap at speeds not much higher than that. This was only true if you didn't want to lose the banner. On those occasions when the banner wouldn't release in the normal way and you tried to drag it off by increasing speed the damned cable wouldn't snap at any price. From Linton-on-Ouse we used to tow on a range just off the coast between Flamborough Head and Filey. The towing was all done at 1500 feet and in the summer it was very pleasant to be able to roll the canopy back and sit in the sunshine imagining you could see all the girls you knew must be milling around in Butlins Holiday camp, so near and yet so far. Then as now, flags would be shot off from time to time, always so it seemed, by the last aircraft to fire on it, so that everybody lost their score. I forgot to mention that four pilots would fire on each banner, three of them using bullets dipped in blue/red/green paint so that hits could be identified. Unpainted was the most popular as you were credited with the hits of anybody whose painted rounds failed to leave sufficient trace.

I can remember only one incident of note connected with towing, and that was the occasion when a 92 Squadron aircraft trying to do a very rapid turn-round so as to get back to the target before the tug had to return to base, took off without having been refuelled. He ran out of fuel while actually shooting on the flag, though at the time he imagined it was just straight engine failure. Fortunately for him, just south of Bridlington there is one of those massive airstrips built during the war to cope with returning damaged bombers, still in good condition in the mid to late fifties and he managed to force land there without any damage to himself or the aircraft.

George Cole

George Cole joined 92 in October '54, and soon afterwards the squadron's Sabres were progressively modified with the extended hard wing, after which a note was attached with "Sellotape" to the aircraft's instrument panel alerting the pilot to the new configuration and the marginal differences in performance conferred by the change. Pilots were sent on familiarization sorties to become *au fait* with the revised handling characteristics, which George Cole considered noticeably improved the Sabre 4's combat flying at high altitude. "However, it made the aircraft fractionally more unstable at low altitude, compared with the unslatted Sabre. The only other problem was on takeoff, when too high a nose position got you into the no climb/no acceleration slot. Otherwise it was OK."

The hard wing extension resulted in redesigned wing root panels and modification of the under-wing drop tank attachment points. Incidentally, Rennie Turner thought that the drop tanks were very slightly offset, i.e. not exactly parallel to the fuselage—an observation with which Canadair may concur?

The squadron continued with its routine tasks for the most part, but occasionally something out of the ordinary would occur, such as the visit by a mixed section of 66 and 92 Sabres to Geilenkirchen in early September '55. For George Cole the day after his return, the 8th of that month, involved a height climb to 47,000 feet—rather higher than normal operating altitude. As many pilots have stated, the Sabre wasn't a star performer in the climb, and it took about 20 minutes to reach even 30,000 feet. For this reason the Linton squadrons used to head west (inland) on the climb-out to gain sufficient altitude before turning east and reaching the usual PI level of 30-35,000 feet out over the North Sea—otherwise they were almost over Holland! Shortly before 92 Squadron relinquished its Sabres in the spring of '56 it put up some neat four- and five-ship formations for the benefit of Air Ministry cameramen who recorded the passing of this much loved aircraft.

BASE: Linton-on-Ouse.
SABRE SERVICE: 24.2.54 (XD727/D)-25.5.56 (XD727 and XB757/R).
REPRESENTATIVE AIRCRAFT: XD709/Z, 719/T, 733/R (initially used by CO S/L Rennie Turner), 769/J; XB694/N, 998/H.
UNIT MARKINGS: Red/yellow chequerboard each side of fuselage roundel. Code letter in yellow, thinly outlined in black above fin flash. Squadron crest initially applied to white centre section of fin flash, and later repositioned beneath the nose (XD779/A had three rows of red/yellow checks around nose while used by S/L Rennie Turner, as already described). Pilot's name often painted in white on canopy sill, usually port side only.
COs: S/L G. Rennie Turner, to Jan. 1955. S/L R.W. Freer, from Feb. '55.

XB931 of 4 Squadron shipped to the UK aboard a Bristol Freighter after being damaged in an accident. (via Roger Lindsay)

4 Squadron

RAF Jever, in North Germany, was the last 2 TAF fighter base to receive Sabres, commencing with 4 Squadron early in March 1954. The first aircraft, XB931, later coded "G," was secondhand, having come from a Bruggen squadron, as did several more of the early deliveries. The squadron was previously equipped with Vampire FB.5s and 9s, the last of which left in May, when 15 Sabres were on strength—rather fewer than other squadrons to receive the type. In common with most of the former Vampire tactical squadrons, No.4 retained its army ground liaison officer, probably because ground attack in support of the troops was still among its tasks,

XB981 of 4 Squadron in 1955. (No.4 Squadron)

280

even if it was now secondary to air defence. The Sabre's tenure with No.4 was destined to be the briefest of all RAF squadrons to operate the type, and after little more than a year, the F-86 was supplanted by the Hunter 4 in August '55.

BASE: Jever.
SABRE SERVICE: 3.3.54 (XB931/G-21.9.55 (XB770/L and 983/S).
REPRESENTATIVE AIRCRAFT: XB773/C, 775/B-M, 854/B-T, 955/W, 980/P, 996/A (used by the CO).
UNIT MARKINGS: Black "sunburst" containing the numeral 4 in red, pierced by a yellow lightning flash, the whole device positioned

BASE: Jever.
SABRE SERVICE: 8.3.54. (XB846)-22.3.56 (XB701/V).
REPRESENTATIVE AIRCRAFT: XB965/X, 726/H, 804/O, 829/D, 833/W, 893/A.
UNIT MARKINGS: Blue rectangle, thinly edged yellow and containing yellow arrowheads pointing forward, on each side of the fuselage roundel. Above the fin flash there was a blue disc containing a yellow escarbuncle (a kind of shield strengthener) adapted from the squadron's crest. The individual code letter appeared on the fuselage ahead of the unit markings, in white or yellow.
CO: S/L R.N.G. Allen, '53-'54, S/L D.F.M. Browne, AFC '55-'57.

Sabre of 93 Squadron with pilots, March 1955. (RAF Museum)

above the fin flash. Initially the unit code letter was applied in pale blue aft of the fuselage roundel, with the individual aircraft letter in the same colour, forward of the roundel. The unit code was later replaced by a black (upper) and red (lower) rectangle diagonally separated by a yellow lightning flash, and outlined in yellow, ahead of which the individual code letter, in pale blue, was retained on the side of the fuselage. On a few aircraft, e.g. XB980/P, this code was in white.
CO: S/L P.W. Gilpin '53-'55, S/L J.R. Chapman '55-'57.

93 Squadron
Receiving Sabres a few days after 4 Squadron at Jever in March '54, No.93's history was very similar, with the exception that it retained Sabres for a longer period, not relinquishing them until January 1956 before they were succeeded by Hunter F.4s.

229 Operational Conversion Unit
Based at RAF Chivenor, in Devon, 229 OCU was primarily responsible for the provision of operational ground-attack training for pilots before their posting to Vampire squadrons. In 1954 the remaining Sabre conversion was transferred from the SCF at Wildenrath to 229 OCU, and this took effect on May 20 with the delivery to Chivenor of six Sabres flown in from 5 MU, Kemble. Between then and early July strength was increased to the full establishment of 22 Sabres, with the first conversion course commencing on August 8. In total 229 OCU ran six full conversion courses, the last starting on January 11, 1955, and there was a special course for more senior pilots to gain swept-wing supersonic experience, in some instances subsequent to "desk flying" tours and prior to postings to fighter units. With the imminent re-equipment of first line squadrons by Hunters (which henceforth formed the main equipment at 229 OCU from 1955 to

'74), the Sabres began to leave Chivenor in April 1955 and were almost all gone by May. During the 12 months of Sabres, only one serious incident occurred, on October 23, 1954, when XB711/S became overdue from a routine exercise over the Bristol Channel, the main training area for Chivenor's aircraft. A land and sea search failed to find any wreckage or clue to the mysterious disappearance, but it was assumed that the Sabre had crashed into the sea.

BASE: Chivenor.
SABRE SERVICE: 20.5.54 (XB641/A plus five others)-30.6.55 (XB813/M).
REPRESENTATIVE AIRCRAFT: XB644/B, 756/D, 821/E, 811/P, 835/T, 763/W.
UNIT MARKINGS: All aircraft carried a white code letter above the fin flash, and most had the nose cone, wing tips and in some instances the fin tip painted in flight colours: B Flt-white (early alphabet codes), C Flt-red (late alphabet codes).

Central Gunnery School, Re-named Fighter Weapons School, on 1.1.55
The role of this unit was to train weapons instructors for RAF fighter squadrons in the UK and overseas, and to provide refresher training in weaponry. Much of the school's work was concerned with air-to-ground attack, with bombs, rockets and guns, over the nearby ranges off the East Yorkshire coast. The main types of operational aircraft used in 1954 were the Venom FB.1 fighter-bomber, Meteor F.8s and various other marks, together with Vampire T.11s, used for dual weapons instruction, but a sprinkling of other aircraft types found their way on to the unit, including a quartet of Sabres, taken on strength by the Trial Flight. These were used in both air-air and air-ground roles, and in the latter case it is believed they tested an automatic bomb release mechanism for which the Sabre had provision, though it was not used by operational squadrons. Their stay was a brief eight months before they departed for 33MU.

BASE: Leconfield.
SABRE SERVICE: 9.7.54 (XB540/A)-23.5.55 (XB546/B).
REPRESENTATIVE AIRCRAFT: XB601/C, 810/D.
UNIT MARKINGS: A large black code letter, outlines in white, on fuselage sides ahead of the roundels.

"Personal" Sabres
It is a requirement of all RAF station commanders (group captain rank) that

XD763 at Linton-on-Ouse, July 24, 1955. The wing commander, W/C Eric W. Wright, has his pennant below the cockpit, and initials on the fin. (via Roger Lindsay)

they should be competent to fly every type of aircraft established on their base, and indeed maintain their personal flying proficiency. In the 1950s when the normal squadron establishment was 16 aircraft (increased to up to 24 in the case of Sabre squadrons), plus hacks, trainers and very often a station flight, in addition to two or more operational squadrons, the station commander and the wing commander (flying) frequently had their "own" aircraft; sometimes this was simply an aircraft drawn at random from one of the based units, but in other situations a particular machine was assigned to

Geilenkirchen wing leader's aircraft (W/C Bob Weighill of 138 Wing). Note W/C's pennant. Checkers were black/white. (via Robin A. Brown)

them personally. The following is a list of such Sabres, together with notes on their "ownership" and markings.

XB893, Bruggen Wing Leader, 21.1.54-29.4.54, to 93 Sq.
XB945, Bruggen Wing Leader, 14.4.54-21.4.54, to 130 Sq.
XB987, Bruggen Wing Leader, 21.4.54-3.4.56, to 71 Sq.
XB948, Jever Wing Leader, 13.4.54-29.7.55, to Geilenkirchen Wing Leader.
XB948, Geilenkirchen Wing Leader, 29.7.55-27.5.56, to UK, black and white chequered nose and fin.
XB886/WL, Oldenburg Wing Leader, 11.11.53-22.9.55, to 20 Sq.
XD736/MP, Linton Station Commander (G/C Mike Pedley), 9.3.54.
XD736/DFS, Linton Station Commander (G/C Dennis F. Spottiswode), 25.4.56, to Westland.
XD763/LM Linton Wing Leader (W/C Lee Mailin from 8.3.54)
XD763/EWW, W/C Eric "Ricky" W. Wright, 25.5.56, to Westland.
XB827, Geilenkirchen Wing Leader, 29.1.54—7.3.55, to 234 Sq.
XB615, Geilenkirchen Wing Leader, 7.3.55-3.5.55, Cat.5 write-off, force-

landed 10 m. from Wildenrath after flame-out.
XB702, Wildenrath Wing Leader, 4.11.53-30.11.55.
XB702, Bruggen Wing Leader, 30.11.55-1.3.56, to 67 Sq.
XB619, Wildenrath Wing Leader, 21.5.53-26.8.53, to 3 Sq.
G/C J.E. Johnson, Wildenrath Station Commander, flew an unidentified Sabre, adorned with his initials and a scarlet fin (possibly XB893).

Aeroplane & Armament Experimental Establishment

The A & AEE at Boscombe Down, Wiltshire, was, and still is, the main test and experimental base for British military aircraft and invariably receives both new prototypes and some of the first examples of any new production aircraft before their entry into the RAF, RN or British Army service. The Sabre was no exception, though the first two examples were USAF F-86As 49-1279 and -1296 which came to the A & AEE on March 1, 1951, after combat evaluation by the Central Fighter Establishment, West Raynham. Both were used by A Squadron, for handling performance and armament trials respectively.

They were passed on to the Royal Aircraft Establishment at Farnborough and there was a gap when no Sabres remained at Boscombe until the delivery of Canadair Sabre XB733 on July 22, 1953. This aircraft, curiously designated Mark 4B, was used to provide swept-wing familiarization to the pilots of C (Naval) Squadron until its departure on March 4, 1955. The final Boscombe Sabre, XB992, saw very brief service, from August 31 to September 28, 1954, and during that month was used by A Squadron to investigate pitch-up characteristics.

Royal Aircraft Establishment, Farnborough

Perhaps the most revered research, development and experimental unit in British aviation, certainly during the 1950s, Farnborough received the two F-86As lent by the USAF and just referred to, the first being 49-1296 which was delivered from the A & AEE to the Aero Flight, RAE, on April 23, 1951. This aircraft was flown by five RAF and one Royal Navy pilot on a wide variety of evaluation flights, until August 14, 1952, when it suffered elevator runaway into full nose-up pitch, causing the pilot, F/L "Taffy" Ecclestone, to abandon it. It was replaced on October 21 that year by the second F-86A, 49-1279, which continued the tests. It was followed by Canadair Sabre 4 XB620, delivered from 5 MU on August 13, 1953, and retained until September 2, 1955, by which time the task of collecting transonic handling data had fallen mainly to high performance aircraft of indigenous design.

RAF Handling Squadron
One of the main tasks of the Handling Squadron, based at RAF Manby, Lincolnshire, was the preparation of Pilots Notes, preparatory to the introduction of new types of aircraft into the British services, and to regularly test aircraft when revisions to these notes, perhaps due to modifications, were required. Although the initial Pilots Notes for the Sabre were partially drawn from their equivalent North American and Canadair documents and from data collected by the A & AEE, one Sabre 4, XB936, was briefly assigned to the Handling Squadron, between November 4 and December 8, 1953, when it was possibly used to evaluate the hard wing.

Central Flying School
The CFS, based at Little Rissington, Gloucestershire, within Flying Training Command not only trained flying instructors but established flying standards for the entire Air Force. The Examining Wing was (and still is) responsible for ensuring that those high standards were maintained, and used to check out instructors on every type of aircraft, whether training or operational, within the RAF inventory. Although no Sabre was permanently on CFS strength, it did borrow Sabres occasionally from other units, notably No.147 Squadron, Benson, and 5 MU, Kemble.

Hawker Aircraft Ltd.
Two Sabres, detailed below, were lent to Hawker, at Dunsfold, for swept-wing familiarization by the company's production test pilots.

XB675, from 5 MU 6.4.55 for one month's loan, returned 25.4.55.
XB997, from 5 MU 28.3.55 for one month's loan, returned 15.4.55.

RAF Maintenance Units
The Service's MUs received new aircraft from the manufacturers and were then responsible for their preparation to RAF standards and issue to the flying units, for storage of those aircraft held as attrition replacements, and for major servicing, repair and modification considered to be beyond the resources of operating units. In the case of the Canadair Sabre, the principal MU was No.5 at Kemble, and it was there that the majority of the species made their final landfall after the transatlantic crossing.

Here post-delivery inspection took place, changes were made to some of the radio equipment appropriate for RAF use in Europe and the majority of fighters received their camouflage paint, actually cellulose dope manufactured by Cellon Ltd. Pre-delivery and periodic test flights would be made, generally by a resident MU test pilot, but sometimes by pilots from a ferry unit or nearby operational base. The main MUs concerned with the Sabres were:

5 MU, Kemble, Gloucestershire.
23 MU, Aldergrove, Northern Ireland.
33 MU, Lyneham, Wiltshire. 431 MU, Bruggen, West Germany (mainly concerned with minor repairs, and modifications, including the introduction of the hard-wing leading edges to RAF Sabres in 2 TAF).

Civilian Contractors
A very important role was also played by several civilian companies in Britain which supported the work of the MUs, particularly with regard to the repair and refurbishment of both RAF and RCAF Sabres; it was these organizations that were almost solely responsible for the overhaul of former RCAF Sabres 2s before their transfer to Greece and Turkey and of the RAF Sabre 4s destined for the air arms of Italy and Yugoslavia. The supply of these Sabres to their new owners was financed from MDAP funds, but the refurbishment work preparatory to their delivery was the financial responsibility of the British government as part of a reciprocal agreement with the United States, which had made a major contribution towards the cost of RAF Hunters, Javelins and Canberras. For this reason, American inspectors were responsible for accepting the overhaul Sabres, even though the British Ministry of Supply had placed the contracts.

Airwork (General Trading) Ltd. was the main contractor in the refurbishment of RAF Sabre 4s and had been involved with Sabre repair work for both the RAF and RCAF since 1953, from its engineering bases at Gatwick (London's second airport), Speke (Liverpool Airport) and Ringway (Manchester Airport). It was joined by two other substantial contractors in Aviation Traders (Engineering) Ltd. at Stansted Airport and Westland Aircraft Ltd. at Yeovil, with a smaller contribution from Hawker Aircraft Ltd. at Dunsfold. The Bristol Aeroplane Co. Ltd. at Filton participated in some of the overhaul and inspection of the J47 engines, and as mentioned earlier had previously provided some of the work parties for on-site installation of the hard-wing leading-edge modification from kits supplied by Canadair.

"The overhaul was quite a thorough affair," recalls Reg Havers, who was an engineer at Stansted with Aviation Traders, which was contracted to refurbish 99 ex-RAF Sabres. "It involved the complete inspection of both airframe and engine, which was removed and stripped at Stansted. Radio, radar, canopy, armament were all dismantled, taken from the airframe and carefully checked. Many thousands of replacement parts were obtained, principally from 61 MU at Cheadle Hulme; I was involved on the procurement side (responsible for ordering parts, stores, stock control and progress) and I wish I had a pound for every demand note I signed. I have absolutely no idea what the contract costs were, but I recall that we were not exactly overpaid! On completion of overhaul to the satisfaction of our own staff, MOS and the US inspectors, they finally authorized the air test by the company test pilot. Initially this was a Mr. Stuart-Smith (who later test flew the ATL Accountant turbo-prop airliner); he was succeeded by Jimmy Evans, who subsequently became a captain with British United, then British Caledonian Airways. After the AT(E)L test pilot had pronounced the Sabre OK, Americans carried out further tests and also ferried the Sabres to Italy, with Pratica-di-Mare near Rome being the most usual destination. One of the two USAF ferry pilots who operated with us at Stansted was killed on January 19, 1957, when his aircraft, XB775/19863, crashed in France. The last 20 airframes were scrapped due to lack of engines; a long wrangle between the MOS and US authorities failed to resolve the dispute as to who would pay for the engines, and after something like a year, during which the aircraft were periodically moved around the hangar, they were towed over to the scrap heap.

The former RAF Sabres were brought up to standard specification, which included the hard wing if not previously incorporated, and were finished in a new coat of gloss camouflage dark green, grey, with cerulean blue undersurfaces with USAF lettering and national insignia, but with the original RCAF serial number on the fin. Stansted was not alone in encountering difficulties, because industrial disputes at Westland resulted in some Sabres being transferred to Speke for completion of overhaul, while others were scrapped. At Gatwick the construction work in progress to enlarge the airport necessitated the transfer of some Sabres to Dunsfold, where they were checked and test flown before delivery to Europe. In total 180 Sabre 4s were allocated to the Italian Air Force and 121 to Yugoslavia; over 70 others never made it any further than various scrap dumps, which included Lasham as a favourite resting place.

The One That Got Away

One Sabre 4 was destined to fly a while longer with RAF roundels. This was XB982, which completed its refurbishment by Westland on March 6, 1957, and was intended to be transferred to USAF custody, but was then selected to flight test the Bristol-Siddeley Orpheus engine. This was the 773rd Canadair-built Sabre, which originally bore RCAF serial number 19873 on its roll-out from Canadair's Plant No.2 in Montreal in June 1953. It was first test flown by Ed Coe October 10 that year, then was transferred to the RAF on October 10. XB982 left Canada on November 9, on Bechers Brook 9, arriving in the UK a few days later for delivery to No.33 MU at Lyneham, where it remained in store until its issue to 92 Squadron at Linton-on-Ouse on July 25, 1955, as a replacement aircraft. When the squadron re-equipped with Hunters, XB982 was flown to Westland on April 16, 1956, for refurbishment. Westland modified it to accommodate the Orpheus 801, with which it flew for the first time on July 3, 1958, subsequently testing the hand-ling of this engine up to an altitude of 47,000 feet, evaluating its performance and calibrating fuel consumption. Later the production Orpheus 803 was installed, and with the completion of that program XB982 was returned from its flight-test base at Filton to Westland Aircraft for the installation of the more powerful Orpheus B.OR.12. Only the "dry" version of this engine was installed because the Sabre's rear fuselage could not accommodate an afterburner without being completely redesigned. Nevertheless the Orpheus 12 endowed the natural metal-finished XB982 with a lively performance because the engine gave 6810 lb. thrust for a dry weight of only 1100 lb., compared to the Sabre 4's original J47-GE13 engine's 5200 lb. thrust for a dry weight of 2590 lb. Following the conclusion of the flight testing program XB982 was withdrawn from use at Filton during 1962 and subsequently scrapped, bringing to a close the final chapter in the story of the Sabre's British service.

XB982, "the one that got away". (Rolls-Royce)

The German Sabre Story

"Richthofen" Swords visit 4 Wing. (Harry Tate via K.M. Molson)

When the post-war Luftwaffe of the German Federal Republic was formed on September 24, 1956, initial plans included formation of four day-fighter wings and one all-weather wing. The plans were ambitious, considering that the new Luftwaffe was starting from scratch—no pilots, no technicians, no administration. In short, not much on which to base a modern air force. At least, not on the surface, for there were wartime veterans, including some highly decorated fighter aces like Barkhorn, Hrabak, Krupinski, Obleser, Steinhoff, and Wehnelt, who would eagerly pitch in, forming the initial cadre of commanders for the first flying units. Even so, the task would be enormous.

The choice of a fighter was one of the lesser problems facing the new Luftwaffe. The best available type was the Canadair Sabre 6, and 225 new examples were ordered in December 1956. These would complement 75

Sabre 5s drawn from the Air Division as the RCAF upgraded its overseas squadrons to the Mark 6. The Mark 5s were flown to Renfrew, where they were overhauled by Scottish Aviation for the Luftwaffe, then ferried by RCAF pilots to Waffenschule 10, the Operational Conversion Unit at Oldenburg. Under the terms of an intergovernmental agreement, Canada also undertook to train 360 pilots to jet standards for the fledgling Luftwaffe.

Check-out at Zweibrücken

On July 2, 1957, OTL Herbert Wehnelt, Hptm Günther "Jolle" Josten and Olt Hans-Ulrich Flade of the new Luftwaffe drove down to Zweibrücken from Fürstenfeldbruck to check out on the Sabre 6 and become the nucleus of instructor pilots for WS 10. Wartime veterans, each had recently had refresher training: Wehnelt on Vampires, Meteors and Hunters in the UK followed by instrument training on

T-33s at "Fursty" (i.e. Fürstenfeldbruck), the others on Harvards at Landsberg, and T-33s at Fursty. Flade later described their conversion to the Sabre:

After a cordial reception by 3 Wing, we were assigned to a squadron. Training began with three familiarization flights in T-33s, so we got to know the local flying area and the three other RCAF bases nearby: Marville, Grostenquin and Söllingen, near Baden-Baden. We also practised procedures in the Sabre simulator.

Our first Sabre flight was in a clean aircraft, being chased by our instructor, F/O Arnie Leiter, a 1200-hour Sabre veteran, and one of 3 Wing's most experienced pilots.

After brake release, the Mark 6 accelerates rapidly and lifts off gently. The gear and flaps are quickly retracted to avoid exceeding speed limits for them. We make a left climb-

F/L Arnie Leiter explains details of the Sabre cockpit to Hptm Josten, Lt Flade and OTL Wehnelt during their initial training on Sabres at Zweibrücken in July 1957. (DND)

would soon be adding to that at Oldenburg. We were all so happy to be able to fly such a wonderful aircraft.

Hans-Ulrich Flade

Needless to say, every Luftwaffe pilot graduating from jets at Fursty dreamed of a posting to Sabres, but not all could be so fortunate. Many were slated for reconnaissance or fighter bomber flying. In the case of Gerhard Joos' course at Fursty, the decision as to who would fly which type was left to the pilots. This led to endless arguments! Joos recalls, "Eventually we agreed that the guys from northern Germany would go to Oldenburg, the others to Erding to fly RF-84Fs. Even today I envy those who made it to Sabres, and wish I had been among them."

Luftwaffe Sabre Markings
After test flying at Canadair, the Luftwaffe Sabre 6s were crated from Montreal to Dornier Werke GmbH in Oberpfaffenhofen near Munich. Dornier was prime contractor for reassembly and testing the new aircraft, and for later maintenance, overhaul and modification. Once accepted by the Luftwaffe, the Sabres were ferried to Oldenburg by young fighter pilots, then temporarily taken over by WS 10 until the Geschwader were ready to equip. So it went for aircraft c/n 1591-1671, but thereafter the Sabre 6s went straight to the Geschwader.

Before arrival of the Mark 6s, WS 10 had accepted the 75 ex-RCAF Mark 5s. These aircraft were used strictly in training until retired in 1962, retaining RCAF camouflage throughout their German careers.

The basic Luftwaffe flying unit is the Geschwader, or wing, as opposed to the squadron of the RAF or RCAF. A Geschwader normally comprises two flying Staffeln, or squadrons, plus supporting units. Fighter wings are Jagdgeschwader (JG). The two Staffeln of each Geschwader have no individual designations, but are always referred to as Erste Staffel and Zweite Staffel (First and Second Squadrons) of the respective Geschwader. Abbreviated, the Staffeln are officially referred to as 1./JG 71 and 2./JG 71 as an example. However, in NATO it is common practice to refer to German Staffeln as 711 or 712 Squadron, similar to other NATO air force squadron numeration, meaning the 1. Squadron of JG 71 or the 2. Squadron of JG 71. Both

ing turn at 350K, and are soon at 15,000 feet. Below is the Rhine and the city of Karlsruhe. For a clean stall I pull the power to idle and extend speed brakes. The Sabre is gaining another 5000 feet while speed is slowly decreasing. It takes some time before the Sabre shows signs of a stall. Then full power for recovery. I repeat the stall with gear and flaps down. Again, the same good-natured reaction. Full power once again, clean up, and climb to 25,000 and repeat the stalls in thinner air. No problems here either. Some steep turns follow—the Sabre rolls like a gyro with a light touch of the stick. Arnie asks for a fuel check—1500 lb. Time to return to base for the first landing.

Over the button the Sabre is pitched into a tight turn, power at idle, speed brakes out. Speed drops from 300K to 185K, and the gear, then flaps, are lowered. I roll into the base turn, bring the power up to 80 per cent, and continue my final turn. Over the

threshold I retard the throttle to idle and the Sabre settles smoothly onto the runway. The nose is slowly lowered. Arnie is beside me to watch my touch-and-go. I apply full power and retract the speed brakes. The Sabre leaps ahead, and like a feather is airborne again. The next landing is a full stop and my first Sabre flight is over.

Training continues with formation flying and high altitude battle formation with GCI support. They call us "Arnie's Air Force" and we operate up towards Belgium and into France. We hassle with F-84s, F-100s, Hunters and Mystères, but none can beat us. Alone and in formation we go up into weather, get down again and are picked up by GCA. The Canadians insist that their Sabre is the best instrument platform. We share their opinion.

Penetration of the sound barrier is unnoticeable in the Sabre, but the Mach meter tells that you are through. Each flight brings something new, like cine gunnery tracking. And aerobatics in the Sabre are simply a pleasure. Step by step we are gaining experience.

On September 6 we said goodbye to our Canadian friends. We had 40 hours of Sabre flying to our credit, and

systems are used in this chapter.

When the Luftwaffe re-equipped in the early sixties, in some cases a third squadron of a wing was temporarily formed. It took over all or some of the "old" fighters in order to maintain combat readiness of the wing while the 1. and 2. Staffeln were busy converting to F-104s or G.91s. Upon full conversion, the third squadrons were disbanded. In the three Sabre wings this procedure was used only with JG 71. During its existence a third squadron was, logically, 3./JG 71, or 713 Staffel. Each unit also had additional aircraft as reserves or on loan from other units. These were given registrations as if belonging to a third squadron.

For the rather large number of aircraft purchased for the German Armed Forces (Bundeswehr), a new registration system was devised: a two-letter unit code and a three-digit squadron and aircraft identification number. The first of the two letters identified the mission of the Geschwader, while the second identified the Geschwader itself. As mission identifier, the fighter wings were thus given the letter J (for Jagd) and conversion units were given the letter B. The first Jagdgeschwader formed, JG 71, thus received the letter A, its aircraft bearing the letters JA.

Mark 6s from WS10 lift off in formation. The tail band was white outlined in black. (E. - D. Bernhard)

Geschwader	Code Letters
JG 71	JA
JG 72	JB
JG 73	JC
JG 74	JD

Waffenschule 10 was assigned letters BB (BA was WS 30, OCU for the F-84F). Sabres of the first squadrons in the operational wings were numbered 101-121, while those of the second squadrons were 231-251. Thus, the first digit of this number indicated the Staffel, the others the actual aircraft number. These numbers were distinct from constructor's numbers (or serial numbers as with ex-USAF types) which were on the fin in tiny figures below the national flag. For larger units like WS 10, the numbering system had to be altered somewhat to cover all aircraft in the inventory.

For third squadrons, normally only the first digit (1 or 2, the squadron designator) was changed to 3. But there were so many exceptions to this rule that even the experts were sometimes confused. For example, spare aircraft assigned to a Geschwader were marked in the 360-379 range. Aircraft so marked were only temporarily with a unit. They changed units without changing registration. Then, in the case of third squadrons, as only a nominal number of aircraft were kept operational, these were also numbered in the 360 and up range. Furthermore, there were sometimes three or four aircraft flying with the same identification numbers! Even worse, different type aircraft of the same unit could fly with identical codes, for example Sabre 6 of 713 Staffel and T-33 of JG 71. To cover all the exceptions and confirm the identity of an aircraft seen in photos of the day is very difficult.

Eventually the Luftwaffe adopted a new numbering system, introduced by Gen Steinhoff on January 1, 1968. By then the Sabre was gone. Only a few used in testing and instructing received new numbering.

Waffenschule 10

To train all future fighter pilots, the Luftwaffe established Waffenschule der Luftwaffe 10, a unit similar to No.1 (F) OTU at Chatham. The order to establish WS 10 came on March 21, 1957, from Der Bundesminister der Verteidigung-Abteilung VI (Luftwaffe). It called for the formation of 1. Staffel Waffenschule 10 at Nörvenich. In early April, 45 men were posted to Fassberg to begin setting up the WS 10 maintenance organization. By August, personnel had moved to Oldenburg. Hand-over of the first Sabre 5s to WS 10 took place at "Oldy" on September 9, 1957, with start-up of training set for October 1. In fact it was November 29 when OTL Wehnelt, the CO, made the unit's inaugural flight. Hereafter activity with the three Staffeln of WS 10 increased. From 15 Sabre 5s in late September 1957, WS 10 grew to 67 Sabre 5s and 25 Sabre 6s by

German Ranks		RCAF Equivalent	USAF Equivalent
Flieger	Flg	Aircraftman 2nd class	Airman 2nd class
Gefreiter	Gefr	Aircraftman 1st class	Airman 1st class
Obergefreiter	Ogefr	Leading Aircraftman	
Hauptgefreiter	Hptgefr		
Unteroffizier	Uffz	Corporal	Corporal
Stabsunteroffizier	Stuffz		
Feldwebel	Fw	Sergeant	Sergeant
Oberfeldwebel	Ofw	Flight Sergeant	First Sergeant
Hauptfeldwebel	Hptfw	Warrant Officer	Master Sergeant
Stabsfeldwebel	Stfw		Staff Sergeant
Oberstabsfeldwebel	Ostfw		
Leutnant	Lt	Pilot Officer	Lieutenant
Oberleutnant	Olt	Flying Officer	First Lieutenant
Hauptmann	Hptm	Flight Lieutenant	Captain
Major	Maj	Squadron Leader	Major
Oberstleutnant	OTL	Wing Commander	Lieutenant Colonel
Oberst	Oberst	Group Captain	Colonel
Brigadegeneral	BrigGen		Brigadier General
Generalmajor	GenMaj	Air Commodore	Major General
Generalleutnant	GenLt	Air Vice Marshal	Lieutenant General
General	Gen	Air Marshal	General

November 22, 1958, the largest of all Luftwaffe Sabre units.

The first WS 10 instructors were 16 pilots from the RCAF under S/L Douglas "Duke" Warren. Warren's title was "Chef Kanadisches Beraterteam Waffenschule 10 Fliegerhorst." His unit was known as the "Canadian Advisory Group." Training priority was given to wartime pilots who, while recruiting for new pilots was going full tilt, were doing refresher training in the US, Canada and Germany. Many of these "retreads" themselves became instructors as soon as they had completed their refresher courses. The first course of post-war student pilots had begun at Landsberg in March 1957, with the young Luftwaffe trainees flying Piper L-18s and Harvard 4s. They received their wings in May 1958, with nine of them then being sent to Oldenburg for Sabre training.

Regular Sabre courses finally began in early 1958 at WS 10, with one new group of students arriving each month. From them would come not only pilots for JG 71, 72 and 73 (all formed at Oldy in 1959-1960), but also the instructor pilots needed by WS 10.

Warren provides some anecdotal history from his days with WS 10. A wartime Spitfire pilot, he had first flown the Sabre at Chatham on April 18, 1952. He commanded 410 Squadron at North Luffenham, and during this time flew Sabres with the USAF in Korea on exchange, though not in combat. In 1956 Warren was posted to Chatham as chief flying instructor. There he worked with a group of the world's best Sabre pilots, including Jim Kasler, a well-known USAF pilot from Korean days. Warren picks up events from here:

In March 1957 Capt Jim Kasler and I went over to the Air Division to liaise with Sabre squadron commanders about the training of pilots we were sending them. After this, I was ordered to report to our embassy in Bonn. There I and four other RCAF officers were tasked to plan a Sabre OTU for the Luftwaffe. In April I returned to Chatham, instructing as usual on Sabres and T-33s. Meanwhile, the Luftwaffe completed its preparations and, unknown to me, had requested me as CO of the RCAF detachment.

Major Obleser accepts welcome flowers from Hptm Bernhard upon delivery to Oldenburg on September 2, 1958, of the first Sabre 6. (H. - U. Flade)

Thus, on very short notice, I was ordered to Oldenburg in August 1957. My last flight at Chatham was on August 13, and my first in Germany (at 4 Wing) on September 19. Between those dates I had my family moved from Chatham to north Germany.

Although it was rather flattering to have the Luftwaffe wanting me for their Sabre operation, I arrived with mixed feelings. After all, I had experienced some bitter fighting during the war, and I still wondered if we were doing the right thing in re-arming the Germans. Even so, I was anxious to meet the German fliers (I had already met General Galland in Bonn), and was enticed by having a new flying position, and further opportunity to fly the Sabre—that's what it was really all about.

WS 10 was rather slow in starting up, and I was the only RCAF officer there for some time. To keep current, I flew Sabres and T-33s with the Air Div. My first trip in a Sabre *"mit dem Eisernen Kreuz"* was on November 29, 1957, and I must say that it was a strange feeling for some time to look out and see those crosses on an aircraft that *I* was flying!

In January 1958 flying commenced at WS 10, and I was involved checking out instructors on the T-33 and Sabre. All of the 16 RCAF instructors under me were post-war pilots, so I was the only Canadian at Oldenburg with combat experience. My staff of pilots, admin, supply and technical people were all of the highest calibre. I recall that in our first briefing I stressed that we were here to do a job, not to talk politics, and not to remind the Germans who had won the war. To my knowledge there was never any friction in that regard.

At this time the Luftwaffe was so short of pilots that if one were to be given a ground job, permission had to be obtained from the Minister of Defence. We had one German pilot on the unit who had been shot down in the Battle of Britain. He waited out the war as a POW and hadn't flown for 17 years. He was a nice chap but rather unsuitable for flying. I liked him and he would have fit ideally in a ground position, but *der Kommandeur* would not hear of it, and insisted that the fellow fly.

On February 10, 1958, I checked out the famous Erich Hartmann in a T-33. He was a smooth pilot, with excellent vision in the air. Surprisingly modest and with a great sense of humour, he was proudest of the fact that he had never lost a number 2, in spite of a combat career that included a personal

These pilots were on the very first course given on Sabres at Oldy. (Bob Flynn)

Maintainers F/L Curtis Barlow and Hptm Erich Schwarskopf talk nuts n' bolts at WS 10. (DND PL 122086)

Wehnelt, commander of WS 10, noted of Warren, "he was especially suited as Commanding Officer of his Advisory Group, and advising partner during the activation of Waffenschule 10." He went on to comment about Warren's outstanding flying abilities, his interest in studying the German language in order to gain a better understanding of the Germans, his ability to run his operation with no friction between German and Canadian, and finished by saying, "I am in the position to give S/L Warren the best testimonial without restriction for the time of his assignment at Oldenburg."

F/O Con Platz of 422 Squadron, and OTL Rolf Ehmling discuss a mission. (DND PL 122058)

score of 352 aircraft shot down. We became very good friends and have kept in touch over the years.

Another pilot at WS-10 was Paul Schauder, who had flown an Fw190 at Dieppe when I was flying a Spitfire there. We both ended the war with a healthy respect for each other's equipment. I visited both Paul and Erich in 1982, the 40th anniversary of Dieppe.

The RCAF technicians had gone to Oldenburg with over a decade of experience on jet aircraft—Vampires, T-33s, Sabres, CF-100s. They were to make an outstanding contribution to the fledgling Luftwaffe. The Luftwaffe technicians showed great respect for us and, once trained themselves, proved highly competent. Our admin staff also managed extremely well, and there were few complaints once the PX lines and gas coupon systems were working smoothly.

Douglas Warren

On July 1, 1960, Warren completed his duties at WS 10. In a letter to the AOC, No.1 Air Division, Herbert

S/L Duke Warren and Major Paul Schauder discuss another time — the day they tangled with each other over Dieppe. (DND PL 122087)

The Canadians at WS 10 were known for their skill and experience, but also for their pranks. One such character was Con Platz. Aware that the Sabre had an oversensitive G-meter which would indicate a hard landing when a perfectly normal one had been made, Platz devised a scheme to get himself some free beer. It was a rule at WS 10 that if the G-meter indicated a

hard landing, thus making an inspection necessary (extra work for the ground crew), the pilot would have to provide the techs and IPs (instructor pilots) with a case of beer. Platz was able to defraud novice pilots of considerable suds by rigging their landings. He would lead his students in for a formation landing at a lower than normal speed which resulted in a positive, though by no means rough landing. This would give a high meter reading and result in the beer donation from the "offending" pilot.

One student, wise to Platz's scheme, cushioned the area between the instrument panel and pedestal with rubber, preventing the two from jolting together on landing (he knew that this caused the high readings). So the wiley Platz was foiled by a wilier student!

Canadian Advisory Group shoulder patch.

Pretty well the entire RCAF complement at WS 10 c. 1959: Red Reiffer, Bill Van Oene, Con Platz, Alex Leslie, Bill Krantz (ATC), Jack McDonnell (Canadair), Al Sherwin, Duke Warren, Jim McCann, OTL Wehnelt, Walt Moore, Lew Mann, Padre Jenks, Reg Heard, Warner Unruh (Admin.), Pete Caws, Glen Hollingshead, Brian Bell, Pete Lenton (ATC), Bob Flynn, Andy Bourdeleau (EO). (via Bob Flynn)

The flight line at Oldenburg on January 22, 1959, showing Sabres of all three squadrons of WS 10. (DND PL 122050)

Another RCAF IP had a way of startling his students. He would trim his Sabre perfectly in close formation, keeping in position with rudder action. At some point the student would glance at his IP, who could be seen with arms resting on the canopy frame and hands nonchalantly folded.

During the WS 10 era, Oldenburg may have been the busiest military airfield in Europe, considering that each of the two WS 10 squadrons had some 50 Sabre 6s. Adding Sabre 5s, F-86Ks and T-33s, there were about 185 jet aircraft on base. Of course, the figure shrank when the Sabre 6s were assigned to the fighter wings, but for a time activity at Oldenburg must have been furious.

OTL Wehnelt led WS 10 until

February 15, 1962, when Oberst Erich Hohagen took command. Sabre training continued until July 1963, with the last official WS 10 Sabre flight taking place July 16—a formation flypast conducted to say farewell to the personnel of WS 10 at Oldenburg when the unit was ready to move to Jever to

Overall view in the barn at Oldenburg with Sabres in various stages of maintenance. (DND PL 122091)

After hours in the flight room at WS 10: Von Sturmer, Arnie Leiter, Bob Flynn, Bob Longhouse, Fritz Obleser and Jolle Josten. (via Bob Flynn)

commence F-104 training. The remaining Sabre 5s were then withdrawn from service to be scrapped, used as targets on the firing range, or relegated as gate guardians. The Sabre 6s were distributed among the three wings which grew out of WS 10, some retaining their BB codes for some years. Fortunately the move to Jever did not mean an end to Sabre flying at Oldy.

Great Fun at Ahlhorn
While serving with WS 10, S/L Duke Warren had an unusual experience which he relates here: "On May 11, 1959, the Swedish firm which made the Safeland barrier was to demonstrate their product at Ahlhorn. The wing there was under command of OTL Hartmann. I forget the reason exactly, but I was asked to participate in the testing which would take place on the main runway. The barrier was like a large tennis net suspended across the runway. The plan was to drive a Sabre down the runway and into the net to show that its strong nylon meshing could safely stop an aircraft. I queried the Swedish engineer about what would happen if the net came over the nose and up past the canopy. He assured me that this could never happen, and explained that when the aircraft went between the two flags marking the centre of the net it would stop smoothly, as he put it, 'like a baby carriage.'

"I must confess that I still had my doubts, and before we went ahead, I talked with Jack McDonnell, the Canadair tech rep, and asked him to put all the pins in the ejection seat, and remove the seat cushion. When all was ready, I taxied out and began my run. I built up speed, then throttled back and flamed out at 120 Kts just short of the barrier, headed right between the two flags. Just before I went into the net I ducked my head low, the Sabre struck the barrier, reared up like a wild horse, left the ground and came back on the tailpipe, breaking the fuselage. The canopy, where my head had just been, was cut clean off!

"As I lifted my head to look out I saw people rushing over. Jack McDonnell was very happy to find me still in one piece, and I looked around for my Swedish friend. I spotted him, and

S/L Duke Warren takes his "bucking bronco" ride in BB-243. The tail is wrinkled, so the picture shows the Sabre after returning to the runway from its short hop. The barrier netting has cleaned off the canopy, and Warren can be seen not a millimetre too low. (Luftwaffe via A.W. Krüger)

when I started towards him to talk about what happened, he just turned and walked quickly away. As it happened, I had been between him and the hangar line, and he headed straight into the middle of the airfield. I never saw him again. Remembering what he had assured me about the system, then seeing what had just happened, he may have feared that I had something in mind a bit more severe than a little chat between professionals."

Jagdgeschwader 71 "Richthofen"
Considered the most popular flying unit of the early post-war Luftwaffe, JG 71's reputation stemmed from the combination of the Luftwaffe's high-spirited young pilots and the unit's popular commander, Maj Erich "Bubi" Hartmann, the greatest fighter ace of all time.

Erich "Bubi" Hartmann, the greatest fighter ace of all time, and the first CO of JG 71 "Richthofen." (JG 71)

Preparation for the formation of JG 71 began at Ahlhorn in 1958, with Hartmann taking over January 19, 1959, assisted by squadron commanders Hptm Schmieder (1. Staffel) and Hptm Druse (2. Staffel). Hart-

291

"Richthofen" Sabres, bare metal and camouflaged, about to launch on a mission, possibly from Sylt. (J. Rack)

Twelve Sabres of JG 71 form their squadron number at the official inauguration of the first post-war Luftwaffe day fighter squadron. (Rolf Batz)

OTL Hartmann checks the new sleeve bands carrying the name "Richthofen" April 21, 1961, the day JG 71 received its historic name. At the same ceremony, JaboG. 31 became "Boelcke" and AG 51 became "Immelmann." General Kammhuber, first Chief of Staff of the post-war Luftwaffe, is at the right. (JG 71)

mann had spent a decade as a POW in Russia and was one of the last prisoners released through the efforts of Chancellor Konrad Adenauer. Once he had recuperated, Hartmann was often urged by friends and fellow pilots in the new Luftwaffe to join up. He resisted for some time, but in late 1956 finally gave in. He did some refresher flying at Landsberg and Fursty, then went to Luke AFB, Arizona, to do an F-84F course. Initially offered a fighter-bomber wing, Hartmann preferred his old fighter pilot trade. He trained on the Sabre at Oldy and became the first CO of JG 71.

The wing was officially formed June 6, 1959, in a ceremony led by General Kammhuber, first chief of the new Luftwaffe. The name "Richthofen" was adopted on April 21, 1961, the 43rd anniversary of the great First World War ace's death.

Hartmann realized how vital it was to bring his young pilots up to standard, and they lived by his motto: "Go flying, go flying and, again, go flying." They flew long, hard and well enough that in a mere half-year JG 71 was declared combat-ready and assigned to NATO within 2ATAF (2nd Allied Tactical Air Force). Hartmann achieved combat readiness for his wing in half the usual time.

Hartmann applied classic fighter pilot training methods, and one of his chief concerns was to train pilots never to lose a wingman. Based on his wartime experiences, he tried to make all training as realistic as possible. As well, he was looking down the road: the F-104 was coming, and the Luftwaffe would need experienced pilots for that.

In June 1961 JG 71 took part for the first time in the NATO gunnery competition for the Guynemer Trophy at Leeuwarden, Holland. Other participants were Belgium, Canada, Denmark, Italy and Norway. Each team comprised four pilots and a spare, and five aircraft. The spare prepared his aircraft for each mission and joined the team immediately if one of the regulars had to abort a mission. Pilots in JG 71's "Foxhound" team were Carstensen, Namyslo, Rack and Wicke, with Batz as spare. Team leader was Maj Schmieder, with Olt Laube as substitute. In preparation for the meet, the team spent some weeks in Westerland on the island of Sylt (the JG 71 "house range"). This was a special treat for the pilots, for they could fly their

Sabres "clean." Usually they operated with 100 Imp. gal. underwing tanks. When a gunnery mission was complete, the pilots could look for some "prey." This was the real fun, for there was no other fighter in the sky to match a clean Sabre, and it was sure to win any dogfight.

JG 71 didn't win the Guynemer— that seemed to be the special privilege of the RCAF, which apparently had a subscription for the trophy! The Germans finished fifth, but it was satisfying enough for the young pilots just to have qualified to be there.

Popularity of the Ahlhorn Wing was enhanced by the rather wild (at least by German standards) paint scheme carried by its Sabres. One day Hartmann had shown one of his pilots a photo of his own Bf 109 carrying the black and white "Tulpenmuster" (tulip scheme) and asked him if he could design something similar for the wing's Sabres. The pilot set to work and soon created an eye-catching scheme. At first it was applied only to the nose of each aircraft, with the intake either in red for the first squadron or yellow for the second. Later, the fin was painted, with the leading edge in the appropriate squadron colour. JG 71's

JG 71 squadron emblem.

scheme produced a mild shock among some high-ranking German officers, who were rather conservative when it came to painting aircraft. But it stuck and the Richthofen Sabres quickly became popular in the Luftwaffe.

In May 1960 a four-ship from JG 71 (pilots Batz, Meinke, Rack and RAF adviser Dickie Millward) sojourned at Son San Juan on Mallorca in sunny Spain. The base was both civil and military, having a detachment of Spanish F-86Fs based there for gunnery training over the Mediterranean. Mallorca was popular with the German pilots, not just because of the hospitali-

The Luftwaffe's Guynemer team at Leeuwarden in 1961: Carstensen, Namyslo, Rack, Wicke, Batz and Laube. (via J. Rack)

JG 71 at the Guynemer meet, Leeuwarden, Holland. The meet took place June 26 - July 6, 1961. Italian F-86Ks are down the line. (Rolf Batz)

The pilots of 712 Squadron c. 1962: Ney, Steenken, Rauzenberg, Gumros, Tuleweit, Kruppa, Meyer, Fischer, Pötter, Empl, Erlemann, Wallner, Bredenkötter, Zirngibl, Holzmann, Busse, Albert, Reich, Wendt, Puls, Pethke. (Archiv G.Joos)

ty of the Spanish Air Force, but also for its fine beaches and the female tourists adorning them. Also for Fundador and Sangria with Paella at Toni's Restaurant, and everything at a bargain.

The Spanish pilots could not be convinced that the wildly-painted German Sabres were not an aerobatic team and insisted that a show be mounted. The Luftwaffe boys tried to explain, but finally had to agree to a little flying display. But first they had to sneak in some sort of practice. This was done on the pretence of test flying the Sabres. So they fuelled up, fired up, and flew away. Out of sight they practised some basic formation manoeuvres, then used their remaining fuel for some low flying over the island which everyone enjoyed very much. There was no traffic around, so the tower cleared them "for everything." They landed, refuelled and put on their aerobatic demonstration, which was a great success. Such was the impact of those Sabre markings!

Erich Hartmann also had designed the first JG 71 emblem: a rising sun and the NATO star with two swords (symbolizing the smallest fighter formation) and the new German pilot's

wings above. The emblem was never applied to the Sabres and was no longer in use by the time the name "Richthofen" had been adopted, after which the "R" badge was used. It was similar to the badge of JG Richthofen Nr. 2 of the Second World War and was applied on the side of the Sabres to complete the JG 71 markings.

Squadron exchanges were common in NATO. 711 Squadron's first exchange was with 444 Squadron at Söllingen, July 6-15, 1960. Another was to 441 Squadron at Marville.

711 Squadron had some eager characters among its pilots. One was a rather short fellow who could lower his seat and hide down near the floor. He used to amuse himself and fellow pilots on 711 by joining other NATO aircraft he had intercepted. Then, with helmet removed, just peeking over the cockpit frame he would fly loose formation. To the other pilot, it looked as if nobody was flying the German Sabre. As a variation on the theme, he would hold a knife between his teeth and make savage-like grimaces at the opposing pilot!

On one occasion a 711 pilot injured a leg falling from a window after a rather wet party. Next day he went flying without reporting the matter—he hadn't wanted to be grounded. After landing, he found that his sore leg prevented him from using the brakes. He sailed off the runway, fortunately without harming the Sabre or himself.

He explained that he had been braking so hard that he hurt his leg, then lost control! It's not likely he expected anyone to believe him, but he still had great fun telling the story.

Another pilot came up with a special flight all his own. He was to ferry a Sabre 6 from Oberpfaffenhofen to the north. At the same time, some relatives were skiing in the Italian Alps, and he figured this was a good opportunity to pay them a visit! He precalculated a flight plan, estimated his fuel requirements, and proceeded with the flight. He flew south at low level, crossed Austria and visited his relatives, then quickly climbed and set course for homebase. Within gliding distance to base, he shut down to save fuel, descended, re-lit at 10,000 feet, and landed normally. The whole flight had been quite illegal, as crossing the German border required diplomatic clearances. The adventuresome pilot's "deviation" from flight plan had not gone unnoticed. An extensive search, with many teletype messages, had been conducted. Fortunately for the pilot, his scheme was not exposed and the incident was closed.

One day two young pilots, just starting to earn their bread as Sabre drivers at Ahlhorn, took off to practice dogfighting. They flew so eagerly that they didn't pay attention to their position. When it was time to return to base, cloud cover prevented a VFR approach. They tuned in the Ahlhorn

NDB (non-directional beacon) but were misled by a Dutch NDB on a similar frequency. They ended up on the Dutch base, from where they called Ahlhorn to explain things to their CO. Then off they went, for yet more dogfighting and, you guessed it, made the same mistake all over again. When they at last got home, there were some sarcastic remarks from the CO about their navigational skills!

JG 71 moved from Ahlhorn to Wittmund in December 1961-January 1962. The new base was refurbished to the latest standards in preparation for the coming F-104s. But the first move to Wittmund was only temporary as runways were being repaired at Ahlhorn. The wing was "home" by July, then back again to Wittmund April 28, 1963, where it remains today.

To maintain NATO commitments during the transition to the F-104, the Luftwaffe combined all JG 71 Sabres into a third squadron (713), commanded by Hptm Erlemann. 713 was transferred to Oldenburg October 18-19, 1963, where it operated alongside G.91s of Aufklärungsgeschwader 54. No. 713 absorbed the Sabres of both 711 and 712 Staffeln. These were renumbered by replacing the first digit of the aircraft number with a "3," retaining the other numerals. This was done to avoid duplicaton with the F-104s operated by the two regular squadrons, which carried the same numbers as the Sabres had done. The Sabres were thus coded JA 301-321 and JA 331-351, with some in the 360-370 range as well.

Most 713 Sabre pilots were already qualified on the F-104, having trained in the US. On their return, there were still insufficient F-104s so the Sabre had to suffice for a time. As Starfighters became available there was a gradual run-down of Sabre activities, but 713 continued to cover JG 71's air defence duties while it re-equipped with F-104s. 713 returned to Ahlhorn in August 1964 and was disbanded September 28.

Erlemann was succeeded by Hptm Böhm on July 15, 1964. OTL Hartmann had remained with JG 71 "R" until May 20, 1962, when he was assigned to staff duties. On May 30, 1962, OTL Josten became the new wing commander and led the unit into the F-104 era. The colourful markings were no longer authorized and disappeared in the fading years of the Sabre, only the "R" badge being used.

Jagdgeschwader 72

Jagdgeschwader 72 was the second day fighter wing to form. Its two squadrons and wing staff formed at Oldenburg, its supporting units at Celle. Flying and support units joined forces in early November 1959 at Leck. On November 11 official inauguration ceremonies were held under General Kammhuber. Wing commander was Maj Erich Hohagen, who had flown the Me 262 with JG 7 during the war. Majors Hans "Easy" Harms and "Charly" Gratz were commanders of 1. and 2. Staffel respectively.

At first the wing faced the usual host of start-up problems, and 10 - 12 hour working days were not unusual. In just about two years, though, JG 72 was ready for NATO assignment, but an internal reorganization at that time set the whole operation back to square one. On November 11, 1961, OTL Hohagen was succeeded by OTL Obleser (he would later become Inspector General of the Luftwaffe until his retirement in March 1983). Like JG 71, which was aided by a Dutch and a British advisor, JG 72 had RCAF advisers. Finally, on June 14, 1962, JG 72 was officially assigned to NATO, and would work closely with the RAF units at Jever, and JG 71 at Ahlhorn in protecting the skies of northern Germany.

Early on, 1. Staffel adopted the name "Vikings," and 2. Staffel, "Foxes," the latter after the mascot of Maj Gratz, who had a real fox (presented to him by his pilots) kept in a cage on base. And not to be outdone by their rivals at Ahlhorn, the boys from Leck soon had their Sabres festooned in colourful markings: large flashes on fuselage, fin and drop tanks. Colours were red outlined in yellow for 1. Staffel, reversed for 2. Staffel. The 1. Staffel badge was the NATO star superimposed by a pilot's helmet bearing Viking horns and a scroll reading "1. Staffel JG 72," while that of 2.

Sabre 6s of JG 72 visit 4 Wing on June 29, 1961. Note 1. and 2. Staffel markings. (Harry Tate via K.M. Molson)

Staffel was a fox emblem carried on both sides of the fuselage about mid position.

Stories abound about the Fox squadron. One tells how the Fox became a Tiger. The second Tiger Meet, a friendly gathering and competition of NATO squadrons having a tiger in their badge, took place in 1962. By then, the Tiger Club had grown to six nations and eight squadrons, including 722 with its fox emblem—not exactly the ticket required to enter the Tiger Club. When 722 applied for membership, an inscription was added around the Fox badge reading "Believe it or not, this is a tiger." This did the trick and is how the Foxes became Tigers.

On another occasion, after night ex-

during the exercise! The fox was not consulted before it was "modified."

On December 19, 1963, OTL Benno Schmieder became CO of JG 72. Also that year, the wing received its new "Geschwaderwappen" or wing badge, presented to JG 72 by Brigadegeneral Wehnelt in a ceremony at Leck. The badge comprised a Viking longboat, NATO star and two stylized fighter aircraft. This badge remains in use by JG 72's successor, JaboG. 43 at Oldenburg. At the same time, all colourful squadron markings disappeared, as did individual squadron badges, as standard Luftwaffe practice was now to display only the wing emblems on its aircraft, these designed according to heraldic principles.

By this time all Sabres were in

evening the Vikings were seen over the Foxes' dispersal with 18 Sabres! As a rule, the Vikings also beat the Foxes in sports, until the prize for winning at soccer became a barrel of beer. Then the Foxes were able to win.

In 1962 a mixed team of pilots from JG 71 and JG 72 was sent to Leeuwarden for the Guynemer meet: pilots Laube, Namyslo and Wicke from JG 71, and Scholz and Schlutter (spare) from JG 72. Helmut Scholz was considered the Luftwaffe's best air-to-air gunner. He had received a citation from General Harlinghausen in 1960 for scoring 41 per cent when average results were 30.6 per cent after gunnery practice at Westerland. His score was especially noteworthy as failures with the A-4 radar gunsight were common

JB-240 of 2/JG 72, fitted with Sidewinder rails, takes off at Marville. Then, JB-107 and JB-244 visiting 4 Wing on September 29, 1961. (John Meuse, Harry Tate via K.M. Molson)

The fox-cum-tiger inscription on a 2/JG 72 Sabre.

ercises, JG 72 Sabres landed at Eggebeck, while RF-84Fs from there (AG 52) went into Leck, all in aid of crossservice training. The mascot of AG 52 was (and still is) a 3-foot sculpted black panther. It had been "acquired" (i.e. stolen) by some pilots at Munich when the wing was building up at Erding. During the exercise in question the Foxes intended to paint the aft portion of the AG 52 panther red. This they tried to do one night, but were surprised by a guard who actually fired a warning shot to break up the mission. Word of these shenanigans reached Leck, where, the following night, the boys from AG 52 shaved off the tail of 722's fox and painted it red—not the least example of good communications

camouflage, though JG 72 retained some individualism: a narrow white outline on aircraft identification numbers. This later became standard on Luftwaffe aircraft. Today the wing is known as Fighter Bomber Wing 43, flying Alpha Jets, and its pilots still bear the historic Fox and Viking emblems on their flying suits. (Squadron numeration was reversed with the advent of the G.91. 1. Staffel "Vikings" became 2. Staffel; 2. Staffel "Foxes" became 1. Staffel.)

There was intensive competition between the Foxes and Vikings, and it was the Vikings who seemed to have the edge in spite of the heroic efforts by the Foxes. The accumulation of monthly flying hours was one area of competition. One evening, after a regular day of busy flying, the Foxes launched 16 Sabres in an effort to surpass the Vikings in hours flown that month. But their triumph was short-lived—next

at the time and pilots often had to depend on visual aiming.

On July 23-31, 1963, 2./JG 72 visited RAF Coltishall, the guests of No. 74 Tiger Squadron. This was the first visit of a post-war Luftwaffe squadron to England, and as such was a major event. Hptm Hans-Joachim Frane led the five German Sabres and much publicity accompanied the visit. On departure day, a low-level Sabre flypast was arranged, but the German leader decided to forgo the offer of radar guidance for a nice line-up. The Sabres took off and the many guests of honour waited for them to return for the flypast. Instead, all that was seen was a neat formation skimming low over the trees on the horizon. Unfortunately the proud formation leader had picked a neighbouring airfield by mistake, making the flypast down its unattended runway. Those at Coltishall never did get their flypast, and some of the Germans there may well have ended up with slightly red ears.

A notable Luftwaffe operation during the JG 72 Sabre era was "Stahlnetz" ("Steel Net"). It was the low-level defence of Schleswig-Holstein up to the Danish border by Sabres flying a precise, timed pattern. "Stahlnetz" was the brainwave of Maj Obleser when he was CO of JG 72 and involved JG 71 as well as JG 72. The idea was to provide gapless air cover by aircraft patrolling the skies for low-level intruders. This required a Sabre taking off every five minutes, then flying to a precise starting point where the pilot began patrolling at 500 feet on east-west-east headings, the heading change being flown with a standard rate turn. Any air traffic encountered had to be investigated. This scheme was costly in terms of aircraft and pilots committed, but was operated from the fall of 1962 to mid-1964. It depended on fair weather but theoretically could provide an impenetrable air defence line. Hence the name "Stahlnetz."

"Stahlnetz" was conducted as a periodic exercise, missions usually being flown early, before the beginning of routine daily activities. These low-flying hunters were intended to supplement the surveillance radar system which could not detect intruders coming in on the deck. "Stahlnetz" got Sabre pilots hoping that their mission in life might be extended, but these were merely sweet dreams.

In late 1964 when 713 Squadron had vacated Oldenburg, JG 72 relocated there from Leck. This coincided with JG 72's change to the fighter-bomber role. It was now Jagdbombergeschwader 43 and was combat ready just six weeks after the move. It became the third Sabre unit to call Oldenburg home, after WS 10 and 3./JG 71. AG 54 had also been based there with G.91s.

JaboG 43 was well settled in by early 1965, with its pilots re-trained and adapted to their new mission. TAC EVAL (tactical evaluation) was completed that summer and the unit declared combat ready. But the days of the Sabre were numbered—JaboG 43 was earmarked for conversion to the Fiat G.91. This began after Oberst Heinz-Günter Kuring replaced OTL Schmieder on January 10, 1966. Kuring recalls: "When I arrived in January 1966 to command the wing at Oldenburg, there was actually not much to do. I had taken over the best wing in the Luftwaffe. Nevertheless, there were the first signs of change: conversion to the 'Minijet' (G.91) had been decided by the Air Force."

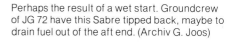

Perhaps the result of a wet start. Groundcrew of JG 72 have this Sabre tipped back, maybe to drain fuel out of the aft end. (Archiv G. Joos)

A JG 72 Sword flies wing to a G.91T3 of AG 53. March 1965. (G. Joos)

"Experience over the past years frequently tempted the merry bunch of fighter pilots to attack from high altitude and, preferably, out of the sun. Using Sabres for fighter-bombers was regarded as a necessary (but not necessarily pleasant) evil. Deep inside, we had hopes of going back to the fighter business with our Sabres. Who couldn't appreciate this, knowing the Sabre for what it was? But hopes and wishful thinking were shattered—the beloved Sabres were sold to Iran. The last exciting event, the coronation of their Sabre career, would be a super trip to Iran for many of the pilots. The last Sabre 6 left the wing on December 22, 1966. The very last we lifted onto a pylon as a monument, after many difficulties, much sweat and donations by all the pilots."

In late 1966 re-equipment with the G.91 was complete, and the wing was redesignated LeKG 43 (Leichtes Kampfgeschwader 43/Light Attack Wing 43). In 1969, when LeKG 43 celebrated its 10th anniversary, its former CO, General Obleser, looked back on the unit's past:

It is difficult to explain in a few words the renown achieved by JG 72 in its relatively short history in tactical air defence operations. In retrospect, it seems we owe much of this success to the balanced harmony of the Sabre weapons system. Airplane, pilot and maintenance were a unity. Viewed from today's impersonal centralization and far-reaching automated mission control, this might sound like an old-time fairy tale. With the change from fighter to fighter-bomber, and the introduction of a new weapon system, the era of the "free fighter pilot" came to an end. Yet, in retrospect, what impressed most was the flexibility and versatility of this Geschwader.

The fighter pilot's stock in trade—total, safe command of his airplane at all altitudes, and complete familiarity with the GCI-system—were developed by JG 72 with the excellent support of the Royal Canadian Air Force. Never during training were the new young pilots so hard and realistically tasked as during their days at WS 10. The Canadian instructor pilots demanded (and demonstrated themselves) perfect mastery of the Sabre and, above all, instilled in their students spirit and enthusiasm. Names like Conny Platz, Walt Moore, Pinky Flynn, Myron Filyk, Alec Leslie and others come to mind, and the wing's history is incomplete without them. Thus the unit was readily integrated into the air defence system.

An RF-84F of AG 51 "Immelmann", and a pair of Fiat-built F-86Ks of JG 74, two contemporaries of the Canadair F-86. The RF-84F was a photo recce aircraft, while the F-86K was the Luftwaffe's sole all-weather fighter of the day. (G. Joos)

298

Sabres of JG 73 standing alert — fuelled and armed. (JaboG.35)

With close cooperation with the RAF fighter wing at Jever, and the JG 71 at Ahlhorn, JG 72 matured in a short time, and today all the problems associated with tactical operations are hardly remembered. ATC, Eider Control, Scramble Signals are just a few key phrases that will take the insider back to those days. We also look back on many coordination visits, the demonstrated will to accept our responsibilities at all levels, the restless duties of squadron and group leaders. But the real test was yet to come: the remarkable moment when the wing was assigned its operational mission within its air defence sector, and had to assume full responsibility in the Lane Control Air Defence System of that time.

As the wing was in the extreme north of the air defence sector, its operational air space was mostly over water —not that the fighter pilot is afraid of water (except at the bar, perhaps) but at that time the chance of survival in the water was very limited. Search and rescue was still in its infancy, sea survival equipment was of more symbolic than practical value, and the navigation equipment in the Sabre was inadequate for such an assignment. But JG 72 not only did an outstanding job completing its mission—it did so

without grumbling, a fact deserving special mention today.

The memories of air defence exercises in those days—of mass dogfights —might make the Sabre pilots melancholic. We think of "Stahlnetz"—low-level defence by fighters. Truly, the decision to procure an aircraft has seldom turned out to be such a lucky one as was the introduction of the Canadair Sabre 6 as the first fighter used by the new German Air Force. We have no such aircraft today, except as monuments on some of our air bases. Fitting monuments indeed.

General Obleser

Jagdgeschwader 73

Formation of the Luftwaffe's third day fighter wing, JG 73, began April 1, 1959, with the first personnel posted to Ahlhorn. Maj Fritz Schröter became the wing's first CO on November 16, and later that month JG 73 transferred to Oldenburg, where it was commissioned by Brigadegeneral Walter of 3. Luftverteidigungsdivision, though the wing was later reassigned to 4. Luftverteidigungsdivision.

JG 73 operated on a reduced scale at Oldenburg for two years, then moved on October 12, 1961, to its permanent base, Pferdsfeld/Sobernheim, as part of 1. Luftverteidigungsdivision, being inaugurated by Generalleutnant Kammhuber on November 11, 1961. Kammhuber had a habit of choosing odd

dates for such occasions—November 11, in this case, being the start of the German Karneval season. Thus the Wing was sometimes jokingly called "Narrengeschwader" — Fool's Wing.

Though JG 73 was now integrated into the NATO air defence system, it would be another year before base infrastructure was fully on stream. Even then things were not perfect. The smooth-surfaced concrete runway was impossibly slippery when wet, resulting in some exciting barrier engagements and otherwise hairy landings. To counter this, an anti-skid layer was applied to its surface, then it had to be completely rebuilt. These difficulties periodically forced JG 73 to wander from home, deploying to neighbouring Luftwaffe or USAF bases. Oberst Schröter recalls those times:

Inauguration of the wing took place in instalments, first in 1960 at Oldenburg. For the parade, our handful of men were lined up to attention in front of all the aircraft we had at the time, four Sabres! The pithy words of the commanding general of Luftwaffengruppe Nord somehow were not quite in relation to that modest beginning.

At first we were to be based at Leipheim, so we got to work with preparations. We endured travelling, conferences and the paper war. But then, to our surprise, higher echelons decided that we were going to Pferds-

299

Quiet scene at Pferdsfeld. (via Jack Forbes)

feld. So we put away the Leipheim files and started all over. Eventually we transferred there, despite strong protests from the local people of Rehbach, who felt that villages near the base would be endangered by noisy, low-flying fighters. (Years later, when the unit got Phantoms, two complete villages were relocated at government expense as a result of the never-ending public outcry.)

Conditions at Pferdsfeld were still in a sad state. The runway was complete, but chemicals had to be applied to improve its surface. These changed the runway during hot or rainy weather into soft soap, causing frequent hairy landings. Radar and other approach aids were either poor or nonexistent. Barracks were primitive, and the hangars had neither water nor heat at first. Again, the wing was "inaugurated," this time with great solemnity and a parade, speeches and *Eintopfessen* in the unheated maintenance hangar. The wing had just 20 Sabres at the time. Any shortage had to be made up by borrowing from other wings.

Improvisation saved the day, and conditions gradually improved when, suddenly, there were rumours that we were to disband! As CO, I discouraged such rumours but, unbelievably, rumour turned to truth. Was all our effort to go down the drain? In the end, we were able to turn the decision

around (though not quite according to official policy). We continued operating, and quite successfully.

We passed two TAC EVALs with good results, something which raised our spirits and confidence. One TAC EVAL critique noted, "L'esprit de corps est recommendable."

Maj Fritz Schröter

On October 25, 1960, JG 73 was involved in an infamous matter. Two of its Sabres on patrol were directed by an RAF GCI controller to investigate an unidentified aircraft near the German-Dutch border. He vectored the Sabres to the target, which was identified as an RAF transport. To everyone's surprise, it soon turned out that this was a VIP flight carrying HRH Queen Elizabeth and HRH Prince Philip back to England from Denmark. Neither controller nor pilots were aware of this. The co-pilot of the Queen's aircraft reported that the Sabres had bounced his aircraft, creating a near-miss incident. The story leaked out and the Press had a field day, reporting that two wild Luftwaffe Sabre pilots had endangered the lives of the Queen and Prince, and the routine exercise snowballed into a diplomatic incident. As the Sabres had been operating from Oldenburg, the CO of WS 10 was arrested! The British demanded and obtained a high-level investigation by a British-German commission, which revealed that the Sabres had violated no rules and that there had been no

danger of collision, as confirmed by GCI evidence. The scandal subsided, the British apologized and the good name of WS 10 and the JG 73 pilots was restored.

Under general reorganization of the Luftwaffendivisions, JG 73 was attached to 5. Luftwaffendivision on July 1, 1963, and plans were made to convert the wing to G.91s in the close support role, with transition to the lightweight fighter starting that fall. The program continued through May 1964 when one squadron had converted to the G.91 and was operating in the reconnaissance role, while the other squadron still flew Sabres. But the wing was then ordered to cease G.91 re-equipment and change back to Sabres, though in the fighter-bomber role. This led to redesignation as Jagd-bombergeschwader 42 on October 1, 1964. Now the Luftwaffe had no more day fighter units flying the Sabre 6. JG 71 was operational on the Starfighter, and JG 72 and JG 73 were fighter-bomber units flying Sabres at low level where they were not best suited.

On April 1, 1966, Oberst Schröter turned over command to OTL Lothar Maretzke. Now began the second transition to the G.91, after some 42,500 hours of Sabre flying by the wing. On May 1, 1967, the unit became Leichtes Kampfgeschwader 42 (Light Attack Wing), as did the other wings flying the G.91 or "Gina" as it became popularly known in the Luftwaffe. In each wing,

Crest of JG 73.

JG-365 and 374 of JaboG.42 prepare to take off on an air-to-ground mission at Deci. Note the practice rocket pods. (Geissler)

Unusual air-to-air photo of JC-233, gear down. Its tanks were white and red. The photo was taken in March 1965. (G. Joos)

one squadron operated on close air support, the other in the recce role.

The JG 73 Sabres carried no special unit markings early on, but later a Geschwaderwappen, a yellow stylized bird on a light blue shield with an iron cross in white, was introduced and carried on the fin of camouflaged aircraft. It is still in use today. As complaints from the populace increased in 1963 about noisy, low-flying NATO aircraft, units of Luftwaffengruppe Süd were ordered to paint drop tanks in colours to help catch offenders. Under this rule, JG 73/JaboG 42 painted its drop tanks red and white, unique among Sabre units.

Jagdgeschwader 74

During the build-up phase, JG 74 had been operating Sabre 6s with the code JD from Oldenburg for several months in 1960-1961 when High Command decided that the existing three wings of day fighters were enough. Thus, JG 74 was disbanded before being commissioned. Its Sabres were spread among the other wings. Meanwhile, the JE-coded F-86Ks of JG 75, also working up at Oldenburg at this time, were re-coded JD and the wing was re-numbered JG 74. It was the sole Luftwaffe all-weather unit until F-104Gs appeared in that role in the mid-sixties.

JC-250 after making JaboG.42's last mission at Pferdsfeld. Pilots and ground crew are smitten with grief and have resorted to drowning their sorrows. The CO, Lothar Maretzke (centre, with right foot turned), joins in the wake. (JaboG.35)

Sabre Alley

When JG 73 Sabres left the runway at Pferdsfeld and turned south, they immediately found themselves in the hottest area for pilots looking for a dogfight. This was the air space dominated by the RCAF Sabre squadrons in France and Germany, and soon it was known as "Sabre Alley." The Canadians were an aggressive bunch of experienced "hunters." They were always looking for prey and bounced any fighter that dared trespass over their territory.

In clear weather one could see the contrails forming over the Rhine valley and hear the muted distant roar of jet engines at full power, a fascinating spectacle. A vertical pull-up was exciting to watch: the contrail went straight up, widened as the fighter slowed, and stopped momentarily as the jet reached the point where the pilot kicked in full rudder and wheeled around starting a dive to build up speed, as he either tried to get on someone's tail or took evasive action. If conditions favoured it, the contrails accumulated and eventually formed their own layer of cloud as the day wore on.

The Canadians revelled in climbing above contrail level to watch for any unwary NATO aircraft penetrating their domain. Then they pounced like hawks, as the young pilots of JG 73 would learn to their dismay and frustration. They had been short of aircraft while building up the wing at Ahlhorn and Oldenburg, and had not accumulated as much experience as they had hoped. So, in order to avoid being clobbered by the RCAF, they devised some tricks of their own. One was simply to climb through the contrail level, then make a quick heading change.

The legends about Sabre Alley were also heard in the north. One eager pilot, Wicke by name, one day got the itch to try the skills of his trade and ventured from Ahlhorn south into Sabre Alley, looking for a hassle. Naturally he could not return home without refuelling, so he stopped at a Dutch base, made a quick turn-around and blasted off again for Ahlhorn. His mission had not been authorized and reflects the spirit of these young German Sabre pilots.

The Last Days

The story of the Luftwaffe Sabres is also one of the birth of an air force. It

The map shows Sabre bases in the Federal Republic of Germany, as well as bases in neighbouring countries. Jever, Oldenburg, Brüggen, Wildenrath and Geilenkirchen were RAF Sabre bases at one time or another during the years 1953-56 before the new German Air Force was formed. Söllingen and Zweibrücken were RCAF bases in Germany. Marville and Grostenquin were RCAF bases in France, and Metz was the RCAF Air Division headquarters.

includes all problems of such a challenge: orders and counter-orders, improvisation, personal engagement throughout the chain of command. The squadrons were very much on their own, with rather a free hand, for the command structure itself had to develop first. But ironically, the day fighter force seemed an unwanted child in the eyes of high command. It was disbanded just as it matured and became effective.

No sooner had the wings produced competent fighter pilots than they were consigned to hill-jumping—a different kind of flying and totally new to the fighter boys. They had had a low-level training mission or two at WS 10, but that was it. More than once a Sabre fighter-bomber pilot said to himself,

"To hell with it, I'm a fighter pilot," as he spotted a contrail, opened up and climbed for the bogey, into the element where his Sabre was really at home.

The Sabre was not ideal for low-level operations. Flying low and fast, its centre of lift moved forward as speed increased, eventually meeting the CG.

This caused instability when the flight path was disturbed by turbulence or an abrupt movement of the control column. The elevator became oversensitive, resulting in porpoising, a fairly rapid oscillation around the pitch axis. This was hazardous near the ground, as counteracting stick movements usually made it worse. The corrective procedure was to extend speed brakes and pull the throttle back (by slowing down, the airplane dampened the porpoising by itself). Canadair recommended a 360 KIAS limit at low level. After all, the Sabre 6 was a dogfighter with an outstanding turning ability designed to meet the enemy high up. In its time, it was superior to all Western fighters (likely, also to those behind the Iron Curtain) except the Hawker Hunter, which turned as well and had better acceleration.

The Sabre wasn't really outdated when phased out by the Luftwaffe. It was a victim of the "missile with a man" outlook which obsessed military planners in the early sixties. Air defence was to be left solely to radar, SAMs and supersonic, missile-armed fighters. Guns were considered obsolete, and there was nothing left to hold airspace over the battlefield clear of enemy fighters. When the F-104 appeared it was for use as a high-speed, low-level carrier of tactical nuclear stores and as a missile-carrying interceptor of the lone-wolf intruder. Dogfights, considered a thing of the past, were actually forbidden to reduce the risk of mid-air collision. Once again, the lessons taught over and over since the First World War were being ig-

nored or forgotten. The Americans learned this again the hard way in Southeast Asia, and the Israelis proved in 1967 that air superiority over the battlefield is absolutely vital. The Luftwaffe especially should have known better, as it had suffered the consequences of losing air superiority in 1944-1945. Only now, in the eighties, do pilots again have aircraft designed for the classic dogfighting role, with special courses to teach fighter pilots the tactics they should never have forgotten. All this 20 years after the Sabre disappeared from European skies.

The Iran Deal

In January 1966 Germany sold Iran 90 Sabres. The Ministry of Defence agreed that the MEREX company would act as agent for the deal and Luftwaffe pilots would ferry the Sabres to Iran. Organization and planning for the operation was done by JaboG 42 at Pferdsfeld under Maj Bernhard. Everyone was eager to get started.

Sabre 6s in Iran on March 31, 1966, with hastily applied Iranian roundels. From the left unknown IIAF officer, Böhm, Ballhorn, Haiplik, Geissler. (Archiv G.Joos)

Routing was straightforward as far as eastern Turkey, but a vast no-man's land devoid of nav aids lay between there and Iran, stretching the Sabre's endurance to its limits. The route was checked out by experienced pilots aboard a Luftwaffe transport. Then the operation got under way, with a plan to move aircraft in eight-plane groups on weekends.

All flights originated at Oldenburg, where the pilots accepted the Sabre from the "Versorgungsregiment" (supply regiment). Each carried a special survival kit for desert use. There was extra concern about the Diyarbakir to Vahdati leg, close along the Soviet border. There pilots would have to get early enough weather reports from Vahdati in order to decide whether to continue or return. Passing beyond Tehran on a southerly course, there was no chance to return if the weather was down at destination, for Vahdati had no approach aids. As an additional safety measure, each formation leader had to have made the trip before.

Two legs were planned for the first day of each trip: Oldenburg across France to Piacenza in northern Italy for refuelling, then to Gioia del Colle in southern Italy for a night stop. Next day took them to Turkey, first to Eskisehir for fuel, then Diyarbakir for a night stop. Stage three was to Iran, first into Tabriz for fuel, then Vahdati, where the Sabres, still in German

German Sabres during their wanderings over Iran. Down below doesn't even look like a nice place to visit. (Geissler)

markings, were accepted by the Imperial Iranian Air Force. The German pilots were ferried to Tehran by IIAF C-130s and travelled home on commercial flights.

This operation, carried out in the summer of 1966, was greatly enjoyed by the Luftwaffe pilots. It was a wonderful opportunity for long cross-country experience, normally beyond the scope of operational flying, and a chance to visit some exotic places.

For this long flight, the Sabres carried 167-gal. underwing tanks. Some of the aircraft on the trip were given non-standard code letters, about which little is known.

Happily, the operation went well, although the last group ran into severe weather in Italy. The Sabres barely made it into Grosseto, with minimum fuel—the last possible place to go. Within moments of their landing, torrential rains struck the area and left the Germans stranded in difficult conditions for two weeks! One unidentified Sabre, parked in a low-lying place at Grosseto, drowned in water up to the canopy. There it was left, so 89 Sabres found their way safely down to Iran. Once in Iran, they hastily received IIAF markings. Oddly, the corners of the Iron Crosses still showed on the green outer circle of the Iranian roundel. Also, the story of these Sabres had not yet ended, for they were quickly transferred to Pakistan, eventually to see combat with India in 1971. German

officials seemed to have had no idea at the time what the real purpose of the deal with Iran was. Pakistan had been looking for a fighter to replace its losses in the 1965 war, and to augment its fleet of F-86Fs. As German policy prevented dealing in arms with countries involved in conflict, or with areas of political unrest, Pakistan had to arrange the Sabre purchase "under the table."

When it became known that former Luftwaffe Sabres were operating with the PAF, there was a stir in the press, notably in India and Germany. Indian Defence Minister Y.S. Chavan alleged that Pakistan was involved in a massive arms build-up following the 1965 India-Pakistan war. Included, said Chavan, were fighters brought in from both China and Germany. Germany replied that it had had Iran's assurance that the Sabres would not be resold to Pakistan. Besides, any resale would be subject to Canadian approval (the Iranian deal had been approved by Ottawa).

Canada drew attention to the Indian reports, but Iran explained by saying that some of the Sabres had to be sent to Pakistan for maintenance and would be returning to Iran. History shows that the Sabres never did return from Pakistan and operated there in the 1971 Indo-Pakistan war. In the PAF the Canadair Sabres were referred to as F-86Es, and last ones were grounded in 1980 for fatigue reasons.

"Jenny" Jensen taxis out in a WS 10 Sabre 6 carrying Sidewinder missiles. The scene is at Oberpfaffenhofen. (Dornier)

The German government acted in good faith throughout the German-Iranian deal. On the surface, there was no indication that the Iranians had other intentions, though it may have seemed a bit odd that Iran, at the time building up squadrons of F-5s, would want such a large number of much older Sabres.

Modifications

The Luftwaffe was quick to design modifications for its Sabre 6s that enabled use of the Sidewinder air-to-air missile. Dornier provided the technical assistance, and BB-188 of WS 10 was the trial aircraft, equipped with launching rails and necessary wiring. Flying characteristics were not changed by the mods.

Sabres were modified at the Geschwader by Luftwaffe technicians, supported by Dornier advisers. JG 72 and JG 73 had their aircraft modified, while JG 71 did not, perhaps because it was to be the initial F-104 wing, so the work may not have seemed worth the effort. The first JG 72 Sabre was modified at Leck in late 1961. It was initially planned that all pilots should make at least one live Sidewinder firing, but in fact only some had a chance to do so.

The pilot familiarization program included a two-ship mission. One

A close-up of the modified canopy opening (canopy raised, not flush with cockpit sill) that was necessary with installation of the Martin Baker ejection seat. Note white outline on airplane number introduced with the ban on individual squadron markings. Kurt Kahl is the pilot. (K. Kahl)

Sabre launched a 5-inch ballistic rocket which became a target for the Sidewinder carried by the other Sabre. Later, one Sabre carried both pieces of ordnance: target rocket and heat-seeking Sidewinder. Considering that the two Sabre wings with Sidewinders were soon to become fighter-bomber units, and the other was awaiting conversion to the F-104, it seems that the costly Sidewinder program was a questionable decision. The whole venture was very short-lived.

The other major German mod to the Sabre was installation of the Martin

Sabre 5 BB-261 during through-the-canopy ejection trials at Oberpfaffenhofen, pending installation of the Martin Baker seats. (Laudam)

Baker Mk.5 ejection seat. The Norwegians had this mod on their F-86Fs, which necessitated an alteration to the opening mechanism for the sliding canopy to increase the clearance for the seat when the canopy moved back. The first M-B seat was installed in JB-102 (c/n 1743), which was flown to Martin-Baker. On August 29, 1959 it was accepted and flown back to Oldenburg by Hptm Flade. Further trials and through-the-canopy test firings were done by Dornier at Oberpfaffenhofen in 1960, in cooperation with Autoflug, the German M-B representative. Sabre BB-261 (c/n 982, previously BB-172) was used in the trials.

JB-102 lands in the UK. It was the first Luftwaffe Sabre modified to take the Martin Baker seat. (Martin Baker Aircraft)

The Sabre was notorious for its weak nose gear. Here a JG 72 bird, Sidewinder rails fitted, bows down. (Archiv Wache AGL)

Although the performance envelope of this seat improved survivability, it was not liked by all pilots. Strapping in was less comfortable than in the old C-2 seat, and rearward vision was restricted, something that would not endear itself to a fighter pilot. To compensate, an additional rear-view mirror was placed at each side of the canopy. It seems that no JG 73 Sabres received the M-B seat mod.

A unique application devised by Maj "Bubi" Hartmann used the Sabre to clear snow from runways. A large deflector held in place by a metal framework was fixed to the Orenda jet pipe of a Sabre with its rear fuselage/tail assembly removed. This "appendage" rested on swivelling wheels. A truck would pull the whole contrap-

Bob Flynn's Sabre sits in the boonies after his bumpy landing at Oldy. (via Bob Flynn)

tion, called a "Bubimat." The Orenda would be running, and its jet blast, directed down through the deflector, would melt the snow and ice. The concept worked effectively, and several Bubimats were rigged up. It seems that most were Mark 5s, though JG 71 used JA-110 in this unusual configuration.

Accidents

The Luftwaffe's Sabres posted a normal accident record (actually better than that of the F-84F). There was no special accident cause unique to the Sabre except that its nose gear tended to collapse easily. One technical flaw was traced to JP 4 fuel with an excess of sulphur, which led to creation of microorganisms in the fuel control units of the Orendas. That, in turn, damaged the high-pressure fuel-pump piston with resultant mechanical failures, causing the loss of at least two Sabres. Late in the Sabre story there were engine failures related to turbine bucket (i.e. blade) failures. Apparently Orenda recommended a fix, but the

Luftwaffe at first turned it down for economy reasons, considering that the Sabre's service days were numbered.

In all, 46 Luftwaffe Sabres were destroyed in crashes or ground incidents. Of 24 ejections (4 with M-B seats), 17 succeeded. Causes of crashes were many and varied: collisions, mechanical malfunctions, weather and pilot factors, etc. Regarding the latter, the Luftwaffe had few "old hands" in their jet operations, so didn't have the experience to lean on that other air forces had. Their pilots were *all* learning the ropes together. While RCAF "sprogs" were learning from instructors who had come up the line on Vampires, T-birds, Sabres and CF-100s, a bare handful of Luftwaffe veterans had flown so much as an Me 262 before 1956. Whilst burdened with admin and other organizational tasks, these few experienced men, like Erich Hohagen, themselves had to master the tricks of the Sabre trade alongside the younger fellows: instrument flight rules and procedures, R/T in English, taking a formation down through weather and so on. Maintenance personnel faced the same problems—everyone was working from scratch.

The Luftwaffe lost its first Sabre (BB-113, c/n 841) on May 19, 1958. F/O R.J. "Bob" Flynn was on a test flight and had a flame-out. He ended by belly-landing at base. After landing long, he bounced into the air, came back down in the overshoot area, then ploughed through some light brush. The plane was a total wreck, but Flynn walked away from it. Later he expressed concern about the safety of the parachute harness in use. These were inspected while WS 10 was grounded for three days. Sure enough, the system was found unsafe—the locks could

give way and release the chute when pulled on with any force.

Bob Flynn was one of WS 10's RCAF instructors. In typical fashion, he had trained on Harvards post-war, done his Sabre OTU in the summer of 1954, then joined 414 Squadron for over three years of flying; and finally joined the original group of Canadians at WS 10. Part of F/O Flynn's report on the crash of BB-113 reads as follows:

I began to level off at 21,000 feet when I experienced a loud explosion, followed immediately by an increase in TPT to 900° plus, and a drop in rpm. Also, smoke filled the cockpit. I immediately stopcocked the engine, and commencing a starboard turn, I informed Oldenburg Approach of my emergency and stated I would attempt to relight. If unable to, or to establish position, I would probably bail out.

Continuing starboard, I caught sight of the ragged hole I had ascended through, and continued in descent to this hole. My first attempt at relighting was above cloud and unsuccessful. My speed at approx. 250 kts, I started to spiral through the hole, increasing my speed to increase rpm at approx. 10,000 feet. I got 15 per cent and attempted another relight, receiving 40 per cent and 800° in idle position. I left my engine in this manner and rolled out of my spiral on approx. 100° and decreased my descent. I was passing in and out of cloud constantly and was unable to establish a positive position.

At about this time, tower informed me GCA had a contact 6 miles east, and he immediately changed it to 4 miles. I caught sight of the Weser River approx. 5 miles ahead, so I commenced a starboard turn and received a steer of 210°. My altitude now 2500 feet and surrounded by haze, I made visual sight of the base. Immediately I flamed out the engine because of the tailpipe temperature which was still 800° plus.

My position seemed to be 1 - 2 miles off the north end of Runway 28, and such that, because of low hanging cloud, I could not establish myself in a positive position for a wheels-down safe forced landing. Electing not to bail out . . . I decided on a wheels-up landing on the runway. Due to the danger of draining the hydraulic system, I did not do any violent turns, and with my dive brakes extended did one small "S" turn before making my final run. I informed the tower which stated field

was clear, and heard Hotel lead state, "You have speed, lower undercarriage!" This I did not do, due to my high speed.

I dove the aircraft at the ground, rounding out sharply over the button, held it about a foot off the runway waiting for speed to drop off. About two-thirds of the length, I felt the tail dragging, so I slammed the aircraft onto the runway in an attempt to help slow it down. It is difficult to describe the remainder of this escapade!

Flynn added that any intentions he had had of ejecting were dispelled "by the uncertainty in my mind of whether or not the parachute release box would sustain the force of the parachute opening."

Bob Flynn

Flynn left WS 10 in July 1960 for a stint instructing at Chatham. Later he flew Clunks with the Electronic Warfare Unit, Voodoos with 425 Squadron, and Falcons with 412. He joined Canadair in 1980 to fly the Challenger at Canadair's Windsor Locks, Connecticut base.

The first Sabre fatality occurred November 7, 1958. Before takeoff, the pilot of BB-129 (c/n 981) had reported trouble with his oxygen mask. He later crashed and the cause of the accident was put down to hypoxia. Jochen "Joe" Rack, today a DC-10 captain, describes his own crash at Oldenburg on January 29, 1959:

I had flown Harvards at Landsberg and T-33s at Fursty on the Luftwaffe's first course of pure beginners; and was just through transition training on the Sabre with 80 hours on type when we were sent to Dornier to ferry our new Sabre 6s back to WS 10. My section leader, No. 3, had been on my course, thus had the same limited experience. As No. 4, I was flying BB-359 (c/n 1619). Weather at Oldenburg was not good but within limits, so the formation leader decided to go.

Just after takeoff I experienced total radio failure—I could neither hear nor transmit. Still, all I had to do was hang on to No. 3. He would take me down OK. Our flight was uneventful, but on arrival my fuel state was getting low, for holding No. 4 position demanded the most frequent power changes. But I had no way of relaying my situation to my leader.

Over the beacon we split into elements of two, and mine was second

F-86 No. 1 Conversion

TIME 1:00
1) Instructor to supervise checks and starting engine
2) Climb to 15,000 Ft (Military Power = 97.5%)
   level off and
   a) practice medium and steep turns
   b) extend D/B at various speeds
   c) stall - wheels and flaps "up"
   d) stall - wheels and flaps "down"
   e) simulate landing pattern at altitude
3) Return to Base when
   "Bingo" = 1,500 lbs of fuel
4) One touch-and-go landing
   one full-stop landing

   approx. 80% RPM - 300 Kt at pitch
   Full stop with at least 900 lbs of fuel

Luftwaffe pilot's check list for first Sabre conversion flight.

in turn. Unknown to me, the weather at Oldy had meanwhile deteriorated considerably and was now down to minimum. We started our let-down, were picked up by radar in the penetration turn, and my section leader executed the GCA approach. The weather was even worse than expected so my leader, also very anxious to land, just pushed the stick forward when he picked up the runway at minimum, and landed in the middle of the runway, forgetting that I was hanging on his wing.

He suddenly dropped from sight and when I saw him again I knew there was not enough runway for me to land safely. There I was, stranded, low on fuel, without radio so unable to execute another GCA, and the weather totally lousy. With nothing left to do I made a go around and started something like a visual circuit, trying to stay below the clouds and within sight of the runway. That left me clearing the chimneys at 200 feet, with no forward visibility due to rain.

I surprised myself by actually getting into position to start my base turn, pulling around as tight as I dared, anxious to keep the runway in sight. But it was not enough. Turning base I knew I would overshoot. But hell! I didn't feel like trying it all over again with nearly empty tanks. I pulled tighter, but now even the Sabre couldn't take it any more. She stalled out. When I felt the buffetting, I reacted instinctively, just as I had learned in training—throttle forward, wings level to try to avoid the worst. I couldn't push the nose down—I was already down! I simply landed straight ahead on the grass and took a hammering as the Sabre headed across soft wet ground for a small building. Just before I hit it, the nose gear collapsed and I stopped. I was unhurt, and, surprisingly, my Sabre was only slightly damaged. It was soon repaired and flew again.

Jochen Rack

On May 22, 1959, four Sabre 6s (two instructors, two students) left Oldy on a cross-country nav exercise to Bandirma, Turkey. A fuel stop was planned at Marseille-Marignane, but weather there on arrival was poor with heavy rain and winds. The 7900-foot runway was wet, and one Sabre (BB-382, c/n 1612), touching down at the 800-foot mark, was unable to stop before overrunning and splashing into the sea at the far end. The pilot was later noticed diving for his personal belongings!

But the Bandirma mission was still not finished with its woes. Instructor Con Platz and student Lt Ehmling were to run into serious trouble. Platz had decided to terminate the cross-country and return to Oldy on May 25. The weather was still bad as they took off into low cloud, Ehmling leading. A 360° turn followed takeoff, and some pilot disorientation (vertigo) seems to have entered the picture. Platz suddenly felt his aircraft buffetting, and a glance at his instruments showed 510 KIAS and a 90° bank. He shouted a warning to the lead, broke off and managed to recover. But Ehmling didn't reply and he crashed fatally. An investigation concluded that, while attemping to pull up, he likely overstressed his Sabre and it disintegrated.

Sabre 6 JD-107 (c/n 1672) was lost August 26, 1960. On approach, the student pilot inadvertently shut down his engine, couldn't re-light and was too low to eject. He crashed through two barracks, barely missing an old lady in her bed, and into a garden. The pilot died and five others were injured.

Another incident was a bit of a comedy of errors. A Sabre 6 (Express 3) of JG 73 hit jet wash while landing at Oldenburg. He flew through and went around. But another Sabre (Whiskey Lead) was by now ahead of him. He followed Whiskey Lead around for base turn. Then the duty officer in the

In a simple picture, the story of Express 3. JC-107 flew again, eventually making it to Pakistan. (Luftwaffe)

mobile tower noticed that Express 3's gear was not down. He grabbed a mike and yelled, "Aircraft on final, negative gear, overshoot!" Unfortunately he had grabbed the wrong mike and Express 3 blissfully continued to approach.

Now the tower also noticed Express 3's state. The controller grabbed a mike from a student controller and yelled, "Whiskey Lead, overshoot!" Wrong call sign! Whiskey Lead was already down. Then the student advised his master controller as to the correct call signs, and the message "Aircraft on final, overshoot" went out. Too late . . . JC-107 (c/n 1674) was just settling nicely onto its tanks. They tore off and exploded, and JC-107 slid 4000 feet to a stop. The pilot quickly evacuated and the firefighters immediately quelled two small fires. Later, when the aircraft was inspected, the landing gear lever was found in the down position! JC-107 flew again and eventually made it to Pakistan.

August 9, 1961, saw two mid-air collisions with the loss of three Sabres and one pilot. Two JG 72 Sabre 6s collided in turbulent air. One landed, but the pilot of JB-362 (c/n 1641) was ejected upon impact, his chute deploying safely. In the other incident, BB-133 (c/n 986) of WS 10 and JA-121 (c/n 1676) of JG 71, were involved. BB-133 was making a practice instrument let-down

at Oldy when JA-121, flown by Olt Hagen Huelfert, who was doing aerobatics, struck it. Jürgen Kamann aboard BB-133 was inadvertently ejected. He parachuted to safety. But Huelfert was thrown clear without his seat and was killed.

Another weather-related incident, on May 15, 1963, involved JB-248 (c/n 1752) flown by Kurt Kahl of 2./JG 72. Kahl relates:

When we took off at Leck for a practice instrument formation mission, the weather was already poor. On our return to recover, we learned that it had deteriorated more, and that the runway was temporarily closed as an aircraft had just engaged the runway barrier. So we set course for Eggebeck, our alternate, only to find that the weather there was just as bad.

We returned to Leck to hold overhead until the runway was reopened. I was No. 2 and it was understood that we would make single-ship landings out of a GCA approach. As wingman, I would land first, while lead would go around for another GCA if a visual landing wasn't possible. I informed lead that my fuel was getting low.

Visibility was poor in heavy rain as we broke out and picked up the runway. Lead checked with me, and I confirmed that I was doing OK. I concentrated on my landing, expecting lead to take it around. But to my surprise, he landed, and straight in front of me. He kicked up a spray that completely obscured my vision. I braked but without much result. In later years we would know why this happened—I was aquaplaning.

The result was that I veered right and off the runway, hitting the 5000-foot marker. In the soft grass my nose gear collapsed, the Sidewinders tore off and I nearly crashed into the GCA radar van. I shut down, jettisoned my canopy and jumped from the cockpit. As I ran from my Sabre I was suddenly jerked to the ground—in my haste to get away I had forgotten to disconnect from the line attaching me to my seat-pack dinghy!

Kurt Kahl

A. Hueller recalls what led to his ejection on August 23, 1963, from JC-104 (c/n 1648):

We were on an IFR training flight from Pferdsfeld as a two-ship formation. We came out of cloud at 27,000 feet and continued to 40,000, where we practised air combat tactics. For the IFR recovery to base, we were cleared to the holding pattern over the Hahn NDB at 26,000 feet by Rhein Information, then changed frequency to Rhein Control and were cleared to 24,000. Meanwhile, the weather had worsened — several aircraft were in the Hahn Holding, so Spangdahlem Control was unable to clear us for penetration at the EAT.

I notified Spang that our reserves were dwindling. Spang asked that I request another flight level for beginning a let-down, and was cleared from Rhein for 22,000 from where we were cleared by Spang for penetration. When we started down, my fuel state

JB-248 of 2/JG 72. This was Kurt Kahl's aircraft. Note the lifeline hanging down from the cockpit with which Kurt nearly hanged himself! (Luftwaffe)

was about 1500 pounds, and while descending I noticed that my ADF indication was unreliable. In the penetration turn, I changed my radio compass to the Pferdsfeld NDB which I received clearly with a steady needle indication. My ADF now showed a heading of 230° to the beacon, a deviation of about 47° to the correct final approach course. I put this down to drift during the holding patterns we had flown, where my ADF appeared unrealiable.

Now, at 4000 feet my identification was identical to that of my wing man. We contacted our GCA and were told to continue to Pferdsfeld NDB at 4000. We seemed to fly much longer compared to other approaches, and since we were in clouds and I could not determine our exact position I declared an emergency. I also switched my IFF to emergency. Now Bitburg tower called, stating they had us by DF, giving me a steer to their base. At the same time, Spang Control also came in and advised that they had us positively on radar and would hand us over to Pferdsfeld GCA. But Pferdsfeld could not accept us as we were not on their scope and they did not yet have an IFF decoder. This was heard by Hahn GCA, which called up and gave us headings to Hahn. Our position was given as 23NM north of Hahn.

After I turned on the given heading I lost radio contact with GCA and could not re-establish it, even on the emergency frequency. So I signalled my wing man to assume lead and we changed positions. I was now really worried about my fuel as all this was happening down low.

We made another turn, so I expected us to be positively under the guidance of Hahn GCA. My leader signalled to drop the landing gear. I checked my speed—it was too high for the gear. I

hesitated momentarily, just long enough to lose sight of No. 1. I caught sight of him again and took position on his wing. Now he pulled up and made a go-around. I tried to follow but lost him again in the rain clouds. To avoid collision, I turned right and tried to climb out of cloud. My fuel was now 300-400 pounds.

I broke into the clear at 9000 and tried finding a hole for a possible visual landing, but there was no chance. My reserves were now burned up and I decided to abandon my aircraft. I ejected near Bernkastel, landing in a potato field, my Sabre crashing into a forest. A farmer got me to a telephone, and a helicopter soon arrived to take me to Spangdahlem. There I was given a medical check, found to be OK and flown by chopper back to Pferdsfeld.

A. Heuller

Of all the Luftwaffe Sabre incidents, one from the annals of JG 73 may be the most humorous. On June 7, 1962, two Sabres were en route Pferdsfeld-Sylt. After they had crossed the coast up north, they decided to continue over water at low level. In one turn, the wing man (BB-174) overshot his leader and came over the beach. On a sand dune in his flight path was a small hut, which turned out to be an outhouse. Before he could pull up, the pilot had driven straight through the outhouse with his Sabre. Unfortunately the "facility" was occupied and though unhurt, the fellow inside was caught literally with his pants down, much to the amusement of all who heard of his plight that day. The Sabre was slightly damaged, but met its doom later on as YA-041 in a yet more amazing incident.

Reinhold Puchert, then an instructor at WS 10, related an incident of November 11, 1963, with JA-305 (c/n 1797): "We were on a high-altitude mission with four Sabres (two instructors, two pilots). During pre-flight, I had found that my left slat did not pop out normally when I pushed it in. The ground crew inspected it and found it acceptable. My takeoff and climb had been normal but in a tight turn my aircraft suddenly snapped into an uncontrollable left roll. In spite of full right aileron I could not correct this, and I went into a wild spiralling dive. Finally, by reducing speed, I got things straightened around. Theo Deyerling, my fellow instructor pilot (IP), came alongside to observe and confirmed that the left slat would not extend.

"I wanted to test the Sabre's stalling characteristics, but feared to, as the cloud base was low, and I didn't want to risk a low-altitude spin. So I carefully reduced speed to see how the Sabre would behave in the landing configuration. I found that control was good down to about 30 knots above normal approach speed with only the right slat extended. I remembered this while approaching to land at Oldy, and all went well. The only snag was that landing fast meant that the Sabre's brakes were sure to overheat. As expected, the hot brakes were fading and I went into the barrier, but it caught the main gear on one side only, thus turning the plane sideways. Fortunately, my speed was already low, so there was only minor damage.

On June 18, 1964, Lt Prinz of 713 Squadron flying JA-338 (c/n 1697) was on an instructor pilot's training mission. Flying wing, he had to chase his IP through traffic circuits and touch-and-goes at Oldy. Upon landing, Prinz felt that he had touched down long, so he added power to start a go-around. His next impression was that he had insufficient runway to get off again. He chopped the power and started to get on the brakes. Then a tire burst and he engaged the barrier (the old net and chain type). Being now one-wing-low, the barrier was deflected on the low side by the drop tank. The Sabre swung violently around and the wing was torn from the fuselage. The latter rolled over and fire erupted. Prinz, still strapped in, was lying face down in a puddle of burning kerosene. Rescue personnel quickly freed him, though he was se-

Olt Prinz's Sabre 6, or remains thereof. (Oldenburg fire brigade via Willi Hahn)

verely burned. After extensive surgery, Prinz recovered and went on to fly the F-104.

JC-104 (c/n 1782) returned to Pferdsfeld with engine trouble on July 16, 1964. As the pilot set up for a simulated flame-out landing pattern, the cockpit filled with smoke. He realized that the best decision was to eject and did so. The Sabre crashed behind the crowded airmen's mess, sending everyone under the tables. The canopy landed close to a group of airmen walking along outside, prompting one witty fellow to complain, "These days they throw just about everything at you!" Nobody was hurt in the whole incident.

On August 27, 1964, "Joe" Detzer took off from Oberpfaffenhofen in YA-041 (c/n 1604). The aircraft was allocated to E-Stelle 61 at Manching and this was an acceptance flight following overhaul at Dornier. Immediately, there was undercarriage trouble, with the nose gear stuck half way. After recycling, the main gear also indicated unsafe. After discussion with the ground, Detzer intended to belly land at nearby Fürstenfeldbruck. But a further visual check indicated gear doors extended, so Detzer decided to eject. He went out safely at 7000 feet, except for a spinal injury often associated with ejection.

Detzer had not shut down the engine before ejecting, and now his Sabre, running at about 85 per cent with lots

BB-161 had been target-towing the day of this mishap. As the pilot came in to drop the flag he lost power so had to put his machine down rather smartly beside the runway at Oldenburg. A rare colour scheme for a Mark 6 — all natural with full unit markings. (Luftwaffe)

BB-383, a Sabre 6 of WS 10, has a drink of sea water at Marseille-Marignane on May 22, 1959. One of the more laughable scenes of Sabre indignation. (Luftwaffe)

of fuel, and in a well-trimmed gentle right turn, began circling Oberpfaffenhofen. As it circled, its bank angle would increase and some lift would be lost. Then the nose would drop a bit, the plane would speed up and, naturally, climb until the cycle began again. But each cycle left it a bit lower, and it was clear that on one of its dives it would crash.

Everyone came out to watch what

JB-110 stalled out during a formation takeoff at Leck on December 5, 1963. Amazingly, this pile of junk was later rebuilt and put on display at Oldenburg. (Luftwaffe)

April 12, 1961, the pilot of BB-269 c/n 1779 used his seat to escape after things went awry. (via Jack Forbes)

was a fascinating demonstration of aerodynamic stability. If only the display were a more harmless one—everyone feared that the Sabre might crash with tragic results. Fortunately, when the moment arrived, it dived steeply into a field beyond the airport perimeter. The whole drama had taken only about 10 minutes.

Early on, the Luftwaffe Sabres had

little engine trouble, but when they became ground attack aircraft, engine failures and fires increased noticeably. Several losses were caused by turbine bucket failures. Of course, it was never known whether failures were caused by the increased stresses put on the engine by the new kind of flying, or simply by aging equipment. However, the loss of three Sabres at Deci in four days during September 1965 may speak for itself. On the 21st, JB-104 (c/n 1791) crashed. The pilot ejected after engine failure and fire coming out the tailpipe. Cause: broken bucket. Two days later JC-367 (c/n 1785) caught fire. The pilot ejected but a severe arm injury prevented him from getting out of his C-2 seat and he did not survive. Another case of a broken bucket.

Next day a flypast was held to honour the dead pilot, and JB-371 (c/n 1813), one of the participating Sabres, had engine failure. The pilot preferred not to eject over a nearby town and made a belly landing at base, severely damaging the aircraft (which is today on display at Oldy).

June 29, 1965, a JaboG. 42 pilot had

an unusual experience. Flying JC-368 (c/n 1780), he had an engine failure near Stuttgart and ejected. He landed in a cornfield and the farmer's wife immediately took him to task for damaging her crop. He eluded her attempts to beat him up and made his way to the US Army detachment at Stuttgart. The friendly Americans put him on an L-20 Beaver to take him home to Pferdsfeld, but it had closed for the day, apparently being unaware of the L-20 coming in. So the army pilot put down in a private field at Domberg, near Pferdsfeld. Here he managed to nose over in the poor light, giving the Sabre pilot his second good fright of the day.

E-Stelle Sabre c/n 1644 bearing the unit's YA code. In later re-numbering, YA-044 became 0106. (via Georges Van Belleghem)

Special Uses
Besides regular air force units, there were some other operators of the Luftwaffe Sabres, one being "Erprobungsstelle der Luftwaffe 61"—E-Stelle, for short—the German test establishment at Oberpfaffenhofen, with some activity later at Manching, near Ingolstadt, where AG 51 was based. These were the YA-coded Sabres, used as chase planes, aerial targets for pilot proficiency, and on other trials and tests.

Messerschmitt also conducted operations at Manching, using Sabres in association with the F-104 program, and as chase planes for their VJ-101 VTOL research program developed by EWR, of which Messerschmitt was a partner. These Sabres were coded KE. Some survived long enough to be renumbered with four numerals, e.g. KE-104 became 0113.

In the mid-sixties the Bundeswehr required towed aerial targets for anti-aircraft gunnery practice. A civil con-

Two E-Stelle Sabres showing different ways of applying the unit numbers. (Peter Nolde, via Peter Keating)

A line-up of Condor Sabres at Westerland on the Island of Sylt. They bear the original colour scheme. (Hans Meinking)

A Sabre flies chase on the VJ-101. (MBB)

tractor, Condor Flugdienst GmbH, was awarded the job. Condor is actually a subsidiary of Lufthansa, but set up a special department for the target towing work.

Sabres, just become surplus, could nicely do the work as fast tow ships, and two (D-9522 and D-9523) were modified by Dornier in 1966. Four were added in June 1967 and, after D-9522 was lost in an accident, a final example was acquired in June 1968. Operatións were based at Westerland Air Base on Sylt, a gunnery base during the Sabre's heyday. Pilots and technicians were an independent organization, totally on their own, far to the north of Condor's Frankfurt HQ.

Mods to the Condor Sabres called for a target launcher atop the left wing, and new radios and other equipment for operating the system. Towing equipment was made in Los Angeles by DELMAR Engineering. The main part of the system was the lightweight RADOP (Radar/Optical) plastic-coated target (FK460A and FK460A-N) with internal radar reflectors made by EMF. The reflectors multiplied incoming radar signals to simulate a four-engined bomber on the radar scope. Detection was possible at 32 km by a fighter and 240

D-9522, ex BB-171, shows the complete DELMAR tow target installation. The winch is below the left wing, target and launcher above. This Sabre was destroyed at Westerland on September 19, 1967. (Hans-Dieter Slawig)

Pilot's view of the launcher and tow target. (Hans Meinking)

313

Condor's D-9541 after the bird strike incident related in the text. (Condor)

km from a ground station. System installation took just 30 minutes. The target could be trailed 8000 m behind the tow plane and reeled in and out on 1-mm piano wire, using a winch powered by a freewheeling propeller. Take-up of the full stretch of wire was a 20-minute operation.

Live firing exercises were conducted over the sea in a restricted zone and at Deci. Delivery of the first Sabre to Westerland was on September 27, 1966, with

A Sabre 6 of 713 Squadron formates with an F-104G Starfighter, its successor. The 104 was on a test flight from Manching, near Ingolstadt, and bears the Messerschmitt code "KE". (Luftwaffe)

operations commencing October 1. Initially heading the Condor target tow group was Hans Meinking.

Of the six Condor Sabres at Sylt, one crashed January 9, 1968, the last Sabre ever lost in Germany (D-9522 c/n 1601). Fifteen minutes after takeoff pressurization was lost in the 167-gal. drop tanks. The pilot returned to base, but after the break he could not advance power beyond idle. Realizing that he could not make the runway, he turned towards an uninhabited area and finished his let-down via Martin-Baker. Later investigation revealed the cause of the crash: failure of the main fuel control.

June 15, 1970, pilot Heinz Buhrmann had just lifted off in D-9541 at Westerland when his Sabre ingested a sea gull. Too low to eject, he had to

push his nose down and get back onto the runway. He braked hard but overshot the barrier before tower people could deploy it. With engine shut down, full flaps, brakes burning and tires blown, Buhrmann finally came to a stop 80 metres beyond the concrete. The compressor blades were damaged by the gull; starter generator crushed; tail pipe deformed by overheating; right flap, left main gear fairing and brakes damaged; and both tires and wheels ruined, all in a matter of moments, but much more was saved by the skill of the experienced pilot.

Interestingly, the G-meter on Buhrmann's Sabre showed +7, −3Gs. Yet no structural damage was caused in this abrupt post-takeoff deceleration. After an engine change and other repairs D-9541 was soon back flying.

When Condor replaced its Sabres in April 1974 with G.91s, they were ferried to Fassberg and handed over to TSLW 3 (Technical School 3), and were still there 10 years later, being used as instructional airframes, kept in excellent condition though never flown.

Condor Sabres

c/n	Reg'n	Luft. Reg'n.	Notes
1601	D-9522	BB-171	w/o 9-1-68
1784	D-9523	JB-234	
1600	D-9538	BB-170	
1603	D-9539	BB-173	
1666	D-9540	BB-185	
1710	D-9541	JB-240	
1740	D-9542	JB-103,BB-266	replacement for D-9522

Sabres around the World

Service in Italy

The Canadair F-86 was the mainstay of Italy's air defences beginning in the mid-fifties. L'Aeronautica Militare Italiana (AMI) received its first of 179 Sabres sometime in late 1954 at its Pratica di Mare base. These were assigned to the 4th Aerobrigata, replacing its Vampires. The 4th was operational on Sabres by the summer of 1956, and that same year formed a Sabre aerobatic team, "Cavallino Rampante" (Rearing Pony), which made its debut at the Paris Air Show that year. In 1957 the 2nd Aerobrigata re-equipped with Sabres. Another aerobatic team, "Lanceri Neri" (Black Lancers), followed in 1958, then a

Italian Sabre Units		
Aerobrigata	*Gruppo*	*Squadriglie*
4	9	95,96,97,98
	10	84,85,86,91
	12	73,74,89,90
2	8	92,93
	13	77,78
	14	21,210,242
—	313	for aerobatic training

permanent national team, "Frecce Tricolori" (Tri-coloured Arrows).

The Canadair Sabre served the numerous AMI squadrons within the Aerobrigata until about the time that the other NATO air forces began modernizing. For the AMI, first came the Fiat G.91 lightweight fighter, which replaced the Sabres in the 2nd Aerobrigata in 1960. In the following three years the 4th re-equipped with F-86K all-weather interceptors and F-104Gs. The Canadair Sabres had been used mainly in training at home and on NATO exercises, and in the ever-popular aerobatic role. Five, though, actually got into a combat theatre. In 1963 these aircraft were sent to the Congo to support UN peace-keeping efforts there, but were actually operated by the Philippine contingent and were fitted out for the air-to-ground role.

The Philippine Air Force Sabres were operated by the 9th Tactical Fighter (Limbas) Squadron-77 personnel under LtCol Jose L. Rancudo. Besides the CO, there were 12 other pilots: Maj Primivito P Mital; Capts Isidro B.

Agunod, Gerardo C. Protacio, Luis J. Diano, Ismael A. Sabarre and Arsenio R. Silva; Lts Isidro S. Calleja, Rogelio J. Censon, and Jose L. de Leon; and 2Lts Edilberto C. Balasso, Tereso J. Isleta and Roberto A. de Peralta. Col Joel R. Hinlo recently explained the role of the 9th TFS: "The contingent operated from February 11, 1963 upon its arrival in the Congo to its departure on June 23, 1963. The unit performed reconnaissance flights, and as a 'show of force' which was necessary as a deterrent measure. The PAF pilots flew their missions for the sector command, covering over 2800 km of road and railroads, and making force demonstrations over hundreds of villages within the operational radius of the aircraft."

AMI Sabre 4s were provided from surplus stock once the RAF began equipping with Hunters. They carried interim USAF markings for ferry purposes, as they were initially funded by the US. This one is seen at Stansted. (Tony Breese via Peter Keating)

The "Lanceri Neri" aero team operated in 1958 with the 2nd Aerobrigata. The fuselage and upper wings/stabilizers paint scheme was black ("Black Lancers") while the under-wings/stabilizers were in Italian tricolours.

19571 of the "Frecce Tricolori", the famed AMI aerobatic team, while attending the air show at Le Bourget, June 16, 1963. (Peter Keating)

Traffic Problems: AMI Prangs

A number of spectacular mishaps involved Italian Sabres. This, of course, was to be expected—dozens of incidents, including many a serious one. On December 1, 1956, 19547 was on a gunnery mission from Pratica di Mare. Near Spalato, Yugoslavia, the pilot ran into a low-fuel emergency. He chose to make a landing on a highway. The Canadair tech rep's summary describes what followed: "After successful wheels-down landing, the aircraft rolled up an incline and was faced with an oncoming bus. Pilot succeeded in getting aircraft airborne and in clearing top of bus, but continued for several 100 yards before striking the auto-strada, tearing off the right wing and aft fuselage, and killing a male cyclist. The severe impact caused the ejection of the pilot who landed uninjured some 500 feet from the wreckage. Aircraft subsequently exploded."

June 26, 1957, 19555 was in a two-ship from Pratica di Mare over the Tyrrhenian Sea. The USS *Forrestal,* one of the USN's major aircraft carriers, was on manoeuvres below and

The "Frecce Tricolori" in neat formation high above rugged Italian terrain. (SMA)

Formation landing by "Cavallino Rampante". (SMA)

(Left) Two photos of AMI Sabres of the 4th Aerobrigata. The close-up photo shows the "Cavallino Rampante" marking on the fin. Note use of original RCAF serial numbers near the tail. (Stato Maggiore Aeronautics)

Formerly XB961, this Sabre 4 is seen in 2nd Aerobrigata code numbers. (SMA)

An unpainted Sabre of the 2nd Aerobrigata, 13th Gruppo. Seen at Cameri, July 14, 1965. (Gordon Macadie)

her F9F-8 Cougars were on patrol above. The AMI Sabres caught two Cougars and bounced them, whereupon they in turn were bounced by more Cougars. In the melée, 19555 collided with a Cougar at 28,000 feet. Both fighters went down and neither pilot escaped. A far worse mid-air occurred October 22, 1958, near Anzio when 19830 collided with a British European Airways Viscount. All 31 aboard the airliner perished. The pilot of the AMI Sabre was hurled from his aircraft during the collision and survived with serious injuries. This was the most disastrous incident ever involving a Canadair Sabre.

On April 16, 1958, AMI Sabre 19851 of the 2nd Aerobrigata was at work on the air-to-ground gunnery range at Brindisi. It crashed, apparently a case of the pilot pushing things too far. The tech rep later reported that on the first pass the Sabre was "so low that the target was blown over by the jet wake." A non-fatal Cat.A at Brindisi involved 19722 on September 23, 1959. While on a target run, the Sabre ingested a ricocheting .50 slug and flamed out, forcing the pilot to punch out.

In summarizing the significance of the Canadair F-86 in the Italian Air

Force, historian Claudio Tatangelo notes: "The Sabre was indeed one of the pillars of the NATO program to upgrade Allied air forces, and it allowed the best Western fighter of its day to be made widely available to NATO air forces. This was a particular leap forward for the AMI, the arrival

An AMI Sabre 4 in UN (ONU) markings. This aircraft was destined for use in the Congo, but crashed while training on March 25, 1960, flying into the ground a half mile short of the runway. Note that 19695 carried the 167 gallon tanks. This was one of the few times that they were used on a Mark 2 or 4. In this case, they may have been fitted for a ferry flight to the Congo. (via Roger Lindsay)

of this new swept-wing generation bringing with it not only improved defensive posture but also new levels of professional performance in many levels of activity from training (brought to its ultimate with the famous national aerobatic team) to logistics, and from tactical doctrine to the organization of fighter units themselves.''

Greece, Turkey and Yugoslavia

Canadair Sabre 2s were used by the Greeks (Royal Hellenic Air Force) and Turks from 1953 to 1966 or so. In the Greek Air Force they equipped 341 and 343 Squadrons of 112 Combat Wing, and later 111 Combat Wing. In 1958 the Greeks formed a Sabre aerobatic team, the Hellenic Flame, using Mk. 2s. In 1961, 343 Squadron re-equipped with F-86D all-weather fighters. The Mk. 2s were finally withdrawn from service on January 4, 1966. Most of the Sabre 2s going to Greece and Turkey were low-time aircraft with 300 hours or less on their airframes. Many were to become quite high-time aircraft by the time they crashed or were phased out. Examples of some which crashed are: 19121 (1276 hours), 19133 (1070), 19142 (1676), 19153 (1879), 19203 (1307), 19213 (1783), 19217 (1897), 19248 (1217), 19293 (1553), 19338 (1837), 19380 (1910) and 19446 (2309 hours). Few RCAF Sabres reached airframe times anywhere near these.

Also under Mutual Aid, a quantity of Sabre 4s was handed over to Yugoslavia in the mid-fifties. At the time the USAF was training the air force there and had already supplied straight-wing F-84s. The Sabres were based at Batajnacica, about 20 miles from Belgrade. The first ones to arrive after overhaul at Bristol in the UK were brought in by USAF pilots. One came in on final with wheels up, so somebody in the tower rushed out with a Very pistol to fire a red warning flare. The problem was he fired a green flare, and the Sabre made an uneventful wheels-up landing. Little is known about the service life of the Yugoslav Sabres, and to this day the country operates on a basis of strict secrecy as far as its military affairs go. It is known, however, that several Yugoslav Canadair Sabres were resold as surplus in the late seventies, and ended up refitted and operating with the Honduras Air Force.

Dan Alton was involved in the RCAF support for the Greek and Turkish Sabres and T-33s. He looks back to those days:

The Sabre aid program to Greece and Turkey started in 1953 when a team of RCAF pilots and technical staff visited these countries to train a core of pilots and ground crew. This was largely a conversion activity since both countries already flew such aircraft as the F-84. The first one or two groups of Sabres

Pilots Bob Simmons (OFU) and Don Simmons (CEPE) with a Sabre 2 at Cartierville just before Bob ferried overseas for the Greeks. This is the first-ever Canadian production Sabre. It pranged in Greece on August 22, 1955, having logged only 256:35 hours. (Canadair Ltd.)

Greek aerobatic Sabre 2 at Le Bourget, June 16, 1963. (Peter Keating)

were delivered by RCAF pilots, the Greeks and Turks flying in the rest.

Canada, through the RCAF, assumed responsibility for logistics support for the over 200 aircraft eventually delivered. This continued for about 10 years. It included supplying everything from engines to bits and pieces of all kinds. Two Canadair tech reps and two from GE were based in Greece and Turkey in the early days of the program to assist and advise the RHAF and TAF on aircraft and gun-firing maintenance. In due course, tech rep support was reduced to one man from Canadair in each country, and they were part of our RCAF logistics support team.

In early 1953, S/L Murray Donaldson was posted to Greece and S/L Matt Dickinson to Turkey. Within a few months, I followed Murray, and WO2 Simmonds joined us in early 1954 to complete our staff of seven. Our base was at Greek AFHQ in downtown Athens.

Most of the early activity was at Elefsis, the first Greek Sabre base, located about 20 miles west of Athens (later, also at Tanagra, north of Athens), and at the supply depot near the municipal airport of Helenekon. We were attached to the Canadian Embassy in a loose way and used their facilities in importing some food and liquor. Most importantly, this arrangement gave us some protection in case of emergency. This we appreciated, as most had families in Greece.

The program in both countries was administered by the Chief of Materiel at AFHQ in Ottawa, and we reported directly to G/C MacKinnon. The Embassy diplomatic bag was used for correspondence.

Aircraft maintenance, especially of the weapons system, presented major problems in the early stages, as both air forces were in the process of developing up-to-date training schools with the help of the USAF, which had a large contingent in each country. Parts were also sometimes a problem. Still, it was keeping the squadrons at the NATO combat readiness level of 80 percent of squadron establishment that was the real problem. The main single problem here was the questionable reliability of the APG 30 radar for the gunsight. The inexperience of Greek and Turkish technicians on the equipment was also a factor, as was to be expected.

Murray was transferred to Germany in 1955 to assist the Luftwaffe in equipping with Sabres, and I replaced him. Upon my return to AFHQ in 1957, the NATO Mutual Aid Program was one of my responsibilities, and I maintained contact with the liaison officers until I retired in 1964. Here are a few things that come to mind in looking back on the program: the friendly and positive approach of Greek officers and others at all levels. We got along very well, and they appreciated Canada's substantial help in providing the Sabres and logistics support. We were often complimented on how we worked as an *ex officio* part of their support system. We were there to help keep the Sabres combat ready, but they were responsible for the level achieved. They were also pleased to see that we had no political agenda, so posed no threat as to the way they chose to operate their program.

Greece, being traditionally a country of classical scholars, had little in technical education. To jump from classical to technical in the 1950s posed a real challenge for them. The Turks, too, had little experience with technology. It is a credit to them that they met the challenge as well as they did regarding the Sabres.

Dan Alton

Phil Perry was part of the small technical and flying contingent which the RCAF sent to Turkey with the first Sabres. He writes: "F/O Danny Kaye and Danny Ray and myself spent about a month in Turkey, where we were to

(Left) Phil Perry (nearest cockpit) with a group of his Turkish students. (Below) A festive mood was the order of the day when the first ex-RCAF Sabre 2s arrived in Turkey, July 17, 1954. (via P.S. Perry, DND PL81135)

Sampling of RHAF Sabre Mishaps					
19121	6-9-60	Rudder case came adrift. Forced landing at base. Suspect bird strike at 420K.	19271	1-11-55	Pilot landed short, then ejected and survived.
19133	1-8-60	Stalled on go-around and crashed.	19344	12-5-57	Severe porpoising. Pilot kept bashing head on canopy and finally ejected.
19209	21-3-56	Crashed into sea with 19423.			
19213	15-1-62	Ejected after fire started in wheel well.	19349	12-5-57	Overran with 19403 and destroyed among rocks in dried-up river bed.
19228	15-4-61	Pilot could not eject in emergency. Climbed from cockpit and struck by fin. Pilot later died after rescue from sea.	19378	3-6-55	Flamed out on final and crashed short.
			19390	9-4-58	Hit mountain south of Corinth along with 19434.

check out some Turkish pilots and train some ground crew on the Sabre. Our task was not an easy one, as there was a lack of equipment and a language barrier. However, after a lot of effort and robbing of parts, we were able to provide Danny Kaye with sufficient aircraft to get a dozen or so pilots checked out.

"The Turks had an engineering officer who drove around in a motorcycle with a side-car. I can still remember him roaring up to the hangar yelling, 'Philip, come quick,' and I would jump into the side-car and we would go tearing off across the field to the flight line. He didn't give a damn for anyone or anything. His only interest was to solve a problem and get the aircraft serviceable—to hell with the traffic.

"Our little contingent worked very hard under difficult conditions in Turkey. The food gave us all dysentery, but the good old Americans came to our rescue, providing US rations which we prepared in our rooms.

"When we finally came to leave, it was a pitiful sight. We had robbed all the aircraft to keep the last one flying, and even it was just about finished, with worn-out brakes. The poor EO had tears in his eyes as we said goodbye. He had no idea what he was going to do now! A few months later, the Turks set up a proper FTTU and finally got some spares to keep the Sabres flying."

Many of the Turkish pilots were trained under the NATO plan in Canada by the RCAF. One was Ziya Ertug, who had joined the air force in 1955. He did some basic training in Turkey on the Miles Magister, T-6 and a Turkish trainer, the Ujur. In 1956 he arrived in Canada, going first to London for language training for six

months. Next he went to Moose Jaw on Harvards, then Gimli on T-33s. He received his wings at Gimli and returned to Turkey for his posting. In September 1957 he was training on Sabres at Chatham. After three months he again went home, this time to a posting on Sabres. The TAF operated three Sabre squadrons, Nos. 141, 142 and 143, with bases at Eskisehir (about halfway between Ankara and Istanbul) and Merzifon (east of Ankara near Amasya). Ertug recalls

that other Sabre training was done at Izmir (a training base on the Aegean Sea), Incirlik (a gunnery base near Adana on the Mediterranean), Diyar-

Turks in the rear, Canucks in front. These RCAF pilots brought Turkey its first Sabres. F/O Kaye stayed on a bit to do some basic flying instruction. Seen in front are Sam Firth, Jerry King, Bob Ayres, Danny Kaye, Jim Fiander and Bill Hind. Ron Fentiman didn't show—he had to belly land in Italy when his engine packed up. (via D. Kaye)

Canadair Sabre of Turkey's aerobatic team. (via Ed Norsworthy)

Sampling of TAF Sabre Mishaps					
19120	1-9-60	Retracted gear too early on takeoff.	19192	25-7-57	Crash landing after fire on board.
19129	2-3-60	Both wings shed during pull-out from dive.	19194	9-6-60	Mid-air with 19236 over Black Sea.
			19248	3-5-58	Disintegrated on gunnery run.
19142	8-8-60	Fuel exhaustion on landing.	19337	3-5-55	Destroyed when struck by careening
19160	29-9-59	Crashed into mountain during test flight.			F-84 at Eskisehir.
19180	10-4-56	Ejected at 9000 feet. Seat hung up in parachute. Pilot OK but seat suffered minor damage!	19410	12-2-58	Compressor stall, crashed on landing.

bakir (an F-84 base in eastern Turkey) and Murted (near Ankara).

Ertug notes that of the three fighters in use by the TAF, the Sabre was best liked and safest. The F-84 was prone to engine failure and in-flight explosions. The F-100 was an excellent fighter, but not quite the pilot's favourite. Ertug later left the air force to fly for Turkish Airlines, then emigrated to the US and finally Canada. He flew briefly with the reserves at St. Hubert while pursuing a career in maintenance with Air Canada.

Republic of South Africa

The F-86 served with the South African Air Force, beginning in the Korean War. At that time South Africa had No.2 "Flying Cheetah" Squadron in Korea, initially flying F-51Ds, and operating under the 18th FBW of the USAF. In early 1953 No.2 re-equipped with F-86Fs, their fins brightly emblazoned with the SAAF tricolour. When the war ended, No.2, no doubt reluc-

tantly, returned its Sabres to the USAF and went home to fly Vampires.

The SAAF realized that it would soon need a Vampire replacement, and after evaluation of available types, the Canadair Sabre 6 was chosen. In February 1956 Capt Larry Eager, Capt Ronnie Nienaber, Lt Edwin Pienaar and another pilot arrived at Chatham to take the Sabre OTU (Course 50). Meanwhile 34 Sabre 6s were quickly being readied at Cartierville for shipment by sea to South Africa and assembly at No.1 Air Depot. They arrived in August and the first, No.350, made its first flight September 4 with Eager at the controls. Nos.1 and 2 Squadrons were equipped, and for the next few years the Sabre was South Africa's primary interceptor. Both Squadrons were based at Waterkloof.

Soon after the Sabres entered service, the SAAF ordered Dassault Mirages for 2 Squadron. It then passed its Sabres on to No.1 in late 1963. In 1967 No.1 moved to Pietersburg, continuing in the air defence business, but it too converted to the Mirage. In 1975 the SAAF withdrew the Sabres from their primary fighter role and reassigned them to OTU status with No.85

Advanced Flying School at Pietersburg, where they operated alongside Mirages and Impalas.

By the late seventies, South Africa's Sabres were growing weary and, of course, there was a shortage of spares for both airframe and Orenda 14. Inevitably, the fighter pilots of the SAAF said goodbye to their beloved Sabres. All remaining examples were grounded on October 10, 1979. On January 12, 1981, a deal was struck between South Africa and a broker whereby 10 SAAF Sabres were sold for some £110,000 Sterling. These were shipped to the United States, where several were soon airworthy again. The Sabres involved were Nos.350, 352, 359, 363, 365, 371, 373, 378, 380 and 382. This left seven Sabres in South Africa: 361 (SAAF Museum), 367 (SAAF Museum at Swartkop), 369 (AFB Waterkloof), 372 (SAAF Museum, AFS Snake Valley), 381 (SAAF Museum, AFS Snake Valley), 383 (Kempton Park Technical School) and 358 (AFB Pietersburg).

Before being camouflaged, the SAAF Sabres were in natural finish. These are seen near Johannesburg. (via Jack Forbes)

No.1 Squadron emblem on a Sabre 6. (SAAF Museum)

Sampling of SAAF Sabre Mishaps

352	24-5-57	Scraped tail pipe on landing.
355	16-10-58	Hit flag during air-to-air firing.
363	20-3-59	Slow roll above limiting roll speed. Twisted airframe.
351	18-4-59	Collided in formation with 358.
383	13-11-59	Damaged by ricochet.
380	21-11-59	Bird strike.
376	16-8-60	Flame-out. Aircraft not refuelled.
371	17-10-60	Dropped rockets on runway accidentally.
350	14-8-61	Struck tree low flying.
371	26-3-62	Damaged in thunderstorm.

Detail of an SAAF Sabre 6 speed brake. (SAAF Museum)

(Above) The Sabre in all its classic beauty, seen here in SAAF markings. (Below) Seven SAAF Sabre 6s ready for work. In 1980 the SAAF finally retired these historic fighters. (Right) Another view of a South African ''Sword''. (Herman Potgieter)

Sabres for Israel

In 1955 Canadair conducted sales talks with Israel, which was interested in a new fighter. Israel was quickly sold on the Sabre 6 as *the* airplane for its needs and a deal was struck for 24. At one point Al Lilly was walking around with a cheque from the Israelis in his pocket for over a million dollars!

Canadair sent Jack MacDonnell, one of its key tech reps, to Israel in anticipation of the IAF deal, and Israeli personnel were soon visiting Canadair. The aircraft were quickly

readied and at least some were painted. Then, faster than the deal had been made, it came to a halt. The Suez war had broken out with Egypt's nationalizing of the canal in 1956. Israel and Egypt were at war, with France and England also involved. The Canadian government, under Prime Minister Louis St. Laurent and its cautious Minster of External Affairs, Lester B. Pearson, wanted no direct Canadian involvement in the Suez fray and promptly squelched the Sabres-to-Israel deal.

In a December 19, 1956, press release, Canadair noted, "In October, delivery of 24 of them (Sabres) to the Israeli government was temporarily deferred by the Canadian government because of trouble in the Middle East." The Sabres never were delivered. The Israelis could hardly put up with delays and quickly re-equipped with French Mystère 4s, functional if less glamorous airplanes than the Sabre 6. The Israelis would make the most of them, while Canadair was forced to eat a bit of crow.

Latin American Sales
Throughout the fifties, Canadair marketed the Sabre in Latin America. Air forces there were just beginning to rebuild, to modernize with their first jets. At the time most were clapped-out operations, flying wartime aircraft, mainly P-51s, but also such a mixed bag as P-38s, P-47s and Corsairs. By 1950 a few F-80s, Meteors and Vampires were beginning to turn up, but major Latin American powers like Argentina, Brazil and Venezuela wanted more current equipment.

Sabre 6 in Israeli Air Force markings, seen at Cartierville. The IAF Sabres were never delivered. Just as well for the Arabs! (George Fuller)

For its part, Canadair assigned Al Lilly the Latin American market, and for several years he travelled throughout the region promoting Canadair products, mainly the F-86. Of course, wherever he went the air force generals were most impressed by the Sabre 6, but Canadair was up against heavy odds in this part of the world, where American influence was all. More than once Lilly's efforts were squelched by powerful US influence. Argentina ordered 36 Sabre 6s, then US representatives there killed the deal by offering refurbished F-86s at give-away prices. How could Argentina refuse? It didn't, and 28 "F"'s were delivered in 1960. There was a similar experience in Venezuela, which received 22 "F"'s. One sale, though, did work out. Dealing with Col Ospina, Lilly was able to complete arrangements to sell Colombia six Sabre 6s. At the time each Sabre was selling for about $300,000, but the package deal to the Colombians totalled some $3,000,000. Ospina sent seven

pilots to Cartierville to check out on the Sabre (these were Capts Rafael Millan, Gilberto Boada and Pablo Duran, 1Lts Juan Gonzalez, Luis Kilby and Leopoldo Piedrahita, and 2Lt Oscar Acero). Several ground crew also came along to do the Sabre ground school and two FAC C-54s, needed to fly personnel, spares, and support equipment back to Colombia also arrived. While the training was going on, Canadair did some major overhaul work on the C-54s.

On May 31, 1956, Col Carlos Uribe accepted the FAC Sabres, and on June 4 they took off for Palanquero, near Bogotá, arriving there June 8. The Sabre then formed 1° Escuadron de Caza-Bombardiero, operating alongside F-80s, A-26s, a lone P-47 and T-33s.

Attrition soon began to bite into the Sabre unit, with the first Cat.A crash occurring in September 1956. In 1970 the FAC began re-equipping with Mirage 5s, and the Sabre era in Colombia became history. During that time, Jim Fitzpatrick was Canadair's field service representative in Colombia and Al Paddon represented Orenda.

Jim Fitzpatrick had joined Canadair

Colombian pilots seen with their Sabre 6s at Cartierville in 1956. (Canadair Ltd.)

The surviving FAC Sabre 6, preserved in Colombia. (via Dan Hagedorn)

straight out of high school in 1951, initially working his way up in the electrician's trade. In time he was promoted into sales and servicing, and when the Colombian deal came up, he accompanied the FAC Sabres on the ferry flight, staging through Greenville (South Carolina), Opalocha (Florida) and Guantanamo (Cuba). When his C-54 arrived at Palanqero he was met by "a beautiful sight"—one of the brand new Sabre 6s had landed short and the gear had been driven up through the wings. So it was straight to work, thanks to Lt Piedrahita!

The Canadair MRP (mobile repair party), of which Fitzpatrick was a part, stayed in Colombia from June to September 1956. Afterwards Fitzpatrick had various duties, including the demonstrations of the Sabre 6 to the Swiss. He returned to Colombia from 1959 to 1961 to keep the FAC Sabres flying. During this period each aircraft

One of the several Honduran Canadair Sabre 4s. These aircraft may still be in service. (N.J. Waters via Dan Hagedorn)

was flying 18-20 hours monthly. With only six aircraft to start with, the FAC needed all the help it could get, but accidents inevitably happened. One day a pilot on short final had the distressing experience of finding a truck driving across the runway in front of him. The Sabre veered just in time, but still glanced off the vehicle. Away went the Sabre in a cloud of dust and debris, and when things cleared up, the Sabre pilot, large stick in hand, could be seen chasing after the "soldado" who had been driving the offending truck.

One odd event Fitzgerald recalled was the day it rained fish and frogs. That day's usual downpour was especially heavy, and out of nowhere appeared vast quantities of swimming fauna. After the rainwater had run off, Palanqero was plastered with slippery critters, and no flying could take place until they had all dried up in the sun and been swept off the runways.

Fuerza Aérea Hondurena

Twenty years ago, the Sabre 2 and 4 era came to an end. In NATO air forces Sabre 2s and 4s had been largely replaced by such types as the G.91 and F-104. Most Sabres have long-since

been scrapped. In Yugoslavia, gradual introduction of MiG-21s meant phase-out of the Sabres, but the process was more prolonged and F-86Ds and Ls and some ancient F-84s survived with the Sabre 2s well into the seventies.

In the late seventies the Honduras air force (FAH) began re-equipping. It was about time, as its WW2 Corsairs must have been getting a bit tired. Super Mystères from Israel and AT-37s from the US were procured, but so was a shipment of at least eight Canadair Sabre 4s. These were ex-Yugoslavian and were likely purchased in a clandestine deal through middle-men arms merchants. Aircraft 19583, '674, '681, '725, '762, '774, '821 and '869 are known to have arrived in Honduras. Refurbishing may have been done on some of these Sabres at Miami, and they were stationed at the FAH base at San Pedro Sula as "Escuadron Sabre." Latin American aviation historian Daniel Hagedorn notes, "I have seen photos in the FAH magazine of at least three Sabres in the air at one time, and they almost certainly are flown by Honduran pilots. Spares must be a problem, however." It has not yet been possible to readily determine which FAH Sabres are Mk. 4s and which are "Fs". The FAH also operated some ex-Venezuelan "Ks" in recent years.

In September 1985 two Nicaraguan helicopters were shot down along the Nicaragua-Honduras border by an FAH fighter. It is possible that the kills were made by a Canadair Sabre, a generation after everyone thought the Sabre's fighting days were over.

Pakistan Air Force - The Canadair Sabre Goes to War

During 1965 and 1971 two brief but furious wars flared up between India and Pakistan. The first lasted 23 days and saw the PAF pitting its F-86Fs, F-104s and B-57s against the IAF's Hunters, Vampires, Gnats, Ouragans, Mystères and Canberras. Losses all round were severe. To recoup its losses, Pakistan took three main steps. Because of an arms embargo, it was cut off from its traditional source of supply, the United States, so turned to France for a limited supply of Mirages (these were too costly for the PAF to obtain in the numbers it needed). It turned to China for a large numer of F-6 fighters. These are a version of the MiG-19 and have been to this day an affordable but reliable (if outdated) aircraft. Finally, Pakistan looked for any available "bargains" and, as it turned out, found an excellent one.

A large batch of Luftwaffe Sabre 6s were currently surplus. Working no doubt with seasoned international arms dealers, Pakistan agents concluded a deal which saw the Sabres purchased by Iran. Some 90 were ferried to that country by Luftwaffe pilots. Once there, so the story goes, they were flown into West Pakistan "for overhaul." They never returned and were soon flying with PAF squadrons. The Sabre 6 was an ideal find for the Pakistanis—it was inexpensive and was readily serviceable; PAF fighter pilots had been brought up on the F-86F, yet the Sabre 6 was a good half-generation advanced over the "F". The Canadair Sabre was to form the backbone of the PAF's day fighter operation in the 1971 war and would fly against vastly superior numbers of IAF fighters, including the Gnat, Hunter, Mystère, HF-24, SU-7 and state-of-the-art MiG-21.

In 1971 East Pakistan was in turmoil and the movement by revolutionaries to reform it as an independent state destabilized the region. In December India launched an all-out invasion of East, then West Pakistan. All the PAF

The very last Canadair Sabre, seen in Pakistani markings. This Sabre was still in Pakistan in 1986. (PAF)

had in the East was a single squadron of Sabres. Too small to take on the Indians offensively, Pakistan had little choice but to try holding on its own frontiers. Unfortunately for the PAF, many of its new F-6s were not yet combat ready. With few Mirages available, it was the Sabre 6s, along with the surviving F-86Fs, that would have to fend off the Indians.

It appears that the first engagement in the air war occurred on November 22, with Gnats and Sabres dogfighting over East Pakistan. One Gnat and two Sabres were lost. From here on activity rose and after the first four days of fighting in December the PAF had claimed 95 enemy aircraft shot down in combat—a high figure, but it has been widely accepted that the PAF made excellent use of its aircraft and did, in fact, establish a high kill ratio against the IAF. A typical day's work was December 6 when five SU-7s, three Canberras and two Hunters were shot down for the loss of two Sabres.

On December 11 PAF Sabres also did well: a supersonic MiG-21 and two SU-7s were bagged. Three days later a MiG fell to an F-6. On the 17th, a Sabre brought down another MiG-21, bringing the PAF tally to 141 enemy aircraft destroyed. That day India agreed to a cease-fire. It is the official Pakistan view that the tenacity of the PAF and the way it established air

F/O Muhammad Shamsul Haq who shot down an Indian SU-7 and two Hunters on December 4, 1971; and F/L Saeed Afzal Khan who shot down a Hunter the same day, but was himself downed in the battle, and taken prisoner. Both were flying Sabre 6s and were later awarded the Sitari-i-Jurat for bravery. (PAF)

superiority led to India's sudden acceptance of the cease-fire. Without control of the skies, India apparently felt that victory couldn't be assured.

By far the most active PAF figher in the 1971 war was the F-86, and it would appear that a large number of Sabre 6s participated and accounted for many of the 141 PAF kills. Thus, in its "declining years," the mighty Sabre 6 had finally been put to work "for real." And the results, for those on the receiving end, proved devastating. PAF records show that 24 Sabre 6s were lost in 1971, most, it is safe to

assume, during the war.

Of course, the IAF deserves its due as well, and its fighters were able to down many PAF aircraft. One of its more potent weapons was its smallest, the Gnat. Barely 31 feet long, the Gnat was fast and well armed. In *Aircraft of the Indian Air Force* it is noted that, "The diminutive fighter earned the appellation 'Sabre Slayer' for it had achieved much distinction, proving capable of outfighting both the F-86 Sabre and the F-104A Starfighter ... Because of its small size, Pak. pilots found the Gnat difficult to see let alone engage ... "

This excerpt from an official PAF paper covers the story of the Sabre 6 and its role in the 1971 war:

The end of 1965 Indo-Pak War entailed a grave challenge as the U.S. military aid to Pakistan was abruptly suspended. Although the suspension of military aid was equally applicable to both India and Pakistan, it hurt Pakistan harder as the Pakistan armed forces had been exclusively equpped with American military hardware within the framework of the then-existing CENTO and SEATO pacts. Pakistan armed forces were thus entirely dependent on American weapons systems. India on the other hand was far less affected in view of her diversified inventory of arms, including a sizable supply from the Soviet Union. Subsequent to the war, India's military needs continued to be met by a substantial and continuous flow of Soviet military equipment and other East European countries, coupled with her own indigenous production of armament.

Obviously, this embargo operated to the great disadvantage of Pakistan and was rightly viewed as constituting *per se* a formidable threat to the territorial integrity of Pakistan. In view of the jeopardized security of the country, the government lodged a strong protest with the U.S.A. for violating existing military pacts. The embargo also accelerated Pakistan's worldwide explorations for new and alternative sources of supply of military equipment along with the search for the badly needed spares for PAF aircraft. This probing for new avenues resulted, between 1966-68, in the acquisition of the Mirage III from France and MiG-19 (F-6s) from China. As an immediate interim reinforcement, however, the year 1966 saw a bulk supply of 90 used

Canadair Sabre Mk. 6s of the German Air Force. The aircraft had already flown for a number of years and were inducted as a stop-gap measure. The 90 Sabres were ferried to Pakistan via Iran, as follows:

April 1966	10
May	20
June	20
July	8
October	12
December	20

These Canadair Sabres (F-86E) belonged to Canada's most widely produced aircraft with approximately 1800 manufactured in all. This epoch-making fighter built under licence by Canada continued to fly in the air forces of a number of countries and was extremely popular in the PAF right up to its phasing out in 1980 due to spares supply having completely dried up ...

PAF's F-86Es were allocated in (the former) West Pakistan to No. 17, 18 and 19 Squadrons and No. 14 Squadron in (the former) East Pakistan (now Bangladesh). In the 1971 Indo-Pak War, air combat operations by F-86Es were of great historical significance and interest. Some selected and salient war events involving the Canadair Sabres are summed up in the following paragraphs.

The resource constraints permitted the PAF to station only a single squadron (No.14) flying F-86Es in the then-Eastern wing of Pakistan. This lone squadron had to face no less than 10 squadrons of the Indian Air Force (IAF) simultaneously, comprising MiG-21s, Gnats and Hunters. The grim but resolute and heroic resistance of No.14 Squadron will go down in air combat history as a glorious chapter of a valiant and determined fight against a vastly superior enemy. It was a no-win situation from the outset, but the squadron put up a fierce fight and continued it against heavy odds. The young and gallant pilots of PAF, with only 100-150 operational hours to their credit, were invariably pitted against eight to ten enemy aircraft at a time.

The story of Flt.Lt. Saeed Afzal Khan, a young pilot decorated for his action in the F-86E, is described in the citation in these words: "On 4th December, 1971, Flt.Lt. Saeed Afzal Khan was flying as No.2 in a formation of two F-86 aircraft when he engaged four Indian Hunters and immediately shot down one. Meanwhile another

formation of four Hunters joined the aerial battle. In the subsequent combat, although facing great odds, he was not deterred from attacking them. He put up a gallant fight with complete disregard to his own safety. Due to his determination and flying skill, he prevented everyone of them from attacking their target, i.e. Dacca airfield."

The citation in fact describes actions very typical of No.14 Squadron's war effort. The objective of the small but dedicated team of PAF men was to protect Dacca airfield from hostile attacks and to keep it safe enough for contineud operations. In this mission their resolute performance was acknowledged even by the adversaries.

With the launching of an all-out assault by Indian forces on East Pakistan on November 22, 1971, the IAF let loose the full combat power of its 10 squadrons against one. The IAF kept on relentless pressure for three days and nights. Dacca Air Base was raided several times by as many as 20 aircraft simultaneously. But for the dogged resistance and will of the PAF, the IAF would have succeeded in achieving their objective within three to four hours of the first day. But the heavily outnumbered but determined pilots of 14 Squadron did not allow the IAF such an easy victory. The PAF F-86s rose repeatedly to meet MiG-21s, SU-7s and Hunters to inflict casualties on the intruders notwithstanding the latter's overwhelming superiority. A memorable dogfight in the defence of Dacca Air Base, amongst the many witnessed by newsmen from the nearby roof of the Inter Continental Hotel, involved the young Flying Officer Shamsul Haq. He alone engaged five enemy aircraft and shot three of them down, two Hunters and one SU-7. F/O Shams, though quite young in flying experience as well as age, engaged each enemy aircraft in turn and got his kills through a blend of aggressiveness and skill. Realizing the ineffectiveness of SU-7s, the IAF effected a qualitative as well as a quantative change in their air element by introducing supersonic and better manoeuvring and more powerful MiG-21s along with the Hunters. This uneven grim tussle for air superiority between the two unequal rivals dragged on until December 8th, when Dacca runway, having been cratered too many times, was irreparably damaged, thus bringing PAF operations to an inevitable end. The Indians, however, failed to destroy No.14 Squadron.

Even when the runway had been rendered non-operational, 11 F-86Es remained intact.

Air war in the then Western wing of Pakistan was a different proposition. The PAF held full sway over her air space and the air superiority gained by the PAF was seldom contested. In the initial 24 hours after the outbreak of war, the IAF suffered the loss of 19 aircraft including 9 SU-7s, 5 Hunters, 3 Canberras, 1 HF-24 and 1 Gnat. In several encounters the F-86E easily outmanoeuvred IAF aircraft and in one case this pilots' favourite shot down even the much faster MiG-21, when the latter attempted unwisely to turn with it, in a tree-top dogfight.

The foregoing brief account is a valuable tribute to the Canadair Sabres which served PAF in good stead. It is also a tribute to those dedicated, brave

Ruins of ex-PAF Sabre 6 No. 1606 in a Bangladesh AF scrap yard. The BAF used several Sabre 6s for a short time following independence from Pakistan. (BAF)

pilots who flew these fighters with aggressiveness and skill. The F-86E is still well-remembered in the PAF.

Pakistan Air Force

Summary of PAF Sabre 6s to 1986

Serial	Fate	Year	Serial	Fate	Year	Serial	Fate	Year
1592	Crashed	1971	1663	,,	,,	1763	Crashed	1971
1594	,,	1969	1665	Scrapped	1976	1764	Extant	
1595	Extant		1669	Crashed	1971	1765	Crashed	1966
1606	Crashed	1971	1670	Museum		1766	,,	1970
1607	,,	,,	1674	,,	1968	1771	Scrapped	1978
1608	,,	,,	1683	,,	1975	1772	Crashed	1971
1614	,,	,,	1689	Crashed	1971	1777	Scrapped	1978
1616	,,	1970	1692	,,	1976	1778	Extant	
1617	,,	1971	1693	Extant		1781	Scrapped	1975
1618	,,	,,	1695	Crashed	1973	1783	Extant	
1621	,,	1972	1701	Extant		1786	Crashed	1971
1622	Scrapped	1979	1702	,,		1787	,,	1975
1623	Extant		1703	Crashed	1971	1788	,,	1980
1624	Crashed	1973	1705	Extant		1789	Extant	
1626	Scrapped	1978	1709	,,		1790	,,	
1627	Extant		1718	Crashed	1971	1792	Scrapped	1980
1629	,,		1719	,,	,,	1794	Extant	
1632	,,		1720	,,	1968	1797	,,	
1634	Scrapped	1980	1722	Extant		1798	Crashed	1974
1636	Crashed	1978	1728	Museum		1800	,,	1972
1639	Extant		1733	Extant		1802	,,	1971
1650	Crashed	1970	1735	Crashed	1971	1803	,,	,,
1652	Scrapped	1968	1738	,,	,,	1804	,,	1975
1653	Crashed	1971	1739	Extant		1808	,,	1978
1655	Extant		1742	Crashed	1968	1809	Scrapped	1977
1656	Extant		1747	Extant		1810	Extant	
1657	Crashed	1971	1749	Crashed	1968	1811	Crashed	1975
1658	,,	1967	1751	Extant		1812	Scrapped	1974
1660	,,	1974	1754	Extant		1815	Extant	
1661	,,	1971	1756	Scrapped	1978			

Old Fighters Never Die

As with all aircraft, it was only a matter of time before the Sabre was finally outmoded by technology. Even while it was coming into its own in Canada, its eventual replacement, the F-104, was already in the air. The prototype F-104 first flew February 7, 1954, and five years later the Canadian government chose it as the Sabre replacement. Canadair was awarded the contract to build 200 CF-104s, while Orenda would build the GE J79 engines. The first CF-104 flew at Palmdale, California, on May 26, 1961, and from Cartierville that August 14. Before long the mighty Sabre 6 would fly no more over Europe. In its place — the CF-104, performing two new roles for the Air Division: nuclear strike and reconnaissance.

But the coming of the CF-104 didn't mean an immediate end for the Sabre, as it did for the CF-100s in NATO. The air force needed an advanced trainer to prepare pilots for their new low-level work with the 104. Thus, at the end of 1961, when the OTU folded up at Chatham, a new unit, the STU (Sabre Transition Unit), opened up for business. Using the ex-OTU Sabre 5s, it began training pilots in the fine arts of low-level navigation and precision bomb delivery. As the Sabre's .50 guns were no longer needed, they were removed.

After their course at the STU, pilots destined for the 104 carried on to No.6 Strike/Reconnaissance OTU at Cold Lake, formed October 1, 1961, under W/C K.C. Lett. There they converted to the 104 and were posted overseas. The STU was to continue until late in 1968. By then, the Sabre was on its last legs, and the OTU at Cold Lake (redesignated 417 (S/R) Operational Training Squadron in March 1967) and a squadron with CF-5s, combined to take on all phases of 104 conversion. As far as the Canadian Forces was concerned, the Sabre had finally outlived

its usefulness. In late 1968 plans were made for a Sabre stand-down thrash at Chatham, and, as a highlight, two Sabres were taken on a commemorative trans-Canada flight. This is the "Sabre Swan" story and is related here by the two pilots involved, G/C A.J. "Arnie" Bauer, base commander at Chatham, and Capt I.F. "Scotty" Campbell. Bauer and Campbell set off from Chatham on December 9, 1968, to work their way westward to Cold Lake flying 23227 and 23363, and returned home December 17.

Though there is no journal of Sabre Swan, there are snapshots of our memories of Canada's farewell to the Sabre. One of the first and strongest impressions is one which denied us the opportunity to take our aircraft right to the West Coast, to Comox, so that old faithfuls there might pay their respects. There had long been an order prohibiting F-86 training trips across the Rockies, and the powers in Air Defence Command were not about to permit us special dispensation. All the more disappointing, for we might have tried to set a new trans-Canada speed record on our return in this old, retiring, but beautiful and still magnificently effective craft.

Sabre Swan quartet: Capt Lundquist and Cpl Treen on maintenance; Col A.J. Bauer and Capt Scotty Campbell doing the flying. (DND)

Snapshot: The reception committees everywhere we landed. Ground crew, air crew, young and old, all lined the sides of the tarmac to wave and cheer our arrivals. This is not to downplay the official, cool-beer, warm-hearted receptions by base functionaries, but to emphasize the love for the Sabre of all airmen who had known her, and even of those who, too young to have known her, had heard all about the Sabre.

We had the great privilege of attending a Wings Parade at Moose Jaw. How proud we were to be there, as representatives of another generation of airmen, to witness the emergence into their careers of youngsters whom we saw as no less steely-eyed and sharp

Bauer's ('363) and Campbell's Sabres while visiting Portage on Sabre Swan. (Bill Ewing)

Flypast of Chatham residents in 1968. The Sword teams up with a T-bird and a 416 Voodoo. (DND)

Ex-RCAF Korean Sabre pilots at the Sabre stand-down thrash. In the rear are Bob Lowry, Bill Bliss and Ernie Glover. Then, Omer Levesque, Bob Davidson, Andy MacKenzie and Eric Smith. (DND)

than we had imagined ourselves to be at our own Wings Parade.

Snapshot: Waking in the middle of the night in Moose Jaw and clearly hearing the Orenda of '227 or '363 spooling up. Was someone out there liberating our aircraft? Would one of us have to walk back to Chatham? Relax! No engine was running. It was only a dream.

Snapshot: "Sabre Swan, Lakehead tower."

"Go ahead, tower."

"Swan, can you do a pass over the city? We have a request from downtown."

"Tower, are you telling us that we're authorized for a low pass over the city?"

STU staff at Chatham late in the game. In back are Terry Elphick, Bill Green, Doug Fraser, Joe Gagnon, Ron Clarkson, Bruce Lundquist, Jim MacKay and Ron Clayton. In front are Don Gregory, Reg Kendrick, Doug Riddell, Bob Massier (OC), Rocky Van Vliet and Scotty Campbell. (DND)

"Affirmative, Swan. Call five out. No local traffic."

Snapshot: After takeoff from Portage into solid December overcast, with Scotty tucked in tight on the starboard wing as usual, we wheel around to the south, behind the hangars, flying comfortably low. As we come back around the corner after our turn, there, right there, is the crowd that's come out to say farewell. Everyone so pleased, proud and nostalgic about their Sabre connection.

Snapshot: The outstanding serviceability of our aircraft during Sabre Swan. Not a single problem with engines, airframes or accessories. Our caretakers, Capt Lundquist and Cpl Treen, did excellent work indeed.

Finale: The long, thoughtfully quiet final leg from Ottawa to Chatham. Each of us carried new memories of a satisfying cross-country trip we were so proud to have made. And we carried all the old memories of the RCAF's pride of fleet—the F-86 Sabre. She had served the air force and her nation with great distinction. She had brought pride and glory, though sometimes tragedy, to airmen at home and in

Europe. She had inspired millions of Canadians at Golden Hawk air shows from coast to coast. She was now going home, her work completed.

A.J. Bauer and I.F. Campbell

At Chatham, on the last weekend of November 1968, 300 Sabre types gathered to bid farewell to their favourite old fighter. The flightline was crowded with Cosmos, Buffalos and Dakotas, proof that loyal old RCAF fighter pilots would travel in anything to bid their goodbyes to the Sabre. A planned flypast of Sabres was chopped at the last minute when the weather refused to cooperate, but that was about the only damper on the weekend. MGen M.E. "Mike" Pollard, Air Defence Command boss, presided over the affair, and began his address, "We are gathered here today to mark the passing from active service of the greatest air superiority jet fighter ever built ...." He finished with a real fighter pilot's testimonial: "Only the fighter pilot can really know the fighter air-

Minor mishap at Chatham (so long as a couple of F-86 wings is "minor"!). (DND)

craft for what it is—a graceful living thing, instantly responsive to the slightest touch, yet an instrument of shattering power ... Its full measure is revealed only to the men who fly alone.''

Things had rapidly wound down around Chatham through November 1968. Sabre 23058 was the last to undergo periodic inspection. The base paper noted in its December issue: ''It had been dismantled and checked. The engine had been removed, checked and run up for performance. The instruments, inverters, meters and radios had been taken to other shops on the base and checked. Every piece had then been gathered together again, and the aircraft re-assembled. 23058 was ready for a test flight and one more month of service.'' November 15, Capt Terry Elphick test flew '058.

In fact, the last training at the STU was conducted on December 13, 1968. Over the unit's seven years of operation, it had trained 403 Canadian pilots and 67 Norwegians, piling up 49,000 flying hours. STU commanders over the years had been W/C L.J. ''Lou'' Hill, W/C C.W. ''Chuck'' Steacy, S/L R.R. ''Bob'' Massier and Maj D.H. Riddell. In early 1969, the STU's 21 Sabre 5s were ferried off to retirement at Mountain View. The Sabre era was history, so far as the Canadian Forces was concerned. Ironically, two years later, Canadair Sabres would be tested in battle for the last time. The scene would be in faraway Pakistan, and the fighter pilot's dream, the Sabre 6, was to acquit itself beautifully.

Flashbacks
Every Sabre pilot has his favourite ''war stories'' to tell, especially when he gets cranked up with some old buddies over a few beers. J.R. ''Jim'' Pugh looks back to a few of his:

First solo: The sheer ecstasy of it all. The power, the terrific roll rate, those well-trained Chatham Swords who took the first solos out and brought them back safely 40 minutes later.

First hi-level formation: Desperately jockeying throttle, speed brakes and all to hang in on the instructor as he methodically dismantled his u/s radio —and showed you each piece.

Flightline views: Watching ''Moose,'' who had taken off with no fuel but a reset densitometer, attempt to make it back to the runway. Too low to make the base, he attempted to land on a country road. But a large rock and

Flightline scene at Chatham in the sixties. (DND)

a team of horses ruined his approach. He hit a tree. The seat let loose, and we didn't have crash helmets in those days.

Again watching a break and landing, and seeing Sam catch his undercarriage in a little ditch near the threshold. The F-86 did a very short roll out and a workman in the ditch was chased by a wheel and phoned in for his pay two days later.

427 Squadron: Two days after signing in, a good friend tried to pull through too low—maybe fighters aren't all fun and games. Picking up your very own Sword at Cartierville— 19422, November 1952.

Leapfrog 2, March 7-April 7, 1953. One week in Goose Bay, snow and all-night poker games. Two weeks in Narsarssuak, snow, million-year-old oily ice in the rum, and powdered eggs stored since 1942. A blown engine on takeoff and, after an all-night engine change, a two-plane to Iceland. One week there, not allowed into town, engine run-ups at 0300, and an introduction to vodka. Three days in Scotland, sightseeing, shilling heaters that quit in the night, and beautiful green after a month of white.

Exercise flying in Germany. After being grounded for five days by WX in Wildenrath, bare minimum takeoff and a low-level formation into Holland. Number 2 lower than other two, transmission lines ahead. Quick radio call, ''Number 3 watch...Never mind.'' Lead and two over lines, three under. Back at base, Bill says, ''What were you muttering about at Eindhoven?'' Never did see the wires.

Rainy day in the Rhone Valley, staying low to avoid having to go IFR. Small yellow French Auster appears ahead. One calls ''Split!'' Wobbly little yellow airplane in rear view mirror.

Away on one-day course June 18, 1953. 19422 flown by our first replacement, crashed on overshoot due to mechanical problems. Pilot killed.

431 Squadron: Formed from aircraft pranged in Canada, repaired by Canadair but not worth flying overseas. Pilots from Air Div and ''newbies''

Famous cartoon done up for the Sabre stand-down in 1968.

from CH. Prairie Pacific air shows flown summer of '54, Winnipeg-Vancouver. Disbanded that October, new pilots overseas, ''old'' ones to Harvards to instruct.

Jim Pugh

Scotty Campbell, who flew on Sabre Swan, adds a note or two from Chatham days: ''The Sabre was such a reliable old bird that it didn't leave me

McEwen Field near Moncton, showing dis-assembled Sabre 5s. (via D. McEwen)

Bob Laidlaw (left) and Dave McEwen pick out 23367 for a rebuild. (via D. McEwen)

with many 'hero' stories. But one does come to mind, and that was my first flame-out. I was on a training flight from Chatham when I mishandled the throttle at 44,000 on a cold winter's morning. I knew the re-start drill, of course, but this time it didn't work till I was down below 12,000. Although we had discussed flame-outs in great detail during ground instruction, nobody ever thought to mention that with no power ice forms quick and thick *inside* the canopy. It was a completely blind trip all the way down, and I found the whole thing quite upsetting. It's the first time I remember my hands and feet nearly frozen while sweat filled my helmet!

"My only other bit of excitement occurred from Chatham in 1959. After I had taken off, my nose wheel stuck at 90 degrees, so couldn't recycle. In the end I became the first pilot at Chatham to land with a strip of foam laid down the middle of the runway. The landing was easy, so my second emergency also had a happy ending."

The Moncton-Mojave Connection

In the mid-sixties, David McEwen of Moncton purchased a large quantity of F-86s and T-33s from Crown Assets Disposal Corp and, thanks to him and his company, Maritime Aircraft Overhaul and Repair (later called Targetair), many of these superb Canadair

aircraft are still active. McEwen had a boyhood fascination with aircraft. His father, Charlie McEwen, was a well known local flier, who had taken flying lessons in the thirties from Al Lilly. And when Dave was a boy, two RCAF Sabre drivers, Bob and Don Simmons, used to visit his father's airstrip outside Moncton, sometimes shooting it up while on flights out of Chatham.

In the fifties, Charlie McEwen had an interest in some surplus RCN Sea Furies. He gave his son the task of cannibalizing them to fulfill a contract to an operator flying target tug Sea Furies in Germany. Dave had just completed his schooling at Northrop's aeronautical institution in Inglewood, and the Sea Fury job provided valuable on-the-

Y'ALL TAKE FAHVE THOUSAN FOR 'IM, CUNNEL?

job training and an insight into the business world.

In the mid-sixties McEwen was purchasing Sabre spares and reselling them mainly to the PAF and SAAF. Inevitably, Sabres themselves were put on the market, and McEwen acquired several at Mountain View. There he stripped them, removed the engines and had the hulks melted down on site.

In 1969 the last batches of Sabres were offered by CADC: 45 at Mountain View and 19 at London, all Sabre 5s. These McEwen purchased on September 8, 1970. The Sabres had their centre sections cut according to government regulations, then were trucked in special jigs to Moncton, an operation that cost several hundred thousand dollars. At McEwen Field, the Sabres were stored outside, and little by little buyers began showing interest in them.

Three were still in original condition; two (23285, 23315) were sold to Leroy Penhall (Fighter Imports, California) and the other (23241) to Lockheed for use as a chase plane. These were delivered to the US from Moncton airport. When 23241 (N8549) crashed at Mojave while Bob Laidlaw was flying it, Laidlaw contacted McEwen and asked if a replacement could be provided. He came up to Moncton, where he and McEwen picked out 23367. It was soon being rebuilt in McEwen's shops, with D.J. "Don" Donovan as chief engineer, and others, like veteran Sabre airframe tech Joe Methot, involved. The rebuild took some 4000 man-hours, and when done, the Sabre was towed to Moncton airport, where Laidlaw test flew it. His impression was that 23367 was a better-than-new aircraft. He then ferried it to California.

A pilotless Sabre 5 (QF-86E) over New Mexico. (via M.J. Kasiuba)

A Canadair Sabre of Flight Systems equipped with a target drogue. (Flight Systems)

About this time the PAF was interested in Sabre 6s and approached Dave McEwen. He determined which of his 5s could be converted to 6s (Orenda 10 to 14) and consulted with Orenda, which agreed to provide the engines. The other major mod would be to install leading-edge slats. Aircraft 23363 was the prototype and was test flown by Scotty Campbell January 30, 1972. But politics soon squelched McEwen's plans: war broke out between Pakistan and India, and Ottawa embargoed the sale of war material to either party.

Coincidentally, the Salvadorean air force was looking for fighters and a representative visited McEwen Field. He was very impressed by the gleaming new Sabre, but no business was completed, apparently also on political grounds. However, Boeing was in a serious buying mood. It wanted a new chase plane to replace 23096, its Mk.5. A Boeing technical team visited Moncton and quickly decided that 23363 would be the perfect aircraft for their needs. McEwen took '096 in as a trade, then sold it to Flight Systems, a company formed in 1968 by W.R. "Bob" Laidlaw.

Laidlaw had been involved with the US Army in target drone negotiations

(Right) A Canadair T-33 carrying stores, and a Sabre 5 take off from Mojave. (Flight Systems)

A Sabre 5 is blasted out of the sky by anti-aircraft fire at White Sands.

and, in cooperation with Dave McEwen, struck a deal whereby he, McEwen and the army collaborated to convert the rest of McEwen's Sabres into pilotless target drones. All the engineering was completed, and on September 30, 1976, McEwen's Sabre modification plant was opened in New Brunswick. At full production, the plant had 10 Sabres under way. Once completed, each was broken down into kit form, crated and trucked to California.

Laidlaw's concept of full-size target drones was based on the premise that there was a growing need for more realistic simulation of airborne threats in the test and evaluation of anti-aircraft weapons. This, plus the growing cost of sub-scale drones like the Firebee, led Laidlaw to pursue his idea, and the military agreed.

The Sabre 5 was ideal for the job. It was available in quantity at affordable prices, was a good serviceable type, and the full range of airframe and engine spares was still on hand. As a drone it could operate up to 45,000 feet at .92M and, under control of the ground stations devised by FSI, act as a fast low-level target down to 200 feet. It could pull as much as 8g, deploy stores, jam electronics and provide other ECM features to attempt disruption of the weapon system under test.

On a mission, the Sabre drone, known as QF-86E, could be shot down, as, over the years, many have been. Others have survived several flights and have even returned with considerable damage from such

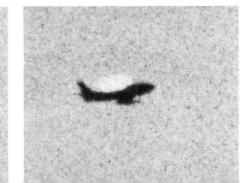

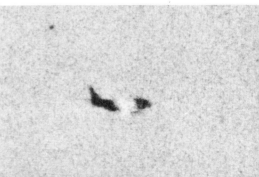

weapons as the Stinger missile and Sgt York anti-aircraft gun. Actual missions are conducted at the White Sands Missile Range in New Mexico, the Sabres being based at Holloman AFB, N.M. After a mission, a chase plane can evaluate damage and then recommend recovery technique. If an aircraft cannot safely be recovered or otherwise must be destroyed, there is a flight termination system built-in that will blow a wing off the Sabre.

Over the years FSI's stock of Sabre 5s has dwindled considerably, and now the US Army and Navy have begun using Sabres imported from places like Japan. Meanwhile, FSI continues flying a number of Sabre 5s and 6s on non-drone contracts which include target towing and the development of new avionics, electronics and ordnance. The company also uses a fleet of Canadair T-33s and such other types as the A-4, F-4 and F-100. Home base is Mojave in the California desert just west of Edwards AFB.

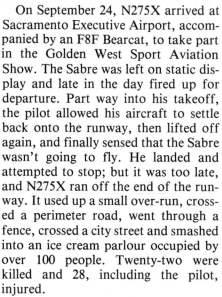

N275X while at Toronto Island. (Peter Keating)

N275X

One of the worst-ever non-commercial civil aviation disasters took place on September 24, 1972, when a Sabre 5, N275X, crashed at Sacramento. The aircraft was formerly 23275 and had been sold to Spectrum Air Inc. in November 1971. It had been stored for a time at Toronto Island Airport, then was ferried to Syracuse, N.Y., for some maintenance. It next flew to the West Coast to be operated by Spectrum.

On September 24, N275X arrived at Sacramento Executive Airport, accompanied by an F8F Bearcat, to take part in the Golden West Sport Aviation Show. The Sabre was left on static display and late in the day fired up for departure. Part way into his takeoff, the pilot allowed his aircraft to settle back onto the runway, then lifted off again, and finally sensed that the Sabre wasn't going to fly. He landed and attempted to stop; but it was too late, and N275X ran off the end of the runway. It used up a small over-run, crossed a perimeter road, went through a fence, crossed a city street and smashed into an ice cream parlour occupied by over 100 people. Twenty-two were killed and 28, including the pilot, injured.

The National Transportation Safety Board concluded "that the probable cause of this accident was the over-rotation of the aircraft and subsequent derogation of the performance capability. The over-rotation was the result of inadequate pilot proficiency in the aircraft and misleading visual cues." The pilot had logged just 3.5 hours of Sabre time when the disaster occurred.

Boeing Sabres

A long-time user of the civilian Canadair Sabre has been Boeing of Seattle. It acquired its first in 1962 when Boeing pilot Tom Edmonds ferried 23096, an ex-Golden Hawks Sabre,

Paul Bennett flies Boeing's chase Sabre while the company's 707 tests the Beech refuelling system. Bennett, who flew Sabres with the 51st FIW in Korea, had some 1300 hours on type by 1986. (Below) The Boeing Sabre accompanies the first 747 during its maiden flight. (Boeing)

Lockheed's Sabre 5 off the wing of the L-1011 Tri Star. (Lockheed)

from Maritime Aircraft Overhaul and Repair in New Brunswick to Seattle, arriving there December 21. The aircraft, registered N8686F, was used frequently as a chase plane, with a typical mission being flown by Edmonds on September 25, 1967, monitoring the first flight of the Boeing 737. On February 9, 1969, it flew chase for the first flight of the 747. The Sabre 5 was finally disposed of by Boeing and was flown away to Flight Systems on July 26, 1974, to be replaced by 23363, a Sabre 5 updated with an Orenda 14 to a Sabre 6, and this aircraft, also registered N8686F, remains in service at Boeing.

Sabres for Sport

In the 1970s the Canadair F-86 began another "lifestyle" when the first few began turning up at air shows in the US bearing civilian registrations and decidedly non-military colour schemes. The Sabre-as-sport-plane era had arrived. Prosperous American businessmen with money to burn and ever on the lookout for the latest in hot warplanes began restoring Sabre 5s and 6s lately made surplus in Canada. Jerry Brassfield, Bob Laidlaw, Gary Levitz and Leroy Penhall in California were the first to show off their Sabre "toys", appearing at Mojave in 1973 to race. Organized by Penhall (later killed in a crash), this was the first closed-course jet race since the military participated at Cleveland and Detroit in the late forties. Besides Sabres, several T-33s were entered. In one race Laidlaw led the Sabre pack in a Mk.6, averaging over 636 mph. In the T-33 field the Canadair-built ones left the US-built machines far behind, and the pilots generally agreed that the T-bird was a far better racer that the Sabre, which for all practical purposes was simply too fast for pylon racing. The sight of jets at an air race was met with mixed feelings by a large crowd of spectators. Their "bag" was the roar of Merlins and other big piston engines powering Mustangs, Bearcats and the like. Most, however, were happy to see the "classic" old jets blazing around the course.

Since the seventies, numerous other jet warbirds have been turning up at North American air shows—Vampires,

Venoms, Meteors, even a Panther—but Sabres and T-birds are still the most numerous. A recent influx of ex-SAAF Sabres has swelled the ranks. One of these belongs to Texan John MacGuire. He added the former SAAF No.365 to his collection (which includes an ex-RCAF T-33) in late 1985. With such interest being shown in these aircraft, it looks as though Canadair will have vintage ambassadors abroad for years to come.

In 1986 Aircraft Unlimited of Chino, California turned out a "new" Sabre made up of a Canadair fuselage with North American wings. The cockpit is "state of the art" with fuel computer, new DME, 2-axis auto pilot and King Gold Crown avionics package. Far cry from the "good ol' days"! (Howard Levy)

Calgary Lawyer Milt Harradence owned this Sabre (CF-AMH) in the sixties, and had it done up in pseudo-Golden Hawk colours. It's seen here at Abbotsford, B.C. in August 1967. (T.R. Waddington via Peter Keating)

(Above) Many Sabres have been preserved throughout Canada and Europe. One, a Sabre 4, is even safely preserved in far off Zaire! This is the original Canadair Sabre, to be seen today at the RCAF Association, 700 Wing in Edmonton. (Jack McNulty)

(Below and left) JC-373 of the Luftwaffe being hauled out of a field for restoration, then seen being raised onto a pylon at Lahr. It bears 444 Squadron markings. 23221 is shown near the shoreline at Kingston, Ontario. (DND, Larry Milberry)

Appendices

Canadair Sabre Production List

The following list includes all 1815 Sabres built by Canadair. It runs in order by Canadair constructor's number (c/n) and includes, wherever known, the following:

RCAF and/or RAF tail number (RAF nos. begin with XB or XD).
RCAF taken-on-strength date (TOS).
RCAF struck-off-strength date (SOS).
First flight (f/f).
Squadrons/units using each aircraft (RCAF first,i.e. 400 series squadrons).
Misc. other operators,e.g. Italy, Honduras, Flight Systems (sometimes military serial nos. shown in brackets,e.g. Italy (2-48).
Category A (RAF Cat.5) accidents (i.e. aircraft written off) indicated by "Cat.A". (No attempt has been made to list the 1000s of other lesser prangs.)
Misc. other bits of trivia included where known,e.g. USAF serials for Mark 4s shown as a 52-series number following RAF serial.
Where known, code letters are given for individual RAF Sabres,e.g. 26/U means aircraft "U" of 26 Squadron.
Where known, RAF delivery dates given. Likewise, dates of transfer of Mark 4s to USAF.

This is considered to be a bare bones list, with data gleaned from many sources, especially pilots' log books. It is by no means "definitive."

Short forms used in production list
AFDS Air Fighting Development School, AAEE Aeroplane and Armament Experimental Establishment, cr crashed, DBR Damaged beyond repair, Fr France, FS Flight Systems, FTU Ferry Transition Unit, FWS Fighter Weapons School, GH Golden Hawks, LRFU Long Range Ferry Unit, MAC Maritime Aircraft Repair and Overhaul, MU Maintenance Unit, NAE National Aeronautical Establishment, OCU Operational Conversion Unit, OFU Overseas Ferry Unit, OTU Operational Training Unit, P Preserved, Pak Pakistan, PWS Pilot Weapons School, RAE Royal Aircraft Establishment, SCF Sabre Conversion Flight, SOC Struck off charge, STU Sabre Transition Unit, TTS Technical Training School, WG West Germany, WS White Sands.

c/n	Tail No.	f/f	TOS	SOS	Notes
1	19101	9.8.50		7.9.65	F-86A, sole Mark 1. To 700 Wing RCAFA 14.7.65. P (Edmonton).
2	19102	31.1.51		29.9.54	410, 431, Greece. Cat.A.
3	19103			20.7.54	410, OTU, Turkey. P.
4	19104			20.7.54	410, 413, OTU, Greece.
5	19105			20.7.54	410, CEPE, OTU, Greece.
6	19106			6.6.56	410. Cat.A. To instructional airframe B592.
7	19107			20.7.54	410, 413, OTU, Greece.
8	19108			4.8.55	431, 441, Greece.
9	19109			20.7.54	416, 430, OTU, Greece.
10	19110			20.7.54	431, Greece. Cat.A.
11	19111			20.7.54	430, OTU, Greece.
12	19112			7.7.52	439. Cat.A.
13	19113			7.5.52	413. Cat.A.
14	19114			4.8.55	439. Greece.
15	19115			3.7.51	410, 441. Cat.A.
16	19116			7.11.52	410, 441, OTU, Cat.A. To Redifon for conversion to simulator.
17	19117			25.4.56	434, Redifon.
18	19118				410. Cat.A. To instru. airframe A593. P (St. Jean, Que.)
19	19119			17.12.53	410, 421, 441, OTU, Cat.A.
20	19120			20.7.54	410, 441, Turkey. Cat.A.
21	19121			20.7.54	410, 421, OTU, Greece. Cat.A.
22	19122			4.4.52	410. Cat.A. To Redifon.
23	19123			3.3.53	410, 430, OTU. Cat.A.
24	19124			4.8.55	421, 441, OTU, Turkey.
25	19125			20.7.54	410, 421, 441, OTU, Greece.
26	19126			20.7.54	421, 441, OTU, CEPE, Turkey.
27	19127			20.7.54	441, OTU, Greece.
28	19128			9.3.55	410, 439, 441, OTU, Greece. Cat.A.
29	19129			20.7.54	410, 421, OTU, Turkey, Cat.A.
30	19130			20.7.54	421, 441, OTU, CEPE, Turkey. Cat.A.
31	19131			31.7.53	441, OTU. Cat.A.
32	19132			12.8.53	441, OTU. Cat.A.
33	19133			18.6.54	430, 441, OTU, Greece. Cat.A.
34	19134			4.8.55	410, 441, Turkey.
35	19135		25.9.51	18.6.54	410, Greece.
36	19136		29.11.51	4.8.55	TTS (Camp Borden), Greece.
37	19137		12.10.51	5.1.54	421, 444. Cat.A.
38	19138		29.11.51	9.3.55	413, 439, Turkey. Cat.A.
39	19139		29.11.51	4.8.55	439, Turkey. Cat.A.
40	19140		6.11.51	29.9.55	421, 439, Greece.
41	19141		5.7.51	18.6.54	410, Greece.
42	19142		5.7.51	29.9.54	410, 427, 441, Greece. Cat.A.
43	19143		5.7.51	25.4.56	441. Cat.A. To instr. airframe A594.
44	19144		16.7.51	18.6.54	410, Greece.
45	19145		16.7.51	24.11.58	410, Cat.A. To instr. airframe B595.
46	19146		16.7.51	29.9.54	413, 441, Greece.
47	19147		20.7.51	4.8.55	410, 441, Turkey. Cat.A.
48	19148		20.7.51	4.8.55	410, 441, Greece.

c/n	Tail No.	f/f	TOS	SOS	Notes	c/n	Tail No.	f/f	TOS	SOS	Notes
49	19149		20.7.51	15.7.54	413, 441, Cat.A.	134	19234		26.11.51	29.12.54	413. Cat.A.
50	19150		23.7.51	29.9.54	410, 439, 441. Turkey.	135	19235		26.11.61	4.8.55	413, 421, 439, Greece.
51	19151		28.8.51	18.6.54	441, Greece.	136	19236		28.11.51	29.9.54	413, 430, Turkey. Cat.A.
52	19152		23.7.51	30.12.53	441. Cat.A.	137	19237		30.11.51	2.6.53	413. Cat.A.
53	19153		27.7.51	29.9.54	410, 441, Turkey. Cat.A.	138	19238		30.11.51	4.8.55	410, 430, 434, 439, Greece.
54	19154		28.8.51	29.9.54	410, Greece.	139	19239		16.5.52	18.6.54	416, 421, Greece.
55	19155		28.8.51	21.4.54	439. Cat.A.	140	19240		30.11.51	31.3.52	439, 441. Cat.A.
56	19156		28.8.51	12.9.52	410. Cat.A. To Redifon.	141	19241		5.12.51	29.9.54	421, Turkey.
57	19157		7.9.51	4.8.55	410, 439, Turkey.	142	19242		5.12.51	4.8.55	413, 431, Turkey.
58	19158		7.9.51	25.8.53	441. Cat.A.	143	19243		5.12.51	29.9.54	416, Greece.
59	19159		28.8.51	9.3.54	410. Cat.A.	144	19244		2.2.52	2.2.52	1st USAF a/c.
60	19160		7.9.51	29.7.54	410, 441, Turkey. Cat.A.	145	19245		21.2.52	21.2.52	USAF.
61	19161		4.9.51	18.6.54	410, Greece.	146	19246		9.1.52	3.2.53	413. Cat.A.
62	19162		4.9.51	4.8.55	410, 441, Turkey.	147	19247		14.12.51	20.7.54	416, OTU, Turkey.
63	19163		28.8.51	19.7.54	441. Cat.A.	148	19248		10.1.52	9.3.55	413, Turkey. Cat.A.
64	19164		28.8.51	4.8.55	439, 441, Turkey.	149	19249		7.1.52	20.7.54	413, Turkey. Cat.A.
65	19165		28.8.51	29.9.54	430, 441, Turkey.	150	19250		14.12.51	29.9.54	416, Greece.
66	19166		4.9.51	4.8.55	439, 441, Turkey.	151	19251		2.2.52	21.2.51	USAF.
67	19167		4.9.51	25.11.53	441. Cat.A.	152	19252		13.6.51	13.6.51	USAF.
68	19168		4.9.51	4.8.55	439, 441, Greece. Cat.A.	153	19253		7.1.52	20.12.54	430, CEPE. Cat.A.
69	19169		4.9.51	18.6.54	410, Greece.	154	19254		10.1.52	29.9.54	413, Greece.
70	19170		4.9.51	9.3.55	410, Greece.	155	19255		12.3.52	19.7.54	430. Cat.A.
71	19171		4.9.51	29.9.54	410, Greece. Cat.A.	156	19256		11.2.52	11.2.52	USAF, Mich. ANG.
72	19172		4.9.51	4.8.55	410, 439, 441, Greece.	157	19257		11.2.52	11.2.52	USAF.
73	19173		10.9.51	18.6.54	410, Turkey. Cat.A.	158	19258		2.2.52	2.2.52	USAF.
74	19174		16.11.51	4.8.55	439, Greece.	159	19259		11.2.52	11.2.52	USAF.
75	19175		10.9.51	9.3.55	410, 439, Turkey.	160	19260		2.2.52	2.2.52	USAF.
76	19176		20.9.51	29.9.54	410, Turkey. Cat.A.	161	19261		21.2.52	21.2.52	USAF.
77	19177		20.9.51	5.6.52	410, 430, 441. Cat.A.	162	19262		21.2.52	21.2.52	USAF.
78	19178		20.9.51	15.9.52	410. Cat.A. To Redifon.	163	19263		11.2.52	11.2.52	USAF.
79	19179		27.9.51	29.9.54	410, Turkey.	164	19264		21.2.52	21.2.52	USAF.
80	19180		25.9.51	4.8.55	410, 439, Turkey. Cat.A.	165	19265		7.1.52	10.7.52	430, Cat.A.
81	19181		26.9.51	5.6.52	410. Cat.A.	166	19266		11.2.52	11.2.52	USAF. Cat.A.
82	19182		4.10.51	18.6.54	410. Greece.	167	19267		10.1.52	29.9.54	413, Greece.
83	19183		4.10.51	4.8.56	441, Turkey. Cat.A.	168	19268		14.2.52	20.7.54	Turkey.
84	19184		4.10.51	29.9.54	410, 441, Turkey.	169	19269		11.1.52	10.6.54	416, Greece.
85	19185		12.10.51	11.12.52	441. Cat.A.	170	19270		10.1.52	4.8.55	434, Turkey.
86	19186		12.10.51	4.8.55	410, Greece.	171	19271		11.1.52	18.6.54	421, OTU, Greece.
87	19187		29.11.51	2.9.52	430, 439. Cat.A.	172	19272		14.2.52	26.4.56	TTS.
88	19188		12.10.51	29.9.54	439, Greece. Cat.A.	173	19273		10.1.52	29.9.54	413, 434, Greece.
89	19189		12.10.51	24.6.52	441. Cat.A. To Redifon.	174	19274		10.1.52	4.8.55	427, 434, Greece. Cat.A.
90	19190		22.10.51	4.8.56	421, 430, 439, Turkey.	175	19275		14.2.52	4.8.55	TTS, Turkey.
91	19191		21.11.51	18.6.54	427, 439, Greece. Cat.A.	176	19276		14.2.52	20.7.53	434, TTS, Greece. Cat.A.
92	19192		19.10.51	4.8.55	439, Turkey. Cat.A.	177	19277		22.1.52	13.4.54	430, 434, Cat.A. To instr. airframe.
93	19193		19.10.51	9.7.53	422, 439. Cat.A.						
94	19194		12.10.51	4.8.55	410, 439, Turkey. Cat.A.	178	19278		22.1.52	20.7.54	OTU, Greece.
95	19195		19.10.51	4.8.55	410, 421, 439, 441, Turkey.	179	19279		4.3.52	4.3.52	USAF.
96	19196		25.10.51	4.8.55	439, Greece.	180	19280		4.3.52	4.3.52	USAF.
97	19197		7.11.51	20.7.54	TTS (Camp Borden), Turkey.	181	19281		22.1.52	20.10.52	OTU. First Sabre del. to OTU (20.2.52). Cat.A.
98	19198		19.10.51	29.9.54	439, 441, Turkey.						
99	19199		19.10.51	29.9.54	439, 441, Greece.	182	19282		21.2.52	21.2.52	USAF.
100	19200	14.6.52			Converted to sole Mark 3 Orenda and f/f 25.9.52 as such.	183	19283		28.1.52	30.4.52	416. Cat.A.
						184	19284		21.2.52	21.2.52	USAF.
101	19201		19.10.51	17.3.54	422, 441, OTU. Cat.A.	185	19285		1.2.52	20.7.54	OTU, Greece.
102	19202		19.10.51	4.8.55	439, Greece.	186	19286		1.2.52	20.7.54	OTU, Turkey.
103	19203		29.11.51	4.8.55	439, Turkey. Cat.A.	187	19287		14.2.52	18.6.54	421, Greece.
104	19204		22.10.51	27.5.53	439. Cat.B and W/O	188	19288		4.3.52	4.3.52	USAF.
105	19205		29.11.51	4.8.55	439, Greece.	189	19289		14.2.52	20.7.55	422, OTU, Turkey. Cat.A.
106	19206		26.10.51	5.8.52	439. Cat.A. to Redifon.	190	19290		14.2.53	8.6.53	OTU.
107	19207		26.10.51	20.7.54	430, OTU, Turkey.	191	19291		2.5.52	20.9.52	430, OTU. Cat.A.
108	19208		6.11.51	4.7.52	413, 439. Cat.A. To Redifon.	192	19292		14.2.52	14.7.52	421. Cat.A.
109	19209		6.11.51	20.7.55	430, 431, OTU, Greece. Cat.A.	193	19293		23.2.52	9.3.55	OTU, Greece. Cat.A.
110	19210		14.11.51	4.8.55	413, 422, 441, Greece. Cat.A.	194	19294		1.3.52	18.6.54	421, Greece.
111	19211		12.1.52	4.8.55	413, 439, Greece.	195	19295		21.3.52	21.3.52	OTU, USAF.
112	19212		6.11.51	18.1.54	430, Greece.	196	19296		21.3.52	21.3.52	USAF.
113	19213		7.11.51	4.8.55	413, 441, Greece.	197	19297		4.3.52	4.3.52	USAF.
114	19214		7.11.51	20.7.54	421, Turkey.	198	19298		28.4.52	21.12.54	421.
115	19215		14.11.51	18.6.54	416, 430, Turkey. Cat.A.	199	19299		4.3.52	4.3.52	USAF. Cat.A.
116	19216		14.11.51	4.8.55	410, 430, Turkey.	200	19300		14.2.52	14.8.53	OTU. Cat.A.
117	19217		29.11.51	18.6.54	416, Turkey. Cat.A.	201	19301		27.3.52	4.8.55	CEPE, Turkey.
118	19218		14.11.51	29.9.54	413, 430, Greece. Cat.A.	202	19302	29.2.52	25.3.52	19.7.54	OTU. Cat.A.
119	19219		14.11.51	19.1.53	OTU. Cat.A.	203	19303		23.2.52	17.9.53	OTU. Cat.A.
120	19220		29.11.51	18.6.54	416, 421, Greece.	204	19304		23.2.52	7.10.53	416. Cat.A.
121	19221		14.11.51	4.10.52	413. Cat.A.	205	19305		23.2.51	4.8.55	OTU, Greece.
122	19222		14.11.51	18.6.54	413, 430, Greece.	206	19306		16.4.52	16.4.52	USAF.
123	19223		20.11.51	20.7.54	430, Turkey.	207	19307		1.3.52	29.9.54	434, Greece.
124	19224		17.12.51	29.9.54	413, Greece. Cat.A.	208	19308		16.4.52	16.4.52	USAF.
125	19225		20.11.51	25.1.54	416, 430, 441. Cat.A.	209	19309		21.3.52	21.3.52	USAF.
126	19226		20.11.51	18.6.54	416, 430, Turkey.	210	19310		21.3.52	21.3.52	USAF.
127	19227		20.11.51	18.6.54	413, 421, Turkey.	211	19311		21.3.52	21.3.52	USAF.
128	19228		17.12.51	4.8.55	410, 439, OTU, Greece. Cat.A.	212	19312		1.3.52	11.3.53	421, Cat.A.
129	19229		17.12.51	3.12.52	413, 441. Cat.A.	213	19313		4.4.52	4.4.52	USAF.
130	19230		20.11.51	20.7.54	OTU, Turkey.	214	19314		4.4.52	4.4.52	USAF.
131	19231		20.11.51	18.6.54	416, Turkey. Cat.A.	215	19315		16.5.52	18.6.54	430, Turkey.
132	19232		23.11.51	18.6.54	413, 434, OTU, Turkey.	216	19316		4.4.52	4.4.52	USAF.
133	19233		26.11.51	18.6.54	430, Greece.	217	19317		28.4.52	29.9.54	410, 416, 421, Turkey. Cat.A.

c/n	Tail No.	f/f	TOS	SOS	Notes
218	19318		28.4.52	18.6.54	430, Turkey.
219	19319		29.4.52	29.4.52	USAF.
220	19320		1.3.52	4.8.55	421, Greece.
221	19321		4.4.52	4.4.52	USAF.
222	19322		4.4.52	4.4.52	USAF.
223	19323		28.4.52	18.6.54	416, Greece.
224	19324		29.4.52	29.4.52	USAF.
225	19325		1.3.52	18.6.54	430, Turkey.
226	19326		2.5.52	17.4.53	OTU. Cat.A.
227	19327		16.4.52	16.4.52	USAF.
228	19328		16.4.52	16.4.52	USAF.
229	19329		16.4.52	16.4.52	USAF.
230	19330		29.4.52	29.4.52	USAF.
231	19331		13.5.52	13.5.52	USAF.
232	19332		29.4.52	29.4.52	USAF.
233	19333		28.4.52	18.6.53	421. Cat.A.
234	19334		29.4.52	29.4.52	USAF.
235	19335		16.5.52	18.6.54	421, Turkey.
236	19336		13.5.52	13.5.52	USAF.
237	19337	23.5.52	16.5.52	20.7.54	OTU,Turkey. Cat.A.
238	19338	22.5.52	31.5.52	29.9.54	416, Turkey. Cat.A.
239	19339	14.5.52	13.5.52	13.5.52	USAF.
240	19340	19.5.52	25.6.52	25.6.52	USAF.
241	19341	23.5.52	28.5.52	28.5.52	USAF.
242	19342	23.5.52	16.5.52	4.8.55	430, Turkey. Cat.A.
243	19343		2.5.52	18.6.53	416. Cat.A.
244	19344		2.5.52	18.6.54	421, Greece.
245	19345		13.5.52	13.5.52	USAF.
246	19346	2.6.52	28.5.52	28.5.52	USAF.
247	19347		30.7.52	29.9.54	413, 434, Greece.
248	19348	27.5.52	28.5.52	28.5.52	USAF.
249	19349	9.5.52	31.5.52	18.6.54	421, Greece.
250	19350	14.5.52	31.5.52	7.1.53	421. Cat.A.
251	19351	20.5.52	28.5.52	28.5.52	USAF.
252	19352	20.5.52	12.5.52	12.5.52	USAF.
253	19353	26.5.52	31.5.52	27.9.54	430, Turkey. Cat.A.
254	19354	22.5.52	14.8.52	18.6.54	421, Turkey, Cat.A.
255	19355	27.5.52	31.5.52	18.6.54	430, Greece.
256	19356	3.6.52	13.6.52	13.6.52	USAF.
257	19357	23.5.52	13.6.52	13.6.52	USAF.
258	19358	3.6.52	25.6.52	25.6.52	USAF.
259	19359	16.6.52	30.7.52	20.7.54	422, OTU, Turkey. Cat.A.
260	19360	4.6.52	13.6.52	13.6.52	USAF.
261	19361	4.6.52	28.5.52	28.5.52	USAF.
262	19362	9.6.52	13.6.52	13.6.52	USAF.
263	19363	31.5.52	10.6.52	20.7.54	OTU, Greece.
264	19364	9.6.52	31.5.52	20.7.54	OTU, Turkey.
265	19365	12.6.52	16.7.52	6.7.53	421. Cat.A.
266	19366	18.6.52	25.6.52	25.6.52	USAF.
267	19367	13.6.52	20.6.52	15.7.52	422, OTU. Cat.A.
268	19368	10.6.52	25.6.52	25.6.52	USAF.
269	19369	18.6.52	25.6.52	25.6.52	USAF.
270	19370	20.6.52	30.7.52	24.10.52	416. Cat.A. To Redifon. Turkey.
271	19371	18.6.54	25.7.52	18.6.54	OTU. Cat.A.
272	19372	18.6.54	31.5.52	19.1.53	OTU. Cat.A.
273	19373	20.6.52	30.7.52	18.6.54	430, Turkey. Cat.A.
274	19374	20.6.52	31.5.52	30.7.54	OTU, Greece. Cat.A.
275	19375	3.7.52	25.7.52	18.6.54	421, Turkey. Cat.A.
276	19376	26.6.52	18.7.52	14.8.55	431, OTU, Turkey.
277	19377	27.6.52	25.7.52	18.6.54	421, Greece.
278	19378	3.7.52	14.8.52	18.6.54	OFU, FTU. To RAF 4.12.52 as XB530. Greece. Cat.A.
279	19379	16.7.52	30.7.52	29.10.54	430, Turkey.
280	19380	11.7.52	16.7.52	18.6.54	416, Turkey. Cat.A.
281	19381	4.7.52	30.7.52	20.7.54	431, OTU, Greece. Cat.A.
282	19382	13.7.52	30.7.52	29.9.55	416, 421, Greece.
283	19383	11.7.52	14.8.52	18.6.54	413, 421, Greece.
284	19384	5.7.52	14.8.52	29.9.52	OFU, FTU, 229 OCU. To RAF as XB531 4.12.52. Cat.A.
285	19385	8.7.52	25.7.52	18.6.54	416, Turkey. Cat.A.
286	19386	6.7.52	16.7.52	18.6.54	421, Turkey.
287	19387	5.7.52	25.7.52	18.6.54	416, Turkey.
288	19388	13.7.52	30.7.52	17.4.55	OTU. Cat.A.
289	19389	6.7.52	16.7.52	29.7.54	421, Turkey.
290	19390	11.7.52	30.7.52	18.6.54	430, Greece. Cat.A.
291	19391	18.7.52	30.7.52	18.6.54	430, Turkey. Cat.A.
292	19392	17.7.52	30.7.52	20.7.54	OTU, Greece.
293	19393	13.7.52	30.7.52	20.7.54	OTU, Greece.
294	19394	13.7.52	14.8.52	29.10.54	434, Turkey.
295	19395	8.8.52	14.8.52	20.7.54	OTU, Turkey.
296	19396	18.7.52	30.7.52	20.7.54	OTU, Turkey.
297	19397	23.7.52	30.7.52	18.6.54	430, Greece.
298	19398	25.7.52	30.7.52	29.9.54	OTU, Greece.
299	19399	19.7.52	14.8.52	18.6.54	413, Turkey. Cat.A.
300	19400	24.7.52	19.9.52	19.5.54	OTU. Cat.A.
301	19401	18.7.52	14.8.52	20.7.54	431, Turkey.
302	19402	18.7.52	14.8.52	25.9.52	434. Cat.A. To Redifon.
303	19403	23.7.52	14.8.52	20.7.54	OTU, Greece. Cat.A.
304	19404	22.7.52	14.8.52	27.9.52	OFU, FTU, CFE, AFDS. To RAF as XB532 4.12.52, Italy (2-19).
305	19405	14.8.52	14.8.52	18.6.54	416, Turkey.
306	19406	1.8.52	14.8.52	4.8.55	430, 439, Turkey.
307	19407	31.7.52	14.8.52	20.7.54	427, 431, Greece. Cat.A.
308	19408	15.8.52	14.8.52	18.6.54	416, Turkey. Cat.A.
309	19409	20.8.52	5.9.52	29.9.54	427, Greece.
310	19410	15.8.52	5.9.52	20.7.55	CEPE, Turkey. Cat.A.
311	19411	20.8.52	19.9.52	20.11.52	427. Cat.A.
312	19412	22.8.52	5.9.52	18.6.54	413, Turkey.
313	19413	15.8.52	5.9.52	20.7.54	431, Turkey.
314	19414	22.8.52	19.9.52	20.7.54	OTU, Turkey.
315	19415	19.8.52	5.9.52	29.9.54	427, Turkey.
316	19416	3.9.52	5.9.52	20.7.54	OTU, Greece. Cat.A.
317	19417	25.9.52	19.9.52	18.6.54	427, 434, Turkey. Cat.A.
318	19418	26.8.52	5.9.52	4.8.55	427, Greece. Cat.A.
319	19419	30.8.52	5.9.52	20.7.54	Turkey.
320	19420	28.8.52	5.9.52	20.7.54	OTU, Turkey. Cat.A.
321	19421	11.9.52	19.9.52	29.9.54	410, Turkey. Cat.A.
322	19422	29.8.52	5.9.52	31.7.53	427. Cat.A.
323	19423	5.9.52	5.9.52	9.3.55	CEPE, Greece. Cat.A.
324	19424	16.9.52	19.9.52	29.9.54	434, Greece.
325	19425	9.9.52	19.9.52	9.3.55	OTU, Greece.
326	19426	18.9.52	19.9.52	28.9.53	OTU. Cat.A.
327	19427	16.9.52	19.9.52	18.6.54	427, Turkey. Cat.A.
328	19428	16.9.52	5.11.52	29.9.54	427, Greece.
329	19429	10.9.52	13.11.52	4.8.55	410, 434, Greece. Cat.A.
330	19430	17.9.52	21.10.52	4.8.55	427, 439, Greece. Cat.A.
331	19431	16.9.52	19.9.52	18.6.54	434, Turkey.
332	19432	16.9.52	22.10.52	4.8.55	427, Greece.
333	19433	20.9.52	21.10.52	29.9.54	410, 427, Greece.
334	19434	25.9.52	21.10.52	29.9.54	434, Greece. Cat.A.
335	19435	25.9.52	5.11.52	20.7.54	421, 431, Turkey.
336	19436	9.10.52	7.11.52	14.5.53	OTU. Cat.A.
337	19437	4.10.52	22.10.52	29.9.54	427, Turkey.
338	19438	26.9.52	22.10.52	29.9.54	427, Greece. Cat.A.
339	19439	23.9.52	22.10.52	4.9.55	439, Turkey.
340	19440	8.10.52	21.10.52	29.9.54	431, Greece. Cat.A.
341	19441	27.9.52	22.10.52	4.8.55	439, Turkey.
342	19442	4.10.52	7.11.52	23.2.54	OTU, Cat.A.
343	19443	17.10.52	7.11.52	4.8.55	427, Greece.
344	19444	4.10.52	7.11.52	18.6.54	427, Greece.
345	19445	16.10.52	7.11.52	29.9.54	427, Turkey.
346	19446	9.10.52	13.11.52	29.9.54	414, 434, Turkey. Cat.A.
347	19447	16.10.52	7.11.52	18.6.54	427, Greece. Cat.A.
348	19448	20.10.52	7.11.52	20.7.54	414, 422, OTU, Greece.
349	19449	17.10.52	7.11.52	29.9.54	434, Turkey.
350	19450	17.10.52	13.11.52	29.9.54	414, 427, Turkey.
351	19451	14.10.52	22.10.52	29.10.54	427, Turkey.
352	19452	16.10.52	13.11.52	20.7.55	414, OTU, Greece. Final F-86 Mk.2.
353	19453/ XB809	28.8.52	11.3.52	1.12.53	To RAF 14.3.54. To USAF (Mutual Aid Plan) 25.10.56. 413, 414. First F-86 Mk.4.
354	19454/ XB816	10.10.52	16.12.52	1.12.53	RAF 22.12.53, USAF 26.2.57. 414, 93.
355	19455/ XB835	20.10.52	16.12.52	1.12.53	RAF 1.3.54. USAF 18.7.56. 414, 229/V, Italy.
356	19456	24.10.56	14.11.52	16.10.53	CEPE. Cat.A.
357	19457/ XB689	22.10.52	13.11.52	1.12.53	RAF 26.4.54, USAF 13.8.57. 413, 414, Yugoslavia (06-051)
358	19458/ XB755	30.10.52	13.11.52	1.12.53	RAF 22.12.53. USAF 14.1.57. 414, 20, 93, Italy.
359	19459/ XB761	5.11.52	13.11.52	1.12.53	RAF 16.6.54. USAF. 414. Yugoslavia. Cat.A.
360	19460/ XB769	25.11.52	13.11.52	1.12.53	RAF 29.6.54. USAF 12.9.56. 414, 444, Italy (4-4). Cat.A.
361	19461/ XB806	25.11.52	16.12.52	1.12.53	RAF 22.2.54. USAF 6.6.57. 413, 414, Yugoslavia (06-11, 11-045).
362	19462/ XB531	10.12.52	16.12.52	3.1.53	414. Cat.A.
363	19463/ XB532	2.11.52	13.11.52	24.3.53	414. Cat.A.
364	19464/ XB533	2.11.52			RAF 16.3.53. USAF 25.9.56. Italy (4-12).
365	19465/ XB534	1.11.52			No.1 LRFU. Cat.A.
366	19466/ XB535	30.10.52			RAF 22.12.52. USAF 14.1.57. 3, 26/L, 234.
367	19467/ XB536	4.11.52			RAF 16.3.53. USAF 21.8.56. 3, 234/N.

c/n	Tail No.	f/f	TOS	SOS	Notes
368	19468/XB537	8.11.52			RAF 22.12.52. USAF 6.7.56. 3/E, FTU, Yugoslavia.
369	19469/XB538	4.11.52			RAF 22.12.52. SOC 19.12.58. 3/F, 67/Z.
370	19470/XB539	1.11.53			RAF 10.11.53. USAF 14.9.56. Italy. Cat.A.
371	19471/XB540	13.11.52			RAF 30.9.53. USAF 9.2.56. 33MU/A, FWS.
372	19472/XB541	13.11.52			RAF 12.3.53. SOC 18.12.58. 3.
373	19473/XB542	28.11.52			RAF 16.3.53. USAF 7.6.57. 66/Z, SCF.
374	19474/XB543	12.11.52			RAF 22.12.52. USAF 7.7.56. 3/G, 26/Z, FTU, OFU, Italy. Cat.A.
375	19475/XB544	8.11.52			RAF 22.12.52. USAF 5.6.57. 3, FTU, OFU, Yugoslavia.
376	19476/XB545	14.11.52			RAF 22.12.52. USAF 11.12.56. 3/J, FTU, OFU, Italy. Cat.A.
377	19477/XB546	17.11.52			RAF 16.3.53. USAF 11.7.56. 33MU/B, FTU, FWS, Italy.
378	19478/XB547	5.11.52			RAF 22.12.56. SOC 18.12.58. 3/K, 20/F, FTU.
379	19479/XB548	14.11.52			RAF 22.12.52. 93, FTU, Cat.A.
380	19480/XB549	25.11.52			147. DBR 10.3.53.
381	19481/XB550	3.12.52			RAF 16.3.53. USAF 30.6.56. 3,67,71/D, Italy (4-76) Cat.A.
382	19482/XB575	18.11.52 ∅			RAF 4.5.53. SOC 28.12.58. 20/Q, 234/N.
383	19483/XB576	18.11.52			RAF 4.5.53. USAF 6.2.57. 93, 112, Italy. Cat.A.
384	19484/XB577	25.11.52			RAF 4.5.53. USAF 10.4.56. 26/V, Italy (4-09). Cat.A.
385	19485/XB578	25.11.52			RAF 7.4.53. USAF 12.9.57. 234/C.
386	19486/XB579	25.11.52			RAF 16.3.53. SOC 19.12.58.
387	19487/XB580	28.11.52			RAF 16.3.53. USAF 28.9.56. 26/D, 67/X, Italy.
388	19488/XB581	25.11.52			RAF 16.3.53. USAF 21.2.57. 3/T, Italy (4-48).
389	19489/XB582	22.11.52			RAF 4.5.53. USAF 8.11.57. 3/R, 234, Yugoslavia (06-045, 06-075, 11-047).
390	19490/XB583	30.11.52			RAF 16.3.53. USAF 9.10.56. 93, FTU.
391	19491/XB584	10.12.52	15.4.53	1.12.53	RAF 12.7.53. USAF 9.11.56. 414.
392	19492/XB585	26.11.52			RAF 16.3.53. SOC 18.12.58. 3/F, FTU.
393	19493/XB586	1.12.52			RAF 16.3.53. USAF 18.3.57. 67/X,Y, Italy.
394	19494/XB587	16.12.52			RAF 16.3.53. USAF 28.6.57. 67/L, SCF, Yugoslavia. (06-042, 11-048).
395	19495/XB588	4.12.52			RAF 3.6.53. SOC 18.12.58.
396	19496/XB589	16.12.52			RAF 13.3.53. SOC 18.12.58. 3, 20/P, 234/D, T, FTU, Italy (4-12).
397	19497/XB590	28.11.52			RAF 16.3.53. SOC 18.12.58. 3/U.
398	19498/XB591	29.11.52			RAF 14.3.53. USAF 5.12.56. SCF, Italy.
399	19499/XB592	3.12.52			RAF 14.3.53. USAF 6.11.56. SCF, Italy.
400	19500/XB593	4.12.52			USAF 13.6.56. 26, 112, SCF, Italy.
401	19501/XB594	31.12.53			USAF 15.3.57. 20/V.
402	19502/XB595	6.1.53			USAF 10.4.56. 26.
403	19503/XB596	19.12.52			USAF 5.10.56. 67.
404	19504/XB597	30.12.52			USAF 9.3.56. 20.
405	19505/XB598	18.12.52			USAF 18.3.57. 67/R, Italy (2-70).
406	19506/XB599	7.1.53			USAF 30.5.56. 71, Italy. Cat.A.
407	19507/XB600	12.1.53			67/W. Cat.A.
408	19508/XB601	31.12.52			USAF 12.10.56. 147, FTU, FWS, Italy (2-12).

c/n	Tail No.	f/f	TOS	SOS	Notes
409	19509/XB602	19.12.52			USAF 15.2.57. SCF, Italy (2-44, 4-24), P (Cameri).
410	19510/XB603	17.12.52			SCF. Cat.A.
411	19511/XB608	6.1.53			USAF 6.11.56. 71, Italy (4-49).
412	19512/XB609	16.12.52			USAF 27.6.56. 3, 26, Italy. Cat.A.
413	19513/XB610	17.12.52			147. Cat. A.
414	19514/XB611	19.12.52			USAF 17.12.57. 71, SCF, Yugoslavia.
415	19515/XB612	7.1.53			SOC 9-57. 3.
416	19516/XB613	23.12.52			USAF 12.11.56. 26/C, Italy.
417	19517/XB614	31.12.52			SOC 18.12.58. 3, 234/J.
418	19518/XB615	31.12.52			234/H. Cat.A.
419	19519/XB616	8.1.53			USAF 5.12.56. 229, SCF, Italy.
420	19520/XB617	6.1.53			USAF 12.7.57. 3, Italy (4-01), Yugoslavia.
421	19521/XB618	31.12.52			USAF 12.9.56. SCF, Italy (4-25)
422	19522/XB619	16.1.53			SOC 18.12.58. 3.
423	19523/XB620	7.1.53			USAF 27.11.56. RAE, Italy (4-50, 13-3). P (Rivolto).
424	19524/XB621	8.1.53			USAF 16.4.57. 3, Yugoslavia (11-051).
425	19525/XB622	5.1.53			USAF 24.4.56. AFDS, Italy.
426	19526/XB623	6.1.53			26/Q. Cat.A.
427	19527/XB624	10.1.53			USAF 16.7.57. 67, 71, Yugoslavia (11-052).
428	19528/XB625	10.1.53			USAF 19.2.57. 67, Italy.
429	19529/XB626	17.1.53			SOC 18.12.58. 67.
430	19530/XB627	21.1.53			67/C. Cat.A.
431	19531/XB628	20.1.53			67/L, 71. Cat.A.
432	XB629	17.1.53			SOC 18.12.58. 3, 93, 112.
433	XB630	22.1.53			SOC 18.12.58. 71/P.
434	XB631	17.1.53			USAF 5.6.56. 71, Italy.
435	XB632	12.1.53			USAF 23.10.57. 67, 71, Italy, Yugoslavia.
436	XB633	12.1.53			3/W. Cat.A.
437	XB634	21.1.53			67. Cat.A.
438	XB635				USAF 27.3.57. 71, SCF.
439	XB636				USAF 31.5.57. 26, Yugoslavia.
440	XB637	9.2.53			SOC 18.12.58. 71.
441	XB638	20.1.53			20. Cat.A.
442	XB639	27.1.53			USAF 20.4.56. 67, Italy (2-05), UN (Congo). P (Kinshasa).
443	XB640	20.1.53			USAF 13.3.57. 3/P.
444	XB641	22.1.53			USAF 12.1.56. 147, 229, Italy.
445	XB642	26.1.53			SOC 18.12.58. 234.
446	XB643	20.1.53			3. Cat.A.
447	XB644	23.1.53			USAF 25.6.56. 3, 229, Italy. Cat.A.
448	XB645	1.2.53			USAF 1.3.57. 20/W, Italy.
449	XB646	23.1.53			SOC 18.12.58. 3, 20/M.
450	XB664	21.1.53			USAF 5.12.56. 67, Italy.
451	XB665	14.4.53			USAF 14.11.56. 67, 71, SCF, Italy (4-30).
452	XB666	10.2.53			USAF 26.2.57. 229, AFDS.
453	XB667	30.1.53			3. Cat.A.
454	XB668	30.1.53			USAF 7.9.56. 67, Italy.
455	XB669	26.1.53			USAF 30.6.56. 71, Italy.
456	XB670	29.1.53			USAF 23.5.57. 3, Yugoslavia.
457	XB671	1.2.53			SOC 18.12.58. 67.
458	XB672	1.2.53			USAF 6.5.57. 3, Yugoslavia.
459	XB673	1.2.53			SOC 18.12.58. 3, SCF.
460	XB674	14.2.53			USAF 4.3.57. 67, Italy.
461	XB675	29.1.53			USAF 23.5.56. SCF, Hawkers.
462	XB676	3.2.53			SCF, DBR 17.6.53.
463	XB677	30.1.53			92, AFDS. Cat.A.
464	XB678	29.1.53			USAF 28.2.57. 67.
465	XB679	6.2.53			USAF 15.2.57. 67, Italy.

c/n	Tail No.	f/f	TOS	SOS	Notes
466	XB680	6.2.53			USAF 14.5.57. 234/G, Yugoslavia.
467	XB681	2.2.53			3. Cat.A.
468	XB682	11.2.53			USAF 3.6.57. 67, 130/V, SCF, Italy, Yugoslavia (11-057).
469	XB683	4.2.53			67/W. Cat.A.
470	XB684	19.2.53			USAF 27.1.56. 3, Italy, Yugoslavia (4-01).
471	XB685	6.2.53			USAF 30.11.56. 3,147, FTU, Italy.
472	XB686	9.2.53			USAF 4.2.57. 71, SCF, Italy (2-36).
473	XB687	10.2.53			USAF 21.9.56. 71, Italy (4-51).
474	XB688	6.2.53			USAF 19.1.57. SCF, Italy, (2-39, 2-52, 4-51).
475	19575/XB825	13.2.53	15.4.53	1.12.53	RAF 8.4.54. USAF 9.10.56. 444, 229/T.
476	XB690	7.2.53			67/Z. Cat.A.
477	XB691	11.2.53			USAF 14.1.57. 71.
478	XB692	7.2.53			USAF 9.10.57. 67, Italy.
479	19579/XB693	13.2.53	11.5.53	1.12.53	RAF 16.6.54. USAF 12.1.57. 414, 67/C, Italy (2-53).
480	XB694	17.2.53			USAF 3.6.57. 92/N, SCF, Italy, Yugoslavia.
481	XB695	20.2.53			USAF 22.3.57. 93/X, Italy. Cat.A.
482	19582/XB696	14.2.53	20.5.53	1.12.53	RAF 26.3.54. USAF 11.7.56. 444, 229/C, Italy (4-82).
483	XB697	14.2.53			USAF 13.6.57. 93, Italy, Yugoslavia (11-059), Honduras.
484	19584/XB698	20.2.53	20.5.53	1.12.53	RAF 22.4.54. USAF 20.3.56. 444, 229/R, Italy (4-07).
485	19585/XB699	19.2.53	15.4.53	1.12.53	RAF 1.3.54. 414, 3, Cat.A.
486	XB700	14.2.53			26/B, 71, SCF. Cat.A.
487	XB701	20.2.53			USAF 22.5.57. 67,93, Italy, Yugoslavia.
488	XB702	14.2.53			USAF 4.3.57. 67/J, Italy.
489	XB703	13.2.53			USAF 9.5.56. 3.
490	19590/XB704	19.2.53	15.4.53	1.12.53	RAF 10.2.54. SOC 18.12.56. 444, 3.
491	XB705	17.2.53			USAF 15.2.57. 67.
492	XB706	20.2.53			USAF 24.6.57. 67, 130/U, Italy, Yugoslavia (11-061).
493	XB707	17.2.53			USAF 29.5.57. 3, 20, 26, Yugoslavia.
494	XB708	21.2.53			USAF 14.9.56. 26/T.
495	XB709	18.2.53			USAF 31.5.56. 20, 26, Italy (4-31).
496	19596/XB710	23.2.53			USAF 21.4.56. 71/J, Italy (4-12, 4-31, 4-46).
497	19597/XB711	6.3.53	15.4.53	1.12.53	RAF 26.3.54. 444, 229/S, Italy (4-12, 4-46).
498	19598/XB712	25.2.53	15.4.53	1.12.53	RAF 8.4.54. USAF 13.3.57. 444, 93/F, Italy.
499	19599/XB713	17.2.53	15.4.53	1.12.53	RAF 26.3.54. USAF 1.3.57. 422, 444, 229, Italy.
500	XB726	21.2.53			USAF 20.3.57. 93, SCF, Italy.
501	19601/XB727	2.1.53	15.4.53	1.12.53	RAF 1.3.54. USAF 6.11.56. 422, 234/Y, Italy.
502	XB728	6.3.53			USAF 27.7.57. 71/V, SCF, Italy.
503	XB729	24.2.53			71. Cat.A.
504	XB730	26.2.53			67/Y. Cat.A.
505	XB731	26.2.53			SOC 18.12.58. 3, 20/J.
506	19606/XB732	25.3.53	15.4.53	1.12.53	RAF 1.6.54. USAF 21.8.57. 414, 130, Yugoslavia (06-055, 11-063).
507	XB733	18.3.53			USAF 25.8.56. AAEE, Italy (4-34, 13-2). To UK as G-ATBF.
508	XB734	6.3.53			26.
509	XB735	18.3.53			234. Cat.A.
510	XB736	10.3.53			USAF 3.10.57. 3, Yugoslavia (11-064).
511	XB737	5.3.53			USAF 13.3.57. 67/A.
512	XB738	8.3.53			USAF 30.6.56. 3, SCF, Yugoslavia
513	XB739	6.3.53			USAF 16.5.57. 71.
514	XB740	18.3.53			USAF 25.7.57. 3.
515	19615/XB741	18.3.53	15.4.53	1.12.53	RAF 28.4.54. USAF 6.5.57. 444, 229/H, Italy, Yugoslavia (06-005, 11-065).
516	19616/XB742	20.3.53	15.4.53	1.12.53	RAF 10.2.54. USAF 10.8.56. 444, 93, Italy. Cat.A.
517	19617/XB743	2.4.53	20.4.53	1.12.53	RAF 29.6.54. USAF 28.3.57. 422, Italy. Cat.A.
518	XB744	6.3.53			USAF 29.3.57.
519	19619/XB745	20.3.53	20.4.53	8.4.54	422. Cat.A.
520	XB746	8.3.53			USAF 5.10.56. 93, Italy.
521	XB747	18.3.53			USAF 5.9.57. 3.
522	XB748	18.3.53			USAF 29.5.57. 234, Yugoslavia.
523	XB749	20.3.53			USAF 20.6.57. 3/A, 20, Yugoslavia.
524	19624/XB750	18.3.53	15.4.53	1.12.53	RAF 12.3.54. SOC 18.12.58. 422, 234/K.
525	XB751	25.3.53			USAF 4.3.57. 26, Italy.
526	XB752	18.3.53			SOC 18.12.58. 20/Y, 234.
527	19627/XB753	18.3.53	11.5.53	1.12.53	RAF 14.6.54. USAF 24.9.56. 422, Italy.
528	19628/XB754	23.3.53	15.4.53	1.12.53	USAF 22.3.57. 414, 67/D, Italy.
529	19629/XB763	20.3.53	15.4.53	1.12.53	RAF 8.4.54. USAF 21.3.57. 422, 229/W.
530	XB756	2.4.53			USAF 4.5.56. 147, 229/D, FTU, OCU, Italy. Cat.A.
531	19631/XB757	23.3.53	15.4.53	1.12.53	RAF 16.6.54. USAF 24.6.57. 414, 444, 92/R, Yugoslavia (06-041).
532	19632/XB758	2.4.53	11.5.53	1.12.53	RAF 12.4.54. USAF 14.12.56. 422, FTU, Italy.
533	XB759	2.4.53			USAF 28.2.56. 26.
534	XB760	27.3.53			71. Cat.A.
535	19635/XB745	25.3.53	15.4.53	18.5.54	RAF 22.7.54. USAF 17.6.57. 422, 30AMB, 3, 130, Italy, Yugoslavia (06-035, 11-069).
536	19636/XB762	25.3.53	15.4.53	1.12.53	RAF 28.4.54. USAF 6.11.56. 422, 444, 229, Italy.
537	19637/XB763	2.4.53	15.4.53	17.3.54	422. Cat.A.
538	XB764	2.4.53			USAF 29.5.56. 26. Italy (4-77).
539	19639/XB765	25.3.53	15.4.53	1.12.53	RAF 30.3.54. USAF 10.1.57. 422, 229/L.
540	XB766	2.4.53			SOC 18.12.58. 234.
541	XB767	2.4.53			USAF 31.10.56. 26/Y, Yugoslavia (11-070).
542	19642/XB768	2.4.53	15.4.53	1.12.53	RAF 10.2.54. SOC 18.12.58. 93/T,Q.
543	19643	2.4.53	21.5.53	18.6.53	414. Cat.A.
544		5.5.53			USAF 20.11.56. 3, 20, 130.
545	XB791	20.5.53			USAF 29.8.56. 20, Italy (4-47).
546	XB792	9.4.53			USAF 20.6.57. 3, 234/X, Yugoslavia.
547.	19647/XB793	14.4.53	20.4.53	1.12.53	RAF 11.3.54. USAF 4.3.57. 422, 229/N, Italy.
548	XB794	8.4.53			USAF 29.4.57. 234/V, Yugoslavia.
549	19649/XB795	15.1.53	20.4.53	1.12.53	RAF 25.3.54. USAF 8.3.57. 422, 66/F, 229/G, Italy (2-60).
550	19650/XB796	27.3.53	15.4.53	1.12.53	RAF 29.6.54. USAF 18.9.56. 444, 71/D,X.
551	XB797	5.5.53			USAF 6.5.57. 444, 20, 130, Yugoslavia.
552	19652/XB798	2.4.53	20.4.53	1.12.53	RAF 15.12.54. USAF 23.7.56. 414, 444, ST, Italy (4-71).
553	19653/XB799	2.4.53	21.5.53	1.12.53	RAF 10.2.54. USAF 31.5.57. 414, 229/K, Yugoslavia (06-025, 11-074).
554	XB800	2.4.53			USAF 6.2.57. 26, 130, Italy.
555	19655/XB801	14.4.53	20.4.53	1.12.53	RAF 22.4.54. USAF 21.3.57. 444, 229/Z
556	XB802	8.4.53			SOC 18.12.58. 112/O, 93.
557	19657/XB803	8.4.53	15.5.53	1.12.53	RAF 30.4.54. SOC 18.12.58. 444, 20, 93, 234/Q.
558	XB804	8.4.53			USAF 4.4.57. 93/O, 112, Italy.
559	19659/XB805	9.4.53	20.4.53	1.12.53	RAF 23.8.54. USAF 30.6.56. 444, ST, Italy.
560	19660/XB806	14.4.53	11.5.53		414. Cat.A.
561	19661/XB807	17.4.53	11.5.53	1.12.53	RAF 30.4.54. USAF 14.3.56. 414, 234/Z.
562	XB808	9.4.53			20, 112. Cat.A.
563	XB551	24.4.53	11.5.53	19.7.54	RAF 22.7.54. USAF 17.5.56. Exchange for 19738. Hawkers.
564	19664/XB810	14.4.53	11.5.53	1.12.53	USAF 27.3.56. 422, CGS/D, FWS, Italy (13-3) P (Capua).

c/n	Tail No.	f/f	TOS	SOS	Notes
565	19665/XB811	14.4.53	20.4.53	1.12.53	RAF 8.4.54. USAF 6.5.57. 444, 229/P, Yugoslavia (06-007, 11-075).
566	XB812	16.4.53			USAF 26.7.56. 93, 112, Italy (4-11, 4-85). P (Rome).
567	19667/XB813	15.4.53	11.5.53	1.12.53	RAF 25.3.54. USAF 9.10.57. 422, 229/M.
568	19668/XB814	22.4.53	11.5.53	1.12.53	RAF 31.5.54. USAF 29.9.56. 422, ST, Italy (13-5). P (Cameri).
569	19669/XB815	22.4.53	11.5.53	1.12.53	USAF 30.8.57. 422, 20/N, Yugoslavia.
570	19670	22.4.53	21.5.53	18.6.53	414. Cat.A.
571	19671/XB817	22.4.53	21.5.53	1.12.53	RAF 17.5.54. SOC 18.12.58. 414, 422, 444, 234/U, Italy.
572	XB818	24.4.53			USAF 29.8.56. 26/M, 112, Italy (4-34).
573	19673/XB819	22.4.53	11.5.53	1.12.53	RAF 1.3.54. 414, 234/Z. Cat.A.
574	19674/XB820	29.4.53	11.5.53	1.12.53	RAF 1.3.54. USAF 20.9.57. 444, 67, Yugoslavia, Honduras.
575	19675/XB821	24.4.53	11.5.53	1.12.53	RAF 10.2.54. USAF 15.3.57. 414, 229/E, Italy.
576	XB822	24.4.53			93, 112. Cat.A.
577	19677/XB823	29.4.53	11.5.53	1.12.53	RAF 12.3.54. USAF 19.9.57. 444, 229, Yugoslavia. Cat.A.
578	XB824	5.5.53			USAF 21.6.57. 93, 130, Yugoslavia.
579	19679	29.4.53	21.5.53	17.3.54	422. Cat.A.
580	19680	5.5.53	11.5.53	1.12.53	RAF 29.6.54. USAF 14.1.57. 414, 444, Italy. (2-37).
581	XB827	24.4.53			USAF 25.5.57. 234, Italy, Yugoslavia (11-079).
582	19682/XB828	24.4.53	11.5.53	1.12.53	USAF 29.3.57. 414, ST.
583	XB829	29.4.53			USAF 11.7.56. 93, 112, 147, Italy (4-19).
584	19684/XB830	4.5.53	21.5.53	1.12.53	RAF 14.6.54. USAF 15.6.56. 444, ST, Italy (4-48).
585	19685/XB831	29.4.53	11.5.53	1.12.53	RAF 29.6.54. USAF 17.5.56. 444, ST, Italy (4-20).
586	19686/XB832	29.4.53	11.5.53	1.12.53	RAF 17.5.54. USAF 21.9.56. 422, 26.
587	XB833	30.4.53			USAF 18.9.56. 93, 130, Italy (4-48).
588	XB834	5.5.53			USAF 13.5.57. 26, 130, Yugoslavia.
589	19689	30.4.53	11.5.53	9.6.53	422. Cat.A.
590	XB836	7.5.53			USAF 27.7.57. 130, 234, Italy.
591	19691	7.5.53	21.5.53	1.12.53	RAF 17.5.54. USAF 27.6.57. 414, 444, 92/K, Italy.
592	XB838	7.5.53			USAF 27.1.58. 130, 234, Italy, Yugoslavia (11-080).
593	XB839	27.5.53			26/X, 130. Cat.A.
594		4.5.53			USAF 14.9.56. 93, Italy (4-44).
595	19695/XB857	5.5.53	21.5.53	1.12.53	RAF 1.6.54. USAF 12.6.56. 414, 422, 444, Italy (4-48). Cat.A.
596	XB858	11.5.53			USAF 11.5.56. 3, 130.
597	XB859	20.5.53			USAF 23.11.57. 3, 130.
598	XB860	19.5.53			234/B. Cat.A.
599	XB861	8.5.53			SOC 18.12.58. 20, 130, 234.
600	XB862	8.5.53			USAF 5.11.57. 20, 26, 130, Yugoslavia.
601	XB863	21.5.53			147. Cat.A.
602	19702/XB864	8.5.53	21.5.53	1.12.53	RAF 17.5.54. USAF 3.10.57. 444, ST, Yugoslavia (06-068, 11-082).
603	XB865	11.5.53			RAF 17.8.54. 26, 112. Cat.A.
604	XB866	20.5.53			26. Cat.A.
605	XB867	12.5.53			SOC 18.12.58.
606	XB868	20.5.53			USAF 13.6.57. 26, Yugoslavia (11-083).
607	XD706/USAF 52-10177	19.5.53			SOC 18.12.58. 66/D.
608	XD707/52-10178	20.5.53			66/B. Cat.A.
609	XD708/52-10179	20.5.53			USAF 6.11.56. 66, Italy.
610	XD709/52-10180	20.5.53			USAF 26.8.57. 92, Italy, Yugoslavia.
611	XD710/52-10181	20.5.53			66. 92/D. Damaged on takeoff at Acklington, 5.4.55.
612	XD711/52-10182	21.5.53			66/U. Cat.A.
613	XD712/52-10183	20.5.53			66/S. Cat.A.
614	XD713/52-10184	20.5.53			92. Damaged on takeoff at Linton-on-Ouse 29.1.55.
615	XD714/52-10185	21.5.53			USAF 29.12.56. 92.
616	XD715/52-10186	25.5.53			USAF 27.7.57. 66/K, Italy.
617	XD716/52-10187	26.5.53			66. Cat.A.
618	XD717/52-10188	22.5.53			66/X. USAF 3.7.57. 92. Cat.A.
619	XD718/52-10189	25.5.53			SOC 12.7.56. 66.
620	XD719/52-10190	25.5.53			USAF 10.1.57. 66, 92/T.
621	XD720/52-10191	25.5.53			USAF 23.5.57. 66, Italy, Yugoslavia.
622	XD721/52-10192	29.5.53			USAF 10.8.56. 66, Italy.
623	XD722/52-10193	29.5.53			66, Italy (4-25). P (Rivolto)
624	XD723/52-10194	28.5.53			USAF 8.11.56. 92 Italy (4-25).
625	XD724/52-10195	27.5.53			USAF 19.12.57. 66, 92, Yugoslavia (11-086), Honduras.
626	XD725/52-10196	26.6.53			USAF 3.7.57. 66.
627	XD726/52-10197	28.5.53			USAF 9.10.57. 92.
628	XD727/52-10198	12.6.53			SOC 18.12.58. 92/D
629	XD728/52-10199	27.5.53			USAF 22.6.56. 92/H.
630	XD729/52-10200	27.5.53			66/J. Cat.A.
631	XD730/52-10201	28.5.53			66/X. Cat.A.
632	XB869	1.6.53			SOC 18.12.58. 67, 71.
633	XB870	28.5.53			USAF 12.4.57. 71, Italy.
634	XB871	29.5.53			SOC 18.12.58. 3, 93, 130.
635	XB872	8.6.53			USAF 30.9.57. 234.
636	XB873	1.6.53			USAF 1.5.57. 234, Yugoslavia.
637	XB874	16.6.53			USAF 4.2.57. 93, SCF.
638	XB875	10.6.53			USAF 5.11.57. 71, Yugoslavia (11-088).
639	XB876	2.6.53			USAF 10.1.57. 444, 71.
640	XB877	1.6.53			USAF 27.5.57. 26.
641	XB878	10.6.53			USAF 28.8.57. 71/X. Italy, Yugoslavia (11-089).
642	XB879	9.6.53			USAF 31.5.57. 71, Yugoslavia. Cat.A.
643	XB880	3.6.53			Cat.A.
644	XB881	9.6.53			USAF 7.11.56.
645	XB882	8.6.53			147. Cat.A.
646	XB883	8.6.53			USAF 5.12.56. 26/A.
647	XB884	10.6.53			112. Cat.A.
648	XB885	10.6.53			USAF 5.10.56. 234/D.
649	XD731/52-10202	10.6.53			USAF 13.9.56. 66, Italy. Cat.A.
650	XD732/52-10203	12.6.53			SOC 18.12.58. 92.
651	XD733/52-10204	11.6.53			92/R. Cat.A.
652	XD734/52-10205	15.6.53			USAF 3.1.57. 92, Italy (4-71). Cat.A.
653	XD735/52-10206	16.6.53			USAF 20.3.57. 66/T. Italy (4-32). Cat.A.
654	XD736/52-10207	7.7.53			USAF 19.2.57. 92, Italy (2-50, 2-52).
655	XD753	15.6.53			USAF 21.8.57. 66/L. Italy, Yugoslavia (11-091).
656	XD754	16.6.53			USAF 31.5.57.
657	XD755/52-10210	16.6.53			66/F. Cat.A.
658	XD756/52-10211	17.6.53			USAF 21.8.57. 92/C Italy, Yugoslavia.
659	XD757/52-10212	18.6.53			USAF 19.8.57. 66,92, Yugoslavia.
660	XD758/52-10213	19.6.53			66/L. Cat.A.
661	XD759/52-10214	23.6.53			SOC 18.12.58. 92.
662	XD760/52-10215	7.7.53			USAF 28.6.57. 92, Yugoslavia (11-094), Honduras.
663	XD761/52-10216	2.7.53			USAF 13.9.57. 66, Yugoslavia.

c/n	Tail No.	f/f	TOS	SOS	Notes
664	XD762/ 52-10217	23.6.53			SOC 18.12.58. 66.
665	XD763/ 52-10218	30.6.53			SOC 18.12.58. 66.
666	XD764/ 52-10219	19.6.53			USAF 19.9.56. 92, Italy (4-50).
667	XD765/ 52-10220	3.7.53			USAF 22.8.57. 66, Yugoslavia (11-096).
668	XD766/ 52-10221	22.6.53			SOC 18.12.58. 92/L.
669	XD767/ 52-10222	7.7.53			USAF 28.5.57. 92.
670	XD768/ 52-10223	2.7.53			66/X. Cat.A.
671	XD769/ 52-10224	2.7.53			SOC 18.12.58. 92/J.
672	XD770/ 52-10225	3.7.53			SOC 18.12.58. 66/M.
673	XD771/ 52-10226	7.7.53			92/K. Cat.A.
674	XB886/ 52-10227	3.7.53			USAF 3.7.57. 20, 26, 93, Yugoslavia (11-097), Honduras.
675	XB887/ 52-10228	9.7.53			USAF 3.9.56. Italy (4-39).
676	XB888/ 52-10229	10.7.53			USAF 4.6.57. 20/T.
677	XB889	9.7.53			SOC 18.12.58. 20.
678	XB890				USAF 29.6.56. 234, Italy (4-32).
679	XB891				SOC 18.12.58. 93, 130, 234/U.
680	XB892	14.7.53			USAF 23.10.56. 20, Italy.
681	XB893	7.7.53			USAF 21.5.57. 93/A, 112, Italy, Yugoslavia.
682	XB894	7.7.53			USAF 12.12.56. 130, Italy, (4-83).
683	XB895	9.7.53			USAF 3.7.57. 20, Yugoslavia (11-099)
684	XB896	9.7.53			USAF 12.12.56. 71, Italy.
685	XB897	14.7.53			USAF 18.12.58. 234.
686	XB898	10.7.53			SOC 18.12.58. 234.
687	XB899	14.7.53			20/B. Cat.A.
688	XB900	9.7.53			20/A. Bristols.
689	XB912	15.7.53			112. Cat.A.
690	XB913	14.7.53			SOC 18.12.58. 3/L, 93, 112.
691	XB914	14.7.53			USAF 12.9.57. 20/S, 112.
692	XB915	16.7.53			USAF 15.10.56. 20/R, 112, Italy (13-1). P (Museo Storico).
693	XD772	21.7.53			66/H. Cat.A.
694	XD773	15.7.53			66/C. Cat.A.
695	XD774	21.7.53			USAF 8.1.58. 66, Yugoslavia.
696	XD775	20.7.53			147. Cat.A.
697	XD776/ 52-10231	21.7.53			66/Z. Cat.A.
698	XD777/ 52-10232	21.7.53			USAF 7.1.57. 66, Italy (2-35).
699	XD778/ 52-10233	20.7.53			USAF 28.3.57. 66.
700	XD779/ 52-10234	28.7.53			USAF 4.11.57. 92/A.
701	XD780/ 52-10235	24.7.53			92, 229, AFDS.
702	XD781/ 52-10236	28.7.53			USAF 23.10.56. AFDS.
703	XB916	19.8.53			USAF 25.9.56. 130.
704	XB917	28.7.53			USAF 12.7.56. 112/A.
705	XB918	30.7.53			SOC 18.12.58. 130/R.
706	XB919	28.7.53			USAF 7.9.57. 112, Italy, Yugoslavia.
707	XB920	28.7.53			USAF 14.6.57. 112/K, Italy, Yugoslavia.
708	XB921	19.9.53			USAF 30.9.57. 4, 71, 130.
709	XB922	19.8.53			USAF 22.10.57. 130, Italy, Yugoslavia.
710	XB923	20.8.53			USAF 20.11.56. 4.
711	XB924	25.8.53			USAF 31.5.56. 130.
712	XB925	19.8.53			147.
713	XB926	26.8.53			USAF 7.1.58. 112, SCF, Italy, Yugoslavia.
714	XB927	18.8.53			130/V. Cat.A.
715	XB928	21.8.53			USAF 25.7.57. 130.
716	XB929	18.8.53			USAF 22.5.57. 130/Q, Italy, Yugoslavia.
717	XB930	19.8.53			USAF 8.11.56. 130.
718	XB931				SOC 9.5.58. 4, 26.
719	XB932				130. Cat.A.
720	XB933	25.8.53			USAF 29.3.57. 130, Italy.
721	XB934	3.9.53			USAF 17.7.57. 112/X, Italy, Yugoslavia (11-106), Honduras.
722	XB935	21.8.53			USAF 24.5.56. 4, SCF, Italy (4-21).
723	XB936	26.8.53			67, Handling Squadron. Cat.A.
724	XB937	21.8.53			4. Cat.A.
725	XB938	31.8.53			USAF 7.11.57. 3, 4.
726	XB939	10.9.53			USAF 29.8.57. 67, 112, Yugoslavia (11-107)
727	XB940	26.8.53			4.
728	XB941	28.8.53			USAF 27.7.57. 4, 66/S, Italy.
729	XB942	4.9.53			USAF 12.6.56. 130, Italy (4-66).
730	XB943	28.8.53			USAF 6.7.56. 71, 130, Italy. Cat.A.
731	XB944	10.9.53			SOC 18.12.58. 112/L.
732	XB945	18.9.53			USAF 21.6.56. 130.
733	XB946	1.9.53			USAF 17.7.57. 112, Italy, Yugoslavia (11-108).
734	XB947	8.9.53			SOC 18.12.58. 112/Q.
735	XB948	3.9.53			USAF 30.10.56. Italy.
736	XB949	2.9.53			USAF 12.6.57. 3, 130/Z, 234, Italy.
737	XB950	11.9.53			112/S. Cat.A.
738	XB951	8.9.53			USAF 22.6.56. 130, Italy.
739	XB952	3.9.53			USAF 15.10.56. 71, 130, SCF, Italy.
740	XB953	12.9.53			USAF 26.9.57. 3, 130, Yugoslavia (11-109).
741	XB954	12.9.53			USAF 7.9.56. 130, Italy (4-44). Cat.A. P (Grazzanise).
742	XB955	11.9.53			USAF 28.9.56. 4/W.
743	XB956	15.9.53			USAF 18.11.57. 112/T, Italy.
744	XB957	11.9.53			USAF 13.6.57. 3, 112, Italy.
745	XB958	11.9.53			USAF 28.2.57. 112.
746	XB959	15.9.53			USAF 19.9.57. 112/V, 130.
747	XB960	15.9.53			USAF 24.5.57. 112/G, Italy, Yugoslavia.
748	XB961	18.9.53			USAF 28.2.57. 4, 26, 130, Italy (2-58).
749	XB973	18.9.53			USAF 19.8.57. 3, 4, Yugoslavia.
750	XB974	18.9.53			USAF 24.6.57. 4, 71/O, Italy, Yugoslavia.
751	XB975	22.9.53			USAF 16.5.57. 130, 234, Italy.
752	XB976	18.9.53			USAF 2.12.57. 112/E, Italy.
753	XB977	18.9.53			USAF 24.8.56. 4/H, 20, Italy.
754	XB647	22.9.53			4. Cat.A.
755	XB648	30.9.53			130. Cat.A.
756	XB649	23.9.53			USAF 27.7.57. 112, Italy.
757	XB650	23.9.53			USAF 16.7.57. 112, Yugoslavia (11-113).
758	XB770	30.9.53			USAF 16.5.56. 4, Italy.
759	XB771	24.9.53			USAF 4.4.57. 112.
760	XB772	28.9.53			USAF 6.5.57. 112, Yugoslavia.
761	XB773	28.9.53			USAF 6.5.57. 4/C, Italy, Yugoslavia.
762	XB774	25.9.53			USAF 5.10.57. 112/D, Italy, Yugoslavia.
763	XB775	13.10.53			USAF 19.1.57. Italy, Cat.A.
764	XB851	1.10.53			USAF 8.5.56. 130.
765	XB852	10.10.53			SOC 15.11.56. 130.
766	XB853	10.10.53			USAF 14.6.58. 130.
767	XB854	1.10.53			USAF 6.5.57. 4, 20, Yugoslavia (11-117).
768	XB855	8.10.53			USAF 10.4.57. 66, 112, Italy.
769	XB978	30.10.53			USAF 29.5.57. 112/N, Yugoslavia (11-118), Honduras.
770	XB979	14.10.53			USAF 26.11.57. 112, Italy.
771	XB980	2.10.53			USAF 9.10.56. 4.
772	XB981	2.10.53			SOC 18.12.58. 4, 71, 130.
773	XB982	7.7.53			USAF 6.3.57. 92. Orpheus test bed.
774	XB983	14.10.53			USAF 30.10.56. 4, Italy.
775	XB984	13.10.53			USAF 8.11.57. 3, Italy, Yugoslavia (11-119).
776	XB985	14.10.53			USAF 5.9.57. 130/V, Italy.
777	XB986	13.10.53			USAF 6.12.56. 130, Italy. Cat.A.
778	XB987	22.10.53			USAF 27.5.57. 71, 130, Italy, Yugoslavia (11-120).
779	XB988	13.10.53			130. Cat.A.
780	XB989	16.10.53			SOC 18.12.58. 4, 71, 147.
781	XB990	14.10.53			USAF 6.12.56. 4, Italy.
782	XB991	30.10.53			USAF 10.2.56. 130.
783	XB992	23.10.53			SOC 18.12.58. AAEE.
784	XB993	8.10.53			USAF 25.4.56. 4, Italy.

c/n	Tail No.	f/f	TOS	SOS	Notes
785	XB994	16.10.53			USAF 9.5.56. 4.
786	XB995	17.10.53			SOC 18.12.58. 4, 71, 112/A.
787	XB996	21.10.53			USAF 14.11.56. 4, Italy, (2-26).
788	XB997	21.10.53			USAF 27.6.56. Hawkers, Italy.
789	XB998	17.10.53			USAF 4.1.57. 92.
790	XB999	21.10.53			USAF 20.8.57. 71, Yugoslavia.
791	23001	30.7.53	24.10.53	29.10.53	Canadair test plane till 10.1.57. Prototype Mk.6. Accepted by RCAF 13.3.58. OTU to Golden Hawks. Cat.A.
792	23002	2.10.53	29.19.53	28.6.57	414, 422, 441, Luft. BB-101. SOC 27.11.61, then instr. airframe.
793	23003	22.10.53	27.10.53	14.12.54	422. Cat.A.
794	23004	1.10.53	24.11.53	28.6.57	441, 422, Luft. BB-102. SOC 7.10.64.
795	23005	30.10.53	24.11.53	18.10.54	444. Cat.A.
796	23006	17.11.53	24.11.53	26.5.60	414, 430, 444.
797	23007	4.11.53	24.11.53	28.6.57	RCAF, Luft. BB-103. SOC 28.3.60.
798	23008	17.10.53	29.10.53	16.1.57	414, Luft. BB-104 NBC Warfare School, to Dornier* 14.10.59.
799	23009	22.10.53	10.2.54	1.11.54	444. Cat.A.
800	23010	18.10.53	24.11.53	25.6.60	414, 439, 441.
801	23011	26.11.53	31.12.53	15.1.57	439, Luft. BB-105, BB-704, (instru. airframe). P (Uetersen museum).
802	23012	30.10.53	24.11.53	26.5.60	
803	23013	30.10.53	28.12.53	26.5.60	422, 430.
804	23014	22.10.53	29.10.53	17.10.56	OTU. Cat.A.
805	23015	30.10.53	24.11.53	26.5.60	414, 439.
806	23016	4.11.53	31.12.53	18.4.55	416, 430. Cat.A.
807	23017*	5.11.53	31.12.53	28.6.57	441
808	23018	30.10.53	24.11.53	26.5.60	413, 422, 441.
809	23019	6.11.53	24.11.53	26.5.60	422.
810	23020	6.11.53	24.11.53	28.1.57	444. SOC 11.11.60, to Dornier 17.1.61.
811	23021	24.10.53	4.1.55		NAE area rule test aircraft. MAC FS(N1049D) Crashed WS 1.2.80.
812	23022	6.11.53	31.12.53	26.5.60	430.
813	23023	24.11.53	24.11.53	26.5.60	422, 439.
814	23024	17.11.53	29.10.53	24.7.56	Loan to Avro, destroyed in hangar fire 22.3.55.
815	23025	23.11.53	25.1.54	8.8.57	RCAF, Luft. BB-137, BB-223. SOC 25.11.58, to Dornier 19.3.59.
816	23026	4.11.53	28.12.53	8.8.57	441, Luft. BB-105. SOC 11.11.60, to Dornier 17.1.61.
817	23027	17.11.53	24.11.53	15.1.57	422, 444, Luft. BB-108. SOC 29.10.59, to Dornier 7.6.60, to "Bubimat".
818	23028	16.11.53	31.12.53	3.2.54	401, 434, MAC FS (N99605). Shot down WS. 12.10.78.
819	23029	17.11.53	31.12.53	28.6.57	422, Luft. BB-112, YA-005 (drag chute trials). SOC 18.1.60, to Dornier 3.12.62.
820	23030	17.11.53	24.11.53	10.1.58	414, Luft. BB-138. To Redifon.
821	23031	16.11.53	28.12.53	28.2.55	414.
822	23032	24.11.53	28.12.53	28.6.57	RCAF, Luft. BB-109. SOC 15.6.59, to Dornier 8.3.60.
823	23033	16.1.53	28.12.53	25.6.60	410, 413, 414.
824	23034	13.12.53	16.2.54		422, 439, FWS. MAC.
825	23035	8.12.53	25.1.54	10.3.55	430. Cat.A.
826	23036	17.11.53	23.12.53		422, 441, OTU, MAC.
827	23037	24.11.53	25.1.54	11.4.63	422, 439. GH.
828	23038	24.11.53	31.12.53	26.5.60	422, 441.
829	23039	24.11.53	31.12.53	26.3.56	421. Cat.A.
830	23040	11.12.53	4.3.54	1.10.54	430. Cat.A.
831	23041	24.11.53	12.1.54	17.9.58	OTU. Cat.A.
832	23042	24.11.53	31.12.53	20.10.64	416, 422, GH.
833	23043	24.11.53	25.1.54	8.8.57	414, 422, 439, 444, Luft. BB-139, BB-238. SOC 9.3.62, to Dornier 18.4.62.
834	23044	24.11.53	28.12.53	28.6.57	416, Luft. BB-110. SOC 11.11.60, to Dornier 24.11.60.
835	23045	26.11.53	31.12.53	28.6.57	414, 441, 444, Luft. BB-111. DBR 29.5.59, to Dornier 19.3.60.
836	23046	24.11.53	31.12.53	2.12.58	421, 430, OTU. Cat.A.
837	23047	23.11.53	29.12.53		401, 414. City of Oshawa 22.6.70. P (Oshawa airport).
838	23048	8.12.53	10.2.54	20.9.57	422, Luft. BB-140, BB-130, ES+ 61. SOC 11.8.59, to Dornier 9.10.60. P (Roth, WG?).
839	23049	17.11.53	16.2.54	26.5.60	413, 422.
840	23050	24.11.53	31.12.53	8.8.57	RCAF, Luft. BB-
841	23051	13.12.53	28.12.53	28.6.57	RCAF, Luft. BB-113, DBR 19.5.58, to Dornier 14.10.59.
842	23052	24.11.53	24.11.53	20.6.61	422, 438, OTU. Cat.A.
843	24053	8.12.53	25.1.54	11.8.54	422, 434. Cat.A.
844	23054	8.12.53	16.2.54	26.5.60	416.
845	23055	13.12.53	25.1.54	28.6.57	414, Luft. BB-114. SOC 9.3.62, to Dornier 22.3.62.
846	23056	11.12.53	28.12.53	8.8.57	422, Luft. BB-142, BB-240. Cat.A.
847	23057	8.12.53	10.2.54	9.12.57	444.
848	23058	23.11.53	8.1.54		430, OTU, STU, MAC.
849	23059	15.12.53	4.3.54	8.8.57	441, Luft. BB-143, BB-241. SOC 9.9.61, to Dornier 22.3.62. Instr. airframe.
850	23060	27.11.53	4.1.54		443, OTU, STU. P (Sidney, B.C.).
851	23061	11.12.53	25-1-54	20.9.57	444, Luft. BB-144, BB-256. SOC 30.11.59, to Dornier 11.7.60.
852	23062	30.12.53	28.12.53	8.8.57	421, Luft. BB-145, BB-248. SOC 29.10.59, to Dornier 7.6.60, to "Bubimat".
853	23063	11.12.53	28.12.53	26.5.60	414, 422.
854	23064	8.12.53	31.12.53	8.8.57	RCAF, Luft. BB-146, BB-242. SOC 17.7.61.
855	23065	11.12.53	10.2.54	11.8.54	434. Cat.A.
856	23066	8.12.53	25.1.54	1.5.64	GH.
857	23067	11.12.53	16.2.54	26.5.60	430.
858	23068	11.12.53	10.2.54	26.5.60	422.
859	23069	8.12.53	25.1.54	14.10.54	434. Cat.A.
860	23070	11.12.53	28.12.53	8.8.57	434, Luft. BB-147, BB-249. SOC 30.11.59, to Dornier.
861	23071	8.12.53	10.2.54	25.7.60	414, 442, CEPE, OTU.
862	23072	13.12.53	16.2.54	26.5.60	413, 444.
863	23073	13.12.53	28.12.53	27.8.59	422, 444, GH. Cat.A.
864	23074	13.12.53	10.2.54	26.5.60	430.
865	23075	7.1.54	4.3.54	26.5.60	430.
866	23076	8.1.54	25.1.54	10.1.58	416, Luft. BB-148. To Redifon.
867	23077	8.1.54	16.2.54	19.7.54	416. Cat.A.
868	23078	8.12.53	28.12.53	26.3.54	444. Cat.A.
869	23079		23.2.54	9.6.66	414, OTU, STU.
870	23080		28.12.53	10.6.60	GH.
871	23081	8.1.54	25.1.54	20.9.57	RCAF, Luft. BB-149, BB-257. SOC 9.3.62, to Dornier 25.4.62.
872	23082	16.12.53	16.2.54	19.1.55	416, 422. Cat.A.
873	23083	8.1.54	11.5.54		413, OTU, STU. Cat.A.
874	23084	23.12.53	10.2.54	25.6.60	430.
875	23085	7.1.54	10.2.54	11.8.54	434. Cat.A.
876	23086	7.1.54	25.1.54	22.9.55	413, 416. Cat.A.
877	23087	17.1.54	10.2.54	15.1.57	RCAF, Luft. BB-119. SOC 30.11.59, to Dornier 24.2.60.
878	23088	15.1.54	25.1.54	7.11.60	442, OTU. Cat.A.
879	23089	24.1.54	10.2.54	26.5.60	414.
880	23090	22.1.54	16.2.54	15.1.57	416, Luft. BB-120, SOC 11.11.60, to Dornier 17.1.61.
881	23091	22.1.54	16.2.54	15.1.57	413, Luft. BB-121. SOC 11.11.60, to Dornier 17.1.61.
882	23092	15.1.54	10.2.54	25.6.60	414, 422, 430.
883	23093	23.1.54	18.3.54	15.1.57	434, Luft. BB-122 (1st Mk.5 for Luft, del. Fassberg 5.57 for use as instr. airframe BB-706). SOC 17.10.64.
884	23084		14.1.54		TTS, STU.
885	23095		8.12.53	12.6.62	TTS.
886	23096	17.1.54	12.2.54	20.9.67	GH, MAC, Boeing, (N8686F), FS (N74100).
887	23097		23.12.53		TTS, FWS, MAC.
888	23098		8.12.53	9.11.60	TTS.
889	23099	17.1.54	16.2.54	3.8.55	416, 430. Cat.A.
890	23100		8.12.53	24.6.60	TTS.
891	23101		8.12.53	12.6.62	TTS.
892	23102		7.1.54		TTS, MAC, FS, (N65331).
893	23103		8.12.53	17.2.60	TTS, CEPE.
894	23104		12.3.55	24.8.59	TTS, 400, 411.
895	23105	17.1.54	10.2.54	8.8.57	RCAF, Luft. BB-150, BB-250. To army logistics school. P (Hamburg-Olsdorf).

c/n	Tail No.	f/f	TOS	SOS	Notes
896	23016	29.1.54	23.2.54		416, OTU, STU, MAC (N5591F).
897	23107	17.1.54	16.2.54	8.8.57	RCAF, Luft. BB-151, BB-243. Arrester net trials at Ahlhorn. To Dornier 23.7.59.
898	23108	29.1.54	28.12.53	8.9.55	413, 430. Cat.A.
899	23109	17.1.54	16.2.54	2.8.55	441, 444. Cat.A.
900	23110	23.1.54	16.2.54	16.8.61	414, 413, OTU. Cat.A.
901	23111	7.2.54	10.2.54	15.1.57	441, 444, Luft. BB-123. Cat.A.
902	23112	29.1.54	4.3.54	26.5.60	430.
903	23113	7.2.54	16.2.54	24.8.54	413, 416. Cat.A.
904	23114	1.2.54	16.2.54	28.6.57	430, 444, Luft. BB-115. SOC 9.3.62, to Dornier 12.4.62.
905	23115	29.1.54	16.2.54	3.10.60	443, 444.
906	23116	7.2.54	16.2.54	26.5.60	413, 430.
907	23117	10.2.54	4.3.54	28.10.54	OFT. Cat.A.
908	23118	7.2.54	3.3.54	26.5.55	444. Cat.A.
909	23119		10.2.54	24.8.54	416. Cat.A.
910	23120		3.3.54	22.6.55	444. Cat.A.
911	23121	9.2.54	16.2.54	18.7.55	430. Cat.A.
912	23122	9.2.54	16.2.54	26.5.60	430.
913	23123	7.1.54	16.2.54	8.8.57	416, 666, Luft. BB-152, BB-244, SOC 9.3.62, to Dornier 18.4.62, then instr. airframe at Fursty.
914	23124	10.2.54	16.2.54	8.8.57	RCAF, Luft. BB-153, BB-245. SOC 9.3.62, to Dornier 23.3.62.
915	23125	10.2.54	16.2.54	8.8.57	RCAF, Luft. BB-154, BB-251. Instr. airframe. SOC 22.11.61. P ?
916	23126	13.2.54	16.2.54	8.8.57	416, Luft. BB-155. SOC 29.10.59, to Dornier 27.6.60, to "Bubimat".
917	23127	13.2.54	16.2.54	8.8.57	RCAF, Luft. BB-156, BB-252. SOC 9.3.62, to Dornier 22.3.62.
918	23128	13.2.54	27.2.54		434, OTU, MAC, FS (N96123). Shot down WS 29.8.80.
919	23129	12.2.54	5.3.54		AFHQ, MAC.
920	23130	19.2.54	4.3.54	3.8.55	416, 430. Cat.A.
921	23131	19.2.54	4.3.54	15.1.57	439, Luft. BB-124. SOC 9.3.62, to Dornier 22.3.62.
922	23132	18.2.54	3.3.54	10.1.58	RCAF, Luft. BB-157. To Redifon.
923	23133	18.2.54	3.3.54		430, 439, OTU, STU, MAC, FS(N96120). Crashed WS 18.5.78.
924	23134	19.2.54	18.3.54	15.7.54	416. Cat.A.
925	23135	18.2.54	9.3.54		444, GH, STU, MAC, FS (N92426). Crashed WS 22.5.79.
926	23136	18.2.54	3.3.54	8.8.57	RCAF, Luft. BB-158, BB-246. Arrester net trials at Ahlhorn. To Dornier 11.5.59.
927	23137	19.2.54	4.3.54	8.8.57	413, Luft. BB-159, BB-253. DBR 24.10.58, to instr. airframe. SOC 24.10.59.
928	23138	18.2.54	4.3.54	8.8.57	RCAF, Luft. BB-160, BB-254. SOC 9.3.62, to Dornier 22.3.62.
929	23139	23.2.54	4.3.54	8.8.57	413, 430, Luft. BB-161, BB-255. SOC 9.3.62, to Dornier 12.4.62.
930	23140	1.3.54	4.3.54	3.12.56	421. DBR 16.3.56.
931	23141	23.2.54	4.3.54	20.9.57	430, 444, Luft. BB-131. ESt 61. to instru. airframe, to gunnery target at Delmenhorst. Scrapped 20.11.81.
932	23142	23.2.54	3.3.54	20.9.57	RCAF, Luft. BB-162, BB-260. To "Bubimat", then to Darnstadt Tech. University.
933	23143	23.2.54	4.3.54	26.5.60	441, 444.
934	23144	22.2.54	4.3.54	15.1.57	RCAF, Luft. BB-125. To Dornier 17.1.62, to instr. airframe at Braunschweig 25.4.63.
935	23145	5.3.54	4.3.54	26.5.60	413, 430.
936	23146	23.2.54	19.3.54		413, MAC, FS. Shot down WS 26.10.82.
937	23147	23.2.54	17.3.54		416, OTU, STU, MAC, FS (N72491). Damaged WS 16.10.79.
938	23148	24.2.54	4.3.54	3.8.54	430. Cat.A.
939	23149	23.2.54	4.3.54	26.5.60	413.
940	23150	13.2.54	16.2.54	7.9.56	430, 434, 444. Cat.A.
941	23151	7.2.54	2.3.54		416, OTU, MAC, FS(N5591L). DBR WS 23.8.82.
942	23152	12.2.54	9.4.54	16.12.59	401, 413, 444, OTU.
943	23153	12.2.54	3.3.54	28.6.57	413, 421, Luft. BB-116. SOC 9.3.62, to Dornier 18.4.62.
944	23154	10.2.54	4.3.54	3.8.55	416. Cat.A.
945	23155	19.2.54	4.3.54	5.3.55	413, 444. Cat.A.
946	23156	10.2.54	16.2.54	25.5.56	430. Cat.A.
947	23157	9.2.54	16.2.54	21.9.54	416, 444. Cat.A.
948	23158	19.2.54	18.3.54	20.9.57	RCAF, Luft. BB-163, BB-259. SOC 25.1.62, then engine test rig.
949	23159	12.2.54	3.3.54	26.5.60	430.
950	23160	19.2.54	2.3.54		OTU, STU, MAC, FS. Shot down WS 21.8.82.
951	23161	22.2.54	4.3.54	21.10.54	427. Cat.A.
952	23162	18.2.54	3.3.54	13.9.62	416, 444, STU. Cat.A.
953	23163	23.2.54	3.3.54	7.1.55	444. Cat.A.
954	23164	20.2.54	7.3.54		GH.
955	23165	1.3.54	4.3.54	20.9.57	414, 422, 439, Luft. BB-164, BB-122. SOC 30.11.59. To instr. airframe.
956	23166	24.2.54	18.3.54	19.5.55	421. Cat.A.
957	23167	22.1.54	4.3.54	4.8.60	443.
958	23168	20.1.54	3.3.54	14.2.56	Cat.A.
959	23169	3.3.54	18.3.54	26.5.60	416, 430.
960	23170	27.2.54	4.3.54	28.6.57	413, Luft. BB-117. To Dornier 10.3.60, then instr. airframe.
961	23171	1.3.54	4.3.54	25.9.58	414, 422, 439, PWS. Cat.A.
962	23172	8.3.54	4.3.54	21.12.55	416. Cat.A.
963	23173	1.3.54	18.3.54	30.9.58	414, 439, Luft. BB-165, BB-262. SOC 9.3.62, to Dornier 23.3.62.
964	23174	9.3.54	18.3.54	28.6.57	413, Luft. BB-118, NBC Warfare School. P? (Sonthofen).
965	23175	12.3.54	18.3.54	26.5.60	413.
966	23176	2.3.54	18.3.54	26.5.60	430.
967	23177	27.2.54	4.3.54	28.6.57	RCAF, Luft. BB-126. SOC 9.3.62, to Dornier 21.3.62, then instr. airframe at Fassberg.
968	23178	10.3.54	18.3.54	28.6.57	413, Luft. BB-127. SOC 29.10.59, to Dornier 27.7.60, to "Bubimat".
969	23179	3.3.54	18.3.54	8.8.57	422, 441, Luft. BB-166, BB-113. SOC 30.11.59, to Dornier 10.2.60.
970	23180	19.3.54	18.3.54	28.2.55	413. Cat.A.
971	23181	8.3.54	18.3.54	28.6.57	422, Luft. BB-128. SOC 9.3.62, to Dornier 21.3.62. At Landsberg AFB for fire training 1977.
972	23182	3.3.54	18.3.54	20.9.57	439, Luft. BB-167, BB-263. SOC 11.11.60, to Dornier 17.1.61.
973	23183	8.3.54	18.3.54	20.9.57	422, 439, Luft. BB-168, BB-134. SOC 9.3.62, to Dornier 18.4.62.
974	23184	5.3.54	18.3.54	20.9.57	416, 430, Luft. BB-169, BB-258. SOC 25.11.58, fuselage to ESt 61.
975	23185	11.3.54	18.3.54	20.9.57	413, Luft. BB-170, BB-264. SOC 30.11.59, to Dornier 12.8.60.
976	23186	15.3.54	18.3.54	26.5.60	414.
977	23187	15.3.54	18.3.54	28.6.57	RCAF, Luft. BB-171, BB-231. SOC 30.11.59, to Dornier 4.5.60.
978	23188	11.3.54	18.3.54	26.5.60	439, 441.
979	23189	17.3.54	18.3.54	26.5.60	413.
980	23190	14.3.54	8.4.54		430, OTU, STU, MAC, FS (N98230). Shot down WS 8.1.80.
981	23191	18.3.54	18.3.54	20.9.57	RCAF, Luft. BB-129. Cat.A.
982	23192	18.3.54	18.3.54	20.9.57	416, 439, Luft. BB-172, BB-261. SOC 9.3.62, then used in seat ejection trials.
983	23193	11.3.54	18.3.54	22.2.55	422. Cat. A.
984	23194	30.3.54	18.3.54	20.9.57	RCAF, Luft. BB-173, BB-135. SOC 12.2.59, to instru. airframe at Fassberg.
985	23195	24.3.54	15.4.54		416, 430, MAC, FS (N5591N).
986	23196	24.3.54	18.3.54	20.9.57	413, Luft. BB-133. Cat.A.
987	23197	24.3.54	6.4.54	29.12.54	427. Cat.A.
988	23198	19.3.54	9.4.54		MAC.
989	23199	24.3.54	18.3.54	28.6.57	RCAF, Luft. BB-174, BB-232. SOC 30.11.59, to Dornier 4.5.60.
990	23200	26.3.54	6.4.54	8.8.57	430, 444, Luft. BB-236. To instru. airframe 18.1.60, to Meppen as target in gunnery trials 31.3.64.
991	23201	22.3.54	4.3.54	9.11.55	430. Cat.A.
992	23202	24.3.54	26.4.54		422, 439, STU, MAC, FS (N55911).

c/n	Tail No.	f/f	TOS	SOS	Notes
993	23203	27.3.54	22.4.54		416, 439, MAC, FS (N201X).
994	23204	29.3.54	22.4.54		400, 411, 416, OTU, STU.
995	23205	1.4.54	6.4.54	29.7.65	414, GH.
996	23206	30.3.54	26.4.54		400, 411, 422, 438, 441, STU, MAC, FS (N5592D).
997	23207	30.3.54	28.4.54		411, 416, 444, MAC, FS (N5592K).
998	23208	30.3.54	26.4.54		411, 414, 441, MAC, FS (N4688J, N46869).
999	23209	30.3.54	28.4.54		401, 422, OTU, MAC, FS (N4688J).
1000	23210	5.4.54	19.5.54	5.6.65	OTU. Cat.A.
1001	23211	7.4.54	15.4.54	2.7.65	OTU, STU. Cat.A.
1002	23212	1.4.54	6.4.54	13.2.65	441, OTU.
1003	23213	5.4.54	6.4.54	9.11.62	441, 444, OTU, STU. Cat.A.
1004	23214	9.4.54	12.5.54	6.3.57	434, OTU. Cat.A.
1005	23215	9.4.54	30.4.54		411, OTU, MAC, FS (N2291B). Shot down WS 27.4.79. OFT. Cat.A.
1006	23216	5.4.54	6.4.54		
1007	23217	9.4.54	6.4.54	22.8.57	439, 441, OTU. Cat.A.
1008	23218	12.4.54	30.4.54	3.11.54	OTU. Cat.A.
1009	23219	19.4.54	6.4.54	3.2.60	414, 439.
1010	23220	8.4.54	6.4.54	25.6.60	400, 422, 439.
1011	23221	13.4.54	30.4.54		441, OTU, STU. P (Kingston, Ont.).
1012	23222	13.4.54	15.5.54		430, 442, MAC, FS (N46882).
1013	23223	23.4.54	6.5.54		414, 439, OTU, STU, MAC, FS (N86EA).
1014	23224	19.4.54	26.8.54		422, 441, OTU, STU, MAC.
1015	23225	21.4.54	12.5.54	16.11.60	OTU.
1016	23226	21.4.54	12.5.54		416, OTU, STU, MAC (N46883).
1017	23227	22.4.54	6.5.54		400, 430, OTU, MAC, FS (N2290R).
1018	23228	21.4.54	11.5.54		414, OTU, STU.
1019	23229	22.4.54	6.4.54	31.5.60	414, 439, OTU. Cat.A.
1020	23230	28.4.54	12.5.54	16.11.60	422, OTU.
1021	23231	23.4.54	11.5.54		MAC, Ronald Reynolds. To N231X.
1022	23232	22.4.54	6.4.54	10.3.55	430, 434. Cat.A.
1023	23233	28.4.54	14.5.54		422, 441, OTU, STU.
1024	23234	26.4.54	6.4.54	27.4.55	444. Cat.A.
1025	23235	28.4.54	12.5.54	16.11.60	OTU.
1026	23236	28.4.54	12.5.54	15.6.55	OTU. Cat.A.
1027	23237	29.4.54	6.4.54	20.4.56	416. Cat.A.
1028	23238	29.4.54	16.6.54		CFS, OTU, STU. To N86EB.
1029	23239		14.5.54	22.6.64	OTU, STU, AFHQ.
1030	23240		12.5.54	18.2.55	OTU. Cat.A.
1031	23241	30.4.54	31.5.54		OTU, MAC 20.10.70, Lockheed (N8544), FS.
1032	23242	30.4.54	12.5.54	24.9.57	OTU. Cat.A.
1033	23243	6.5.54	12.5.54	13.3.57	OTU. Cat.A.
1034	23244	6.5.54	12.5.54	28.7.54	OTU. Cat.A.
1035	23245	6.5.54	12.5.54		OTU. Instr. airframe No. 634B. To 428 Wing RCAFA 26.10.70. P (Peterborough, Ont. as 23428).
1036	23246	5.5.54	12.5.54	16.11.60	OTU.
1037	23247	5.5.54	12.5.54	22.3.55	OTU. Cat.A.
1038	23248	12.5.54	12.5.54	16.11.60	OTU.
1039	23249	6.5.54	12.5.54	4.5.55	414, OTU. Cat.A.
1040	23250	13.5.54	12.5.54	9.11.61	TTS (Instru. airframe No. 658), OTU.
1041	23251	13.5.54	12.5.54	25.7.60	OTU, STU.
1042	23252	12.5.54	26.8.54		430, MAC, FS (N96122). Shot down WS 8.11.79.
1043	23253	12.5.54	12.5.54	8.11.55	OTU. Cat. A.
1044	23254	13.5.54	12.5.54	23.12.55	OTU.
1045	23255	19.5.54	12.5.54	16.11.60	OTU.
1046	23256	14.5.54	12.5.54	17.11.54	OTU. Cat.A.
1047	23257	18.5.54	11.6.54		OTU, STU, Town of Trenton 23.2.67. P (CFB Trenton).
1048	23258	18.5.54	12.5.54	16.11.60	OTU, STU.
1049	23259	31.5.54	2.7.54		OTU, MAC, FS. To N98250.
1050	23260	31.5.54	12.2.54	7.10.54	OTU. Cat.A.
1051	23261	26.5.54	12.2.54	30.5.56	OTU. Cat.A.
1052	23262	20.5.54	12.2.54	19.7.55	OTU. Cat.A.
1053	23263	26.5.54	12.2.54	22.8.57	OTU. Cat.A.
1054	23264	26.5.54	12.2.54	1.2.57	OTU. Cat.A.
1055	23265	25.5.54	12.2.54	18.2.55	OTU. Cat.A.
1056	23266	31.5.54	12.2.54	26.11.65	OTU, STU. DBR 1.9.65.
1057	23267	31.5.54	12.2.54	1.5.64	OTU.
1058	23268	7.6.54	8.7.54		OTU, STU, MAC, FS (N96125). DBR WS 16.8.78.
1059	23269	7.6.54	12.2.54	25.3.65	OTU.
1060	23270	7.6.54	2.7.54		434, OTU, STU.
1061	23271	7.6.54	12.2.54	11.4.56	OTU. Cat.A.
1062	23272	7.6.54	12.2.54	8.8.60	OTU.
1063	23273	8.6.54	22.7.54		434, OTU, STU. Cat.A.
1064	23274	10.6.54	12.5.54	16.11.60	OTU.
1065	23275	8.6.54	14.10.54		City of Oshawa 22.6.70, CEPE, N275X. Cat.A.
1066	23276	15.6.54	12.5.54	16.5.63	OTU, STU. Cat.A.
1067	23277	10.6.54	15.7.54		OTU, STU.
1068	23278	15.6.54	12.5.54	21.6.55	OTU. Cat.A.
1069	23279		12.5.54	19.1.61	OTU, GH. Cat.A.
1070	23280		11.8.54		OTU, STU, MAC, FS (N2290V).
1071	23281	16.6.54	22.7.54	27.6.55	OTU, PWS. Cat.A.
1072	23282	16.6.54	12.5.54	9.11.54	OTU. Cat.A.
1073	23283	17.6.54	30.7.54		PWS, Avro, OTU, STU, MAC, FS (N22902).
1074	23284	18.6.54	11.8.54		OTU.
1075	23285	19.6.54	11.8.54		OTU, MAC, FS (CF-BKG, N8686D).
1076	23286	19.6.54	12.5.54	27.10.55	OTU. Cat.A.
1077	23287	21.6.54	28.7.54	29.7.65	411, OTU.
1078	23288	5.7.54	28.7.54	29.7.65	OTU.
1079	23289	23.6.54	5.8.54		PWS, MAC, FS (N99594). Shot down WS 16.8.78.
1080	23290	21.6.54	28.7.54	23.2.65	OTU, STU. Cat.A.
1081	23291	28.6.54	18.8.54		OTU, STU, MAC, FS (N70726).
1082	23292	5.7.54	28.7.54	24.8.56	OTU, PWS. Cat.A.
1083	23293	30.6.54	18.8.54		OTU, STU, PWS, MAC, FS (N4689H).
1084	23294	6.7.54	28.7.54	24.5.55	OTU. Cat.A.
1085	23295		15.7.54		TTS.
1086	23296		30.6.54	3.11.61	TTS, OTU, STU.
1087	23297	8.7.54	28.7.54	29.7.65	OTU.
1088	23298	9.7.54	28.7.54	8.5.64	OTU.
1089	23299	12.7.54	2.7.54	15.11.55	430. Cat.A.
1090	23300	5.8.54	3.9.54		413, 422, CFS, MAC, FS (N4724A).
1091	23301	15.7.54	27.8.54		443, GH. P (Picton, Ont.).
1092	23302	3.8.54	2.7.54	29.6.55	441. Cat.A.
1093	23303	6.8.54	27.8.54		438, STU, MAC.
1094	23304	16.7.54	23.8.54		430, OTU, STU. Cat.A.
1095	23305	3.8.54	2.7.54	20.9.57	410, Luft. BB-132. SOC 9.3.62, to Dornier 20.3.62.
1096	23306	5.8.54	25.8.54		411, 416, MAC, FS (N306X). Shot down WS 22.7.78.
1097	23307	6.8.54	2.9.54	17.1.54	CEPE. Cat.A.
1098	23308	6.8.54	2.9.54		411, MAC. To N4724N.
1099	23309	9.8.54	3.9.54		441, STU, MAC, FS (N92473).
1100	23310	17.8.54	9.9.54		430, 443, MAC.
1101	23311	10.8.54	2.7.54	24.4.59	439, 443, OTU. Cat.A.
1102	23312	12.8.54	2.7.54	29.7.65	400, 411, 434. OTU.
1103	23313	17.8.54	2.7.54	7.3.61	438, OTU, GH. Cat.A.
1104	23314	13.8.54	14.9.54		441, AFHQ, STU, MAC, Air Sabre Inc. (CF-BKH, N8687D).
1105	23315	17.8.54	14.9.54		401, OTU, MAC, FS (N72492).
1106	23316	18.8.54	14.9.54		430, 442, STU.
1107	23317	19.8.54	2.7.54	28.3.55	430. Cat.A.
1108	23318		2.7.54	6.4.55	OFU. Cat.A.
1109	23319		2.7.54	26.5.60	
1110	23320		14.10.54		434, GH, MAC, FS (N74170 "Bessy"). Shot down WS 29.8.80.
1111	23321	25.8.54	2.7.54	8.8.57	439, Luft. BB-131, BB-237. SOC 9.3.62, to Dornier 21.3.62. P (Wahn, WG ?).
1112	23322	27.8.54	2.7.54	26.5.60	
1113	23323	26.8.54	20.9.54		441, STU, FWS, MAC, FS (N98279).
1114	23324	1.9.54	2.7.54	26.5.60	410.
1115	23325	8.9.54	2.7.54	26.5.60	413, OTU.
1116	23326	1.9.54	2.7.54	26.5.60	441.
1117	23327	3.9.54	2.7.54	8.8.60	RCAF, Luft. BB-134, BB-235. SOC 8.6.60, to Dornier 24.11.60 after prang.
1118	23328	3.9.54	2.7.54	29.6.55	410. Cat.A.
1119	23329	8.9.54	30.9.54	26.5.60	439.
1120	23330	9.9.54	5.10.54		OTU, MAC, Flight Int'l (N86FN).
1121	23331	10.9.54	5.10.54		439, OTU, AFHQ, MAC, FS (N46901).
1122	23332	9.9.54	30.9.54	25.3.65	438, 439, OTU.
1123	23333	21.9.54	30.9.54	20.8.56	410, 434, OTU. Cat.A.
1124	23334	23.9.54	30.9.54	26.5.60	413.
1125	23335	14.9.54	15.3.55	29.7.65	434, OTU.

c/n	Tail No.	f/f	TOS	SOS	Notes
1126	23336	15.9.54	30.9.54	19.5.55	439. Cat.A.
1127	23337	15.9.54	30.9.54	5.7.63	439, 441, OTU.
1128	23338	28.9.54	9.11.54		416, CEPE, OTU, STU, MAC, FS (N4689N).
1129	23339	23.9.54	13.10.54		441, AFHQ, MAC, FS (N46791). Destroyed WS 25.7.81.
1130	23340	1.10.54	30.9.54	28.2.57	401, 430, OTU. Cat.A.
1131	23341	1.10.54	14.10.54	28.8.57	OTU. Cat.A.
1132	23342	8.10.54	25.2.55	8.5.64	400, OTU.
1133	23343	28.9.54	30.9.54	26.5.60	414.
1134	23344	5.10.54	28.10.54		439, 441, OTU, MAC. To N86EC.
1135	23345	1.10.54	30.9.54	26.5.60	414.
1136	23346	5.10.54	30.9.54	22.7.60	401, OTU. Cat.A.
1137	23347	5.10.54	2.11.54		434, 439, AFHQ, MAC.
1138	23348	6.10.54	30.9.54	8.8.57	439, Luft. BB-136, BB-234. SOC 9.3.62, to Dornier 25.4.62.
1139	23349	13.10.54	14.10.54	29.7.65	434, OTU.
1140	23350	8.10.54	30.9.54	13.4.60	434, 439, 441, CFS. Cat.A.
1141	23351	21.10.54	9.11.54		439, OTU, STU, MAC. To N86ED.
1142	23352	14.10.54	2.11.54		439, MAC, FS. To N98270.
1143	23353	19.10.54	30.9.54	16.11.60	439, GH.
1144	23354	15.10.54	2.11.54		OTU, STU.
1145	23355	15.10.54	16.11.54		439, STU. P (Chatham, N.B.).
1146	23356	18.10.54	30.9.54	22.7.60	438, OTU. Cat.A.
1147	23357	28.10.54	30.9.54	9.1.58	400, 439. Cat.A.
1148	23358	25.10.54	15.11.54		410, 439, OTU, STU, MAC. To N4690J.
1149	23359	22.10.54	30.9.54	9.4.59	439, 441, 443, GH. Cat.A.
1150	23360	22.10.54	30.9.54	15.6.65	439. Cat.A.
1151	23361	28.10.54	26.11.54		OTU, STU.
1152	23362	25.10.54	14.10.54	8.5.64	OTU.
1153	23363	28.10.54	26.11.54		OTU, MAC, FS. To N74180, Boeing (N8686F), FS. Last Sabre to leave Chatham (19.2.69).
1154	23364	1.11.54	14.10.54	16.11.60	400, OTU.
1155	23365	28.10.54	14.10.54	11.4.56	OTU. Cat.A.
1156	23366	5.11.54	13.12.54	16.11.60	OTU.
1157	23367	5.11.54	26.11.58		OTU, STU, MAC, FS N92402, N86FS.
1158	23368	5.1.54	13.12.54	24.5.57	OTU. Cat.A.
1159	23369	5.11.54	14.10.54	8.5.64	OTU.
1160	23370	9.11.54	13.12.54	8.5.64	OTU. Last Mark 5.
1161	23371	19.10.54	30.12.54	12.5.64	414. First production Mark 6.
1162	23372	5.11.54	30.12.54	22.6.55	OFU. Cat.A.
1163	23373	9.11.54	30.12.54	10.11.61	444. Cat.A.
1164	23374	10.11.54	30.12.54	21.4.61	421. Cat.A.
1165	23375	22.12.54	31.12.54	3.6.63	416, 444, CEPE.
1166	23376	17.12.54	3.12.54	26.4.56	434. Cat.A.
1167	23377	12.11.54	30.12.54	28.9.62	STU.
1168	23378	20.12.54	14.1.55	1.8.63	421, 434.
1169	23379	22.12.54	31.3.55	10.7.62	444.
1170	23380	20.12.54	14.1.55	8.7.59	421. Cat.A.
1171	23381	5.1.55	14.1.55	5.10.62	413.
1172	23382	22.12.54	14.1.55	20.11.63	439.
1173	23383	22.12.54	14.1.55	1.8.63	421, 422, FWS.
1174	23384	10.1.55	14.1.55	16.1.57	413. Cat.A.
1175	23385	14.1.55	14.1.55	7.2.61	
1176	23386	10.1.55	10.3.55	1.8.63	414.
1177	23387	10.1.55	14.1.55	23.9.57	422. Cat.A.
1178	23388	14.1.55	24.3.55	2.5.62	414, 434.
1179	23389	10.1.55	14.1.55	12.5.64	439.
1180	23390	14.1.55	6.4.55	19.11.56	434, 444. Cat.A.
1181	23391	20.1.55	6.4.55	28.6.62	444.
1182	23392	10.1.55	14.1.55	1.3.53	422, 444.
1183	23393	19.1.55	14.1.55	13.3.56	427. Cat.A.
1184	23394	24.2.55	24.3.55	8.3.63	413, 434.
1185	23395	20.1.55	24.3.55	17.4.63	444.
1186	23396	21.1.55	24.3.55	10.6.57	434. Cat.A.
1187	23397	31.1.55	14.1.55	25.6.57	422. Cat.A.
1188	23398	3.2.55	14.1.55	12.5.64	434.
1189	23399	22.12.54	14.1.55	17.12.62	413.
1190	23400	20.1.55	14.1.55	26.3.56	OFU. Cat.A.
1191	23401	4.1.55	14.1.55	28.9.62	434.
1192	23402	10.1.55	14.1.55	28.9.62	413, 444.
1193	23403	10.1.55	24.3.55	2.2.56	413, 430. Cat.A.
1194	23404	4.1.55	31.12.54	9.9.63	CEPE. Cat.A.
1195	23405	11.1.55	24.3.55	28.9.62	
1196	23406	10.1.55	20.6.55	17.6.60	414, 422. Cat.A.
1197	23407	14.1.55	14.1.55	11.9.62	414, 444. Went missing 4.7.62.
1198	23408	20.1.55	6.4.55	28.9.62	
1199	23409	19.1.55	6.4.55	6.3.61	444. Cat.A.
1200	23410	10.1.55	31.3.55		434, GH.
1201	23411	20.1.55	24.3.55	12.5.64	414.
1202	23412	19.1.55	14.1.55	6.2.57	427. Cat.A.
1203	23413	19.1.55	6.4.55	6.2.57	444. Cat.A.
1204	23414	20.1.55	6.4.55	7.9.62	422, 434.
1205	23415	19.1.55	24.3.55	7.8.58	434.
1206	23416	20.1.55	6.4.55	28.9.62	414.
1207	23417	20.1.55	6.4.55	20.3.63	434.
1208	23418	28.1.55	6.4.55	28.11.63	
1209	23419	18.2.55	14.1.55	24.6.63	422, 434, 439. Cat.A.
1210	23420	28.1.55	4.8.55	29.3.61	427, 434. Cat.A.
1211	23421	26.1.55	14.1.55	1.8.63	434, 444.
1212	23422	2.2.55	14.1.55	17.4.63	422.
1213	23423	31.1.55	14.1.55	17.4.63	413.
1214	23424	31.1.55	14.1.55	13.8.65	414, 434, GH, Air Museum of Canada (Calgary) 9.8.65, later N186X. Cat.A.
1215	23425	26.1.55	6.4.55	30.8.62	
1216	23426	28.1.55	24.3.55	14.6.63	413, 434.
1217	23427	24.2.55	24.3.55	1.8.63	422, 444.
1218	23428	24.2.55	4.6.55	1.3.63	422, 434, 441. Tail no. later inappropriately used on 23245.
1219	23429	24.2.55	24.3.55	28.9.62	414, 434, 439.
1220	23430	24.2.55	24.3.55	28.9.62	427.
1221	23431	3.2.55	24.3.55	7.1.57	422. Cat.A.
1222	23432	18.2.55	24.3.55	16.1.63	439, 441.
1223	23433	24.2.55	25.3.55		434.
1224	23434	18.2.53	24.3.55	17.4.58	422, 434. Cat.A.
1225	23435	24.2.55	24.3.55	28.9.62	GH.
1226	23436	25.5.55	24.3.55	31.3.58	413, 441. Cat.A.
1227	23437	18.2.55	20.6.55	31.1.57	416, 430. Cat.A.
1228	23438	24.2.55	6.4.55	1.8.63	414.
1229	23439	24.2.55	24.3.65	9.3.56	422. Cat.A.
1230	23440	24.2.55	24.3.65	28.11.63	414, Avro.
1231	23441	7.3.55	6.4.55	28.10.59	414, 434, 441. Cat.A.
1232	23442	14.3.55	24.3.55	17.4.63	414, 416.
1233	23443	8.3.55	6.4.55	15.11.57	434. Cat.A.
1234	23444	10.3.55	6.4.55	21.2.57	434. Cat.A.
1235	23445	14.3.55	24.3.55	9.3.56	444. Cat.A.
1236	23446	15.3.55	4.8.55	17.12.62	434.
1237	23447	15.3.55	24.3.66	28.9.62	
1238	23448	14.3.55	6.4.55	1.8.63	421, 441, 444.
1239	23449	14.3.55	24.3.55	24.4.59	416, 421, 434. Cat.A.
1240	23450	14.3.55	24.3.55	28.9.62	414.
1241	23451	14.3.55	24.3.55	12.5.64	422, 439.
1242	23452	14.3.55	6.4.55	4.9.58	414, 439. Cat.A.
1243	23453	14.3.55	6.4.55	23.11.61	422, 444. Cat.A.
1244	23454	24.3.55	6.4.55	13.8.65	RCAF, Air Museum of Canada (CF-AMH) 9.8.65, later N186F, FS. DBR WS 17.5.78.
1245	23455	24.3.55	20.6.55		444. P (Ottawa).
1246	23456	24.3.55	6.4.55	24.11.61	444. Cat.A.
1247	23457	25.3.55	1.7.55		414, 444, GH. P (Trenton, Ont.).
1248	23458	25.3.55	6.4.55	2.5.62	427.
1249	23459	24.3.55	24.3.55	25.3.63	
1250	23460	24.3.55	6.4.55	27.6.62	
1251	23461	24.3.55	6.4.55	25.11.57	444. Cat.A..
1252	23462	25.3.55	20.6.55	12.5.64	422.
1253	23463	29.11.55	7.10.55	11.10.62	
1254	23464	24.3.55	6.4.55	5.6.62	
1255	23465	30.3.55	28.6.55		416, GH.
1256	23466	25.3.55	20.6.55	24.9.63	414.
1257	23467	25.3.55	6.4.55	29.11.55	444. Cat.A.
1258	23468	31.3.55	24.3.55	28.9.62	414.
1259	23469	30.3.55	11.7.55		422, 439.
1260	23470	31.3.55	21.6.55		444, GH.
1261	23471	31.3.55	27.6.55	3.6.63	430, 434.
1262	23472	1.4.55	20.6.55	3.6.63	444.
1263	23473	4.4.55	6.4.55	1.3.63	414.
1264	23474	5.4.55	6.4.55	4.6.56	427, 434. Cat.A.
1265	23475	5.4.55	6.4.55	16.1.63	434.
1266	23476	5.4.55	6.4.55	1.4.61	434.
1267	23477	12.4.55	6.4.55	17.4.63	
1268	23478		18.3.55	21.2.57	434. Cat.A.
1269	23479	18.4.55	20.6.55	2.5.62	434, 444.
1270	23480	11.4.55	6.4.55	3.6.63	434.
1271	23481	18.4.55	20.6.55	28.11.62	414.
1272	23482	12.4.55	18.11.55		
1273	23483	20.4.55	20.6.55	9.3.56	422. Cat.A.
1274	23484	18.4.55	4.8.55	23.4.57	427. Cat.A.
1275	23485	18.4.55	20.6.55	16.1.63	422.
1276	23486	20.4.55	20.6.55	28.9.62	414.
1277	23487	18.4.55	15.11.55		434, GH.
1278	23488	22.4.55	20.6.55	6.3.61	444. Cat.A.
1279	23489	27.4.55	27.6.55	28.9.63	422, 434.
1280	23490	27.4.55	20.6.55	11.1.62	434, 444.

c/n	Tail No.	f/f	TOS	SOS	Notes
1281	23491	29.4.55	11.7.55	27.11.58	441. Cat.A.
1282	23492	27.4.55	27.6.55	6.4.62	
1283	23493	29.4.55	20.6.55	11.9.57	422. Cat.A.
1284	23494	27.4.55	20.6.55	15.6.56	444. Cat.A.
1285	23495	3.5.55	24.6.55	3.6.63	441.
1286	23496	3.5.55	4.8.55	11.10.56	439. Cat.A.
1287	23497	10.5.55	27.6.55	17.11.60	422, 441. Cat.A.
1288	23498	3.5.55	27.6.55		414, 444.
1289	23499	3.5.55	27.6.55	1.3.63	422, 434.
1290	23500	4.5.55	27.6.55	17.12.62	422, 434.
1291	23501	4.5.55	27.6.55	16.1.63	413.
1292	23502	5.5.55	27.6.55	17.12.62	422.
1293	23503	10.5.55	4.8.55	16.1.63	439, 441, AFHQ.
1294	23504	11.5.55	17.11.55		RCAF, Age of Flight Museum 16.11.65, to US in 1969.
1295	23505	11.5.55	4.8.55	17.5.56	413, 434. Cat.A.
1296	23506	18.5.55	8.10.55	3.10.55	
1297	23507	10.5.55	20.6.55	12.10.62	422.
1298	23508	26.5.55	20.6.55	17.4.63	422, 444.
1299	23509	20.5.55	4.8.55	3.1.63	422, 444.
1300	23510	18.5.55	23.9.55	29.7.65	410, 434, GH.
1301	23511	27.5.55	4.8.55	24.5.62	416, 434.
1302	23512	10.6.55	4.8.55	20.11.63	439, 441.
1303	23513	2.6.55	4.8.55	8.7.63	421, 439. Cat.A.
1304	23514	30.5.55	4.8.55	21.6.57	416, 421. Cat.A.
1305	23515	26.5.55	27.6.55	22.4.60	421. Cat.A.
1306	23516	30.5.55	4.8.55	21.3.57	421. Cat.A.
1307	23517	2.6.55	27.6.55	16.1.63	434, 439.
1308	23518	2.6.55	20.6.55	3.6.63	414.
1309	23519	3.6.55	27.6.55	27.11.58	441. Cat.A.
1310	23520	29.5.55	27.6.55	17.4.63	422, 434, 444.
1311	23521	3.6.55	20.6.55	28.9.62	434, 439.
1312	23522	9.6.55	20.6.55	12.5.64	427, 434, 439
1313	23523	15.6.55	27.6.55	1.3.63	422, 444.
1314	23524	16.6.55	27.6.55	9.3.56	422.
1315	23525	15.6.55	27.6.55	3.6.63	434.
1316	23526	15.6.55	20.6.55	7.5.63	416, 439.
1317	23527	22.6.55	27.6.55	18.1.61	441.
1318	23528	17.6.55	27.6.55	28.11.63	422, 439.
1319	23529	27.6.55	27.6.55	3.5.58	422, 434. Cat.A.
1320	23530	28.6.55	27.6.55	7.5.57	441. Cat.A.
1321	23531	4.7.55	27.6.55	11.1.57	434. Cat.A.
1322	23532	8.7.55	4.8.55	11.12.62	439.
1323	23533	6.7.55	27.6.55	19.12.56	422. Cat.A.
1324	23534	5.7.55	27.6.55	17.12.62	434.
1325	23535	5.7.55	27.6.55	13.12.56	421. Cat.A.
1326	23536	8.7.55	27.5.55	16.1.63	
1327	23537	6.7.55	11.10.55	12.4.62	430. Cat.A.
1328	23538	6.7.55	16.8.55	20.11.63	439.
1329	23539	6.7.55	15.7.55		Avro.
1330	23540	8.7.55	27.6.55	12.5.64	439.
1331	23541	12.7.55	4.8.55	13.10.61	413, 421, 434. Cat.A.
1332	23542	11.7.55	27.6.55	17.12.62	434.
1333	23543	14.7.55	27.6.55	21.8.56	427. Cat.A.
1334	23544	12.7.55	20.7.55	29.7.59	CEPE.
1335	23545	15.7.55	27.6.55	1.8.63	434, 439, 441.
1336	23546	2.8.55	4.8.55	10.8.60	422, 434. Cat.A.
1337	23547	19.7.55	4.8.55	20.11.63	439.
1338	23548	4.8.55	4.8.55	1.8.63	421, 439.
1339	23549	3.8.55	5.11.56	20.11.63	439.
1340	23550	2.8.55	4.8.55	1.3.63	416, 434, 444.
1341	23551	8.8.55	15.11.55		413, 434, 441, GH.
1342	23552	8.8.55	4.8.55	11.12.62	
1343	23553	12.8.55	4.8.55	7.1.64	
1344	23554	22.8.55	4.8.55	20.11.63	416, 421, 439. CEPE.
1345	23555	18.8.55	11.8.55	16.12.58	441, CEPE. Cat.A.
1346	23556	26.8.55	7.10.55	26.2.58	441. Cat.A.
1347	23557	23.8.55		24.9.63	441.
1348	23558		4.8.55	12.5.64	434, 439.
1349	23559		12.10.55		CEPE, AFHQ.
1350	23560		7.10.55	16.1.63	439.
1351	23561	24.8.55	3.4.56	6.3.58	439. Cat.A.
1352	23562	7.9.55	7.10.55	28.9.62	
1353	23563	2.9.55	7.10.55	28.5.62	
1354	23564	23.8.55	4.8.55	3.6.63	434.
1355	23565	24.8.55	2.10.56	12.5.64	441.
1356	23566	26.8.55	23.9.55	3.6.63	
1357	23567	1.9.55	7.10.55	29.11.56	427. Cat.A.
1358	23568	2.9.55	7.10.55	28.10.59	439. Cat.A.
1359	23569	16.9.55	7.10.55	28.9.62	434.
1360	23570	29.9.55	4.8.55	20.11.63	439.
1361	23571	29.9.55	7.10.55	23.7.58	427. Cat.A.
1362	23572	21.9.55	7.10.55	20.11.63	434, 439.
1363	23573	21.9.55	7.10.55	16.1.63	439, 441.
1364	23574	16.9.55	7.10.55	17.12.62	
1365	23575	1.9.55	7.10.55	28.9.62	
1366	23576	29.9.55	7.10.55	25.3.63	430.
1367	23577	29.9.55	7.10.55	12.12.62	413, 441.
1368	23578	21.9.55	7.10.55	1.8.63	430, 441.
1369	23579	29.9.55	7.10.55	28.9.62	439.
1370	23580	29.9.55	7.10.55	28.9.62	
1371	23581	29.9.55	3.4.56	21.2.57	439. Cat.A.
1372	23582	14.10.55	7.10.55	3.6.63	422.
1373	23583	5.10.55	7.10.55	28.9.62	
1374	23584	11.10.55	3.4.56	23.4.57	439. Cat.A.
1375	23585	11.10.55	7.10.55	1.3.63	444.
1376	23586	11.10.55	7.10.55	3.6.63	430.
1377	23587	7.12.55	3.4.56	17.4.63	439.
1378	23588	13.12.55	3.4.56	1.8.63	416, 421.
1379	23589	18.1.56	3.4.56	17.4.63	439, 444.
1380	23590	1.12.55	3.4.56	23.2.60	441. Cat.A.
1381	23591	9.12.55	11.6.56	16.1.63	
1382	23592	16.12.55	11.6.56	17.12.62	
1383	23593	7.12.55	7.10.55	23.8.63	416, 430, 441. Cat.A.
1384	23594	16.12.56	3.4.56	17.4.63	439, 444.
1385	23595	7.12.55	3.4.56	17.4.63	413, 416, 421, 444.
1386	23596		2.10.56	13.8.62	444.
1387	23597	9.12.55	11.6.56	1.8.63	421, 434.
1388	23598		11.6.56	17.4.63	416, 430.
1389	23599		3.4.56	20.11.63	439, 441.
1390	23600		6.1.56		422, 441, GH. Was CF-JJB May 1957.
1391	23601	7.12.55	7.10.55	10.2.60	422, 444. Cat.A.
1392	23602	9.12.55	7.10.55	16.1.63	441.
1393	23603	9.12.55	7.10.55	24.9.63	441.
1394	23604	13.12.55	3.4.56	18.3.63	421, 439, 441.
1395	23605	13.12.55	3.4.56	17.4.63	439, 444.
1396	23606	20.12.55	3.4.56	1.8.63	439.
1397	23607	23.12.55	11.6.56	24.9.63	441.
1398	23608	23.12.55	11.6.56	1.8.63	434.
1399	23609	23.12.55	1.10.56	16.1.63	434.
1400	23610		23.8.56		
1401	23611	18.11.55	9.1.56	8.2.61	416, 430, 434. Cat.A. First Mk.6 with re-introduced "6-3" wing.
1402	23612	16.12.55	3.4.56	17.12.62	439.
1403	23613	16.12.55	9.1.56	17.12.62	Was CF-JJC May 1957.
1404	23614	6.1.56	9.1.56	12.5.64	413.
1405	23615	20.1.56	3.4.56	12.5.64	416.
1406	23616	18.1.56	3.4.56	3.6.63	416.
1407	23617	18.1.56	9.1.56	17.12.62	416.
1408	23618	5.1.56	3.4.56	12.5.64	434, 439, 441.
1409	23619	18.1.56	9.1.56	22.4.60	416, 439. Cat.A.
1410	23620	21.1.56	9.1.56	1.3.63	416, 434, 444.
1411	23621	21.1.56	19.9.56	28.9.62	
1412	23622	24.1.56	9.1.56	3.6.63	421, 427, 430.
1413	23623	1.2.56	9.1.56	21.11.57	416, 421. Cat.A.
1414	23624	31.1.56	7.10.55	16.1.63	413, 434, 441.
1415	23625	21.2.56	3.4.56	20.11.63	439, 441.
1416	23626	9.2.56	9.1.56	17.12.62	416.
1417	23627	9.2.56	9.1.56	18.3.63	
1418	23628	21.12.55	18.10.56	17.12.62	Was CF-JJB. (41 flights by Swiss Air Force Feb. 18-Mar. 1, 1957).
1419	23629	31.1.56	9.1.56	16.1.63	416, 439.
1420	23630	9.2.56	9.1.56	16.1.63	416, 434.
1421	23631	24.1.56	9.1.56	28.9.62	416.
1422	23632	16.2.56	9.1.56	16.1.63	416.
1423	23633	9.2.56	3.4.56	24.8.62	439.
1424	23634	17.2.56	9.1.56	30.10.61	416, 434.
1425	23635	6.1.56	13.12.56	28.9.62	444, CEPE.
1426	23636	18.1.56	9.1.56	24.9.63	413, 416, 441. GH.
1427	23637	30.12.55	9.1.56	17.12.62	416.
1428	23638	19.1.56	9.1.56	17.12.58	421. Cat.A.
1429	23639	5.1.56	9.1.56	20.11.63	439.
1430	23640		9.1.56	1.3.63	441.
1431	23641	6.1.56	29.3.56		441, GH. City of Belleville 20.12.66. P (Belleville, Ont.).
1432	23642	18.1.56	19.3.56		421, 434.
1433	23643	18.1.56	9.1.56	25.3.63	414, 416.
1434	23644	24.1.56	9.1.56	24.9.63	416, 434, 444.
1435	23645	18.1.56	3.4.56	1.3.63	439, 444.
1436	23646	27.1.56	9.1.56	30.3.60	416, 434. Cat.A.
1437	23647	1.2.56	9.1.56	17.12.62	416.
1438	23648	25.1.56	9.1.56	17.4.63	416, 421, 444.
1439	23649	31.1.56	3.4.56		416, GH, 426 Wing RCAFA, P (Brockville, Ont.).
1440	23650	16.2.56	9.1.56	20.11.63	416, 421.
1441	23651	1.2.56	3.5.56		GH. P (Ottawa).
1442	23652	10.2.56	9.1.56	1.8.63	439.
1443	23653	16.2.56	3.4.56	28.9.62	421, 439.
1444	23654	10.2.56		28.8.56	421, 441. Cat.A.

c/n	Tail No.	f/f	TOS	SOS	Notes
1445	23655	22.2.56	3.4.56	27.12.60	416, 421, Cat. A.
1446	23656	16.2.56	3.4.56	3.6.63	416.
1447	23657	16.2.56	3.4.56	17.4.63	416, 434.
1448	23658	20.3.56	13.4.56	24.9.63	441.
1449	23659	16.2.56	3.4.56	6.3.57	441. Cat. A.
1450	23660	15.3.56	9.1.56	13.1.61	416, 434. Cat. A.
1451	23661	19.3.56	3.4.56	1.3.63	439, 444.
1452	23662	21.3.56	11.6.56	16.1.63	430, 439.
1453	2021	21.5.56			del. 8.6.56. Cat. A.
1454	2022	28.5.56			del. 8.6.56. Cat. A.
1455	2023	24.5.56			del. 8.6.56. P (Bogota).
1456	2024	23.4.56			del. 8.6.56.
1457	2025	27.4.56			del. 8.6.56. Cat. A.
1458	2026	24.3.56			del. 8.6.56. Cat.a.
1459	350/ 23669	28.2.56			del. 29.9.56. 1/A.
1460	351/23670	28.2.56			del. 29.9.56. 1/B. Cat. A.
1461	352/23671	19.3.56			1/B, 2/C. To N38301.
1462	353/23672	25.3.56			1/S, 2/D. Cat. A.
1463	353/23673	19.3.56			del. 2.10.56. 1/T, 2/A. Cat. A.
1464	355/23674	20.3.56			del. 29.9.56. 1/C, 2/G. Cat. A.
1465	356/23675	23.3.56			del. 24.11.56. 1/E. Cat. A.
1466	357/23676	21.3.56			1/D,Z, 2/C. Cat. A.
1467	358/23677	20.4.56			del. 16.11.56. 1/N. P (Pietersburg).
1468	359/23678	1.5.56			del. 11.10.56. 1/U, 2/F. To N3831B.
1469	360/23679	22.3.56			del. 11.10.56. 1/W, 2/B. Cat. A.
1470	361/23680	6.4.56			del. 11.10.56. 1/F. P (SAAF Museum Swartop).
1471	362/23681	22.3.56			del. 2.10.56. 1/R, 2/L. Cat. A.
1472	363/23682	21.3.56			1/V, 2. P (South Africa), later N3842H.
1473	364/23683	6.4.56			del. 2.10.56. 1/R. Cat. A.
1474	365/23684	23.4.56			del. 11.10.56. 1/Q, 2/O.
1475	366/23685	20.4.56			del. 12.11.56. 1/G. Cat. A.
1476	367/23686	20.4.56			del. 12.11.56. 1/E, 2/E. P (SAAF Museum Snake Valley).
1477	368/23687	23.4.56			del. 2.10.56. 1/K. Cat. A.
1478	369/23688	20.4.56			del. 13.12.56. 1/H. P (Waterkloof).
1479	370/23689	30.4.56			del. 2.10.56. 1/D, 2/H. Cat. A.
1480	371/23690	8.5.56			del. 11.10.56. 1/M. To N3842J.
1481	372/23691	9.5.56			del. 11.10.56. 1/X, 2/P. P (SAAF School of Technical Training).
1482	373/23692	17.5.56			del. 11.10.56. 1/AD, 2/X. To N3844E.
1483	374/23693	9.5.56			del. 9.10.56. 1/Y, 2/N. Cat. A.
1484	375/23694	9.5.56			del. 11.10.56. 1/L. Cat. A.
1485	376/23695	11.5.56			del. 11.10.56. 1/Q. Cat. A.
1486	377/23696	15.5.56			del. 11.10.56. 1/O. Cat. A.
1487	378/23697	10.5.56			del. 7.10.56. 1/J. To N38453N.
1488	379/23698	17.5.60			del. 11.10.56. 1, 2/Q. Cat. A.
1489	380/23699	15.5.56			del. 11.10.56. 1/AB, 2/R, 85AFS. To N3846J.
1490	381/23700	17.5.56			del. 11.10.56. 1/AC, 2/J. P (SAAF Museum).
1491	382/23701	23.5.56			del. 11.10.56. 1/P. To N3847H, then N87FS.
1492	383/23702	24.5.56			del. 11.10.56. 1/L, 2/M. P (Kempton Park Tech. College, RSA).
1493	23663	7.6.56	11.6.56	28.9.63	
1494	23664	7.6.56	3.4.56	1.3.63	441, 444.
1495	23665	7.6.56	11.6.56	28.9.62	413, 434, 441.
1496	23666	7.6.56	11.6.56	26.3.63	439, 441.
1497	23667	12.6.56	11.6.56	1.3.63	441.
1498	23668	11.6.56	17.8.56		422.
1499	23669	12.6.56	11.6.56	11.9.57	416, 430. Cat. A.
1500	23670	26.6.56	27.8.56		421.
1501	23671	26.6.56	2.10.56		441.
1502	23672	11.7.56	27.8.56		421, 441.
1503	23673	28.6.56	11.6.56	11.9.57	430. Cat. A.
1504	23674	4.7.56	11.6.56	12.5.64	413, 434, 439, 441.
1505	23675	3.8.56	11.6.56	12.5.64	416, 430.
1506	23676	14.8.56	11.6.56	10.4.63	
1507	23677	2.8.56	11.6.56	24.9.63	430.
1508	23678		11.5.65	16.10.58	434. Cat. A.
1509	23679		11.6.56	17.12.62	
1510	23680		11.6.56	28.2.62	422.
1511	23681	22.8.56	11.6.56	28.9.62	
1512	23682	21.8.56	11.6.56	9.1.62	422.
1513	23683	22.8.56	11.6.56	17.4.63	416.
1514	23684	16.8.54	11.6.56	28.2.64	421, 422, 444.
1515	23685	27.8.56	11.6.56	9.2.59	434. Cat. A.
1516	23686	24.8.56	11.6.56	17.4.63	
1517	23687	4.9.56	19.9.56	28.9.62	
1518	23688	29.8.56	19.9.56	16.1.63	434, 444.
1519	23689	27.8.56	11.6.56	20.11.63	416, 439.
1520	6030 +	5.9.56			
	23753	1.5.57	23.4.57	24.9.63	441.
1521	23690	12.9.56	19.9.56	28.9.62	
1522	23691	10.9.56	19.9.56	28.9.62	
1523	6031	13.9.56			
	23754	23.4.57	23.4.57	20.11.63	439.
1524	6032	19.9.56			
	23755	18.3.57	23.4.57	24.9.63	
1525	6033	19.9.56			
	23756	19.3.57	23.4.57	21.2.61	439. Cat. A.
1526	6034	25.9.56			
	23757	30.4.57	23.4.57	11.10.63	
1527	23692	11.10.56	19.9.56	28.9.62	434.
1528	23693	26.9.56	19.9.56	27.10.59	
1529	23694	10.10.56	19.9.56	1.3.63	444.
1530	23695	28.9.56	9.1.57	16.1.63	434, 439.
1531	6035	10.10.56			
	23758	7.5.57	23.4.57	25.7.60	
1532	6036	15.10.56			
	23759	7.7.57	23.4.57	24.9.63	434.
1533	23696	18.10.56	19.9.56	3.6.63	421.
1534	6037	15.10.56			
	23760	19.3.57	23.4.57	16.1.63	434.
1535	23697	19.10.56	19.9.56	28.9.62	
1536	23698	26.10.56	19.9.56	28.9.62	
1537	23699	5.11.56	19.9.56	28.9.62	441.
1538	23700	5.11.56	19.9.56	3.6.63	
1539	23701	5.11.56	19.9.56	31.5.60	421. Cat. A.
1540	23702	5.11.56	19.9.56	15.6.62	
1541	23703	18.12.56	28.1.57		434.
1542	23704	10.11.56	6.2.57	7.1.64	439.
1543	23705	14.11.56	19.9.56	24.9.63	441.
1544	23706	4.12.56	19.9.56	16.1.63	434.
1545	23707	18.12.56	19.9.56	10.4.62	434. Cat. A.
1546	23708	4.12.56	17.1.57		
1547	23709	4.12.56	19.9.56	1.3.63	
1548	23710	19.12.56	19.9.56	16.3.62	434. Cat. A.
1549	23711	21.12.56	19.9.56	17.4.63	444.
1550	23712	14.11.56	4.3.57		
1551	23713	20.11.56	20.12.56	11.10.63	441.
1552	23714	2.1.57	1.3.57	17.12.62	
1553	23715	21.12.56	19.9.56	1.8.63	
1554	23716	13.12.56	19.9.56	3.6.63	
1555	23717	19.12.56	19.9.56	1.8.63	434.
1556	23718	8.1.57	19.9.56	4.4.62	
1557	23719	14.1.57	19.9.56	28.9.62	
1558	23720	11.1.57	18.2.57	1.3.63	444.
1559	23721	11.1.57	19.9.56	1.3.63	
1560	23722	28.1.57	1.3.57	17.4.63	
1561	23723	31.1.57	1.3.57	1.3.63	434.
1562	23724	31.1.57	26.4.57	21.11.61	Cat. A.
1563	23725	31.1.57	1.3.57	1.3.63	444.
1564	23726	8.2.57	1.3.57	16.10.61	
1565	23727	31.1.57	11.3.57	1.3.63	
1566	23728	8.2.57	1.3.57	28.9.62	
1567	23729	14.2.57	16.4.57		421.
1568	23730	19.2.57	26.4.57	1.3.63	
1569	23731	21.2.57	1.3.57	17.12.62	
1570	23732	18.2.57	6.5.57		
1571	23733	21.2.57	10.5.57		
1572	23734	28.2.57	26.4.57	16.1.63	439.
1573	23735	1.3.57	1.3.57	1.3.63	444.
1574	23736	18.3.57	1.3.57	17.12.62	
1575	23737	18.3.57	1.3.57	17.12.62	441.
1576	23738	22.3.57	26.4.57	17.12.62	
1577	23739	25.3.57	26.4.56	1.3.63	
1578	23740	3.4.57	1.3.57	3.6.63	
1579	23741	26.3.57	1.3.57	17.4.63	
1580	23742	3.4.57	26.4.57	17.4.63	434.
1581	23743	9.4.57	26.4.57	1.3.63	444.
1582	23744	15.4.57	5.6.57		Avro.
1583	23745	16.4.57	26.4.57	7.1.64	439.
1584	23746	10.4.57	26.4.57	28.9.62	
1585	23747	15.4.57	26.4.57	1.8.63	
1586	23748	24.4.57	26.4.57	29.8.60	422, 434. Cat. A.
1587	23749	24.4.57	26.4.57	18.3.63	444.
1588	23750	30.4.57	26.4.57	16.1.63	434.
1589	23751	7.5.57	5.6.57		421, 434.
1590	23752	7.5.57	26.4.57	17.12.62	434.

c/n	Tail No.	f/f	TOS	SOS	Notes
1591	JA-101	4.6.57			Later BB-161, BB-261, YA-005, 0101. To Hayden-Baillie Aircraft and Naval Collection in UK, 1979.
1592	BB-162	3.6.57			BB-362. Pak.
1593	BB-163	30.5.57			YA-043, 0102. To MBB as instr. airframe. Later FS N1039B, N81FS.
1594	BB-164	6.6.57			BB-364. Pak, cr.
1595	BB-165	30.5.57			BB-365, JB-122. Pak.
1596	BB-166	6.6.57			JB-360.
1597	BB-167	11.6.57			BB-167.
1598	BB-168	10.6.57			JB-362, YA-041.
1599	BB-169	11.6.57			BB-369. Cat.A.
1600	BB-170	17.6.57			D-9538, FS N1039C, N82FS.
1601	BB-171	20.6.57			Later D-9522. Cat.A.
1602	BB-172	27.6.57			Cat.A.
1603	BB-173	27.6.57			D-9539.
1604	BB-174	27.6.57			YA-041. Cat.A.
1605	BB-175	27.6.57			BB-275, KE-201, KE-102, 0103, to MBB as instru. airframe. P (Baden as 23605).
1606	BB-176	4.7.57			BB-276, BB-376. Pak. cr.
1607	BB-177	8.7.57			BB-277. Pak. cr.
1608	BB-178	10.7.57			BB-278. Pak., Bangladesh. Last flight 21.1.72.
1609	BB-179	1.8.57			BB-279. Pak., Bangladesh.
1610	BB-180	1.8.57			BB-280, BB-380, JB-123.
1611	BB-181	6.8.57			BB-281, JB-371. P (WG).
1612	BB-182	7.8.57			BB-282, BB-382.
1613	BB-183	16.8.57			BB-283, YA-042, 0104. P (Stuttgart).
1614	BB-184	16.8.57			BB-284, JC-105. Pak. cr.
1615	BB-185	16.8.57			BB-285, JC-249. Cat.A.
1616	BB-186	19.8.57			BB-286. Pak. cr.
1617	BB-187	22.8.57			JB-255, KE-202. Pak., Bangladesh. Last flight 28.9.72.
1618	BB-188	4.9.57			BB-288. Pak. cr.
1619	BB-359	6.9.57			JC-360, JC-288. Cat.A.
1620	BB-	6.9.57			
1621	BB-	9.9.57			JA-107. Pak. cr.
1622	BB-	13.9.57			Pak.
1623	BB-	13.9.57			Pak.
1624	BB-	15.9.57			JA-310. Pak. cr.
1625	BB-	23.9.57			
1626	BB-	24.9.57			JA-112. Pak.
1627	BB-	3.10.57			Pak.
1628	BB-281	3.10.57			JD-249. Cat.A.
1629	BB-	9.10.57			JD-243. Pak.
1630	BB-	11.10.57			JA-116.
1631	BB-	15.10.57			JB-250, JA-321.
1632	BB-	22.10.57			Pak.
1633	BB-	21.10.57			
1634	BB-	28.10.57			Pak.
1635	BB-	28.10.57			
1636	BB-	31.10.57			Pak. cr.
1637	BB-	6.1.57			JD-240. Cat.A.
1638	BB-	6.11.57			JC-373. P (Lahr as 23444).
1639	BB-279	7.11.57			JD-241. Pak.
1640	BB-	12.11.57			JA-234. Cat.A.
1641	BB-	18.11.57			JD-239, JA-363, JB-362. Cat.A.
1642	BB-	17.12.57			JB-361.
1643	BB-382	26.11.57			JB-110, JB-374. P (Utersen, WG).
1644	BB-	25.11.57			JD-235, JA-369, JB-363, JC-360, JC-246. Later instr. airframe at Celle.
1645	BB-	26.11.57			JA-232, JA-332.
1646	BB-	2.12.57			JA-247.
1647	BB-	2.12.57			JA-101, JA-301. To fire brigade at Sylt.
1648	BB-	17.12.57			JC-104, JD-249. Cat.A.
1649	BB-	27.12.57			JA-373, JD-233. Cat.A.
1650	BB-294	17.12.57			Pak. cr.
1651	BB-	17.12.57			JA-334, JA-339, JD-334.
1652	BB-289	23.12.57			JB-252. Pak.
1653	BB-	23.12.57			JB-253. Pak. cr.
1654	BB-	23.12.57			BB-292, JD-119. Cat.A.
1655	BB-	24.12.57			JB-248. Pak.
1656	BB-	9.1.58			Pak.
1657	BB-	9.1.58			Pak. cr.
1658	BB-291	9.1.58			Pak. cr.
1659	BB-	9.1.58			YA-048, KE-105, 0105. P (German Museum, Munchen).
1660	BB-169	20.1.58			Pak. cr.
1661	BB-296	23.1.58			JB-254. Pak. cr.
1662	BB-	10.1.58			JB-121.
1663	BB-	20.1.58			Pak., Bangladesh.
1664	BB-186	24.1.58			JD-112, YA-044, 0106. P (Neubiberg?).
1665	BB-184	5.2.58			Pak.
1666	BB-185	6.2.58			D-9540. Later FS N1039D, N83FS.
1667	BB-	24.1.58			BB-277, JA-235.
1668	BB-	6.2.58			0107.
1669	BB-	6.2.58			BB-298. Pak., Bangladesh. Last flight 26.9.72.
1670	BB-	6.2.58			JB-105. Pak. P (Lahore).
1671	BB-	6.2.58			Pak. cr.
1672	JD-107	5.2.58			Cat.A.
1673	JA-108	5.2.58			JC-116.
1674	JC-107	11.2.58			Pak. cr.
1675		11.2.58			KE-104, 0113. Later FS N1039K, N80FS.
1676	JA-121	20.2.58			JD-101. Cat.A.
1677	JA-236	11.2.58			JA-336. Cat.A.
1678	JC-117	5.3.58			
1679	JC-108	19.3.58			Suspected Cat.A.
1680		11.3.58			
1681	JB-361	11.3.58			
1682	JC-106	25.3.58			
1683		11.3.58			Pak. cr.
1684	JC-112	25.3.58			
1685		25.3.58			
1686		13.3.58			
1687		25.3.58			
1688	BB-182	13.3.58			JC-231. Cat.A.
1689		19.3.58			Pak. cr.
1690		26.3.58			
1691		19.3.58			
1692		1.4.58			Pak. cr.
1693		27.3.58			Pak.
1694	JC-250	1.4.58			Cat.A.
1695		3.4.58			Pak. cr.
1696	JC-101	1.4.58			
1697	JA-238	10.4.58			JA-338. Cat.A.
1698	JC-110	25.3.58			
1699		1.4.58			
1700	JC-249	3.4.58			
1701		10.4.58			Pak.
1702		3.4.58			Pak.
1703		9.4.58			Pak. cr.
1704	JC-240	15.4.58			P (Budel, Netherlands).
1705		9.4.58			Pak.
1706	JC-241	15.4.58			
1707	JA-239	16.4.58			Cat.A.
1708	JC-246	15.4.58			Cat.A.
1709		15.4.58			Pak.
1710	JB-240	18.4.58			D-9541. Later FS N1039L, N89FS.
1711		18.4.58			YA-049, 0108, D-FADE. Crashed north of Frankfurt on 1970 ferry flight.
1712	JC-233	24.4.58			
1713	JC-238	24.4.58			Cat.A.
1714	JC-114	24.4.58			P (Hohn, WG).
1715		25.4.58			0109. To flight simulator.
1716	JC-235	24.4.58			
1717		5.5.58			
1718		30.4.58			Pak. cr.
1719	JB-241	1.5.58			Pak. cr.
1720	JC-236	2.5.58			Pak. cr.
1721		5.5.58			
1722		5.5.58			Pak.
1723		10.5.58			
1724	JB-251	14.5.58			Instr. airframe.
1725	JC-118	11.5.58			Cat.A.
1726	JB-242	14.5.58			JC-117. Instr. airframe at Fassberg.
1727		12.5.58			
1728	JB-231	10.5.58			Pak., P (Lahore).
1729	JB-239	15.5.58			
1730	JB-114	21.5.58			P (Jever as BB-103).
1731	JB-116	23.5.58			
1732	JB-107	20.5.58			JC-104. Instr. airframe. P (Goslar, WG as GS-338)
1733		20.5.58			Pak.
1734	JB-110	21.5.58			JC-110. Cat.A.
1735	JB-120	26.5.58			Pak. cr.
1736	BB-175	27.5.58			JB-238.
1737	JA-242	27.5.58			JA-342. Cat.A.
1738	JB-109	23.5.58			Pak. cr.

c/n	Tail No.	f/f	TOS	SOS	Notes
1739	JB-232	3.6.58			Pak.
1740	JB-103	2.6.58			0110, D-9542. Instr. airframe at Fassberg.
1741		3.6.58			
1742		3.6.58			Pak. cr.
1743	JB-105	6.6.58			JC-105. Cat.A.
1744	JB-121	6.6.58			Cat.A.
1745	JB-235	9.6.58			Instr. airframt at Fassberg.
1746	JB-246	12.6.58			YA-046, 0111. To flight simulator.
1747	JA-243	9.6.58			Pak.
1748	JB-245	12.6.58			
1749	JB-102	12.6.58			Pak.
1750	JB-111	12.6.58			
1751		18.6.58			Pak.
1752	JB-101	18.6.56			JB-248.
1753	JB-250	18.6.58			Cat.A.
1754	BB-176	3.7.58			JB-234. Pak.
1755	JB-244	19.6.58			Suspected Cat.A.
1756	JB-108	26.6.58			JB-244. Pak.
1757	JA-244	26.6.58			JB-344. Cat.A.
1758	JB-247	22.6.58			
1759	BB-273	9.7.58			JB-241. Cat.A.
1760	JB-113	3.7.58			YA-057, 0112.
1761	JB-233	14.7.58			Instr. airframe at Fassberg.
1762		14.7.58			
1763	BB-274	10.7.56			Pak. cr.
1764	BB-272	14.7.58			Pak.
1765		14.7.58			Pak. cr.
1766	JB-119	11.8.58			Pak. cr.
1767	JB-236	17.7.58			
1768	JB-237	17.7.58			
1769		12.8.58			
1770	JB-118	12.8.58			Instr. airframe at Fassberg.
1771	JB-364	12.8.58			Pak.
1772	BB-180	12.8.58			JB-106. Pak. cr.
1773	JB-104	13.8.58			
1774	JC-364	13.8.58			Suspected Cat.A.
1775	JB-112	12.8.58			JB-370. Instr. airframe P (Ahlhorn).
1776		14.8.58			
1777	JB-363	13.8.58			Pak.
1778		19.8.58			Pak.
1779	BB-269	15.8.58			JB-231. Cat.A.
1780	JA-248	22.8.58			JA-348, JC-366. Cat.A.
1781	JB-115	20.8.58			Pak.
1782	JB-116	22.8.58			JC-104, JC-361. Cat.A.
1783	BB-178	22.8.58			JB-124.
1784		27.8.58			D-9523. Instr. airframe at Fassberg.
1785	JA-249	27.8.58			JA-349, JC-367. Cat.A.
1786		26.8.58			Pak. cr.
1787		3.9.58			Pak. cr.
1788	BB-177	2.9.58			JC-246. Pak. cr.
1789	BB-267	3.9.58			Pak.
1790	JB-125	3.9.58			Pak.
1791	JB-104	5.9.58			
1792		12.9.58			Pak.
1793	JB-103	12.9.58			
1794		19.9.58			Pak.
1795		19.9.58			
1796	JA-121	19.9.58			Cat.A.
1797	JA-105	19.9.58			JA-305. Pak.
1798		19.9.58			Pak. cr.
1799		23.9.58			Suspected Cat.A.
1800		23.9.58			Pak. cr.
1801		19.9.58			
1802	JB-365	24.9.58			Pak. cr.
1803		26.9.58			Pak. cr.
1804		26.9.58			Pak. cr.
1805	JA-102	29.9.58			JA-302, JC-361. Fire brigade at Wahn.
1806		2.10.58			
1807	BB-188	17.10.58			JB-366.
1808	JB-367	21.10.58			Pak. cr.
1809	JB-117	17.10.58			Pak.
1810	JB-368	11.11.58			Pak.
1811	JB-369	17.10.58			Pak. cr.
1812	JB-370	22.10.58			Pak.
1813	BB-293	3.11.58			JB-377. P (Oldenberg as JB-371).
1814	BB-194	12.11.58			JC-247, JC-376. Cat.A.
1815		21.11.58			Pak.

BT-495 of 441 Squadron and IG-661 of 439
formate with other 1 Wing types: a CF-100 of
445 and an Instrument Flight T-33.
(via Lou J. Hill)

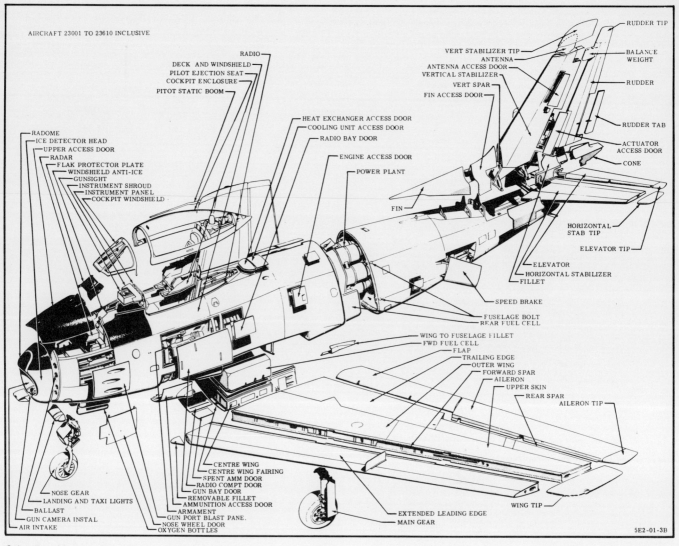

Sabre 5 and 6, exploded view

5E2-01-3B

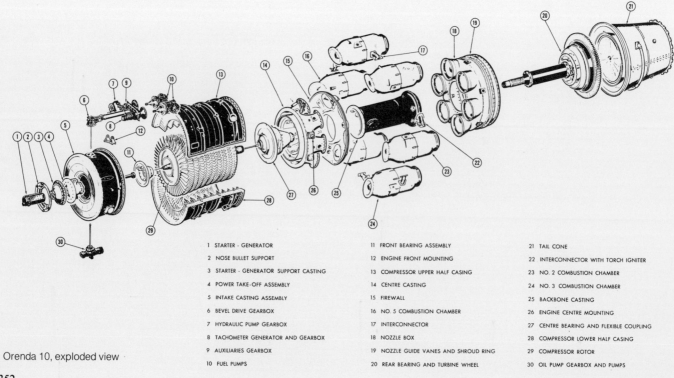

Orenda 10, exploded view

1 STARTER - GENERATOR	11 FRONT BEARING ASSEMBLY	21 TAIL CONE
2 NOSE BULLET SUPPORT	12 ENGINE FRONT MOUNTING	22 INTERCONNECTOR WITH TORCH IGNITER
3 STARTER - GENERATOR SUPPORT CASTING	13 COMPRESSOR UPPER HALF CASING	23 NO. 2 COMBUSTION CHAMBER
4 POWER TAKE-OFF ASSEMBLY	14 CENTRE CASTING	24 NO. 3 COMBUSTION CHAMBER
5 INTAKE CASTING ASSEMBLY	15 FIREWALL	25 BACKBONE CASTING
6 BEVEL DRIVE GEARBOX	16 NO. 5 COMBUSTION CHAMBER	26 ENGINE CENTRE MOUNTING
7 HYDRAULIC PUMP GEARBOX	17 INTERCONNECTOR	27 CENTRE BEARING AND FLEXIBLE COUPLING
8 TACHOMETER GENERATOR AND GEARBOX	18 NOZZLE BOX	28 COMPRESSOR LOWER HALF CASING
9 AUXILIARIES GEARBOX	19 NOZZLE GUIDE VANES AND SHROUD RING	29 COMPRESSOR ROTOR
10 FUEL PUMPS	20 REAR BEARING AND TURBINE WHEEL	30 OIL PUMP GEARBOX AND PUMPS

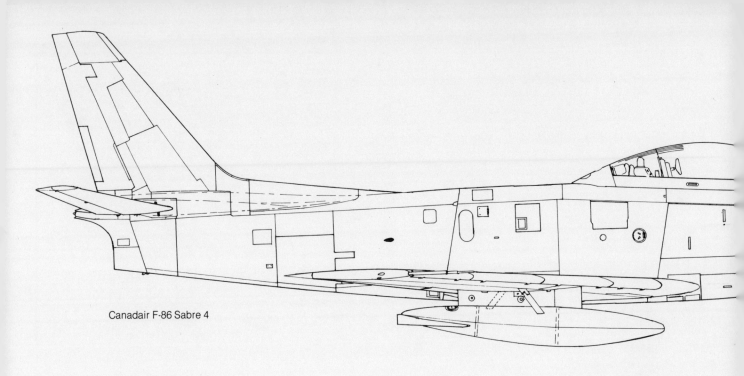

Canadair F-86 Sabre 4

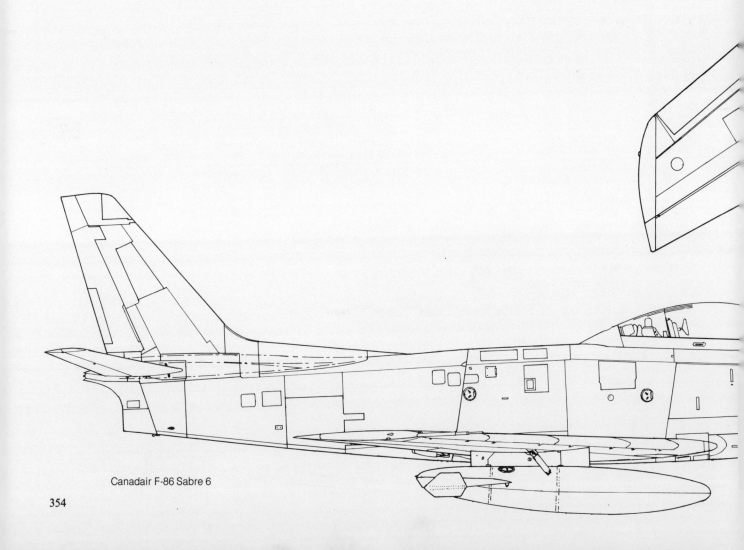

Canadair F-86 Sabre 6

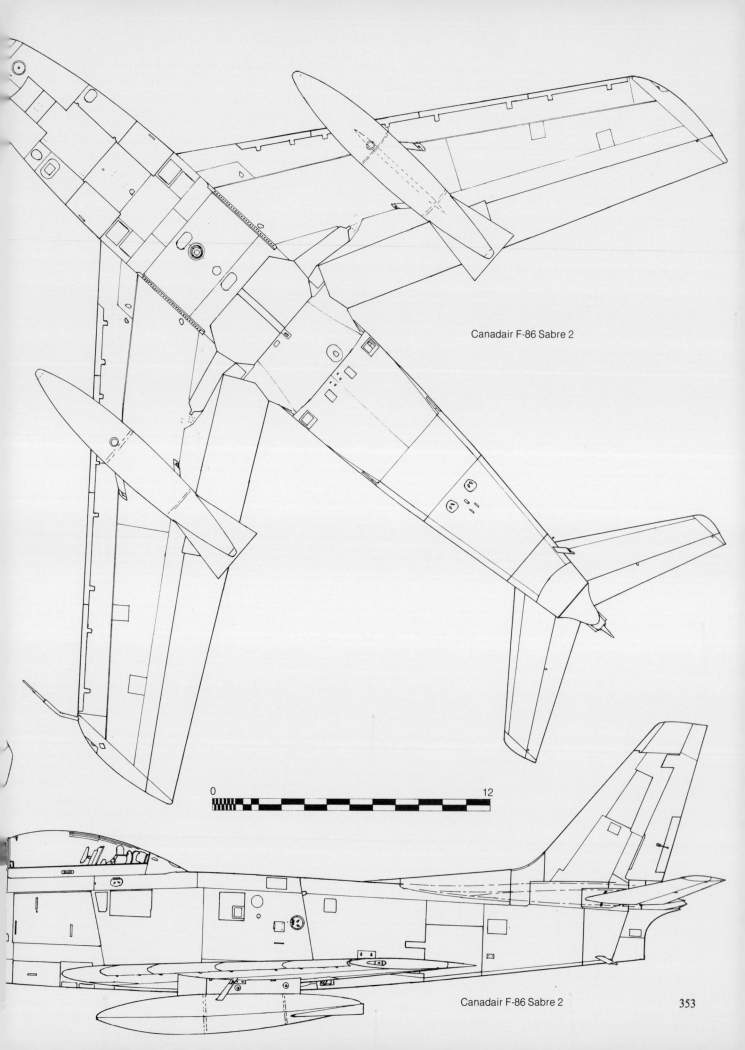

Canadair F-86 Sabre 2

0   12

Canadair F-86 Sabre 2

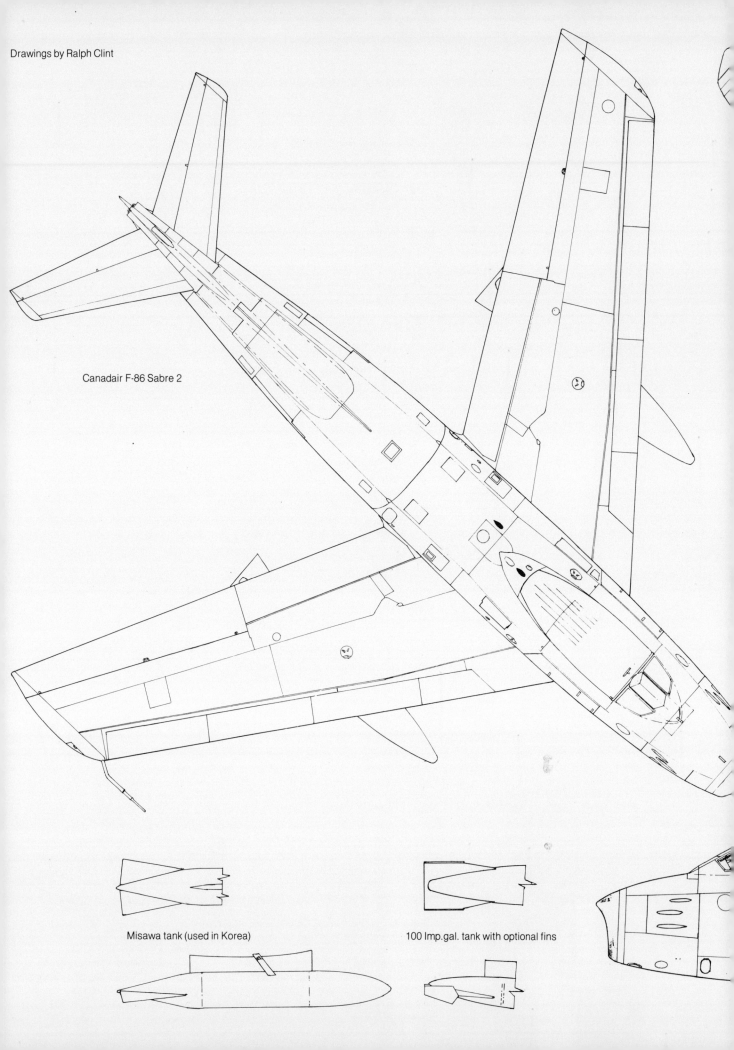

Drawings by Ralph Clint

Canadair F-86 Sabre 2

Misawa tank (used in Korea)

100 Imp.gal. tank with optional fins

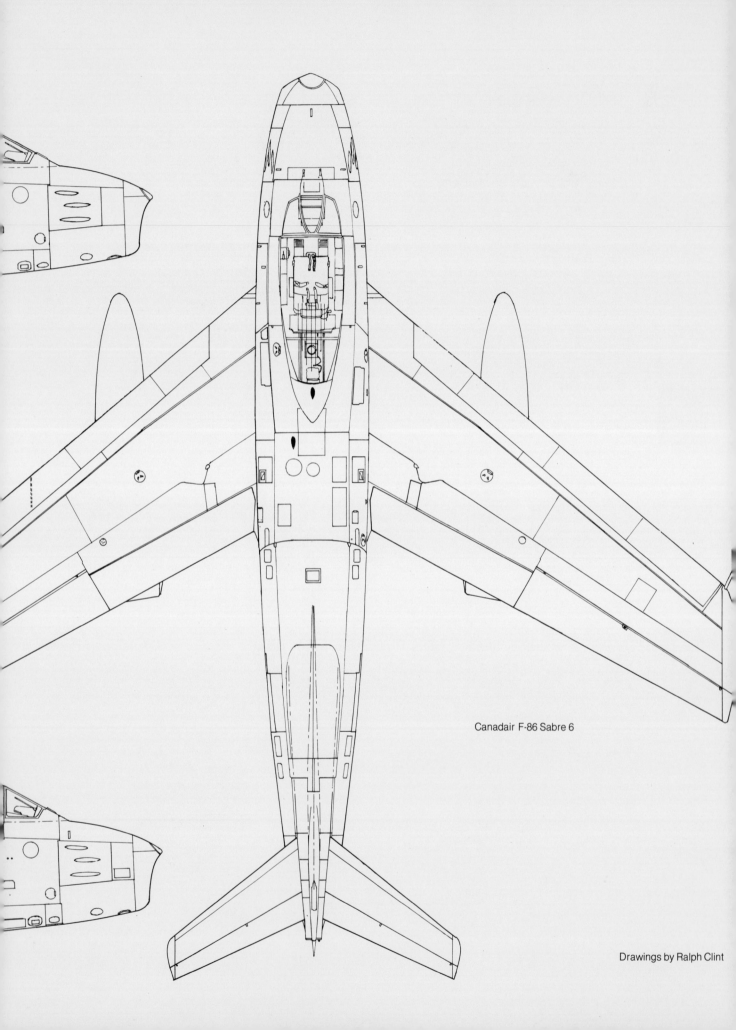

Canadair F-86 Sabre 6

Drawings by Ralph Clint

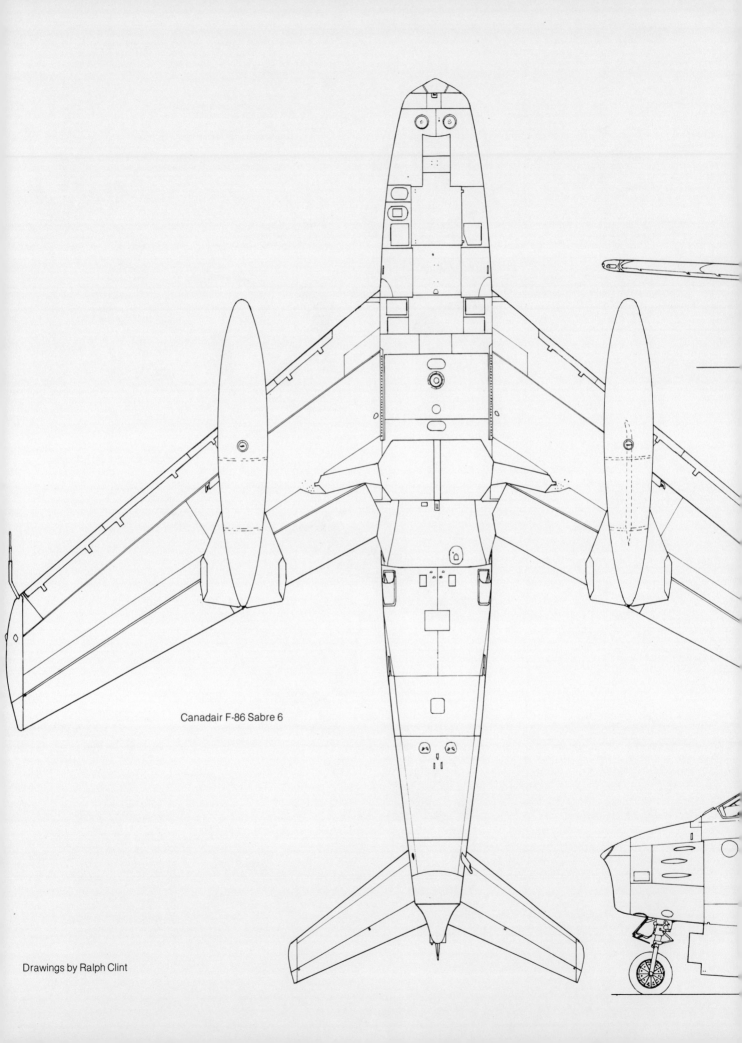

Canadair F-86 Sabre 6

Drawings by Ralph Clint

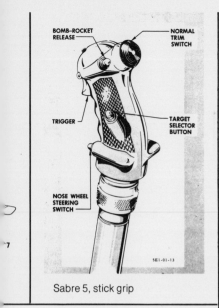

BOMB-ROCKET RELEASE

NORMAL TRIM SWITCH

TRIGGER

TARGET SELECTOR BUTTON

NOSE WHEEL STEERING SWITCH

5E1-01-13

Sabre 5, stick grip

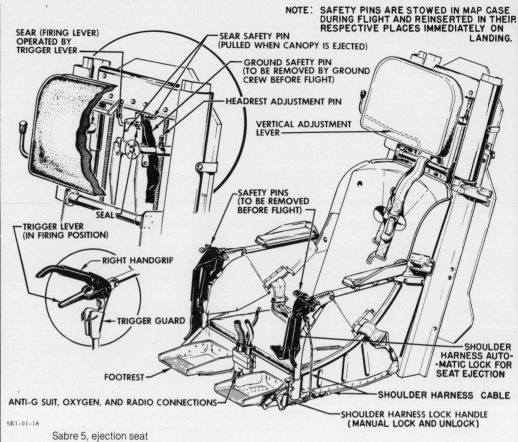

NOTE: SAFETY PINS ARE STOWED IN MAP CASE DURING FLIGHT AND REINSERTED IN THEIR RESPECTIVE PLACES IMMEDIATELY ON LANDING.

SEAR (FIRING LEVER) OPERATED BY TRIGGER LEVER

SEAR SAFETY PIN (PULLED WHEN CANOPY IS EJECTED)

GROUND SAFETY PIN (TO BE REMOVED BY GROUND CREW BEFORE FLIGHT)

HEADREST ADJUSTMENT PIN

VERTICAL ADJUSTMENT LEVER

SAFETY PINS (TO BE REMOVED BEFORE FLIGHT)

SEAL

TRIGGER LEVER (IN FIRING POSITION)

RIGHT HANDGRIP

TRIGGER GUARD

FOOTREST

ANTI-G SUIT, OXYGEN, AND RADIO CONNECTIONS

SHOULDER HARNESS AUTO-MATIC LOCK FOR SEAT EJECTION

SHOULDER HARNESS CABLE

SHOULDER HARNESS LOCK HANDLE (MANUAL LOCK AND UNLOCK)

5E1-01-18

Sabre 5, ejection seat

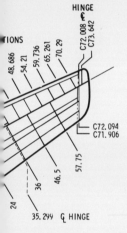

HINGE ℄

C72.008
C73.642

TIONS

48.686
54.21
59.736
65.261
70.29

C72.094
C71.906

57.75

46.5

36

35.299 ℄ HINGE

24

RIZONTAL STABILIZER STATIONS

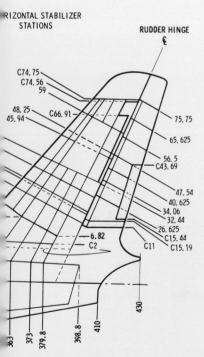

RUDDER HINGE ℄

C74.75
C74.56
59

48.25
45.94

C66.91

75.75

65.625

56.5
C43.69

47.54
40.625
34.06
32.44
26.625
C15.44
C15.19

6.82
C2
C11

430

363
373
379.8
398.8
410

5E3-01-40A

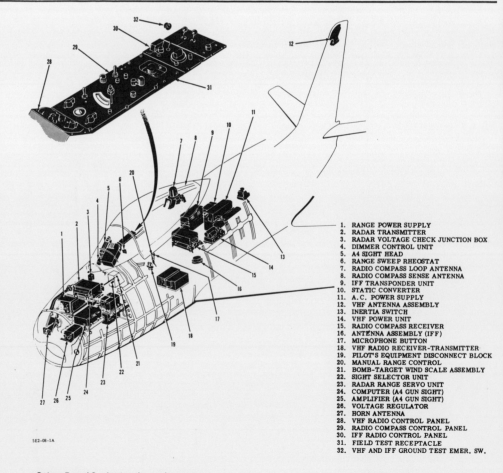

1. RANGE POWER SUPPLY
2. RADAR TRANSMITTER
3. RADAR VOLTAGE CHECK JUNCTION BOX
4. DIMMER CONTROL UNIT
5. A4 SIGHT HEAD
6. RANGE SWEEP RHEOSTAT
7. RADIO COMPASS LOOP ANTENNA
8. RADIO COMPASS SENSE ANTENNA
9. IFF TRANSPONDER UNIT
10. STATIC CONVERTER
11. A.C. POWER SUPPLY
12. VHF ANTENNA ASSEMBLY
13. INERTIA SWITCH
14. VHF POWER UNIT
15. RADIO COMPASS RECEIVER
16. ANTENNA ASSEMBLY (IFF)
17. MICROPHONE BUTTON
18. VHF RADIO RECEIVER-TRANSMITTER
19. PILOT'S EQUIPMENT DISCONNECT BLOCK
20. MANUAL RANGE CONTROL
21. BOMB-TARGET WIND SCALE ASSEMBLY
22. SIGHT SELECTOR UNIT
23. RADAR RANGE SERVO UNIT
24. COMPUTER (A4 GUN SIGHT)
25. AMPLIFIER (A4 GUN SIGHT)
26. VOLTAGE REGULATOR
27. HORN ANTENNA
28. VHF RADIO CONTROL PANEL
29. RADIO COMPASS CONTROL PANEL
30. IFF RADIO CONTROL PANEL
31. FIELD TEST RECEPTACLE
32. VHF AND IFF GROUND TEST EMER. SW.

5E2-08-1A

Sabre 5 and 6, electronic equipment

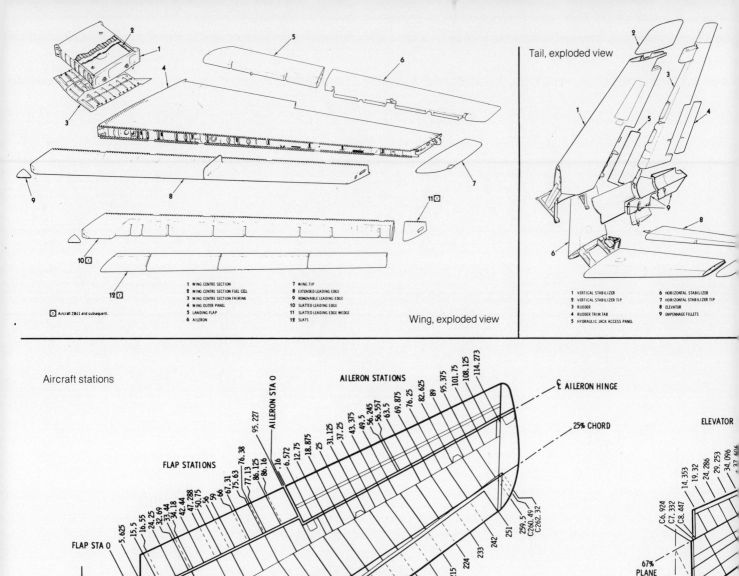

Tail, exploded view

1	WING CENTRE SECTION	7	WING TIP
2	WING CENTRE SECTION FUEL CELL	8	EXTENDED LEADING EDGE
3	WING CENTRE SECTION FAIRING	9	REMOVABLE LEADING EDGE
4	WING OUTER PANEL	10	SLATTED LEADING EDGE
5	LANDING FLAP	11	SLATTED LEADING EDGE WEDGE
6	AILERON	12	SLATS

① Aircraft 23611 and subsequent.

Wing, exploded view

1	VERTICAL STABILIZER	6	HORIZONTAL STABILIZER
2	VERTICAL STABILIZER TIP	7	HORIZONTAL STABILIZER TIP
3	RUDDER	8	ELEVATOR
4	RUDDER TRIM TAB	9	EMPENNAGE FILLETS
5	HYDRAULIC JACK ACCESS PANEL		

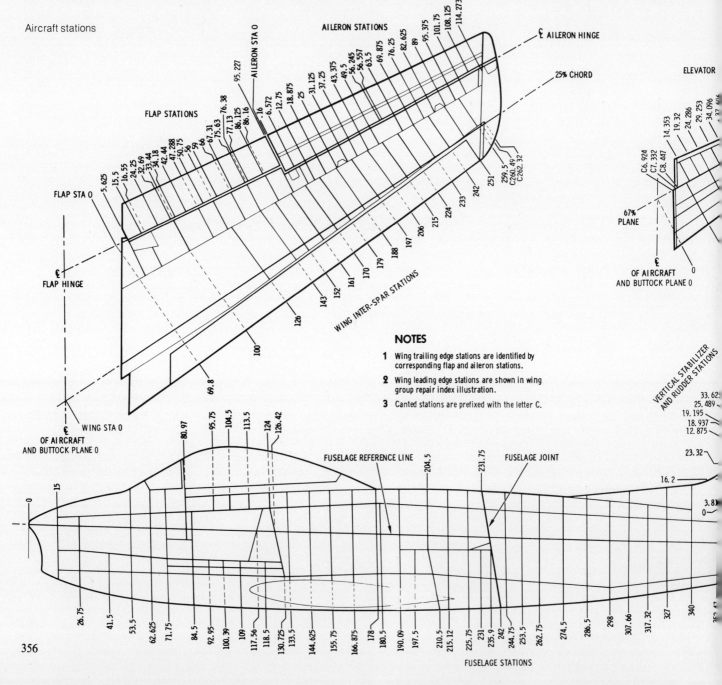

Aircraft stations

NOTES

1 Wing trailing edge stations are identified by corresponding flap and aileron stations.

2 Wing leading edge stations are shown in wing group repair index illustration.

3 Canted stations are prefixed with the letter C.

FUSELAGE STATIONS

356

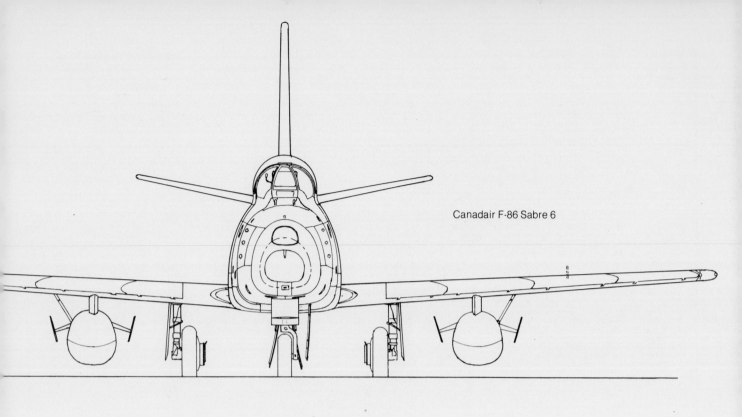

Canadair F-86 Sabre 6

0 ⬛⬛⬛⬛⬛⬛⬛⬛⬛⬛⬛⬛ 12

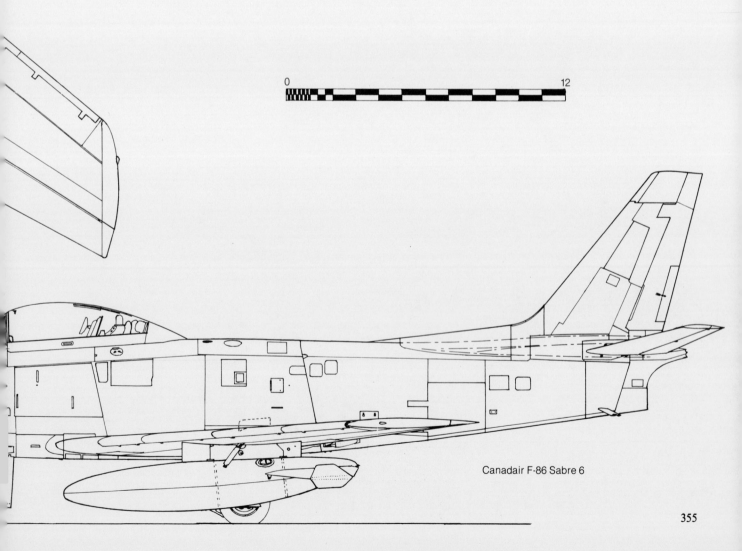

Canadair F-86 Sabre 6

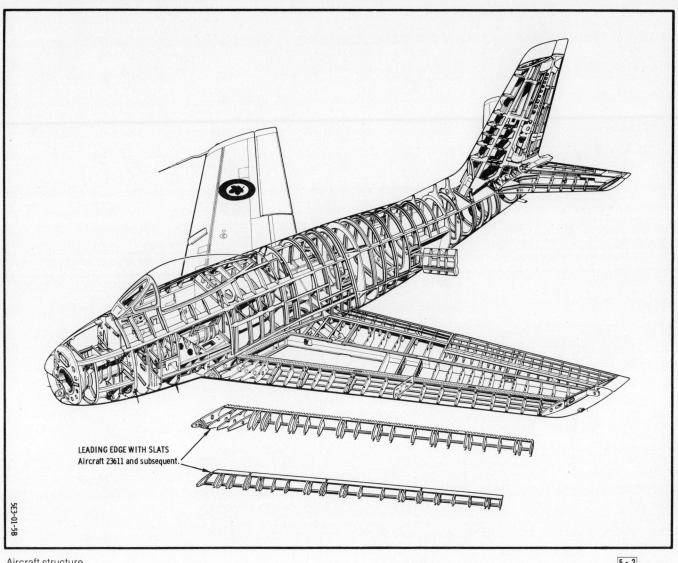

5E3-01-5B

LEADING EDGE WITH SLATS
Aircraft 23611 and subsequent.

Aircraft structure

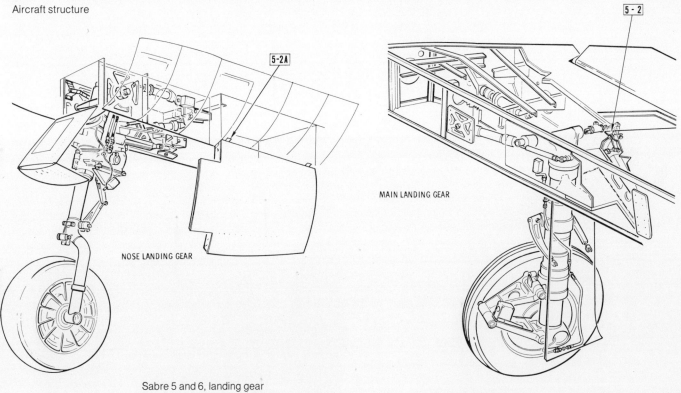

5-2A

NOSE LANDING GEAR

5 - 2

MAIN LANDING GEAR

Sabre 5 and 6, landing gear

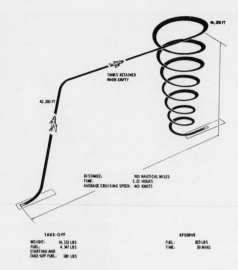

DISTANCE: 983 NAUTICAL MILES
TIME: 2.22 HOURS
AVERAGE CRUISING SPEED: 443 KNOTS

TAKE-OFF		RESERVE	
WEIGHT:	16,122 LBS	FUEL:	823 LBS
FUEL:	4,347 LBS	TIME:	20 MINS
STARTING AND TAKE-OFF FUEL:	180 LBS		

Typical ferry mission.

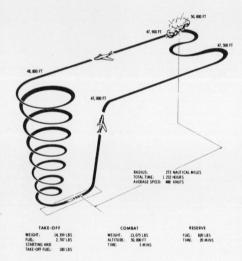

RADIUS: 273 NAUTICAL MILES
TOTAL TIME: 1.212 HOURS
AVERAGE SPEED: 488 KNOTS

TAKE-OFF		COMBAT		RESERVE	
WEIGHT:	14,359 LBS	WEIGHT:	13,075 LBS	FUEL:	820 LBS
FUEL:	2,787 LBS	ALTITUDE:	50,000 FT	TIME:	20 MINS
STARTING AND TAKE-OFF FUEL:	180 LBS	TIME:	5 MINS		

Typical combat mission.

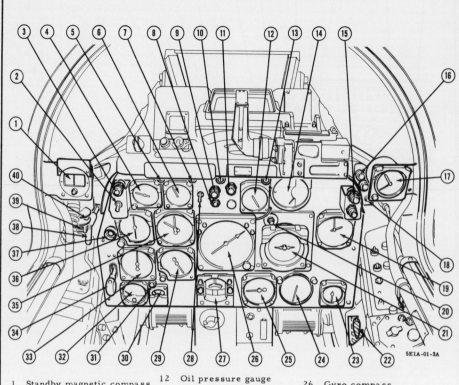

1 Standby magnetic compass
2 Emergency fuel control switch
3 Emergency fuel control warning light
4 Accelerometer
5 Main instrument inverter warning light
6 Hydraulic pressure gauge
7 Both instrument inverters warning light
8 Gyro compass fast slave button
9 Alternate flight control light
10 Main radar inverter warning light
11 Low fuel pressure warning light
12 Oil pressure gauge
13 Trim take-off position indicator light
14 Exhaust temperature indicator
15 Drop tanks empty warning lights
16 Fire warning lights
17 Clock
18 Fire warning light test button
19 Tachometer
20 Artificial horizon fast erection button
21 Artificial horizon
22 Alternate canopy jettison release
23 Cabin altimeter
24 Fuel contents gauge
25 Rate-of-climb indicator
26 Gyro compass
27 Turn and bank indicator
28 Hydraulic pressure gauge selector switch
29 Altimeter
30 Loadmeter
31 Generator off warning light
32 Voltmeter
33 Machmeter
34 Landing gear selector handle
35 Airspeed indicator
36 Radio compass
37 Landing gear emergency up button
38 Parking brake handle
39 Tow target jettison switch (Aircraft 23371 to 23430 incl.)
40 Canopy actuating switch

Cockpit, forward view, Sabre 6.

Target Tow. With these friends, who needs enemies?

Low-level Air Div war games

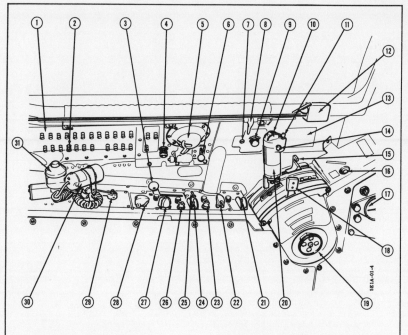

1 Left circuit breaker panel.
2 Landing gear control circuit breaker
3 Cockpit air outlet selector.
4 Windshield anti-ice overheat warning light.
5 Cockpit sidewall air outlet.
6 Windshield anti-ice control.
7 Rocket release indicator dial.
8 Canopy and windshield auxiliary defrost control.
9 Rocket release control.
10 Speed brake switch.
11 Gunsight gyro caging button.
12 Tow target emergency release. (Aircraft 23371 to 23430 inclusive.)
13 Fuel specification placard.
14 Microphone button.
15 Jet pipe temperature limiter override tell tale.
16 Bomb-rocket-tank jettison button.
17 Oxygen regulator.
18 Wing flap control.
19 Throttle friction wheel.
20 Throttle control lever.
21 Flight control switch.
22 Longitudinal alternate trim switch.
23 Rudder trim switch.
24 Cockpit pressure control switch.
25 Lateral alternate trim switch.
26 Cockpit pressure schedule switch.
27 Cockpit temperature control rheostat.
28 Cockpit temperature control switch.
29 Drop tank pressure shut-off lever.
30 Console floodlight.
31 Anti-G suit valve

Cockpit, left side, Sabre 6.

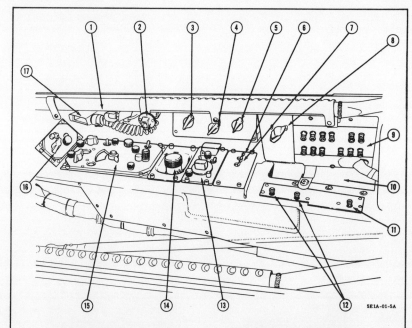

1 Cockpit sidewall air outlet control. (behind console light).
2 Console floodlight mount.
3 Instrument panel primary light rheostat.
4 Instrument panel auxiliary light rheostat.
5 Console and panel light control rheostat.
6 Air intake duct pitot heater switch.
7 Drop tanks empty lights switch.
8 N-9 camera lens aperture selector.
9 Right circuit breaker panel.
10 Map case.
11 Fire warning circuit breaker.
12 Instrument inverter circuit breakers.
13 IFF control panel.
14 Gunsight test plug.
15 Radio compass control panel.
16 VHF control panel.
17 Console floodlight.

Cockpit, right side, Sabre 6.

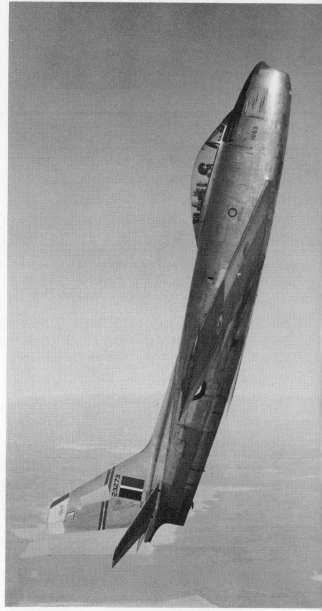

A Sabre of the Central Flying School, RCAF Station Trenton, goes into a loop over the Bay of Quinte. Photo by Cpl Barry Herron. (DND)

Daily Highlights . . .

Canadair Sabre Category "A" Crash List

These aircraft were destroyed (or severely enough damaged in accidents) so as to be struck off strength. Few Cat.A. incidents have been missed, except those in Yugoslavia for which data was not available at time of printing.

Additional short forms: AMI (L'Aeronautica Militare Italiana), CEPE (Central Experimental and Proving Establishment), CFS (Central Flying School), F (fatal), FAC (Fuerza Aérea Colombiana), G (Greece), N (non-fatal), RSA (Republic of South Africa), T (Turkey), Y (Yugoslavia), lndg (landing), t/o (take-off).

	C/N	Tail No.	Unit	Date	Notes
1.	2	19102	G	22.8.55	Crashed on lndg. N
2.	6	19106	410	2.8.51	Dorval. Crashed on lndg with cocked nosewheel. F/O A.E. 'Art' Rayner. N
3.	10	19110	G	20.10.55	Athens. Heavy lndg. N
4.	12	19112	439	8.7.52	Engine quit, ejected over The Wash. F/O Al Seitz. N
5.	13	19113	413	7.4.52	Flame-out on flight from Bagotville, crash landed in woods. F/O Ray Peterson. N
6.	15	19115	410	20.6.51	Engine trouble. Crashed through ILS shack at Dorval. F/O Ron Found. N
7.	16	19116	441	31.10.52	Chatham. Undershot. F/O S.A. Miller. N
8.	17	19117	434	30.11.52	Controls seized, wheels up lndg near Manotick, Ont. F/O Thorleifson. N
9.	18	19118	410	18.7.51	Heavy lndg at Dorval. F/O Knox-Leet. N
10.	19	19119	OTU	26.11.53	Fuel exhaustion, hit trees in crash lndg near Summerside, P.E.I. F/O A.D. Lockhart. N
11.	20	19120	T	1.9.60	Eskisehir. Gear retracted prematurely on t/o. N
12.	21	19121	G	6.9.60	Ankhilos. Rudder came adrift from top hinge, wheels-up lndg. Suspect bird strike. N
13.	22	19122	410	21.2.53	North Luffenham. Landed short. F/O Knox-Leet. N
14.	23	19123	OTU	3.3.53	Chatham. Crashed on t/o. F/O Fox. N
15.	26	19126	T	1.9.55	Eskisehir. Crashed 1 mile short. N
16.	28	19128	G	8.5.59	Athens. Ejected. N
17.	29	19129	T	2.3.60	Merzifon. Wings folded up during pull-out from dive. F
18.	30	19130	T	16.8.57	Black Sea. Mid air with 19138. F
19.	31	19131	OTU	22.7.53	Newcastle, N.B. Fuel exhaustion, ejected. F/O McLeod. N
20.	32	19132	OTU	15.7.53	Mars Hill, Maine. Became lost, ejected. F/O Cushing. N
21.	33	19133	G	1.8.60	Tanagra. Stalled on go-around. N
22.	37	19137	439	16.12.53	Loughborough, England. Fuel exhaustion, unable to eject but climbed from a/c to attempt parachuting. F/O D.G. Tracey. F
23.	38	19138	T	16.8.57	Black Sea. Mid-air with 19130. F
24.	39	19139	T	27.6.56	Eskisehir. Ran off runway. N
25.	42	19142	T	8.8.60	Eskisehir. Fuel exhaustion while lndg. N
26.	43	19143		13.8.51	St. Hubert. Burned on start up. N
27.	45	19145	410	22.8.51	Dorval. Fuel exhaustion on t/o. F/O J. Donald. N
28.	47	19147	T	26.8.63	Murted. Control problem. F
29.	49	19149	413	23.6.54	Zweibrücken. Flame-out on lndg, hit posts. F/O Ron Fentiman. N
30.	52	19152	441	26.11.53	Wells, England. Ejected from spin. F/O H.D. Klein. N
31.	53	19153	T	18.5.62	Murted. Emergency lndg after fire. N
32.	55	19155	439	8.4.54	North Luffenham. Engine trouble, landed short. F/O L.J. Elphick. N
33.	56	19156	410	24.6.52	Stamford, England. Fire in ammunition bay, emergency lndg. F/O L.J. Bentham. N
34	58	19158	441	20.8.53	Off Cromer, England. Fuel exhaustion. Ejected into sea. F/O Les Benson. N
35.	59	19159	410	21.2.54	North Luffenham. Landed short. F/O Knox-Leet. N
36.	60	19160	T	29.9.59	Merzifon. Crashed into mountain while on test flight. F
37.	63	19163	441	17.5.54	North Sea. Failed to return to base. W/C W.F. Parks. F
38.	67	19167	441	6.10.53	North Luffenham. F/O Haran. N
39.	71	19171	G	18.6.58	Tanagra.
40.	73	19173	T	17.4.61	Merzifon. Crashed on t/o. N
41.	76	19176	T	6.5.58	Merzifon. F
42.	77	19177	410	18.4.52	Mid air with 19181 over The Wash. F/O J.A.L. Kerr. F
43.	78	19178	410	25.8.52	North Luffenham. Crash landing while overshooting. F/O Johnson. N
44.	80	19180	T	10.4.56	Eskisehir. Controls froze, ejected at 9000'. N
45.	81	19181	410	18.4.52	Mid air with 19177 over The Wash. F/O A.B. Rayner. F
46.	83	19183	T	22.8.66	Merzifon. Crashed on t/o. N
47.	85	19185	441	5.12.52	North Luffenham. Landed short. F/O K.A. Branch.
48.	87	19187	439	1.7.52	Crashed into sea, fuel exhaustion. F/O R.J. Conti. F
49.	88	19188	G	12.7.57	Tanagra. Crashed on t/o. N
50.	89	19189	441	12.6.52	Engine trouble, wheels-up deadstick lndg in potato field. S/L MacKenzie. N
51.	92	19192	143	25.7.57	Merzifon. Fire after t/o, crashed during emergency lndg. N
52.	93	19193	439	3.6.53	Boston, Lincs. Dove straight in. F/O J.J.R. Bedard. F
53.	94	19194	T	9.6.60	Eskisehir-Black Sea. Mid air with 19236. F
54.	101	19201	OTU	23.2.54	Shediac Bay, N.B. Dove straight in from 35000'. P/O R.N. Fiala. F
55.	103	19203	T	11.11.60	Ankara. Mid air with 19450. N
56.	106	19206	439	3.3.52	Uplands. Crash lndg after flame-out. F/O Cheesman. N
57.	108	19208	413	26.6.52	Chatham. Crashed on lndg. F/O Dan Kaye. N
58.	109	19209	112W	21.3.56	Elefsis. Crashed into sea with 19423. F
59.	113	19213	G	15.1.62	Ankhilos. Fire after t/o, ejected. N
60.	115	19215	T	1.4.59	Eskisehir. Dove straight in 30 mi. east of base. F
61.	117	19217	T	26.11.62	Murted. Flame-out on lndg, crashed beside runway. N
62.	118	19218	G	2.11.59	Tanagra. Mid air with 19293. F
63.	119	19219	OTU	5.1.53	Gardiner Point, N.B. Dove straight in. F/O J.R. "Tiny" Thomson. F
64.	121	19221	413	19.9.52	Thedford Mines, Que. Dove straight in from 41000' en rt. Bagotville-Toronto. F/O R.J. Moncrieff. F
65.	124	19224	G	22.7.57	Tanagra. Crashed on t/o. N
66.	125	19225	416	16.1.54	Grostenquin. Crash landed on go-around. F/O S.J.G. Telford. N
67.	128	19228	G	15.4.61	Ankhilos. Crashed into sea. F
68.	129	19229	413	28.11.52	Bagotville. Fuel exhaustion, ejected. W/C C. Hull. N.
69.	131	19231	T	21.7.59	Blew tire on t/o, destroyed by fire. N
70.	134	19234	137(T)Flt	14.12.54	Ringway. Crashed into high ground near Huddesfield. F/O P.V. Robinson. F
71.	136	19236	T	9.6.60	Black Sea. Mid air with 19194. N
72.	137	19237	413	28.11.52	Fuel exhaustion after became lost, crash landed (had dud seat). F/O R.J. Barnett. N

	C/N	Tail No.	Unit	Date	Notes
73.	140	19240	439	12.3.52	Uplands. Rt. gear collapsed. N
74.	146	19246	413	21.2.52	Dolbeau, Que. Crashed, located 1.5.53. F/O R.V. Snow. F
75.	148	19248	T	3.5.58	Eskisehir. Disintegrated on gunnery range east of base. F
76.	149	19249	T	15.4.63	Merzifon. Crashed just after t/o. N
77.	153	19253	CEPE	6.12.54	Cartierville. Engine quit on t/o, crashed and burned. F/L Deans. N
78.	155	19255	430	12.5.54	Lelling Moselle, Fr. Flame-out in circuit, inadvertent ejection after crash lndg. F/O G.D. MacDonald. F
79.	165	19265	430	24.6.52	North Bay. Flame-out at 5000' crashed near Callendar. F/O C.W.A. Troke. F
80.	166	19266	USAF	20.2.52	Langley, VA. Hit water on final. F
81.	169	19269	G	11.5.55	Athens. Crash landing after fire. N
82.	171	19271	G	1.11.55	Athens. Landed short. N
83.	172	19272		11.1.55	Crashed Aylmer, Ont. N
84.	174	19274	114W	20.12.57	Tanagra. Electrical failure, crash landed. N
85.	176	19276	G	2.2.62	Athens. Collided on t/o with 19430. F
86.	177	19277	434	21.10.52	Crashed Sarsfield, Ont. F/O J.C. Richardson. N
87.	181	19281	OTU	29.9.52	Chatham. Hit drogue target, crashed into sea near Neguac Beach, N.B. F/O D.W. Laubman. F
88.	183	19283	416	9.4.52	Uplands. Ejected from spin. First to eject from jet in Canada. F/O H. Hrischenko. N
89.	189	19289	USAF	11.7.55	Dijon, Fr. Crashed on UK-Turkey ferry flight near Chaumont, Fr. F
90.	190	19290	OTU	25.5.53	Burnsville, N.B. Control problems. Ejected. F/O M.B. "Mike" Sutherland. N
91.	191	19291	OTU	26.8.52	Chatham. Flame-out after t/o, crashed trying to return to base. F/O Collingwood. F
92.	192	19292	421	24.6.52	Chateauguay, N.Y. Fuel exhaustion after became lost, crash lndg in field. F/O Northrop. N
93.	193	19293	G	2.11.55	Tanagra. Mid air with 19218. F
94.	199	19299	USAF	28.9.53	Indian Springs AFB. F
95.	200	19300	OTU	29.7.53	Chatham. Ran off runway on t/o. F/O Day. N
96.	202	19302	OTU	1.6.54	Dove into Gulf of St. Lawrence. F/O R.M. Cairney. F
97.	203	19303	OTU	1.9.53	Chatham. Crashed on t/o F/O Webber. N
98.	204	19304	416	21.5.53	Grostenquin. Crashed on t/o F/O Morgan. N
99.	212	19312	421	4.2.53	Grostenquin. Crashed on go-around. F/O Northrop. N
100.	217	19317	T	17.10.55	Eskisehir. Mid air with 19165, ejected. N
101.	226	19326	OTU	17.3.53	Crashed on Miramichi Bay with 19388. F/O K. Nicholls. F
102.	233	19333	421	24.3.53	Grostenquin. Suspected broken fuel line on landing. Crashed on field. F/O G.J. "Jerry" Tobin. N
103.	237	19337	T	3.5.55	Eskisehir. Destroyed when struck by crashing F-84. N
104.	238	19338	T	15.10.62	Murted. Mid air, ejected. N
105.	242	19342	G	30.8.59	Ankara. Mid air with 19353. F
106.	243	19343	416	21.3.53	Grostenquin. Landed short. N
107.	244	19344	G	20.9.54	Athens. Severe porpoising, ejected. N
108.	249	19349	G	12.5.57	Athens. Overran on landing at Hassani. N
109.	250	19350	421	6.11.52	Sculthorpe, England. Electrical failure, emergency lndg. F/O Buzik. N
110.	253	19353	G	30.8.59	Ankara. Mid air with 19342. F
111.	254	19354	T	15.10.59	Eskisehir. Fuel exhaustion, landed short. N
112.	259	19359	T	24.10.57	Merzifon. Prematurely retracted gear. N
113.	265	19365	421	9.6.53	Grostenquin. Crashed 12 mi. from base, ejected too low. F/O J.G. Cloutier. F
114.	267	19367	OTU	21.5.53	Chatham. Flame-out on t/o, crash landed. F/O L.J. Redman. N
115.	270	19370	416	11.10.52	North Luffenham. Flame-out and wheels up lndg. F/O G.J. Carpenter. N
116.	272	19372	OTU	30.12.52	Chatham. Flame-out and wheels up lndg. F/O Coulter. N
117.	273	19373	T	26.10.54	Eskisehir. Stalled on approach. F
118.	274	19374	G	25.6.57	Tanagra. Compressor stall, crash landed in field. F
119.	275	19375	G	28.4.64	Merzifon. Crashed in mountains with 19446. F
120.	278	19378	G	3.6.55	Elefsis. Flame-out on final, crash lndg. N
121.	280	19380	T	31.7.62	Murted. Crashed on t/o. N
122.	281	19381	G	22.4.60	Tanagra. Crashed on t/o. F
123.	285	19385	T	10.5.56	Adana. Crashed on lndg. N
124.	288	19388	OTU	17.3.53	Crashed on Miramichi Bay with 19326. F/O D.G. Allen. F
125.	290	19390	G	9.4.58	Athens. Hit mountain south of Corinth with 19434. F
126.	291	19391	G	8.3.55	Eskisehir. Flame-out on lndg. N
127.	299	19399	T	23.11.55	Eskisehir. Crashed into mountain with 19417. F
128.	300	19400	OTU	3.5.54	Dove into Miramichi Bay, F/O G.R. "Gar" Brine. F
129.	302	19402	434	22.8.52	Fuel exhaustion. Crash landed Ashton, Ont. F/O R.J. Childerhose. N
130.	303	19403	G	12.5.57	Athens. Overran. N
131.	306	19406	430	17.6.54	Marville. Ran off runway while landing. N
132.	307	19407	G	11.10.60	Pagasitikos Kolpos. Dove straight in. F
133.	308	19408	T	6.5.58	Merzifon. Mid air with 19176. F
134.	310	19410	T	11.2.58	Merzifon. Compressor stall on lndg. N
135.	311	19411	427	3.11.52	Dove straight in St. Mathias, Que. F/O J.C. "Jimmy" Peterson. F
136.	316	19416	G	13.3.57	Athens. Flamed-out and landed short. N
137.	317	19417	T	23.11.55	Eskisehir. Crashed into mountain with 19399. F
138.	318	19418	G	3.10.57	Tanagra. Engine trouble, crashed on lndg. F
139.	320	19420	USAF	11.7.55	Dijon, Fr. Crashed on UK-Turkey ferry flight with 19289. F
140.	321	19421	T	21.10.60	Merzifon. Landed wheels up. N
141.	322	19422	427	18.6.53	Dove in on fire near Pirmasens, W.G. F/O G.D. "Bud" Foxton. F
142.	323	19423	112W	21.3.56	Elefsis. Crashed into sea with 19209. F
143.	326	19426	OTU	15.9.53	Crashed 28 mi. from base, ejected too low. F/O S.I. Banks. F
144.	327	19427	141	12.2.57	Eskisehir. Crashed into mountain. F
145.	329	19429	G	28.10.58	Tanagra. F
146.	330	19430	G	2.2.62	Athens. Collided on t/o with 19276. F
147.	334	19434	G	9.4.58	Athens. Hit mountain south of Corinth with 19390. F
148.	336	19436	OTU	25.4.53	Chatham. Crashed on landing. F/O Venus. N
149.	338	19438	G	18.4.60	Tanagra. Burned on ground after drop tanks jettisoned and ignited. N
150.	340	19440	G	18.8.60	Nea Ankhilos. Inadvertently riddled with .50 cal. on ground from nearby F.86. N
151.	342	19442	OTU	1.12.53	Failed to return to base. P/O J.A. Menzies. F
152.	346	19446	T	29.4.64	Merzifon. Crashed in mountains with 19375. F
153.	347	19447	G	26.1.55	Tanagra. Crashed on t/o. N
154.	356	19456	CEPE	19.9.53	Toronto. Crashed at CNE airshow. S/L W.R. Greene. F
155.	359	19459	Y	8.8.56	Belgrade. Wheels up lndg by USAF instructor. N
156.	360	19460	AMI	31.8.57	Fire on start-up. N
157.	362	19462 XB531	414	22.1.53	Bagotville. Forced landing. F/O Lyon. N

	C/N	Tail No.	Unit	Date	Notes
158.	363	19463 (XB532)	414	5.3.53	Fuel exhaustion. Ejected. F/O Heiliger. N
159.	365	XB534	LRFU	19.12.52	Prestwick. Dove straight in. F
160.	370	19470	AMI	25.10.56	Crashed on lndg. N
161.	374	19474	AMI	15.6.59	Frosinine. F
162.	376	19476	AMI	21.2.58	Gatlinara. Mid air with 19877. Ejected. N
163.	379	XD548	93	3.8.55	Jevers. Crashed on gunnery range at Meppen. F
164.	381	19481	AMI	6.11.58	Dove into sea off Netuno. F
165.	384	19484	AMI	11.10.58	Exploded near Anzio. F
166.	399	19499	AMI	8.1.58	Landing mishap. N
167.	406	19506	AMI	14.7.56	Fire warning. Ejected near Decima. N
168.	407	XB600	67	22.3.54	Wildenrath. Electrical failure, wheels-up lndg. N
169.	410	XB603	SCF	15.6.53	Wildenrath. Hard lndg when lost power. N
170.	412	19512	AMI	24.7.57	Brindisi. Crashed after flame-out. F
171.	413	XB610	147	5.4.53	Kinloss. Instrument failure. Hit high ground soon after t/o. S/L Cole. F
172.	415	XB615	234	3.5.55	Flame-out, forced lndg 10 mi. from base. N
173.	426	XB623	26	26.4.55	Oldenburg. Hit snowbank on t/o. N
174.	430	XB627	67	7.9.54	Wildenrath. Got lost and ran out of fuel. Crash lndg near Leige, Belgium. N
175.	436	XB633	3	26.6.55	Geilenkirchen. Crashed in wake turbulence on t/o. N
176.	437	XB634	67	5.4.55	Wilendrath. Mid air with Anson TX238 on lndg, 3 killed. F
177.	441	XB638	20	5.8.54	Oldenburg. Hit trees short of runway. N
178.	446	XB643	3	24.2.54	Crashed with XB667 in bad weather, Henri-Chapelle, Belgium. F
179.	447	19547	AMI	1.12.56	Crashed near Spaloto, Jugoslavia, killing one. N
180.	755	XB648	130	3.6.54	Burst tire on t/o. N
181.	453	XB667	3	24.2.54	Crashed with XB643 in bad weather, Henri-Chapelle, Belgium. F
182.	455	19555	AMI	26.6.57	Mid air with USN Cougar over Tyrrhenian Sea. F
183.	463	XB677	92	24.6.55	Linton-on-Ouse. Crashed on t/o. N
184.	464	XB678	AMI	27.10.54	Bafini, W.G. Mid air with XB729. N
185.	467	XB681	3	10.2.54	Geilenkirchen. Crashed on lndg. N
186.	469	XB683	67	17.9.53	Ejected from spin near Liege. N
187.	476	XB690	67	6.11.53	Mid air near München Gladbach with XB730. N
188.	481	19581	AMI	16.4.58	Brindisi. Crashed on gunnery range. F
189.	485	XB699	3	16.5.55	Crashed near Lontzen, Netherlands. Ejected too low. F
190.	497	XB711	OCU	23.10.54	Presumed crashed at sea. F
191.	503	XB729	71	26.10.54	Mid air with XB628 near Krefeld, W.G. Pilot thrown out. N
192.	504	XB730	67	6.11.53	Mid air near München Gladbach with XB690. F
193.	509	19609	AMI	2.9.55	Brindisi. Flame-out and crashed on approach. F
194.	516	19616	AMI	11.3.57	Pratica-di-Mare. Flame-out and crashed on landing. N
195.	517	19617		.55	Crashed on t/o at Turin. F
196.	519	19619 XB745	422	28.12.53	Crashed near Beauvechain after engine failure. Ejected. N
197.	527	19627	AMI	24.3.60	Mid air with 19630. Ejected. N
198.	530	19630		24.3.60	Mid air with 19627. N
199.	534	XB760	71	4.2.55	Dove straight in near Julich, W.G. F
200.	537	19637 XB763	422	2.3.54	Fuel exhaustion. Ejected over Belgium. F/O F.K. Axtell. N
201.	543	19643	414	15.6.53	Bagotville. Flame-out on lndg, hit tree. F/O Jim Giles. N
202.	560	19660	414	9.6.53	Bagotville. Dove straight in. F/O G.C. Hall. F
203.	562	XB808	20	16.8.55	Meppen. Crashed on gunnery range. F
204.	570	19670	414	12.6.53	Bagotville. Engine trouble, landed short. F/O Neill. N
205.	573	XB819	234	29.6.54	Engine failure, forced landing near Julich, W.G. N
206.	576	XB822	112	1.10.55	Jever. Engine failure and landed short. N
207.	577	19677	Y	26.11.57	Belgrade. F
208.	579	19679	422	2.3.54	Fuel exhaustion. Ejected over Belgium. F/O G. Brennand. N
209.	589	19689	422	27.5.53	Ejected near Aylmer, Que., after control loss. Suspected assymetric slats. F/O Carruthers. N
210.	593	XB839	26	10.2.55	Oldenburg. Ejection at 600', possibly inadvertent. F
211.	595	19695	AMI	25.3.60	Pratica-di-Mare. Crashed on final while instructing pilot in 19749. F
212.	598	XB860	234	29.10.54	Broke up soon after t/o, crashed near Sittard, Netherlands. N
213.	601	XB863	147	5.6.53	Lost in cloud. Crashed St -Felix de Valois, Qué. F
214.	603	XB865	26	23.7.54	May have lost canopy in flight, crashed near Hede, W.G. Ejected too low. F
215.	604	XB866	26	24.2.54	U/s compass, crashed into sea in cloud. F
216.	608	XD707	66	22.7.54	Flew into hill top in Pinnines, with XB730. F
217.	612	XD711	66	16.6.54	Mid air with XD716. Ejected. N
218.	613	XD712	66	16.6.55	Broke up over North Sea during practice dog fight. F
219.	617	XD716	66	16.6.54	Mid air with XD711. Ejected near Hornsea, Links. N
220.	623	19722	AMI	23.9.59	Brindisi. Crashed after own bullets ricocheted into air intake. N
221.	630	XD729	66	25.1.56	Linton-on-Ouse. Crashed during landing on wet runway. N
222.	631	XD730	66	22.7.54	Flew into hill top in Pinnines with XD707. F
223.	643	XB880	26	15.7.55	Bruggen. Stalled in turn on lndg. F
224.	645	XB882	147	18.7.53	Inadvertent ejection near Dundeen, Scotland. N
225.	647	XB884	112	16.6.54	Bruggen. Electrical failure. Ejected. N
226.	649	19749	AMI	25.3.60	Pratica-di-Mare. Crashed on final. F
227.	651	XD733		21.9.54	Struck high ground at night, Easingwold, Yorks. F
228.	652	19752	AMI	26.8.58	Cameri. Hit wires on final. N
229.	653	19753	AMI	28.3.59	Cameri. Crashed on t/o. F
230.	657	XD755	66	16.3.55	Stalled on approach to Driffield. F
231.	660	XD758	66	22.7.54	Fire warning. Ejected near Helmsley, Yorks. N
232.	670	XD768	66	10.8.54	Crash landing at Full Sutton after engine failure. N
233.	673	XD771	92	29.9.54	Belly landed in field after engine failue. N
234.	677	XB899	20	22.9.54	Belly landed Schleswigland, W.G. N
235.	689	XB912	112	3.3.54	Bruggen. Crashed into trees on go-around. N
236.	693	XD772	66	29.11.54	Ejected at 35000' when engine failed, Kelstern, Lincs. N
237.	694	XD773	92	13.5.54	Flame-out on final. F/L Jed Gray. N
238.	696	XD775	147	18.8.53	St. Hubert. Crashed after stabilizer malfunctioned. Ejected. N
239.	697	XD776	66	27.8.54	Fire in ammunition bay. Ejected SW North Luffenham. F/L Jed Gray. N

	C/N	Tail No.	Unit	Date	Notes
240.	701	XD780	92	14.5.55	Stalled on landing and crashed at Linton. N
241.	714	XB927	130	29.10.54	Bruggen. Undershot after engine failure. N
242.	719	XB932	130	12.7.55	Bruggen. Undershot. N
243.	723	XB936	67	4.3.54	Wildenrath. Stalled on t/o. Hit approach light posts. N
244.	724	XB937	4	8.10.54	Dove straight into sea near Sylt during tail chase. F
245.	730	19830	AMI	22.10.58	Mid air with BEA Viscount (31 killed) near Anzio. N
246.	737	XB950	112	5.7.55	Engine fire and dove straight in, Heerlen, Netherlands. F
247.	741	19841	AMI	31.7.58	Pratica-di-Mare. Crashed on t/o, jet wash. N
248.	754	XB647	4	8.7.54	Jever. Stalled on lndg. F
249.	763	19863	USAF	19.1.57	Etain AFB. Broke up near Thumerville, Fr., while on UK-Italy ferry. F
250.	777	19877	AMI	21.2.58	Gatlinara. Mid air with 19476 (XB545). F
251.	779	XB988	130	19.10.54	Dove straight in on night flight near Kassel, W.G. F
252.	793	23003	422	29.11.54	Baden. Engine failed on approach. Ejected too low. F/O M.L. MacEachern. F
253.	795	23005	444	29.9.54	Baden. Crashed on lndg. F/O L.J. Redman. N
254.	799	23009	444	20.10.54	Baden. Dove in on fire 30 mi. west of base. F/O R.J. Christoffersen. F
255.	804	23014	OTU	1.10.56	Chatham. Stalled during final. F/L D.D. Ashleigh. N
256.	806	23016	430	7.4.55	Grostenquin. Fuel exhaustion. Ejected. F/O R.L. MacDonald. N
257.	811	23021	US Army	1.2.80	White Sands Missile Range - Drone, crashed when ground station malfunctioned.
258.	814	23024	Avro	22.3.55	Burned in hangar fire at Malton, Ont.
259.	818	23028	US Army	12.10.78	White Sands. Drone, destroyed by Patriot missile.
260.	821	23031	414	5.11.54	Baden. Crashed on t/o, crossed ailerons. F/O "Bruno" Brunette. N
261.	825	23035	430	3.3.55	Grostenquin. Mid air at 44000' with 23232, Saar Guemines, WG. F
262.	827	23037	129AFF	10.4.63	Dorval. F/O R.M. Jones. N
263.	829	23039	421	16.3.56	Baden. Swung on emergency landing, hit 23140 and 23048. N
264.	830	23040	430	16.7.54	Grostenquin. Crashed on t/o. N
265.	831	23041	OTU	2.9.58	Chatham. Engine failed. Ejected at 800'. F/O R.K. Flavelle. N
266.	833	23043 (BB-238)	GAF	26.6.61	Oldenburg. Crashed on t/o. N
267.	836	23046	OTU	6.11.58	Chatham. Fire in radios. Ejected 50 mi. south of Chatham. F/L J.F. Fitzgerald. N
268.	841	23051 (BB713)	WS10	19.5.58	Oldenburg. Flame-out on lndg, wheels up. N
269.	842	23052	OTU	12.6.61	Chatham. Ejected. F/O Johnson. N
270.	853	23053	434	30.7.54	Zweibrücken. Engine trouble. Ejected. F/O W.M. Day. F
271.	846	23056 (BB-240)	WS10	13.7.59	Crashed Oldenburg. Engine failure. F
272.	855	23065	434	1.8.54	Zweibrücken. Mid air with 23085. 3 killed on ground. F/O D.W. McCombs. F
273.	859	23069	434	29.9.54	Zweibrücken. Crashed into hill turning final. F/O P. Baron. F
274.	863	23073	G.H.	9.8.59	Mid air at Calgary with Tripacer in circuit. F/L G.J. Kerr. F
275.	866	23076	416	29.12.55	Crashed on landing. F/O C Cherewick. N
276.	867	23077	416	8.6.54	Grostenquin. Fuel exhaustion. Ejected near Tenteling, Fr. F/L D.O. Evjen. N
277.	868	23078	444	15.3.54	Baden. Suspected inadvertent ejection at 800' while making forced lndg after engine failure. W/C H.F. Darragh. F
278.	872	23082	416	13.1.55	Grostenquin. Fuel exhaustion. Ejected. Petit Tenquin, Fr. F/L G.W. Patterson. N
279.	873	23083	STU	23.10.67	Chatham. Last RCAF Sabre crash. G/C W.R. Cole. F
280.	875	23085	434	1.8.54	Zweibrücken. Mid air with 23065. F/O Pete Cunningham. F
281.	876	23086	416	9.9.55	Grostenquin. Fuel exhaustion when lost. Ejected. F/L E.C. Tuckey. N
282.	878	23088	OTU	25.10.60	Chatham. Ejected. N
283.	889	23099	416	21.7.55	Grostenquin. Mid air with 23154. F/O E.A.J. Noel. F
284.	897	23107	EST61	11.5.55	Ahlhorn. Crashed during runway barrier trials. BB243
285.	898	23108	413	2.9.55	Zweibrücken. Spun in 35 mi. from base. F/O E.S. Oliver. F
286.	899	23109	441	21.7.55	Marville. Stalled on landing. Thierville, Fr. F/L E.L. Fine. N
287.	900	23110	OTU	20.7.61	Chatham. Collided on runway with 23162. N
288.	901	23111 (BB123)	WS10	26.9.58	Oldenburg. Hit trees on gunnery range. Ejected 1200'. N
289.	903	23113	416	18.8.54	Grostenquin. Dove in near Baumholder, W.G., after dog-fighting. F/O F.G. Robins. F
290.	907	23117	OTU	15.10.54	St. Hubert. Crashed on t/o. F/O J. Gaudry. N
291.	908	23118	444	17.5.55	Baden. Crashed Karlsruhf, W.G., while force lndg. F/O R.A. Grant. F
292.	909	23119	416	11.8.54	Grostenquin. Dove in near Greutzweld Moselle. Ejected too low. F/O G.L. Beaulac. F
293.	910	23120	444	11.6.55	Baden. Rolled in turning final. Suspected right aileron hinge failure. F/O R.W. Kostiuk. F
294.	911	23121	430	19.7.55	Grostenquin. Flame-out on final. F/O Adams. N
295.	918	23128	US Army	29.8.80	White Sands. Drone, shot down by DIVADS AA gun.
296.	920	23130	416	21.7.55	Grostenquin. Crashed Faulquemont. F/L G.L. Howarth. N
297.	923	23133	US Army	18.5.78	White Sands. Drone, crashed due to control malfunction.
298.	924	23134	416	25.6.54	Zweibrücken. Stalled at 50' and crashed onto runway. F/O J.H. Volfing. N
299.	925	23135	US Army	22.5.79	White Sands. Drone, crashed on landing.
300.	936	23146	US Army	26.10.82	White Sands. Drone, destroyed by Patriot missile.
301.	938	23148	430	25.7.54	Grostenquin. Crashed on t/o. F/O Belliveau. N
302.	940	23150	430	29.8.56	Grostenquin. Ejected from flat spin, Saarbrücken. F/O W.V. Closs. N
303.	941	23151	US Army	23.8.82	White Sands. Drone, crashed on recovery.
304.	944	23154	416	21.7.55	Grostenquin. Mid air with 23099. F/O B.G. Donald. F
305.	945	23155	413	19.2.55	Zweibrücken. Mid-air with 23180 near Bolanden, W.G. F/O D.A. "Rick" Mace. F
306.	946	23156	430	18.5.56	Grostenquin. Control problem. Dove straight in from 38000', ejected. F/O C.J. Simpson. N
307.	947	23157	416	12.9.54	Grostenquin. Stalled on t/o from Rabat. F/O J.H. Volfing. F
308.	950	23160	US Army	21.8.82	White Sands. Destroyed by Stinger missile.
309.	951	23161	427	4.10.54	Zweibrücken. Crashed on lndg at Rabat. F/O "Barney" Hunter. N
310.	952	23162	OTU	24.8.62	Chatham. Ejected. F/O Paquette. N
311.	953	23163	444	30.12.54	Baden. Engine failure. Ejected. F/L A.J. Bauer. N
312.	956	23166	421	4.2.55	Grostenquin. Fuel exhaustion. Ejected near Saarburg. F/O Dea. N
313.	958	23168	416	27.1.56	Grostenquin. Ejected at 5000' when landing gear malfunctioned. F/O L.B. Marion. N
314.	961	23171	PWS	12.9.58	Macdonald. Crashed while landing. S/L J.G.G. Guerin. F
315.	962	23172	416	13.12.55	Grostenquin. Fuel exhaustion. Ejected. F/O J.R. Allingham. N
316.	970	23180	413	19.2.55	Zweibrücken. Mid air with 23155 near Bolanden, W.G. F/O Algimantos Navikenas. F
317.	980	23190	US Army	8.1.80	White Sands. Drone, destroyed by Sidewinder missile.
318.	981	23191 (BB129)	WS10	7.11.58	Crashed Augustfehn. Suspected hypoxia. F
319.	983	23193	422	1.2.55	Baden. Ejected off Valencia en rt. Rabat-Baden. F/O Ray Carruthers. N

	C/N	Tail No.	Unit	Date	Notes
320.	986	23196 (BB133)		9.8.61	Mid air with JA-121. F
321.	987	23197	427	21.12.54	Zweibrücken. Lost oil pressure. Ejected. Lembach, W.G. F/O Brian Peters. N
322.	991	23201	430	31.10.55	Grostenquin. Ejected after flame out. F/O Jack Hubbard. N
323.	1000	23210	OTU	22.5.56	Chatham. Ejected after flame out, Bathurst, N.B. F/O R.A. Crouch. N
324.	1001	23211	STU	17.6.65	Chatham. F/L J.M. Craig. F
325.	1003	23213	STU	9.10.62	Chatham. Ejected. F/L J.B. England. N
326.	1004	23214	OTU	18.2.57	Chatham. Ejected at 10000' from spin, Upper Blackville, N.B. F/L Steacy. N
327.	1005	23215	US Army	27.4.79	White Sands. Drone, destroyed by Patriot missile.
328.	1006	23216	OFU	21.2.55	St. Hubert. Destroyed when jumped sandbag chock at Keflavik. Rammed 23318 and 23356. N
329.	1007	23217	OTU	6.8.57	Chatham. Engine compressor casing failure caused fire and aborted t/o. S/L L.P. Frizzle. N
330.	1008	23218	OTU	20.10.54	Chatham. Engine failure. Ejected near St. Quentin, N.B. Parachute failed to deploy. F/O A.E. Roberts. F
331.	1019	23229	OTU	14.4.60	Chatham. F/O B.C. Todd. F
332.	1022	23232	430	3.3.55	Grostenquin. Mid air with 23035, Saar Guemines, W.G. F
333.	1024	23234	444	12.4.55	Baden. Inadvertently closed throttle on lndg. S/L J.B. Lawrence. N
334.	1026	23236	OTU	11.3.55	Chatham. Failed to return to base. Wreck found by hunters 23.11.56 McGivney Junction, N.B. P/O J.A. Muirhead. F
335.	1027	23237	416	12.4.56	Grostenquin. Ejected after control failure. F/O B.W. Cherewick. F
336.	1029	23239	STU	13.4.64	Chatham. Low-flying, hit trees. F/L C.W. Warrian. N
337.	1030	23240	OTU	8.2.55	Chatham. Mid air near Beaverbrooke Stn., N.B. with 23265 while air fighting. P/O P.A. Standen. F
338.	1032	23242	OTU	13.8.57	Chatham. Crashed while lndg. F/O N.S. Granley. N
339.	1033	23243	OTU	28.2.57	Chatham. Pilot thrown out in severe buffeting, Rexton, N.B. F/O Pickett. N
340.	1034	23244	OTU	15.7.55	Chatham. Lost power on final, hit pole. P/O K.R. Williams. N
341.	1037	23247	OTU	9.3.55	Chatham. Flame-out at 15000' on gunnery exercise. Ejected. F/O J.O.H. "Joe" Gagnon. N
342.	1039	23249	OTU	18.4.55	Chatham. Crashed off a loop during aerobatic practice. F/O W.F. "Ted" Griffin. F
343.	1042	23252	US Army	8.11.79	White Sands. Destroyed by Patriot missile.
344.	1043	23253	OTU	19.10.55	Chatham. Flame-out and ejected, Blackville, N.B. F/L H.M. Lepard. N
345.	1046	23256	OTU	29.10.54	Chatham. Broke up in flight when overstressed. F/O E. Levine. F
346.	1050	23260	OTU	14.9.54	Chatham. Wing hit water in turn, Point Escuming, N.B. F/O J.T. Mitchell. F
347.	1051	23261	OTU	15.5.56	Chatham. Flame-out, landed on dirt road but cartwheeled. F/L D.H. "Steve" Atherton. F
348.	1052	23262	OTU	7.7.55	Chatham. Compressor blades failed on t/o. F/O G.P. McCully. N
349.	1053	23263	OTU	9.8.57	Chatham. In-flight fire. Stalled turning final. F/O R.N. Lakins. N
350.	1054	23264	OTU	15.1.57	Chatham. Ejected at 10000' from spin near Burton, P.E.I. Parachute failed to deploy. F/O W.H. Johnston. F
351.	1055	23265	OTU	8.2.55	Chatham. Mid air with 23240. F/O R.F. Slee. F
352.	1058	23268	US Army	16.8.78	White Sands. Drone, damaged by Roland missile and DBR on recovery.
353.	1061	23271	OTU	29.3.56	Chatham. Collided in dogfight with 23365. Ejected. F/O L.W. Swanston. N
354.	1063	23273	STU	5.5.64	Chatham. F/O B.A. Mannion. F
355	1065	23275	Spectrum Air	24.9.72	Crashed Sacramento, killing 22 on ground. R.L. Bingham.
356.	1066	23276	STU	19.3.63	Chatham. 2nd Lt. A. Novelstrud, Nor. A.F. F
357.	1068	23278	OTU	31.5.55	Chatham. Fire warning and ejected. F/O M.A. MacKinnon. N
358.	1069	23279	OTU	5.1.61	Chatham. Engine packed in. Ejected. F/O W.C. "Bill" Stewart. N
359.	1071	23281	PWS	11.6.55	Stalled turning final at Calgary. F/O R.H. Aitken. N
360.	1072	23282	OTU	9.11.54	Chatham. Engine failure and stalled turning final for deadstick lndg. F/O A.R. Hart. F
361.	1076	23286	OTU	1.8.56	Chatham. Flame-out. Crashed into Bay of Chaleur. 2nd Lt. Inalakdere, Turkey. F
362.	1080	23290	STU	4.2.65	Chatham. Did loop over survival camp and crashed. Newcastle, N.B. F/L J.W. Faulds. F
363.	1082	23292	OTU	1.8.56	Chatham. Hit tree on Ex. Morningstar while flying low near Gagetown, N.B. F/L I. Gordon-Johnson, RAF. F
364.	1084	23294	OTU	13.5.55	Chatham. Mid air with 23291. F/L D.O. Evjen. F
365.	1089	23299	430	26.10.55	Grostenquin. Stalled turning final. F/O R.O. "Bob" Linklater. F
366.	1092	23302	441	23.6.55	Marville. Stalled turning final. F/O J.H. Johnson. N
367.	1094	23304	STU	27.7.67	Chatham. F/L F.M. Constantine. F
368.	1096	23306	US Army	22.7.78	White Sands. Destroyed by Roland missile.
369.	1097	23307	CEPE	28.10.54	Namao. Stalled soon after t/o and dove in. F/L C.L. Hull. F
370.	1101	23311	OTU	13.4.59	Ejected low level near Chatham. F/O J.G. Westphal. N
371.	1107	23317	430	17.3.55	Grostenquin. Engine failed on approach. F/O R.A. Robertson. F
372.	1108	23318	OFU	21.2.55	Rammed at Keflavik by 23216. N
373.	1110	23320	US Army	29.8.80	White Sands. Destroyed by DIVADS AA gun. First drone shipped out by Target Air. Was CF-CLM, N74170.
374.	1117	23327 (BB235)	WS10	8.6.60	Oldenburg. Belly landing. N
375.	1118	23328	410	25.6.55	Crashed on Ex. Carte Blanche while chasing Vampire. F/O A.G. McCallum. F
376.	1123	23333	410	13.8.56	Mid air with 23543, Bitburg, W.G. F/O R.H. Roden. F
377.	1126	23336	439	11.5.55	Fuel exhaustion. Ejected over Luxemburg. F/O F.B. Davis. N
378.	1129	23339	US Army	25.7.81	White Sands. Drone, destroyed by ground control after malfunction.
379.	1130	23340	401	16.2.57	Ejected too low from spin. F/L J.V. Karr. F
380.	1131	23341	OTU	13.8.57	In-flight fire. Ejected too low. F/O H.G. Sereda. F
381.	1136	23346	OTU	6.7.60	Mid air with 23356. Ejected. F/O R.R. Webber. N
382.	1140	23350	CFS	23.5.60	Saskatoon. Engine failure on approach. F/L G. Brennand. N
383.	1146	23356	OTU	6.7.60	Mid air with 23346. F/O G.S. Hanson. F
384.	1147	23357	400	14.12.57	Downsview. Flame-out and crashed on lndg. F/O McKay. N
385.	1149	23359	GH	12.3.59	Chatham. Hit trees recovering from 5500' loop. F/L L.M. "Sam" Eisler. F
386.	1150	23360	439	7.6.55	Marville. Crashed on lndg. F/O S.R. Easson. N
387.	1155	23365	OTU	29.3.56	Collided in dogfight with 23271. Ejected. F/O R.E. Wrather. N
388.	1158	23368	OTU	6.5.57	Chatham. Inadvertent flame-out on approach. F/O J.W.R. Arsenault. N
389.	1162	23372	OFU	7.6.55	St. Hubert. Flame-out and made belly lndg short of runway. F/O "Red" Hettrick. N
390.	1163	23373	444	26.8.61	Baden. Overran. F/O J.E.B. Currie. N
391.	1164	23374	421	18.4.61	Fuel exhaustion. Ejected near Homburg, W.G. F/O Bill Slaughter. N
392.	1166	23376	434	13.4.56	Zweibrücken. Crashed while trying to direct rescue party to crash of 23505. F/O J.D. Ross. F
393.	1170	23380	421	26.6.59	Crashed 50 mi south of Prestwick. F/O R.G. Starling. F
394.	1174	23384	413	9.1.57	Generator failure, ejected at .85M/28000' near Beersdorf, W.G. F/O W.J. Tunstad. N
395.	1177	23387	422	31.8.57	Fuel exhaustion while towing drogue at Sardinia. Crash landed 2.5 mi from Deci. F/O R.W. Jupp. N
396.	1180	23390	444	5.11.56	Dove straight in from 41000'. F/O D.E. Elliott. F
397.	1183	23393	427	11.2.56	Engine seizure, ejected near Ramstein, W.G. F/O S.L. Corning. N
398.	1186	23396	434	31.5.57	Zweibrücken. Doing visual check of landing gear on 23463 when stalled and crashed. W/C H.C. Stewart. F
399.	1187	23397	422	12.6.57	Mid air at 30000' with 23514, near Stuttgart. F/O J.L. Robinson. F
400.	1190	23400	OFU	19.2.56	Flame-out and crash landed on frozen lake 70 mi NW Goose Bay. F/L R.D. Himmelman. N
401.	1193	23403	413	23.1.56	Zweibrücken. Flame-out. F/O R.G. Horn. F

	C/N	Tail No.	Unit	Date	Notes
402.	1196	23406	422	20.5.60	Mid air with 23701. Ejected. S/L R.G. Murray. N
403.	1197	23407	444	4.7.62	Failed to return to base. F/O R. Baltins.
404.	1199	23409	444	23.2.61	Mid air with 23488. W/C R.V. Smith. F
405.	1202	23412	427	15.1.57	Zweibrücken. Crashed short on lndg. F/O A. Leiter. N
406.	1203	23413	444	9.1.57	Mid air with 23677 and lost 4' of port wing. Ejected. F/O M.R. Henderson. N
407.	1209	23419	439	16.5.63	Marville. F/O M.L. McKibbin.
408.	1210	23420	434	14.3.61	Fuel exhaustion. Ejected. F/O E.W. Moss. N
409.	1214	23424 (N186X)		19.6.68	Crashed Cantil, California. Ejected.
410.	1221	23431	422	22.12.57	Baden. Hydraulic failure. Crashed on t/o. F/O P.A. Hayes. N
411.	1224	23434	422	11.4.58	Ejected from 400'. F/O D.P. Davidson. N
412.	1226	23436	441	24.3.58	Engine trouble. Ejected near Rhein Main. N
413.	1227	23437	430	22.1.57	Seized controls. Ejected at 20000'. F/L Wilson. N
414.	1229	23439	422	2.3.56	Crashed near Strassbourg with 3 other a/c (Skylancers). F/O F.K. Axtell. F
415.	1233	23443	434	8.11.57	Crashed soon after t/o. F/O R.G.H. Rolston. F
416.	1234	23444	434	31.1.57	Mid air with 23478 near Hornback, W.G. Ejected. F/O J.R. Allingham. N
417.	1235	23445	444	2.3.56	Crashed near Strassbourg with 3 other a/c (Skylancers). F/O J.H. Adams. F
418.	1239	23449	421	12.5.59	Both wings torn off in low level flight. F/O Dave Smith. F
419.	1242	23452	444	29.8.58	Baden. Stalled turning final. F/O R.C. Rosart. F
420.	1243	23453	422	14.11.61	Baden. Flame-out. Crash landed at base. F/O L.F. Best. N
421	1244	23454	US Army	17.5.78	White Sands. Drone, crashed during recovery.
422.	1246	23456	444	19.11.61	Nose gear collapsed on t/o. F/O C.H. Elgie. N
423.	1251	23461	444	18.11.57	Baden. Engine failure. Ejected, Sardinia. F/O R.E. Clarkson. N
424.	1257	23467	444	9.11.55	In-flight fire. Ejected near Istres. F/O T.L. White. N
425.	1264	23474	427	24.5.56	Flame-out near Achern, W.G. Ejected too low. F/O T.B. Griffith. F
426.	1268	23478	434	31.1.57	Zweibrücken. Mid-air with 23444. Ejected. F/L W.C. Frye. N
427.	1273	23483	414	2.3.56	Crashed near Strassbourg with 3 other a/c (Skylancers). F/O J.D. McLarty. F
428.	1274	23484	3W	1.4.57	Zweibrücken. Crashed practicing dumbell over base. F/O A.R. Cushing. F
429.	1278	23488	444	23.2.61	Zweibrücken. Mid-air with 23409. F/O E.D. Payne. N
430.	1281	23491	441	17.11.58	Fuel exhaustion. Ejected near Frankfurt on Ex. Soft Spot. N
431.	1283	23493	422	2.9.57	Flame-out and crashed attempting forced lndg. F/O Coleman. F
432.	1284	23494	444	7.6.56	Engine failure. Ejected near Phalsbourg, Fr. F/L K.A. McLeod. N
433.	1286	23496	439	28.8.56	Marville. Flame-out on overshoot. Ejected at 1000'. F/O M.T. Tillotson. F
434.	1287	23497	441	9.11.60	Marville. Crashed on t/o. F/O R.A. Duffie. F
435.	1295	23505	434	13.4.56	Zweibrücken. Engine trouble. Crashed near base. F/L J.C. Richardson. N
436.	1303	23513	421	3.7.63	Ejected. F/O Eric Stewart. N
437.	1304	23514	421	12.6.57	Mid-air at 30000' with 23397 near Stuttgart. F/O Van Oene. N
438.	1305	23515	421	8.4.60	Mid-air at 42000' with 23619. Ejected. F/O W.L. Riley. N
439.	1306	23516	421	14.3.57	Dove in from 25000' near Weisbaden. Ejected. F/O W.B. Wilson. F
440.	1309	23519	441	17.11.58	Fuel exhaustion. Ejected near Frankfurt on Ex. Soft Spot. N
441.	1314	23524	414	2.3.56	Crashed near Strassbourg with 3 other a/c (Skylancers). F/O E. Welters. F
442.	1319	23529	434	20.2.58	Flame-out. Landed short at Grostenquin. F/O B.M. Ferris. N
443.	1320	23530	441	2.5.57	Flame-out at 21000' and crashed attempting deadstick lndg at base. Ejected at 400'. P/O H.A. Davidson. F
444.	1321	23531	434	3.1.57	Lost hydraulics. Ejected at 1100'. F/O B.C. Dixon. N
445.	1323	23533	422	10.12.56	Flew into hill. F/L F. Konrad. F
446.	1325	23535	421	10.12.56	Flame-out. Ejected, crashed into building in Saarbrücken. F/O Geo. B. Shorey. N
447.	1327	23537	430	30.3.62	Overran and wrecked in swamp. F/O T.F. Hallett. N
448.	1331	23541	421	6.10.61	Grostenquin. F/O R.C. MacKay. F
449.	1333	23543	427	13.8.56	Mid-air with 23333, Bitburg, W.G. F/O Z.B. Tothpal. F
450.	1336	23546	434	1.8.60	Mid-air with Norwegian A.F. a/c, Rygge, Norway. F/O McNicol. N
451.	1345	23555	441	20.11.58	Crashed at Deci. F/O D.H. Barnes. F
452.	1346	23556	441	10.2.58	Fire warning. Ejected at 40000' near Angele, Fr. F/O K.R. Morash. N
453.	1351	23561	439	27.2.58	Marville. Controls froze. Ejected 3 mi N. of base. F/O J.L. Olson. N
454.	1357	23567	427	16.10.56	Ejected from spin at 15000' near Hahn, W.G. F/O J.E. Noga. N
455.	1358	23568	439	17.7.59	Marville. Crashed 2 mi from base. S/L C.J. "Hap" Day. F
456.	1361	23571	427	17.7.58	Crashed near Bruchsal, W.G. F/O J.B. Talbott. F
457.	1371	23581	439	4.2.57	Engine explosion. Ejected. F/O F.P. Luettger. N
458.	1374	23584	439	1.4.57	Marville. Stalled on approach. F/O Tidball. N
459.	1380	23590	441	12.12.59	Marville. Crashed in fog at base. F/O T. Koch. N
460.	1383	23593	441	10.8.63	Controls seized at 30000'. Ejected 10000'. F/O J.A. Davidson. N
461.	1391	23601	444	21.12.59	Baden. Exploded during high speed pass over base. F/O R.J. Chalmers. F
462.	1409	23619	439	8.4.60	Mid-air with 23515 near Zweibrücken. Ejected. F/O R.W. Hallworth. N
463.	1413	23623	421	15.11.57	Grostenquin. Hit jet wash on final. F/L H.T. Hoar. N
464.	1428	23638	421	2.12.58	Grostenquin. Flame-out on t/o. Ejected too low. F/O M.H.P. "Mike" Fitt. F
465.	1436	23646	434	10.3.60	Compressor casing contracted in squall. Ejected and parachuted into Rhone R. F/L Rodger Ritchie. N
466.	1444	23654	441	20.8.56	Dove straight in near Rheims. F/O D.E. Bradley. F
467.	1445	23655	421	5.12.60	Jammed control column. Ejected at 1000'. 2 killed on ground. F/L H.H. Schoning. N
468.	1449	23659	441	27.2.58	Flame-out. Caught fire, crashed on taxiway at Etain AFB. F/O Tidball. N
469.	1450	23660	434	20.12.60	Ejected near Sembach, W.G. N
470.	1453	2021	FAC	6.9.61	Palanquero, Colombia.
471.	1454	2022	FAC	22.6.60	F
472.	1455	2026	FAC	18.9.56	F
473.	1460	351	RSA	5.6.62	Mid-air with 382 near Pienaar's Riugr. 2 Lt. J.A. de Bruine. F
474.	1462	353	RSA	26.4.66	Crashed 30 mi N. Rustenburg. Lt. Day. F
475.	1463	354	RSA	11.6.68	Crashed near Pietersburg during rocket attack. Lt. Viljoen. F
476.	1464	355	RSA	19.11.70	Mid-air with 370 near Turfloop. Ejected. N
477.	1465	356	RSA	2.11.61	Mid-air with 375. Ejected. 2 Lt. H.H. Meter. N
478.	1466	357	RSA	11.5.66	Crashed Waterkloof. Lt. Roos. F
479.	1469	360	RSA	29.6.65	Crashed near Louis Trichardt. Lt. Schlesinger. F
480.	1471	362	RSA	18.2.71	Flamed-out. Landed 3 mi short, Pietersburg. 2 Lt. W.J. Hartogh. N
481.	1473	364	RSA	14.4.61	Stalled on landing, Pietersburg. Capt. J.M. Moolman. N
482.	1475	366	RSA	29.10.687	Crashed near Banderleirkop. 2 Lt. C.F. du Toit. F
483.	1477	368	RSA	26.11.69	Engine failure on t/o. Ejected Pietersburg. Maj. Brits. F
484.	1479	370	RSA	10.4.75	In-flight fire. Ejected. Capt. F.W.C. Brits. F
485.	1483	374	RSA	22.6.71	Engine failure. Ejected. 2 Lt. J. Allison. N

C/N	Tail No.	Unit	Date	Notes
486.	1484	375	RSA	2.11.61	Mid-air with 356. Ejected. 2 Lt. C.C. Basson. N
487.	1485	376	RSA	16.8.60	Flame-out near Pretoria. Aircraft not refuelled, ejected. 2 Lt. C.N. Venter. N
488.	1486	377	RSA	26.3.71	Engine failure. Ejected near Blouberg Strand. 2 Lt. B.H. Arnold. N
489.	1488	379	RSA	15.7.60	Mid-air with 354 near Port Elizabeth. Ejected. Lt. H.J.W. Botha. N
490.	1499	23669	430	28.8.57	Mid-air with 23673. F/O Myers. F
491.	1503	23673	430	28.8.57	Mid-air with 23669 near Saarbrücken. Pilot thrown clear. F/O Larry Moser. N
492.	1525	23756	439	2.2.61	Seized controls. Ejected Chaloh-sur-Marn. F/O R.W. Hallworth.
493.	1528	23693	430	15.10.59	Mid-air with 23749. F/O H.A. Bacon. N
494.	1539	23701	421	20.5.60	Mid-air at 30000' with 23406. Ejected. F/O R.C. McKay. N
495.	1545	23707	434	21.3.62	Zweibrücken. Crashed on lndg. Jet wash. S/L Arnold. N
496.	1548	23710	434	6.3.62	Zweibrücken. Exploded on t/o. Ejected. F/O J. Swallow. N
497.	1562	23724	422	16.10.61	Baden. Flame-out on lndg. Ejected. S/L P.R. Higgs. N
498.	1586	23748	422	17.8.60	Dove in on night flight. F/O J.F. Baxter. F
499.	1597	BB-167	WS10	20.9.62	Flame-out at Oldenburg. Ejected. N
500.	1599	BB-369	WS10	25.5.59	Crashed after t/o from Marseille. Lt. Ehmling. F
501.	1601	D-9522	Condor	9.1.68	Lost power on approach to Westerland. Ejected. N
502.	1602	BB-172	WS10	18.10.60	Mid-air near Groningen, Netherlands, with BB-273. Lt. Holtgrewe ejected. Other pilot killed.
503.	1604	YA-041	EST61	27.8.64	Undercarriage problems. Ejected Oberpfaffenhofen. Joe Detzer. N
504.	1615	JC-249	JG42	27.11.64	Flew into trees in bad weather north of Büchel AFB. Thought following wrong radar instructions. F
505.	1619	JC-238	JG42	14.2.66	Engine failure in icing conditions. Ejected near Bad Kreuznach. Jochen Rack. N
506.	1628	JD-249	JG71	12.1.61	Mid-air near Nordhorn with JD-240, and RNAF a/c also damaged. Horst Arnoldt killed. Stabsunteroffizier Uwe Fischer ejected. Dutch a/c landed.
507.	1637	JD-240	JG71	12.1.61	Mid-air with JD-249.
508.	1640	JA-231	JG71	13.6.62	Crashed SE Helgoland. Stabsunteroffizier Bert Luthmer. F
509.	1641	JB-362	JG72	9.8.61	Mid-air in turbulence, ejected. Stabsunteroffizier Dieter Kelle. N
510.	1648	JC-104	JG73	23.8.63	Fuel exhaustion in bad weather. Ejected near Bernkastel-Kues. J. Hueller. N
511.	1649	JA-373	JG71	15.5.62	Crashed SE Helgoland. Lt. Rudolf Rohde. F
512.	1654	JD-119	JG72	3.9.64	Crashed on approach to Husum-Schwesing, ejected too low. Oberleutnant Peter Hoffman. F
513.	1667	JA-235		24.7.59	Overstressed (11Gs).
514.	1672	JD-107		26.8.60	Crashed after engine failed, Oldenburg-Ohmstede, killing pilot plus five. F
515.	1676	JA-121	JG71	9.8.61	Mid-air with BB-133 near Hölingen/Ostersehlt. Oberleutnant Hagen Hülfert. F
516.	1677	JA-336	JG71	7.7.64	Hydraulic trouble. Ejected near Seefelderaubendeich. Feldwebel Schuster. N
517.	1688	BB-182		22.4.63	Engine trouble. Ejected. N
518.	1694	JC-250		8.7.64	Flame-out over Sardinia. Ejected. N
519.	1697	JA-338		18.6.64	Barrier engagement, Oldenburg. Prinz. N
520.	1707	JA-239		7.12.60	Engine fire. Ejected. N
521.	1708	JC-246		5.8.64	Loss of control. Ejected near Edenkoben. Oberleutnant Liftel. N
522.	1713	JC-238		12.6.62	Aborted t/o at Lechfeld and overshot.
523.	1725	JC-118	JG73	7.4.64	Hit trees on low level flight near Binger Wald. Oberleutnant Frank Sedelitz. F
524.	1734	JB-110	JG72	5.12.63	Stalled and crashed on formation t/o at Leck. Stabsunter-offizier Joachin Hetzel. F
525.	1737	JC-372		18.5.65	Engine failure on approach to Pferdsfeld. Ejected. N
526.	1743	JB-105	JG72	9.5.61	Mid-air with JB-121 near Owschlag. Lt. Beckmann and Stabsunteroffizier Schluter ejected. N
527.	1744	JB-121	JG72	9.5.61	Mid-air with JB-105. N
528.	1753	JB-250	JG72	15.9.60	Crashed W. of Hamburg on flight from Leck. Stabsunteroffizier Rolf Hermann. F
529.	1757	JA-344	JG71	7.8.63	Crashed into flak emplacement at Brockzetel killing pilot plus five soldiers. Feldwebel Eckhardt Wendt. F
530.	1759	BB-273	WS10	18.10.60	Mid-air with BB-172.
531.	1779	BB-269	WS10	12.4.61	Compressor stall. Ejected. N
532.	1780	JC-368	JG73	29.6.65	Flame-out. Ejected near Gomaringen. Oberleutnant Jörg Jonatzke. N
533.	1782	JC-104		16.7.64	In-flight fire. Ejected at Pferdsfeld. N
534.	1785	JC-367		23.9.65	Engine fire after t/o Sardinia. Ejected. F
535.	1791	JB-104		21.9.65	Engine fire, Sardinia. N
536.	1793	JB-103		19.3.64	Engine failed. Ejected near Leck. N
537.	1796	JA-121	JG71	12.6.60	Crashed in North Sea following airshow at Husum-Schwesing. Stabsunteroffizier Egon Osenberg. F
538.	1814	JC-246		14.7.66	Lost power on approach to Pferdsfeld and crashed on runway. N
539	942	23152	OTU	3.12.59	F/O R.R. Webber.

N.B. List does not include Sabre 2s and 6s lost in Korea and Pakistan due to accident or combat.

Summary of Canadair Sabre Marks

Mark	Span	Length	Height	Wing Area* sq.ft.	Empty Wt. lb	Max. Wt. lb	Max. Speed (Sea Level) mph	Cruise Speed mph	Initial Climb fpm	Service Ceiling ft	Combat Radius mi.	Max. Range mi.
1	37.12'	37.54'	14.74'	287.4	10093	15876	679	533	7250	48000	320	1052
2	"	"	"	"	10434	17750	"	537	"	47100	"	1022
3	"	"	"	"								
4	"	"	"	"	11000	17750	"	"	"	47200	"	"
5	"	"	"	302.3	10662	17581z	696	552	9700	50700	"	1220
6	"	"	"	"	10638	17560z	698	"	12000	54100	360	1486

Mark	First Flight	No. Built	Engine	Thrust lb
1	8-8-50	1	GE J47	5200
2	31-1-51	350	"	"
3	29-9-52	1	Orenda 3	6000
4	28-8-52	438	GE J47	5200
5	30-7-53	370	Orenda 10	6500
6	19-10-54	655	Orenda 14	7440

Mark	Constructor's No.	RCAF No.	No. Built	Cumulative
1	1	19101	1	1
2	2-99	19102-19199	98	99
3	100	19200	1	100
2	101-352	19201-19452	252	352
4	353-790	19453-19890	438	790
5	791-1160	23001-23370	370	1160
6	1161-1815	23371-23760[1]	655	1815

[1]plus SAAF, Colombia, Luftwaffe

Standard Armament
All marks: 6 x .50 mg with 267 rounds per gun; up to 2000 lb bombs and rockets.

Mark	Operators
1	RCAF (1)
2	RCAF (350), Greece (106+), Turkey (107+)
3	RCAF (1)
4	RCAF (71**), RAF (438), Italy**(180), Yugoslavia**(121), Honduras(8)***
5	RCAF (370), Luftwaffe++ (75)
6	RCAF (390), Luftwaffe (225), SAAF (34), Colombia (6), Pakistan+++ (90)

* Mark 1,2,3,4, up to and including c/n 700 built with original wing (287.4 sq.ft.); c/n 701 and on built with "6-3 wing" (302.3 sq.ft.). Mark 1,3 and surviving 2s and 4s retrofitted with "6-3 wing".
\+ From original RCAF batch
** From original RAF batch
*** From original RAF batch via Yugoslavia
++ From original RCAF batch
+++ From original Luftwaffe batch
z Max.wt. from Canadair specs, with 2 x 167 Imp.gal.

Summary of Canadair Sabre Variations

1-150	Fibreglass nose ring for radar transmission.
151 and subsequent	Ring replaced by fibreglass nose cap.
1-70	Inboard sway brace on underwing tanks.
71 and subsequent	Sway brace deleted, fuel level indicators changed from gallons to pounds.
1-352	Taxi light on left, landing light on left.
353 and subsequent	Left light, land and taxi. Landing light on right.
2-352	Sabre 2s could carry 166 Imp.gal. drop tanks, but only with strict adherence to flight limitation.
353 and subsequent	166 Imp.gal tanks for ferry use only. Oxygen filler valve relocated from lower left nose to upper right forward fuselage. Dual rear latches on radar compartment. Normal and alternate flight controls hydraulic power systems filler relocated from left dive brake well to underside rear fuselage. IFF antennae relocated from fin tip to under fuselage (Stn.152).
365 and subsequent	Changed from A-1C to A-4 gunsight.
401-1221	Provision for target towing.
701-1400	Slats deleted, "6-3" leading edge substituted.
791 and subsequent	166 Imp.gal. standard fitting, 100 gal. tanks optional.
791-1000	One lower position light.
791-1280	Ice detector in intake duct.
1001 and subsequent	Upper ident. light may be deleted. Two wing lights and one tail light (right side) standard.
1401 to 1815	Slats re-installed on "6-3" wing.

Mark 6 Breakdown

Constructor's No.	No.	No. Built	Cumulative	Operator
1161-1452	23371-23662	292	292	RCAF
1453-1458	2021-2026	6	298	Colombia
1459-1492	350-383	34	332	SAAF
1493-1519	23363-23689	27	359	RCAF
1520	23753*	1	360	RCAF
1521-1522	23690-23691	2	362	RCAF
1523-1526	23754-23757*	4	366	RCAF
1527-1530	23692-23695	4	370	RCAF
1531-1532	23758-23759*	2	372	RCAF
1533	23696	1	373	RCAF
1534	23760*	1	374	RCAF
1535-1590	23697-23752	56	430	RCAF
1591-1815		225	655	Luftwaffe

*Originally Israeli AF Nos.6030-6037

Summary of RAF Sabres

RAF Serial	RCAF Serial (441 A/C)
XB530-XB551	*19378, *19384, *19404, 19464-19481, 19663.
XB575-XB603	19482-19510.
XB608-XB650	19511-19549, 19854-19857.
XB664-XB713	19550-19574, 19457, 19576-19599.
XB726-XB776	19600-19618, 19635, 19620-19628, 19458 19630-19634, 19459, 19636, 19629, 19638-19642, 19460, 19858-19863, 19644.
XB791-XB839	19645-19659, 19461, 19661/19662, 19453, 19664-19669, 19454, 19671-19678, 19575 19680-19688, 19455, 19690-19693.
XB851-XB900	19864-19868, 19694-19706, 19732-19748, 19774-19788.
XB912-XB961	19789-19792, 19803-19848.
XB973-XB999	19849-19853, 19869-19890.
XD706-XD736	19707-19731, 19749-19754.
XD753-XD781	19755-19773, 19793-19802.

*Mk.2's loaned to RAF.

RAF Sabres Diverted to RCAF (71 A/C)

19453-19463, 19491, 19575, 19579, 19582, 19584, 19585, 19590, 19597-19599, 19601, 19606, 19615-19617, 19619, 19624, 19627-19629, 19631, 19632, 19635-19637, 19639, 19642, 19643, 19647, 19649, 19650, 19652, 19653, 19655, 19657, 19659-19661, 19663-19665, 19667-19671, 19673-19675, 19677, 19679, 19680, 19682, 19684-19686, 19689, 19691, 19695, 19702. (Crashed in RCAF Service) 19456, 19462, 19463, 19619, 19637, 19643, 19660, 19670, 19679, 19689 (10 A/C)

Sabre Squadrons of the RCAF, 1951-1963

Squadron	Name	Wing	Code	Station(s)	F-86 in Service	Current
400	City of Toronto	(2 Group)	GW	Downsview	Mk.5 Oct.1956-Oct.1958	CH-136
401	City of Westmount	(1 Group)		St. Hubert	Mk.5 Oct.1956-Oct.1.1958	CH-136
410	Cougar	1	AM	St. Hubert May 1951 North Luffenham Nov. 1951 Baden-Söllingen Nov.1954 (TD) Marville Apr.1955-Oct.1956	Mk.2 May 1951-Nov.1954	CF-18
411	County of York	(2 Group)	KH	Downsview	Mk.5 Oct.1956-Sep.1958	CH-136
413	Tusker	3	AP	Bagotville Aug.1951 Zweibrücken Apr.1953-Apr.1957	Mk.2 Nov.1951-Jun.1954 Mk.5 Jun.1954-Sep.1955 Mk.6 Sep.1955-Apr.1957	Buffalo, CH-113
414	Black Knight	4	AQ	Bagotville Nov.1952 Baden-Söllingen Sep.1953-Jul.1957	Mk.4 Nov.1952-Nov.1953 Mk.5 Feb.1954-Aug.1955 Mk.6 Jul.1955-Jul.1957	Challenger,Falcon T-33,Voodoo
416	Black Lynx	2	AS	Uplands Jan.1951 Grostenquin Oct.1952-Jan.1957	Mk.2 Mar.1952-Mar.1954 Mk.5 Mar.1954-May 1955 Mk.6 Apr.1955-Jan.1957	
421	Red Indian	2	AX	St. Hubert Dec.1951 Grostenquin Oct.1952-Aug.1963	Mk.2 Dec.1951-Mar.1954 Mk.5 Mar.1954-Jun.1956 Mk.6 Jun.1956-Jul.1963	
422	Tomahawk	4	TF	Uplands Jan.1953 Baden-Söllingen Sep.1953-Apr.1963	Mk.2 Jan.-May 1953 Mk.4 Apr.1953-Dec.1954 Mk.5 Jan.1955-Sep.1955 Mk.6 Sep.1955-Apr.1963	
427	Lion	3	BB	St. Hubert Aug.1952 Zweibrücken Apr.1953 Grostenquin Jun.1962-Dec.1962	Mk.2 Sep.1952-Jun.1953 Mk.5 May 1953-Sep.1955 Mk.6 Sep.1955-Dec.1962	CH-135, CH-136
430	Silver Falcon	2	BH	North Bay Nov.1951 Grostenquin Oct.1962-May 1963	Mk.2 Nov.1951-Jun.1953 Mk.5 Jun.1953-Jun.1957 Mk.6 May 1957-May 1963	CH-135, CH-136
431				Bagotville	Mk.2 Jan.-Oct.1954	Tutor
434	Bluenose	3	BR	Uplands Jul.1952 Zweibrücken Apr.1953-Jun.1962 Marville Jun.1962-Jan.1963	Mk.2 Jul.1952-Nov.1953 Mk.5 Oct.1953-Jan.1957 Mk.6 Jan.1957-Jan.1963	CF-5
438	City of Montreal	(1 Group)	BQ	St. Hubert	Mk.5 Oct.1956-Nov.1958	CH-136
439	Sabre Tooth Tiger	1	IG	Uplands Sep.1951 North Luffenham Jun.1952 Marville Apr.1955-Nov.1963	Mk.2 Nov.1951-Feb.1955 Mk.5 Mar.1955-Jul.1956 Mk.6 Jul.1956-Oct.1963	
441	Silver Fox	1	BT	St. Hubert Mar.1951 North Luffenham Mar.1952 Zweibrücken Dec.1954 (TD) Marville Apr.1955-Sep.1963	Mk.2 Jun.1951-Jun.1955 Mk.5 Jan.1955-Aug.1956 Mk.6 Aug.1956-Sep.1963	
442	City of Vancouver	19(Aux)	SL	Sea Island	Mk.5 Oct.1956-Aug.1958	
443	City of New Westminster	19(Aux)	PF	Sea Island	Mk.5 Oct.1956-Aug.1958	
444	Cobra	4	VH	St. Hubert Mar.1953 Baden-Söllingen Sep.1953-Mar.1963	Mk.4 Mar.1953-Mar.1954 Mk.5 Feb.1954-May 1955 Mk.6 May 1955-Mar.1963	CH-139

Other Units

No.1(F)OTU				Chatham	Mk.2 Feb.1952-mid 1955 Mk.5 mid 1955-Oct.1961	
No.1 OFU				St. Hubert	Oct. 1953-Jul.1957	
Sabre Transition Unit				Chatham	Mk.5 Nov.1961-Nov.1968	
Golden Hawks				Chatham	Mk.5/6 Mar.1959-Feb.1964	

Air Armament Evaluation Detachment (Cold Lake), AFHQ Practice Flight (Uplands), Central Experimental and Proving Establishment (Uplands), Central Flying School (Saskatoon, Trenton), National Aeronautical Establishment No.129 Test and Ferry Flight (Trenton), Station Flight (Macdonald, Gimli).

RCAF/CF Sabre Hours Flown and Accidents

Year	Hours flown		Accidents (Category A-E)		Write-offs	
	By yr.	Accum.	By yr.	Accum.	By yr.	Accum.
1950/51	26	26	1	1	0	0
51/52	6002	6,028	50	51	4	4
52/52	36497	42,525	139	190	37	41
53/54	62269	104,794	190	380	30	71
54/55	80550	185,344	144	524	44	115
55/56	96479	281,823	99	623	39	154
56/57	108450	390,273	101	724	32	186
57/58	91027	481,300	103	827	25	211
58/59	85766	567,066	70	897	13	224
59	77440	644,506	83	980	11	235
60	74162	718,668	88	1068	16	251
61	72829	791,497	57	1125	13	264
62	67457	859,044	37	1162	5	269
63	32046	891,090	23	1185	5	274
64*	10503	901,593	2	1187	1	275
65	7937	909,530	3	1190	2	277
66	5884	915,414	0	1190	0	277
67	5569	920,983	2	1192	2	279
68	4647	925,630	1	1193	0	279
69	37	925,667	0	1193	0	279

*"D" Category accidents not included 1964-1969

Relight

Index

The old and the new. A Flight Systems Canadair Sabre with drogue flies with an F-15 Eagle near Holloman AFB, New Mexico. (Flight Systems Inc.)